Writings of Charles S. Peirce

Volume 1

From the Harvard Class Album of 1859

Writings of
CHARLES S. PEIRCE

A CHRONOLOGICAL EDITION

Volume I

1857–1866

MAX H. FISCH, *General Editor*
CHRISTIAN J. W. KLOESEL, *Associate Editor*
EDWARD C. MOORE, *Associate Editor*
DON D. ROBERTS, *Associate Editor*
LYNN A. ZIEGLER, *Textual Editor*
NORMA P. ATKINSON, *Research Associate*

Indiana University Press   Bloomington

Preparation of this volume has been supported in part by grants from the Program for Editions of the National Endowment for the Humanities, an independent federal agency, and the National Science Foundation.

CENTER FOR
SCHOLARLY EDITIONS

AN APPROVED EDITION

MODERN LANGUAGE
ASSOCIATION OF AMERICA

Harvard University Press holds the copyright to those parts of this volume that first appeared in *Collected Papers of Charles Sanders Peirce* (Vols. 1–6 edited by Charles Hartshorne and Paul Weiss, 1931–1935; 7–8 by Arthur W. Burks, 1958); Mouton Publishers to those that first appeared in *The New Elements of Mathematics by Charles S. Peirce* (4 vols. in 5 edited by Carolyn Eisele, 1976).

Manufactured in the United States of America

Library of Congress Cataloging in Publication Data

Peirce, Charles Santiago Sanders, 1839–1914.
Writings of Charles S. Peirce.
1. Philosophy—Collected works.
B945.P4 1981   191   79-1993
ISBN 0-253-37201-1

CONTENTS

Preface

The writings Peirce himself published run to approximately twelve thousand printed pages. At five hundred pages to the volume, these would make 24 volumes. The known manuscripts that he left unpublished run to approximately eighty thousand handwritten pages. If, on the average, two manuscript pages yield one book page, it would take 80 additional volumes for the unpublished papers and a total of 104 volumes for his complete works. Every previous letterpress edition of Peirce's writings might therefore fairly be entitled "Selected Papers," with a subtitle indicating the scope of the selection. The present edition is no exception. What follows is a statement of the aims and editorial policies that have governed the selections for the *Writings of Charles S. Peirce: A Chronological Edition.*

Our primary aim is to facilitate the study of the historical development of Peirce's thought. The Peirce corpus extends over sixty years, and Peirce returns again and again to his most difficult problems. To understand the positions he finally reached it is necessary to understand the problems he discovered along the way and to see why he felt forced to resolve them as he did. For that reason the present edition brings Peirce's writings into a single chronological order according to date of publication or, in the case of unpublished papers, date of composition.

To distinguish the papers Peirce published, the place and date of publication are given immediately following the title, while unpublished writings are identified by a manuscript number and the date of composition as noted by Peirce himself or as determined from other evidence. For papers datable only within a year or two, some latitude was taken in placing them in relation to dated papers. The new manuscript numbers were assigned after all of Peirce's papers, except his correspondence, were reassembled and completely rearranged in chronological order. This task, which took over three years to accomplish, was carried through primarily by Christian Kloesel.

The second aim of our edition is to demonstrate the degree of coherence and systematic unity of Peirce's thought at each stage of its development. Accordingly, it was necessary to depart occasionally from the strict chronological arrangement in order to present series of papers as uninterrupted units. There are few excerpts in A *Chronological Edition;* when an incomplete papers appears, it is, unless otherwise indicated, Peirce's complete fragment. It is hoped that these procedures will preserve the integrity of the efforts Peirce made to give an orderly and more or less complete exposition of his views.

Our third aim is to include as high a proportion of previously unpublished papers as possible. In all cases of material not published by Peirce himself, we have returned to the original manuscripts and edited them anew. Overall, we plan to present roughly one-half new material, that is, papers that have not previously appeared in printed form.

Recently an increasing proportion of readers of Peirce have come to him from semiotics, the general theory of signs, and think of him as one of the founders of that science, often as *the* founder, or at least as the American founder. Peirce from the beginning conceived of logic as coming in its entirety within the scope of the general theory of signs, and all his work in logic was done within that framework. At first he conceived of logic as a branch of semeiotic (his preferred spelling). Later he distinguished a narrow and a broad sense of logic. In the broad sense logic was coextensive with semeiotic. Eventually he abandoned the narrow sense, and the comprehensive treatise on which he was working in the last decade of his life was entitled "A System of Logic, considered as Semeiotic." The present edition is the first to give prominence to this development and to facilitate the tracing of it in detail.

In choosing papers for A *Chronological Edition,* preference was in general given to the more significant writings in the philosophy of science, in logic, and in metaphysics. Although fewer purely technical writings in science and mathematics are included, we have not overlooked the fact that Peirce's professional career was in science, not in philosophy. Peirce made original contributions to an extraordinarily wide range of the physical sciences, to pure mathematics as well as to mathematical pedagogy, and to the history of science and mathematics. Accordingly, some technical papers have been included when they seemed most useful to our purpose. Because of the work that others have done on Peirce's scientific papers, we believe that twenty volumes will allow us to accomplish the goals we have set for the present edition.

Each volume will contain a brief historical introduction giving an account of the activities of Peirce within its time span, including the work he was doing in the sciences, in mathematics, and in the history of science. Each volume will also include a single chronological list of all the papers Peirce wrote within the period covered by that volume. Thus readers who wish to make a thorough study of Peirce's work will find within each volume a guide to the complete Peirce corpus for the years of the particular volume. The historical introduction near the beginning and the chronological list near the end of each volume will serve as a frame for the papers that appear between them. It is hoped that reference to these additional materials will provide a comprehensive sense of Peirce's work in mathematics, the sciences, and philosophy.

Our editorial policies and practices have been established with the help of the Board of Advisors and the Editorial Board, whose advice and encouragement have carried us through the darker days.

EDWARD C. MOORE

Indianapolis
June 1980

Acknowledgments

We are indebted to Indiana University, the National Endowment for the Humanities, and the National Science Foundation, for their continuing support of the Project; to the Harvard University Department of Philosophy for permission to use the original manuscripts, and to the officers of the Houghton Library, where the Charles S. Peirce Papers are kept, for their cooperation; to Harvard University Press, Mouton Publishers, and Philip P. Wiener, for permission to re-edit materials first published in the *Collected Papers, The New Elements of Mathematics,* and *Values in a Universe of Chance,* respectively; to the IUPUI Interlibrary Loan department for service beyond the call of duty; to all those scholars who have given us expert help at particular points; to Don L. Cook, chairman of the Modern Language Association's Committee for Scholarly Editions, for helpful counsel on editorial policies and procedures; and especially to Webb Dordick for his invaluable research assistance in the Harvard libraries.

For permission to use duplicates of its annotated electroprint copy of Peirce's manuscripts—the next best thing to the originals—we are indebted to Texas Tech University's Institute for Studies in Pragmaticism.

Introduction

1. How Peirce Defined His Object in Life

When Peirce graduated from Harvard College in 1859, he was not yet twenty. Shortly before graduation, each member of his class wrote an entry in the Harvard Class Book of 1859. Peirce's was a humorous autobiography-in-miniature, with a sub-entry for each of the years from 1839 through 1859. The last was: "1859. Wondered what I would do in life." In a private notebook, "My Life written for the Class-Book" is continued through 1861. The last sub-entry reads: "1861. No longer wondered what I would do in life but defined my object." What was the reason for the wonder of 1859, and what had happened by 1861 to dispel that wonder and define the object?

In the male line, Peirce was descended from a John Pers (ca. 1588–1661) who came from Norwich, England, in 1637, and settled in Watertown, Massachusetts. For four generations, the Peirces were craftsmen, shopkeepers, or farmers. Then Jerathmiel (1747–1827) married Sarah Ropes, settled in Salem, entered the East India shipping trade, prospered, and built the elegant Peirce–Nichols house at 80 Federal Street. His son Benjamin (1778–1831) graduated from Harvard College, married Lydia Ropes Nichols, entered the shipping trade with his father, became a state senator, and, when Salem's shipping trade declined, became Librarian at Harvard, published a four-volume *Catalogue* of the library's holdings, and wrote a history of the university, which was published shortly after his death. *His* son Benjamin (1809–1880) graduated from Harvard College in 1829, taught for a time at the Round Hill School at Northampton, Massachusetts, and married Sarah Hunt Mills, daughter of Elijah Hunt Mills, a lawyer, co-founder of a law school there, and immediate predecessor of Daniel Webster as United States senator from Massachusetts. *This*

Benjamin Peirce, father of our Charles S. Peirce, became professor of astronomy and mathematics at Harvard, and was the leading American mathematician of his day. He was active in the Lazzaroni, an informal group of "beggars" for federal support of scientific research, and in the movement for a national university. He published several mathematical textbooks of high quality. His major works were *Analytic Mechanics* (1855–57) and *Linear Associative Algebra* (1870). He was president of the American Association for the Advancement of Science in 1853–54, and one of the founders of the National Academy of Sciences in 1863. Just beyond our period, he was superintendent of the U. S. Coast Survey from 1867 to 1874. His brother Charles Henry Peirce was a physician, and his sister Charlotte Elizabeth Peirce had kept school and taught privately, and was at home in German and French literature.

A sister of Benjamin Peirce's wife married Charles Henry Davis, who after seventeen years in the Navy (1823–1840) took up residence in Cambridge, studied mathematics with Benjamin, joined the Coast Survey, and in 1849 became the first superintendent of the American Ephemeris and Nautical Almanac.

Benjamin and Sarah had five children: James Mills (1834–1906), Charles Sanders (1839–1914), Benjamin Mills (1844–1870), Helen Huntington (1845–1923), and Herbert Henry Davis (1849–1916). James Mills (Jem), after graduating from Harvard in 1853, spent a year in the Law School, was tutor in mathematics for several years, graduated from the Divinity School in 1859, spent two years in the ministry, returned to the teaching of mathematics, and eventually succeeded to his father's professorship. Benjamin Mills, after graduating from Harvard in 1865, studied at the Paris School of Mines and later at the Lawrence Scientific School, became a mining engineer, and compiled *A Report on the Resources of Iceland and Greenland*, which was published by the U.S. State Department in 1868; but he died early in 1870 at Ishpeming in northern Michigan. Helen married William Rogers Ellis, who went into the rolling mill business and eventually into real estate. Herbert, after some years in the interior decorating and other businesses, became a diplomat, was secretary of legation at the U.S. embassy in St. Petersburg, then Third Assistant Secretary of State, and later minister to Norway.

The full range of the learned professions of law, medicine, divinity, and higher education, as well as business, engineering, politics, and diplomacy, was represented in the immediate family or by near relatives. Literature, the theater, and other arts were cherished if not represented. Benjamin Peirce, Charles's father, was a member of the Saturday Club, along with Emerson, Longfellow, Lowell, Oliver Wendell Holmes, and other literary figures. The Peirces were devotees of the theater, attended plays in Boston, and entertained actors in their home. Amateur theatricals were a common form of home entertainment. But what stood out for Charles in looking back from later years was that he had grown up in the Cambridge "scientific circle." The biologist and geologist Louis Agassiz lived but a stone's throw from the Peirces, and was a frequent visitor. Peirce, Agassiz, and Davis were leading members of the Cambridge Scientific Club. That club had at least fifteen meetings in the Peirce home before Charles defined his object, and another five during the years 1861–66. The Cambridge Astronomical Society (1854–57), which met every two weeks, began with Benjamin Peirce as president and Joseph Winlock as recording secretary. It was succeeded by a Mathematics Club presided over by Benjamin Peirce, which met on Wednesday afternoons for several years. It was attended by all the members of the Nautical Almanac staff. To that club Charles himself presented a paper on the four-color problem in the 1860s.

The items in the Class Book entry that shed most light on Charles's intellectual development are all extra-curricular: (1) "taking up the subject of Chemistry" (1847); (2) "Wrote a 'History of Chemistry'" (1850); (3) "Worked at Mathematics for about six months" (1854); (4) "Read Schiller's *Æsthetic Letters* and began the study of Kant" (1855).

We begin where Charles began, with chemistry. His father was one of the moving spirits behind the establishment within Harvard University of the Lawrence Scientific School in 1847. Eben Norton Horsford had then recently returned from two years at Giessen studying chemistry under Liebig, who combined laboratory instruction with demonstration experiments during lectures. To Liebig more than to anybody else it was due that the experimental method of teaching was more highly developed in chemistry than in any other science, so that the study of chemistry offered at that time the best entry into experimental science in general. Horsford was now made professor of chemistry in the Lawrence Scientific School, where he established, on the Liebig model, the first laboratory in America for analytical chemistry. Charles's uncle, Charles Henry Peirce, until then a practicing physician in Salem, became Horsford's assistant and was encouraged by him to translate Stöckhardt's *Die Schule der Chemie* for textbook use. Charles's aunt, Charlotte Elizabeth Peirce, whose German was excellent, did most of the actual work of translation. During the years in which the chemical laboratory was being established and the translation was in progress, Charles's uncle and aunt helped him set up a private laboratory at home and work his way through Liebig's hundred bottles of qualitative analysis. In 1850, when the translation appeared, Charles, then eleven, wrote a "History of Chemistry" (which has not been found). In the same year, his uncle became federal inspector of drugs for the port of Boston, and two years later, in 1852, published *Examinations of Drugs, Medicines, Chemicals, &c., as to their Purity and Adulterations*, giving some of the results of his official labors. Not long before Charles entered Harvard College in 1855, his uncle died, and Charles inherited his chemical and medical library. Charles's college teacher of chemistry was Josiah P. Cooke, the initiator of laboratory instruction at the undergraduate level. The textbook he used was Stöckhardt's, as translated by Charles's aunt and uncle under the title *Principles of Chemistry, Illustrated by Simple Experiments*.

One episode not recorded in his Class Book entry, but more often recalled in later life than any that is recorded there, was that of his introduction to logic, within a week or two of his twelfth birthday, in 1851. His older brother Jem was about to enter upon his junior year at Harvard College and had bought his textbooks for the year. Among them was Whately's *Elements of Logic*. Charles dropped into Jem's room, picked up the Whately, asked what logic was, got a simple answer, stretched himself on the carpet with the book open before him, and over a period of several days absorbed its contents. Since that time, he often said late in life, it had never been possible for him to think of anything, including even chemistry, except as an exercise in logic. And so far as he knew, he was the only man since the Middle Ages who had completely devoted his life to logic.

In his freshman year at college, Charles began intensive private study of philosophy with Schiller's *Aesthetic Letters*. From that he moved on to Kant's *Critic of the Pure Reason*. In his later college years, while continuing with Kant, he added modern British philosophy. In his junior year, he had to recite on Whately's *Elements of Logic,* as Jem had done six years before him. But all the while, as he later said, he "retained . . . a decided preference for chemistry," and it was taken for granted in the family that he was headed for a career in that science. The obvious next step after graduating would have been to enter the Lawrence Scientific School. But he felt the need of experience at earning his own living, and he had suffered so from ill health during his senior year that an interval of outdoor employment in science seemed desirable before he proceeded further. His father's friend, Alexander Dallas Bache, superintendent of the Coast Survey, offered him a place in his own field party in Maine in the fall of 1859, and in another field party around the delta of the Mississippi in the winter and spring of 1860. In early August 1859, before joining Bache's party, Charles spent a week at Springfield reporting sessions of the American Association for the Advancement of Science for six issues of the Boston *Daily Evening Traveler.*

On 18 December 1859 Charles wrote Jem, who was then a minister, a long letter from Pascagoula, Mississippi, in which he sought Jem's counsel. A man's first business, thought Charles, is to earn a living for himself—and for his family if he has any. Scientific research is for such leisure as that may leave him; society cannot be expected to pay for what it may have for nothing. It would appear, then, that his wondering in the Class Book what he would do in life meant wondering how he would earn a living, whether he would marry, what leisure he would have for science and for the logic of science. Jem replied at great length on 10 January. Society does pay for science, he wrote, at least if the scientific man has a practical side to his profession. And if one has a strong preference for science, one will never be happy in any other occupation. "I have often thought what a fine thing it would be if you & Benjy & I should go into different departments of science: Chemistry, Natural History, & Mathematics."

During Charles's absence in Maine and Louisiana, Darwin's *Origin of Species* appeared, and also a separate edition of Agassiz's *Essay on Classification.* Chemistry was an experimental but also a classificatory science. Biology was the chief other classificatory science. The differences between these two sciences were being brought into focus by the controversy between supporters of Darwin and supporters of Agassiz. In the latter half of 1860, while serving as proctor and tutor at Harvard College, Charles was for six months a private student of Agassiz's, to learn his method of classification. One of the tasks that Agassiz set him was sorting out fossil brachiopods.

In the spring of 1861 Charles at last entered the Lawrence Scientific School. Two and a half years later he graduated as a *summa cum laude* Bachelor of Science in Chemistry. But during his first term the Civil War had begun, and his father had lost, by resignation, the computing aide who assisted him in his chief service to the Coast Survey, that of determining the longitudes of American in relation to European stations from occultations of the Pleiades by the moon. Charles asked his father to obtain that appointment for him. His father wrote Superintendent Bache that he had at first urged his son to "keep to his profession and wait until he could get money by his chemistry—to which he replied that he wants to get the means to buy books and apparatus and devote himself longer to the study of his profession." Bache authorized Charles's appointment as aide beginning 1 July 1861, and he was launched on the career that occupied his next thirty and a half years and took him from chemistry into astronomy, geodesy, metrology, spectroscopy, and other sciences. Some measure of his attainments in them may be found in the facts that his father proposed him for the chair of physics at The Johns Hopkins University to which Henry Augustus Rowland was appointed, and that he was the first modern experimental psychologist on the American continent.

Throughout those thirty and a half years and on beyond them, however, when he had occasion to state his profession, or even his occupation, he continued to call himself a chemist. His first professional publication, in 1863 at the age of twenty-three, was on "The Chemical Theory of Interpenetration." In later years he found in Mendeleev's work on the periodic law and table of the elements the most complete illustration of the methods of inductive science. And he took satisfaction in having, in June 1869, when he was not yet thirty, published a table of the elements that went far in Mendeleev's direction, before Mendeleev's announcement of the law, a little earlier in the same year, became known in western Europe and America. At that year's meeting of the American Association for the Advancement of Science it was remarked that Peirce "had greatly added to the illustration of the fact of pairing by representing in a diagram the elements in positions determined by ordinates representing the atomic numbers."

At the end of 1891, after thirty-one and a half years in the service of the Coast and Geodetic Survey, his appointment was terminated, and he set up in private practice as a chemical engineer, thereby returning to the profession to which he had committed himself before he entered the Survey, and from which his career in the Survey had been in some sense a diversion.

It was not until 1906, in the first edition of *American Men of Science*, that for the first time in any biographical reference work, logic was named as the chief field of his investigations. In the first five editions of *Who's Who in America*, from 1899–1900 through 1908–1909, his profession appears as that of lecturer and engineer. In the sixth edition, that of 1910–1911, for the first time in any reference work, it appears as that of logician. Only after his death did he begin to be called a philosopher.

How then had he defined his object when in 1861 he no longer wondered what he would do in life? There are no letters or other records of that year from which an explicit, complete, and confident answer can be drawn. We are reduced therefore to piecing together the few indications we have from that time, and filling them out from subsequent events and from Peirce's later recollections and autobiographical remarks.

Chemistry at that time offered the best entry into experimental science in general, and was therefore the best field in which to do one's postgraduate work, even if one intended to move on to other sciences and, by way of the sciences, to the logic of science and to logic as a whole. Moreover, chemical engineering was then the most promising field in which to make a living by science, if one had no opportunity to do so by pure science or by logic.

That Peirce had no intention of confining himself to chemistry appears from his spending six months in private study of zoological classification under Agassiz before entering the Lawrence Scientific School. It appears also from his oration on "The Place of Our Age in the History of Civilization" (1863) and from "Shakespearian Pronunciation" (1864). It becomes fully evident from the two courses of lectures on the logic of science which he delivered in the spring of 1865 and the fall of 1866, and from the course on the history of logic in Great Britain which he delivered in 1869–70. The first and third of these courses were "University Lectures" at Harvard, each a part of an extensive program of such courses intended primarily for graduates of the college, and each offered but once. One of the men who attended the third course, along with others given in 1869–70, described them many years later as "The Germ of the Graduate School." Both in the university and in the Lowell Institute, in which the second course was given, each lecturer was expected to devote his lectures to the field and topics of his greatest competence, or on which he had most to offer that was new.

The most striking evidence, however, may be found in Peirce's election in January 1867 to the American Academy of Arts and Sciences, and in April 1877 to the National Academy of Sciences. To the former academy, in March, April, May, September, and November 1867 he presented five papers, all in logic, and all his subsequent papers in the *Proceedings* and *Memoirs* of that academy were in logic. Before his election to the National Academy, he was asked to send a list of his scientific papers, but sent instead the titles of four of his papers in logic and said he wished to be judged by those alone; and after his election he wrote to the secretary expressing his gratification at the implied recognition of logic as a science. Of the thirty-four papers he presented to the National Academy from 1878 to 1911, nearly a third were in logic. Others were in mathematics, physics, geodesy, spectroscopy, and experimental psychology; but in none of these fields did the number approach that in logic.

In connection with Peirce's private study of zoological classification under Agassiz, we mentioned that biology, like chemistry, is a classificatory science. We may add now that logic also is a classificatory science; that in Peirce's first series of published papers in logic, which will appear early in our second volume, the second paper was called "On a Natural Classification of Arguments"; that his first privately printed paper in logic, his "Memoranda Concerning the Aristotelean Syllogism," near the end of the present volume, contained his first original contribution to the classification of arguments; that he at that time conceived logic to be a branch of semeiotic, the general theory of signs; that he later adopted a much broader conception of logic in which, if it was not coextensive with semeiotic, it was so nearly so that for some time to come logicians were likely to be the chief cultivators of the general theory of signs; and that, in his own lifetime as a whole, he devoted more labor to the classification of signs than to any other single field of research. His pragmatism, for example, lay wholly within its scope.

How then had Peirce defined his object in 1861? Somewhat as follows, we may safely infer from all the evidence, early and late. In mathematics and in as wide a range of the sciences, physical and psychical, as possible—including the history of science and of mathematics—he would reach the point of carrying out and publishing original researches. He would begin with chemistry, the open sesame to the experimental sciences. He would earn his living by science as far as possible, so that his hours of employment as well as of leisure should further his object. He would prefer employment that gave him scope for diversity of researches over a period of years. His researches in sciences other than logic would in the first place be for the sake of those sciences themselves, but all would be brought to a second focus in logic, as including both the logic of mathematics and the logic of science, and eventually as including the general theory of signs. By bringing logic (and thereby metaphysics) abreast of the exact sciences in which he had been bred, he would at the same time serve the several sciences at a second and higher level.

But *why* should Peirce have supposed that by first making positive contributions to mathematics and to a wide range of the sciences he would then become a better contributor to logic? Because a scientific logic must take full account of the reasonings of mathematics and the sciences and because the traditional logic has failed to do so. It has failed in part because mathematicians who are not logicians, and logicians who are not mathematicians, are not fully competent to analyze the reasonings of mathematicians; and because scientists who are not logicians, and logicians who are not scientists, or who are scientists in only a single science or in but two or three closely related sciences, are not fully competent to analyze the reasonings of scientists.

If we think of the literature of the logic of science as including on the one hand Descartes's *Discourse on the Method of Rightly Conducting the Reason and Searching for the Truth in the Sciences,* and on the other Bacon's *Novum Organum* and Whewell's *Novum Organon Renovatum,* it will seem at least an hypothesis worth trying that a logician's ability to contribute to the logic of science may be enhanced by extending the range of his scientific researches. For Whewell had done just that, and had also written and published a three-volume *History of the Inductive Sciences* (1837), before publishing his two-volume *Philosophy of the Inductive Sciences, Founded Upon Their*

History (1840). His *Novum Organon Renovatum* (1858) was Part 2 of the third edition of the latter work.

In his 1865 Harvard University Lectures on the Logic of Science, in the present volume, Peirce speaks of Whewell as "man of science," "historian of science," and "the most profound writer upon our subject." But he speaks at much greater length in the lecture on Whewell in his Harvard University Lectures of 1869 on the British Logicians, which will appear in volume 2. That may be our best evidence of the way in which Peirce had defined his object in life.

But whether in fact, and to what extent, Peirce's contributions to the logic of science can be traced to the diversification of his scientific researches is still to be determined, and it is one of the aims of the present edition of his writings to open the way toward answering that question.

2. The Categories

When Bacon gave the title *Novum Organum* to the second part of his major work, *The Great Instauration,* and when Whewell gave the title *Novum Organon Renovatum* to the second part of his major work in its third edition, they thereby claimed to be making great advances in logic, the science founded by Aristotle in his *Organon.* Advances not in the whole range of the *Organon,* to be sure, but only in the logic of science; more exactly, in the theory of how the inductive and especially the experimental sciences are advanced. But the *Organon* itself began with a treatise on *Categories,* in which ten were listed and discussed; and Peirce began where the *Organon* began.

Aristotle's categories were substance, quantity, quality, relation, place, time, position, state, action, and passion. Many lists differing more or less from his were drawn up by later logicians. In Peirce's time the best known of these were Kant's short list of twelve and the long list of Hegel's *Encyclopedia of the Philosophical Sciences.* Bacon had used the phrase "Transcendentals, or Adventitious Conditions of Essences." Whewell used the phrase "Fundamental Ideas" but offered no inclusive list; it was for the future progress of the sciences to evolve one.

Looking back from 1898, Peirce wrote: "In the early sixties I was a passionate devotee of Kant, at least as regards the Transcendental Analytic in the *Critic of the Pure Reason.* I believed more implicitly in the two tables of the Functions of Judgment and the Categories than if they had been brought down from Sinai." In Meiklejohn's translation of 1855, which Peirce owned and used beginning not later than 1856, the two tables appear six pages apart. To facilitate comparison, we present them here in parallel columns.

[TABLE OF JUDGMENTS]   TABLE OF THE CATEGORIES

I	I
Quantity of judgments	*Of Quantity*
Universal	Unity
Particular	Plurality
Singular	Totality

II	II
Quality	*Of Quality*
Affirmative	Reality
Negative	Negation
Infinite	Limitation

III	III
Relation	*Of Relation*
Categorical	Of Inherence and Subsistence (substantia et accidens)
Hypothetical	Of Causality and Dependence (cause and effect)
Disjunctive	Of Community (reciprocity between the agent and patient)

IV	IV
Modality	*Of Modality*
Problematical	Possibility—Impossibility
Assertorical	Existence—Non-existence
Apodeictical	Necessity—Contingence

For the present we shall confine our attention to the Table of the Categories. It is obvious at once that three of Aristotle's ten categories appear as heads of three of Kant's four triads, and two or three others appear in modified forms within them. Hegel remarked that the four headings that Kant used for his triads were in fact categories of a more general nature. Kant himself had remarked that in each triad the third category arises from the combination of the second with the first. Peirce will later make a similar observation about Hegel's three stages of thought, which he will call Hegel's universal categories, as distinguished from the particular categories of the *Encyclopedia*. He will also say that his own three categories correspond both to Hegel's universal categories and to the three categories implicit in each of Kant's four triads.

Volume 2 will include the five papers in logic that Peirce presented to the American Academy of Arts and Sciences in 1867. The third of them offered the following "New List of Categories":

BEING,
　　Quality (Reference to a Ground),
　　Relation (Reference to a Correlate),
　　Representation (Reference to an Interpretant),
SUBSTANCE.

Peirce soon reduced the five to three by sloughing off Being and Substance. We note at once that two of Aristotle's categories reappear in Peirce's triad as well as in the headings of two of Kant's triads. Only representation is new. But that is novelty enough. It is the first list of categories that opens the way to making the general theory of signs fundamental in logic, epistemology, and metaphysics.

Peirce's paper "On a New List of Categories" was presented to the academy on 14 May 1867. In his private Logic Notebook, on 23 March, Peirce wrote:

I cannot explain the deep emotion with which I open this book again. Here I write but never after read what I have written for what I write is done in the process of forming a conception. Yet I cannot forget that here are the germs of the theory of the categories which is (if anything is) the gift I make to the world. That is my child. In it I shall live when oblivion has me—my body.

And thirty-eight years later, in a draft of a letter to Mario Calderoni, he could still write that

on May 14, 1867, after three years of almost insanely concentrated thought, hardly interrupted even by sleep, I produced my one contribution to philosophy in the "New List of Categories" . . . . My three categories are nothing but Hegel's three grades of thinking. I know very well that there are other categories, those which Hegel calls by that name. But I never succeeded in satisfying myself with any list of *them*.

Readers of the present volume will bring to it numerous questions the editors cannot hope to anticipate. It seems safe to assume, however, that readers wishing to understand Peirce on his own terms will be more numerous than those who approach him with the same particular question or group of questions of their own. On that assumption, our primary aim in volume 1 has been to include in their chronological places the writings in which the reader can trace the steps by which Peirce arrived at his new list of categories, and at the first published forms of his general theory of signs and his sign theory of cognition; and in subsequent volumes the steps by which he moved through successive modifications of all three toward his last great undertaking, "A System of Logic, considered as Semeiotic." But we include every paper of comparable originality, whether directly relevant or not to this primary aim. No range of his work will be left unrepresented.

3. *I, IT, and THOU*

We turn now to a few of the less obvious early episodes in the search for the categories within the period of the present volume.

Charles Russell Lowell (eldest brother of the poet James Russell Lowell) and his wife, Anna Cabot Jackson Lowell, were neighbors of the Peirces. Their home was a center of hospitality. It was there that Peirce met Chauncey Wright, the ablest philosopher with whom he was personally acquainted in his early years. Shortly before he entered college, Mrs. Lowell had lent Peirce a copy of John Weiss's translation of *The Aesthetic Letters* of Friedrich Schiller. As a result of alphabetic seating in their college classes, he and Horatio Paine ("noble-hearted, sterling-charactered," "almost the only real companion I have ever had") became intimate friends. Schiller's book interested them more than anything they were required to read in college, and they "spent every afternoon for long months upon it, picking the matter to pieces as well as we boys knew how to do." From Schiller they proceeded to Kant's *Critic of the Pure Reason* (as Peirce later rendered the title), and Peirce continued the study of the *Critic* until he almost "knew it by heart in both editions."

One of the assigned "themes" in their sophomore year was on a sentence from Ruskin's *Modern Painters:* "It has been said by Schiller in his letters on aesthetic culture that the sense of beauty never farthered the performance of a single duty." Peirce was well prepared to defend Schiller against Ruskin's misunderstanding. He gives an account of the three impulses distinguished by Schiller—the *Formtrieb, Stofftrieb,* and *Spieltrieb.* In response to a comment on his theme by their professor, Francis J. Child, Peirce added at the end: "I should say that these were the I impulse and faculty, and the IT impulse and faculty; and also the THOU impulse and faculty which (it seems to me) is what Schiller regards as that of beauty."

Readers familiar with Martin Buber's *I and Thou* will be struck by the prominence of I, IT, and THOU in the early stages of Peirce's search for the categories. If Kant's categories come in triads, and if the Hegelian dialectic moves in triads of thesis, antithesis, and synthesis, and if Schiller finds only three fundamental drives or faculties, we may well be moved to try the hypothesis that Aristotle's ten categories and Kant's twelve are reducible to three. If, further, we expect the categories to manifest themselves in language as well as in thought, it may strike us that in the language we speak there is nothing more prominent than the three persons of the verb and the corresponding pronouns. (Some readers will recall at this point that Peirce later held that nouns are substitutes for pronouns, not, as their names assume, pronouns for nouns.)

If we then try finding our categories in, or deriving them from, the personal pronouns, our first trials are likely to take them in the order I, THOU, IT; and that is what Peirce does in his earliest surviving table, as well as in a theme comparing Michelangelo and Raphael, both written in 1857. In the table, he is already connecting his pronominal categories with Kant's triads; for that purpose he changes the order of the second and third categories in two of Kant's triads, and we wonder why he does not do so in the third as well.

By January 1859, if not earlier, he has settled on the order I, IT, THOU. In that month he begins a book on "The Natural History of Words," in which the first page of text reads:

THE PERSONS

I

I me
The first person, the ego, the I, the Me, subject, self   Not-I non-ego
Subjective, my, mine
to me

IT

He him she her it they them, third person
Being, Thing, τὸ ὄν, thing in itself, *noumenon*
be is are were was been

THOU

Thou, thee, ye, you; O!
Second person,
thine, yours, thy, your.

It is assumed throughout that semeiotic, the general theory of signs, including words and other symbols, is a classificatory science, like chemistry and biology; and we are starting with words, and, among words, with those associated with the three persons of the verb, and with the names I, THOU, and IT for those persons. It is made emphatic that the logical or categorical order of these names is different from the traditional grammatical order of the persons, but the reason for the difference is not stated.

On 1 June 1859 Peirce constructs an octagonal table of subcategories of the IT, including all of Kant's categories with some puzzling alterations. Kant's first triad appears as Infinite Qualities of Quantity, his second as Influxual Dependencies of Quality, his third as Necessary Modes of Dependence, and his fourth as Perfect Degrees of Modality. These are followed by four other triads, the last of which brings us back to Kant's first.

In the spring of 1861 Peirce begins a book entitled, "I, IT, and THOU." "I here, for the first time," he writes, "begin a developement of these conceptions. . . . THOU is an IT in which there is another I. I looks in, It looks out, Thou looks *through*, out and in again." For the first time, it becomes emphatic and clear that THOU presupposes IT, and IT presupposes I. That is the reason for the difference between the categorical and the grammatical order.

In the next year, 1862, William James writes in one of his notebooks:

> The *thou* idea, as Pierce calls it, dominates an entire realm of mental phenomena, embracing poetry, all direct intuition of nature, scientific *instincts*, relations of man to man, morality &c.
>
> *All analysis* must be into a triad; *me* & *it* require the complement of *thou*.

In his oration on "The Place of Our Age in the History of Civilization," delivered at a reunion of the Cambridge High School Association on 12 November 1863 and published in the *Cambridge Chronicle*, Peirce says: "First there was the egotistical stage when man arbitrarily imagined perfection, now is the idistical stage when he observes it. Hereafter must be the more glorious tuistical stage when he shall be in communion with her."

In 1891 Peirce defines *tuism* for the *Century Dictionary* as "The doctrine that all thought is addressed to a second person, or to one's future self as to a second person." The *Oxford English Dictionary* later quotes this definition in its own entry. There and in its *illeism* entry, it is recorded that Coleridge had used the terms *egotism, illeism,* and *tuism,* but not in any systematic or technical way.

Though by 1867 Peirce has abandoned I, IT, and THOU as *names* for his categories, it is only because he has found better technical terms for what he has meant by those more colloquial ones.

4. *From Unitarianism to Trinitarianism*

The main substance of the present volume is in the two series of lectures on the logic of science—the Harvard University Lectures in the spring of 1865 and the Lowell Institute Lectures in the fall of 1866. Though a few extracts from both series have been published, the present volume contains for the first time as near an approach to a complete letterpress edition of the two as the surviving manuscripts make possible. It also enables us to attend both series with the benefit of prior acquaintance with several years of the young lecturer's life and work, and thereby prepares us for the second and subsequent volumes.

We are tempted to say on the one hand that in these two courses Peirce has for the most part unfolded his thoughts before us with such fullness that any editorial introduction would be superfluous, and on the other hand that an adequate introduction will be possible only after several years of detailed examination by Peirce scholars and by historians of logic.

If some readers find his metaphysics more interesting than his logic, we invite their attention to the last of the Lowell Lectures, on the advantages of "adopting our logic as our metaphysics." If we learn our logic from Peirce, we shall thereby be led, for example, not only to the sign theory of cognition but also to the sign (more exactly the symbol) theory of man, and to a metaphysics akin to trinitarian theology. Near the end, the lecturer is saying:

Here, therefore, we have a divine trinity of the object, interpretant, and ground. . . . In many respects, this trinity agrees with the Christian trinity; indeed I am not aware that there are any points of disagreement. The interpretant is evidently the Divine *Logos* or word; and if our former guess that a Reference to an interpretant is Paternity be right, this would be also the *Son of God*. The *ground*, being that partaking of which is requisite to any communication with the Symbol, corresponds in its function to the Holy Spirit.

This becomes intelligible only in the light of biographical details more intimate than those we have so far cited.

Peirce was brought up a Unitarian. The family attended services at the College Chapel. Frederic Dan Huntington's appointment as Plummer Professor of Christian Morals and Preacher to the College began with Peirce's freshman year and continued a year beyond his graduation. It was under Huntington that Peirce in his freshman year studied Richard Whately's *Lessons on Morals* and *Christian Evidences*. Huntington was a Unitarian, but he became an Episcopalian early in 1860 and therefore resigned his professorship. (He later became the first Episcopal bishop of Central New York, with diocesan headquarters at Syracuse.)

Among the Harvard classmates of Peirce's father was Charles Fay, who became an Episcopalian clergyman, married a daughter of John Henry Hopkins, the first Episcopal bishop of Vermont, and since 1848 had been rector of St. Luke's Episcopal Church at St. Albans, Vermont. The eldest daughter of the Fays, Harriet Melusina, usually called Zina, was a passionate feminist deeply concerned from adolescence about the role of women in society. In the summer of 1859 she arrived at an interpretation of the doctrine of the trinity according to which the Holy Spirit is the feminine element in the triune godhead: "a Divine Eternal Trinity of Father, Mother and Only Son—the 'Mother' being veiled throughout the Scriptures under the terms 'The Spirit', 'Wisdom', 'The Holy Ghost', 'The Comforter' and 'The Woman clothed with the sun and crowned with the stars and with the moon under her feet'."

After her mother's death in 1856, Zina had been in correspondence with Ralph Waldo Emerson, and it was on his advice that in the fall of 1859 she entered the Agassiz School for Young Ladies, in the Agassiz home just across Quincy Street from the Peirces. Perhaps it was there that Charles and Zina met, in the winter of 1860–61 if not earlier. He made his first formal call upon her in January 1861. Several of his metaphysical writings from 1861 onwards are marked "For Z. F.," and probably most if not all of them were written for her. In the summer of 1861 he made the first of several extended visits to Zina and her family in St. Albans. His "Views of Chemistry: sketched for Young Ladies," written for Zina and her younger sisters, were begun during that visit. When he defined his object in that year, it probably included marriage with her. By the spring of 1862 they were engaged. It seemed to his parents that for the first time he was taking religion seriously. In the evening of 24 July, in the chapel of the Vermont Episcopal

Institute in Burlington, in the presence of Zina and several members of her family, Charles was confirmed by her grandfather, Bishop Hopkins. On 16 October Charles and Zina were married by her father at St. Luke's in St. Albans. (They had no children. After fourteen years together, she separated herself from him. He divorced her in 1883 and took a second wife. Zina did not remarry.)

Peirce's conversion to Episcopalianism entailed of course a conversion from unitarianism to trinitarianism. Though not always an active communicant, he remained an Episcopalian and a trinitarian to the end of his life. And as late as 1907 we find a distant echo of Zina's feminist version of the trinity. In outlining a draft of what turned out to be his best account of pragmatism within the framework of his general theory of signs, he then wrote: "A Sign mediates between its *Object* and its *Meaning*. . . Object the father, sign the mother of meaning." That is, he might have added, of their son, the Interpretant.

5. The Classification of Arguments

Though Peirce's categories are meant to be universally applicable, and he did so apply them, his most frequent single application of all three together is in the definition of a sign. In his many definitions, early and late, the nearest to a constant is that a sign is a first something so determined (limited, specialized) by a second something, called its object, as to determine a third something, called its interpretant, to determination by the same object. That is, sign action or semeiosis (as distinguished from dyadic mechanical action) involves an irreducibly triadic relation between (1) a sign, (2) its object, and (3) its interpretant.

His most frequent single occasion for defining a sign is that of a logician for whom logic is "the critic of arguments" and arguments are a kind of signs. After defining a sign, his most frequent next three moves, each a reapplication of his categories, are: (1) dividing signs into icons, indexes, and symbols; (2) dividing symbols into terms, propositions, and arguments; and (3) dividing arguments into retroductions, inductions, and deductions. He is then ready for the main business of logic, that of determining the relative validity or strength of each kind of arguments.

(In the present volume, he uses "representation" and "representamen" in approximately the senses in which he will later use "sign," and by "sign" he usually means what toward the end of the volume he begins calling "index." What in this volume he calls "likeness," "copy," "image," or "analogue," he will begin calling "icon" in 1885. "Abduction" and "retroduction" are his later and more technical terms for what he here calls "hypothesis" or "inference *à posteriori*." For a short while he tries "subject" and "correspondent" for what, toward the end of the volume, he begins calling "interpretant.")

Logic is for Peirce a science, and its definition must therefore place it in relation to other sciences. That calls for a classification of the sciences. No logician—no philosopher—ever attached more importance, or devoted more attention, to classifications of the sciences than Peirce did. The most general and the most familiar classification was that which John Locke, in the last chapter of his *Essay Concerning Human Understanding* (1690), ascribed to the Greeks: φυσική or natural science, πρακτική or moral science, and σημειωτική or "*the Doctrine of Signs*, the most usual whereof being Words, it is aptly enough termed also λογική, Logick." Peirce objects that, of the three kinds of signs, logic deals only with symbols, and with them only in relation to their objects, and only in respect of truth and falsity. Moreover, of the three kinds of symbols, it has little to say of terms and propositions except as they enter into arguments. So logic is at most but a third part of a third part—that is, a ninth part—of semeiotic. It might be defined as objective symbolistic.

By the mid-1880s, however, Peirce will have come to realize that logic cannot do business without icons and indexes and that it must take account of all three kinds of symbols both in themselves and in relation to their interpretants as well as in relation to their objects. In the 1890s he will distinguish a narrow sense in which logic is still concerned only with arguments and only in relation to their objects, and a broad sense in which it is coextensive with semeiotic in the sense of "the *general* theory of signs," leaving room for an indefinite number of more specialized semeiotic sciences. He is thus halfway back to Locke. By 1902, he will abandon the narrow sense altogether, or use Locke's term *critic* rather than *logic* as the name for it; and the semeiotic trivium will become the logical trivium of speculative grammar, critic, and speculative rhetoric or methodeutic; and by 1909 he is drafting "A System of Logic, considered as Semeiotic." It has taken him most of his productive lifetime to come all the way back to Locke. With this in mind, it should not surprise us that, over that lifetime,

Peirce devoted more study than any other major logician has done to "the doctrine of signs."

Returning now to the classification of arguments, we remark that though the title of Peirce's Harvard University Lectures of 1865 was simply "On the Logic of Science," that of his Lowell Institute Lectures of 1866 was "The Logic of Science; or, Induction and Hypothesis." The latter title would have been read at the time as if it had been written "The Logic of Science; or, Induction—*and Hypothesis!*" The common assumption was that the logic of mathematics was the logic of deduction, and the logic of science that of induction. Though it was obvious that the advancement of the empirical and experimental sciences depended on the forming and testing of hypotheses, hypothesis was not (and is not yet) understood as a distinct kind of inference or argument.

But Peirce's three categories led him to expect to find three distinct kinds of arguments. (He later intimated that the chief single purpose of his work on the categories had been to have a guide to the classification of arguments.) The problem was to identify, distinguish, and name them. He began where Kant began in his major work, whose title Peirce proposed to translate "Critic of the Pure Reason"; namely, with the distinction between two kinds of "judgments": (1) analytic or explicative and (2) synthetic or ampliative. Peirce first adopted the second term of each pair. He then turned the distinction between explicative and ampliative judgments into the distinction between explicative and ampliative arguments or inferences. A possible way of coming out with three kinds instead of two was to divide one or the other into two. He would later distinguish two kinds of mathematical demonstration, corollarial and theorematic, but he had as yet no inkling of that. Even if he had already worked it out, the difference between them would not have seemed to him so radical as that between the two kinds of ampliative inference which he now readily found; the difference, that is, between induction more strictly speaking on the one hand, and on the other reasoning *to* a hypothesis that will both account for puzzling data already obtained and serve to predict results of experiments not yet tried or observations not yet made.

Peirce next connected explicative arguments with the first of the three Aristotelian figures of the syllogism, and more particularly with the mood *Barbara*. He then tried connecting hypothesis with the second figure, and particularly with the mood *Baroco;* and induction with the third figure, and particularly with the mood *Bocardo.* In the order of the validity or strength of the three kinds of arguments, from the weakest to the strongest, the connections thus became: (1) first category, hypothesis, second figure; (2) second category, induction, third figure; (3) third category, deduction, first figure.

But connecting the three kinds of inference with the three Aristotelian figures of the syllogism was open to two lines of attack. (1) What about the fourth figure? Having adopted as his "primary conceptions" those of rule, subsumption or case, and result, Peirce rejects the fourth figure and "all its moods not as being invalid but as being indirect, and unsyllogistic." (2) But since syllogisms in the second and third figures are reducible to syllogisms in the first, must we not concur with Kant in his early tract *On the False Subtlety of the Four Syllogistic Figures?* That question led Peirce to his first major discovery in logic; namely, that every such reduction takes the logical form of an argument in the figure from which the reduction is made. He thought enough of this discovery to have his essay on it privately printed in time for distribution at his Lowell Lectures in November 1866, under the title *Memoranda Concerning the Aristotelean Syllogism;* and he mailed copies to logicians at home and abroad. Augustus De Morgan in London received his copy on 29 December 1866. By the end of the period covered by the present volume, Peirce had thus joined the small international community of professional logicians.

MAX H. FISCH

Writings of Charles S. Peirce

Volume 1

My Life
written for the Class-Book

MSS 51 and 63:
May 1859 and 10 September 1860

1839
September 10. Tuesday. Born.

1840
Christened.

1841
Made a visit to Salem which I distinctly remember.

1842
July 31. Went to church for the first time.

1843
Attended a marriage.

1844
Fell violently in love with Miss W. and commenced my education.

1845
Moved into new house on Quincy St.

1846
Stopped going to Ma'am Sessions and began to go to Miss Wares—a very pleasant school where I learnt much and fell violently in love with another Miss W. whom for distinction's sake I will designate as Miss W'.

1847

Began to be most seriously and hopelessly in love. Sought to drown my care by taking up the subject of Chemistry—an antidote which long experience enables me to recommend as sovereign.

1848

Went to dwell in town with my uncle C. H. Mills and went to school to the Rev. T. R. Sullivan, where I received my first lessons in elocution.

1849

In consequence of playing truant and laving in the frog-pond, was taken ill. On my recovery, I was recalled to Cambridge and admitted a member of the **Cambridge High School.**

1850

Wrote a "History of Chemistry."

1851

Established a printing-press.

1852

Joined a debating society.

1853

Set up for a fast man and became a bad schoolboy.

1854

Left the High School with honor after having been turned out several times. Worked at Mathematics for about six months and then joined Mr. Dixwell's school in town.

1855

Graduated at Dixwell's and entered College.

Read Schiller's *Æsthetic Letters* and began the study of Kant.

1856

SOPHOMORE. Gave up the idea of being a fast man and undertook the pursuit of pleasure.

1857

JUNIOR. Gave up the pursuit of pleasure and undertook to enjoy life.

1858

SENIOR. Gave up enjoying life and exclaimed "Vanity of vanities! All is vanity!"

1859

Wondered what I would do in life.

———

Appointed Aid on the Coast Survey. Went to Maine and then to Louisiana.

1860

Came back from Louisiana and took a Proctorship in Harvard. Studied Natural History and Natural Philosophy.

1861

No longer wondered what I would do in life but defined my object.

Private Thoughts
principally on the conduct of life

MS 55: 7 June 1860 to 17 March 1888

III

1853

Love is the foundation of everything desirable or good.

VI

Every truth may be infinitely extended, but when all truths are expanded to universal principles they make a parallelogram of forces which can't be calculated. Hence the need of particular rules.

IX

1853

Poets see common nature.

XIX

1857

	I	Reason Faith	Goodness	Love of Order	Unity	Reality	Permanence
Faculty } The Soul	THOU	Affection Love	Beauty	Love of Men	Totality	Limitation	Causality
Impulse	IT	Sensation Hope	Truth	Love of World	Plurality	Negation	Community

XXII

1860 June 23

The difference between Wisdom and Knowledge is this:—Knowledge is that which we get empirically but Wisdom is wrought by the unfolding of the mind.

XXIV

1860 June 11

Errare est hominis

Observations may be wrong, but still it is not very likely they are quite the contrary of the fact, and as long as they are not, they are not essentially false; they only need additions and modifications.

So likewise, logical fallacies produce propositions, false, indeed, as they were intended, but yet with a modified meaning, true. This is obviously the case with the Illicit Process. In the cases of the Undistributed Middle, Negative Premisses, and Ambiguous Middle, a modification of one of the premisses will always make a conclusion possible.

This fact, that human errors are always those which addition or amendment will rectify, has given rise to the common saying that "genius never errs" and to the philosophers' boast "that science has never been in the wrong." The fact is, essential error can only arise from perversion, from wickedness, or from passion. Sincere and philosophic production have no other falsity than that which is inseparable from every human proposition.

This reflection should teach us the inhumanity of a polemic spirit and should teach us still to revere a great man notwithstanding his mistakes. In reading his books we can silently add and modify, altho' in writing again a conviction that words and the meaning of words have always been the great source of heresy, may well make us as precise as possible with our own phraseology.

XXV

1860 July 12

The terms of every proposition are presupposed to be comprehended; therefore no proposition can give us a new conception, and Wisdom is not learnt from Books.

XXVI

1860 July 13

Metaphysics is the study of form. In the study of matter we have at least some idea of our subject and therefore are never wholly in the wrong, but a modified form is in no degree the same as the unmodified form, therefore in metaphysics we are never partly right.

XXXVI

1859

It is impossible for a man to act contrary to his character.

It is foolish for him to try to do it; he would be no better man for doing it since the character makes the man.

The Very Law of the Growth of Character is contained in the Character.

XXXVII

1860 August

The essential of a thing—the character of it—is the unity of the manifold therein contained. *Id est,* the logical principle, from which as major premiss the facts thereof can be deduced.

What are called a *man's* principles however are only certain beliefs of his that he may or may not carry out. They therefore do not compose his character, but the general expression of the facts—the ACTS OF HIS SOUL—does.

What he does is important.

How he feels is incidental.

XXXVIII

1860 September 16

It is on account of man's finite nature that he has a free will. His will is free only when he is in doubt—only therefore in certain critical moments. Hence the practical part of Ethics is the study of these critical moments.

XLI

1856 August 12

The "soul" is that which can move. According as a soul is *greater* or *less,* it possesses more or less of this power. According as at any time it is exercising this power or moving, it is more or less "excited."

When the soul is in an active state the repetition or continuance of the same thought or notion (to be distinguished most carefully from many notions which leave to each little weight) will pass that notion naturally *up through* the soul.

But what puts the soul in this active state? *Beauty.* In this (which I shall term the *Automatic*) method of excitement, it is necessary that the *patient* notion should outweigh all others—which can happen in two ways:—First, by the superiority of the Notion itself [a thought is *caeteris paribus* superior to an idea] and

2nd by the attention given to it.

In order that our Automatic Method may be of any use it will be necessary to devise some means by which in practice

All superior notions may be expelled

The principal part of the attention may be given to the *patient*. That is to say

1st That the attention may be drawn from all other notions

(2nd) to the patient notion.

Now then we have decided that 3 things are to be done: 1 to render the soul sensitive and active, 2 to empty the attention, 3 to put the Patient Notion in.

XLIII

1858

When a child burns his finger at the candle, he has not only excited a disagreeable sensation, but has learnt also a lesson in prudence. Now the mere matter cannot have given him a notion since it had none to give; therefore, it must have been God who at the creation of the world put this thought into nature. Now this heat was a form, and all powers are forms. And matter we know nothing of.

All forms are also powers, since to affect is to effect, and are therefore spiritual manifestations. If this is so every form must have a meaning. But since all phenomena are forms, all things must have meanings. The transparency of the drop of water must actually convey a meaning to our conscious *affections* as truly as the Whole Sea itself.

XLVI

1859

Prayer

I pray thee, O Father, to help me to regard my innate ideas as objectively valid. I would like to live as purely in accordance with thy laws as inert matter does with nature's. May I, at last, have no thoughts but thine, no wishes but thine, no will but thine. Grant me, O God, health, valor, and strength. Forgive the misuse, I pray of thy former good gifts, as I do the ingratitude of my friends. Pity my weakness and deliver me, O Lord; deliver me and support me.

XLVII

1854?

It is almost impossible to conceive how truth can be other than absolute; yet man's truth is never absolute because the basis of Fact is hypothesis.

It has been proved that the probability of the premisses is always greater than that of the conclusion, or that these starting hypotheses are the truest of facts. How the consciousness humbles the arrogance of intellect that the most plausible truths at which it has arrived are the ones at which it has guessed.

XLIX

1859

On the Classification of the Human Faculties

Who will give us the true one at last? Here is one which I offer as presenting some merits:

Man   1 awakens and rouses himself
     2 he sees
     3 he thinks
     4 he desires
     5 he does
     6 he enjoys and suffers
     7 he respects and loves

I have elsewhere advanced the classification of the I-impulse, the it-impulse and the Thou-impulse, but that is not a classification according to faculties. That the present classification includes everything needs no proof, everything is there which has been inserted into any other system.

2 Every faculty is a real one.

3 No faculty is the same as another, for arousing is not volition, nor enjoyment perception.

LI

1859

However immense our science may become, we are only burrowing light into an infinitude of darkness. Once an infinitude, always an infinitude.

LIV

1860 November 25

Every man his own Metaphysician.

LV

1860 November 25

I have come to the conclusion that our primary conceptions are not simple but complex; that our elementary conceptions are not independent but linked complexedly together; that nevertheless properly speaking we have no *à priori* synthetical propositions, and that axioms are only definitions.

LXIV

1864 March 27

Just as Science cannot advance without Philosophy—because (to use Kant's expressions) Induction pure is Blind—so Philosophy cannot exist without science—because Deduction pure is Void.

Science and Philosophy must advance together. If science casts aside Philosophy it will become Chinese. If philosophy does not study science, it will remain what it is.

If philosophy has the question on hand, whether things are in themselves unknown, or whether they are knowable through their attributes, let it look at the question thus. Substance is that which is permanent in events. *Mass* is permanent *actually*, hence it is *really* substance. But it is *supposably* transient, hence it is *nominally* accident.

Let philosophy analyze the conceptions of zoological classification, and extract the essential.

Nature suggests and the mind thinks out the suggestion.

LXX

1866 Nov. 20

What is not a question of a possible experience is not a question of fact.

LXXII

1867 June 18

Man is nature's first essay towards the production of an intellectual animal. He is not that, but is a prophecy of it, perhaps.

LXXIII

1868 Feb. 17

Positively the most important part of the most advanced sciences, Mechanics and Astronomy, has been merely metaphysical, twisting things into shape. So morphology.

LXXV

1888 March 17

The best maxim in writing, perhaps, is really to love your reader for his own sake.

The Sense of Beauty never furthered the Performance of a single Act of Duty

MS 12: 26 March 1857

"Schiller, in his Esthetic Letters, observes that the sense of beauty never furthered the performance of a single act of duty" (Ruskin).

Is it possible that the great philosophical poet of the age has contented himself with an "observation" on such a subject—an observation, too, so contrary to daily experience? Ruskin is one of those who, without pretending to understand what they term the "German Philosophy," yet presume to censure it.[1] If he had read the letter which follows the one to which he refers he would have found the words: "Beauty is in the highest degree fruitful with respect to knowledge and morality." We must go nearer to the fountain-head, then, if we seek Schiller's view of the matter, and I think I cannot do better than to devote this Theme to a most brief exposition of the doctrine of the *Esthetic Letters,* so far as it relates to our present subject.

The first thing to be done is to define beauty. This is Schiller's definition:

All things which can ever be objects of perception may be considered under four different relations. A fact can relate directly to our sensuous condition (our existence and well-being), that is its *physical* quality. Or it can relate to the *understanding* and furnish us with knowledge; that is its *logical* quality. Or it can relate to our will, and be considered as an object of choice for a rational being; that is its *moral* quality. Or finally, it can relate to the entirety of our different powers, without being a definite object for any single one of them; that is its *æsthetic* quality. A man may recommend himself to us with his obligingness; we regard him through the medium of his conversation; he may inspire us with respect for his character, but finally, independent of all

---

1. I fear I may fall under this reproach in the present instance.

this, and without having regard in our judgement either to any law or any design, he may please us, in pure contemplation, through his empirical expression.

Experience affords unanswerable arguments both for the moral utility and moral evil of a cultivated taste; there seems, then, to be a false beauty which sometimes misleads experience. We must seek then a pure idea of beauty, by which we can test experience. Such an idea of beauty, if it exists, is to be inferred from what our nature renders possible, and beauty will discover itself to be a necessary condition of humanity. It will be necessary, then, in the first place, to develope the purely *à priori* idea of humanity.

Man consists of Person and Condition—analysis can go no further. Now, from these elements of humanity arise two impulses; from Person, the impulse which produces form, which insists on absolute formality and would resolve every thing that is mere world[2] into itself, and bring harmony into all its mutations; from Condition, the *sensuous impulse*, which insists upon absolute reality, and would convert all pure ideas into manifold realities, and make all dispositions apparent. The first impulse gives *laws*, the second creates *cases*.

At first sight these impulses, because contrary seem contradictory, but this is not the case. It is true no third *fundamental* impulse reconciling the two is possible, but since they do not conflict in the same objects they can easily coexist, and in perfect harmony, whence arises a third impulse, the result of the perfect balance of the other two, which since it is the condition of a complete humanity and relates to the entirety of our different powers, thus coinciding with our original definition, may be regarded as the impulse which creates beauty. Schiller calls it the play-impulse, because play, that which is neither internally nor externally constrained and, while we are in the esthetic state, the balance of the two fundamental impulses, produces perfect freedom.

Having thus analyzed beauty it merely remains for us to apply our idea of it to answering the question, "what are its results with respect to morality?"

Now it will be observed that beauty gives the mind no particular direction or tendency—hence it can have no result either for the intellect or the will, and can help us to perform no single duty. On the other

2. The formless contents of time.

hand, it places the mind in a state of "infinite determinableness" so that it can turn in any direction and is in perfect freedom, hence, beauty is in the highest degree fruitful with respect to knowledge and morality.

It may be compared to sleep. Sleep, like beauty, puts us in a state of ability to do our duty, but it does not further the performance of it. Sleep is unlike beauty, inasmuch as the latter is an active and the former a passive state.

I have thus given Schiller's view of the matter; I have not attempted an analysis of the *Esthetic Letters*, but merely given such arguments as applied to this subject arranged according to the requirements of the subject.

I shall add nothing more. Schiller seems to have said everything which can be said, and it is difficult to repeat his thoughts, without the splendid language in which he has clothed them recurring to and occupying the mind.

Raphael and Michael Angelo
compared as men

MS 21: 22 October 1857

[I have hardly changed a word in this theme since Thursday, but I have added a synopsis, and am surprised myself to find how much method there is in it.]

SYNOPSIS

INTRODUCTION. Necessity for this comparison, on account of the near approach of both minds to the Golden Mean.—Their faults almost hidden by opposite virtues. PRELIMINARY OBSERVATION. What Qualities should be omitted from this comparison. PROPOSITION. Pith of my comparison, that Michael Angelo's was a masculine and Raphaello's a feminine mind. DEFINITION. What the above difference consists in. ARGUMENT. Illustration drawn from Good-Will as it appeared in each. OBJECTION ANSWERED, that I am making Michael Angelo the greater man. Why Raphael had more artistic Genius. CONCLUSION. Sum of my comparison.

Raphael and Michael Angelo seem to have been made to be compared. Their virtues are easily enough seen but the faults and imperfections of each would quite elude us if the superior excellencies of the other did not point them out. Certain shades of difference, too, in those good qualities which they possess in common will be brought out more clearly by comparison; for they are very different men. Especially the mind of each is so well balanced that I am sure it is only the other's which enables us to see any preponderance from the Golden Mean in either.

Thus, in their best days, Michael Angelo was old, Raphael young, and we can discern, by comparing them together that they have corresponding faults.

Michael Angelo, for instance, seemed (at this time[1]) to want self-confidence: he feared to undertake the painting of the Sistine Chapel, a task which I need not say he proved equal to. Raphael never would have hesitated in such a case; he erred the other way, a fact which we never should know, however, if he had not attempted to imitate Michael Angelo. But observe how Michael Angelo in his old age is still young; he retains his vivacity, he retains his power, and when he can no longer hope to improve and sees himself outdone by a stripling, envy, which would seem almost inevitable, finds no place in his bosom. Raphael, too, is old in his youth, which is very well proved by the fact that the heat of his temperament in nowise retarded the maturity of his mind.

By their very greatness, these men have much in common; but I must remember that my object, in a comparison, is to exhibit their relations to each other and this can only be done by showing their differences not their similarities. Their great difference, then, is this,—Michael Angelo's was a masculine, Raphaello's a feminine mind; nor is this a difference of intellect, alone; it extends to their taste, as exhibited in their productions and to their morals.[2] This is a common observation. May I venture, now, to question the usual statement of the difference between the male and female nature?

The common notion, I believe, is that

$$\text{The Understanding:Man} = \text{The Heart:Woman}$$

hence,

$$\text{The Understanding} + \text{Heart:Man} + \text{Woman} = \text{The Understanding:Man}$$

but the understanding is supposed to be the essential faculty of men; now the understanding *plus* the heart is not the essential faculty of men with women or humanity, that is, if the word *heart* is used with any definiteness.

1. Not certainly in his Youth.
2. Connected with this, perhaps, is the fact that M. succeeded better with male, R. with female faces.

The *heart* is that which loves; which flies toward a fellow being, as such. The sensibilities do not do this, neither do they conceive; hence they are a distinct element of the soul. In my opinion

1. The Intellect &c. or that which says I,
2. The Heart &c. or that which says THOU,
3. The Sense &c. or that which says IT,

compose the inward nature. Why I think these include everything, I will not detail here, thus much I have been obliged to say as a key to what follows. Now I cannot think that the element marked 2. which includes that charity which is the foundation of christianity has been given to one class of persons, naturally, more than to another. At any rate, I think, that as a fact, it is the element marked 3. which is the real characteristic of women; men have as much *love* though not so much *affection* as they.[3] Both these qualities come under the general head of good-will. Let us then examine and compare the good-will of Michael Angelo and Raphael.

Michael Angelo had the reputation of being a stern man, which is no wonder though he by no means deserved the name. Like all strongly masculine minds, he worked hard and worked in solitude, but no one can read his letter to Urbino on the death of his servant, for instance, and still think he wanted, I will not say heart, but affection. Raphaello's was one of those natures that seem to contradict the saying—"that among great men there is not one who has been transported to a mad degree by love." Yet really he does not contradict it. His affection for the Fornarina, deep as it was, was sufficiently subdued by his love for his art never quite to run away with his understanding. In place of the ready popularity and absolute inability to displease[4] which held Raphael, Michael Angelo possessed affections which his reason controlled; no one could compel him to love by idle flattery. Raphael needed no *Angelo* in his name,—the trait was obvious enough; perhaps, too, he deserved the name less than Michael for he could not help being

3. This leads me to the following remarkable result. Since 1. is the essential quality of man, and 3. of woman; and since 2. though not $1 + 3$ results necessarily from their union (just as in arithmetic 7 results from 3 and 4, though not the same as three with four) then man + woman do not make humanity but their sum does. N.B. = is not the same as *is* though it amounts to the same thing.

4. It is said he could not draw an ugly face.

amiable nor could he keep from unworthy likings on the one hand, nor, on the other, from envy usually considered as the mark of a small mind. On Michael's freedom from envy, I have already remarked. I will add, here, that all his impetuosity never led him beyond perfect purity—that, too, in an age consecrated to vice.

The exact difference then between Michael Angelo and Raphael, I should state to be this: Michael Angelo was intellectual, Raphael sensitive, so I should expect that one to talk of his *ideas* of beauty, justice, truth, etc., this of his *sense* of beauty, justice, &c. I should expect that one to excel in understanding, this in making use of his understanding. As to largeness of view, Michael Angelo had more grandeur, Raphael more variety; as we say, the one represented the Sublime, the other the Beautiful. Raphael was inferior to Michael Angelo in power on account of their difference in kind. Self was a centre for the latter; his intellectual faculties were *self*-directed, *self*-poised, *self*-ordered. In the former there is a conglomeration of the finest qualities—sympathies and sensibilities without a centre.

As to morality Michael Angelo was one of those men who might as well be an atheist, as far as outward relations go; but this was because of a deep-seated principle of morality which would have rendered it impossible for him not to believe. Raphael was a man very sensitive to religion but he had none of that stern unrelenting morality whose *"must"* is as strong as a physical *"must."* He fell away but never very far, his heart being too genuine. In short, Michael Angelo was a really moral man, Raphael was not this but he was really a religious man.

Finally, as to artistic genius, Raphael's was beyond cavil greater than Michael Angelo's whose mind was stronger but less flexible and docile. He was a man characterized by gravity and earnestness, but nevertheless both gentle and fiery, too. Raphael, beside other men almost superhuman, was after all a mere boy to Michael Angelo. And this perhaps was the cause of his greater success. He could absorb the styles of other artists and enter into their spirit. Michael Angelo, though remarkable for his powers of imitation, could never assimilate other artists into himself nor could he produce from himself alone anything beginning to equal the results which Raphael thus arrived at.

This ends this unskillful comparison of Raphael the artist and Michael Angelo the *man*.

A Scientific Book of Synonyms

MS 20: November–December 1857

Preface

Most works of this kind have proved to be little better than failures, and the reasons seem not very difficult to point out. The differences of the only synonyms one would ever take the trouble to refer to a vocabulary for are of such a delicate and evanescent character that, like the flavor of a fine wine, when we try to notice them they are gone; so that when a man sits down to write about them he is puzzled about words which he could never use amiss. The differences no longer suggest themselves to him, but he has to suggest them to himself. Now as it is commonly said that no two words have exactly the same meaning, so it is also true that none have exactly the same force *in any respect*. Of course, then, the writer no sooner suggests a difference to himself than he finds it accords with the facts; but in this way he entirely misses the object of the work which is to note the *important* differences.

Moreover writers do not make it sufficiently clear in each case whether the two words refer to different objects, or to the same object regarded as a function of different variables, or whether their difference consists merely in the style of the words themselves. For instance, I open Graham's *Synonymes* at random and read

Actual qualifies what is done, and refers to a previous act; *real* refers to what simply exists as an object of thought. The former is active, the latter passive in meaning. When we speak of the actual condition of the country, we signify the condition into which it has been brought by previous acts; when we speak of its real condition, we mean the state in which it exists as an object of contemplation. Actual is opposed to supposititious; real is opposed to imaginary, feigned, or artificial. An actual fact, a real sentiment.

I fear to comment on this article as it is a thousand times less clear than the difference in meaning of the words. I would explain them thus:—

Whatever is actual is real, viz. that which is a possible object of sensation. But, as we shall presently see, actuality refers to the relation of
the object to our understanding, reality to the existence of the object
itself. An examination of their opposites will best explain this. Reality
is opposed to shadowiness and non-existence. By shadowiness I mean
a sort of half-way between existence and non-existence, *in the object
itself. Actuality* stands between Possibility and necessity, and therefore
refers you see to the modality of the conception. The same difference
exists between asserting and affirming between being and existing (not
strictly observed) subsisting again meaning dependent existence, predicating corresponds to it. Now let us try another work Whately's
Synonyms.

> To be, To exist: These two verbs are often used in a nearly similar sense:
> but to exist refers more to the original nature of things than to be. If we say
> there could not be freedom of the press under a despotic government we
> merely imply that it would not be allowed; but the phrase freedom of the
> press could not exist under a despotic government would imply an inherent
> incompatibility in the *nature* of the two institutions.

This is certainly much better than Graham's "active and passive" existence. But if the reader examines the example given he will see that
in this case all the difference in meaning arises from the fact that here
we put the emphasis on *exist* because it is a long and unusual word.
In general this manner of illustrating synonyms is very poor. The following is an example of a better way. If we say "not only that, it *is*"
evidently "it may be" has been suggested; if we say "not only that, it
exists" "it seems to be" has preceded; if we say "at any rate, it *is*" =
whether there is any argument or necessity for it or not, "at any rate, it
exists" does not suggest anything as having very certainly preceded.

In looking in a dictionary under some common word, we are struck
by the great diversity of meaning there laid down though we had never
observed the slightest ambiguity in the use of the word. If the dictionary were arranged on the principle of Passow's *Greek Lexicon*—that is,
if the meanings were arranged in chronological order with dates of
arising and disappearance—a synonym-vocabulary would hardly be
required. But as it is the dictionary serves rather to confuse than in-
struct and a book of synonyms becomes necessary in order to make a
synthesis of the meaning which has been analyzed in the dictionary.
How is this to be done? We have only to look out the same word in

two books of synonyms and then compare it with our own //impression/notion// to be convinced that no guess-work however plausibly sustained in its results by facts will //do/answer// here, but a strict scientific induction is necessary. The process I have followed was this. The first thing to be done was to select words. I began with Metaphysical terms, taking the transcendental philosophy throughout but in cases of importance explaining them according to other systems, also. I then took up the arts and sciences, grammar, rhetoric, &c., and miscellaneous terms. Then I proceeded to words expressive of our feelings, and lastly considered the conjunctions, prepositions, &c.

After having got a word to be explained I generally looked into Roget's *Thesaurus* for as large a number as possible of words of similar meaning.

Next I made general sentences like those above under *is* and *exist*, only of the greatest possible variety for each word, and from these inferred the differences in the meaning of the words.

I then looked up examples in modern authors where I could of the different words and tested my result by them. Lastly I traced where I could the way in which the words came to have the signification I had given to them.

Think Again!

P 1: Harvard Magazine
4 (*April 1858*): *100–105*

> He that knows better how to tame a shrew,
> Now let him speak; 't is charity to show.

MR. EDITOR:—

A writer in the *Magazine* has already awaked to the fact that Shakespeare is not what he is cracked up to be, and proclaims himself a reformer accordingly. But his business will be no very difficult task, if undertaken with characteristic modesty; for few of us either love or read the works of Shakespeare much. As for the *Iliad* and *Odyssey*, they have long been detested by Juniors and Freshmen generally, and the Vedas are now held up by professors to be laughed at by students. Yet these three have been considered the sublimest poems out of the Bible. Does all this show that the delicacies of Tennyson and Browning, or else the inevitable progress of the mind, have given us a distaste for the rudeness and meagreness of these old poets? No. At no time since Shakespeare's day, at least at no time since Nicholas Rowe, have they been so well appreciated. Johnson and Pope, for example, had no kindred feeling with either the Greek or the English poet. This will hardly be questioned, but I will support it by an example or two. Johnson never could wade through Homer, although he was well read on most other branches of Greek literature. He has the following criticism on *Cymbeline:*—

This play has many just sentiments, some natural dialogues, and some pleasing scenes; but they are obtained at the expense of much incongruity. To remark the folly of the fiction, the absurdity of the conduct, the confusion of the names and manners of different times, and the impossibility of the events in any system of life, were to waste criticism upon unresisting imbecility, upon faults too evident for detection and too gross for aggravation.

Pope's perversion of the Homeric spirit in his translation of the *Iliad* is well known; while the absurdity of many of his emendations of Shakespeare, as proved by Theobald, shows that he had no appreciation of that poet.

Compare such critics with Goethe, Schlegel, Coleridge, Hazlitt, Wilson, Douce, Knight, Collier, White, and Wolf, Lachmann, Mure, Tyler, and Gladstone. All of these sit rather as disciples than judges of the authors they criticise; all recognize their unvarying truth. It is not, then, to the age of the world, but to the age of the critics, that we must ascribe a distaste for Homer and Shakespeare in College.

Some devout writer says that almost every healthy mind must be an atheist in one stage of its progress; and it is at least true, that there is a time when we must either apply ourselves to imbibing trustfully the spirit of sublime minds, or rest content with being scoffers. This time comes to most of us in College. If we adopt the latter course, we must turn round; if the other, we are already on the right track. A young man feels sure he sees something unreasonable in Milton or Bacon, or else in the study of natural science in general, or of the dead languages in general, and he is tempted to admire too much his own imitation of the pig's squeal. This ought to be a sign to him that he does not comprehend the author or the science, and he should throw himself into the study of him or it with the more *abandon*.

The argument of the critic of the *Taming of the Shrew* is this:—

Shakespeare makes a radical change occur in the character of one of his heroines.

Radical changes of character never do occur in real life.

Ergo, Shakespeare is not true to nature.

He then suggests to Mr. Shakespeare how he was led into so great a blunder, wherein it lies, and how he might have avoided it.

First, for the origin of the error, he says: "We shall find, I think, that this truly artistic design, so clearly shown in the afterpart of the drama, was an *afterthought*, irreconcilable with Katharina's conduct in the earlier scenes."

Then for the error itself: "Violent she might have been, easily roused to any burst of passion, but there should be no unprovoked outbreak. But listen to her, and judge if Shakespeare has not so far overstepped the line, there can be no consistent return," &c.

Then for the means of avoiding it: "It is the true, masterly, central idea of the play. But was it Shakespeare's idea? It should have been, that is clear. If, however, we refuse to believe that it was, because it ought to have been, his design," &c. That is, if the readers of the *Magazine* will refuse to believe that it was clear to Shakespeare because it is clear to this critic, he is in a condition to proceed with his argument. The wonder is that a masterly idea occurred, even as an afterthought, to so stupid a block as Shakespeare is represented to be.

But it is useless to quote all this. I deny his major premise. Radical changes of character are certainly improbable, but it is unnatural for improbabilities never to occur. They are extraordinary, but a play in which there are no extraordinary workings of character is simply commonplace. Every one of Shakespeare's plays contains something improbable or extraordinary. The delineation of Hamlet's character, which your critic seems to approve, is so extraordinary, that its meaning is not now settled.

I cannot think why he selected so insignificant a field for the exhibition of this great principle of ethics,—that nothing can change the character,—which is unexpressed indeed, and which perhaps suggested itself as an afterthought to the critic, but which is, in fact, the true, masterly, central idea of his article. His argument would have applied very well to the parable of the Prodigal Son. He might say: "Disclaiming all affected singularity, I feel called upon to present a minority report on one of the parables ascribed to our Lord. A bad man never can turn round and become good. Thus Paul by his own account, even before his conversion, still acted according to his ideal of right, and, as he thought, to the glory of God. The prodigal son, therefore, ought to be represented as acting under a mistaken notion that it was his duty to travel; that is clear. But if we refuse to believe that it was, because it ought to have been the Evangelist's account, and critically examine, requiring the parable to prove its own excellence, instead of resting on its reputation, we shall find, I think, that this truthful design, so clearly shown in the after-part of the story, was an afterthought, irreconcilable with the prodigal's conduct in the earlier scenes. Zealous he might have been, but there should be no wickedness. But listen, and judge if Luke has not made him so far overstep the line of propriety, that there could be no consistent return. If so, it is proved that the parable never came from the lips of our Saviour."

Now, if Shakespeare brought about an extraordinary result, he also used extraordinary means; namely, the power of love, which has worked a miracle with every Christian.

We condemn the writer's verbal criticisms as much as his general one. People who like gaudy poems had better shelve Shakespeare, and take up Alexander Smith, the Brownings, and Tennyson. And I am afraid they will be disgusted to find that even these poets, except the first, try to avoid showiness, and have a real sympathy with Homer and Shakespeare and the Vedas.

If your critic has a different reason for not admiring certain passages and plays, we suggest that he publish a new and improved edition of Shakespeare,—since he hints he could sometimes do better than he. Those admired passages of which he "ventures to say the sapient critic" (who is this?) "might do as well himself," should be rewritten, and as for the *Taming of the Shrew*, let that be made over again, according to its true, masterly, central idea. The thing has already been attempted by Dryden and others, but it has never succeeded, and we should rapturously hail a really improved Shakespeare.

We are not afraid to meet the critic's arguments, but even if we could not, they are not worth answering. It is an important lesson that must some time be learnt, that our reason must govern, sometimes curb itself. Now our business here in College is not, it is true, to stop originating, for thus we should lose the faculty, but to learn from master-spirits and originate with them, not to controvert them and originate against them. We are not yet men, and are not to arrogate the office of men. A contrary spirit is not one of progress. Thus, a young man thinks he ought to have no model, under the impression that, if he does, he never will have an ideal of his own. A chemist might as well resolve that he never would read a chemistry, in order that he might bring a fresh mind into the department.

When the writer has acquired some understanding of Shakespeare, we shall be happy to discuss the question of whether Shakespeare had a plan, of whether Mrs. Clarke understands Katharina, or of whether Shakespeare's images are commendable. At present, this is all we shall say on the subject.

THE NORMAL MAN.

P.S. (*Afterthought.*) After all is said, I must confess your critic's argument is plausible, and if his theory can really be established,—as I must say I think it needs to be,—it will shed much light on Shakespeare's mode of writing and of living. It is well known that Shakespeare founded his play upon an old comedy, called the *Taming of the*

Shrew, published in 1594 (again in 1607, and again by Steevens in his *Six Old Plays*). This also represents the Shrew as reduced to entire subjection, so that, since this idea presented itself to Shakespeare as an afterthought, we have come at once upon the astonishing fact that Shakespeare began to rewrite plays before he had once read them, seen them played, or knew the plot.

This will lower the authority of Shakespeare, which the writer truly represents as an unfair advantage which Shakespeare has over himself. His *quasi* claim rests, not, as the writer says, on his reputation, but upon his accuracy. But if he wrote plays so that an afterthought so important could occur to him, his accuracy amounts to nothing. Authority, however, is at best an unfair advantage, and it is but charitable to be a little inaccurate.

Analysis of Genius

MS 42: 19 March 1859

It is important to observe that we have been desired to discuss not the meaning of the *word* "genius" but the question what genius itself consists in; it is not the question whether Dr. Johnson applied the word "genius" to the right thing, but whether the thing to which he applied it consists in "large general powers accidentally determined in a particular direction." Hence it would not be enough to say for instance that genius is contemplative heroism for this is not an explanation but merely an exposition of the admitted conception of genius and could form the basis of no discussion whatever.

Much less should I have a right to take the ground that genius consists in activity of mind or that genius is talent combined with the moral sense, because in either case it would be evident that I applied the word to a different class of minds from that which Dr. Johnson gives to it; and his application of the word we are required for the nonce to admit. Dr. Johnson gives in one sentence a definition and an analysis of genius. As a definition we admit it, but as an analysis we doubt it, we criticise it, we discuss the whole subject and if need be present an analysis of our own.

We must take care to stick to the definition; to call genius genius and to call nothing else that. For this purpose it will be well to compare our final result with some standard intellect as an example of what genius is, and luckily enough English literature furnishes us with the very thing in the mind of Samuel Johnson. "A mind of large general powers accidentally determined in a particular direction." The definition is pat, the instance is truly normal. And I now see what the great fault of *The Lives of the Poets* is. Instead of being written by a man cut out for just that, they are by a man who only had a genius for the pursuit.

I am now going to begin with a remark that sounds like a definition. A FACULTY *is an original power of doing a* SPECIAL *thing.* I will not venture to state positively that this is the meaning established by usage. I only wish to use it so, myself. I will therefore write the word in blue ink through the remainder of the forensic, to avoid introducing a general abuse of the term.[1] Otherwise my class-mates might hear my definition and adopt it, the College might adopt it from them, the alumni might adopt it from them, America might adopt it from them; and if it went on any further all would be well. But suppose that those who use the word with more propriety should here make a vigorous stand against the encroachments of the new definition. The contest would wax high. A score of mediators would come forward with new definitions and the end would be that the word would be so loaded with contradictory definitions as to be utterly useless and would be discarded by the wise and degenerate into a slang or meaningless word. To be sure as I am writing a forensic the danger of this result could hardly be called imminent, but if it were a dictionary I were making, only what has happened to *genius* would occur again if in College and the world faculty were to become a thing without a name.

I will elucidate my definition a little. I did not say that Faculty is an original power of doing a particular thing. I might as well have said so but in order to be more emphatic I said A faculty is an original power of doing an especial thing. Dr. Johnson says the man of genius has only general powers. I say he has special powers. He admits his general powers are *accidentally* determined in a particular direction. I insist he has special powers inborn—**faculties.** Dr. Johnson must believe that man in general is destitute of **faculties** otherwise he makes his man of genius *peculiar* in not having them, whereas he says the only essential difference between him and other men is in the possession of larger general powers.

Now I am aware and I acknowledge before going a step further that whoever disbelieves the doctrine of innate ideas must disbelieve that man has **faculties.** Which is unfortunate as I am to be read by but one person and he in that class. No matter. I shall endeavor to counterbalance that by showing that all who do believe in innate ideas must also believe in **faculties.** So that for them Dr. Johnson is wrong.

Mental **faculties** I should have said; for bodily, it is very evident we

---

1. The fun of this consisted in the fact that Bowen was color blind.

have **faculties.** I have a **faculty** of bending my arm in one direction and have none of bending it in any other. Indeed it is obviously inevitable that whatever has organs has **faculties;** and so it is with those actions which are on the boundaries between the mental and the corporeal but which still depend upon or are connected with a complexity of organism, as seeing, remembering and recollecting.

The longest vibrations which the eye perceives measure $\frac{1}{40,000}$ of an inch; the shortest vibrations which the ear perceives measure $\frac{1}{2}$ an inch. Supposing the eye were delicate enough to perceive any of the intermediate vibrations we should *see* them. Supposing the ear delicate enough to perceive the same vibrations we should *hear* them. Accordingly we not only have bodily organs for receiving certain vibrations, but also in ourselves faculties of seeing and of hearing. And it is not difficult to see that this must hold good in all cases that special functions always imply speciality of organism or of faculty.

To resume our argument to the noölogist. All our conceptions the noologists admit are produced are occasioned by experience. Even in dreams in the wildest flights of fancy, every element of thought is an experience simply contained by the memory or reproduced by the imagination. Thus I have in my mind's eye a shade blue such as I have never seen—but the elements of it (*blue, shade,* and *degree*) are elements of actual experiences; and so it is evident that every fancy must be entirely made up of elements of actual experiences. And so it must be with our innate ideas and so the noölogists admit it to be. They deny however that any peculiarity of the object enters into these; so that, admitting they are produced by thinking an object, and denying they are produced by the object, the only thing left to them is to consider they are produced by the very act of thinking—itself.

Now thinking is in its nature a single act, but whenever a plurality of effects is produced by a single cause there must be a complexity of organism—it is a case of speciality of functions which we have just seen implies special faculties.

I have now proved that the question under discussion depends on our opinions on innate ideas. And having arrived at this point I seem to have an excuse for laying down my pen. I will however confess that I believe in innate ideas because I have seen no sufficient refutation of the argument from universality and necessity.

The necessary is that whose actuality is determined by the universal conditions of experience—whether these be regarded as conditions of knowing or conditions of being. But the actuality of nothing which is entirely independent of experience can be determined by the conditions (as such) of experience. Now that which is given by experience, the empirical, is independent of experience. That is the argument from necessity; the argument from universality is just like it.

The universal is that which is made *one* by our contemplation of its plurality. The unity of the empirical does not depend on our thought hence it cannot have any universality *à priori*.

Certain conceptions as relation, dimension, &c., are universal and necessary hence they are not given by experience.

There are two answers to be made to those who try to find an exceptional kind of experience to which the above does not apply. The first is that such power of knowing if it were found would indeed be peculiar, for it must comply with these two conditions, first itself must determine the actuality of its object, second if we choose to think its objects one that must make them so. The second answer is that if the consciousness of volition did indeed give the conceptions of universality and necessity—not to a man here and there merely but to the whole human race and by necessity then these conceptions would be derived *à priori* from the constitution of the human mind—which accords with the definition of an innate idea.

But independently of the argument from universality and necessity, I still cannot see how relative knowledge differs from knowledge in general. Knowledge of a thing is having it in my consciousness—not the thing itself surely—what then but something to which the thing is related? This related thing—this *idea*—is born of my consciousness and of the object—and was produced partly by the object partly by me; now in so far as it took its origin in my mental constitution it is an innate idea.

I must now consider the question solved as well for those who accept the doctrine of innate ideas as for those who reject it. But for persons unsettled on that point it becomes necessary to adduce an entirely different argument.

It seems to me that to show one person has a special disability for performing certain acts shows that the rest of mankind have a faculty for performing it. And I think that it is a fact which can be established that a not very small proportion of the human race are abnormal with respect to certain special functions of judgement, and that there is nothing accidental which suffices to account for it. I admit it will be very difficult to establish this; that much, that nearly all will be left to the reader. And I contend that it *must* be very hard to establish such a conclusion because it can only be done by nice observation within one's own circle. All that I can do is to point out what kinds of facts to look for.

In the first place then one must not expect to find persons through whom any simple conceptions can never be rammed. They are seldom or never wholly deficient in the powers to perform certain acts, only they do them with special difficulty. Which special difficulty implies a special power to do them in other people. They do them with special difficulty although their education must have been on these points no different from usual—showing an original special power in other people.

The power of regarding a *case* as singular as *sui generis*, one would suppose belonged alike to all men. Yet observation reveals enormous differences of this power. The accidental educational differences are very great. One man has a tendency to regard everything as *sui generis;* another will never do it except in the plainest cases. Sometimes this is owing to a ridiculous dislike to certain conceptions. This is very far from being always the case. On the contrary very frequently a man is dazzled by ideas however common-place to other people which seldom present themselves to his own mind. Notwithstanding that so large a proportion of the cases of eccentricity with regard to that function can be put down and often traced to accidental determinations, a few are not to be accounted for on any such hypothesis. So it is with the kindred functions of regarding cases as exceptional and regarding them as forming a total as *making* a law.

No one has any right to say with regard to this—as though it were a theory—that it is likely or unlikely. They know nothing about it until they have made the observations, for these differences are seldom glaring.

An acquaintance has a deficiency of the faculty of taking a half-way ground. He can easily assert or deny but he hardly knows what is meant by predicating something somewhat.

Many persons doubt *free will*. The normal man cannot doubt it. There is no question that these people have as many data as we, but they have a partial deficiency in the faculty of seizing the fact of *free will*. It cannot be an accidental determination. They have had presented to them the same arguments *pro* as the normal man has. He *can't* be argued away from the position; they have been. It is necessary to assume they are deficient in some way. You may put the deficiency where you please. If it is a deficiency of faith—we have a faculty of faith; if of seeing himself—we have a faculty of inner sense. If of logic, it still indicates a faculty.

I will now run over the course of my argument.

I wished to show Dr. Johnson was wrong. I began by showing that unless he was, man has no faculties—because the man of genius hasn't and he doesn't differ in that respect from other men.

The Axioms of Intuition
After Kant

MS 50: May 1859

All Intuitions are Extensive Quantities.

An extensive quantity is that wherein the representation of parts renders possible (and therefore necessarily antecedes in the synthesis) the representation of the whole.

Axiom I

Space has three dimensions.

Proof. Space is the form of the external sense. Our knowledge of external things can only be of qualities; and since all knowledge is discrimination I can only know them by their difference of quality. And this difference of quality must exist at each moment of time. It cannot be a mere difference in quantity, because different quantities differing also in quality must be observable at the same time. And difference in quality necessitates the possibility of entire difference of quality; and this therefore must be expressed in the conditional form of intuition. But since space and time are the only forms of intuition, there can be no difference in the universe except difference in space and difference in time. This entire difference in quality therefore is a difference in space not a difference in quantity—an entire difference in position with no difference in distance—in short is dimension.

Space therefore must have two dimensions to represent the qualities of things. Now, again, our knowledge of things can be only relative. Hence, we must be able to perceive a difference between the relations of things to us and to each other. This implies the possibility of an entire difference in relation, which must exist in position, and occasions the third dimension. ∴ &c.

Axiom II

A straight line is the shortest way between two points.

Proof. Let a and b be extensive quantities. Now since 1 A part is that which is formed by the synthesis of units—or is a unit. 2 A whole is that which is formed by the synthesis of parts. 3 Units are similar things—the units of any extensive quantity must be similar and similar to the whole. Therefore an extensive quantity must possess all its qualities in the same intensity throughout. Let then

β_b = the degree to which any quality β
    is realized in each unit of b

β_a = the degree to which any quality β
    is realized in each unit of a

$$\text{And suppose } b\beta_b = a\beta_a$$

Then if $\beta_b > \beta_a$	But if $\beta_b = \beta_a$
$b < a$	$b = a$

Let now a and b be lines, as they can be since lines are intuitions; and let β be the quality of running in the direction of b. Since this quality is possessed in uniform intensity, the lines must be straight. Now we further suppose, in accordance with the first equation that both lines run just as far in the direction of b. Then the interpretation of the other equations is that if the lines are oblique or perpendicular b is the shortest, but that if they are parallel they are of the same length.

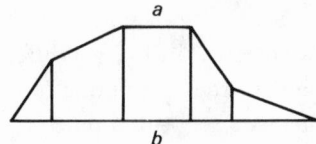

Now in the case of two ways between two points, if a is not straight, it can be divided into lines which are oblique to b and those which are parallel to b, and it runs just as far (as much) as b in the direction of b. Now of those parts which are oblique to b they must all be longer than the corresponding parts of b and of those parts which are parallel to b they can none be shorter than b. So that, taking the sum, $a > b$. $\therefore$ &c.

Axiom III

Two lines cannot enclose space.

Proof. By this is meant that they cannot enclose a portion of space having two dimensions.

To do this they must have different directions (otherwise dimension would not be introduced) and must have two points in common, otherwise nothing would be enclosed.

That which is formed solely by the synthesis of units must depend for its existence solely upon the existence of units. But since lines and units of lines are mere representations, the line *AF* which is formed solely

ABCDE⅂

by the synthesis of the units *AB* &c. must depend for its representation upon the representation of the units, and is an extensive quantity. Hence no quality can exist in the line *AF* which did not exist in some degree in the lines *AB* &c. And the point *F* can have no relation to *A* which was not had in some degree by the points *D C B* &c. Hence ⅂ has the same direction from *A* as *B* has; and *AF* must have the same direction as *AB*. Now by definition *AB* has the same direction as *B* from *A* hence the direction of ⅂ from *A* must be that of the line *AF*. Now the direction of *F* from *A* does not vary; therefore two straight lines drawn between *F* and *A* cannot vary in direction. ∴ &c.

/Three Essays on
Infinity and God/

An essay on the Limits of Religious thought written to prove that we can reason upon the nature of God

MS 53: August 1859

I

What can we discuss? Can we discuss nothing we do not comprehend? Can we not even discuss that which has no existence in nature or the imagination? We can discuss whatever we can syllogise upon. We can syllogize upon whatever we can define. And strange as it is we can give intelligible comprehensible definitions of many things which can never be themselves comprehended.

I will give two instances of this; one simple and the other practical. Suppose somebody should talk about an OG and when you asked him what he meant he should say it was a four-sided triangle. You would proceed to show that he had no such conception that nobody had. You would reason upon that which you could not conceive of. This instance is too elementary. Suppose someone should tell me he could imagine two persons interchanging identities. I should proceed to reason on the pretended imagination and show that it was inconceivable.

We can therefore comprehend definitions, when we cannot conceive of that which they define. That is to say; a synthesis of some conceptions cannot be made. Now in all cases there is but one cause of this, and that is that our faculties will not make the synthesis. Nevertheless, the reason divides the cases into two, and these I shall speak of hereafter. It is sufficient at present to conclude that whatever can be defined can be discussed.

II

Can the infinite be defined? Is it not a simple conception? The term *simple conception* has not its metaphysical sense in Logic. In Metaphysics it signifies one that is formed by the energy of a single faculty. And in this sense most simple ideas may be defined. For they may have complex and crossing relations by which we can draw their coordinates. And in this way I propose to define the infinite.

Let us think and consider the object of our thought (for convenience sake) as an event. Every event is a relation or dependency. The motion of a ball through the air, for example, is a complex event composed of an indefinite number of elementary events each of which is the relation of the ball at any moment to itself at the previous moment. Every dependency has one of three necessary modes. The first is community. This is where there is no dependency and therefore no event at all, as two balls at the same instant of time. The second necessary mode is causality, which is the mode of dependence everything at each moment has upon things at the last moment. The third necessary mode is influx which is the mode of the dependence substance to form, character to acts, things to qualities. I call these the necessary modes of dependence. It is merely a more true and philosophical expression for the modes of necessary dependence.

Not the necessary modes of dependence only but all modality whatever has one of three perfect degrees. The first is Possibility; this is where we merely think a thing and it really exists in no mode whatever. The second perfect degree is Actuality; this is where the thing is or occurs. The third perfect degree is Necessity, where it could not have been otherwise. I call these *perfect* degrees because, not meaning by possibility, numerical probability nor by necessity syllogistic sequence, —nothing subjective but something objective—I consider them as standing for those degrees of modality.

Not only the perfect degrees of modality, but all degree whatsoever has one of three successive stages. The first is nullity, the second Positivity, and the third Perfection. I call these successive and not retrogressive or contemporaneous because they are stages towards perfection.

Not only the successive stages of degree but all stage whatever has one of three temporal expressions: Retrogression, Contemporaneity, succession.

There are three formal intuitions of expression: Consciousness, Space, and Time.

There are three total quantities of intuition: Notion, substance, form. All notions I call "notion" &c.

There are three infinite qualities of quantity: Unity, Plurality, Totality. Infinite because possessed beyond limitation.

Lastly there are three Influxual Dependencies of Quality viz.:— Negation, Reality, Infinity.

I have run through the categories in this way in order to show precisely what infinity is and where in the scheme of conceptions it stands. It is only qualities which can be infinite, and infinity is to be defined in two ways: either we can say that which is to be predicated of Unity, Plurality, and Totality as Qualities of Quantity. Or we can say it is that Influxual Dependency of Quality which surpasses Reality.

This explains how though we cannot think Infinity we can judge about it. For we either predicate something of it which is common to Reality or which is not. An instance of the first is where we say that $\frac{1}{2}$ an infinite line is half the length of that line. Here we take as a premiss Infinity is an influxual dependency of quality. An instance of the second is where we say Infinitesimals may be neglected. Here the premiss is Infinity surpasses reality.

Such being infinity what idea have we of it and how does that idea differ from our idea of all the quantities of intuition?

I wish now to draw the distinction I referred to before between the two classes of thinkables. When an object is presented to us we immediately perform the following analysis. But first I will give the common and erroneous enumeration of the elements

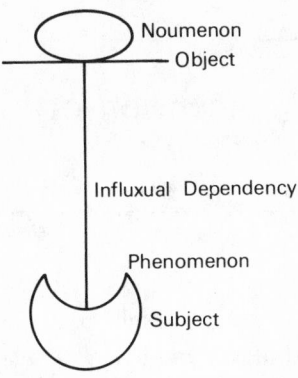

The objection to this representation is that while the phenomenon alone is what we are conscious of, mental elements enter into all but the noumenon, and the influxual dependency is really between the object and the noumenon not between the phenomenon and the object. I represent the analysis thus

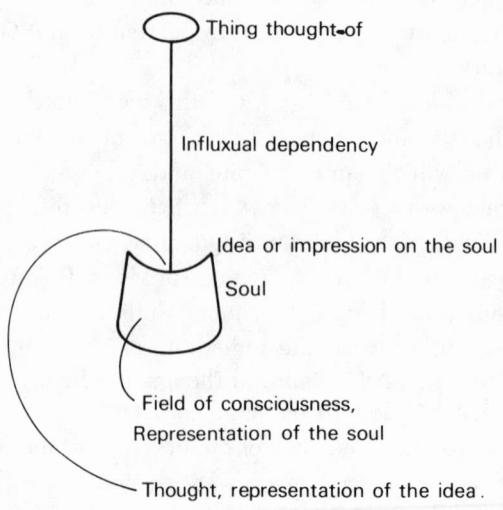

That which may be thought-of—which is a source of influx—I call a thing. Whatever is not a thought I call unthought.

/The Conception of Infinity/

MS 53: August 1859

What can be discussed? We can syllogise on whatever we can define. We can define many things of which we cannot conceive. What we define is never a thing but an idea or a pretended or supposed idea.

Now we can define ideas which we cannot think. Thus a four-sided triangle is a defined pseudo-idea. We can reason upon it and show that it is an absurdity.

What is infinity? How is that defined? What is infinity? It is not the conception of a thing, neither is it the conception of the quality of a thing. If we can think of a good man, it is because in the first place we have a notion of man and in the second place we have the conception of good and in the third place we can combine one conception with the other. When this is done, I express the synthesis by saying that an influxual dependency of *good* upon *man* is conceived of. Influxual dependency has three degrees. 1st It may be negative as when we say *the man is not good.* 2nd It may be real as when we say *the man is more or less good* or *pretty good* or *very good,* in short when he has goodness in degree. And 3rd it is infinite when we say *he is perfectly good.* Then he has goodness beyond degree. Infinity then is only to be predicated of qualities and only of qualities conceived to be possessed. We can therefore analyse the conception of infinity; we can state its relations to other conceptions although the conception itself we never have.

Infinity is that influxual dependency of quality which is further from negation than reality is; and it is clear that every proposition we make about infinity is deduced from this. Thus, Twice an infinite line is twice as long as a finite line depends on the premiss that infinity is a positive influxual dependency of quality. Infinitely small quantities may be neglected depends on the fact that infinity surpasses reality.

Pseudo-conceptions or conceptions that we cannot think are of two kinds. The first is where the conceptions into which we analyze it in definition refuse to be combined, where they are contradictory of themselves or the soul's nature. And here for the sake of system I might give a formal proof that such conceptions are conceptions of no *thing.*

The second case is where the elementary conceptions do not refuse to be combined, but where our power of synthesizing is inadequate, so that the combination never can be completed. Pseudo-conceptions of this kind may or may not have objective validity; in this respect they stand just where real conceptions stand. Their truth in any particular case however is not susceptible of positive proof; we can never be certain that what we think *infinite* is anything more than *very.* In this respect, however, they stand precisely where negative conceptions stand; and whenever we suppose a negative we do in effect suppose a negative infinite.

Where, then, in the mind, stands this conception of infinity. It is certainly not in the region of consciousness, any more than the four-sided triangle. The four-sided triangle is not in the soul at all; is Infinity? If not what follows?

This is not a philosophical question, and to allow the answer to influence our theory would be a proceedure like that of the realists; and the result we shall find to be a realistic theory.

When a thing influences the soul its effect comes into the field of consciousness or not. In the former case we call the modification of consciousness a true thought; in the latter case we may call its influence an unconscious idea. Now FAITH says, the infinite does influence the soul—as infinite. It follows that we have an unconscious idea of it. There then is where the infinite belongs.

When we think of a mind thinking of a thing, our thought has 5 elements. Common analysis enumerates them thus. 1st the *noumenon* or the thing regarded simply, 2nd the *object* or the thing regarded as thought of, 3rd the act of thinking, 4th the *phenomenon* or thought, and 5th the thinker or *Ego*.

Why we can Reason
on the Infinite

MS 53

1859 October 25

What can be discussed? We can syllogise on whatever we can define. We can define many things of which we cannot conceive. What we define is never a thing but an idea or a pseudo-idea. Now we can define ideas which we cannot think; thus a four-sided triangle is a defined pseudo-idea, and we can reason upon it and show that it is an absurdity.

What is infinity? How is that defined? What *is* infinity? It is not the conception of a thing, neither is it the conception of the quality of a thing. If we can think of a good man, it is because in the first place we have a notion of *man* and in the second place we have the conception *good* and in the third place we can form the synthesis of these two. This synthesis I express by saying that an influxual dependency of good and man is conceived of. Influxual dependency is of three kinds:—1st Negative as when we say the *man is not good*, 2nd Limited as when we say *he is good*, third infinite when we give the conception good in all its extent to *man*. Infinity, then, is only to be predicated of qualities, and only of qualities conceived to be possessed. We can therefore analyze the conception of infinity—we can state its relations to other conceptions although the conception itself we never have.

Infinity is that influxual dependency of qualities which is farther from negation than limitation is; and it is clear that every proposition we lay down about infinity is deduced from this. Thus, "twice an infinite line is twice as long as that line" depends on the premiss that infinity is a positive influxual dependency of quality. And in the same way, that Infinitesimals may be neglected depends on the fact that infinity surpasses limitation.

Pseudo-conceptions or conceptions that we cannot think are of two kinds. The first is where the conceptions into which we analyze the pseudo-conception in definition refuse to be combined and are contradictory. And I will in another place give a *formal* proof that such conceptions represent no thing and are not had.

The second case is where the elementary conceptions do not refuse to be combined, but where our power of synthesizing is inadequate and the combination never can be completed. Such are the four grand ideas

Unity
Reality or Infinity
Substance
Necessity.

Pseudo-conceptions of this kind may or may not be true; in this respect they stand just where limited conceptions stand. On the other hand their truth is not susceptible of positive truth; we never can be certain that what we think is *infinite* is anything more than *very*. In this respect, however, they stand precisely where negative conceptions stand; and whenever we suppose a negative we do in effect suppose an inverse infinite.

Proof of the Infinite
Nature of the Creator

MS 61: Summer 1860

The Necessary Sequence of Cause and effect is inseparable from time, therefore, this began when time began and therefore time also was *created* when the Universe was created. Therefore this whole sequence of Causation in time has the dependence of Creation, which is Influx. Therefore since the Universe has been a-going from everlasting the amount of Spiritual Manifestation is *Infinite*. Q.E.D.

I, IT, and THOU
A Book giving Instruction in
some of the Elements of Thought

MS 65: Spring 1861

Introduction

If conceptions which are incapable of definition are simple, I, It, and Thou are so. Who could define either of these words, easy as they are to understand? Who does not perceive, in fact, that neither of them can be expressed in terms of the others?

I here, for the first time, begin a developement of these conceptions hoping that this will be accompanied with a developement of the souls of those who read.

I! How simple and sublime! It! how protean and comic! *Thou!* how beautiful and pathetic!

Though they cannot be expressed in terms of each other, yet they have a relation to each other, for THOU is an IT in which there is another I. I looks in, It looks out, Thou looks *through,* out and in again. I outwells, It inflows, Thou commingles. I is self-supported, IT leans on a staff, THOU leans on what it supports.

Chapter I

The Three Persons have nothing in common.

True   The I may be IT—as when we think of ourselves objectively
        The IT may become THOU—in apostrophe
        The THOU may become IT—in cruelty or rather hardness
        The IT may even become I—in Pantheism
        The THOU become I—in Love
        Or the I become THOU

Yet in all these cases

The IT of the I contains nothing which either the I of the I contains, nor which the THOU of the I contains. Nor have these anything in common with each other.

The THOU of the IT contains nothing which either the IT of the IT contains, nor which the I of the IT contains. Nor have these anything in common with each other.

The IT of the THOU contains nothing which either the THOU of the THOU contains or which the I of the THOU contains; nor have these anything in common with each other.

The I, the IT, and the THOU are therefore in Three different worlds.

The Modus of the IT

MS 66: Spring 1861

There are three Celestial Worlds. 1 that whose heaven is a speck, or the manifold of sense, 2 that whose heaven is of extensive manifestation or the world of consciousness, 3 that whose heaven is of immense manifestation or the world of abstraction.

Consciousness is the only one of the worlds which is real and tangible to us. How shall sense become consciousness? This is not meant as a skeptical question; I ask it of faith.

The relations of the triad being apprehended, it will be clear that which is in the sensible world can only enter the mental world by having in it a *revelation* which is in the abstract world. Now there are three abstract revelations, 1 that whose abstraction is in a world of time or arbitrariness, 2 that whose abstraction is in a world of space or dependence, and 3 that whose abstraction is in a celestial world or absoluteness. Of these only dependence is revelation to us. Why was the abstraction spatial not temporal, the revelation dependence not arbitrariness? Because to the arbitrariness was joined absolute existence. [An absolute existence is one which is determined indeed but determined by its very self; it is so utterly determined as to become, as it were, arbitrary again.]

Now there are three kinds of absolute existence: for if the absoluteness is only a revelation in the world of sense, the existence is mere possibility—feasibility; if the absoluteness is of mental revelation then the existence is actuality; and if the absoluteness is abstract absoluteness the existence is necessity. Of these only actuality is existence *to us*. And why did the absoluteness reach mental and not mere sensual revelation? Because conjoined with the feasibility was necessary form of fact or mode. Form of fact is the way in which a fact is, that mode which by being in it is. A necessary mode is one whose non-actuality is not feasible. Clearly therefore for mere feasibility to become actuality it must have in it a necessary mode.

Now there are three kinds of necessary mode, 1 that whose necessity is a logical necessity i.e. of arbitrary existence so that this mode is company, community. 2 that whose necessity is a physical one i.e. of dependent existence—the mode, causality. 3 that whose necessity is absolute, and self-dependent or the mode of existence of a quality, *influx*. Of these only causality is a mode for us, and why should the necessity have been physical instead of merely logical, why should there have been not mere company but causation? Because the phenomena which were in community had also an influxual derivation or sequence so that fortuitousness disappeared.

But there are three kinds of influxual derivation. 1 that whose influx is of possible mode or negation, 2 that whose influx is of actual mode or reality, and 3 that whose influx is of necessary mode (the possibility and actuality being coextensive) or infinity.

Of these only reality is anything to us. Why was the influx actual and the derivation more than negation? Because into the negation was worked an infinite quality which since in it all that was possible was actual turned the negation to a reality.

Now there are three kinds of infinite quality but all relate to quantity since it is that which everything must have in order to be 1 *unity* which is an infinite quality indeed since the influx of its derivation is necessary and yet its infinity is derived from the community since it would be a total which is another thing were it not for a denied plural. 2 plurality which is an infinite quality (even a unity being a plural by continued existence) and yet one whose infinity is derived from the steps of the counting process hence from causality. 3 totality which is an infinite quality (every thing being a total in itself) and whose infinity is of that sort of derivation the necessity of whose mode is of self-dependent existence.

Of these only plurality belongs to the mental world. But the Unity took Total shape to become plurality. Now shape is that subsidiary form which a thing takes up for the sake of being itself form and which though not its true form exactly coincides with that. A total shape is one the diversity of which is so great that it ceases to have any diversity but every thing which has the shape has it in all its diversity.

There are three total shapes. The first is that whose totality is a negative quality. It is mere point, elementariness. The second is that whose totality is a real quality. It is extension. The third is that whose totality is an infinite quality. It is immensity.

Of these only extension is in the world of consciousness. But Elementariness has become extension by taking on Immense manifestation.

There are three immense manifestations. That whose immensity is a Unitary Shape or Time. That whose immensity is of plural shape or space. That whose immensity is of total shape or Heaven.

Time becomes space by conjunction with a heavenly world. That of consciousness.

And this turns the IT to THOU.

Views of Chemistry:
sketched for Young Ladies

MS 69: Summer–Fall 1861

No. 1. Kinds of Matter

Chemistry is the Science of **Kinds of Matter.** I shall devote the first number to a sketch from this far-distant upland.

No modern science is the study of the material, but of the immaterial contained in the material. Once, men were contented with facts and names and uses. Now, we always ask What is the meaning of this thing? Now the *meaning of a thing is what it conveys.* Thus, when a child burns his finger at the candle, he has not only excited a disagreeable sensation, but has also learned a lesson in prudence. Now the mere matter cannot have given him this notion, since matter has no notions to give. Who originated it, then? It must be that this thought was put into nature at the beginning of the world. It must have been *meant* because it was *conveyed.* Further, what is the necessary condition to matter's conveying a notion? It is that it shall present a sensible and distinct form. It must obviously possess a form, since formless matter is chaos,—is matter untouched by mind. It must be sensible in order to be anything *to us,* and it must be distinct or distinguished in order to be a form *to us.* There is a gentleman in England who has shown by an ingenious research that everything appears green to him. Green however is not a refreshing color to him, because it is undistinguished.

Thus it is the form of a thing that carries its meaning. But the same thing conveys different meanings to the different faculties. So there are different orders of meaning in nature. The poet with his esthetic eye reads the secret of the sea. Solomon with his moral eye reads the secret of the ant. The man of science with the eye of reason reads the secret of Nature as a system. He sees nature as a system because he studies the relations of things and he must study the relations of things in order to distinguish their forms. The meaning that *he* sees may be termed the idea of the thing. Natural History, therefore, which is one great division of Natural Science studies the Ideas of things and therefore their *forms* or *kinds*. A branch of this, of course, is the study of the *kinds* of matter. The very Nomenclature of Chemistry puts this in a very strong light. In Worcester's *New Dictionary* a whole column is devoted to the explanation of the word *Salt* and yet how do you think the whole thing is summed up—

A term applied to a very large class of compounds, having no character-istic property common to them all, consisting each of two components, simple or compound, and possessing properties materially different from those of either of its components.

Now, all the chemists in the world use the word *salt* in one perfectly determined sense and they all would recognize that definition as inade-quate. If you ask why it is that the lexicographer could not define *salt*, I answer 'It is because the word indicates an idea which it requires the salt itself to convey'. Here is the way in which the idea arose.

1. GLAUBER put some common Sea-Salt into a retort with some oil of Vitriol and distilled. White fumes were given off and a sharp spirit came over which he called the Spirit of Sea Salt. Meantime, the salt in the retort had become transformed into a substance with the same general properties but of a sickish taste and of valuable medical prop-erties—the *sal admirabile* (Glauber's Salt).

2. When he dropped the Spirit of Sea Salt into some Mineral Alkali and evaporated he *regenerated* the sea salt.

Sea Salt + Oil of Vitriol *gave* Glauber's Salt + Spirit of *Sea Salt*

Spirit of Sea Salt + Mineral Alkali *gave* Sea Salt + Water

3. When spirit of Sea Salt was dropped into Fixed Vegetable Alkali (the twin brother of Mineral Alkali) a body was obtained by evapora-tion so strongly resembling sea-salt that in a work I have just been referring to published by the Royal Society in 1753 the two are con-founded. Is not this then to be called a salt?

Spirit of Sea Salt + *Mineral* Alkali *gave* a Solution of Sea Salt

Spirit of Sea Salt + *Vegetable* Alkali *gave* a Solution of this

It might be called Salt of Vegetable Alkali, might it not? It has gone by the names—Digestive Salt, doubly refined culinary salt, *Sal Silvii*, &c.

4. Moreover if we distill this culinary salt with oil of Vitriol as we before did the sea-salt, the spirit of sea salt goes over as before and there is left in the retort a salt so strongly resembling the *sal admirabile* that Boerhaave devotes a paragraph to showing that they are not identical. It has been known as *Tartarus Vitriolatus*.

Sal Silvii (culinary salt) + oil of Vitriol
gave Tartarus Vitriolatus + Spirit of Sea Salt

5. Now this *Tartarus Vitriolatus* may also be made by Mixing Vegetable Alkali and Oil of Vitriol and evaporating to dryness. That is

Tartarus Vitriolatus = Vegetable Alkali
+ Oil of Vitriol − Water evaporating.

Or letting K^+ stand for the Vegetable alkali *minus* so much of the water as came from it and V^- stand for the Oil of Vitriol *minus* so much of the water as came from it, we may represent the *Tartarus Vitriolatus* by

$$\boxed{K^+ \ V^-}$$

Then the *Sal Silvii* or culinary salt made in Exp. 3 and decomposed in Exp. 4 will be (if we let Cl^- represent the Spirit of Sea Salt minus its share of water)

$$\boxed{K^+ \ Cl^-}$$

Then the decomposition will be thus

$$\boxed{K^+ \ Cl^-} \ + \ V^- + \text{share of Water of } V^-$$
Sal Silvii   Oil of Vitriol

$$= \quad \boxed{K^+ \ V^-} \ + \ Cl^- + \text{share of Water of } V^-$$
Tartarus Vitriolatus   Spirit of Sea-Salt.

The relation of the Sal Silvii and the Tartarus Vitriolatus may be shown by writing them thus

K+	V−
Cl−	

In the same way if Na+ stand for Mineral Alkali, Sea Salt (regenerated Exp. 2) will be

Na+	Cl−

And Sal admirabile Glauberi will be

Na+	V−

Which may be added to the diagram, thus

Na+	Cl−
V−	K+

It is thus seen that Tartarus Vitriolatus has nothing in common with Sea Salt. Yet it is connected with such links that we cannot refuse to call it a *Salt*. Whatever is thus linked with Common Salt is a salt.

But—"what is the meaning of this thing?"—is not the question every science puts to nature. "What makes the rainbow? What makes the top stand up?" are the kind of inquiries belonging to Mechanics, Optics, Acoustics, and all the branches of Physics. They are questions of force. Force is that in every change which causes that the change unless stopped shall keep itself up and expend itself on its own continuity. Force must be wherever matter is known, since matter is known by the affections of our senses which must be effects of force. The science of kinds of matter must then treat questions of force—it is therefore a branch of Physics. For instance, in the case of salts it is obvious that there must be a certain force which makes the spirit of sea salt and mineral alkali transform themselves to *salt*. Now if 35 parts of spirit of sea salt neutralizes 40 of Mineral Alkali and 50 of Vegetable Alkali and if it requires 50 parts of Oil of Vitriol to neutralize 40 of the former, it follows that it contains just force enough to neutralize 50 of the latter. And so we find it and this same amount of force is in every salt.

Thus it appears that the Science of the Kinds of Matter through treating of *matter* belongs to Natural Philosophy; through treating of *kinds* belongs to Natural History, and thus unlike the other sciences treats alike of form and force,—of the *worth* and the *expense* of the spiritual manifestations of nature. Indeed, as that very expression shows, the form and the force are but the same thing from different points of view. (One is the Spirit seen by its Influxual relations the other by its Causal relations.) The peculiarity of Chemistry is that it embraces both views in one.

Now we have viewed the science in a preliminary way, and I must say something respecting that of which it treats—*matter* and the *kinds* of matter.

Since we only know matter through force and since this force conveys to our brain not matter but the immaterial forms of matter—how do we know that there is any matter at all? Why not say with Bishop Berkeley that the force going out from me reaches you on its own wings and that this *vehicle* of matter is a mere fiction? Because we know that every quality belongs to a substance. This substance has quantity. We feel it. Some matter is more difficult to move than others; it has more *mass*, more inertia. This *mass*, this inertness is not force, is not any spiritual thing but is the necessary condition to there being any spiritual manifestation in nature, for the greater the mass moved the greater the *exhibition*, then if there were no mass there would be no exhibition. If it required no exertion whatever to produce a phenomenon, how much would the phenomenon convey?

There is, then, matter. But the idea of it is a perfectly simple one; how can it have kinds? It can have quantity—it can even have quality. But this quality is a form, a force, a phenomenon, an excitation in the mind which perceives it. Suppose we say that the different kinds of matter are owing to its varying susceptibility to different kinds of force. But different kinds of force are forces producing different kinds of change; now, in space but one kind of change is possible, namely *motion*. [This is somewhat abstruse as an axiom but it must go as such since its proof is metaphysical and long.] How then can matter be susceptible to one motion and not to another? Here we must stop. This question I cannot answer. We must be satisfied with the Natural History of the chemical Elementary bodies without as yet explaining their physics. We must not assume that they do not exist because we cannot explain them. That would be to go back to the old Fire, Water, Earth, and Air theory which tried to explain everything by making the only differences in substances their *heat, moisture, weight,* and *volatility.* From this theory the alchemists made the first movement when they said that all things were composed of Sulphur, Salt, and Mercury.

No. 2. Chemical Method

To discover the true method of science we must know distinctly what science is. Last time, we agreed that it was the study of the immaterial in the material. And that this was divisible into the study of forms and the study of forces. But are the resemblances of clouds to lions, camels, and whales, which are certainly forms, and the sequence of defeat to an attack, or of being drowned (for little boys) to swimming *on a particular day of the week,* which is a force of course, matters of science? and if not why not? No, because they are imaginary, you will say. But even if all matters of this kind were false, which I do not admit, still they are *forms* and *forces* in the imagination and they are derived from the Material; why then are they not matters of science? Of course they are not. Nature is a book which science interprets, and yet all its poetry which is a form and all its pathos which is a force are foreign to science.

She walks in beauty like the queen of night.

This line contains a poetical image. Is it in the ink? Yet no Englishman can look at this ink without the form and the thrill coming to him can he? Not if he can read. What is this reading? It is an interpretation according to a system agreed upon beforehand. That establishment, then, contains the elements of the form;—it was the establishment of a correspondence between material forms and the forms of the imagination. Natural language by which we read the poetry of nature is a natural correspondence between material forms and the forms of the imagination. This correspondence cannot lie. Therefore, forms of beauty are merely perceptions of another mind and not material at all. In scientific proceedure, then, we must establish rules to prevent our taking forms of the imagination and forces of passion for material forms and forces.

These are 1. We must derive our data for obtaining forces and forms from no metaphysical axiom however true, from no religion, and from no authority; but only from nature. 2. We must not take our data as they seem to us, but as they are. That is, they must not be relations of the material to the intellectual, but of the material to the material. By these rules we collect our data.

We must then collate the analogous instances. We must then reduce these analogous instances to one form. This can only be done precisely by precision in the original observation; hence, one important reason for the necessity of *measurement* in science. Having got thus far, it is time to seek a **Law** for this phenomenon. To get this we must, as you can easily see, go back to axioms again. And axioms we must draw from mental sources.

To illustrate this point, I will take the case of Rust. Rust is a combination of Iron with *Oxygen* and *Water*. It is red, amorphous, and insoluble in water. If it is heated intensely it gives off its water and becomes difficultly soluble in acids. Iron rusts even when dissolved in acids. The solution quickly absorbs oxygen, turns brown, and deposits rust on the sides of the bottle. Platinum, Gold, Copper, Mercury, Zinc, Lead, Silver, Arsenic, Antimony, Bismuth, and Tin exhibit no such property. Manganese, Nickel, and Cobalt, in solution, rust. The rust of these metals is similar to that of Iron in the above-mentioned properties. Chromium also rusts but its rust is Green. We easily see that these metals resembling iron in other respects, resemble it also in rusting as no others do. But when we throw these metals into a *Class*, in consequence of which rusting is the characteristic, we have obviously drawn upon a synthetical faculty allied to the Imagination, and have not derived the idea *purely* from experience.

We have been logical but we have not confined ourselves to experience. Yet we have not gone out of nature. We have only recognized the immaterial in nature.

But to go further, and say that all Iron metals must rust and that all rust must have similar properties or allied properties to Iron rust is obviously a step which even this new mode of proceedure will not warrant. Yet science must have universal laws in order to be useful. At the same time, a universal law would imply a perfection of knowledge to which we cannot attain.

The problem is, then, to throw the imperfection somewhere else— to get a universal law and yet not to get it perfectly. This is accomplished by so considering rust that we shall not call it by that name unless it obeys the law. And then to proceed again to nature to learn what *rust* is.

/A Treatise on Metaphysics/

MS 70: 21 August 1861–30 March 1862

PREFACE

This book it is my intention to write in a syllogistical style, because in metaphysics we should not take the smallest step without caution. The remarks interspersed are intended to furnish the germs of ideas to be used hereinafter.

1861 August 21

CONTENTS

INTRODUCTION

BOOK I.—Principles

BOOK II

The whole will take about 100 pages.

INTRODUCTION

Chapter First

The Domain, the Basis,
and the Fabric of Metaphysical Thought

The word *metaphysics* is derived from the title of a work of Aristotle which treats, according to its author, of that science "which is desirable on its own account and for the sake of knowledge," and which is pre-eminent over the others (Aristotle *Metaphysics* 1.2.7).

In the following three sections, I shall be forced to consider metaphysics in three lights; viz.

in §1 As Philosophy

in §2 As a Branch of Psychology

in §3 As the Analytics of Conceptions.

§1. On the Definition of Metaphysics

"Definition," says Sir William Hamilton, "is the resolution of the comprehension of a notion into its parts."

I say that Definition is the statement of equivalence in conception.

———————

By his system of nomenclature, Sir William Hamilton has conferred an immense boon not alone on his own school but on all English philosophers who believe in anchoring words to fixed meanings. I deeply regret that I am not one of these. That is the best way to be stationary, no doubt. But, nevertheless, I believe in mooring our words by certain applications and letting them change their meaning as our conceptions of the things to which we have applied them progress.

———————

a. No definition proper states more than the signification of its object. But Sir William Hamilton would have it state of what its object is composed. Perhaps, this is making it state too much.

b. A definition must either be of a thing, a word, or a notion; and to state what either of these is, is to give its equivalence in conception. But all mankind acknowledge that, in Aristotle's words, "a definition is a sentence signifying what a thing is"; hence my definition of Definition is correct.

[The best discussion of Definitions is in Kant's *Critique of Pure Reason.* "Doctrine of Method," Ch. 1, Sect. 1.]

Any science got from observations may be subsequent to some other.

No subsequent thing can be preëminent over [i.e. ruler of] a previous thing.

∴. Metaphysics is not got from observations. And knowledge obtained *à priori* is preëminent over all other knowledge. *A priori* science is also desirable for itself. It is also necessary for knowledge. ∴. Metaphysics is coëxtensive with science *à priori*. Yet this is not a definition of metaphysics, for the notion contained in "*à priori*" is derived from metaphysics; but no notion is equivalent to anything subsequent to itself.

A Philosophy is a science no part of whose proceedure is observation. Metaphysics is therefore coextensive with philosophy. Yet, though the notion of philosophy is not metaphysical, this again is not a definition of metaphysics. For "philosophy" cannot suggest "metaphysics" without an intermediate process of thought, but

Equivalent notions are those which may suggest each other without any mediating conceptions.

This intermediate thought is that philosophy is a condition of all science, that it deals with what we immediately know, and that it progresses from elements. Metaphysics, therefore, is the philosophy of primal truths. This is my definition.

It is absolutely necessary that that which is metaphysics should be science, should not be drawn from experience, that it should deal with truths, and that these truths should be primary conditions of all science. But this is no more than the definition states.

Moreover all philosophy of primal truths is desirable on its own account and on account of knowledge and is preëminent over all other sciences.

Therefore, my definition neither omits anything essential nor asserts anything contingent. Therefore, it is correct.

Let me not be misunderstood as claiming that this definition is perfect. That is a thing, says Kant, which in philosophy should be the end of our labor rather than the beginning of it; and I am so far from falling into that mistake that it is upon this account that I have felt compelled to take three distinct views of metaphysics in order to see what it is. In this first section I regard it subjectively, in the next objectively, and in the third in a way which is as nearly expressed by—practically—as any other word.

It is also because I feel the arbitrary impossibility[1] of an apodictic deduction of metaphysics that so much discursive remark is permitted in this chapter.

Of the Usefulness of Metaphysics as a Study. Is not *meditation* metaphysics? Is not the unfolding of the mind the same process as meditation? Is not Wisdom the unfolding of the mind?

To understand a proposition it is necessary to comprehend the terms of it. The conceptions of a proposition are contained in its terms. Hence, the primal philosophy is not to be learnt from propositions nor from books which are series of propositions, but from meditation. That meditation which gives us new conceptions is a *cultivation* resulting in a growth of thoughts, and the result of a growth of the mind as displayed in the thoughts is called Wisdom.

Why is metaphysics so hard to read? Because it cannot be put into books. You may put suggestions towards it into books but each mind must evolve it for himself—and every man must be his own metaphysician.

§2. On the Fundamental Distinction of Metaphysics

It is usually conceded or assumed that all metaphysics is based on some fundamental distinction. The fact is that every new system of metaphysics has some particular merit which is based on some particular distinction. The distinction upon which my system is based is between the potentially *thought* and the potentially *thought-of*. The common, and as I think, erroneous view of the relation of the Thing known to the Person knowing is as follows:—First, there is the Subject, the *Ego*. The thing known, is known by an *affection* of the consciousness, consequently only by its effect. Therefore, a distinction is drawn between (2) the *Noumenon* or thing as it exists which is entirely unknown (except, according to some philosophies, by reason), and (3) the Object or *thing as thought*. (4) There is the affection of the consciousness or Phenomenon and (5) there is the relation of Causality between the Object and the Phenomenon.

The objections to this view are these.

a. If the *noumenon* is thought of it is known. If it is not thought of, it has no relation to the consciousness. But it is represented as both totally unknown, yet the *ground* of knowledge.

---

1. Arbitrary impossibility = accidental, chance impossibility.

b. "Thing as thought" contains mental elements, but the mind does not really affect the things that it knows. Hence the word *object* like noumenon is a mere logical form, incapable of comprehension.

I represent the relationship as follows:—(1) There is the soul (2) There is the field of consciousness in which we know the soul (3) There is the thing *thought of* (4) There is the power it exerts on the soul (5) There is the Idea or impression it makes on the soul (6) There is the *thought* or the idea as it appears in the consciousness.

Above these partial views, however, it is obvious that the possibility and the utility of each science must be based on a distinction of the primal philosophy. I may illustrate this by examples to the point.

In the first place, the possibility and the utility of philosophy in general, that is of the application of the Understanding to experience, depends on our having besides the facts of experience, certain truths *à priori* on the objects of experience.

Again, the fundamental distinction of psychology is between the soul and the body. To show that this is a metaphysical distinction. The soul is that which moves itself; the body is that which moves but does not move itself. When I say, by the way, that the soul moves itself, I do not mean that it originates any force, but that a certain amount of force which is in it always moves in it and never out from it[2] (so that every force passing through it is subjected to modification by a force within it and belonging to it). All force, however, must manifest itself in change of some kind, but there is no change in space, there is no manifestation of things outwardly except in space, and it is only forces in substances that make those substances manifest; hence, The soul is that which is manifested interiorly. In a body, on the other hand, every force which is at one instant in one atom at the next instant is in another atom. Hence, there is no unity in the manifestation of a body. Hence the body can only manifest itself in such a form of intuition as admits of *extension*. But this the inner sense does not. Hence, the body is that which is manifested exteriorly only.

Since philosophy in general rests on one metaphysical distinction, and Psychology a branch of it on another, on what Metaphysical distinction does that branch of Psychology the science of the thoughts—Metaphysics itself—rest? Metaphysics is the philosophy of all that we immediately know? Its basis is obviously the distinction between what

2. Plato in the *Phaedrus* calls the soul that which moving itself never ceases to be moved since it does not abandon itself.

we immediately know—the thought, and what we *mediately* know—the thought-of—or that by which we know the thought-of the of-thought.

The distinction upon which *All* PHILOSOPHY is based, lies between Images *à priori* and Images *à posteriori*

The distinction upon which *Psychology* is based, lies between Inner Images and Outer Images

The distinction upon which *Metaphysics* is based, lies between Images as Images and Images as Representations.

How purely mental are these distinctions! In the former section in a subjective view metaphysics was considered as all philosophy of which psychology is a branch. In our objective view it appears as a branch of psychology and in our final view it will appear to be nothing else than Psychology itself. Yet I have based each of these sciences on a separate distinction. How to reconcile them. Perhaps it will turn out that Images *à priori* are only Images *à posteriori* viewed as Images, that those *à posteriori* are only those *à priori* excited as Representations, that to view an image as an image it must indispensably have come from within and that such as do so come we cannot regard as representations but as immediate consciousness.

The Real Worth of Metaphysics must lie, of course, in its practical application. Now if there be any knowledge that we can neither find in the outward world nor in ourselves, which we have not got *à priori* and cannot receive *à posteriori,* and which consequently we can never have as a representation—

> If the deep says it is not in me
> And the sea says it is not in me—

but which nevertheless lies in our immediate consciousness, it is obvious that neither Physics, Cosmology, nor Science nor any other Philosophy or Psychology than metaphysics, but that and that only can find it out. Now there is such a knowledge; that of the PERFECT. Accordingly, all the higher life is strengthened by metaphysics. And we find metaphysicians are generally Holy Men.

A second, negative, advantage of metaphysics is that on another side, that of *pure religion,* it has no practical bearing and cannot have.

The efficacy of prayer, for example, a man's intellect might not endorse; but when the intellect has the ascendency, we do not wish to make use of that. When we feel no confidence in her, we pray. Besides, pure metaphysics, studying images as images and not as representations, must recognize the facts of consciousness for on them it is founded but does not inquire into their *reality,* at all.

If metaphysics can make no attack on *religion in general,* neither can religion sustain one against *metaphysics in general.* For what could religion do but show a contradiction? But in metaphysics contradictions are the only manifestations of imperfection, from which metaphysics, no more than any human belief, is exempt. Religion would tell us, then, no more than we knew before; for we perfectly recognize that every metaphysical system must be full of contradictions. But the only way to pick a flaw in metaphysics is by going over the ground and picking the flaw.

§3. On the Treatment of Metaphysics

In one view, metaphysics is a branch of Psychology while in another psychology is but applied metaphysics. This suggests two modes of treating metaphysics, one starts by drawing the conceptions from the system of psychology and reasoning to their logical relations and meaning; the other draws the conceptions from no system but from the thoughts as they present themselves in their logical form—examining them logically—and finally puts them in their right place in the mind. The latter is the only proper course, since it is only after understanding these truths that we can find their logical relations. It may be called the Logical in opposition to the Psychological Treatment of Metaphysics.

The logical method will consist only in a study of the logical relations of conceptions since definition is itself a statement of relation.[3] A part of this process will be a complete analysis of the conceptions. And it will be the whole, for conceptions cannot have a logical relation (that is one that is contained in the very thought itself) unless they are complex. Hence metaphysics is the analysis of conceptions.

If there is any positive science of psychology—that is the science of the mind itself—it must be that the mind is more than a *unit.* It must have parts, and these will be faculties. Each of these faculties will have special functions and these functions will be simple conceptions. We

3. Thus, $3 = 2 + 1$ is a statement of the relation of 3 to 2 and to 1.

can only know faculties, however, through their functions; accordingly the knowledge of simple conceptions will be the knowledge of the mind itself and the analysis of conceptions will be psychology. Moreover, if the mind has these faculties, every thought will be an action of the faculties by whatever means excited, and there must always be an occasion for such excitation. Hence, in one view all thoughts are *à priori*, in another all are *à posteriori*. This abolishes, *as real*, the distinction upon which all philosophy is based and makes metaphysics the whole of reasoning; and, indeed, it is obvious that the logical examination of truths is the same as the practice of Logic.

The following consideration also will show that all reasoning is applied metaphysics and psychology. All proveable propositions have for their ancestors a major premiss and a minor premiss, a major premiss and a minor premiss, a major premiss and a minor premiss untill we come to their very progenitors which are primal truths. Where do these primal truths come from. Some, perhaps, from experience; but the original major premiss cannot come to us so, for a major premiss distributes the middle term, and must therefore be either universal or negative. Now experience *unreasoned upon* (which has no ancestry) cannot be universal. Neither can it be negative; for instance, the proposition This is not Green cannot be an experience, for it is a thought of Green and that thought Green experience, by the very statement, did not give. It is only minor premisses, then, that nature affords us; for all Universal, Negative, Unconditional, and Necessary Truths exist and *have their truth* in the mind. They, being true without proof, can have but one basis and must be independent of nature.

Nothing can be more important, therefore, than that Primal Truths should be tested by normal minds; but lamentably most minds are upon most subjects or upon most subjects about which there is any question, abnormal. Nothing is more certain than that Salt-Junk does not go with molasses. No salt Junk ever can. This is not derived from experience merely, but is a truth founded in the constitution of the human mind. Yet most eaters of salt-junk are heretics on this point. True, no one doubts that the shortest way between two points is in a straight line, because the ideas of the whole world are perfectly clear upon this point. The Sailor's Judgement on the salt-junk is falsified not only by his inaccurate distinctions of taste but also by his uneducated esthetic ideas. Humanity always agrees upon the *à priori* propositions when the ideas are perfectly analyzed; when they have not been they have occasioned the most fruitless controversies.

To learn how to analyze ideas, therefore, and to analyze them will be *par excellence* **education.**

Metaphysical—*Odi Profanum Vulgus*—1862 March 30

INTRODUCTION

Chapter II

On the Insufficiency of Dialectics

§1. The Position of the dialectician

The First Chapter attempted a developement of the true idea of metaphysics. The triplicity of the conception, and the impossibility of achieving the synthesis of it, creates naturally three true schools of metaphysics:—the dogmatical, the psychological, and the logical schools. The proceedure of each of these, depending as it does on a partial conception, is liable to abuse, although that must be in reality contrary to the normal mode of the very view assumed. I shall designate these errors as follows—

The abuse of dogmatism, I call dialectics
  ”   ”   ” psychology, ”   ”   transcendentalism
  ”   ”   ” logic,   ”   ”   rationalism.

To the two former, I shall devote one chapter each of the introduction; but as I myself belong to the logical school, the abuse of it will be the constant topic of Book I, and need not be specially considered here.

When the notion that metaphysics is philosophy antecedent to all other science is carried so far as to produce a denial that it is the study of our own consciousness merely and also of the fact that it adds nothing to our knowledge but only analyzes it, this notion produces *dialectics*, that is to say, a system which seeks to investigate truth by elaborate reasoning from *first principles*. Dialectics is thus a genuine outgrowth of dogmatism only, but it may nevertheless be pursued by a psychologist or a logist.

The ground of *dogmatical dialectics* is that the light of necessary truths is a participation of the infinite reason.

Proof. According to dogmatical dialectics, that which is antecedent to science is itself science; that is, there are certain major premisses from which (by means of the minor premisses of experience) all other knowledge is deduced.

No knowledge can be deduced from premisses the truth of which is not given. ∴ The truth of the first principles is given.

No truth can be given by that which is deduced from it.

∴ The truth of a first principle must be given in the very proposition itself. A fact whose statement carries its own necessity with it must either have its predicate implied in its subject or else it must as a fact have an existence which is self-dependent. But the predicate of *science* goes beyond what the subject implies.

∴ Hence first principles must (as facts) have a self-dependent existence.

Nothing has a self-dependent existence but the Divinity.

∴ These first principles are statements concerning Divinity.

To know, from our own nature the Divine is to partake of the divine nature,

∴ According to dogmatic dialectics we partake of the divine nature in the inward light of reason.

Axioms do indicate a participation in the Divine Reason.

Proof. Axioms are thoughts.

> All thoughts come to us from God.
> We cannot have them by nature without certain qualities of the mind from which they come.
> Participation of qualities is participation of nature.
> Unity of substance is essential to the Divine Nature.

The above is, in a general way, the view of Leibnitz.

The ground of *psychological dialectics* is that the consciousness contains not mere images of the object thought of but is an immediate seizing of the object itself.

Proof. Psychological dialectics affirms that the sheer study of consciousness is not a mere study of impressions but also a science of things themselves.

The consciousness makes assertion only of what is in it.

∴ This system implies that the things themselves are taken into the consciousness.

This is the theory of Immediate Perception.

The ground of *logical dialectics* is that some abstractions are realities.

Proof. It asserts that the science of abstractions gives the knowledge of fact.

This cannot be true if abstractions are mere negations.

Some abstractions are realities.

Proof. We have a conception of a necessary being.

The necessary is that whose actuality is given by the conception itself.

∴ There is an abstraction which of itself gives actuality to existence. This is the argument of Anselm and DesCartes.

§2. Refutation of Dialectics

A. As a System

I. Philosophical Objection. There can be no science except so far as a previous principle has permitted it. Our eyesight affords knowledge only if the principle of optics is valid.

1. Metaphysics is the principle previous to all science. It cannot, therefore be science itself, for in this case, it must itself have a previous principle, so that it would no longer be the principle previous to all science.

2. Metaphysics is the science of consciousness. The dialectician asserts that in this study we find knowledge of outward fact. But the first knowledge thus arrived at must have a previous principle asserting its validity, this cannot be found in metaphysics since such a principle would be knowledge of outward fact and we search for something previous to the first knowledge of that kind obtained from metaphysics. Nor can the previous principle of metaphysics afford it, for this only asserts the validity of the science of consciousness.

3. Metaphysics is the analysis of conceptions. All science is synthetical (predicate goes out of subject). Every previous principle of synthetical truth is synthetical for it goes beyond the subject—the representation of the fact—to state its correspondence with something beyond itself, the fact. The previous principle of analysis is analytical for it is nothing but

the general principle of identity—All *A* is *A*. Hence neither analysis nor its previous principle can afford any basis for synthetical science.

II. Psychological Objection. All our knowledge of things as they exist, is by and in the modifications of our own consciousness.
1. Metaphysics is antecedent to all other science. Hence metaphysical knowledge is by and in modifications of our own consciousness, antecedent to all other modifications. This antecedence is an antecedence of principle. But no one phenomenon is antecedent to another in the sense of being its principle. Hence, metaphysics does not afford science.
2. Metaphysics studies only the consciousness as such. But if only as such, it refers to nothing else and can be knowledge of nothing but what is in the consciousness; that is what we already know.
3. Metaphysics is the analysis of conceptions. Hence metaphysical knowledge is by and in modifications of consciousness produced by analyzing what we were conscious of before. Such a modification can be produced by no new fact, hence it is the knowledge of no new fact.

III. Logical Objection. The conclusion of a syllogism never transcends the premisses.
1. Metaphysics is all that is antecedent to all other science. Hence, if it were a set of propositions, from it could all other science logically be deduced. Hence it must contain all other science but to say that all science is previous to itself is absurd. Hence metaphysics is no science.
2. Metaphysics relates to the human consciousness merely. Hence its conclusions contain nothing we were not already conscious of.
3. Metaphysics is the analysis of conceptions. Hence its conclusions have no synthetical content.

In answer to these objections it may be said
1. That there is a science, that of the Divine, which is previous to all science. Metaphysics is all which is previous to all other science. ∴ Metaphysics is a knowledge of the Divinity.
2. That in the human consciousness itself is manifest its Creator although he is not in the consciousness. Metaphysics is Psychology. ∴ Metaphysics is knowledge which transcends consciousness.
3. There is a certain conception, that of a necessarily existing Being which in itself goes out of itself to necessitate its real existence. Metaphysics is Analysis of Conceptions. ∴ Metaphysics affords science of positive content.

The logic of this reply is formally correct, but the rejoinder is that any such argument relating to the Divinity would depend on these facts:—

1. That there is such a science of the Divine. But this fact is not previous to all science, but is clearly subsequent to the science spoken of.
2. That the consciousness is a manifestation of its Creator. But this fact cannot be discovered in the consideration of the pure consciousness.
3. That there is a conception of a necessary Being. But this is not an analytical proposition.

Hence the basis of such an argument is not purely metaphysical and consequently the argument belongs to *applied* rather than to *pure* metaphysics. Now in all science

1. There is an application of that which necessarily precedes science.
2. There is some supposition as to the trustworthiness of human consciousness.

3. There is an analysis of the predicate from the subject. Hence *all* science is applied metaphysics and to say that we can discover a thing by an *application* of metaphysics means nothing at all, except that we can discover it.

B. As a tendency

Systematic dialectics pretends to take strictly metaphysical premisses. I have refuted the validity of such a system and have shown moreover that its actual premisses are not strictly metaphysical, but are if you please matters of common sense. Dialecticians thus cease to be metaphysicians but as they call themselves so and their claim is generally admitted, I suppose I must say a few words on Dialectics as a tendency of investigation.

1. The first thing which suggests itself is the liability to error in this sort of premisses. The subjects are those which are most difficult to think correctly about, because they are abstract and we cannot figure an abstraction to our imagination but have to clothe it so that we are actually thinking of specialties whose properties may not be in all respects the same as their generals.

But men are very apt to neglect this toilsome work of examining abstractions; they forget to clothe them and thus talk of words instead of abstractions. The Hamiltonian school, according to me, are chargeable with this fault.

But even if we are very diligent and conscientious we can hardly hope to outgo human liability to error. We make mistakes in all investigation, but in thinking of the concrete, if we err, it is by a measurable distance from the truth. In the world of abstraction, on the contrary, there is no extension and consequently the slightest error is as absolute as the greatest.

2. The second consideration is the fact that in abstract reasoning *à priori* we cannot have but two premisses to each syllogism. This follows from the fact that there are not, in the abstract world, *two* propositions of *the same meaning*. Dialectical investigation has herein an enormous disadvantage in comparison with the Baconian method because in the latter proceedure the errors of a multitude of data neutralize each other in all probability.—None hits the bull's eye but their centre of gravity nearly corresponds with it.

Moreover, the probability of the premiss is to some degree determined by the amount of variation from it of the discrepant observations, and also the magnitude of the probable error and no opinion can be held scientifically and justly till we know (what we can never know in dialectics) what degree of certainty it reaches.

To leave a premiss to stand alone on one datum is an unknown rashness in physical science. Think how many observations establish gravitation, how many any chemical reaction, how many the cycle of the seasons, &c. Now if a premiss rests on a thousand data each of which has one chance in ten of being worthless, the chance of the premiss itself being false is one out of twenty octillion nonillion vigintillion vigintillion vigintillion vigintillion vigintillion vigintillion vigintillion vigintillion vigintillion vigintillion vigintillion vigintillion vigintillion vigintillion vigintillions.

3. The third consideration is the extreme length of dialectical arguments. Syllogism must be strung onto syllogism to make a long chain any link of which breaking the conclusion falls. [A probability of 1. is certainty; a probability of 0.5 is mere unsupported hypothesis.] If we

deduce a conclusion from a chain of 15 syllogisms—the probability of each premiss being .9 and of each logical process being performed without fallacy .9 the probability of the conclusion is .519 that is there is only one chance in 26 that we have proved it. Even if we make the probability of each premiss .99 the probability of the conclusion is only .588—scarce enough to bet on!

Moreover, there is no dialectical argument which is not met by others from some other source. Suppose our argument of probability = .588 be opposed to that of probability = .519. Its probability is then reduced to .570—one chance in 7 of having proved it.

Probability is ultimately a matter of judgement. For my part I should not assign to any dialectical conclusion of a single argument a higher probability than .57 to .60.

The existence of a God as metaphysically defined and on metaphysical considerations, is perhaps not more than .93.

No other dialectical conclusion is so high as .75, perhaps not more than .68.

Compare this with the results of Bacon's method!

C. As an Intention

I have now shown that Dialectics must be lowered from a system to a tendency, and that it cannot even be a true tendency but only an intention. In this view also it is fundamentally wrong for three reasons.

1. It seeks to substitute common-sense or what we know already for observation of what we have still to learn. Thus, it is lazy.

2. It substitutes human speculation for fact. It is arrogant.

3. It thinks by dividing knowledge to add to it. It is trifling.

§3. Inference Regarding True Dogmatism

We thus see that although axioms do indicate a participation in the divine Reason, nevertheless Philosophy is not science. We must infer, therefore, that no axioms are first principles but that they are derived from inspirations upon which and not upon propositions, our knowledge rests. Attention to these inspirations will give us a power of Truth. This attention consists in distinguishing them from themselves and each other through the cognitive elements they afford. In other words it is the analysis of conceptions.

Second: although we perhaps have the object thought of in our consciousness, nevertheless the study of consciousness tells us nothing we did not already know. The reason is that pure consciousness, though it has faculties for thinking the different thoughts, thinks nothing before experience. Yet if we arrange what we already know, it will be more easy to arrive at new experience. This arrangement is the analysis of conceptions.

Abstractions are revealed in consciousness and in the world, and our studies of them in one place hold good in the other. There is that much truth in dialectics.

INTRODUCTION

Chapter III

On the Uselessness of Transcendentalism

§1. *The Stand-point of the Transcendentalist*

When the view that metaphysics is the study of the human consciousness is carried out in a one-sided way, in forgetfulness that it is as truly Philosophy and also the Analysis of Conceptions, it produces Transcendentalism (better named Criticism), which is the system of investigation which thinks necessary to prove that the normal representations of truth within us are really correct.

Transcendentalism is thus the peculiar disease of psychology, but dogmatists and logicians may become transcendentalists. The first phase of modern transcendentalism was dogmatical, but the psychological form sprang up, at once.

Psychological transcendentalism reasons thus:—Experience as well as speculation, is the result of the working of the object and the working of the mind. Hence there are two elements of belief, the *mental* and the *real* element; and we can *know* nothing until we can say what validity for truth the mental element has. There is no possible way of answering such a demand from *external* studies; consequently we must study the action of consciousness in order to solve the problem *quid juris:* If it cannot be solved in this way, then it is insoluble and we cannot attain cognition. This is Kant's idea.

Dogmatical transcendentalism reasons thus:—Every cognition depends on a chain of syllogisms of which the first major premiss is philosophical. Our knowledge is incomplete unless we can show ground for that premiss. It must be shown that is a matter of fact; in what cases can this in the nature of things be done? This is Hume's idea (somewhat extended).

Logical transcendentalism reasons thus:—Every proposition is a compound of conceptions. Now just as no proposition can be true which contradicts what is truly predicated of the same subject, so the conceptions of which it is composed cannot have even a general validity if they universally imply a contradiction. And just as we test every proposition by common logic, so we must test every abstraction by a critical examination in order to see whether it is consistent or not. This is the idea which springs from Hamilton's system much as Hume's sprang from Locke's.

The dogmatical transcendentalist regards philosophy as psychology and the logical transcendentalist regards logic as psychology.

§2. *Refutation of Transcendentalism*

I. Psychological Objection
   Metaphysics is the Science of the Consciousness.
1. Psychological transcendentalism says that the results of metaphysics are worthless, unless the study of the consciousness produces a warrant for the authority of consciousness. But the authority of consciousness must be valid within the consciousness or else no science, not even psychological transcendentalism, is valid; for every science supposes that and depends upon it for validity.
2. Dogmatical transcendentalism says that we cannot, in metaphysics, assume premises without warrant. But since our premisses merely state how our own consciousness is modified if they are an undue assumption, transcendentalism also is since it assumes that premiss.
3. Logical transcendentalism says that metaphysics cannot proceed with certainty, unless it shows that the elementary principles upon which it reasons are not self-contradictory. But since a contradiction is that which cannot be taken into the consciousness, it follows that the principles cannot contradict, if the proceedure has been normal.

II. Philosophical Objection
   Metaphysics consists of the major-premises of all science.
1. Psychological transcendentalism says that metaphysics depends for its premisses upon the testimony of our impressions, and demands a

reason for accepting that testimony. But no logical support can possibly be given to an ultimate major premiss; to demand it therefore is to overthrow all science.

2. Dogmatical transcendentalism says that there must be a reason for accepting the premisses of metaphysics. But this is an arbitrary assertion which, if true (since it would be a *petitio principii* to draw this reason from any thing) would destroy all certainty owing to the want of foundation for the principles of truth.

3. Logical transcendentalism asserts that metaphysics depends upon the nature of certain abstractions and that it must be shown that none of these abstractions are self-contradictory. But if an abstraction may be self-contradictory, it may be inadmissible into philosophy, without being self-contradictory, which destroys all philosophy and all science.

III. Logical Objection
    Metaphysics is the analysis of conceptions.

1. Psychological transcendentalism asserts that metaphysics must show the authority whereby consciousness decides the nature of abstractions. But conceptions are determinations of abstractions and so far are of the same nature.

2. Dogmatical transcendentalism asserts that metaphysics must prove its premisses. But metaphysics has no premisses. It is pure analytics. If the analytic itself be a premiss, it is one which all reasoning involves.

3. Logical transcendentalism asserts that analysis may not be applicable to abstractions because they may be self-contradictory. But 'self-contradictory' is only applicable to certain supposable predicates which are unrealizable and therefore necessarily false. The abstraction itself then cannot be self-contradictory for falsity does not belong to objects but to judgements. It must, therefore, be our conception which is false. But a conception cannot be contradictory in the right use of reason, for No *A* is not-*A*.

§3. *On Faith*

A. Need of It

I shall show
α. that the Transcendentalists conclude with a return to Faith.
β. that the use they make of it in their own proceedure is the source of all that is valuable in their investigations.

γ. that while their own faith is necessarily blind, their reasoning is not so close as to leave no room for demonstrably trustworthy faith.

I. *Kant's Work*

An inference is involved in every cognition.

Proof. Relative cognition is the recognition of our relations to things.

All cognition of objects is relative, that is we know things only in their relation to us.

Every cognition must have an object (the subject of the proposition). The faculties whereby we become conscious of our relation to things are known as perceptions or sense.

∴ Every cognition contains a sensual element.

Now the information of mere sensation is a chaotic manifold, while every cognition must be brought into the unity of one thought.

∴ Every cognition involves an operation on the data.

An operation upon data resulting in cognition is an inference. ∴ &c.

This demonstration is extracted from Kant. It does not extend to the cognition "*I think.*"

Nothing is certain except what rests on the combined testimony of the senses and *I think.*

Proof. All knowledge, as we have just seen, is an inference from sensual minor premisses. In metaphysics, all inferences have major premisses. All knowledge is inferential except the *I think.* No cognition is certain which rests only on what is inferential. ∴ &c.

Such is Kant's reasoning. He then proceeds to test all our Conceptions as to objective validity by finding whether they are anything but particular expressions of the *I think* or of sensuousness. The following he makes objectively valid:—

> The Form of the External Sense—Space
> The Form of the Internal Sense—Time

The Conceptions of the Understanding

I	II
Of Quantity	*Of Quality*
Unity	Reality
Plurality	Negation
Totality	Limitation

III	IV
Of Relation	*Of Modality*
Substantia et Accidens	Possibility—Impossibility
Causality	Existence—Non-existence
Action and Reaction	Necessity—Contingency

The following can never enter into any certain thought:—

The Ideas of Reason.

1. The Immateriality, Incorruptibility, Personality, Animality[4] of the Soul.

2. The Nature of the World as to
$$\begin{cases} \text{Limitation} \\ \text{Compositeness} \\ \text{Fate} \\ \text{Createdness.} \end{cases}$$

3. God.

α. Though Kant cannot demonstrate the validity of the Ideas of pure reason, yet he chooses to believe it. Although there is not to him one whit more probability that they are true than that they are false, still he *trusts* in them,—he has Faith.

β. He also takes the validity of sensibility and of the *I think* for granted. Yet only by doing so has he made any solid work.

γ. A part of his argument is that nothing which rests only on what is inferential can be certain. This is not axiomatic nor demonstrable. It therefore leaves hope of proving the contrary which establishes the validity of faith.

II. *Hume's Work*

Hume separates cognitions into Impressions (as when we see, hear, will, love, &c.) and Thoughts (reflections, remembrances, &c.).

All Thoughts are copies of Impressions.

Proof. The conclusion never goes beyond the premisses. But *thoughts* are conclusions from impressions as premisses.

☞ This premiss is an *induction;* it is true whether the thoughts are properly applied to the matter-in-hand or not. ∴ &c.

---

4. Animality = existence as a principle of life in matter.

In reflection the mind travels from the impression by three paths of "Association of Ideas," viz.:—Resemblance, Contiguity, Causality.[5] It is necessary to inquire whether all pretended thoughts exist in the nature of things as manifested in impressions or mere experience. Resemblance and Contiguity are not examined. Causality has the idea of Necessary Connection. Necessity cannot be discovered in any external or internal impression. Hence causality or power is no thought at all.

α. Hume nevertheless confesses that belief in causality is perfectly unavoidable and allows that it has equal *authority* with reason.

β. All reasoning from experience depends on Hume's causality; all causality with him depends on Faith; and his prime principle that all thoughts are copies of impressions depends on experience.

γ. Hume shows that Faith in power is usually seemingly blind, but he does not inquire what rational grounds there may be either for it or for Impressions regarded as evidence. Should it turn out that they both stand upon the same ground, he must give up criticism in order to avoid pure scepticism.

III. Mansel

Mansel's scepticism consists in denying that the unconditioned is either A or not-A.

α. He concludes with a system of credulity.

β. While his conclusion is that something is neither A nor not-A, his argument nevertheless depends upon a presupposition of logic one of whose principles is the contrary of this, and consequently he must accept logic without reason or on faith.

γ. His criticism does not apply to any new system because new systems do not admit contradictions in themselves.

B. Reason of Faith

Unfaith is either total or partial scepticism.

The different faculties have different realms by which they are distinguished. No faculty is to be trusted out of its own realm. ∴ Hence no faculty can derive any support from another but each must stand upon its own credibility. No one faculty has more inherent credibility

---

5. Hume uses 'cause' in a wider sense than I do to include all that can any ways be said to be the origin of another. For instance the earth would be the cause of the stone's falling, of its own qualities, of the impossibility of another body's occupying that space.

than another. ∴ Partial scepticism is inconsistent. Total scepticism condemns itself. ∴ Faith is the only consistent course.

The argument has the following advantages.

1. It puts faith on the same ground as all certitude.

2. It does not make it so sure that it is no longer faith.

3. By showing that faith is inherent in the very idea of the attainment of truth, it makes its acceptance *axiomatic*, and thus explains how we were already sure before we had reasoned about Faith.

C. Nature of Faith

I. What Faith is Not

1. It is not a purely intellectual principle; it is an unaccountable impulse to confide in certain truths.

This is forgotten by those who are over-anxious about the details of evidence in religion. They forget that with the highest certitude of inspiration and of history, belief still depends on an internal impulse. For, some things we should not believe though the angel Gabriel told us, while true religion is instinctively accepted by the ingenuous mind.

2. Faith is not peculiar to or more needed in one province of thought than in another. For every premiss we require faith and nowhere else is there any room for it.

This is overlooked by Kant and others who draw a distinction between *knowledge* and *faith*. Wherever there is knowledge there is Faith. Wherever there is Faith (properly speaking) there is knowledge.

3. There is no such thing as having immediate faith in the statements of others, be they men or angels or what. For whenever we believe statements, it is either *because* there is something in the fact itself which makes it credible or *because* we know something of the character of the witness. In either case there is a because whose major premiss is some principle concerning general characters of credibility. To believe without any such 'because' is mere credulity.

II. What Faith is

1. It is the recognition by consciousness of itself. It is the strength of that faculty by which abstractions are conceived.

2. It is the hearing of the testimony of consciousness, which developes into trust in every man till there is reason for distrust and a spirit of obedience to the Law of God.

3. It is the vigour of that part of the mind which is in communication with the eternal verities. By this, mountains are moved.

III. Effect of faith on Transcendentalism

1. *Criticism* is entirely swept away as useless.

2. *Transcendentalism* as a study of the out-reaching of the human mind retains its full value.

3. This study of consciousness is the examination of abstractions by analysis of conceptions.

BOOK I.
PRINCIPLES OF METAPHYSICAL INVESTIGATION

Chapter I. *Man the Measure of Things*

In the Introduction we have considered the Nature of Metaphysics, and have rejected certain false notions of its proceedure.

In our investigations, metaphysics is to be taken as the analysis of Conceptions.

We need not ask the critical question; but still there is a question of uncritical transcendentalism with which every method of philosophy must open. It is, How should the conceptions which spring up freely in our minds by virtue of the constitution thereof be true for the outward world?

In this question we detect three leading conceptions *Truth, the Innateness of Ideas, Externality*. Let us analyze each of these.

§1. Of Truth

True is an adjective applicable solely to representations and things considered as representations. It implies the agreement of the representation with its object.

A. The simplest kind of agreement of truth is a resemblance between the representation and its object. I call this *verisimilitude,* and the representation a *copy.*

Resemblance consists in a likeness, which is a sameness of predicates. Carried to the highest point, it would destroy itself by becoming identity. All real resemblance, therefore, has a limit. Beyond the limits of resemblance, verisimilitude ceases. ∴ Verisimilitude is partial truth.

Whatever claims to be a representation (a portrait for example) is a representation. Truth is that which, claiming to be a representation, is a representation. ∴ Truth has no absolute antithesis.

Falsehood also claims to be a representation
It is an imperfect *copy* of truth
∴ Verisimilitude is falsehood.

From Chapter III of the Introduction, it follows that there is no falsehood in our conceptions.
∴ The truth of conceptions is not *verisimilitude*.

B. A representation agreeing with its object, without essential resemblance thereto, is a sign. The truth of a sign, I denominate *veracity*.

Veracity consists in a constant connection between the sign and the thing; for if the sign sometimes goes without the thing, then it may speak falsely, and if the thing goes without the sign, it may be belied in negative cases. Moreover a sign cannot exist as such the first time it is presented, because it must *become* a sign.

Conceptions claim as much truth the first time they are presented as they ever do.
∴ The truth of conceptions is not *veracity*.

C. The objection to verisimilitude's being the truth of conceptions is its limitation as to completeness; the objection to veracity's is its limitation in beginning. Neither is open to the objection against the other. But veracity was called that kind of truth which was not verisimilitude.

Conceive, however, veracity to be perfect—to be founded not upon convention but upon the very nature of things and what have we?
1. The nature of a thing is that which it derives from its origin. Derivation not in time is the relation of accident to substance. Hence, an invariable connection in the nature of things is unity of substance.
2. The qualities of things are founded in the nature of things; hence, unity of substance implies perfect correspondence of qualities.
3. Hence perfect veracity is of a distinct character from cognizable veracity and it approaches quite as nearly perfection of verisimilitude. I will call it *verity*, and the representation a *type*.
4. Since conceptions perfectly correspond with qualities and since they have a connection therewith in the nature of things, they are *types* of things.

§2. Innateness of Notions

In the phrase 'Innate Ideas', Idea is used in an improper sense instead of *representation*, which is the proper word. I used the word *notion,* because that has no definite signification, and I wish to direct attention to the quality of Innateness.

The nature of a product is derived from its producer. When we think of a thing (whether present or absent), our thought is a product of the action of the thing on the mind.

The acting of one thing upon another is a state of things which has three elements:—1st The state of the agent, 2nd the state of the patient, 3rd the static relation of agent to patient.

The state of a thing has two elements 1st The nature of the thing and 2nd its relations.

∴ Every thought has three elements and possibly a fourth

1 The Nature of the Thing
2 The Nature of the Mind
3 The Relations of the Thing to the Mind
4 The Occult Relations of the Thing and of the Mind.

The nature of the thought-of as an element of thought is Truth, which we considered in §1. The second element, to be considered now, is Innateness. The third element is Externality, the subject of §3. The possible fourth element will be considered in the conclusion to this Chapter, for the present we must suppose this not to exist. The effect of supposing unknown influences not to exist is to give an account of how things would be supposing them not to exist. If this accords with fact, it is clear those influences do not exist; but if it does not, it is only necessary to determine what modification it requires in order to accord with fact, in order to find what these influences effect. Our conclusion will therefore be a synthesis of the elements of our analysis.

The Innate Element is distinct from the others; from this we infer

1st That it has no *Truth* nor Falsehood. Any predicate, however, which can be predicated is either true or false, unless it may always be predicated. Hence the Innate Element may be predicated of anything without altering the fact.

2nd That the Innate Element has no externality but is entirely subjective. It is not even thought of as external.

If now we wished to make a determinating analysis of Innateness, since it is the constitution of the mind as an element of thought, we should consider what the Constitution of the Mind is so far as it thinks *of* anything. The prime element in it is clearly its receptivity. Receptivity enters into of-thought as mere sensation. Sensation has neither truth nor falsehood for whether it be predicated or not doesn't alter the fact. It is not even thought of as external. Sensation then is the first category of Innateness.

This analysis, however, is not necessary now. It suffices to consider that in each element of motion of the mind, a faculty is exerted in the only manner in which it is constructed to act.

In this action of the faculty, therefore, the constitution of the mind is manifested.

Each element of thought is a motion of the mind.

∴ In each element of thought it is Innate.

It is innate in its possibility.

It is true in its actuality.

§3. Externality

Proposition. All unthought is thought-of.

Proof. We can sometimes think of the unthinkable as thought; we have, for instance, a conception of the conception Infinity, though we cannot attain that conception.

To think of a thing is to think in such a way that our conception has a relation to that thing. When we think of a thing's being blue, we think of blue things, in general. When we think of a thing's being long, we have a reference to those that are short. In the same way, any unthought which is not thought of as thought, is by the relation of complete negation, negatively thought of as unthought.

Cor. I. Only the phenomena can be thought of as thought, the things in themselves are thought of as unthought.

Cor. II. All *noumena* (things-in-themselves) are unconditioned because they cannot even be thought of as thought.

Cor. III. All thought is thereby thought of, for it would not be in our consciousness unless we were conscious of it. Hence, all things in heaven and earth are thought of, however small our experience may be.

Cor. IV. Whatever is unthought is apprehended, for as I showed before all falsehood is partial truth.

Whatever is thought-of can be normally thought of. Normal thought is true.

∴ All the unconditioned is apprehended and may be so without error. To formulate it: Whatever is unintelligible is true.

Idealism. The only possible definition of the person (self) is that which one thinks of when he closes his senses and excludes all thought but simple consciousness. That is, it is the thought-of, when the only thought-of is the thought. By Cor. III nothing external to the self exists.

Materialism. Matter is substance whose existence is not subject to mental conditions. By Cor. II Nothing but matter exists and the soul is matter.

Realistic Pantheism. From Idealism, it follows that nothing exists which is not of-thinkable as thought. From Materialism, it follows that nothing but the unthought exists. That which being unthinkable is of-thinkable as thought is Perfection. In Chapter III of the Introduction, it was shown that Perfection is God. Hence, nothing exists but God.

Here then we have three worlds Matter, Mind, God, mutually excluding and including each other, as I showed was possible in one of my letters.

Synthesis

Let us now restate the problem and see whether it answers itself. Given three worlds completely unrelated except in identity of substance. Everything which springs up freely in one of these, the Mind, does so from the very nature and substance thereof. Verity is unity of substance. It is clear that these data answer the question How Innate Notions can be True to External Fact. The connection between mind and matter is thus a preëstablished Harmony.

Metaphysical

Chapter II. Nature of the Perfect

§1. Composition of Abstractions

Proposition. There are elementary conceptions.
Proof. Every thing is either simple or composed of parts. A conception is simple or complex according as it is composed of other conceptions or not.

A simple conception is an elementary one.

∴ Every conception is either elementary or composed of elementary conceptions.
Proposition. Every conception is of boundless complication in its own nature.
Proof. The only ways in which two thoughts can be compounded are

1 by being both thought at the same time
2 by one's being a thought of the other
3 by both being thought through a third.

In the last case the third thought thinks of the others in the second mode. It can only think of two through their being compounded. ∴ The 3rd way is reduced to the first and second.

We can think two thoughts at the same moment.

[*Example*]

∴ Conceptions can only be compounded by one's being a thought of the other.

[A thought of a thought may differ from the thought itself; but they must both belong to the same abstraction.]

That the of-thought should be true, it must be dependent upon the thought. It has a relation thereto of secondary to primary.

When one thing has a relation to another, that wherein it has the relation must be complex, and the related members must have something in common.

Hence two simple thoughts cannot have any relation in their own natures.

∴ All thoughts are complicated as far as they are compounded and there can be no plurality of elementary thoughts.

Proposition. The field of thought is extensive.

Proof. An extensive field is a total which has subjective elements *ad libitum* all of which are perfectly related to the others and any one of which supposes all the others. Such are time and space.

There are elementary conceptions.

Whatever is thought at once is an elementary conception.

Conceptions are infinitely complicated and every conception related in its very conception to every other. ∴ &c.

Since conceptions are typical of abstractions the world of abstractions is constructed in the same way.

§2. The world composed of numbers

The final elements of abstraction since they contain in themselves the relations to one another can contain nothing else (being simple) and hence are nothing but relations.

The final elements being relations contain the idea of numbers; and hence can contain nothing else.

Hence for every number there can be but one simple relation.

For 1. Ego.

Two-fold. Primary and Secondary.

Fourfold. Metaphysical Mathematical Dynamical Physical.

§3. Nature of the Perfect

Analysis of Creation

MS 71: Fall–Winter 1861

Whence are these thoughts, sensations, and passions? Or to substitute an abstract for concrete terms whence is modification of consciousness? A feeling or thought pure simple and perfect divested of all that is special, accidental, or external becomes such things as *Causality, Space, Love*—which are abstractions. An abstraction, however, is no longer a modification of consciousness at all, for it has no longer the accident of belonging to a special time, to a special person, and to a special subject of thought. Abstraction, therefore, to become modification of consciousness needs to be combined with that which modification of consciousness as yet unrelated to any abstraction is, that is to the perfectly unthought manifold of sensation. Well, how shall abstraction be combined with manifold of sensation? By existing as a form for matter, by *expression*. The first condition of creation is then expression.

I shall formularize the mode by which this conception has been arrived at in order that there may be no doubt regarding the sequence of thought.

Formula of Thought. 1 Whence is B. 2 B pure simple perfect is A. 3 A is no longer B. Why. 4 A to become B must be joined to B in its *null* form C. What C is. 5 What is the process by which A is combined with C? It is B^{2nd}.

Examples of the Necessity of Expression

1. Nobody can think pure abstraction on account of the necessity of doing it at a particular time &c. The abstraction to be realized must be a form of the thought, passion, or sensation in which it is realized.
2. If we have instead of one person, two people in conversation or correspondence the abstraction must be the form of a speech or deed.
3. Even religion must exist in some forms or rites in order to find the least realization.

§2

1 Whence is expression? That is what are the conditions of its existence? 2 Expression perfectly free from the extraneous and accidental
is mere meaning, which is of course no longer expression at all, because it will be shorn of its matter altogether. Expression is form but
mere form in its purity being deprived of matter is only form because
the intellect regards it as such and not really. Meaning to become
expression needs to be combined with that which expression is before
it has any meaning, or Language. This Language is not matter but is
a partial form which permits the existence of that ideal form Meaning
to become a realizable form. The means therefore by which meaning
enters into language, is the determination, the *regulation* of language.

Examples of the Necessity of Regulation

1. No one can have a thought of an abstraction which does not belong
to some subject. For instance, we cannot think of length without thinking of a line of space or time. Here the space or time is our language—
unthinkable without length. By the determination or regulation of the
time we introduce length as the meaning. So plurality must be thought
through imagining a plural of dots or something else—This plural need
not be thought very accurately it will have a variable character, at one
moment appearing before the mind's eye

thus   ⠿   then   ⠿   then   ⠿   &c.

2. Nothing can be clearer than the necessity of the regulation of Language, meaning the mode of expression between man and man, by
Meaning—whether this Language consists of gestures or speech or
music or what.
3. A prayer is not a prayer so long as the prayerfulness is wanting;
neither is it one before prayerfulness regulates some rite, or at least
some inward movement.
4. A curve is an expression, in which the meaning regulates the language—which is geometrical form.
5. The animal kingdom is a Language. The four types are the regula-
tions of that Language by the Meaning.

6. The human life is a language. The character is the regulation by the meaning, which is the principles of action.

7. The minds and hearts of two people is a language capable of expressing a meaning which regulates them by virtue of their ratio.

§3

How is this regulation possible? Regulation carried to perfection becomes in the case of the curve a straight line, thus in the illustration 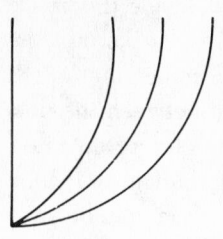 the meaning of the curve is regularly increasing increase but when this is carried out in the language to the utmost the curve becomes a straight line where the idea is no longer conveyed. So the plurality of dots must have no unitary interspace, hence it would cease to be a plural. The long line can have no breadth and thus ceases to be a line. The language must cease to have any mere grammatical forms and thus ceases to be language. The gestures must do away with the accidents of flesh and blood. The music with Laws of time &c. The prayer with all forms of service, speech, or thought. The human character with all constitutional frailty, thus becoming a mere mechanism. The lovers will become literally one. This perfect regulation ceasing to be regulation I will call Normality. Normality to become Regularity must have formality—or the regularity of meaningless language. The mode in which this must take place is by the introduction of an element into language which shall be unaffected by the meaning simply—such an element of language I will call diflection.

Examples of the Necessity of Diflection

1. To think length we must think of a long line of a certain breadth. To think plurality, of a unitary interspace between dots. To think force we must think of a body having inertia.

2. To speak we must have syllables. To make signs a body which remains the same in all gesticulations. In music we must have the scale &c.

3. That the mind may turn to the absolute it must turn also to the factitious.

4. That a curve should express increasing increase it must have a dimension perpendicular to that increase.

5. The Types of the animal kingdom must be carried out in classes.
6. Greatness of soul emerges from frailty of flesh.
7. Love exists through difference of natures.

§4

By diflection we do not mean the diametric element, itself, of language but the influence, the inworking of this element. If this diflection is carried to perfection the language becomes as incapable of expressing the meaning as though there were no diflection and the difference between the two cases will be merely subjective. If we make our line pure breadth instead of pure length, the breadth becomes the length and the result is the same. If we make the interspace between the dots absolutely unbroken, the result is the same as if there were no interspace. If a body has no resistance, forces can no more influence it than if it had absolute inertia, and one conception contains the idea of force no more than the other. If there were no peculiar laws of language *per se* we should have the same inarticulate result as though language were wholly influenced by laws for itself. If the body is absolutely under physical and physiological control there is no more gesture than if there were no fixity of body at all. If the mind tries to turn to the Manifold of sense wholly there is the same negation of thought that there would be if it tried to turn wholly to the Absolute. If the second dimension of a curve is infinitely drawn out a straight line is produced just as if it had no second dimension. If human frailty were absolute we should be mere machines, so we should if human principles were absolute. Lovers would be as indifferent if they had nothing in common as they would if they had everything in common. Obviously the diflection perfect and the diflection null are to be combined by coördination. But as one of these is coincident with the tendency of the meaning and the other opposed to it, this coördination is tantamount to an ordination in the meaning expressed.

Examples of the Necessity of Ordination

1. On account of breadth, we can only think elongation to a certain degree. On account of interspace a certain amount of plurality; on account of inertia a certain intensity of force.
2. On account of the machinery of language we must be content to express ourselves with what terseness and strength the language admits

of. On account of our joints and muscles we are limited to a few elementary gestures. Scales and times limit us as to melodies.

3. An algebraic curve must have a certain order or degree.

4. Our prayers are imperfect because we cannot get along without forms.

5. A limited amount of virtue is attained by a frail being.

6. A limit to love is the incompatibility of natures.

7. The Types of the animal kingdom are limited by the Classes to certain orders.

§5

What is the condition of ordination. Ordination pure simple and perfect which I will call *inordination* would have this effect. The long line would have a breadth but would be inconceivably long. The plural would have interspace but would be inconceivably numerous. The dynamic condition of the body would be that of inertia made inconsiderable by the inconceivable force applied.

The language would possess a machinery but it would be utterly inadequate to express the meaning. The joints of our arms would prevent the expression of the gesture. The scales and times would be too contracted for our music.

The curve would be reduced to an ⊢⊣ with the uprights infinitely long.

The resistance to temptation would become merely formal.

The difference of nature of the lovers would be mere difference of individuality.

All this is not ordination, and that it should become such it must be joined to what I call *coördination*. That is, that lowest degree of ordination which gives the long line length but no breadth except at one point where it runs out inconceivably toward the sides; which reduces the plurality to a ring; (?) Which gives the moving body infinite force and infinite inertia. (?) Which reduces the curve to two lines crossing at right angles. Now it is observable that in all these instances of inordination and coordination there is wanting (and this is the difficulty) that element of form which the diflection seemed to introduce. The diflection remains, but not uniformly. Centralization, formity, *conformity*, must be the process by which Inordination and coördination unite to form ordination. We shall have a clearer idea of what this conformity is by noting the effect of its introduction. To think length we must imagine a line through the conception of parallelogram, oval, or arrow-head, which conception, quite distinct from the idea conveyed, yet so far as it goes determines the whole image. To imagine a plural we must conceive it as a *group* which conception determines the manifestation without calling any further upon the original idea. So force must be conceived through the conception of motion of a mass, merely.

So increase of increase can only be expressed geometrically by giving the curve a *focus*, its relations to which completely determine its form.

It is clear that *Conformity* has a certain intimate connection with diflection.

§6

Whence this conformity? In its perfect state it would become eccentricity simply and no longer be conformity. On the other side uniformity. They both want particularization of the influence of parts which would make uniformity conformity and eccentricity conformity.

We seemed to have introduced this particularization in regulation.

MS 72: Winter 1861–1862

Quantities applied to things

S   Unity
    Plurality } are the kinds of Quantity that we must regard a
    Totality   //thought-of/thing// as having

Predicates applied to Qualities

P   Negation
    Reality   } are the different extents to which a Quality may be
    Infinity   possessed

Amounts of time applied to Relations

Q   Community
    Causality } are the different Dependencies a Quality can have,
    Influx   dependent on the *time* of the relation

Position in the Intellect applied to forms of fact

R   Possibility
    Actuality } indicate the thoughts belonging to the Imagination,
    Necessity   Perception, or Reason

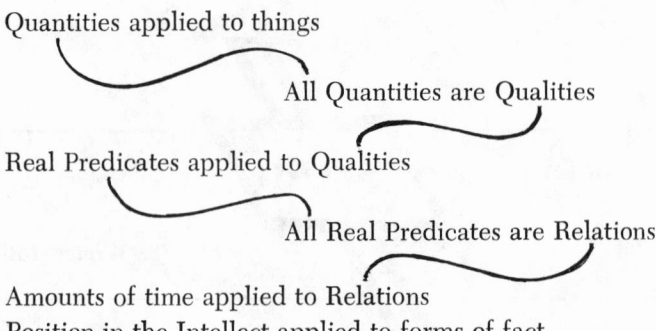

Quantities applied to things

All Quantities are Qualities

Real Predicates applied to Qualities

All Real Predicates are Relations

Amounts of time applied to Relations
Position in the Intellect applied to forms of fact.

Quantities viewed how are qualities? Transcendentally. Separated from their things and viewed in their relation to the thing.

Real predicates viewed how are relations? Transcendentally. Taken away from the quality so as to see their manner of affecting the quality.

Now how does the Amount of time stand to the Relation? View the world first with the relations of things in it as all one momentary thing. How is it with the relations now? They are purely *formal* and forceless. Let us now introduce time. Now from one fact another follows in time, the relation is now *real* and *forcible*. The further we go back in time the more and more is the cause the origin of the effect, the greater and greater is the dependency through there being more and more Spiritual Exhibition, till we arrive at the *first* cause; this, since our faculty cannot think of a *first in time* (which, indeed, is not), becomes that which *sustains* this whole train of cause and effect—that from which all things *perpetually emanate*. Now the dependency is Absolute, through the spiritual exhibition being real. Now what is time that it should enable a spirit a-hold of matter and by it in connection with another spirit to communicate itself thereto? It is action-room, is it not?

We have now

All quantities are qualities	Negation Reality Infinity are applied to qualities
All Real Predicates are relations &	Community Causality Influx are applied to relations
All times are forms of fact	Possibility Actuality Necessity to forms of fact.

Well Quantity is Infinite qualities
Real Predicates are Influxual relations
Times are Necessary Forms of fact.

What does reasonableness give to form of [fact? Remove] all reasonableness and it is merely possible th[ought, a pure] form unfilled
up by the matter of fact which [has no verity.] Give to the form of fact
the reasonbleness of [perception] and it has verity—positive limited
verity. Give to [form of fact] the reasonableness of reason; it is necessary, it has a perfect verity. WHAT IS REASONABLENESS THAT
IT SHOULD GIVE VERITY TO FORM OF FACT? This is a *Question!* Now you see we come to something *new*,—new to the school of
philosophy from which we have emerged. We have risen to a Cartesian,
Platonic atmosphere—quite above the conceptions of Aristotle, Locke,
or Hamilton. Express the answer to this question how you please, you
must give utterance to Idealism. The identity of mind and matter [is]
that they are the same thing from different points of view.

Let us go back and try another road. You will notice that there are
three kinds of Infinity—The Infinity of Unity—the Infinity of Plurality—
and the Infinity of Totality. Bear in mind what infinity is, The *perfect*
influxual dependence of a quality. Now Unity, plurality, totality all
being perfectly dependent are Infinite. Yet the dependence is not the
same.

> A *unit* is one of a number
> A *plural* is an incomplete series
> A *total* is a series viewed as *one*,
>   the perfect number.

The *unity* depends not merely on the thought of its own substance
but on other coëxistences. Dependence on coexistences is communitive
dependence. The infinity of unity therefore is a communitive or conditional infinity.

Plurality depends on the previous pluralities of the series. In
thinking

          • • • • • • • •

I run them up some such way as this

    •
   • •
  • • •
 • • • •
• • • • •
• • • • • •
• • • • • • •

Or this

```
           O

      +    O    +

 •  +  •   O   •  +  •
```

In any case the quality is dependent on previous qualities—but this constitutes causality. The dependency of Plurality therefore is Causal infinity.

In like manner Totality which emanates from a thing relating to a plurality at once has Influxual Infinity.

Thus the Category of Q (Community Causality Influx) is drawn from the definition of S.

There are also 3 kinds of Influx. That of Negation which is Possible Influx, that of Reality which is Actual Influx, that of Infinity which is Rational or Necessary Influx. Thus R is obtained from P.

There are further three kinds of Necessity. The necessity of Community which is Intellectual or formal simply. That of Expense which is forcible and that of Creation, where the whole force is reduced to a form, the absolute necessity.

This gives a fifth category of Formality, Intellectuality or Arbitrariness, Forcibleness, and Absoluteness; where it is obvious that much more than usual is meant by the words.

The Chemical Theory
of Interpenetration

P 11:
American Journal of Science and Arts
2d ser. 35 (*January* 1863)*:78–82*

Physicists are now rapidly doing away with all theories which demand peculiar shapes and kinds of matter in favor of those which demand peculiar vibrations. At this day, the arrow-shaped particles of the old theory of light seem grotesque. There is a good reason for this tendency. We require an explanation of forces. Now a force is only a mathematical function of a change, and a change in space can only be conceived of *a priori* as a motion. To explain a thing is to bring it into the realm of our *a priori* conceptions. Hence, whenever we endeavor to explain any force of nature by means of hypothetical shapes and properties of matter these only help us so far as they are conditions of certain motions. These motions are the real explanation; and if we can succeed in getting the motions without the peculiarities of matter, our hypothesis will be so much the smaller.

The object of the present article is to apply this principle to the Atomic Theory.

I. In the first place, it is necessary to show that the hypothesis of atoms, in itself, explains nothing.

That which the atomic theory undertakes to explain is the connection of integral numbers with chemical equivalents.

An explanatory hypothesis is one which, being admitted, necessitates all the phenomena. The laws to be explained are as follows:

1. The Law of Equivalents, or that if *a* units of one body combine with *x* of a second and *y* of a third; and if *x* of that second combines

with b of a fourth, that y of the third will also combine with b of the fourth.

The explanation is that these are the weights of the atoms and that bodies combine atom by atom. But how should we know that they combine atom by atom? This is an addition to the hypothesis.

2. The Law of Multiple Proportions.

How should we know that atoms will mix in any simpler ratios than black and white beans would if stirred up together?

3. The Law of Combining Volumes of Gases.

The explanation is that the atoms of all gases are equally distant. A new hypothesis.

4. The Law of Volumes of Isomorphous Crystals. Another hypothesis needed.

5. The Law of Thermal Equivalents of the Elements.

Explanation: All atoms have the same capacity for heat. Still another hypothesis, which moreover does not apply to compounds.

6. The Thermal Equivalents of Isomorphous Crystals.

7. Kopp's Law of Boiling Points. How is this explained?

8. Prout's Law as modified by Dumas.

The only atomic weights which have been determined with sufficient accuracy to test the law, beside those of Stas, are the following:—
   Carbon 6.01 Berzelius; 6.00 Dumas and Stas; 6.00 Erdmann and Marchand; 6.06 Liebig and Redtenbacher; 6.03 Strecker. C is not more than 6.004.
   Lithium, Diehl 7.026 (prob. error $\pm.006$); Troost 7.01; Mallet ($S = 16.03$, Na $= 23.05$, Mg $= 12.0125$) 7.027. Mean 7.02.
   Calcium 20.002 ($C = 6.004$) Erdmann and Marchand.
   With less accuracy we have
   Iron, Svanberg and Norlin (after rejecting two discordant experiments according to Peirce's criterion) 28.048; Berzelius, 28.024; Erdmann and Marchand, 28.012; Maumené, 28.000. Mean 28.017.
   Combining the first three atomic weights with those determined by Stas, we have:—

	Experiment.	Law.	Difference.	Dif.÷Exp.
K	39.154	39.25	−.096	$\frac{1}{400}$
Na	23.05	23	+.05	$\frac{1}{500}$
Ag	107.94	108	−.06	$\frac{1}{1600}$
Pb	103.45	103.5	−.05	$\frac{1}{2000}$
Cl	35.46	35.5	−.04	$\frac{1}{900}$
N	14.04	14	+.04	$\frac{1}{350}$
S	16.03	16	+.03	$\frac{1}{500}$
H	1.005	1	+.005	$\frac{1}{200}$
Li	7.02	7	+.02	$\frac{1}{400}$
Ca	20.002	20	+.002	$\frac{1}{10000}$
C	6.004	6	+.004	$\frac{1}{1500}$

K is an unexplained anomaly, but the probability of only one difference out of thirteen being greater than $\frac{.25}{4}$ is .0000087, while the
effect of the residual influence which carries K out of this limit is only
$\frac{1}{1200}$ of the atomic weight. Omitting K, the sum of the above differences
is +.001; the probability of this being so small is .035; hence, upon this
consideration, the probability of the law is .782.

The probability is, therefore, still in favor of the law. The last column in the table shows how small the residual phenomena are; and
they may be made still smaller by making the unit by which the atomic
weights are measured a little larger.

This law presents another example of the connection between
chemical equivalents and integral numbers, and must probably be
capable of a common explanation with the rest. Yet it is clear that the
atomic hypothesis never can explain it.

9. It is impossible for the atomic theory to explain why the mono-
atomic radicles combine together without condensation in the gaseous
form; while the diatomic radicles lose their own volume, the triatomic
one more than their own volume, &c., in combining with the mono-
atomic. Why in acetic ether, for example, $\left.\begin{array}{c} CO.CH_2.H \\ 2CH_2.H \end{array}\right\} O$ the dibasic
radicles occupy no space at all.

II. I shall now attempt to show that the facts of chemistry are explicable by the view of Kant, that matter is not absolutely impenetrable

and that chemical union consists in the interpenetration of the constituents.

1. The law of definite proportions is capable of demonstration without any hypothesis. We can conceive of no event in space which does not consist of a motion. Nothing can be the cause of a motion except a motion; hence every force is a motion. And every quality of matter is either a motion or some element of the mental analysis of the conception of a body moving in some way or other. Hence, when the force of one body acts on the quality of another to produce an event, it is merely one motion modifying a second to produce a third. Motion is never stationary, but always communicates itself from the moving particle to all others which are in communication with that. Accordingly, when one body acts on another *through a difference of quality*, the latter will also act on the former and there will be a tendency to produce homogeneity of quality throughout the two. This homogeneity is actually established, or it is not. If it is not, the amount of force which holds back the two forces from their natural action must be just as strong as the forces themselves. It is clear, therefore, that when the force of the acting body equals that of the body acted upon, all the force will be exhausted in preventing the homogeneity. Probably, however, it might be proved that the homogeneity is always established; and if it is, it cannot be established through both motions existing at the same time without interference. For, if they had not interfered, they could not have acted upon one another. They must, therefore, destroy each other (producing a new motion) and when they are equal the peculiarities by which they acted will be neutralized and there will be no further action. Now the same kind of matter under the same dynamical conditions possesses always the same amount of force proportionally to its mass; hence when one kind of matter acts on another through being of a different kind, it can only act on a definite amount of that matter, the dynamical circumstances remaining the same.

2. Let us call the reciprocal of the Atomic Weight the Chemical Intensity. This represents the force which causes bodies to combine. It remains the same under all dynamical circumstances. Hence, it must be something inherent in matter and unaffected by all vibrations. In gases it is proportional to the elasticity, and in elementary bodies generally it is equal to the specific heat, which is the elasticity of the

medium of heat-vibrations. We conclude, then, that the Chemical Intensity is the molecular or substantive elasticity. (B. Peirce.)

When heat expands the body, it is the elasticity which restores it. Any motions of vibration in a homogeneous elastic medium may be resolved into expansions and contractions. Hence, if we assume that heat produces the expansions, this elasticity is an active condensing force.

If two bodies interpenetrate it is clear that this force may hold them together. This explains the law of definite proportions, the law of vapor densities, and the law of thermal equivalents.

3. It is geometrically self-evident that interpenetration must take place between equal volumes and must result in a condensation to one half, unless some other action takes place. Accordingly we find that wherever there is no condensation there is only a double decomposition.

4. In one volume of a compound there is one equivalent of chemical intensity. Hence there is nothing to prevent its combining with one volume more, &c. This explains the law of multiple proportions, which it is to be observed has no place where the bodies unite without condensation.

5. The solid and liquid states result from the action of cohesion. Now cohesion is an attraction properly so called and acts at a distance, for if it did not it would not vary with the state of condensation. Hence it is a force affecting molecules and not matter in its continuity. This explains why the above reasonings from the state of gases are not invalidated by the facts relating to liquids and solids.

6. If we suppose, with the metaphysicians, that all the kinds of matter are derived from one, since this must have become condensed by the law of equal volumes, all the equivalents of the elements will be multiples of that of the original matter. This explains Prout's law. If, moreover, we admit that the different elements are distinguished by different elasticities, and accept the recent view that the lines of the spectroscope are only produced by elements in their free state, it will follow that every element except sodium is a mixture of several. We have no reason to suppose that these are present in equivalent pro-

portions. So that this consideration gives room for large discrepancies from Prout's law.

7. It is observable that tribasic radicles frequently behave like monobasic ones, as N in $\mathrm{C_2H_2(NO_2)O \brace H}$ O and in $\mathrm{H \brace NO_2}$ $\mathrm{O_2}$, and that monobasic radicles frequently behave like tribasic ones, as Cl in ICl_3. There is the same confusion between dibasic and tetrabasic radicles, as in CO. Hence we infer that the distinction between even- and odd-basic is altogether superior to that between monobasic and tribasic, dibasic and tetrabasic.

Now if a body can enter into double decomposition with hydrogen (that is, combine without condensation) it is obvious that it must be odd-basic; for in that case it will form a compound which being of two volumes cannot combine with another volume of H unless it combines with two volumes. If it does thus combine it will be tribasic, otherwise monobasic.

On the other hand, if a body cannot enter into double decomposition with the monobasic radicles, it must be even-basic; for in this case, since its volume after combination will be the same as before, there is no reason why it should not either combine with condensation with a new volume of the monobasic radicle (in which case it will be four or more basic) or else enter into double decomposition with it, in which case it will be dibasic. This explains why the dibasic radicles always lose their own volume in combining with the monobasic; why the tribasic lose twice their own volume, &c.

8. A radicle being a constituent in combination, it follows that its internal forces do not come to equilibrium of themselves, and this accounts for the fact that monobasic radicles cannot exist free. This fact is determined by reactions and not by vapor-density, for according to the present theory the volume fixes neither the atom nor the molecule but the *equivalent*, that is to say, the amount of matter containing a unit of chemical intensity. The dibasic radicles may exist in the free state because, since in combining they are condensed, it follows that there is some disturbance of their internal forces.

9. An odd-basic radicle being in itself out of equilibrium in this way, it follows that the addition of it to another radicle will change the basicity of that radicle from odd to even or from even to odd; while the addition of an even-basic radicle will have no such effect.

Cambridge, Mass., Dec. 1862.

[The Place of Our Age in the History of Civilization]

P 12: **Cambridge Chronicle**
21 November 1863, p. 1

Extracts from an Oration, Delivered at the Reunion of the Cambridge High School Association, Thursday Evening, Nov. 12, 1863

Ladies and Gentlemen of the High School Association:—In attempting to address you, I feel keenly the disadvantage of never having made any matter of general interest a special study. I am, therefore, forced to select a topic on which I have scarcely a right to an original opinion—certainly not to urge my opinion as entitled to much credit. I beg you, then, to regard whatever I say on THE PLACE OF OUR AGE IN THE HISTORY OF CIVILIZATION, as such a suggestion as might be put forth in conversation, and nothing more.

By *our age* I mean the 17th, 18th, and 19th centuries. There are those who, dazzled by the steam-engine and the telegraph, regard the nineteenth century as something *sui generis*. But this I think is doing injustice to ourselves.

Bring Bacon or Newton here, and display to him the wonders our century has to show, and he will tell you, "All this is remarkable and deeply interesting, but it is not surprising. I knew," he will say, "that all this or something very like it must come at this time, for it is nothing more than the certain consequence of the principles laid down by me and my contemporaries for your guidance." Either of them will say this. But now let us turn from the Century to the Age (reckoning from the settlement of Jamestown). Let us bring the sublimest intellect that ever shone before, and what would Dante say? Let him trace the rise of constitutional government, see a down-trodden people steadily bend a haughty dynasty to obedience, give it laws and bring it to trial and execution, and finally reduce it to a convenient cipher; let him see the most enthralled people under the sun blow their rulers into a thousand pieces and establish such a terror that "all the kings of the earth, and the great men and the rich men and the chief captains and the mighty men and every bondman and every freeman hide themselves in the dens and in the rocks of the mountains"; let him see the human mind try its religion in a blazing fire, expose the falsity of its history, the impossibility of its miracles, the humanity of its revelations, until the very "heavens depart as a scroll when it is rolled together"; and then let him see the restless boundary of man's power extending over the outward world, see him dashing through time, conversing through immense distances, doing violence to the lightning, and living in such a fire of activity as less salamandrine generations could not have endured; and he who viewed Hell without dismay would fall to the earth quailing before the terrific might of intellect which God has scattered broadcast over this whole age. This century's doings taken apart are mere jugglery—clever feats—but this age is that in which "the sun becomes black as sack-cloth of hair, and the moon becomes as blood, and the stars of heaven fall unto the earth even as a fig-tree casteth her untimely figs, when she is shaken of a mighty wind." I equally disagree with those who think we are living in the age of the reformation. I do so on the ground that there was nothing rationalistic in the tendency of that age. In our time, if we wish to found a new government, religion, or art, we begin at first principles, consider the philosophy of our object and follow it out. But the reformation, as its name implies, was an attempt to suppress abuses in existing institutions without doing away with the institutions themselves. In religion, they reformed the church, but still they had a church. In our times, new denominations cast aside the church, at least. In politics, they resisted the growing power of royalty, but only in favor of the ancient system. Even their great inventions, gun-powder, printing, and the compass were not the results of original research but were heard of in old books. The discovery of America, itself, was suggested by a study of the ancient geographers. The passion for antiquity was intense,—inconceivable to us, except by remembering that the age which had preceded them, that of the crusades, was far more magnificent than theirs, and that the Greeks were both in mind and manners most evidently their superiors.

Then there was another great difference between them and us: their attempts at emancipating the human mind either from mistake or insufficiency were always failures; their republics were swept away,

the power of royalty was more firmly established than ever, their no-
blest arts perished, and the churches which they had set up gave no
more room for freedom of thought than mother Rome herself. There
was a stifled cry for liberty,—a blind groping for the light, backward
instead of onward.

The Reformation was a struggle of humanity to regain its rightful
master; in our day the aim is absolute liberty. We have *Tracts for the
Times* in England, a strict Lutheran party in Germany, the Empire in
France; but who will say that these are primary tendencies of the age?
They are rather reactions against the extravagancies of the times. From
the moment when the ball of human progress received its first impetus
from the mighty hands of Descartes, of Bacon, and of Galileo,—we
hear, as the very sound of the stroke, the decisive protest against any
authority, however venerable—against any arbiter of truth except our
own reason. Descartes is the father of modern metaphysics, and you
know it was he who introduced the term "philosophic doubt," he, first,
declaring that a man should begin every investigation entirely without
doubt; and he followed a completely independent train of thought, as
though, before him, nobody had ever thought anything correctly.
Bacon, also, respects no philosophers except certain Greeks *whose
works are lost;* Aristotle he scouts at, and maintains that there has been
no science before his time and that nothing has ever been discovered
except by accident.

The human mind having been emancipated by these great sceptics,
works of great originality were speedily produced, so that the same
century saw the productions of Hobbes, Cudworth, Malebranche,
Spinoza, Locke, Leibnitz, and Newton. The effect of these works was
stupendous. Every question that the human mind had to ask seemed
at once answered, and that too by works of such greatness of thought
and power of logic, that the attention of every reasoning mind was
engrossed by them. Their vastness, indeed, was overwhelming; so complete were they, so true, so profound, that, at first, they seemed to
check originality. In the first half of the eighteenth century scarcely
anything new seems to have been produced.

At last, however, the ball of progress was struck again. And by
whom? By another, more powerful doubter, the immortal Hume. In his
day, the philosophical world was divided between the doctrines of
Leibnitz and Locke, the former of whom maintained the existence of
innate ideas while the latter rejected them. Hume, accepting the latter

doctrine, which was prevalent in England, asked "How do we know that every change has a cause?" He demonstrated by invincible logic, that upon Locke's system, it was impossible to prove this, and that it ought not to be admitted as a principle at all. Of course, the doctrine of a first cause and the very idea of miracles, vanish with the notion of causality.

Immanuel Kant was reposing in a firm belief in the metaphysics of Leibnitz as theologized by Wolff when he first read the book of Hume. How many scholastics, nay how many theologians of our own day would have done otherwise than say "Behold the fruit of our opponent's system of philosophy!" This mean, degraded spirit, which is eager to answer an opponent and still remain the slave of error, was far from being Kant's. He set about asking his own philosophy the question that Hume had asked of Locke's. "We say that this and the other are innate ideas," he said; "but how do we know that our innate ideas are true?"

The book in which he embodied the discussion of this question is, perhaps, the greatest work of the human intellect. All later philosophies are to be classified according to the ideas contained in it, for it is all the direct result of this production. And in these later philosophies, whether we consider their profundity or their number, our age ranges far above all others put together. This wonderful fecundity of thought, I say, is the direct result of Kant's *Kritik;* and it is to be explained by the fact that Kant presented a more insoluble doubt than all the rest, and one which has not been answered to this day, for while he showed that our innate ideas of space, time, quantity, reality, cause, possibility, and so on are true, he found himself utterly unable to do this respecting the ideas of Immortality, Freedom, and God. Accordingly, all metaphysicians since his time have been endeavoring to remove this difficulty, but not altogether with success. Hegel's system seemed, at first, satisfactory, but its further development resulted in Strauss' *Life of Jesus,* against which the human soul, the datum upon which he proceeded, itself cried out; the sense of mankind, which he had elevated into a God, itself repudiated the claim. We thus see, however, that all the progress we have made in philosophy, that is all that has been made since the Greeks, is the result of that methodical scepticism which is the first element of human freedom.

I need not repeat the political history of the last 250 years, to prove the predominance of the spirit of liberty in that sphere. You will find an ever-increasing irreverence toward rulers, from the days of Hampden to ours, when some of the more advanced spirits look forward to the time when there shall be no government. If, then, all the glory of our age has sprung from a spirit of Scepticism and Irreverence, it is easy to say where its faults are to be found.

Modern progress having been detached from its ancient mother by the dark ages, that fearful parturition, has since now lived a self-sustaining life. Its growth, its outline, its strength are all its own; influenced to some degree, by its parent, but only through an exterior medium. The only cord which ever bound them, and which belonged to either, is Christianity. Since the beginning of Christianity the growth of civilization has had six stages.

The 1st is the Age of the Rise of Christianity, the 2d is the age of the Migrations of the Barbarians, the 3d is the Age of the Establishment of Modern Nations, the 4th is the age of the crusades, the 5th is the age of the Reformation, and the 6th is our own age, or as we are fond of calling it, the Age of Reason. Now, briefly to indicate these periods, we may take them of equal length. Make them, 320 or 325 years apiece, and it will suffice for my purpose. Let us see what each of these ages has done for civilization.

The age of the Rise of Christianity presents no other event which has had any influence upon the destinies of mankind. The whole era must be interpreted according to that central fact. For what do we see? A complete centralization of power in the Emperor, so that subjects had *no* rights whatever. Here is a very remarkable thing, that Rome, so distinguished for her ethical ideas, should have lost sight of the reciprocity of right and duty, altogether. Who could fail to see that this corruption of theory was to be accounted for by the corruption of practice? Vice had gone to greater lengths and spread more widely than ever before or since. I cannot with decency describe a state of affairs in which virtue in any station was certain ruin. The extraordinary virtue displayed by the early Christians in the persecutions throughout this period was in wonderful contrast to the vices of the heathen; it gained them positions of trust and honor, even in that age, and indicated some divine influence working within them. A philosophical, candid, and humane observer, therefore, even in that age, must I think have been convinced that Christianity was the hope of the world. The church was defined in this age. The conception of the messianic kingdom had been already indicated; this age saw its relations established to those outward institutions, doctrines, and works in which it embodies itself. It is that "beginning" of the church which has generally been made its standard in later ages.

The age of the migrations of the barbarians witnessed the entire sweeping away of the vestiges of ancient civilization. The new people were without history, without Pagan prejudice and were full of the spirit of freedom. The Roman Empire and its modes of thought melted at their breath. To the church which appeared in those troublous times as the sole preserver of the arts of peace as well as of spiritual health, they bowed and quickly knelt. This institution, while the civil confusion was becoming greater, consolidated its internal government more and more, spread its external influence wider and wider through all the affairs of life, and in the night of ignorance which ensued, the only intellectual movement of Europe was that of the church.

The next age is one of establishment. The new languages grew up. The feudal system arose from small beginnings until it formed the one law of Europe. The Empire of Charlemagne was established and soon separated into the three nations of France, Germany, and Italy; while all the other nations of Modern Europe received their separate governments. Even learning began to glimmer through the Pyrenees, the universities of Paris and Oxford were founded, and philosophy began to take root. The condition of the church was humiliating; her spiritual power was vastly increased, the temporal power began to arise, and at first the promise was that the head of the church should be the head of Christendom. And had the clergy kept the high spiritual post that naturally belonged to them, it might have been so. Unfortunately, they began to love their power, and as a consequence they became ambitious. Their ambition generated corruption; corruption, sneaking vice, intrigue, rebellion, and ruin. John the XII, the Pope, was deposed by Otho, the Emperor, for murder, incest, and plots against the State; and a few years later we witness the now familiar spectacle of a Pope kept in his place by the arms of an Emperor. What a lesson is this of obedience to the conditions which God has imposed upon the church!

The next age is that of the Crusades. For four hundred years, God had been preparing another civilization, with which that of Christianity might be compared; namely, that of the Mahommedans. Christianity now presented its most imposing aspect. The magnificence of Rome finds its parallel in that of Solomon; Scholasticism, the only thoroughly

Christian form of philosophy, was at its height; a grand Christian architecture was flourishing; and the whole civilization of Europe seemed to have reference to the church, while that of Islam was thoroughly Mahommedan. And now—wonder of wonders!—the whole of Christendom, men, women, and children, swarmed forth to Palestine, passing through Rome on their way, in order to compare the two civilizations. Upon the result of this comparison on the mind of Europe, I need not dwell. Modern times, modern breadth of thought, and modern freedom from ecclesiastical superstition followed the crusades, in place of the mediæval narrowness and fondness for ignorance which had preceded them. The great idea which emerged was that the church is a great and good thing, but that it should not be allowed to override all the other means and appliances of civilization.

We have now come down to the age of the Reformation, the character of which I need not sketch. It seems to me apparent that all this civilization is the work of Christianity. If it is not so clear respecting the progress of our own age, it is because we have not seen the termination of it, and do not understand the philosophy of it.

* * * * *

Christianity is not a doctrine, or possible law; it is an actual law—a kingdom. And a kingdom over what? "All things shall be put under his feet." What then does it not include? Do you assert that liberty is of any value? "His service is perfect freedom." We are accustomed to say that these phrases are hyperbolical. But that is an unwarrantable assumption—a mere subterfuge to reconcile the statement with the fact. The Jews were given to understand by every token that language or the miraculous course of their history could convey, that they were to be taken care of and saved as a nation. I say that no human being however spiritually minded could have read those Jewish prophecies and have got any other idea from *them* than that the Messiah there promised them was a Prince, seated upon the throne of his fathers, conducting the affairs of the nation, and leading them on to national glory as much as to individual immortality. When the promise was extended to the Gentiles, it meant the same thing for them. If therefore we are Christians it seems to me we must believe that Christ is now directing the course of history and presiding over the destinies of kings, and that there is no branch of the public weal which does not come within the bounds of his realm. And civilization is nothing but Christianity on the grand scale.

In a mimic history—a well-constructed play—the developement of the plot has a regular course.

It begins with a prologue, or semi-lyrical speech of one of the characters, displaying the general idea of the play, putting the audience in the right state of mind. This accomplished, the drama proper begins. First, the materials and elements of the plot are displayed, the situation, characters, etcetera in which the idea is to be embodied. Next, the idea is presented, at work among these elements. The plot is *actualized*. Next, it is necessary that we should see the causes, the means, the conditions by virtue of which the plot is actualized. Otherwise, we could see no developement in the play. Fourth, comes the display of the passion in full operation, neither over- nor under-drawn, but well marked, definite, and human. This is the middle of the play. Next, fifthly, if the play is an instructive one relatively to the working of the idea it embodies, there must be a counterplot, or plurality of plots, all having reference to the same conception. Thus, in *Othello*, after the treachery of Iago has been displayed fully towards Othello and his jealousy depicted, we have some scenes in which the action of the same double-dealing is shown towards Cassio, Roderigo, and Bianca. Sixthly, comes the grand climax, showing the idea, no longer working in the heart and mind merely, but in material effects; and then comes the conclusion, in which the whole plot is wound up, and the whole ends with an address to the audience, as it had begun, with a soliloquy.

Now let us see if Christianity, the plot of History, does not follow determinate laws in its developement, so that from a consideration of them we can gather where we are and whither we are tending.

Religion ought not to be regarded either as a subjective or an objective phenomenon. That is to say, it is neither something within us nor yet altogether without us—but bears rather a third relation to us, namely, that of existing in our communion with another being. Nevertheless, religion may be revealed in either of the three ways—by an inward self-developement, or by seeing it about us, or by a personal communication from the Most High. An example of revealed religion in the first way is natural religion. A man looks upon nature, sees its sublimity and beauty and his spirit gradually rises to the idea of a God. He does not see the Divinity, nor does nature prove to him the existence of that Being, but it does excite his mind and his imagination until the idea becomes rooted in his heart. In the same way, the continual change and movement in nature, suggest the idea of omnipresence. And finally, by the events of his own life, he becomes persuaded of the relation of that Being with his own soul. Such a religion, where all is hinted at, nought revealed, is natural religion. Of much the same character is the religion of the Jews. Though they had miracles, so it appeared did the Egyptians and Canaanites; so that these miracles did not *prove* their religion. Nowhere did they actually see, for that is not possible except to an already developed spiritual insight, the intimate union of man with God. Their wonderful history led them to believe it, and their prophets told them of it; but all this only amounted to suggestion. And by these suggestions it was impressed.

This inward or subjective revelation of religion, in our dispensation, cannot be said to exist in its pure form. For, in consequence of our being in a christian community, we no sooner get to recognize religion, than we learn from people of higher attainment, as out of a book.

Religion through immediate revelation is what we hope for in the millennium. It certainly cannot be said to exist now, for though there have been revelations the cases have been very few, and the mass of christians receive only sufficient grace to understand a portion of prophecy.—Christianity is objectively impressed, being wholly inculcated by our great example. We learn it by contemplating it in its full manifestation in Him, and in the lesser lights of the church. In order therefore to understand the history of christianity or civilization, we must seek to know the successive conditions of the developement of religion in man by seeing it in an example.

Every object is obliged to appear under a certain set of forms. The most familiar exemplification of these is found in a *proposition*. Every statement may be regarded as an object, that is it is something outside of us which we can know, and the grammatical analysis of a statement exemplifies I say more familiarly than anything else the laws of objective presentations. Hence, in order to trace the laws of the objective presentation of religion, I shall try to embody it in a proposition. The first condition of a statement is that it shall state something,—that it shall have a predicate. But this again implies a whole series of conditions previously to the statement of the proposition, which shall enable you to comprehend the notion which I wish to convey as well as the language in which I convey it. Before a man can read a book, he must understand the meaning of terms, that is, he must already have the elements of the thought which the book propounds. In the same way, before a man can hear the voice of God or even comprehend an example of religion he must have a notion of what religion is, and that implies that he must previously have had an inward revelation of religion. In compliance with this condition, both heathen and Jews, before the birth of Christ, had attained to the idea of an intimate union of humanity with Deity, such that they should be brought into an ordinated harmony, in which the creature should be so completely in unison with the creator that all his motions should be brought under law, as much as inanimate natures are, and yet that man should in this very subjection and passivity find his highest freedom, activity, and rounded completion. This, then, is the predicate of the formula by which I propose to express Christianity—and I will call it the Kingdom of heaven. The Jews had besides this, a complicated ritual delivered to them, a system of purification which as the epistle to the Hebrews argues never could effect anything, and a temple and feasts which were perpetually calling their attention to vacant forms. All this was symbolic. It was the grammar of christianity without its substance. It was the fulfillment of that other condition, that a man to understand what I tell him must have not only the comprehension of ideas but an acquaintance with the language in which they are to be put.

After the inward revelation, comes the objective revelation, and the latter must itself be the culmination of the former, for bearing as it must a higher message it must itself act suggestively in order that its meaning may be perceived. This culminating point will be the phenomenon of perfection in such a form that man can see and know it; that is, it must be perfection in human form. The first condition, therefore, the enunciation of the predicate, was fulfilled at the birth of Christ.

(The orator here proceeded to analyze the formula "The Church is the Kingdom of Heaven"; and endeavored to show what part each age had played in its enunciation.)

This division of history into ages suggests another reflection. That there is an analogy between the course of ancient Grecian and of modern history. If we had our migration of peoples, so had they theirs, 2000 years before. Corresponding to our age of chivalry, they had the Argonautic expeditions and Trojan war. Our Reformation is very imperfectly represented by a reform of another kind, that of the governments of the Grecian States. But these ages have another curious coincidence, it is that one dawns in Homer, the other in Dante. But doubtful as the analogy of these last ages is, that between the Greece of two thousand years ago and our own times, is truly remarkable. The resemblance, indeed, is so complete as to tempt one to follow it into detail.

The most striking tendency of our age is our materialistic tendency. We see it in the developement of the material arts and the material sciences; in the desire to see all our theories, philosophical or moral, exemplified in the material world, and the tendency to value the system only for the practice. This tendency often seems to be opposed to another great movement of our age, the idealistic movement. The idealist regards abstractions as having a real existence.—Hence, he places as much value on them as on things. Moreover, by his wide and deep study of the human mind he has proved that the knowledge of things can only be attained by the knowledge of ideas. This truth is very distasteful to the materialist. His object being the ideas contained in things, there is nothing that he would more carefully eradicate than any admixture of ideas from our own minds; so that it seems to him like overturning natural science altogether to tell him that all truth is attained by such an admixture. He thinks at least that nothing more than common sense should be admitted from the mind. This amounts to admitting the loose ideas of the untrained intellect into his science, but to refuse admission to such as have been exercised, strengthened, and developed. He retorts that the conjunction of speculation with science has constantly led to error. Be it so; but then it is only by means of idealism that truth is possible in science. Human learning must fail somewhere. Materialism fails on the side of incompleteness. Idealism always presents a systematic totality, but it must always have some vagueness and thus lead to error.—Materialism is destitute of a philosophy. Thus it is necessarily one-sided. It misunderstands its relations to idealism; it misunderstands the nature of its own logic. But if materialism without idealism is blind, idealism without materialism is void. Look through the wonderful philosophies of this age and you will find in every one of them evidences that their novel conceptions have been to a very large extent suggested by physical sciences. In one point of view indeed, pure *a priori* reasoning is a misnomer; it is as much as to say analysis with nothing to analyze? Analysis of what? I ask. Of those ideas which no man is without. Of common sense. But why *common* sense? Metaphysics stands in need of all the phases of thought of that uncommon sense which results from the physical sciences in order to comprehend perfectly the conceptions of the mind. So much so that I think that a due recognition of the obligations of the idealists to natural science will show that even their claims will receive a just award if we interpret the whole greatness of our age according to this materialistic tendency.

See too, what truth, and what peculiarly christian truth there is in this tendency. There are two fields of human learning, the science of outward things and the science of the mind itself. Now materialism opposes itself to this latter; not as an ornamental study, a regulative study, or an educative study, but as having any value or truth in itself. It is the assertion that man was not made to turn his eye inward, was not made for himself alone, but for the sake of what he should do in the outward world. And I will now ask how christianity will appear if we look upon it from a materialistic point of view? There is one aspect which it certainly will not present; there will be no German refining away of Christ into a class or into self. It will be inclined to slight the subtleties of dogmas and look upon dogmas in a common sense way. True religion, it will think, consists in more than a mere dogma, in visiting the fatherless and the widows and in keeping ourselves unspotted from the world. It will say that christianity reaches beyond even that, reaches beyond the good conscience, beyond the individual life; must transfuse itself through all human law—through the social organization, the nation, the relationships of the peoples and the races. It will demand that not only where man's determinate action goes on, but even where he is the mere tool of providence and in the realm of inanimate nature Christ's kingdom shall be seen.

Our age is brilliant; and apparently confident of its own eternity. But is it never to end, as the Greek age merged in the Roman? The human mind cannot go on eon after eon with always the same characteristics, for such monotony is too poor for it. Is our age never to end? Are we then to go on forever toying with electricity and steam, whether in the laboratory or in business, and never *use* these means in the broad field of humanity and social destiny? I seem, perhaps, to sneer at what you respect. And I confess we have utilized a little surplus energy in the business of philanthropy on our triumphant road to wooing *things*. But I agree with the man who says of this age that

The horseman serves the horse;
The neatherd serves the neat;
The merchant serves the purse;
The eater serves the meat.
'Tis the day of the chattel; web to weave
    and corn to grind.
Things are in the saddle, and ride mankind.

The fulcrum has yet to be found that shall enable the lever of love to move the world. Is our age never to end? As man cannot do two things at once, so mankind cannot do two things at once. Now Lord Bacon, our great master, has said, that the *end* of science is the glory of God, and the use of man. If then, this is so, action is higher than reason, for it is its purpose; and to say that it is not, is the essence of selfishness and atheism. So then our age shall end; and, indeed, the question is not so much why should it not, as why should it continue. What sufficient motive is there for man, a being in whom the natural impulse is—first to sensation, then reasoning, then imagination, then desire, then action—to stop at reasoning, as he has been doing for the last 250 years? It is unnatural, and cannot last. Man must go on to use these powers and energies that have been given him, in order that he may impress nature with his own intellect, converse and not merely listen.

First there was the egotistical stage when man arbitrarily imagined perfection, now is the idistical stage when he observes it. Hereafter must be the more glorious tuistical stage when he shall be in communion with her. And this is exactly what, step by step, we are coming to. For if you will recur a moment to my dry analysis of the formula of Christianity, you will perceive that the conclusions of the preceding ages have answered three kinds of questions concerning that proposition. Two were metaphysical, what is its predicate and what is its subject? two were dynamical; is it hypothetical or actual, and is it categorical or conditional? two were mathematical; what is its quality, and what is its quantity?

And now there are questions of but one kind more that remain to be asked, and they are physical. And they are two. The first is, is christianity a fact of consciousness merely, or one of the external world? And this shall be answered by the conclusion of our own age. The second is, is this predicate true to the understanding merely, or also to the sense? And this, if we may look forward so far, will be answered by

Christ's coming to rule his kingdom in person. And when that occurs, religion will no longer be presented objectively, but we shall receive it by direct communication with him.

When the conclusion of our age comes, and scepticism and materialism have done their perfect work, we shall have a far greater faith than ever before. For then man will see God's wisdom and mercy, not only in every event of his own life, but in that of the gorilla, the lion, the fish, the polyp, the tree, the crystal, the grain of dust, the atom. He will see that each one of these has an inward existence of its own, for which God loves it, and that He has given to it a nature of endless perfectibility. He will see the folly of saying that nature was created for his use.— He will see that God has no other creation than his children. So the poet in our days,—and the true poet is the true prophet—personifies everything, not rhetorically but in his own feeling.—He tells us that he feels an affinity for nature, and loves the stone or the drop of water. But the time is coming when there shall be no more poetry, for that which was poetically divined shall be scientifically known. It is true that the progress of science may die away, but then its essence will have been extracted. This cessation itself will give us time to see that cosmos, that æsthetic view of science which Humboldt prematurely conceived. Physics will have made us familar with the body of all things, and the unity of the body of all; natural history will have shown us the soul of all things in their infinite and amiable idiosyncrasies. Philosophy will have taught us that it is this *all* which constitutes the church. Ah! what a heavenly harmony will that be when all the sciences, one as viol, another as flute, another as trump, shall peal forth in that majestic symphony of which the noble organ of astronomy forever sounds the theme.

Letter Draft,
Peirce to Pliny Earle Chase

L 82a

Cambridge 1864 April 4.

Dear Sir

I saw this morning for the first time your *Intellectual Symbolism* with which I was greatly interested for a reason which may perhaps interest you in hearing from me.

I have myself been studying Kant's categories for several years, and have called them the categories of the IT—an obvious name for them but suggesting the existence of other categories. I have added other categories of the IT and have thus made a circle of which Kant's form an arc. Thus my circle stands in the same position as your 2nd circle. But unfortunately there is very little resemblance beyond that. My circle is the result of hard study: so, I suppose, is yours. In my view of the matter, their being different would not prove either to be false. Nevertheless, I have no great confidence in either circle.

As our general views are very similar, I should esteem it a great favor, if you would consent to discuss the matter with me, in order that we may separate some error. In the hope of your thinking well of this I send you now (before reading your book) some thoughts of mine intended to discover *how we ought to investigate the categories.*

The first and fundamental question is What is metaphysics? To answer this, I must consider it in three different lights.

The first of these views is that of Aristotle—which is the freshest and most pregnant—that metaphysics is that science "which is desirable on its own account, and for the sake of knowledge," and which is preeminent over the others. This is about what we express by "Philosophy."

The second view is that Metaphysics is Psychology.

The third view is that it is Analysis.
The first view distinguishes between

Images *à priori*   and   Images *à posteriori*

The second distinguishes between

Inner Images   and   Outer Images

The third between

Images as Images   and   Images as Representations

These distinctions are involved in the three definitions of Metaphysics, according to these different views. Now I regard these views as equally true, because I am satisfied that the 3 distinctions amount to the same thing. Images *à priori* are only Images *à priori* recalled as Images, while Images *à posteriori* are only Images *à priori* excited as representations. An image to be viewed as an Image must have come from within and to be viewed as a representation must have come from without. The proof of this, I omit. These 3 views lead to 3 methods of investigation, each one-sided; each needing the influence of the other two to keep it right.

[Shakespearian Pronunciation]

P 13: North American Review *98*
(*April 1864):342–69*

1. *Lectures on the English Language.* By George P. Marsh. First Series. New York. 1862. Lecture XXII. "Orthoepical Change in English."
2. *The Works of William Shakespeare, &c.* By Richard Grant White. Boston. 1861. Appendix: "Memorandums of English Pronunciation in the Elizabethan Era."
3. *The English of Shakespeare illustrated in a Philological Commentary on his Julius Cæsar.* By George L. Craik. London. 1857.

It has come to pass that in our day we have two separate languages, —English spoken and English printed. The works of some of our authors were composed on paper; when they are read aloud, they sound almost like translations; they may not lack rhythm and euphony, but it is a rhythm and a euphony that the eye can see. Another class, on the other hand, among whom Shakespeare is pre-eminent, can only be quite comprehended, appreciated, and accompanied in the spoken language; the print may give an indication of what that is, but it is only in that that the words breathe and are quick. It cannot, then, be useless to point out precisely how Shakespeare pronounced. It may be a small portion of the commentary upon his works, but no sincere disciple of his will despise labor bestowed even on this small object. And a knowledge of the old pronunciation is not merely a curious thing; it leads to other knowledge, highly important. It suggests many corrections of the text, and renders many previous emendations far less credible. By showing, in many places, puns hitherto unnoticed, it gives us an understanding of lines hitherto unintelligible. Besides this, it helps us in discovering the derivations of words; and finally, it renders clear and indisputable the fact that our forefathers possessed a more rational, though less constraining, system of orthography than our own.

Two methods of investigating this subject have been proposed. One is by means of rhymes, puns, misspellings, and other such indications. This is the process of Mr. White and Professor Craik. Its value is best estimated by applying it to the literature of our own day. Thus Thomas Hood is a peerless master of puns, yet, excluding those which present an identity in spelling, one out of three of his are imperfect in sound. So the "Voices of the Night" and "In Memoriam" will compare in point of polish with any poems of Shakespeare's day; yet in the former the proportion of imperfect rhymes is one in nine, and in the latter one in seven. We are aware that a notion is rife that such rhymes were not allowed in the Elizabethan era; but some extracts from Spenser, printed phonotypically by the tutor of Milton, display fully the modern proportion of them; that is to say, the lines frequently do not rhyme to the eye, as they should do when so printed, and as they are sometimes forced to do by the editor's spelling one of the words differently from his usual way. As for bad spelling, it is usually utterly irrational, or, if it be phonetic, it is the phonetics of a man whose pronunciation and ear are as rude as his spelling. Doctor Johnson observes that every language has two pronunciations: one, which is regular and sedate, is its true orthoëpy; the other, existing in colloquial and vulgar use, is merely a corruption of the former. Now it is to this latter only that researches like Mr. White's can be directed, and it is an extremely interesting subject of antiquarian research; but it must be evident to every reader that the study of that which is irregular and various can only be successfully prosecuted when founded upon a thorough knowledge of that more stable thing about which it shifts and veers. Moreover, the conclusions to which this method has led have been very strange, and have been very frequently corrected or reversed by their authors.

The other method consists in collecting the positive statements of original orthoëpical and phonetical writers of the sixteenth and seventeenth centuries. This is the process of Mr. Marsh, whose chapter on this subject is admirable both for the skilful conduct of the inquiry and for the undogmatical manner in which its conclusions are presented. Let it not be supposed that authorities are wanting for such an examination. No less than six phonographical systems of Shakespeare's day are preserved to us.[1] Here are their titles:—

---

1. A seventh, by one Wade, is referred to by an old writer as exhibiting a very vulgar pronunciation; writing, for instance, 'Lŭndŭn' or 'Lŭŭn' for 'Lundon',—"like the linkboys and bargemen."

1568. Sir Thomas Smith. *De recta et emendata linguæ Anglicæ scriptione Dialogus.* Paris. 4°.

1569. John Hart. *On Orthographie: conteyning the due order and reason how to write or paint thimage of mannes voice, most like to the life or nature.* London. 8°.

1580. [William] Bullokar's *Booke at large, for the amendment of Orthographie, for English speech; wherein a most perfect supplie is made for the wantes and double sound of Letters in the Olde Orthographie, with Examples for the same. With easie conference and use of both Orthographies to save expence in Bookes for a time, until this amendment grow to a generall use, for the easie, speedie, and perfect reading and writing of English, (the speech not changed, as some untruly and maliciously, or at least ignorantly blow abroad,) etc.* London. 4°.

Æsops Fables in true Ortography with Grammar Notz. Herunto ar also cōioined the shorte Sentencez of the wyz Cato, imprinted with lyke form and order, etc. London. 1585. 8°.

1590. Peter Bales. *Writing Schoolemaster; conteining three Bookes in one; the first, teaching Swift Writing; the second, True Writing; the third, Faire Writing.* London. 4°.

1619. Alexander Gil. *Logonomia Anglica. Quâ Gentis sermo facilius addiscitur.* London. 4°.

1633. Charles Butler. *The English grammar or the institution of letters, syllables, and words in the English tongue.* Oxford. 4°.

The Feminin' Monarchi', or the histori of bẽẽs. Shewing their admirable Natur', and Propertis; their Generation and Colonis; their Government, Loyalti, Art, Industri; Enemi's, VVars, Magnanimite, &c. together with the right ordering of them from tim' to tim' and the swẽẽt' Profit arising ther'of. Written out of experienc'. Oxford. 1634. 4°.

It is often said that from these works we can ascertain what words were pronounced alike, but not what sounds they had. The mode of removing this difficulty is as follows. We should first consider, in a general way, the amount of change that the language has undergone in two hundred and fifty years. This certainly is not very great. We find that almost all words which now have a peculiar pronunciation are peculiarly represented in these phonetic systems. Such, for instance, as *lieutenant, Coteswold, iron, subtile, of, borough,* etc. Hence, no very great amount of change can be admitted. We must also consider in what directions the language is changing, and how its present pronunciation differs from the Saxon. Then, with regard to each sound, we must consult the grammars from our own time backward to the time of Shakespeare, noting what changes have occurred in their rules for the sounds of the letters, and in their statements of the equivalency of our sounds with those of other languages. This process can hardly ever deceive us. Let us exemplify this mode of procedure by an actual study of the sounds. We shall be able to refer to but three of the above-mentioned phonotypical authors,—Smith, Butler, and Gil; the last is, however, probably the best of them all.[2]

In this article, words will be put under one head, which, *with us*, convey the same sound. The mode in which we shall indicate the vowel-sounds is that of Mr. Jennison, in his admirable introduction to Hillard's *Reader;* it is best explained by an example: 'pl*ai*n' means the vowel-sound in 'plain'. Let the reader understand, therefore, when a word is enclosed in single quotation-marks, with certain letters italicized, that what is denoted is simply the sound of the italicized letters.

Of the Consonantal Sounds

J. The substitution of *y* for *j* in old authors has occasioned the assumption that *j* was pronounced by them, as in some parts of Europe now, with the force of *y*.[3] Gil's testimony is very exact. He says:—

G before *a, o,* or *u,* is pronounced with the pure and German sound, as it is before consonants, in *gloria* and *gratia;* before *e* or *i,* for the most part, as by the Italians in *gentile* and *giovane;* for even so we sound a *giant,* a *gibet, ginger, gentle, changed,* and other words. Some nations may perhaps express this sound by *dzy,* we by simple g before *e* or *i,* but before *a, o,* and *u* always by *j* consonant; for in *Jason, Geffrey, Ginger, Joseph,* and a *Judge,* the g and *j* have the same pronunciation; the *dg,* even, following the *u* in the latter word, having the same sound as the *j* preceding it.[4]

Judah was pronounced 'Yuda'.

2. The last work we found in the library of Harvard College, which is very rich in school-books, new and old. The tract of Smith, and the *Feminine Monarchy* of Butler, were kindly lent to us by the trustees of the Boston Public Library. Mulcaster's *Elementarie,* and Coote's *English Schoole-Master,* were obtained from private libraries.

3. White's *Shakespeare,* Vol. VII, p. 141.

4. *Logonomia Angl.,* p. 2. See also B. Jonson (Gifford's ed., 1816), IX, 265; and Wallis, p. 38.

Q. Mr. White has taken the ground that *qu* was pronounced "like simple *k*, and often represented by it in many words in which the full sound of the former combination is now heard."[5]

Sir Thomas Smith summarily ejects the letter from his alphabet, as beggarly, false, servile, infirm, and lame, having no power without its staff *u*, and with *u* no better than *k*.[6] Baret in his *Alvearie*, or Bee-Hive, doubtless the most charming dictionary of our language, leaving the alphabet to be reformed "by better learned men," contents himself with the following animadversion:—

Q hath long bene superfluouslie used in writing English wordes, whereas the Greekes never knew it, neither could the English Saxons ever abide the abuse thereof, but alwaies used K when such occasion served. . . . And surelie, I thinke reason, and the verie judgement of the eare will teach a young beginner, that Quest, Quarrell, etc. maie be as well, and as easilie spelled with K, and Kuest, Kuarrell, &c., for it appeareth that Q is no single letter, but compounded of K and U, which soundeth Q.[7]

Cʜ. There is abundance of testimony that this digraph was pronounced precisely as at present. "It is the peculiarity of the English tongue," says Gil, "to express by *ch* that sound that the Italians give to *c* in *piacevole*."[8] White thinks that in *speech, beseech*, &c., it had the *k* sound; but Mulcaster observes, "The strong *ch* is mere foren, and therefore endeth no word with us, but is turned into *k*."[9] He speaks here of his own system of orthography. Now he has *speche, beseche, eche, breche, leche*.[10] He also says, "For *ch*, where it is strong the number is not manie, and therefor it maie well abide the perpendicular accent over the coplement, as 'charact, ar'changell."[11] Now he does not use this accent over any *ch* not now pronounced *k*. Mr. White must have come upon a provincialism of "the Scotch and Transtrentane English" noticed by Sir T. Smith.[12]

5. White's *Shakespeare*, II, 320 and XII, 430.
6. fol. 29.
7. *Alvearie*, 2d ed., 1580, *sub lit.* Q. See also *Gatakerus de Diphthongis* [1646], ed. 1698, p. 20 E; Gil, p. 9; Wallis, *Grammatica Linguæ Anglicanæ*, 1653, p. 40.
8. Smith, fol. 21 *et seq.*; Gil, p. 2; Jonson, IX, 285; Wallis, p. 39.
9. p. 127.
10. p. 128.
11. p. 152.
12. fol. 23.

GH. The sound of this guttural must have been atonic and faint, for Baret, Smith, and Jonson make it equivalent to *h*.[13] But Bullokar and Gil assign to it a separate character. Its sound must have been disappearing in Shakespeare's time, for in 1653 it was a provincialism.[14] Smith and Gil sound it in almost all words, but never in *delight* and not always in *high*.[15] Coote, in his *English Schoole-Master*, 15th ed., 1624, one of the most valuable of our authorities, says:—

(*Gh.*) Comming together, except in *Ghost*, are of most men but little sounded, as *might, fight*, pronounced as *mite, fite:* but in the end of a word some countries sound them fully, others not at all: as some say, *plough, slough, bough:* other, *plow, slow, bow.* Thereupon some write *burrough*, some *burrow:* but the truest is both to write and pronounce them.[16]

Gil mentions that the common pronunciation was in many respects ambiguous; and instances *enough* and *enuf*.[17] Smith sometimes spells 'laugh' *laf*.[18] It is probable that *f* was frequently substituted for *gh*.

SH was equivalent to the French *ch* and German *sh*.

SMITH. I say that its sound comes nearer to *s* and *y* than to *s* and *h*; and that you may understand more clearly what I mean, first sound our word for the infernal regions. QUINTUS. *Hel.* SMITH. Preserve that sound entire, and prefix an *s*. QUINT. *Shel.* SMITH. You see that that does not make our word for conch. But now sound *y–e–l*. QU. *Yel.* SMITH. And prefix an *s*, preserving the former sound and making one syllable. QU. *Syel.* SMITH. I put it to you now, Quintus, which of these sounds comes nearer to the word *shell*.[19]

The pronunciation of *tion, sion, tial*, &c., is shrouded with difficulty and doubt. They seem in many instances to be dissyllabic in pronunciation; but Professor Craik inclines, with some hesitation, to the belief that such lines as

But for your private satisfaction

are to be regarded as truncated lines; and has, on the whole, no doubt that words ending in 'tion' and 'sion' had in the age of Shakespeare already come to be sounded exactly as at the present day.[20] The un-

---

13. Baret's *Alvearie, sub lit.* H; Smith, fol. 25; Jonson, IX, 285.
14. Wallis, p. 31.
15. For *delight*, Gil, pp. 21, 114, 141. For *high*, Gil, pp. 21, 34, 74, 98, and 24, 34, 83, 100.
16. Coote, p. 21.
17. p. 19.
18. fol. 24.
19. fol. 40.
20. *English of Shakespeare*, p. 168.

abbreviated notation of these endings in the phonetic system of Gil shows that he regarded them as dissyllabic, and we are not therefore surprised at his statement that words of these terminations are *sometimes* contracted by synæresis. Sidney, in his *Defence of Poesie,* also gives 'motion' and 'potion' as instances of English dactyls, and Puttenham instructs us that 'remuneration' makes two *good* dactyls.[21] Are we then to infer, with Mr. Marsh, that 'motion' and 'potion' were pronounced 'mo–shi–on' and 'po–shi–on'? To this Mulcaster would answer:—

T kepeth one force still saving where a vowell followeth after, *i,* as in *action, discretion, consumption,* whereas, *t,* soundeth like the full *s,* or strong [weak] *c,* so the words where it is so used, be altogether strangers.[22]

In fewer words, Wallis:—

T before *i* followed by another vowel is sounded like the hissing *s,* . . . but in *question, mixtion,* and wherever else *t* follows the letter *s* or *x,* it retains its pure sound.[23]

These authorities, with a number of others, seem to bear out the view that *t* was pronounced in these words as in modern French.[24] It seems improbable that 'tion', even in its contracted form, was pronounced 'shun', as the forms *shon* and *shun* are never met with in the old books and manuscripts, although we continually meet with *scion, syon, cyon,* and *son.* Could the present aspirated pronunciation have existed in the popular speech, and have failed to manifest itself in the infinitely varied cacography of the time,—especially when it is considered that in 1675 the aspirated spelling of 'tion' was the prevalent form in which the juvenile depravity manifested itself?[25] We must, however, confess that the weight of direct authority upon this point is weakened by the following consideration. The whole vocal interval between *sh* and *si* is filled up with innumerable possible sounds, which, both with respect to their formation in the mouth and the sound itself in the ear, differ not at all in *kind,* but only in *degree,* resulting from the greater

21. *Apud* Marsh, p. 530.
22. *Elem.,* p. 122.
23. p. 47.
24. Baret, Coote, Ben Jonson, Gataker, and Gil. See also Percival's *Spanish Grammar,* edited by the English Minsheu, and prefixed to his *Spanish Dictionary,* London, 1623, p. 8. Also, Cotgrave's *French Dictionary,* 1607.
25. Nat Strong, *England's Perfect School-Master,* 10th ed. (enlarged), 1704. Licensed, 1675. pp. 28–30.

or less proximity of the tongue to the palate and teeth. The sound of *tion* was once undoubtedly *si–on,* but during the progress to *shun* it probably rested for generations on some of these intermediate semivocals. Now, in all grammars and dictionaries, down to the *middle of the last century,* '-tion' and '-sion' are still described as sounding *shon* or *syon,* although, from a chance remark in De la Touche's *L'Art de bien Parler Français* (Amsterdam, 1704), we discover that ever since that was written, at the least, they have been pronounced exactly as they now are. Moreover, the orthoëpists of those days used ordinarily to describe *sh* as equivalent to *sy.*[26] How natural, then, for them to call what was really near *shi, si.* We therefore conclude,—1st, that *-tion* and *-sion* are dissyllabic, but could be contracted to one syllable; and, 2d, that they had nearly, if not quite, the modern French sound.

TH. The arguments used by a writer in the *Atlantic Monthly,* Vol. III, p. 241, seem to us to demonstrate that this "couplement" had its two modern sounds. Wallis, whose descriptions of the sounds, renowned as they are, are even more accurate than has been imagined, says:—

> In pronouncing *T,* if the breath go forth more thickly, the Greek *Theta* is formed, the Hebrew *Thau* aspirated, and the Arabic *The;* this is the English *Th* in the words *thigh, thing, thin, thought, throng,* etc. The Anglo-Saxons used to write it with a Spina. . . . In pronouncing the letter *D,* if the breath breaks forth more grossly, and as through a hole, the Arabic *Dhal* is formed, the aspirated Hebrew *Daleth,* and the Spanish *d* soft as that letter is used in the middle and end of words, as *Majestad, Trinidad,* etc. The English represent this sound in the same way as the one mentioned above, namely by *th,* as in the words *thy, thine, this, though,* etc.

Mr. White thinks the sound of the French *t* in *meurtre,* and the Irish *th* in *further* is the sound indicated. But it cannot be a French or Irish sound, for both those peoples are represented, both in the plays and grammars of the period, as unable to pronounce the *th.*[27]

Th was probably vulgarly and provincially interchanged with *t.* At least the cacography of the period seems to indicate this, and Gil says, "Certainly, where the dialect varies, I readily suffer the writing itself to be least consistent; as, *further* or *furder; murther* or *murder.*"[28] But

---

26. Wilkins's *Essay towards a Real Character,* p. 372. Wallis, pp. 38, 65.
27. See Davenant's *Playhouse to be Let,* and Jonson's *Irish Mask;* also, Palsgrave, p. 20; and Smith, fol. 5, where, however, the phrase is ambiguous.
28. Gil, Preface.

this looseness must not be exaggerated. Of the hundred words given by Gil in which the *th* sound now occurs, only *author, Arthur,* and certain ordinal numerals have the *t;* while *murder* is the only word in which his *th* would now be *d* or *t.* Mulcaster's general table contains one hundred and sixty-five words now sounded with *th.* Of these only *author, authority, authentic,* and some ordinals, have the *t.* And the only words he gives with *th* which now have the sound of *t,* are *nostril* and *t'other.* These authorities are entirely independent; the later of them speaks of the other as a man who had "wasted much time and good paper."[29] Their agreement demonstrates that, notwithstanding the popular looseness, there *was* a correct pronunciation of words containing *th* which very nearly coincides with the orthoëpy of our times.

We will pass over the other consonants, and proceed to the

Silent Letters

E final was, of course, silent. It remained silent when the word it ended was compounded with another; to this rule the only well-established exception was *commandement.* The vowel of the termination *-ed* was familiarly omitted, but was also frequently heard. The notion that the "usual pronunciation" of *shuffled* was "shuffleëd" is entirely unsupported, except by an argument which, if valid, would show that that was the usual spelling also. 'Handès' for 'hands' is mentioned by Gil as a poetical license.[30] The *l* in such words as *talk, calm, folk, half,* &c., had long been silent (though Gil says that certain "eruditi non ejiciunt *l*"), and this rule extended to *fault.*[31] The sound of *l* lingered much longer in *would, should, could.*[32] A *b* following an *m* at the end of a word, or preceding a *t,* was silent, as now. The same may be said of a *g* before *n,* but Gil sometimes writes *benign* and *condign, beningn* and *condingn. H* was silent in *honor, hour, honest,* and also in *hyssop* ("ïzop"), but apparently was sounded in *herb.* In *ha'penny, two, whole, Worcester,* the same letters were silent that are so now. But *k* before *n,* and *w* before *h,* would seem to have been invariably sounded.[33] *Iron* was sounded as at present.

29. Gil, Preface.
30. p. 137.
31. Preface.
32. Smith and Gil.
33. *Ibid.*

The Vowel-Sounds

The use of the final *e* to lengthen the preceding vowel was even more common then than now. All those words we have now, in which, though the spelling indicates a long vowel, the pronunciation is short, such as *logic, valor, spirit,* etc., were short then; and to these we must add *ăge*[34] (sometimes long), *chănge,*[35] *cĭder* (?),[36] *dĭămond,*[37] *dĭvers* (?),[38] *făvor* (?),[39] *ŏver,*[40] *sĭlent.*[41] Saturn, however, *been,*[42] sometimes *have, mischief, mĭnūte,* sometimes *ire* final, *ai* in a final syllable, and a number of words in *ea,* had their vowels long. So, on the other hand, words now pronounced long, though spelt short, were then long; but to this we except *angel*[43] and *chamber.*[44] Challenge was spelt with one *l* and had the *a* long.

SHORT VOWELS. 1. 'Good'. All words spelt with *oo* had the long sound, and properly took the final *e;* except *blood,*[45] *flood,*[46] *good,*[47] *hood,*[48] *wood,*[49] and *wool.*[50] Woman[51] and Worcester[52] had the 'good' sound; but *could, would, should,* were long.[53]

2. 'Up'. There is ample evidence that, in the reign of Charles II, *ŭ* had the same sound we now give it; and Mr. Marsh is of opinion that it was so pronounced in Shakespeare's day. This scholar, whose reasons are usually so direct and unerring, seems here to have made a curious mistake. He founds his conclusion solely upon the following words of Gil: "V, *est tenuis, aut crassa: tenuis* v, *est in Verbo* tu vz USE: *crassa brevis est* u, *ut in pronomine* us *nos.*" He does not translate this, but he evidently understands it thus: "U is thin or thick; the thin *u* is in the verb 'to use', the thick *u* is short, as in the pronoun *us.*" But had he

34. Gil, pp. 92, 98, 112.
35. *Ib.,* pp. 12, 20, 28; Smith, fol. 44.
36. Gil, p. 38.
37. *Ib.,* pp. 79, 91, 107.
38. *Ib.,* p. 93.
39. *Ib.,* p. 82.
40. *Ib.,* pp. 24, 30, 70, 98, etc.
41. *Ib.,* pp. 48, 110.
42. *Ib.,* pp. 56, 57, 58, 63, 65, etc. For the three following words see Gil.
43. *Ib.,* p. 24.
44. *Ib.,* pp. 23, 24.
45. *Ib.,* pp. 4, 38, 106, 110; Smith, fol. 24.
46. Gil, pp. 119, 124.
47. *Ib.,* pp. 12, 25, 39, 68, 115, etc.; Smith, fol. 25, 43.
48. Smith, fol. 25.
49. Gil, pp. 10, 22, 39, 113, 142; Smith, fol. 19, 42.
50. Gil, pp. 39, 70; Smith, fol. 19.
51. Gil, pp. 41, 94, 117.
52. *Ib.,* pp. 70, 81.
53. *Ib.,* pp. 55, 56; 17, 24, 53; 54, 85.

turned over the page, he would have found the sentence finished thus: "*aut longa* ū: *ut in verbo* tu ūz OOSE *scaturio, aut sensim exeo more aquæ vi expressæ.*" Gil is in this chapter describing his own orthography. Now he has three characters for *u;* namely, v, which takes the place of our *u* long, u (short), which takes the place of ŏŏ and of ŭ short, and ū (long), which takes the place of ōō long. He says, then, "U is thin or thick; the thin '*u*' occurs in '*use*'; the thick, when short, is 'u' as in 'us', when long, is 'ū' as in 'ooze'." He thus states directly that the *u* in 'us' is the short sound of the *oo* in 'ooze'.[54] In another place he says: "So in *Bucke* and *Booke;* nor have these any other difference in sound but that which is perceived in quantity."[55] The reader must remember that the *oo* in Book was long. In these statements Gil is fully supported by the other authorities.

Ben Jonson. "In the short time more flat and akin to *u;* as

cozen,   dozen,   mòther,
bròther, lòve,   pròve.

Note. *Ut* oo, *vel* ou Gallicum." (IX, pp. 266, 267.)

Coote. "You shall find some words written with (e) and (o) single, when they should be written with the dipthongs *ee, oo,* as he, be, she, me, do, mother; for hee, bee, mee, doo, &c." (p. 22.)

Butler. "For as *i* short hath the sound of *ee* short, so hath *u* short of *oo* short." "U short into oo short (which sound is all one)." (pp. 8, 9. *Apud* White's *Shakespeare,* Vol. IV, p. 101.)

This sound of *oo* short extended to all the words which we now pronounce with '*up*', whether spelt with *u, o,* or *ou.*

The only exceptions that we have met with are *among, nothing,*[56] with the sound of *o* short, and *none* and *one* with the sound of *o* long. It is noticeable that this class of words includes nearly all those which end with *om* and *on.* The French *o* nasal was anciently pronounced 'soon'. It is by means of this tendency to pronounce *om* 'oom', that the puns between *Rome* and *room* are to be explained. At any rate, it is certain that, when Pope wrote these lines,—

From the same foes, at last, both felt their doom,
And the same age saw learning fall, and Rome,—

he meant both words to be pronounced 'ooze', for Granville Sharp's

<hr>

54. Marsh's *Lectures,* 1st Series, 4th ed., p. 484 *et seq.* Gil, pp. 7, 8.
55. "Sic in *Bucke* hic dama, et *Booke* liber: neque in his ulla soni differentia est, præter illam quæ in quantitate percipitur."—*Log. Angl.,* p. 3.
56. Gil, pp. 32, 38, 39, &c.

Short Treatise, an excellent work on English orthoëpy (London, 1767), says, "in *lose, move, prove,* and *Rome, o* is commonly pronounced like *oo.*" The word *one* was commonly pronounced as spelt, down into the middle of the last century. Nevertheless, the pronunciation of the *w* is very ancient.

In 1650, *u* short had acquired its present sound, and even those words spelt with a *oo,* mentioned under the last heading, changed into 'gud', 'hud', 'sut', 'blud', 'flud'; but *good, hood, soot* (*wood, foot,* and *wool*) afterward recovered their regular pronunciation, to correspond with the many words in *oo* long, which, in consequence of the omission of the final *e,* were becoming short.

3. '*on*'. A Yankee pronunciation of 'whole' and 'coat' bears the same relation to their true sounds that "b*u*ll" does to "r*u*le," and the question arises whether *o* short, as well as *u* short, has undergone a change in sound. One thing is very clear, that, in the middle of the seventeenth century, '*on*' had the same pronunciation as now, for Wallis and Wilkins describe it without ambiguity as the short sound of *a* in 'fall' and 'ball'. The latter author also states that no short sound corresponding to *o* rotund existed in the language.[57] Previous to the Rebellion, Gil is our sole authority. He makes no distinction in his phonotypy between the *o* in 'hop' and 'hope', except by the long mark, but still he fails to tell us expressly that they are the same in sound, although he *does* say so of *e* short and *e* long, of *i* short and double *e,* of *u* short and double *o.* He remarks, in general, that, "although in a long or short syllable the time in pronunciation is different, the vicinity of the sound is not; still the same vowel sometimes sounds broader, sometimes sharper, as in *hall, hale,* and *Hal.*"[58] Perhaps by *vicinity* of sound he did not mean *identity.* This matter must, therefore, remain in doubt.

Words in which *a* now has the sound of *o* short, as 'was', 'what', and 'quality', were formerly pronounced regularly.[59] Numerous words, as 'hot', 'moth', 'cloth', which are found in books of about the date 1600 spelt 'hoate', 'moathe', and 'cloathe', were nevertheless, in the year 1621, as we learn from Gil, pronounced as at present. Mr. White would place more reliance on the spelling, as an indication of the sound, than on the orthoëpist. *O* short following *i* short was silent in a few words, as in the lines,—

57. *Essay toward a Real Character,* p. 363.
58. *Log. Angl.,* p. 3.
59. Gil.

A carrion crow sat on a tree.

To grace in captive bonds his chariot wheels.[60]

"In the last syllables," says Ben Jonson, "before *n* and *w, o* frequently loseth its sound; as in *person, action, willow, billow*." These
last words remind one of Chaucer's *herberw*, and the Yankee pronunciation 'willer'.

4. 'can'. Ben Jonson, following Mulcaster, whom indeed he ever
closely copies, distinguishes *a* short from *a* long by calling the former
flat and the latter sharp.[61] Wallis describes the present sound in an unmistakable manner.[62] It may be safe to assume that the sound has
not changed for three hundred years. In this case, it is a defect in Gil's
system, that it does not distinguish between the *a* in 'cat' and that in
'cart'. This error is an easy one, for Webster's *Unabridged Dictionary*
gives to 'grass', 'dance', etc., the sound of 'cart', while his smaller Dictionaries assign to the same words the sound of 'cat'. *Have* was sounded
either long or short. *Shall* was sounded generally as at present, but
sometimes with the *au* sound. *Than* was spelt and pronounced with
an *e*.

5. 'End'. This sound has undergone no perceptible change. *Any*[63]
and *many*[64] had the sound of *a* short. *Friend*[65] had the sound of *i* short,
and so generally had *yet*,[66] *yes*,[67] and *yesterday*.[68] These are now all
Hibernicisms.

6. 'In'. Words to which we now give this sound had in general the
same pronunciation in Shakespeare's day. *Women*,[69] *busy*,[70] and
breeches[71] were sounded as at present. *Build* was pronounced either
'byūld', 'bīld', 'bōōld', 'bĭld', or 'beeld', according to Gil.[72] *Y* or *ie* at the
end of a word had indifferently its present sound, or that of the long
diphthongal *i*.

---

60. Gil.
61. B. Jonson, IX, 261; Mulcaster, *Elem.*, p. 110.
62. p. 8.
63. Gil, p. 95.
64. *Ib.*, pp. 34, 39, 75, 87, 91, etc.
65. *Ib.*, pp. 69, 81, 90, 117, 139, etc.
66. *Ib.*, p. 10; Smith, fol. 18.
67. Gil, pp. 149, 150; Smith, fol. 17, 18, 37.
68. Gil, p. 77; Smith, fol. 17.
69. Gil, p. 41.
70. *Ib.*, p. 91.
71. *Ib.*, p. 17.
72. *Ib.*, pp. 4, 19, 105, 111.

LONG VOWELS. 1. *'ooze'*. This sound we derive from the Saxons, and it has been in the language ever since. Wallis describes it accurately, and Baret remarks:—

But that which we call double *o*, (*oo*) I thinke in English is much mistaken, and abused. For how can *oo* have the name of *o*, when it chaungeth his sound (which is as it were his name) and doth degenerate into the nature and name of an other vowell? hop, hope, hoop. A diphthong, I thinke, it cannot be: for that no vowel can be compounded in a diphthong with itselfe. . . . Some thinke such wordes should be rather written with *u*.[73]

As Mr. White says, the original use of a doubled vowel was the expression of the long, pure sound. This was one of the uses of the *oo* in 1530, for Palsgrave says of the French:—

The soundyng of the *o*, which is most generall with them is lyke as we sounde *o* in these wordes in our tonge, 'a boore, a soore, a coore', and such lyke, that is to say, lyke as the Italians sounde *o*, or they with us that sounde the latine tong aright.[74]

'Move', 'tomb', 'prove', 'lose', 'do',[75] and 'two',[76] were sounded as at present. And 'who' was called *'whoe'*[77] the *w* being sounded.

2. 'herd'. A difference seems to have existed between the sounds of 'fur' and 'fir', for Coote tells us that 'durt', 'gurt', 'hur', 'sur', in place of 'dirt', 'girth', 'her', and 'sir', were a part of "the barbarous speech of your country-people." So with Wallis, *ter ter* is different from *turtur*, and *iter* from *itur*. This was owing to the distinctly consonantal pronunciation of the *r*. 'Heard' is pronounced 'hārd' by Gil, but 'hărd' by Baret, Coote, and others. 'Worm', 'work', 'word', 'worth', 'worse', were pronounced 'wŏŏrm', etc.

3. 'dance', 'daunt', 'dawn'. These three vowels, which, in Mulcaster's phrase, "entermedle with each other" so much, will be conveniently considered under one head. Indeed, the three words given as their representatives all had the same vowel-sound in 1600. The sound 'daunt' did not exist unless in such words as 'car'; for *father*,[78] *rather*,[79] and

---

73. *Alvearie, sub lit. O.*
74. p. 7.
75. Gil, pp. 50, 53; Smith, fol. 42.
76. Gil, pp. 13, 37, 70, 89; Smith, fol. 12, 24.
77. Smith, fol. 20; Gil, *passim*.
78. Gil, pp. 76, 80, 81.
79. Or *răther*, Gil, pp. 121, 122.

water[80] (in the last century 'wahter') took the sound of long *a*, while *aunt, daunt, calf, half*, etc., had the vowel of 'dawn'.[81] Words now sounded like 'dance' had indifferently the *a* of 'fat' and 'fall'.[82]

What, then, was the sound of *au* which belonged to all these words? The grammars will tell us that it was that of the French and German *a*. Here follow a few citations, with dates and authors prefixed.

1633. *Ben Jonson.* "When [*a*] comes before *l* in the end of a syllable, it obtaineth the full French sound, and is uttered with the mouthe and throate wide opened and the tongue bent back from the teeth."

1653. *Wallis.* "Neither do the *Germans* alone, but the *French* and some other nations most commonly pronounce their *a* with the same sound."—p. 6.

1673. *Festeau* says that the French pronounce their *a* like the English *aw*. (p. 1.)

1698. *Berault.* "A se prononce encore comme en Français quand il est fermé par une ou deux consones: Example. *Fat*, gras; *mad*, enragé; *all*, tout; *call*, appelle."—p. 214.

It is established, then, that our *au* and the French *a* were nearly enough alike to be described as equivalent. The next step is to obtain some further information respecting the French *a*, and here we shall find that though the resemblance to the English *au* is still perceived, yet that, aside from that statement, the grammarians, after the year 1700, tell a very different story from those previous to that date. Thus:—

1710. "Les Anglois donnent quelquefois à *oi* le son de *ai* comme *toil*." De la Touche, *L'Art de bien Parler Français* (Amsterdam, 9th ed.), Vol. I, p. 44. Here French *a* is made equivalent to our *o* short.

1745. "A is pronounced as in English in these words, War, that, tall; as academie, Academy; abattre, to pull down, &c. they must always be pronounced full and plain, as *aw*."—Taudon, *French Grammar*, 4th ed., p. 1.

1767. "*a* in *Water* is commonly pronounced like the French *a*, or English *aw*; in *Father*, and the last syllable of *Papa, Mamma*, it has a medium sound between *aw* and the English *a*."—Sharp on the English Pronunciation, p. 5.

80. Sometimes *wǎter* and even *wauter*, Gil, 10, 23, 24, 38, 69, 81, 118.
81. Gil, Preface.
82. Mulcaster, pp. 128, 129, 137; Gil, Preface. The following is from Coote:— "*Robert.* What spelleth *b, r, a, n, c, h?* *John.* Branch. *Robert.* Nay, but you should put in (*u*). *John.* That skilleth not, for both ways be usuall." (p. 29).

1784. "It is the legitimate sound of the long *a* in the French language; but I do not know that it is to be met with at all in the Italian."—Nares on Orthoëpy, p. 7.

We thus see that, after 1700, the French *a* was not the Italian *a*, but was the *o* in 'toil', or *fully and plainly* aw. Now let us consult a few of the older grammarians.

1530. "The soundyng of *a* whiche is most generally used through out the frenche tonge, is . . . lyke as the Italians sound *a*, or they with us that pronounce the latine tonge aryght.

"If *m* or *n* followe next after *a* in a frenche worde, all in one syllable, than *a* shall be sounded lyke this diphthong *au*, and something in the noose, as these wordes *ámbre, chámbre, mandér, amánt, tant, parlánt, regardánt*, shall in redynge and spekynge be sounded *aumbre, chaumbre, maunder*, &c."—Palsgrave, p. 2.

And on the next page he lets us know what this Italian *a* is:—

"If *m* or *n* folowe next after *e* all in one syllable, than *e* shall be sounded lyke an Italian *a* and some thynge in the noose."—p. 3.

1623. "A is sounded plainly with opening the mouth, as in Latine, French, and Italian, as in English man, can, so in Spanish man*a*da, ens*a*lada."—Richard Percival, *Spanish Grammar* affixed to the *Dictionary*, edited by Minsheu.

1650. "A in the *English* Toung, and in no other, hath two differing sounds, the one open and cleer, as *Balaâm*, the other pressing and as it were halfe-mouth'd and mincingly, as *Stale Ale;* In French 't is alwaies pronounced as in the first, cleer and ouvert."—Cotgrave's *Dictionary*, by Howell.

It is true that Strong (1698), E. Coles (1701), and Bailey (2d ed., 1733) say that *Baal* and *Bawl* are pronounced alike, but this proves but little with regard to Balaam; and is it probable that, with *Bawl*, &c. directly in his path, Cotgrave would have sought out an uncommon proper noun to illustrate the French sound, unless he had perceived that it answered his purpose better?

1660. "*Of the Pronunciation of the Netherdutch Letters. a* is pronounced more fully and broader than ours, as the French *a* with an open mouth, or as *ah* in English."—Hexham's *Dictionary*.

There are three reasons for thinking that Hexham here meant to give the French *a* nearly its present sound. The first is, that he refers to the French *a with an open mouth* as though he wished to distinguish it from some other sound of *a* in French. This can only mean the nasal sound (which is even now pronounced *aw,* though some of the modern grammars do not say so). But this would not differ from the ordinary *a* if the the latter was *aw;* therefore the orthoëpy must have been like that of Palsgrave's time. The second reason is, that this French *a* is made equivalent to our interjection *Ah!* Is it credible that this was ever *aw?* Thirdly, it is said to equal the Dutch *a.* For the sound of that see Sewel's *Wegwyzer,* 1705: "In some words, however, *a* in English is pronounced nearly as in Dutch; as, *Man, animal, bastard, singular, particular, mutual,* . . . *apply, arrest, assist,* &c." (p. 8).

1690. "A is the most open of the letters, as well as the simplest and the easiest to pronounce; whence it comes that it is with this that children begin to form sounds."—Pomey's *Royal French Dictionary.*

We have now collected authorities of every generation, from 1600 to 1800, and from them we conclude:—1. That in the time of Henry VIII the French *a* was pronounced as it is now. 2. That as we advance into the seventeenth century, the statement that it is pronounced 'daunt' is less and less distinctly enunciated, and its equivalency to the English *aw* is more frequently noticed. 3. That from 1700 until after the Revolution, it was pronounced 'dawn'. But what conclusion shall we draw respecting the English *au,* which the grammarians of the seventeenth and eighteenth centuries alike concur in representing to be the same as the French *a?* The inference that it also changed, and that at the same time as the French *a,* would be preposterously improbable. For inferring a change at any other time sufficient reason is wanting. We must, therefore, endeavor to explain our facts on the presumption that its sound underwent no change. Now this can only be done by supposing that the French *a,* from 1620 to 1690, represented such a sound as might at once be described as 'daunt' and be made equivalent to 'dawn'. Such a sound is, perhaps, given to 'balm' in Georgia and Alabama. Soon after 1690 it took another step in the same direction as that which was taken after the wars of the Huguenots, perhaps, and now bore no resemblance to the *a* in *father.* It appears, however, that this change had not struck completely into the provinces, for, as the Revolution gradually passed off, this orthoëpy also died out, and left the pronunciation as it was during the reign of Francis I. If we accept this theory, our conclusion respecting the English *aw* will be that it was always pronounced as at present.

The 'daunt' sound we have always had in English in a few such words as 'car' and 'star'; probably also in one mode of pronouncing *dance, France,* &c.; but its present use in *daunt, aunt, father,* and others arose between 1660 and 1737, when Saxon[83] first states that the *u* in *aunt* is silent. The remarkable absence of original grammars during the fourscore years before the last date renders it difficult to assign any particular period to this change,[84] but it is natural to think that it took place after the Revolution, when many new customs arose, and when other vowels altered their sound. Still later, and in fact very recently, the sound we give to words like *dance* branched off from that of 'daunt', and now the prevalent vulgarism is to call *dance* like 'damsel'; in all which stages one tendency of growth is manifest,—1. 'dawn', 2. 'daunt', 3. 'dance', 4. 'damsel'.

4. 'Ale', 'air'. A long had a sound nearly like 'ale'. A single extract will suffice to show this. It is from *An Introductorie for to lerne to rede, to pronounce, and to speke the French trewly,* 1532, by Giles Du Guez, the tutor of Queen Mary Tudor.

> Ye shal pronounce your *a,* as wyde open mouthed as ye can; your *e,* as ye do in Latyn, almost as brode as ye pronounce your *a* in englysshe.[85]

A in 'Ale', as now sounded, ends with a very short *i* sound, as *o* in 'old' does with a *oo* sound; and it is an important but difficult question to determine whether this vanish existed or was invariably used in Shakespeare's day. Gil uses three characters in places where we sound 'ale'; they are, ā, ai, āi. The two latter, which are used indifferently where the *a* is followed by an *i* or *y* in common spelling, he regards as diphthongs. And in speaking of the peculiarities of the Lincolnshire speech he says, "In *ai, abjiciunt i, ut pro* pai *solvo,* pā; *pro* sai *dico,* sā."[86] This shows that he really distinguished the sound of *pale* and *pail, pain* and *pane, gait* and *gate.* Sir Thomas Smith's remarks are even more explicit; thus:—

> The consideration of the diphthongs follows the vowels. Now a diphthong is any sound compounded of two vowels: as AI, *pai, dai, wai, mai, lai, say, esai, tail, fail, fāin, pain, disdain, claim, plai, arai.* In these both letters are

83. *English Schollar's Assistant,* 2d ed., p. 10.
84. Sewel (*Korte Wegwyzer,* p. 8) gives the sound of *particular* to *water, was,* and *altar,* and the sound of 'dawn' to *aunt, daunt, August.* Strong (*Perfect School-Master,* 1698) gives the 'dawn' sound to Draught, Haunt, Laugh, Taunt, Vaunt (p. 35). In his table of words of like sound he has "*Walter* came by *Water*" (p. 56). But he makes *aunt* different from *ant.* These authorities are not sufficient to fix the date.
85. Same vol. as Palsgrave.
86. p. 17.

short among more cultivated speakers. The country-folk produce a dense, odious, and too greasy sound, by sounding both vowels, or at least the latter one, long. *Pāi, dāi, wāi, māi, lāi.* So those who pronounce these words very delicately, young ladies especially, exhibit plainly the Roman diphthong *æ*. *Æ Latin diphthong. Pæ, dæ, wæ, mæ, læ.* Scotch and some Transtrentane English pronounce these words with the improper Greek diphthong *ạ*, so that neither *a* nor *e* is heard, unless very obscurely. *A, improper Greek diphthong. Pā, dā, wā, mā, lā.*[87]

There was then a decided difference between *ai* and *a*. Had, then, the latter a diphthongal termination as now? Sir Thomas Smith, speaking of the relation of *mad* and *lad* to *made* and *lade*, says:—

It is certain that there is no difference between these words except in the length and shortness of the vowel, as any one who is willing to listen and consult his ears, unless his are more ἀμούσας than those of an ass, can readily understand.[88]

And Wallis, whose knowledge of phonetics is not to be questioned, says:—

With the larger opening is formed the *a* of the English, that is, *a* thin, such as is heard in the words, *bat, bate, pal, pall, Sam, same, lamb, lame, ban, bane*, etc. This sound differs from the German *â* thick or open; in that the English raise the middle of the tongue, and thereby compress the air in the Palate; while the Germans depress the middle of the tongue, and thereby compress the air in the throat. The French almost give *that* sound where *e* precedes the letter *n* in the same syllable, as *entendement*, &c. The Welsh are accustomed to pronounce their *a* with *this* sound.[89]

Now the Welsh *a* is 'cat' when short, and when long the same elongated without a vanish, or nearly 'care'. There was then no vanish to the long *a*, and *ai* was a true diphthong, more resembling our *a* long than our *i* long. *Ea* had a peculiar pronunciation, which we shall presently consider.

5. 'old', 'ore'. Having seen that *a* wanted the vanish, we are ready to believe that the same was the case with *o*, since we find the old phonotypists indicating it. There was, besides, the diphthong *ou*, formed of the long *o* and *u*, which was heard in all those words in which *ou* and *ow* are now sounded 'old', and also wherever *o* long was followed by *l*; this sound must have been the same with which the Irish now pro-

87. fol. 14, *et seq.*
88. fol. 10.
89. p. 8.

nounce the word '*bold*'. *Court* was pronounced *cŏŏrt*.[90] *Door*,[91] *quoth*,[92] *shew*,[93] *pour*,[94] were sounded exactly as spelt, the last word differing only from 'power' in spelling.

6. '*Eve*', '*deer*'. There can be no doubt that this sound was heard in almost all the words where it now occurs, including 'people'[95] and '-shire'[96] in combination, for Gil gives to all these words the long sound of the short *i*. The principal exceptions were words in *ea*, several in *ei*, *Cæsar*,[97] *cedar*,[98] *equal*,[99] *fierce*,[100] *Grecian*,[101] *interfere*,[102] *these*,[103] etc., which had the peculiar sound of *ea*.

The sound of ea. It was a great puzzle to Mr. White, when considering rhymes and puns, to decide whether *ea* was sounded like long *a* or double *e*. Mr. Marsh, looking at the grammars, at once discovered that it was neither one nor the other, but an intermediate sound, like the *e* in *met*, prolonged. This view is sustained by the following extract from Wallis:—

In the same place, also, but with a *middling* opening of the mouth, is formed the *é* masculine of the French: which sound the English, Italians, Spanish, give to this letter; a vivid and sharp sound. It is a sound intermediate between the preceding vowel and that which is to follow [*ā* in *pane* with a *greater* opening, and *ee* with a *less* opening of the mouth]. This sound the English express by *e*, and when long not infrequently by *ea*, and sometimes

90. Gil, 22. So *courteous*, p. 67, *courtesy*, p. 82. With reference to the distinction between *o* and *ou*, Mr. White quotes Shakespeare's "Not on thy soale: but on thy soule, harsh Jew," and argues from this that the two words were pronounced alike. What does the reader say to this inference? Will some future antiquarian apply the same reasoning to Hood's lines on the learned pig?

> Of what avail that I could spell
>   And read just like my betters,
> If I must come to this at last,
>   To litters, not to letters?

91. Gil, p. 95; Smith, fol. 24. But the present pronunciation also existed. Gil, pp. 118, 122.
92. Or '*koth*'. Gil, p. 64.
93. Gil, pp. 12, 98.
94. Also like '*poor*'. Gil, p. 21; Smith, fol. 43.
95. Gil, pp. 21, 22, 41, 78.
96. *Ib.*, 70, 81, etc.
97. Or with *e* short. Gil, pp. 43, 78, 82.
98. *Ib.*, 105.
99. *Ib.*, 84.
100. *Ib.*, 99.
101. *Ib.*, 73, 74.
102. *Ib.*, 33.
103. *Ib.*, 13, 14, 45, and Wallis quoted below.

ei. As *the, there, these, sell, seal, tell, teal, steal, set, seat, best, beast, red, read* (lego), *receive, deceive,* &c.[104]

Many words in *ea,* which now receive the short sound, in Shakespeare's day were long. Of these we have noted the following: *bread,*[105] *deadly,*[106] *death,*[107] *deaf,*[108] *dread,*[109] *heavy,*[110] *lead* (the metal),[111] *meant,*[112] *pleasant,*[113] *pleasure,*[114] *spread* (present tense),[115] *sweat* (present tense),[116] *threat,*[117] *weapon.*[118] The following were pronounced both ways: *dead,*[119] *health,*[120] *heaven,*[121] *ready,*[122] *sweat* (noun),[123] *thread,*[124] *tread,*[125] *treasure.*[126] The following were, as now, short: *breadth,*[127] *breast,*[128] *breath,*[129] *cleanly,*[130] *cleanse,*[131] *endeavor,*[132] *feather,*[133] *head,*[134] *leads* (noun plural),[135] *leather,*[136] *read* (past),[137]

104. p. 9.
105. Gil, pp. 24, 37, 73; Smith, fol. 11, 41. So Coote also.
106. Butler's *Feminine Monarchy,* p. 20. Butler evidently distinguishes between *ea* short and *ea* long, for his spelling is uniform and consistent with Gil's.
107. Gil, pp. 12, 116, 118, 119, 122; Butler, pp. 13, 15, 20, 22, 24, etc.
108. Smith, fol. 24.
109. Butler, p. 129.
110. Gil, p. 119; Butler, p. 43.
111. Butler, pp. 43, 44.
112. Butler, p. 51.
113. *Ib.,* pp. 27, 51, 76, 160.
114. Gil, pp. 89, 144; Butler, pp. 19, 24, 46, 55, 104, etc.
115. Butler, pp. 90, 118.
116. Smith, fol. 20; Gil, pp. 48, 111.
117. Gil, p. 99.
118. Butler, pp. 8, 60.
119. So says Gil, *errata;* Smith, fol. 24, has it long; Butler, p. 50, has it long, but in pp. 3, 4, 5, 9, 24, etc., has it short.
120. Long, Gil, p. 21. Short, Butler, p. 138.
121. Long, Gil, pp. 22, 99, 118, 121. Short, *ib.,* pp. 23, 24, 98, 110.
122. Long, Butler, p. 150. Short, Gil, pp. 84, 93; Butler, pp. 4, 15, 18, 32, 36, etc. See also White's *Shakespeare,* XII, p. 427.
123. Long, Butler, p. 58. Short, Smith, fol. 20.
124. Long, Smith, fol. 38. Short, Butler, pp. 35, 37, 41, 91, 92, etc.
125. Long, Smith, fol. 38; Butler, pp. 81, 89. Short, Butler, pp. 117, 118, 119.
126. Long, Gil, p. 126. Short, *ib.,* p. 77.
127. Butler, pp. 13, 18, 43, 44.
128. Gil, pp. 104, 127; Butler, pp. 9, 15, 122.
129. Gil, p. 125; Butler, pp. 11, 136.
130. Butler, p. 64.
131. *Ib.,* pp. 53, 84.
132. *Ib.,* p. 49.
133. *Ib.,* pp. 6, 9, 154, 157.
134. Smith, fol. 41; Gil, pp. 27, 38, 103, 104; Butler, pp. 5, 7, 9, 10, 13, 23, etc.
135. Butler, p. 23.
136. *Ib.,* p. 10.
137. Smith, fol. 11; Gil, pp. 48, 52, 117; Butler, pp. 16, 137.

Reading,[138] *spread* (past),[139] *sweat* (past),[140] *wealth,*[141] *weather.*[142]
Several words now written *ear* had then the sound of *eer;* they were,
appear,[143] *clear,*[144] *year,*[145] and sometimes *near*[146] and *rear.*[147] Consequently these words did not rhyme with the following: *bear* (noun and
verb),[148] *fear,*[149] *hear,*[150] *tear* (verb).[151] *Instead* was often called 'in-
steed'.[152] *Heard* had the sound 'hare',[153] and *heart* was pronounced as
at present.[154] When *ea* is found rhymed with *ai,* it is owing to a common mispronunciation of the latter diphthong noticed by Gil. The *ei*
in *receive, deceive,* etc., was a diphthong in Gil's time; it was used interchangeably with *ai,* as both Smith and Mulcaster observe. The latter
says:—

Ai, is the man's dipthong, and soundeth full: *ei,* the woman's, and soundeth finish in the same both sense, and use; a woman is deintie, and feinteth
soon; the man fainteth not, bycause he is nothing daintie.[155]

DIPHTHONGS. 1. 'Ice', 'ire'. It is the characteristic peculiarity of
English speech, that all transition from one note or tone to another is
made, not by a sudden change, but by what in *pitch* is called a slide.
Accordingly, none of our diphthongs are combinations of two vowels,
but run from the first sound to the last through an infinite number of
gradations. 'Ice', according to this view, instead of being *ah–ee,* is more
nearly *ah, up, err, end, in, eve.*[156] But it is not to be supposed that any
abrupt change was made from the Saxon *i* long to this very complex

138. Butler, p. 35.
139. Gil, p. 106; Butler, pp. 92, 95, 97, 109, 148.
140. Gil, p. 48.
141. Gil, pp. 39, 77, 85, 87, 89; Butler, pp. 2, 20, 138, 139, 141.
142. Butler, pp. 2, 3, 4, 9, 11, 15, 16, etc.
143. Gil, pp. 87, 94; Butler, pp. 13, 15, 16, 23, 51, etc.
144. Butler, pp. 160, 161.
145. *Ib.,* pp. 23, 29, 30, 31, 32, etc.
146. *Ea* sound, Gil, pp. 34, 104. *Ee* sound, Gil, p. 84; Butler, pp. 14, 18, 28, 30,
34, etc.
147. *Ea* sound, Smith, fol. 30; Butler, pp. 29, 42, 47, 86, 97. *Ee* sound, Butler,
p. 87.
148. Gil, p. 50; Butler, pp. 54, 139.
149. Gil, pp. 20, 22, 98, 99, 109, etc.; Butler, pp. 15, 29, 48, 65, 84, etc.
150. Gil, p. 27; Butler, pp. 14, 15, 114.
151. Smith, fol. 30; Gil, p. 107; Butler, p. 119.
152. Butler, pp. 5, 8, 18, 144. Gil, however, gives it the long sound of *ea,*
p. 103.
153. Gil, pp. 21, 23, 80; Butler, p. 150; White's *Shakespeare,* XII, 427.
154. Gil, pp. 21, 23, 24, 79, 99, 119; Butler, pp. 15, 25, 33, 150.
155. p. 119.
156. Mr. J. Jennison in Hillard's *Reader.*

combination. It is more rational to suppose that the sound grew up by insensible gradations somewhat in this way:—

1.   *eve*;
2.   *in–eve*;
3.   *end–in–eve*;
4.   *err–end–in–eve*;
5.   *up–err–end–in–eve*;
6. *ah–up–err–end–in–eve*.

The grammars do not afford us that full and exact information which we should desire upon so interesting a subject; but it would seem that in the time of Palsgrave the change from *eve* to *ice* was but half completed.

I, in the frenche tong hath II dyverse maners of soundynges [: 1.] Like as the Italians sounde *i*, whiche is almost as we sound *e* in these wordes: "a bee, a flie; a beere, for a deed corps; a peere, a felowe; a fee, a rewarde"; a litell more soundynge towardes *i*, as we sounde *i* with us. [2.] If *i* be the first letter in a frenche worde, or the laste, he shall, in those two places, be sounded lyke as we do this letter *y* in these wordes with us, "by and by, a spye, a flye, awry," and suche other, as in *ymage, converty, ydole, estourdy*, in whiche the *y* hath suche sounde as we wolde gyve hym in our tonge.

I reken *ui* also among the diphthonges in the frenche tong, whiche, whan they come to gether, shalle have suche a sounde in frenche wordes as we gyve hym in these wordes in our tong: "a swyne, I dwyne, I twyne"; so that these wordes, *aguyser, aguyllon, conduyre, deduyre, aujourdhuy, meshuy*, and all suche lyke shall sounde theyr *u* and *i* shortly together, as we do in our tong in the wordes I have gyven example of, and nat eche of them distinctly by hymselfe.[157]

The unmistakable drift of these citations is to the effect that 'ice' was pronounced like *i* in 'wind', or perhaps 'end–in–eve'. During the next half-century the pronunciation underwent a further change, as is evident from Mulcaster's remarks upon 'wind' and 'kind' quoted below.

Some phonotypists in the time of Baret thought that *ei* should take the place of long *i*; but Gil says that *i* long differed slightly from *ei* (that is, probably, 'err–in'); and because *i* long had a sharper sound than this combination, he adopted into his system the character *j* as its representative.[158] Wallis regards 'ice' as compounded of French *e* feminine, that is, *e* in 'stranger', and *i* short, pronounced like the Greek *ei*,

---

157. Palsgrave, pp. xviii, 6, and 16.
158. *Logonomia*, pp. 7 and 16.

and almost like *ai* in the French words 'main' and 'pain'.[159] This description may not appear strange when the process by which 'point' came to
be pronounced 'pint' is explained. The analysis of 'ice' by Wallis may
be thought to be that of numbers four or five in our table, but it is not
to be asserted that this is or is not the case. It may be doubted whether
Shakespeare pronounced this sound like ourselves; but, until stronger
evidence is produced than that of Gil and Wallis, we should hardly be
justified in believing that its pronunciation has become essentially
changed since 1600. Even at this day so excellent an orthoëpist as Smart
is confident that '*ur–i*' is the true analysis of *i* long. This resolution
differs but little from that of Wallis.

'Mice', 'lice', and 'kine' were pronounced as now; but Jonson informs
us that the old sounds 'meece', &c., were also allowable.[160] The Pals-
gravian pronunciation of '*ice*', in words where the *i* is now sounded
long, appears to have been confined, with Mulcaster, to a few words
ending in *nd*. "Wind, frind, bind," he laconically remarks, "and with the
qualifying *e*, kinde, finde, &c."[161] So Coote, who, however, like Gil, preferred the longer pronunciation in all words of this class, not excepting
'wind'. "And some pronounce these words, bl*i*nd, f*i*nd, beh*i*nd, short:
others bl*i*nde, f*i*nde, beh*i*nde, with *e*, long."[162]

'Height' and 'sleight' were pronounced 'hate' and 'slate' by Mulcaster, but by Gil as they are now. 'Eye' was also sounded like *I* by
Gil, who, however, refers to Mulcaster's pronunciation, which was
nearly that of *a* long.

2. 'oil'. There were two different sounds of this diphthong in Shakespeare's day, the present sound and that of '*oo*il'. This duplicity of
sound is thus referred to by Mulcaster:—

> Thirdlie, *oi*, the diphthong sounding upon the o, for difference sake, from
> the other, which soundeth upon the u, wold be written with a y, as *joy, anoy,
> toy, boy,* whereas *anoint, appoint, foil,* and such seme to have an u. And
> yet when, *i,* goeth before the diphthong, tho it sound upon the u, it were
> better oy, then oi, as *joynt, joyn,* which theie shall soon perceive, when theie
> mark the spede of their pen: likewise if oi with i, sound upon the o, it maie
> be noted for difference from the other sound, with the streight accent.[163]

---

159. Wallis, pp. 38 and 60.
160. B. Jonson, p. 301.
161. *Elementarie*, p. 133.
162. Coote, p. 19.
163. *Elementarie*, pp. 117, 118.

Mulcaster, therefore, in the system of orthography in which his work is written, the most marked characteristic of which is the employment of *e* in place of *ee*, places a straight or acute accent upon *oi*, or rather *oy*, sounded upon the *o* in this position. While treating of the proper diphthongs, Gil, in confirmation of Mulcaster, remarks: "Sometimes we indifferently foist ū in the place of o before i. For we say toil or tūil, broil or brūil, soil or sūil."[164]

During the thirty-four years which intervened between the publication of Gil's and Wallis's Grammars, the '*ooze*' sound in '*oil*' shortened into '*up*'; and we are instructed by the latter author, that in *oi*, sometimes *o* short, as in 'boy', and sometimes *o* or *u* obscure, as in 'oil' or 'ŭyl', 'toil' or 'tŭyl', is the first part of the combination.[165] This pronunciation soon degenerated into that of *i* long, the almost universal orthoepy for nearly a century. Even as late as 1784 Nares says: "The banished diphthong seems at length to be upon its return; for there are many who are now hardy enough to pronounce *boil* exactly as they do *toil*, and *join* like *coin*."[166]

3. '*out*'. The combination *ou* is said by the old grammars to have had two sounds. One might, perhaps, be so hasty as to make the same remark now, though in fact it has seven,—'*touch*', '*trough*', '*ought*', '*group*', '*should*', '*mould*', and '*thou*'. The sounds it most frequently had are spoken of in the following quotations from Palsgrave and Mulcaster:—

Ou in the frenche tong shalbe sounded lyke as the Italians sounde this vowell *u*, or they with us that sounde the latine tong aright, that is to say, almost as we sounde hym in these words, "a cowe, a mowe, a sowe," as *oultre, soundayn, oublier:* and so of suche other.[167]

O is a letter of as great uncertaintie in our tung, as e, is of direction both alone in vowell, and combined in diphthong. The cause is, for that in vowell it soundeth as much upon the u, which is his cosin, as upon the ó, which is his naturall, as in *còsen, dòsen, mòther*, which o, is still naturallie short, and, *hósen, frósen, móther*, which o, is naturallie long. In the diphthong it soundeth more upon the, u, then upon the, o, as in *found, wound, cow, sow, bow, how, now*, and *bów, sów, wróught, óught, mów, tróugh*.[168]

164. *Logonomia,* p. 15.
165. Wallis, pp. 37, 63.
166. *Elements of Orthoëpy,* p. 74.
167. Palsgrave, p. 15.
168. *Elementarie,* p. 115.

An acute accent placed upon the last six words indicates that they were sounded on the *o*. Sounding upon the *u* in all cases in Mulcaster means sounding *oo*, whether long or short. In another passage he says, "*Hoop, coop*. If custom had not won this, why not ou? . . . *Houl, coul, skoul*. Why not as well with oo?"[169] It would appear from these quotations, that in 1582 *ow* was pronounced like *oo*. There are several puns in Shakespeare, as that of 'fowl' and 'fool', which depend upon this identity in sound.

Jonson copies Mulcaster; Gil says:—

We place before the vowel u, either o short as in bound, sound; or ō long, as in blōun, thrōun. So a bou *bough* differs from a bōu *bowe*, and a boul from a bōul *bowle*.

That this language can only be construed as teaching a pronunciation different from that of Mulcaster is made still more evident by Gil's mode of spelling certain words regarded by Wallis as exceptions to the general sound of *ou*, as yū for you, yūr for your, wūnd for wound, cūrt for court, cūld for could, &c.

Wallis seems to contradict both Mulcaster and Gil; he says:—

Ou and *ow* are pronounced with an obscure sound; to wit, a sound composed of *o* or *u* obscure and *w*. As *house, mouse*.

This is not an accurate description of the present sound, but what is intended must be left to others to determine.

4. '*use, ure*'. The pronunciation of '*use*' is described with some unanimity, as that of the French *u*, as indeed it may well have been once; but that certainly was not its sound in Shakespeare's day, for Baret describes it in terms of more than ordinary clearness as being a diphthong compounded of *e* and *u*. Palsgrave mentions two sounds of *eu*, one occurring in "adewe, ashewe, afewe," the other in "trewe, glew, rewe, amewe." Most of the latter words afterwards changed their spelling. Gil has *eu* with short *e*, and *ēu* with long *e*. The latter occurs infrequently, as in *few, ewe, ewer, sewer*. The former *eu* differed from *u* in '*use*', apparently in beginning with the vowel 'end' instead of the consonant *y*. Wallis says:—

Eu, ew, eau are sounded by *e* clear and *w*. As in *newter, few, beauty*. Still some pronounce them a little more sharply, as if written *niewter, fiew,*

---

169. *Ibid.*, p. 136.

biewty, or *niwter, fiw, biwty,* especially in the words *new, knew, snew.* But the first pronunciation is more correct.[170]

The old pronunciation of the terminations 'rue' and 'ure' in unaccented syllables has been mooted by verbal critics. Gil is not uniform. He spells 'scripture' and 'venture' respectively 'scriptur' and 'venter', but to 'creature', 'measure', 'nature', and 'treasure' he assigns their present sound, representing their *u* by v, the character in his alphabet which stands for *u* in 'use'. Mulcaster, on the other hand, classes 'future' with such words as 'writer' and spells it 'futer'. He also writes 'conjectur', 'conjur', 'creatur', 'figur', 'measur', 'misconster', 'natur', 'nurtur', 'pastur', 'pictur', 'scriptur', 'statur', 'treasur', and 'ventur'. With this catalogue, flattering to Yankee lips, we end our account of the olden orthoëpy.

170. Wallis, p. 63.

Analysis of the Ego

MS 78: Spring 1864

This investigation seeks an answer to this question: How does any-thing which exists, exist? or What are the conditions of subjectivity?

The first thing to be said is that it exists by virtue of being whatever it is. Thus, Gold *is*, by virtue of being heavy and yellow. The subject is subject by being an incarnation of a predicate. Every subject is the incarnation of a predicate, which is an abstraction, and which when incarnated in the consciousness is called a conception or in its relation to the exterior incarnation an idea. It is only, then, by its idea, that any thing exists. Of most things we do not know th[e] ideas, of none wholly. Subjects are either monads or collective subjects or universal subjects. No monad is known to exist, for all subjects which w[e] know have extension. Extension is infinite; thus, all collective subjects are partial subjects. The Universal subject we only know through conceptions and partial subjects. This explanation, perhaps not in place here, is made to remove the objection which would arise to my saying that artificial objects exist through the qualities they are intended to embody, *namely* that I have not explained the existence of the subject but only the form. Now, I reply that it is the formed substance only of which we have any knowledge; and I say that it is by the form or collective quality that the collective substance exists, for it is by the quality that substance in general, exists. At the same time, that the final cause of an artificial body is only partially its cause. I shall occupy no more space with this point although the objection will probably not be effaced from the mind, but will content myself with pointing out that it is a purely meta-physical question of the mode of existence of the *noumenon* and can never affect any scientific conclusions, for empirically speaking capacity for containing fire is the subjective condition of the existence of a fur-nace. The difficulty of conceiving this matter rightly arises from the circumstance which I shall mention next.

But, first, let us notice that it is only by means of this circumstance that every concretion is the product of some abstraction that we can classify things, for classification consists in ranging things under their predicates. Is classification arbitrary? To a certain extent it is, for we can classify a body according to any of its predicates. But here again we must distinguish between the quality in the body and the representation of that quality in sensation and in conception. It is by the representation that we classify bodies and the classification will be just, according as the representation is just. Were the representation *perfect,* it would represent the idea of the body fully, so that the body would have no predicate which this representation failed to express; and classification according to *such* a representation would have nothing arbitrary in it. It is this classification which is the infinitely distant point at which we aim. I will now name some subjects which I propose to classify, showing their relations to other things. I will select all sorts of things, so as to test the applicability of my method.

List of Substances

α 1. Charles S. Peirce
β 2. The orbit of the earth
γ 3. The idea of *substance*
δ 4. The stars of heaven
ε 5. The piano in this room
ζ 6. A certain dog—"Scott"
η 7. The Great Organ in Boston
θ 8. A computing scale I have before me
ι 9. The Government of the United States
κ 10. The Tragedy of Othello
λ 11. A retort
μ 12. The bodies HCl, H_2O, NH_3, SO_3, NO, CN, ClS, &c.

Idea of α. The idea of Charles S. Peirce is that of a created soul (not excluding body). Without undertaking therefore to say precisely what that is, because it doesn't happen to be necessary, but remembering Plato's definition that it is something which moving itself does not cease to move because its motion does not pass beyond itself, and Swedenborg's idea of a bud upon the Almighty, we may be content with saying he is a *living being.*

Idea of β. The orbit of the earth according to all previous philosophy is not a substance. But I, seeing that there are no substances in the ordinary sense, except the universal and incomprehensible substance, regard all subject as substance. The idea of the orbit of the earth is an *external geometrical line.*

Idea of γ. The idea of an idea. The idea of a conception is *the realization of an abstraction in the consciousness.*

Idea of δ. This subject is so little understood that it might be classified in several ways but as a whole we know so little of the firmament that we shall do best to regard it a plural or *multitude,* simply.

Idea of ε. The idea of a piano, is its final cause, namely *a sonorous vibrating instrument.*

Idea of ζ. The idea of the dog Scott is that of an *animal,* whatever that may be.

Idea of η. Same as ε.

Idea of θ. The idea of the computing scale, is that it measures the relations of numbers.

Idea of ι. The idea of a Government is its definition (for here the final cause may be doubtful). That is, the centre of the force in the organization of a society.

Idea of κ. The idea of a Tragedy, is that of a Dramatic representation.

λ. The idea of a retort is, a vessel capable of holding a boiling liquid, tight to prevent escape of vapors and with a neck for drawing them off.

Before passing to μ let us consider the above 11 instances. ε, η, θ, κ, λ are artificial. ι is historical. β, γ are Subjective. α, δ, ζ are natural.

Of the artificial subjects, the idea of ε and η, was simply the final cause, expressed as a predicate of these subjects. If anything was added thereto, it was owing to the fact that music may be made without sonorous vibrations in the instrument itself; and if this be so, then the idea was stated too narrowly.

The idea of θ, was stated as merely the final cause, without being expressed as a predicate thereof. This seems to be a defect in the statement, but I feared to attempt to improve it in this respect for fear of limiting the statement to some particular kind of computing scale.

Why did I say sonorous vibrations neither embracing the whole scale of vibrations nor limiting myself to stringed or discrete instruments and why did I limit myself to measurements of *numbers* and yet not to logarithmic measurements?

To the first of these questions the answer is perhaps not difficult. The final cause of an organ or a piano widely stated is to exalt the aesthetic nature and to produce remote effects upon the whole nature of man and thus to improve the condition of the universe. But all that this instrument can in itself do is to make the sounds when placed within an atmosphere of proper density, and otherwise favorably circumstanced, and on being worked. Hence, the instrument must be regarded simply as a producer of vibrations. It is true that were there any other material means which affected the same faculties as music they must be included, but this I take it is not the case. The indefiniteness that now remains is owing to our imperfect knowledge of the final cause of the musical instrument.

The object of a computing scale is the solution of a series of problems (all within certain limits) *à posteriori* that might be solved *a priori* by putting the principle of them all into the machine in its manufacture. I have then two categories of classification here

1st   All such instruments

2nd Limitation by the different series of problems.

The 1st indicates the idea. But all such instruments are really numerical; hence, I inserted that word. The idea κ is obviously its final cause.

λ may be viewed in more aspects than one. A retort may be regarded as an element of the chemical laboratory. But it is not so necessarily, and in itself is not a chemical apparatus, any more than a stone in the bladder is an animal. The only object that is *really inherent in it*, is distillation.

We thus see that the idea of artificial objects is their inherent purpose expressed as inherent. This is in all cases the most general definition that can be applied to an artificial object. And hence forms the largest category of their classification.

The purpose of a government may be doubtful but its idea as I have expressed it is that which it performs. Not the particular things which it performs, but the general statement of any thing which it can perform without the limitations actually seen in the object.

The idea of the orbit of the earth is place during time, or a portion of space belonging to a substance. This is what the orbit *marks*.

The idea of a conception, regards the conception a realizer and expresses its realization.

The metaphysical ideas suggested under a express the function of the living being.

An animal is probably the same thing.

The idea of the stars I have taken to be that which they convey to the mind.

In general, therefore, the idea regards the subject as doing or expressing something—as working itself out—and expresses the particular working out that it does. It disregards the abstraction worked out and it disregards that in which it is worked out, and looks to the identity or difference of the working out function itself. We may therefore discard the vague term *idea* and substitute for it *Function*.

I will now ask what is the idea of the objects of Chemical Study. We must first know what these objects are. They are not the forms or motions of things, they are not mere phenomena. But they are the properties of things, that is the phenomena, forms, motions, etc., which *inhere* in things. Matter then is the object of chemistry, and would remain so were it proved that there were no matter in its present sense in the universe, but that all was pure force. To matter we attach the most definite notion as a subject. It is the subject of motion. Mobility, then, is the idea of matter. Here a difficulty occurs. Motion itself, also moves. This difficulty cannot always be removed in practice, but theoretically it can be. Motion moves because it is mere predicate and not subject, for if it made any resistance to motion it would be the subject of motion. But whenever it moves, the predicate of its motion is itself; it never is moved. Matter on the other hand never moves but always is moved; it might be still and remain the same matter; or if under given circumstances it moved less it would only make it more matter; but motion could not under given circumstances move less, or if it does it is only by diminishing the motion. The capacity for being moved then is the function of a chemical object. The only question is whether I ought not to say that in which motion can *reside*.

§2. When that incarnation of a predicate which we have called Function becomes Perfect, we have no matter left, in the sense of an impressed thing, so that there is no longer an incarnation but rather a Carnification of the predicate. What this is we shall define better later in the course of our inquiry. It is easy to see that this is not a subject except so far as the abstract predicate itself is its own subject; hence it is entirely beyond our present field of thought. The incarnation reduced to a nullity is merely the Function of Function, and may be called Linguification because meaningless language is the function of expression reduced to zero; or it may be called Materiafication.

Incarnation may be regarded as a Combination between Carnification and Materiafication. And how can this occur? By the determination of the Material by its Idea. Let us apply this to the same examples as before.

The piano. The material is rendered sonorous by making it elastic. We must not say by making it into elastic strings for it is enough that it should be elastic.

The organ. Here the material itself is not necessarily elastic but it is rendered sonorous by its arrangement for striking the air in its cavities.

The Computing Scale. This is a logarithmic scale. Here then the *à priori* principle is worked experimentally, not by allowing it to operate directly but by a device, which consists in marking the relationship between the principle that actually operates and that which is conceived as operating. Our scale, therefore, belongs to the branch which marks this relationship.

The Tragedy of Othello. The *function* of a tragedy is the representation of human life. The method of introducing that function is by rendering it a *copy* of men and women.

The Retort. The *function* of a retort is the holding a boiling liquid so as to allow the fumes to separate themselves without being lost. This is done by having a heatable *body* and a *neck*.

The Government. The plan is to bestow upon an institution definite rights and duties and to place in its grasp the material resources of the community for carrying them into effect.

The Orbit of the Earth. The function is to be the place of a body. The material is determined by this idea by making the body pass through this space.

The idea of substance. The material of a conception is thought or the consciousness. The determination of this material by its being a realizer of an abstraction consists in the direction of the attention or subject-selecting capacity to that particular element of the thought which if abstracted would be the given abstraction.

C. S. Peirce. Plato's definition itself contains both function—"that which moving itself does not cease to be moved"—and determination of material—"because it never moves out of itself."

The Dog. The function of an animal is perhaps hard to state. But certain partial statements put into the equation of equilibrium have determined 4 forms of material as conditions of this function. The forms are recognized as standing for the four branches of the animal kingdom —although the naturalist would state the characteristics of these branches in a different way. Still, it is hereby clear that the Branch is the determination of the material with reference to the general Function of the kingdom.

The Stars. The function should rather have been stated as the esthetic quality. And the determination of the material is the plurality of masses.

In all these instances we see very clearly that it is the actual quality which constitutes the Function which we have been determining. It has been well called the Plan. It is the *root* of the equation, which is given as a problem in the Function. Hence it is a question of equality or equilibrium.

If the regulation in a *plan* be conceived of simply and absolutely, that is if the determination of the material by its function be fully carried out, it will cease to have any substantiality. If it is not carried out but only conceived of, it will have a merely formal existence. Thus take the function *force-carrying.* The plan is *moveability.* But if moveability becomes perfect there can be no force. If it is reduced to *zero* the case is the same. Yet there is no sufficient reason for any intermediate condition. The function must not determine the purely substantive material but the latter must be subjected to other functions as conditions and the function must *apply* itself to them. There must be *application;* or there must be equations of condition to satisfy, and these must standing in place of the material receive the *plan.* The different applications of the same plan constitute its classes. They do not have reference to different materials but different applications to material generally speaking.

PIANO. The plan of the piano is to be *vibratory.* The application is that it is vibratory (not in plates or bells but) in strings. The elasticity or vibratoriness is essentially the same thing in bells, plates, or strings. But in every case the vibration resides in the form of the matter, it is an affair of form; indeed, when sonorousness was planned it was as much as saying what it should be in the matter, whether change of form or motions with reference to the air, which should receive a determination having the required result. A predicate of matter, to be determined was selected; and now this predicate must be determined. What the determination of the form is other wise than as regards the vibra-

On the Doctrine of Immediate Perception

MS 81: August 1864

I hold the Doctrine of Common Sense to be well fitted to Reid's philosophical calibre and about as effective against any of the honored systems of philosophy as a potato-pop-gun's contents might be against Gibraltar.

By Common Sense is meant according to Sir William Hamilton "the complement of those cognitions or convictions which we receive from nature; which all men profess in common; and by which they test the truth of knowledge and the morality of actions." The doctrine is that these convictions are cognitions.

Now my objections to making this principle the corner-stone of philosophy are two.

The first is that it is ambiguous. It is defended in one sense, in which it is a truism. But it is inevitably applied in another sense in which it will not bear its own test.

The second is that the test is not capable of being directly applied, and that the trial is as difficult as the original problem.

I will first endeavor to show that this doctrine taken strictly is a truism. It will be admitted that if anyone has denied it, it is Kant. And yet he has not done so, even with respect to the speculative employment of Pure Reason. On the contrary the whole gist of his argument is that the ideas of pure reason, having no relation to any possible experience, could not possibly be employed to test our knowledge; and he equally insists that as *speculative* (not *practical*) ideas they have no bearing on the morality of actions. So in his Deduction of the Categories,—where the course of his reasoning is obscure only to those who can understand no portion of his work,—Kant only overrides Hamilton's Law by never requiring any test further than compliance with the conditions of the possibility of cognition. And by these conditions of cognition he means the conditions of judgement. And he rejects other conceptions (such as *fortune, fate,* &c.) because they cannot be tests of the truth of knowledge. It is absurd, therefore, to say that he questions the tests of the truth of knowledge; on the contrary, he applies them. But is it not a truism to assert that those convictions must be accepted which no man can resist?

But that there is a significance in making this truism the principle of investigation, I admit. It is in restricting us to one line of inquiry, namely that of finding what convictions are native to the mind and what are abnormal results of experience. Now there is no criterion by which it may be determined whether a given conviction is normal or not. The test of universality and necessity only determines whether a proposition may be derived from real observation, but clearly not whether it is true. The consciousness in giving us a proposition, confines itself to that without disclosing its origin. Hence the application of the rule is only possible by indirect reasoning *à posteriori.*

Now I do not deny that this process may sometimes be used with success. But to make it our one principle of investigation, never to dogmatize, to proceed from acknowledged axioms as all natural sciences do, never to analyze so as to find what is simple in thought and not merely what is primitive, is not only to throw away two-thirds of our means of investigation, but is to sow the seeds of the overthrow of that principle of faith with which we set out.

Let us now come to the celebrated application of this principle to the theory of perception. It is said to be a fact that consciousness testifies to our perceiving the non-ego. This is put forward as opposed to the doctrine that our knowledge of the non-ego is inferential.

This pretended testimony of consciousness must either be given in the act of perception itself, or it must be an axiom concerning perception. On the former alternative every perception itself involves and contains a proposition. A proposition is the thinking a predicate of a subject; the universal usage of speech argues that this is a natural conviction. Accordingly, we have the testimony of consciousness that the subject is not *thought* but *thought of,* that it does not enter into the field of consciousness. If the other alternative is adopted that the doctrine in question is an axiom, what does this axiom explain and how is it suggested? A genuine axiom is a proposition which arises in the mind in view of a manifold of phenomena, and which enables us to connect this manifold into a unity. It is necessary, therefore, that an axiom should explain something; but this principle so far from doing that renders the connection of ego and non-ego, which is otherwise explicable, demonstrably inexplicable. Now a theory which renders any fact demonstrably inexplicable is in opposition to that fact.

Both these alternatives, therefore, must be given up. And there is no other. It seems to be imagined that this immediate perception may be a matter of observation but in the first place truths of observation cannot be natural and inalienable convictions, and in the second place we cannot have any such observation upon pure perception since this faculty is never exercised alone, but always in conjunction with others.

Perception is in fact a mere residuum of analysis and what belongs to it is not a question of common sense but of analytic simplicity.

All the cognitions which we actually have experience of are propositions, in which the non-ego enters only as something to which certain predicates are referred, these predicates being in themselves modifications of consciousness. Here is the observed fact, and genuine common sense will not oppose it.

Letter, Peirce to
Francis E. Abbot

Francis E. Abbot Papers

1865 Feb. 5
Cambridge

Dear Abbot

As I am going to make a slight reference to Kant's theory of Apprehension in Intuition in some lectures next term, I have been led to re-
examine your objections to his doctrine and would like to submit to
you some of the difficulties I still find in comprehending them.

In reference to the distinction between Space and Extension, I am
inclined to agree with you that Kant did not intend it even in his early
paper on the *Metaphysical Principles of Natural Science.* Space, in fact,
is as you say known, if at all, by pure intellect; and therefore the con-
ception· of it would be utterly false (transcendent) according to Kant.
He would probably say that it was the supposition of an object to correspond to the form of intuition; and as he says (Rosencrantz' Ed.,
p. 236), "The mere Form of Intuition, without Substance, is in itself
no object, but the mere formal condition of it (as Phenomenon), as the
pure Space and pure Time (*ens imaginarium*) which certainly are
something, as Forms for Intuiting, but are themselves no objects which
can be intuited." His Space as an image is, therefore, your extension.
But you will ask how he can speak of a pure intuition of space by
which you say (p. 103) that he means "the mental image of empty
space." You seem not to have noticed that in the Transcendental Aesthetic he is not considering the mode of Apprehension in Intuition but
only the questions "Whether and how Space and Time can be objectively valid?" He has accordingly treated the subject of Apprehension
separately in the 1st Edition of his *Kritik* (p. 93) and in a wonderfully
acute manner, and in the second Edition this being omitted he explains

(p. 753) that to avoid a complication he allowed a loose statement in the Esthetic in regard to Space as an object. It fully appears in both editions (as also in the phrase *ens imaginarium*) that this image of space is a product of imagination not of sense, and that it involves the imagination of an object and requires a previous experience. So much for his speaking of an intuition of space as an image. Now for the adjective *pure*. I need not say that the fundamental and central idea of the whole critic, is that all cognitions whatsoever are cognitions of objects of a possible experience. But it occurs to me that the manner in which this view is carried out, slipped your mind when you say, on page 105, that Kant did not foresee the difficulty that intuited triangles are still not general cases and will not lead to general propositions; for Kant devotes a whole chapter (pp. 122–130) to explaining this point. I will therefore go on to say that these pure cognitions are simply cognitions contained in the experience of objects in general, that is to say, as much in any one object as in any other. A straight line is the shortest distance between two points. True, a straight line is not even ever given as such, but this proposition is deducible from any experience as explained rather briefly in the section on "Axioms of Intuition" (p. 761).

I return then to my opinion that your extension is Kant's image of space. And your space is his form of space. The first difference between you and him is that you adopt the theory of immediate perception; that is to say (as I understand it) you *do not ask the question* how the representation of a continuum can have validity, contenting yourself with the presumption of common sense,—a presumption indeed which Kant himself fully admits to be satisfactory as far as (his) Space goes (p. 85); and asks the question *quid juris* only on account of such suppositions and Ideas as transcend experience. I cannot make out whether you go any further than this and hold that extension is given in the impressions of the senses. If so, I think that a consideration of the argument from universality as illustrated by the curious anatomy of the retina would entirely convert you.

The other difference between you and Kant in regard to extension is that you regard it as a congeries of units. You may be right and I do not feel sure that Kant's criticism on that opinion is entirely sound. Though I should reject it for other reasons. Kant says,

It will always remain a remarkable phenomenon in this history of philosophy, that there has been a time, when Mathematicians even, who were also Philosophers, began to doubt not certainly the correctness of their geometri-

cal principles, so far as they concerned merely Space, but the objective validity and application of this conception itself and all its geometric determinations to Nature, since they supposed, that a line in Nature might well consist
of Points and consequently the pure space in Objects of simple parts, although the Space which the geometers have in thought can nowise be so
constituted.

But I foresee that you will say this begs the question and a discussion
of it would come round to the mathematical infinity again.

It seems to me however that both your refutations of Kant' are
defective; and if I am mistaken I earnestly desire to be set right if
you think you can do it in a small time.

The question Kant has in view may be stated thus. The present instant is felt, the past is remembered, the future is expected with certainty. How can the phenomena of memory and feeling be connected
into one continuum seeing that there is feeling in each instant of time
though in this instant is no continuum? How can pre-remembered time
and future time be known; if they can be known? The same with reference to Space. Here are some prerogative instances of space-perception.
The eye can easily see objects which make smaller images on the retina
than the distances of the nerve-points. The finger can feel finer texture
in moving than when still. The retina is not a field for a picture but a
bundle of tubes each containing a nerve point.

Yours very truly   Charles S. Peirce

P.S. My letter is already long but I will add another sheet in order
to notice a few more apparent misconceptions of Kant's doctrine.

You seem to think (p. 101) that Kant's division of the pure and
impure cognition is contrary to the relativity of knowledge. In order to
comprehend Kant, you should consider that he would associate your
doctrines with those of scholastic realism. Your space is an intelligible
form and as it is always a subject, it is a sort of *forma substantialis*
which you consider to be *real*. There seems to be a similar difference between your and his conception of a general judgement. Kant in
common with most modern philosophers does not regard this abstraction as being the whole of any act of thought. The judgement that two
straight lines cannot enclose a space is merely an element of the whole
act. He holds for instance that in abstraction we are conscious of the
element abstracted as well as of that which remains (*Werke* vii. p. 16
et seq.). When he says therefore that a conception or judgement is

purely *à priori* he means that it is one of the elements of thought, no part of which is logically determined by experience.

Observe the derivation of *à priori;* that which determines another this, *quod ponit praedicatum cum exclusione oppositi,* is prior to that other. Any representation then determines its object, *in representation.* So far then as representation relates to peculiarities of this or that object, in so far is it determined by this object; that is to say it is determined to be different from what it otherwise would be by that which it does itself in representation determine; hence it is determined *à posteriori.* In so far on the other hand, as its character would not be altered by the difference of the object, as in the character of *extension* &c., it is determined *a ratione* or *à priori.* When therefore you say (p. 104) "We admit unconditionally, that mere induction from experience can never possess these characteristics [universality and necessity]," you are mistaking the terms *à priori* and *à posteriori* as used by Kant, if you suppose that you are here admitting any doctrine of his. All the principles *à priori* are in his view, not it is true logical inductions, nor yet partial scientific inductions, but material inferences from *every and any* experience. An attentive study of the Transcendental Deduction of the Categories will show this. Let me express myself a little more precisely. Scientific men when they adopt hypotheses excuse themselves by saying that it is only by so doing that the facts can be comprehended (that is brought to a logical unity) and they say they do not believe these hypotheses as facts in themselves but only so far as they do bring the facts to a unity. In the same way Kant admits universals on the ground they are indispensible for bringing to the unity of consciousness, not facts merely, but the very impressions of sense. And he also refuses to accept them any further than this, into speculative philosophy or science, whatever practical *presumption* there may be in their favor and however admissible they may be into the *court* of conscience. According to Kant then material inference from experience is the very thing which alone can give validity to synthetic judgements *à priori.*

I will next refer to your observation (p. 98) that to say that the form of sensation is not itself sensation is irremediably vague. This is a charge not upon Kant merely but upon almost all the philosophers whom we are accustomed to respect. Is there such a contemptible obscurity in the general distinction between form and matter or only in this particular application of it? We see extension as a continuum; that is a matter of fact. All argument that it is divisible into units is a matter not of intuition but of thought. The structure of the eye (not that the illustration is necessary to the argument) shows, however, that sensations contain no continuum; consequently, we have in intuition what is given in sensation and the synthesis of it. The synthesis results in predicating extension of the body. This extension is the *quid*. The reason postulates as you say an underlying Space; a receptacle, a condition of the possibility of extension. This, then, is *quod explicat quid res sit;* that is, it is the Form of the intuited object in general. Here is the vagueness in other words which is irremediable.

I observe you complain of the technicality of Kant's terminology. He did not invent all these terms or give them their modern meanings at one jump. For many years the truly scientific spirit of Germany had been producing and developing this philosophical language. Every science in a vigorous state must have a language of its own; it is pedantry to confine oneself to classical language when one ought to have post-classical ideas. Kant seized the elements of this young language and brought them to full developement introducing very little absolutely new but generally going to the scholastic storehouses. But it is fine, now, to object of everything Kantian as new-fangled. Cousin, I remember, says that his two categories of *Realität* and *Daseyn* are all one. As though St. Thomas who said that substantial forms were *in posse* not *in actu* (= not, *dem Daseyn nach*) was not a Realist. Very likely you will sweep away some of my objections; though I cannot say I hope so, since I have a personal enthusiasm for Kant. C.S.P.

P.S. You have noticed I presume that a *representation* is not necessarily conscious (*Kritik* p. 258).

ON THE LOGIC OF SCIENCE

[Harvard Lectures of 1865]

Lecture I

MS 94: February–March 1865

Though I ask your attention to one of the studies of the ancient Trivium—a study therefore according both to etymology and long prejudice, trivial—I trust I need not at this day defend it from the charge of piddling. It is now pretty plain that though modern science has scorned the scholastic terminology it has either continued to employ or has been forced to relearn the ideas that terminology conveyed, having simply thrown away the advantage of exact expressions. Logic in itself, however, has never been contemned by profound minds. It was a particular scheme of logic and not the science itself against which Bacon protested (see Aphorism XI); hence, he proceeds at once to substitute for that scheme another of his own,—and that intended to be a strictly logical one as I shall hereafter show. In the same way the reform of Ramus, the reform of Kant and all the reforms of science have been logical reforms. The Ramists sneered at the scholastics, the modern natural theorists sneer at both, and certain persons are now beginning to sneer at the natural theorists. Another reform seems to be coming: it is in the air. Several logical questions are already under discussion by scientific men. Naturalists are divided into two classes, more according to Lyell upon a logical question than anything else. An eminent mathem[atic]ian has proposed a reform of the most important part of the theory of probabilities on logical grounds. And physicists ought not to feel too secure of the logical character of the hypothesis of impenetrability and its consequences which has already been attacked by men of high standing. On this account, I believe that there are not *now* many thoughtful men of science who will think that the investigation of the logical character of scientific reasoning is a needless or unimportant inquiry.

These lectures will take up two points in order,
1st The degree and character of the certainty of scientific ratiocination.

2nd The degree and character of the certainty of scientific primitive principles.

The first point will be considered in this order.

1st The conception of logic.

2nd A theory of induction developed out of Aristotle's, which I prefer.

3rd The study of the modern theories of Boole, Apelt, Herschel, Gratry, Whewell, and Mill.

4th The theory of Bacon.

The second point will be considered in this order.

1st The full presentation of Kant's theory of this subject.

2nd Consideration of the effect of modern researches in modifying this theory.

The one great source of error in all attempts to make a Logic of Science has been utter misconception of the nature and definition of logic. All the pure and formal logicians agree upon that. What then is logic? Of course, the definitions of a subject which has been pursued with ability for two thousand years and more have been very various. They may however be divided into two classes; those which do not and those which do give to logic a psychological or human character.

Of the unpsychological views there are several that occur to me as interesting. In the first place, there is the definition attributed rather doubtfully to Aristotle that Logic is the science of Demonstration. Spalding in the *Encyclopaedia Britannica* declares that it is the "theory of inference" which comes to the same thing. But apart from the narrowness of this view in identifying Logic with Syllogistic, these are mere word-definitions since they do not explain the nature of inference or demonstration. St. Augustine calls it the science of truth. Several writers of the *renaissance* (Peter Molyneux, Vossius) and at least one modern one Reimarus (1790) have advocated this definition. There is great merit in the view, but it is too broad; for logic does not consider how an object or idea may be presented but only how it may be represented; *eyesight*, that is to say, and *inspiration* are both beyond the province of logic. Another curious definition is that of Hobbes. "Ratiocination is Computation." A very remarkable and profound conception.

Of the psychological definitions, the commonest is that of Cicero which was adopted by Ramus. "Dialectica est ars se tradere bene disserendi." The Hindoo definition agrees with this. This identification of logic with the art of discussion, is at once the narrowest and lowest view of the subject which has ever been taken. But Melanchthon's definition "Ars et via docendi" is scarcely better. Another definition once in high favour is "ars dirigendi mentem in cognitione rerum." This is a step higher but is radically faulty in making it a collection of maxims instead of inviolable laws. Since Kant, there has been a vast majority of the suffrages of logicians in favor of his definition which is as follows —the science of the necessary laws of the Understanding and Reason —or what is the same thing—the science of the sheer Form of thought in general. Observe the two branches of this statement the former more psychological the latter scarcely at all so; one has two faculties and their capacities; the other thoughts as *objects* with forms. This is certainly the best definition yet given. It has been more or less modified in one way or other by subsequent logicians but not essentially by any-one who knows logic. One may say it is the science of the normative laws of human cognition. Another that it is the science of the relations of Conceptions. Another that it is the science of the laws of formal thinking. There are some erratic persons whose views differ as much from Kant as they do from each other. Thus Mr. Mill says "Logic is the science of the operations of the understanding which are subservient to the estimation of evidence." Duval-Jouve says it is the science of the facts of the intellect, of its laws, and of the rules which serve to //regulate/guide// its exercise. Krause says it treats of the law of the activity of the soul in thought. De Morgan says it is that "branch of inquiry in which the act of the mind in reasoning is considered."

All such statements as these last are worse than erroneous, in the extreme. Logic has nothing at all to do with operations of the understanding, acts of the mind, or facts of the intellect. This has been repeatedly shown by the Kantians. But I will go a step further and say that we ought to adopt a thoroughly unpsychological view of logic, and that we may do so without entirely overturning established ideas. For this purpose, suppose I write this syllogism on the board

> All conquerors are Butchers
> Napoleon is a conqueror
> ∴ Napoleon is a butcher.

Now this has a particular logical character to me as I write it; it has the same to all of you as you read it; it will have the same if you read it tomorrow; and while it remains on the board it will retain the same character to whoever can read it. Now is this logical character a form of *thought* only? My thought when I wrote it was a different event from each one of your thoughts, and your thoughts will be each different if you read it again from what they were when you read it just now. The thoughts were many, but this form was one. For that which was written on the board remained the same. What is written, therefore, is the continual determinator of this form. Now a continual determinator of a form is that in which the form inheres by the definition of the relation of *substantia et accidens*. Hence, this logical character belongs to what is written on the board at least as much as to our thought. To this reasoning, there are at least three intelligent objections. The first is, that if this which is on the board were rubbed out and written again the logical character would remain the same &c. So that the form would then inhere in the memory. I admit this objection and all its consequences; but it does not touch my point which was that the logical character does not belong to thought, *peculiarly.* The second objection is that though what is written has a logical character, it only has it because it can be understood and thought. This, also, I entirely admit. In the same way, those letters are white. There is no doubt the whiteness inheres in the chalk. Yet they are only white in so far and because they can be seen. There are ten words there—that is to say ten conglomerations of writing. Yet there are ten only because by a mental process we distinguish ten objects. Indeed there is no form which could be unless the mind could think it. Form is as much determined by the *subject* or *I* as it is by the *object* or *IT;* but it is the IT which constitutes its matter and in fact matter may be defined as the //pure/sheer// IT and the analogous word *substance* may be defined as the absolute IT. Hence the objection that this form is such only because it may be thought entirely fails of its object. The third objection is that by a form of thought is meant a form of thought in general not of this or that particular thought; and that this thought in general is in fact the genus of thought, and hence an abstraction not capable of being thought in its generality. This objection also I very nearly agree to. That which I set out to prove was that the psychological character of the Kantian definition was not an essential character. There is no difference amounting to the slightest contradiction between the two views. The psychological view is that these forms are only realized in thought, and that language is essential to thought. The unpsychological view is that they are forms of all symbols whether internal or external but that they only are by virtue of possible thought. In short, I say that the logical form is already realized in the symbol itself; the psychologists say that it is only realized when the symbol is understood.

If the two views are so nearly alike why should the new one be pressed? What are its advantages? I answer that it has three. 1st It is philosophically more perfect. A definition of a science should not include conceptions foreign to that science. For instance, according to the generally received view space is the form of the external sense. If this be true, it would not be false to call geometry the science of the formal laws of the external sense. It would, however, be bad as a definition, because geometry regards extension simply as an object without any reference to its psychological or ontological character whatsoever. In the same way logic needs no distinction between the symbol and the thought; for every thought is a symbol and the laws of logic are true of all symbols.

2. The second advantage of the unpsychological view is that it affords a most convenient means for exploding false notions of the subject. Take for example, Mr. Mill's definition of logic: "It is the science of the operations of the understanding which are subservient to the estimation of evidence." The psychological character of this is essential. This shows that the view is not merely false but wholly false. Accordingly, it is no exaggeration to say that Mr. Mill's logic is no more like what has been understood by that term than is Locke's *Essay Concerning Human Understanding*. *Again*, in almost all logics the subject of fallacies has occupied a prominent place. It has been supposed that the laws of logic might be broken. That they say "Thou ought" not "thou shalt," that in short they are statements not of *fact* but of *debt*. But what page of man's ledger does this "ought" refer to? Thought *debtor* to what? It is impossible to say. But why ought we to be logical? Because we wish our thoughts to be representations or symbols of fact. It is evident therefore that logic applies to the thought only in so far as the latter is a symbol. It is to symbols, therefore, that it primarily applies. Now by recognizing this fact it becomes plain at once that the objects of these laws cannot but comply with the laws; and hence that the whole idea of their being "normative" laws is false. *Again* the Kantians have one and all assumed that since the laws of logic are laws of thought, they do not apply to that which cannot be thought. Hence, some make out that there is some thing of which it is not true that A is not not-A. Now the unpsychological view makes that systematically evident, which it would seem were otherwise sufficiently axiomatic,

that these laws apply not merely to what can be thought but to whatever can be symbolized in any way. And hence extends their validity to all subjects of argumentation whatever.

The third advantage of the unpsychological view is that it points to a direct and secure manner of investigating the subject. The psychologists are continually asking do we think thus and so or not, and they find this a very difficult question to answer because these thoughts which they speak of, if not fictitious, are, at least, not in the mind in that unmixed state in which they talk of them. But if the view I have taken is correct, these forms may just as well be studied in the sensible representation as the mental. The psychologists are very apt to fall into notions which are only compatible with regarding logical truths as derived empirically from the observation of the mind. But this is not in accord with their own system. To make this clear, let us refer for a moment to metaphysics. The inner and the outer worlds as represented in common opinion and even sometimes by philosophers are two completely separate experiences, as distinct as two chambers; but this representation is a metaphysical fiction. Nothing is more common than for the philosophizing intellect in attempting to state clearly some view of the natural common-sense, to fall into a great error; and then this clear but false view displacing the true but undefined one produces a popular error. But having once eat of the tree of knowledge, there is no remedy but to eat more. We first draw a distinction and draw it badly; then the only way is to push on our analysis and draw it well. In the present instance it becomes important to distinguish two kinds of self-knowledge—two selves, if you please, one known immediately and the other mediately. The mediate knowledge of self is not the inner world with which we are at present concerned, is not something presented to us but is a mere product of active thought. We find that every judgment is subject to a condition of consistency; its elements must be capable of being brought to a unity. This consistent unity since it belongs to all our judgments may be said to belong to us. Or rather since it belongs to the judgments of all mankind, we may be said to belong to it. But the world of self, the world of the feelings does not contain such a unity. Much rather does this unity contain the feelings. The world of feelings then is not a world of self but of instances of self. We know our feelings immediately; we also know what is before us in space immediately. But nevertheless we do not distinguish what is within from what is without immediately; for this distinction implies an act of comparison the product of which requires to be known before we can judge that the inner is not the outer. But however this may be, whether this judgment is immediate or not; one thing will be admitted namely that the representation of the distinction between the two is a judgment. Furthermore it is a judgment which involves abstraction. Under all circumstances we have outward and inward feelings at once; that is to say we have a mixed feeling. We cannot then separate this feeling into two parts one of which is in space and the other not. For the feeling is all connected with space if any of it is. We can separate the relations of its parts according as they are of space or not. But surely all relations not of space as for instance that of light and dark are not inward relations. No; the inward world must have a positive definition. Now everything within is known by memory except the mere point of present consciousness. But unless we could compare our consciousness by memory we could attain no consciousness of ourselves. An immediate knowledge of the past is contradictory in the same sense in which an immediate knowledge of the distant is. In both cases some machinery is requisite for bringing them into the present. The past of which we have an immediate knowledge is a remembered past, but memory is a mere mechanical faculty without any feeling or active consciousness. And when we say knowledge is immediate we do not mean to exclude mechanical media. The inward world is then the world of memory for it is clear that we can remember nothing except what is within. But the world of *memory* is the world of time; hence the inward world and the world of time are the same. Taking it for granted, then, that the inner and outer worlds are superposed throughout, without possibility of separation, let us now proceed to another point. There is a third world, besides the inner and the outer; and all three are coëxtensive and contain every experience. Suppose that we have an experience. That experience has three determinations—three different references to a substratum or substrata, lying behind it and determining it. In the first place, it is a determination of an object external to ourselves—we feel that it is so because it is extended in space. Thereby it is in the external world. In the second place, it is a determination of our own soul, it is *our* experience; we feel that it is so because it lasts in time. Were it a flash of sensation, there for less than an instant, and then utterly gone from memory, we should not have time to think it ours. But while it lasts, and we reflect upon it, it enters into the internal world. We have now considered that experience as a determination of the modifying object and of the modified soul; now, I say, it may be and is naturally regarded as also a determination of an idea of the Universal mind; a preëxistent, archetypal Idea. Arithmetic, the law of number, *was* before anything to be numbered or any mind to number had been created. It *was* though it did not *exist*. It was not *a fact* nor a thought, but it was an unuttered word. Ἐν ἀρχῇ ἦν ὁ λόγος. We feel an experience to be a determination of such an archetypal Logos, by virtue of its //*depth of tone*/logical intension//, and thereby it is in the *logical world*.

Note the great difference between this view and Hegel's. Hegel says, logic is the science of the pure idea. I should describe it as the science of the laws of experience in virtue of its being a determination of the idea, or in other words as the formal science of the logical world.

In this point of view, efforts to ascertain precisely how the intellect works in thinking,—that is to say investigation of internal characteristics —is no more to the purpose which logical writers as such, however vaguely have in view, than would be the investigation of external characteristics.

Some reasons having now been given for adopting the unpsychological conception of the science, let us now seek to make this conception sufficiently distinct to serve for a definition of logic. For this purpose we must bring our *logos* from the abstract to the concrete, from the absolute to the dependent. There is no science of absolutes. The metaphysical logos is no more to us than the metaphysical soul or the metaphysical matter. To the absolute Idea or Logos, the dependent or relative *word* corresponds. The word *horse*, is thought of as being a word though it be unwritten, unsaid, and unthought. It is true, it must be considered as having been thought; but it need not have been thought by the same mind which regards it as being a word. I can think of a word in Feejee, though I can attach no definite articulation to it, and do not guess what it would be like. Such a word, abstract but not absolute, is no more than the genus of all symbols having the same meaning. We can also think of the higher genus which contains words of all meanings. A first approximation to a definition, then, will be that logic is the science of representations in general, whether mental or material. This definition coincides with Locke's. It is however too wide for logic does not treat of all kinds of representations. The resemblance of a portrait to its object, for example, is not logical truth. It is necessary, therefore, to divide the genus representation according to the different ways in which it may accord with its object. The first and simplest kind of truth is the resemblance of a copy. It may be roughly stated to consist in a sameness of predicates. Leibniz would say that carried to its highest point, it would destroy itself by becoming identity. Whether that is true or not, all known resemblance has a limit. Hence, resemblance is always partial truth. On the other hand, no two things are so different as to resemble each other in no particular. Such a case is supposed in the proverb that Dreams go by contraries,—an absurd notion, since concretes have no contraries. A false copy is one which claims to resemble an object which it does not resemble. But this never fully occurs, for two reasons; in the first place, the falsehood does not lie in the copy itself but in the *claim* which is made for it, in the *super-scription* for instance; in the second place, as there must be *some* resemblance between the copy and its object, this falsehood cannot be entire. Hence, there is no absolute truth or falsehood of copies. Now logical representations have absolute truth and falsehood as we know *à posteriori* from the law of excluded middle. Hence, logic does not treat of copies.

The second kind of truth, is the denotation of a sign, according to a previous convention. A child's name, for example, by a convention made at baptism, denotes that person. Signs may be plural but they cannot have genuine generality because each of the objects to which they refer must have been fixed upon by convention. It is true that we may agree that a certain sign shall denote a certain individual conception an individual act of an individual mind, and that conception may stand for all conceptions resembling it; but in this case, the generality belongs to the *conception* and not to the sign. Signs, therefore, in this narrow sense are not treated of in logic, because logic deals only with general terms. The third kind of truth or accordance of a representation with its object, is that which inheres in the very nature of the representation whether that nature be original or acquired. Such a representation I name a *symbol*. To clear up the vagueness of this statement let us consider for an instant, our words. Every human word was once the sign of an individual conception,—a sign in the narrow sense. But does it always retain this character? On this point I will read a few paragraphs from Locke.

§4. *Words often secretly referred,*
First, to the Ideas *in other mens minds.*
But though words, as they are used by men, can properly and immediately signify nothing but the *ideas* that are in the mind of the speaker, yet they in their thoughts give them a secret reference to two other things.

First, They suppose their words to be marks of the ideas *in the minds also of other men with whom they communicate:* for else they should talk in vain, and could not be understood, if the sounds they applied to one *idea,* where such as by the hearer were applied to another; which is to speak two languages. But in this men stand not usually to examine whether the *idea* they and those they discourse with have in their minds, be the same: but think it enough that they use the word, as they imagine, in the common acceptation of that language; in which they suppose, that the *idea* they make it a sign of, is precisely the same, to which the understanding men of that country apply that name.

§5. *Secondly, to the Reality of things.*

Secondly, Because *men* would not be thought to talk *barely* of their own imaginations, but of things as really they are; therefore they *often suppose their words to stand also for the reality of things.* But this relating more particularly to substances, and their names, as perhaps the former does to simple *ideas* and modes, we shall speak of these two different ways of applying words more at large, when we come to treat of the names of mixed modes, and substances in particular: though give me leave here to say, that it is a perverting the use of words, and brings unavoidable obscurity and confusion into their signification, whenever we make them stand for any thing, but those *ideas* we have in our own minds.

§6. *Words by use readily excite* Ideas.

Concerning words also it is farther to be considered, *First,* That they being immediately the signs of men's *ideas,* and by that means the instruments whereby men communicate their conceptions, and express to one another those thoughts and imaginations they have within their own breasts, *there comes by constant use* to be such *a connection between certain sounds, and the* ideas *they stand for,* that the names heard, almost as readily excite certain *ideas,* as if the objects themselves, which are apt to produce them, did actually affect the senses. Which is manifestly so in all obvious sensible qualities; and in all substances, that frequently and familiarly occur to us.

§7. *Words often used without signification.*

Secondly, That though the proper and immediate signification of words are *ideas* in the mind of the speaker, yet because by familiar use from our cradles we come to learn certain articulate sounds very perfectly, and have them readily on our tongues, and always at hand in our memories, but yet are not always careful to examine, or settle their significations perfectly; it *often* happens that *men,* even when they would apply themselves to an attentive consideration, *do set their thoughts more on words than things.* Nay, because words are many of them learned, before the *ideas* are known for which they stand; therefore some, not only children, but men, speak several words no otherwise than parrots do, only because they have learned them, and have been accustomed to those sounds. But so far as words are of use and signification, so far is there a constant connection between the sound and the *idea,* and a designation that the one stand for the other; without which application of them they are nothing but so much insignificant noise. (Book iii, Ch. 2, §§4.5.6.7)

I have adduced Locke, as a good authority on questions of fact. His critic, however, is wholly inadequate and false. It is enough to state this, because it is now a thing of the past. He here states the natural conceptions of the Human mind. He thinks them illusions; I shall accept them as valid. I ask you therefore to attend to his facts and to consider my interpretation of them. His first fact is that "a word as it is used by a man can immediately signify nothing but the idea that is in the mind of the speaker." This is true; but we are not now dealing with words in their use, but with *words in themselves.* Upon this latter point he makes two observations. "First that men suppose their words to be marks of ideas in other men's minds." This opinion that the individuality of the mind which has the idea corresponding to a word is of no account, shows that the idea is regarded as belonging to mind in general, to the universal mind, and that words are considered, however obscurely, as determinations of the pure idea. "Secondly, men suppose their words to stand for the reality of things." That is, they regard that intelligible form of the word wherein its agreement with the conception and with the fact consists to be also a form of the fact and not merely of the conception; this agreement of form constituting, in short, the *truth* of both word and conception. These two observations of Locke repose on the truth that the representative character of a word is naturally expressed in two ways, first as determined by the idea of the universal mind and second as determined by the abstract form of a possible object; this idea and this pure form being one and the same. Locke now makes two other observations which bear more precisely upon my expression of "symbolization by nature." "Concerning words also it is farther to be considered," he says, "that there comes by constant use to be such a connection between certain sounds and the ideas they stand for, that the names heard, almost as readily excite certain ideas as if the objects themselves, which are apt to produce them, did actually affect the senses." Now this readiness of excitation obviously consists in this; namely, that we do not have to reflect upon the word as a sign but that it comes to affect the intellect as though it had that quality which it connotes. I call this the acquired nature of the word, because it is a power that the word comes to have, and because the word itself without any reflection of ours upon it brings the idea into our minds. "Secondly," says Locke, "it often happens that men even when they would apply themselves to attentive consideration do set their thoughts more on words than things." It would be no wonder if men fell into error when they think of mere marks or sounds having nothing in common with the object of discussion. The wonder would be how they ever could advance one step. And yet in all //analytical/ abstract// thought, not only do men more often think of words than things, but I venture to say they seldom think of the things at all, except in reference to their geometry owing to space being more easily thought than the words. How often do we think of the thing in algebra? When we use the symbol of multiplication we do not even think out the conception of multiplication, we think merely of the laws of that symbol, which coincide with the laws of the conception, and what is more to the purpose, coincide with the laws of multiplication in the object. Now, I ask, how is it that anything can be done with a symbol, without reflecting upon the conception, much less imagining the object that belongs to it? It is simply because the symbol has acquired a nature, which may be described thus, that when it is brought before the mind certain principles of its use—whether reflected on or not—by association immediately regulate the action of the mind; and these may be regarded as laws of the symbol itself which it cannot *as a symbol* transgress.

I may mention in passing that if the symbolic nature is original it is more like a copy and that instances of such symbols are hieroglyphs, geometrical symbols, emblems, parables, &c., as well as conceptions or mental symbols. On the other hand if the symbolic nature is acquired the symbol is more like a sign as ordinary letters, language, and algebraical symbols. Locke says that the use of words in this symbolical way is attended with danger of ambiguity and that the only safety lies in using them as signs of recognized conceptions. That may be. But I believe it is demonstrable that attempts to define words, in the sense of determining the conceptions which correspond to them, are attended with some peculiar dangers. It is true, that the essence of philosophy is definition; but it is a trite remark that there is danger of error in philosophizing. It is substituting complex machinery for simple; artificial machinery for simple; it is walking on stilts. It is true that this machinery however dangerous is indispensible. Still I believe that there is a far better way of acquiring the *use* of our words; namely, the way in which we acquire the use of our arms, by exercise, by *selected exer-*

cise. And even for *communicating* the use of words, what can be more perfect than the method of examples?

But not to follow this subject too far, we have now established three species of representations; *copies, signs,* and *symbols;* of the last of which only logic treats. A second approximation to a definition of it then will be, the science of symbols in general and as such. But this definition is still too broad; this might, indeed, form the definition of a certain science which would be a branch of Semiotic or the general science of representations which might be called Symbolistic, and of this logic would be a species. But logic only considers symbols from a particular point of view.

A symbol in general and as such has three relations. The first is its relation to the pure Idea or Logos and this (from the analogy of the grammatical terms for the pronouns I, IT, THOU) I call its relation of the first person, since it is its relation to its own essence. The second is its relation to the Consciousness as being thinkable, or to any language as being translatable, which I call its relation to the second person, since it refers to its power of appealing to a mind. The third is its relation to its object, which I call its relation to the third person or IT. Every symbol is subject to three distinct systems of formal law as conditions of its taking up these three relations. If it violates either one of these three codes, the condition of its having either of the three relations, it ceases to be a symbol and makes *nonsense.* Nonsense is that which has a certain resemblance to a symbol without being a symbol. But since it simulates the symbolic character it is usually only one of the three codes which it violates; at any rate, flagrantly. Hence there should be at least three different kinds of nonsense. And accordingly we remark that we call nonsense meaningless, absurd, or quibbling, in different cases. If a symbol violates the conditions of its being a determination of the pure Idea or logos, it may be so nearly a determination thereof as to be perfectly intelligible. If for instance instead of I am one should say *I is. I is* is in itself meaningless, it violates the conditions of its relation to the form it is meant to embody. Thus we see that the conditions of the relation of the first person are the laws of grammar.

I will now take another example. I know my opinion is false, still I hold it. This is grammatical, but the difficulty is that it violates the conditions of its having an object. Observe that this is precisely the difficulty. It not only cannot be a determination of this or that object, but it cannot be a determination of any object, whatever. This is the whole difficulty. I say that, I receive contradictories into one opinion or symbolical representation; now this implies that it is a symbol of nothing. Here is another example: This very proposition is false. This is a proposition to which the law of excluded middle namely that every symbol must be false or true, does not apply. For if it is false it is thereby true. And if not false it is thereby not true. Now why does not this law apply to this proposition. Simply because it does itself state that it has no object. It talks of itself and only of itself and has no external relation whatever. These examples show that logical laws only hold good, as conditions of a symbol's having an object. The fact that it has often been called the science of truth confirms this view.

I define logic therefore as the science of the conditions which enable symbols in general to refer to objects.

At the same time *symbolistic* in general gives a trivium consisting of Universal Grammar, Logic, and Universal Rhetoric, using this last term to signify the science of the formal conditions of intelligibility of symbols.

In the next lecture I shall give the general theory of induction.

Lecture II

MS 95: February–March 1865

Having now, as I believe, successfully surmounted the great difficulty in the way of understanding the logic of science namely the adequate conceiving of logic itself, we may proceed at once to discover the elementary processes which lie at the bottom of all scientific reasoning. This subject is necessarily dry and abstract; but its importance is so obvious that I hope you will be willing to tax your attention as heavily as is necessary to attain a thorough and fundamental comprehension of it.

Hamilton and Mansel tell us that the consideration of scientific induction is without the province of logic. But there is certainly some reason in it; and yet to state this reason has been found very difficult;

there ought to be some science to point it out, therefore. These gentlemen have abandoned this problem altogether; inasmuch as they have thrown the inference from induction—into the form of a premiss;—and this without any attempt at demonstrating that there is no logic behind this premiss. To solve this problem, whether it be logical or extralogical, is the object of these lectures; and the solution which I offer is a logical solution arising directly out of the Aristotelic doctrine.

Aristotle says that "Induction and the syllogism from Induction is the syllogizing one extreme as a predicate to the middle through the other extreme." This demands some explanation. Take this example—

> All carnivora are mammals
> All mammals are vertebrates
> ∴ All carnivora are vertebrates

In this ordinary deductive syllogism, the symbols of the three classes are the three *terms*. [Repeat] Of these terms, *carnivora* is the least extensive and is called the minor extreme; *vertebrates* is the most extensive and is called the major extreme; *mammals* is intermediate in extension and is called the middle. The syllogizing consists in the synthesis in the inferred proposition of the two terms not united in either of the given propositions. I will add that I shall take the word *conclusion* to mean the proposition which follows apodictically from the other two, in contradistinction to *inference* which I shall use to mean the proposition inferred. And *premisses* shall mean the two propositions from which another apodictically follows, in contradistinction from *data* which shall mean the propositions from which something is inferable. The sense of this distinction will be made clear by an example.

> Neat and deer are herbivora
> Neat and deer are cloven-footed
> Hence   Cloven-footed animals are herbivora.

This you recognize as an induction, because it infers the character of the whole from the character of the parts. The first two propositions are the *data*, and the third is the *inference;* but this *inference* is not related to these *data* as *conclusion* to *premisses* because it does not follow apodictically. But if we transpose the propositions thus

> All cloven-footed animals are herbivora
> Neat and deer are cloven-footed
> Neat and deer are herbivora

it becomes apparent that there is among these propositions a conclusion of which the others are the premisses.

This example will also serve to illustrate Aristotle's definition, for *herbivora* is here our most extensive or major extreme, *neat and deer* is the minor extreme, and *cloven-footed* is the middle; and our inductive inference has consisted as he says of the syllogizing of the major extreme as a predicate to the middle through argument from the other extreme. I will read Aristotle's own illustration however to show that this is really what he means. I must observe that he denotes the major extreme by *A*, the middle by *B*, and the minor extreme by *C*. His example in both the above forms is as follows:—

C	*A*	*B*	*A*
Man horse and mule is long-lived		What is without gall is long-lived	
C	*B*	*C*	*B*
Man horse and mule is without gall		Man horse and mule is without gall	
B	*A*	*C*	*A*
What is without gall is long-lived		Man horse and mule is long-lived	

He says, "Let *A* be long-lived, *B* without gall, and *C* everything long-lived as man horse mule." He does not state the inference, but there is no doubt that it is that Everything without gall is long-lived, because the same argument is used seriously in one of his physiological discussions. He then continues (referring to the right-hand form) thus, "*A* then belongs to the whole of *C*; for everything without gall is long-lived [major premiss] but *B* also, or what is without gall, inheres in the whole of *C* [minor premiss]." He then attempts to state the condition of the validity of the inductive inference thus, "Now if *C* and *B* reciprocate and each is all the other, it follows necessarily that *A* inheres in all *B*. But we must regard *C* as made up of *all* the individuals; for induction has its inference from all." This sufficiently exhibits the doctrine of Aristotle.

That induction is through simple enumeration or, at least, that there is such an induction is the doctrine of all logicians. I object to this, however, *in toto*. Aristotle evidently supposes that a general term is equal to a sum of singulars. But this is easily refuted. Singulars are not symbols but only signs. Even if they have extension they have certainly no intension. By that I mean that their truth does not depend on any quality of the object. For instance, if I name a girl Richard, Richard is

her name, previous usage notwithstanding. Owing to this meaningless-
ness, singulars come under general terms only by accident, not by the
implication of the words themselves. But the comprehension of a general term consists in the total of all possible things to which it is applicable and not merely to those which actually occur. So that singulars
never can fill up this extension. 'All men', in logic, means man in general. I might perhaps enumerate all the men who have been, but I never
can know that I have enumerated all who are to be. So 'all the letters
on this page' is not limited in logic to the letters there at any one inspection or at any plural of inspections; and such a limitation of its
meaning would simply deprive it of all its generality and leave it a
mere sign. In short, the logical comprehension, is a total of possibles
and possibles have no total of enumeration.

But this error of making generals composed of singulars was long
ago noticed; and though individuals are still sometimes called *infimæ
species* it is customary now to speak of the enumeration of particulars
and not the enumeration of the singulars composing a whole of comprehension. The word *particular* in its strict use refers to an indefinite
limitation, as in '*some* men'. The word 'some' is a true symbol referring
to a general class or quality, though indefinitely and indirectly; it is in
fact not the symbol of a class or quality, but the symbol of such a symbol. But the word has, of course, a different sense in the phrase enumeration of particulars, and means simply the division of logical genus
into species. This division must be made, if at all, either 1st by induction or 2nd by the implication of the Species themselves, or 3rd in some
other way. Neither of these, however, will answer to account for the
datum of the formula of induction. For as to division by induction; that
bare supposition cannot explain or clear up induction itself. As to division by implication—it will not lead to induction but only to the
dilemma; because induction is by *enumeration,* and enumeration the
representation of terms successively, one by one, from first to last;
whereas in *dilemma* when all the horns but one have been represented
the last one is already implicitly represented as distinctly as it is explicitly afterwards. As to any other way of dividing the genus, if relevant
it can only be enumeration; now to this the objections urged to enumeration of singulars apply with full force. It follows that this complete
datum of induction which has always been taken for granted by the
pure logicians, is not within the range of logical possibility. And inasmuch as all logical explanations of induction have been based upon
this postulate, the real explanation can never have been reached.

The consideration of this imperfect datum leads us to make a fundamental observation; namely, that the problem how we can make an induction is one and the same with the problem how we can make any general statement, with reason; for there is no way left in which such a statement can originate except from induction or pure fiction. Hereby, we strike down at once all such attempts at solving the problem as involve the supposition of a major premiss as a datum. Such explanations merely show that we can arrive at one general statement by deduction from another, while they leave the real question, untouched. The peculiar merit of Aristotle's theory is that after the objectionable portion of it is swept away and after it has thereby been left utterly powerless to account for any certainty or even probability in the inference from induction, we still retain these *forms* which show what the *actual process* is.

And what is this process? We have in the apodictic conclusion, some most extraordinary observation, as for example that a great number of animals—namely neat and deer, feed only upon vegetables. This proposition, be it remarked, need not have had any generality; if the animals observed instead of being all *neat* had been so very various that we knew not what to say of them except that they were *herbivora* and *cloven-footed*, the effect would have been to render the argument simply irresistible. In addition to this datum, we have another; namely that these same animals are all cloven-footed. Now it would not be so very strange that all cloven-footed animals should be herbivora; animals of a particular structure very likely may use a particular food. But if this be indeed so, then all the marvel of the conclusion is explained away. So in order to avoid a marvel which must in some form be accepted, we are led to believe what is easy to believe though it is entirely uncertain.

Besides the form of induction given by Aristotle, there are two others which seem never to have been noticed. The first, is as if we should infer in the example that no carnivora are cloven-footed and here would be a mere difference of form. The second is as if the neat and deer observed to be cloven-footed were not the same ones as those noticed to be herbivora, their sameness being merely of character and not of observation. The logical character of these forms is essentially the same as that of Aristotle's form. The difference is that his is the inference of the major premiss of a syllogism of the first figure while these are inferences of the major premisses of syllogisms of the second and third figures. Syllogisms of the first figure, are characterized by having the middle term subject of one premiss and predicate of the other. Those of the second figure, have the middle for the predicate of both premisses. Those of the third figure, have the middle for the subject of both premisses. Induction, then, is in general the inference of a major premiss.

There is a large class of reasonings which are neither deductive nor inductive. I mean the inference of a cause from its effect or reasoning to a physical hypothesis. I call this reasoning *à posteriori*. If I reason that certain conduct is wise because it has a character which belongs *only* to wise things, I reason *à priori*. If I think it is wise because it once turned out to be wise, that is if I infer that it is wise on this occasion because it was wise on that occasion, I reason inductively. But if I think it is wise because a wise man does it, I then make the pure hypothesis that he does it because he is wise, and I reason *à posteriori*. The form this reasoning assumes, is that of an inference of a minor premiss in any of the figures. The following is an example.

Light gives certain fringes	Ether waves give certain fringes
Ether waves give these fringes	Light is ether waves
∴ Light is ether waves	∴ Light gives these fringes.

The whole of these forms of reasoning is conveniently illustrated by the following table. [Give it.]

In reference to my employment of the terms *à priori, à posteriori,* and *inductive,* I will confess that it is not according to usage for the simple reason that the distinction itself is not according to usage; but this usage professes to adhere to the original and strict sense of the words and this I altogether deny and insist that this original sense is justification enough for the very distinct and useful definitions which I have given to the words. I shall hereafter show that to [vi]ew so-called *à priori* conceptions and principles in this way is in the strictest harmony with the Kantian philosophy on the one hand and with empirical speculations on the other hand, and is in fact the only avenue by which the Idealists and Empiricists can ever come to understand each other.

In the further discussion of these kinds of reasoning; two points remain to be investigated 1st Whether these kinds of inference are really entirely different and 2nd What is the *rationale* of each.

The difference in their general character between the three kinds of reasoning is strongly marked. A consequent is inferred *à priori*, an antecedent *à posteriori*, and the nexus between them inductively. The question is whether these differences may not shade into one another and whether in this way it may not happen for example, that one and the same inference is both inductive and *à posteriori*. Here for instance is an inductive inference. I give it in the deductive form

> *All positions of* Juppiter *are on an ellipse*
> These positions are positions of *Juppiter*
> These positions are on an ellipse

And we may also make the following inference *à posteriori:*

> Whatever moves over this ellipse passes through these points
> Juppiter *moves over this ellipse*
> *Juppiter* passes through these points.

These inferences seem nearly the same; but there is an essential difference between them, in that the inductive inference *restricts Juppiter* to the ellipse without opposing a further restriction, while the inference *à posteriori extends* his motion over the ellipse without opposing a further extension.

No inference can be drawn from the same premisses in two different ways, unless its division into two terms is the same in both cases. For otherwise its terms could not be combined with middle terms so as to give equivalent propositions in the two cases unless one of those propositions were like this 'all rational mortals are rational'. Now such propositions as this are in fact no propositions at all. This is quite different from saying 'all men are rational' because this last case supposes some act of thought or symbolization; but the proposition 'all rational mortals are rational' is of merely grammatical and not in the least of logical import. It is not an analytical proposition because no analysis is performed; it is what is called an identical proposition, that is the mere empty formula of a proposition. Upon our conception of logic, everything of the nature of immediate inference is referred to grammar, because it depends on the relations of symbols to each other without reference to their relations to their objects. I repeat then, that if the same proposition may be inferred in two different ways from the same premisses, it must be inferred in the same form in both cases.

The simplest way of finding whether this can be done is to make a table of all inferences with broadest conclusions and narrowest premisses. In the centre of this table, let us enter that proposition of each syllogism which has its subject like that of one of the others and its predicate like that of the third. At the top, let us enter the proposition which it has its predicate like; and at the side, let us enter the proposition that it has its subject like. The reason for constructing the table in this way is that this will give us a table of data and inferences. In the middle will be all the inferences of whatever kind which are drawn from data whose eliminated term is both subject and predicate, and these data will be at the top and side. At the side will be all the inferences from data whose eliminated term is only predicate and these data will be at the top and middle. And at the top will be all the inferences from data whose eliminated term is only subject and these data will be at the middle and side. Further; we will denote universal affirmatives by A, universal negatives by E, particular affirmatives by I, and particular negatives by O. In order to make the table symmetrical we must observe symmetrical rules in arranging the letters along the top and side. Take these for instance

> Universals at the top, particulars at the bottom
> Affirmatives at the left, negatives at the right

As there is no top or bottom on the top line nor no left or right along the side line we will suppose that the middle part of each bulges out a little. Then we shall have this arrangement.

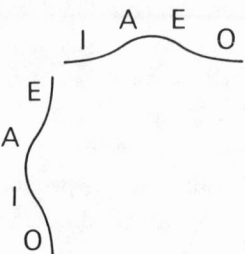

Now we enter the first figure s, the 2nd m, the 3rd s. *Darapti* and *Felapton* must be omitted, as having their premises too broad.

		E	A	
I	A	E	O	
A	I	O	E	
		O	I	

In this table you will perceive that the three figures are entirely separated. The middle part is the 1st figure, the top and bottom wings the 2nd figure, and the side wings the 3rd figure. Consequently, there can be no inference in two ways from the same data. This is made still more clear if we have three tables instead of one so as to bring the inferences into the middle in all cases. The symmetry is thereby made very striking.

We come now to the question, what is the *rationale* of these three kinds of reasoning. And first let us understand precisely what we intend by this. It is clear then that it is none of our business to inquire in what manner we think when we reason, for we have already seen that logic is wholly separate from psychology. What we seek is an explicit statement of the logical ground of these different kinds of inference. This logical ground will have two parts, 1st the ground of possibility and 2nd the ground of proceedure. The ground of possibility is the special property of symbols upon which every inference of a certain ki[nd] rests. The ground of proceedure is the property of symbols which makes a certain inference possible from certain premisses. The ground of possibility must be both discovered and demonstrated, fully. The ground of proceedure must be exhibited in outline, but it is not requisite to fill up all the details of this subject, especially as that would lead us too far into the technicalities of logic.

As the three kinds of reasoning are entirely distinct, each must have a different ground of possibility; and the principle of each kind must be proved by that same kind of inference for it would be absurd to attempt to rest it on a weaker kind of inference and to rest it on one as strong as itself would be simply to reduce it to that other kind of reasoning. Moreover, these principles must be logical principles because we do not seek any other ground now, than a logical ground. As logical principles, they will not relate to the symbol in itself or in its relation to equivalent symbols but wholly in its relation to what it symbolizes. In other words it will relate to the symbolization of objects.

Now all symbolization is of three objects, at once; the first is a possible thing, the second is a possible form; the third is a possible symbol. It will be objected that the two latter are not properly objects. We have hitherto regarded the symbol as *standing for* the thing, as a concrete determination of its form, and addressing a symbol; and it is true that it is only by referring to a possible thing that a symbol has an objective relation; it is only by bearing in it a form that it has any subjective relation, and it is only by equaling another symbol that it has any tuistical relation. But this objective relation once given to a symbol is at once applicable to all to which it necessarily refers; and this is shown by the fact of our regarding every symbol as *connotative* as well as *denotative*, and by our regarding one word as standing for another whenever we endeavor to clear up a little obscurity of meaning. And the reason that this is so is that the possible symbol and the possible form to which a symbol is related each relate also to that thing which is its immediate object. Things, forms, and symbols, therefore, are symbolized in every symbolization. And this being so, it is natural to suppose that our three principles of inference which we know already refer to some three objects of symbolization, refer to these.

That such really is the case admits of proof. For the principle of inference *à priori* must be established *à priori;* that is by reasoning analytically from determinant to determinate, in other words from definition. But this can only be applied to an object whose characteristics depend upon its definition. Now of most things the definition depends upon the character, the definition of a symbol alone determines its character. Hence the principle of inference *à priori* must relate to symbols. The principle of inference *à posteriori* must be established *à posteriori*, that is by reasoning from determinate to determinant. This is only applicable to that which is determined by what it determines; in other words, to that which is only subject to the truth and falsehood which affects its determinant and which in itself is mere *zero*. But this is only true of pure forms. Hence the principle of inference *à posteriori* must relate to pure form. The principle of inductive inference must be established inductively; that is by reasoning from parts to whole. This is only applicable to that whose whole is given in the sum of the parts; and this is only the case with things. Hence the principle of inductive inference must relate to things.

Finally, these principles as principles applying not to this or that symbol, form, thing, but to all equally, must be universal. And as grounds of possibility they must state what is possible. Now what is the universal principle of the possible symbolization of symbols? It is that all symbols are symbolizable. And the other principles must predicate the same thing of forms and things.

These, then, are the three principles of inference. Our next business is to demonstrate their truth. But before doing so, let me repeat that these principles do not serve to prove that the kinds of inference are valid, since their own proof, on the contrary, must rest on the assumption of that validity. Their use is only to show what the condition of that validity is. Hence, the only proof of the truth of these principles is this; to show, that if these principles be admitted as sufficient, and if the validity of the several kinds of inference be also admitted, that then the truth of these principles follows by the respective kinds of inference which each establishes.

To prove then, first, that all symbols are symbolizable. Every syllogism consists of three propositions with two terms each, a subject and a predicate, and three terms in all each term being used twice. It is obvious that one term must occur both as subject and predicate. Now a predicate is a symbol of its subject. Hence in all reasoning *à priori* a symbol must be symbolized. But as reasoning *à priori* is possible about a statement without reference to its predicate, all symbols must be symbolizable.

2nd To prove that all forms are symbolizable. Since this proposition relates to pure form it is sufficient to show that its consequences are true. Now the consequence will be that if a symbol of any object be given, but if this symbol does not adequately represent any form then another symbol more formal may always be substituted for it, or in other words as soon as we know what form it ought to symbolize the symbol may be so changed as to symbolize that form. But this process is a description of inference *à posteriori*. Thus in the example relating to light; the symbol of 'giving such and such phenomena' which is altogether inadequate to express a form is replaced by 'ether-waves' which is much more formal. The consequence then of the universal symbolization of forms is the inference *à posteriori*, and there is no truth or falsehood in the principle except what appears in the consequence. Hence, the consequence being valid, the principle must be accepted.

3rd To prove that all things may be symbolized. If we have a proposition, the subject of which is not properly a symbol of the thing it signifies; then in case everything may be symbolized, it is possible to replace this subject by another which is true of it and which does symbolize the subject. But this process is inductive inference. Thus having observed of a great variety of animals that they all eat herbs, if I substitute for this subject which is not a true symbol, the symbol 'cloven-footed animals' which is true of these animals, I make an induction. Accordingly I must acknowledge that this principle leads to induction; and as it is a principle of objects, what is true of its subalterns is true of it; and since induction is always possible and valid, this principle is true.

Having discovered and demonstrated the grounds of the possibility of the three inferences, let us take a preliminary glance at the manner in which additions to these principles may make them grounds of proceedure.

The principle of inference *à priori* has been apodictically demonstrated; the principle of inductive inference has been shown upon sufficient evidence to be true; the principle of inference *à posteriori* has been shown to be one which nothing can contradict. These three degrees of modality in the principles of the three inferences show the amount of certainty which each is capable of affording. Inference *à priori* is as we all know the only apodictic proceedure; yet no one thinks of questioning a good induction; while inference *à posteriori* is proverbially uncertain. *Hypotheses non fingo*, said Newton; striving to place his theory on a firm inductive basis. Yet provisionally we must make hypotheses; we start with them; the baby when he lies turning his fingers before his eyes is testing a hypothesis he has already formed, as to the connection of touch and sight. Apodictic reasoning, can only be applied to the manipulation of our knowledge; it never can extend it. So that it is an induction which eventually settles every question of science; and nine-tenths of the inferences we draw in any hour not of study are of this kind.

The three figures of *à priori* inference are as follows:—

All A is B	All A is B	X is B
X is A	X is not B	X is A
$\therefore X$ is B	$\therefore X$ is not A	$\therefore$ Some A is B

The first figure consists in taking as a predicate the predicate of another predicate. Every predicate is a symbol of its subject. So that this inference depends on the fact that the symbol of the symbol is itself a symbol of the same object. Now the most that a symbol of a symbol can contain is the symbol itself; hence if all this can be predicated, any other symbol of the symbol may be; but the proposition 'A which is $A = A$' is the law of identity. The second figure depends in the same way on the equivalent law of contradiction, There is no symbol whose symbol is not a symbol. The third figure depends upon the law of excluded middle, A symbol is a symbol or not according as it coincides with its object.

The principles of the three inductive inferences of the three major premisses of the above forms are, 1st The symbol of an object has the same predicates as its object, 2nd Nothing which is not the symbol of an object has the same predicates as its object, 3rd A predicate applies to an object or not according to its predicability of the symbol of that object. Were these principles of easy application induction would have as much certainty (though of a different kind) as inference *à priori*. But, unfortunately, they never can be applied, directly. For they require us to find a symbol which shall have the same predicates as an object of which we have not already a symbol. This is never possible, since we do not know the predicates of objects except through symbols. It remains to be seen why this circumstance does not destroy induction altogether.

The three principles of the inferences *à posteriori* of the minor premisses of the above forms are as follows. 1st The symbol which embodies any form is predicable of the same subjects as the form itself. 2nd The form embodied in a symbol is nothing of which the symbol is denied. 3rd A form is in any subject or not according as any symbol of it is affirmed or denied of that subject. These principles, also, labor under the difficulty of impracticability, for we only know forms in symbols yet these require us to substitute for a symbol which does not express explicitly its form another which does.

In order to understand how these principles of *à posteriori* and inductive inference can be put into practice, we must consider by itself the substitution of one symbol for another. Symbols are alterable and comparable in three ways. In the first place they may denote more or fewer possible differing things; in this regard they are said to have *extension*. In the second place, they may imply more or less as to the quality of these things; in this respect they are said to have *intension*. In the third place they may involve more or less real knowledge; in this respect they have *information* and *distinctness*. Logical writers generally speak only of extension and intension and Kant has laid down the law that these quantities are inverse in respect of each other. For example, take *cat*; now increase the extension of that greatly—*cat* //or/and// *rabbit* //or/and// *dog*; now apply to this extended class the additional intension *feline*;—feline cat //or/and// feline rabbit //or/

and // feline dog is equal to cat again. This law holds good as long as the information remains constant, but when this is changed the relation is changed. Thus *cats* are before we know about them separable into *blue cats* and *cats not blue* of which classes *cats* is the most extensive and least intensive. But afterwards we find out that one of those classes cannot exist; so that *cats* increases its intension to equal *cats not blue* while *cats not blue* increases its extension to equal *cats*. Again, to give a better case, *rational animal* is divisible into *mortal rational animal* and *immortal rational animal;* but upon information we find that no *rational animal* is *immortal* and this fact is symbolized in the word *man*. *Man*, therefore, has at once the extension of *rational animal* with the intension of *mortal rational animal,* and far more beside, because it involves more *information* than either of the previous symbols. *Man* is more *distinct* than rational animal, and more *formal* than mortal rational animal. Now of two statements both of which are true; it is obvious that that contains the most truth which contains the most information. If two predicates of the same intension, therefore, are true of the same subject, the most formal one contains the most truth. Thus, it is better to say Socrates is a man, than to say Socrates is an animal who is rational mortal risible biped &c. because the former contains all the last and in addition it forms the synthesis of the whole under a definite *form*. On the other hand if the same predicate is applicable to two equivalent subjects, that one is to be preferred which is the most *distinct;* thus it conveys more truth to say All men are born of women, than All rational animals are born of women, because the former has at once as much extension as the latter, and a much closer reference to the things spoken of.

Let us now take the two statements $\frac{S \text{ is } P}{\Sigma \text{ is } P}$; let us suppose that Σ is much more distinct than S and that it is also more extensive. But we *know* that S is P. Now if Σ were not more extensive than S, Σ is P would contain more truth than S is P; being more extensive it *may* contain more truth and it may also introduce falsehood. Which of these probabilities is the greatest? Σ by being more extensive becomes less intensive; it is the intension which introduces truth and the extension which introduces falsehood. If therefore Σ increases the intension of S more than its extension, Σ is to be preferred to S; otherwise not. Now this is the case of induction. Which contains most truth *neat* and *deer* are herbivora or cloven-footed animals are herbivora?

In the two statements $\begin{array}{c} S \text{ is } P \\ S \text{ is } \Pi \end{array}$, let Π be at once more *formal* and more *intensive* than P; and suppose we only *know* that S is P. In this case the increase of formality gives a chance of additional truth and the increase of intension a chance of error. If the extension of Π is more increased than its intension, then S is Π is likely to contain more truth than S is P and *vice versa*. This is the case of *à posteriori* reasoning. We have for instance to choose between

> Light gives fringes of such and such a description
> and   Light is ether-waves.

Lecture III

MS 96: February–March 1865

Closely allied to the subject of logic, if not actually a part of it, is the theory of probabilities,—or doctrine of chances. It is a matter with which it is of considerable advantage to have a practical acquaintance. But there are two obstacles to acquiring a thorough knowledge of it; the first is that the more complicated problems tax the resources of the mathematician; and the second and more serious is that the mere putting a problem of chances into equations or bringing it to the point where the mathematical work first begins requires the subtlety of a metaphysician. Fortunately the late Professor Boole has entirely overcome this second difficulty by means of a distinct calculus; which is very readily comprehended and may be applied with the utmost facility. Everyone can master this curious branch of mathematics in a short time; and as the knowledge of it enables us to solve readily all simple questions of probability and to understand the general principles of solution of the most difficult ones, I propose to devote this lecture and the next to the exposition of it.

The first point is that instead of writing words, we write letters. Thus instead of horses we write h, instead of black b, and so forth. h stands not for one horse but for all horses,—the whole class of horses collectively. b stands for all black things.

Then, if we wish to write *all black horses*, it will be natural to put bh—black horses. This is analogous to multiplication in arithmetic for as three times two means *three twos* and six times seven, six sevens, so we may say that *black horses* are black into horses. Three times two implies a *three* ⋮ each of whose units is a two ⋮ . In the same way *black horses* implies all black things each of which is a horse. Perhaps you will think this analogy fanciful; I do not say that it is not. But it will serve our purpose very well as you will see.

Suppose c represents cows. Then how shall we represent all horses and all cows together. Clearly it is horses added to cows or $h + c$.

Suppose w stands for Washington City and u for the Capital of the United States. How shall we say that Washington City and the capital of the United States are the same? By writing $w = u$, w equals u. By equality then we mean, in this case, not mere identity in respect to number but complete identity.

In arithmetic any number added to naught remains the same.

$$3 + 0 = 3$$
$$4 + 0 = 4$$

Now in this new calculus which we are studying we have as yet not introduced any *naught*. Let us introduce it, with such a meaning that such equations as these shall hold. Let

$$h + 0 = h$$
$$c + 0 = c$$

Or all horses together with *naught* constitute all horses. And all cows together with *naught* constitute all cows. What, then, does *naught* mean? It plainly means nothing; not nothing in respect to one measure merely as it does in arithmetic but absolutely nothing.

You can now see the real appropriateness of making *black* multiplied by *all horses* mean all black horses. For in Arithmetic, any number multiplied by naught is naught.

$$3 \times 0 = 0$$
$$4 \times 0 = 0$$
&c.

Now just in the same way in the Calculus of Logic, Horses which are nothing are nothing; horses which do not exist are nothing

$$h \times 0 = 0$$

and so for any other letter

$$c \times 0 = 0$$
$$b \times 0 = 0.$$

In arithmetic, any number multiplied by *one* gives that number

$$3 \times 1 = 3$$
$$4 \times 1 = 4$$
&c.

Now thus far we have not adopted any meaning at all for *one* in our Calculus of Logic. We may therefore assign to it any convenient meaning. Let us, then, take it in such a sense that these equations shall hold. So that for instance

$$h \times 1 = h$$
$$c \times 1 = c$$
&c.

Now what meaning must *one* have? The product of two letters, represents those objects which are common to both the two classes represented by the letters multiplied together. Now *one* represents that class which multiplied by any other gives that other; that is it is that class which has the whole of the objects of every class under it. In other words it is *everything* or *whatever is*. $h \times 1 = h$ means that whatever horses *are* are the same as all horses. $c \times 1 = c$ means that whatever cows *are* are the same as all cows. *One* then means all that *is*. Just as h means all horses, c all cows, &c.

I must now draw your attention to one of those peculiar and original proceedures which characterize Professor Boole's work. $h + c$ means horses and cows, *besides*. Now you cannot take anything beside itself; you cannot say horses and horses besides; although you can say nothing and nothing besides. And, therefore, if you meet with such an expression as $a + a$, or a and a besides, you may be sure that a is nothing. Thus the mere addition of a thing to itself, in this system, quite contrary to the whole analogy of mathematics, determines what the value of that thing is.

As $a + a$ makes $a = 0$ so does $a + a + a$, $a + a + a + a$ and so forth or in other terms $2a$ $3a$ $4a$ make $a = 0$ &c. Now this determines the meaning of all the other numbers besides *one* and *zero*. These numbers mean that that which they are multiplied by is nothing.

We thus see that in this Boolian calculus no letter can have any numerical value except 1 (unity) and 0 (zero). But unity means *all things* and zero means nothing. It is plain then that h which stands for all horses, since it is neither all things nor nothing, has a value which is *not numerical*. This, again, is a very peculiar and interesting point. Every letter, unless it denote everything or nothing, has a value which is not numerical. At the same time we may have a general expression, in numbers, for a class. For since

$$h \times 0 = 0$$
$$c \times 0 = 0$$
$$b \times 0 = 0$$
$$\&c.$$

If we divide these quantities by *zero*, we have

$$h = \tfrac{0}{0} \qquad c = \tfrac{0}{0} \qquad b = \tfrac{0}{0}$$

Zero divided by zero then denotes any class—without discriminating and determining what class. This meaning of zero divided by zero is similar to its meaning in arithmetic. In arithmetic one number divided by another is the number of times a pail which holds the number of quarts denoted by the divisor can be emptied into a pail which holds the number of quarts denoted by the dividend. Now suppose neither pail holds anything, suppose the sides of both have been cut down till nothing but the bottom is left, then the number of times that one can be emptied into the other is *zero* divided by *zero*. But how many times is that? We cannot say; it is indeterminate. Just so in the calculus of logic *zero* divided by zero is an indeterminate class, we cannot say what one.

If we have $a + b = c$—that is, if the classes a and b together make up the class c—then $c - a = b$, that is b is c except a or the class c after the class a is taken away. Let b denote everything black and $\overline{b}$ denote everything not black; then, $b + \overline{b} = 1$, that is everything black and everything not black make up everything; then $\overline{b} = 1 - b$ or everything not black is denoted by b subtracted from 1, or everything except what is black.

In the same way $1 - h$ stands for all that is not a horse and so with every letter.

The peculiarities of the system may all be summed up in one form of equation, $b(1 - b) = 0$ or that which is black and is not black is nothing. $h(1 - h) = 0$ or that which is a horse and is not a horse is nothing. Observe that there are only two numbers *zero* and *one* which will satisfy such an equation, for since the product of b and $(1 - b)$ is
$$b = 0$$
zero either b is *zero* or $(1 - b)$ is zero $1 - b = 0$. If $1 - b = 0$, $b = 1$ so that this equation itself implies that b has only two numerical values *one* and *zero*.

I have now given explanations of the signification of the more simple combinations of letters; but for the benefit of those who may have lost a word here and there I will briefly repeat what I have said.

In this logical mathematics, then, the single letters denote the whole collection of individuals under a class. Thus, m may be taken to stand for all men, w for all women, a for all animals, o for all that is old, d for all that is dead. *Secondly* 1 minus a letter, or the difference between one and a letter, stands for the whole collection of things which do not belong to the class denoted by the letter. Thus $1 - m$ will stand for all things not men; $1 - w$ for all things not women, and so forth. *Thirdly*, one class multiplied by another stands for those things which belong to both of the two classes. Thus dm stands for dead men, $(1 - d)m$ for men not dead, $d(1 - m)$ for everything not men that are dead, ow for all old women, $a(1 - w)$ for all animals not women, and so forth. *Fourthly* one letter added to another, stands for all things denoted by the first together with all the things denoted by the second besides; and implies that there are no things which belong to both classes at once.

Thus $m + w$ stands for all men together with all women. $d + (1 - d)$ stands for all things dead and all things not dead. $dm + (1 - d)w$ stands for all dead men and all women not dead. *Fifthly* 1 or as we often write it $\frac{1}{1}$ stands for all that *is;* and consequently $\frac{1}{1} m$ stands for all the men there are, that is for all men; the same as m. *Sixthly* 0 or as we often write it $\frac{0}{1}$ stands for what is *not*, or nothing, hence $\frac{0}{1} m$ stands for no men, and is the same as $\frac{0}{1}$ alone. *Seventhly* $\frac{0}{0}$ stands for some class we know not what, perhaps for all things, perhaps for nothing, perhaps for some things. Accordingly $\frac{0}{0} m$ stands for *some, all,* or *no men.* $\frac{0}{0} w$ for *some, all,* or *no* women and so forth. *Eighthly* any number except *one* and *zero* when multiplied by any letter implies that there is no such class as is denoted by that letter. Thus $2d(1 - d)$ implies that the class of dead things which are not dead, does not exist. Instead of writing a number we generally write $\frac{1}{0}$ so that

$$\frac{1}{1} \quad \frac{0}{1} \quad \frac{0}{0} \quad \frac{1}{0}$$

are the four numerical forms which have a use in this system. *Finally* every letter and every combination of letters is equal to *one* or *zero* or else has no numerical value. This is expressed by the equations

$$m(1 - m) = 0$$
$$w(1 - w) = 0$$
$$d(1 - d) = 0$$
$$a(1 - a) = 0$$
$$o(1 - o) = 0$$
$$\&c.$$

Supposing, then, that so much is firmly fixed in the mind, I proceed to explain how we can interpret the meaning of complicated expressions such as $\frac{a}{m}$, $\frac{w}{w+m}$, $\frac{1-d}{a+wd}$, and so forth.

We will begin with expressions which contain only one letter, such as $\frac{m}{m}$ or $\frac{1+m}{2-m}$. Now if we can reduce such an expression to the form $\frac{1}{1} m + \frac{1}{1}(1 - m)$ or $\frac{1}{0} m + \frac{0}{0}(1 - m)$ or $\frac{0}{1} m + \frac{1}{1}(1 - m)$ or any form where we have m and $(1 - m)$ separately multiplied by $\frac{1}{1}, \frac{0}{1}, \frac{0}{0}$, or $\frac{1}{0}$ and then added; I say if we can show that any expression has the same meaning as such an expression as this, we can tell what that meaning is. For we know what $\frac{1}{1} m, \frac{0}{1} m, \frac{1}{0} m$, and $\frac{0}{0} m$ stand for and what $\frac{1}{1}(1 - m)$, $\frac{0}{1}(1 - m)$, $\frac{1}{0}(1 - m)$, and $\frac{0}{0}(1 - m)$ stand for.

$\frac{1}{1}m$ stands for all men $\frac{1}{1}(1-m)$ for all things not men

$\frac{0}{1}m$ for no men $\frac{0}{1}(1-m)$ for no things not men

$\frac{0}{0}m$ for some, all, or no men $\frac{0}{0}(1-m)$ for some, all, or no things not men

and $\frac{1}{0}m$ implies that there are no men $\frac{1}{0}(1-m)$ implies that there are no things not men

We know what each of these means and we know what addition means, and therefore we know what any such expression as $\frac{1}{1}m + \frac{0}{0}$ $(1-m), \frac{0}{1}m + \frac{1}{1}(1-m)$ means. The first means all men together with *some, all, no* things not men. The second means all things not men.

We may denote such an expression in a general way by $Am + B$ $(1-m)$. That is, m is multiplied either by $\frac{1}{1}$ or $\frac{0}{1}$ or $\frac{0}{0}$ or $\frac{1}{0}$ but as we do not know which, we put A, merely to show that it is one or the other of these, and we put $B(1-m)$ for the same purpose.

Now I can give you a very simple rule by which you can reduce any expression to this form $Am + B(1-m)$ for if I write down this form twice—

$$Am + B(1-m) \qquad\qquad Am + B(1-m)$$

and on one side put 1 instead of m and on the other put 0 instead of m

I have $A \times 1 + B(1-1)$ and $A \times 0 + B(1-0)$

Now A times one is A and 1 *minus* 1 is nothing so that on that side we have $A + B \times 0$ or as B times nothing is nothing, it is simply A. On the other side $A \times 0$ is nothing; and 1 minus *zero* is 1 so that we have $B \times 1$ or simply B. So we have A on the side where 1 was put instead of m, and B on the side where *zero* was put instead of m. Now we have only to write in the m's and

$$A \qquad B$$

becomes $Am + B(1-m)$ which is the original expression. Now suppose we perform this same process on an expression of a different form; say $\frac{m}{m}$

$$\frac{m}{m} \qquad\qquad\qquad \frac{m}{m}$$

$$\frac{1}{1} \qquad\qquad\qquad \frac{0}{0}$$

$\frac{1}{1}m + \frac{0}{0}(1-m)$ and this shows that $\frac{m}{m}$ stands for *all* men and some, all, or none of the things not men. Now I can show you in a different way that this is what $\frac{m}{m}$ stands for. $am = m$, that is all men who are animals are the same as all men. Now divide by m and we have $a = \frac{m}{m}$, but all animals are $a = m + \frac{0}{0}(1-m)$ and therefore $\frac{m}{m} = m + \frac{0}{0}(1-m)$. The general rule then for reducing an expression to a form we can understand is to put it down twice side by side; and put 1 for the letter on the left and *zero* for the letter on the right and then write the letter after the first and 1 minus the letter after the second and connect them with the sign +.

What does $\frac{1-m}{3-m}$ stand for?

$$\frac{1-m}{3-m} \qquad\qquad \frac{1-m}{3-m}$$
$$\frac{1-1}{3-1} \qquad\qquad \frac{1-0}{3-0}$$
$$\frac{0}{2} \qquad\qquad\qquad \frac{1}{3}$$

For $\frac{0}{2}$ put $\frac{0}{0}$ and for $\frac{1}{3}$ put $\frac{1}{0}$ which mean the same;

$$\frac{0}{0}m \qquad + \qquad \frac{1}{0}(1-m)$$

Now let us consider expressions which contain two letters. Take for instance $\frac{mw}{m+w}$. We may treat it first as though m were the only letter.

$$\frac{mw}{m+w} \qquad\qquad \frac{mw}{m+w}$$
$$\frac{w}{1+w} \qquad\qquad \frac{0}{w}$$
$$\frac{w}{1+w}\,m + \frac{0}{w}(1-m)$$

Now what does this mean? We can answer this if we know first what $\frac{w}{1+w}m$ means and then what $\frac{0}{w}(1-m)$ means. 1st what does $\frac{w}{1+w}m$ mean? Let us treat it as if w were the only letter.

$$\frac{w}{1+w}m \qquad\qquad \frac{w}{1+w}m$$
$$\frac{1}{1+1}m \qquad\qquad \frac{0}{1}m$$
$$\frac{1}{0}mw \qquad + \qquad \frac{0}{1}m(1-w)$$

This is what $\frac{w}{1+w}m$ means that there are no men who are women and it includes none of the men not women. Next what does $\frac{0}{w}(1-m)$ mean?

$$\frac{0}{w}(1-m) \qquad \frac{0}{w}(1-m)$$
$$\frac{0}{1}(1-m) \qquad \frac{0}{0}(1-m)$$
$$\frac{0}{1}(1-m)w + \frac{0}{0}(1-m)(1-w).$$

This is the equivalent of $\frac{0}{w}(1-m)$. It includes no women not men and some, all, or none of the things which are neither women nor men.

Now if we add together the expressions for $\frac{w}{1+w}m$ and $\frac{0}{w}(1-m)$ we have the equivalent of $\frac{mw}{m+w}$ because this is the same as $\frac{w}{1+w}m + \frac{0}{w}(1-m)$. $\frac{mw}{m+w}$ then is

$$\tfrac{1}{0}mw + \tfrac{0}{1}m(1-w) + \tfrac{0}{1}(1-m)w + \tfrac{0}{0}(1-m)(1-w)$$

That is it is the class which includes some, all, or none of the things which are neither men nor women and none of the women not men and none of the men not women and it implies further that there are no men who are women.

Now I can give you a shorter rule for getting the same result. We start with $\frac{mw}{m+w}$. Write it down four times.

$$\frac{mw}{m+w} \qquad \frac{mw}{m+w} \qquad \frac{mw}{m+w} \qquad \frac{mw}{m+w}$$

First we put $\begin{matrix} m=1 \\ w=1 \end{matrix}$ then $\begin{matrix} m=1 \\ w=0 \end{matrix}$ then $\begin{matrix} m=0 \\ w=1 \end{matrix}$ then $\begin{matrix} m=0 \\ w=0 \end{matrix}$

This gives $\qquad \frac{1}{1+1}$ or $\frac{1}{0} \qquad \frac{0}{1} \qquad \qquad \frac{0}{1} \qquad \qquad \frac{0}{0}$

Then wherever we put *one* for m write an m and wherever we put *zero* for m write $1-m$. And so with w. And we have

$$\tfrac{1}{0}mw + \tfrac{0}{1}m(1-w) + \tfrac{0}{1}(1-m)w + \tfrac{0}{0}(1-m)(1-w)$$

which is the same result we had before.

I will give one more example of this process. What does $\frac{m}{a}$ stand for?

$$\frac{m}{a} \qquad \frac{m}{a} \qquad \frac{m}{a} \qquad \frac{m}{a}$$

$$\begin{matrix} m=1 \\ a=1 \end{matrix} \qquad \begin{matrix} m=1 \\ a=0 \end{matrix} \qquad \begin{matrix} m=0 \\ a=1 \end{matrix} \qquad \begin{matrix} m=0 \\ a=0 \end{matrix}$$

$$\frac{1}{1} \qquad\qquad \frac{1}{0} \qquad\qquad \frac{0}{1} \qquad\qquad \frac{0}{0}$$

$$\tfrac{1}{1}ma \quad + \quad \tfrac{1}{0}m(1-a) + \tfrac{0}{1}(1-m)a + \tfrac{0}{0}(1-m)(1-a).$$

Suppose we have the equation

$$1 = \tfrac{1}{1}xy + \tfrac{1}{1}x(1-y) + \tfrac{0}{0}(1-x)(1-y)$$

This reads that all things consist of all those things which are both x and y, of all which are x and not y, and perhaps of some that are neither x nor y. Observe that it is not implied that there are any things which are both x and y; or that there are any that are x and not y. But as something certainly exists, there must be something of one or other of these two classes.

When then we have 1 made equal to anything; it is asserted 1st that something among all the classes multiplied by $\frac{1}{1}$ *exists*, 2nd that nothing among all the classes multiplied by $\frac{0}{1}$ exists, and 3rd it is left in doubt whether anything among all the classes multiplied by $\frac{0}{0}$ exists. In the same way it might be shown that if we have such an expression as the following

$$\frac{xy + x(1-y) + (1-x)y + (1-x)(1-y)}{xy + x(1-y) + (1-x)y + (1-x)(1-y)} = 0$$

or any other expression derived from this by striking out any term or terms from numerator or denominator or both that—

1st No individual among all the classes appearing in the numerator exists.

2nd Some individual among all the classes not in the numerator but in the denominator exists.

Hence if we wish to say

$$\text{All men are animals we write } \frac{m(1-a)}{ma + m(1-a)} = 0$$

$$\text{No men are women } \quad " \quad " \quad mw = 0$$

$$\text{Some men are kings } \quad " \quad " \quad \frac{0}{mk} = 0$$

I will now explain how reasoning is to be conducted upon this system. To do this we wish to be able to strike any letter out of an equation. Suppose for instance we have $ab + c(1-b) = 0$ and wish to get rid of b

$$
\begin{array}{cccc}
ab + c(1-b) & ab + c(1-b) & ab + c(1-b) & ab + c(1-b) \\
b + (1-b) & b & (1-b) & 0 \\
1 & & & 0 \\
ac & + \quad ba(1-c) & + (1-b)(1-a)c = 0 & \\
& ac = 0 & &
\end{array}
$$

Now this result may be got also by writing

$$ab + c(1-b)$$

Put $b = 1$ and $=$ zero

$$a \qquad\qquad c$$

$$ac = 0$$

Now let us put an argument into syllogisms.

All men are Animals $\frac{m(1-a)}{ma+m(1-a)} = 0$

Socrates is a Man $\frac{s(1-m)}{sm+s(1-m)} = 0$

$$\frac{m(1-a)}{ma+m(1-a)} + \frac{s(1-m)}{sm+s(1-m)} = 0$$

As I know your minds must be wearied with this mathematics, I will now postpone the further consideration of it for another lecture and will take up now a lighter subject.

The art of Logic began with the conflict of pantheistic and sensational philosophies. This conflict led to acute arguments on the one side to show the contradictions involved in the doctrine that many things exist. And to curious instances on the other side to show that there is no absolute truth. Those who took this latter ground were called Sophists; and the purpose of their sophistry was to show that valid argument contradicts itself and that therefore truth is nothing more than what any man believes. Aristotle was brought up in a school that for two generations had rejected the conclusions of the sophists. Their sophisms, therefore, were to him merely matters of curiosity. They are useful to philosophy, he says, for two reasons; 1st because they generally arise from ambiguities of speech and, therefore, are instructive in reference to the nature of propositions and arguments and 2nd because practice in detecting them makes us less liable to deceive ourselves with false arguments. I believe that it was in fact from the study of these bits of sophistry, which smaller minds pass over as unworthy of serious attention, that Aristotle was led to the knowledge of the true laws of reasoning. To illustrate: An ancient philosopher Melissus had advanced this argument to prove that the world had no beginning:—

> Everything born has a beginning   A
> The universe is not born   E
> ∴ The universe has no beginning.   E

Now Aristotle quotes this argument and remarks that it is not conclusive because it does not follow that every thing which has a beginning is born; from the fact that everything born has a beginning. In fact, it is easy to see that if we could say

	Everything which has a beginning is born	A
then from the fact that	The universe is not born	E
it would follow that	The universe has not a beginning	E

Thus Aristotle would be led by the consideration of this deceptive argument or paralogism to make a distinction between two figures of reasoning, in the first of which the mood A E E is bad; though in the second it is good. It seems to me, therefore, that Aristotle's remarks upon the advantages of picking to pieces even the most obvious fallacies and detecting precisely where the fallacy lies, are exceedingly just; and that the contempt with which such things are commonly received is only another instance of what will be found a general rule, that the unintellectual man considers the objects to which the intellectual man applies himself as too trifling to bestow any attention upon. But, in fact, as Aristotle says, the analysis of sophisms not only sharpens the wits and makes us wary in inferring, but is also the great means for the discovery of logical forms.

On that account, I propose to consider some of the ancient sophisms and also some which I have invented myself.

I will begin with one which I find in a commentary upon Aristotle but whose origin I cannot trace. It runs thus:—It is impossible for a person who is silent to speak; but this man is silent; therefore it is impossible for this man to speak. Yet this man has spoken and will speak. This is to be explained in this way. When we say it is impossible that a person who is silent should speak, we mean that without considering whether in fact any one exists who is silent, if in any state of things whatever such a person should exist he would not speak. Or in other words whenever any person is silent he is not speaking. This is the expression of a general rule. Now when we say that this person is silent, we subsume a case under that rule, and the result follows that this person is not speaking. We ought not to infer that this person would never speak; for we have not said that this person would always be silent. Thus we see that if for our rule we have *I* would always be *C* and for our case *D* is *I*, the result is not *D* would always be *C* but *D* is *C*. To infer *D* would always be *C* we must have *D* would always be *I* for our case. The proposition

$$S \text{ would be } P \qquad \text{is termed a } necessary \text{ one}$$
$$S \text{ is } P \qquad \text{a contingent one.}$$

This is the established meaning of the word *necessary*. When we say that a straight line is necessarily the shortest distance between two points we mean that it is so not merely in this or that state of things but in every state of things. It always has been so, it is so; and it always will be so. When we say that all men are sinful; we make a merely contingent assertion because we generally allow that there was a state of innocence in Eden and that there will be another in the Millennium. In this case, therefore, we speak only of existing men; and the proposition is contingent. This is what philosophers have generally meant by necessary. But, of late, an entirely different meaning has been given to the word. It has been said that that is necessary whose contradictory we cannot conceive. Thus we cannot conceive of a straight line which should not be the shortest distance between two points, and therefore every straight line is necessarily the shortest distance between two points. Now this is to confound what we necessarily think with what we think to be necessary. It is a question whether what we *do* think necessary we need think necessary. A great philosopher has laid down the principle that nothing is observed to be necessary. For instance, we have observed that trees have roots; but we have not observed that they have roots under all circumstances, for the simple reason that all circumstances are not within the range of our experience. Mr. John Stuart Mill thinks he has triumphantly refuted this principle by adducing the following instance. The ancients could not understand how people could be upon the other side of the earth and therefore thought it impossible. You will wonder how he supposes that this is inconsistent with the principle laid down, since he must admit that they had not observed that there were no antipodes. He thinks it bears on the matter in hand first because he understands that philosopher to hold that whatever we have tried in vain to imagine is false; and second because he thinks the ancients tried in vain to imagine antipodes. But neither one nor the other of these propositions is true. No one ever meant to say that we can be sure that further discipline will not enable us to imagine what we cannot now imagine; nor were the ancients unable to imagine antipodes. They thought antipodes were impossible, but a race who had produced the science of geometry were certainly able to imagine a man in what they thought an impossible position, as the very existence of the word *antipodes* in their tongue proves. Such are the reflections which are suggested by this first sophism.

The next argument which I shall take up is one which was not intended to be fallacious but was urged seriously. It runs as follows.

Whatever moves in an instant must move in the place in which it is at that instant or in a place in which it is not in that instant. But nothing can move in the place in which it is at an instant nor in any place in which it is not during the motion. Hence nothing moves in an instant. But whatever has been moving at no instant has not been moving at all. Hence nothing has ever moved at all. The nature of the fallacy here is best shown by a parallel case. No one man constitutes a nation; but it is not true that all men do not make many nations. In the same way no instant contains any motion; but all instants contain motion. No thing moves in an instant but it may be moving at that instant. Motion is the difference in the positions of one thing. There is no difference in the position of the same thing at one instant; but the position of a thing at one instant may be different from its position at another instant. The fallacy in this example then is that the predicate of the case is not the subject of the rule.

Here is another example;

That which a man is now without but once had, he has lost
This man had once ten dollars and has now only nine
Therefore he has lost ten dollars.

In fact he has lost the collection of ten; at least he has if what is here said is true, that he has lost whatever he once had but now has not. But he has not lost every unit which made up that ten. Therefore the error is that the subject of the case "ten dollars" is taken in a different sense as the subject of the result.

A much more difficult case to resolve is this. Every proposition is either true or not true and is not both. The proposition

What is here written is not true

if it be true—is not true for it says it is not true; but if it be not true—is true for it says it is not true. Now ask yourselves *Is* this true? It either is or it is not; and it can't be both. If it is true then *what is here written is true* but the proposition contradicts this and therefore contradicts what is true. Therefore if it is true it is not true. But suppose it is not true, then what is true is that what is here written is not true; but this is just what is said; therefore, if it is not true, it is true. Again, suppose it is true, then what it *says* is true, but it says it isn't true; therefore, it isn't true. But if it isn't true what it says isn't true; but it says it isn't true; therefore it is true. Do you say then that it is true or not? That it is not true? What is not true, what is here written or what is here written about what is here written? Because if what is here written is not true, what is here written about what is here written is true; and if what is here written is true, what is here written about what is here written is not true. But after all what is here written is identical with what is here written about what is here written, for nothing is here written about anything except what is here written.

We have then

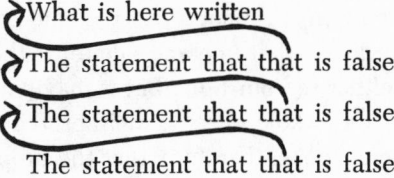

and we have

and so on to infinity

and moreover what is here written is a statement that something is false and thus we go to infinity in the other direction also. Now what all the statements are about if they are about anything is the last one of this infinite series. But there is no last one and therefore they are about nothing and have no meaning at all. The statement here written then is not true because it has no meaning; and therefore it is true, after all because it says so. We can say; this proposition so far as it is spoken about by itself is false but so far as it speaks about itself is true. But this is a distinction without a difference. The question is whether this proposition is in all respects true. If it is not in all respects true, then it is in all respects true; for two reasons 1st because what it says cannot in that case be altogether true, and what it says is that it isn't in all respects true and 2nd because it is seen to accord precisely with what is in all respects true; namely, that it isn't in all respects true. The fact is that in this proposition truth and not truth—affirmative and negative —this and other—coincide. It stands upon the boundary of the true and the false; and is therefore in both.

Here is a sheet of paper of which one part is red and the other blue. Every point is either red or blue. The boundary between them forms a line; now is that line red or blue? You cannot say it is red on one side and blue on the other unless like Hudibras you can distinguish and divide a hair twixt south and southwest side. A line is not double and has not different strips of color. It is all red or all blue or all both at once or all neither. It is plainly as much either one as it is the other. We must therefore say that it is *both* or neither. Most persons will say that it is neither; because colour can only reside in surfaces not in lines, but that is to fall into an ambiguity similar to that between motion in an instant and motion at an instant. It is true that a surface is required to constitute colour; but we apply the term to every point of that surface. In the same way a community is requisite to make a city but every individual of that community is called a citizen. If that line is not red it lies without the red part of the sheet; therefore if I simply draw away the red portion, I cannot affect the color of that line which lies without it. Accordingly that line and whatever the moving boundary passes over is neither red nor blue; but it may pass over the whole sheet and therefore the whole sheet is neither red nor blue. But it clearly is blue. It seems to me, therefore, that the proper answer is that the boundary is both red and blue;—the distinction between them vanishing at this point. And this is the answer which was made by Hegel and which mathematicians give to similar questions. It seems to me that this is a parallel instance to the proposition we have on the board. We cannot say that this proposition is neither *true* nor *not true*. That is self-contradictory. It is not self-contradictory to say that it is both true and not-true because this is a special case when the difference between affirmation and negation vanishes. Now these questions may seem trifling and puerile; but I have no hesitation in saying that I know of none upon the correct solution to which man's happiness depends more; for the paradoxes which beset our highest practical interest—our religion—the puzzles of free will, of divinity, of immortality are precisely of such a character as these.

Lecture on the Theories of Whewell, Mill, and Compte

MS 99: *March–April 1865*

I purpose to occupy this lecture and the next one with the consideration of several modern theories of the logic of science. To-day I shall speak of Whewell, Mill, and Compte whose views are intimately connected with the systems of metaphysics they support. Next Friday I shall give some account of the contributions made by Waddington, De Remusat, Gratry, and Apelt to our knowledge of the subject.

Dr. Whewell has usually been considered as a Kantian. Up to a certain point this is true. He accepts Kant's division of the matter and form of our knowledge and also his theory of space and time but he seems to have cast away from the doctrine of the limits of our knowledge which is the essence of the critical philosophy and speaks of causality as carrying our knowledge beyond the bounds of experience. The following aphorism which he often repeats sounds very Kantian:—

Fact and *Theory* correspond to Sense on the one hand, and to Ideas on the other, so far as we are *conscious* of our Ideas: but all facts involve ideas *unconsciously;* and thus the distinction of Facts and Theories is not tenable, as that of Sense and Ideas is. (p. 6, Aphorism V)

This is precisely what Kant would say. We cannot form an objective judgment without introducing either the conception of substance or of cause or of action and reaction all of which are conceptions involving necessity in the most obvious manner and therefore all of them are *theories* which cannot be given in the matter of experience nor can cases of them be given.

It is entirely impossible to understand Whewell's theory of induction or even his definition of it without taking into consideration his transcendental opinions. He says that "the two processes by which science is constructed are the *Explication of Conceptions* and the *Colligation of Facts.*" This is almost axiomatic; for the latter process, the colligation of facts, is simply gathering and placing in juxtaposition the matter of science; while the former process, the explication of conceptions, is the developement of the form of science. All cognition has its matter and form which is the unity of its matter. To obtain both and put them together is science. "Induction," he says, "is a term applied to describe the *process* of a true colligation of facts by means of an exact and appropriate conception."

An Induction is not the mere *sum* of the Facts which are colligated. The Facts are not only brought together, but seen in a new point of view. A new mental Element is *superinduced;* and a peculiar constitution and discipline of mind are requisite in order to make this Induction. (p. 71, Aphorism XV)

Mill objects altogether to this definition of induction on the ground that this colligation of facts is merely a new description of the phenomena. But this is merely as much as to object to Whewell's Kantian metaphysics. He holds that the facts from which the induction is drawn, already transcend the phenomena absolutely. He holds that the superinduction of a conception upon sensation already made in these facts carry them infinitely beyond the mere matter of sensation. Every new mental element added gives a still greater extension to the judgment. Take the example, Webster died, Stonewall Jackson died, John Jacob Astor died, therefore all men die. The very conceptions of a Webster, a Jackson, an Astor as individual objects as anything more than fleeting phantasmagoria carry us quite into the open sea of theory, and include suppositions not of millions of unseen facts merely but of an infinite number of them. Thus it is that every conversion of a fact to one which is more mental, more abstract, by a simple law of formal logic, adds to its extension. Mr. Mill's objection, therefore, is an exceedingly awkward one; and Dr. Whewell's definition is perfectly consistent with his fundamental principles and applicable to all cases of induction which his opponent could adduce.

The historian of science, resolves the process of induction itself into three steps: the selection of the Idea, the construction of the conception, and the Determination of the Magnitudes. You will notice that he uses the words *Idea* and *Conception* in a sense peculiar to himself. His ideas are Kant's conceptions—general representations—and his conceptions seem to be Kant's schemata. "We have given the appellation of *Ideas*," he says, "to certain comprehensive forms of thought—as *space, number, cause, composition, resemblance*—which we apply to the phenomena we contemplate. But the special modifications of these ideas which are exemplified in particular facts, we have termed *Conceptions;* as *a circle, a square number, an accelerating force, a neutral combination of elements,* a *genus*." By selecting an Idea, then, he means looking at a subject in a particular light; by constructing a conception he means getting definite general notions of the matter in hand when viewed in that light. As an instance of all three steps he gives the following:—

when Hipparchus found that the distance of the bright star Spica Virginis from the equinoxial point had increased by two degrees in about two hundred years, and desired to reduce this change to a law, he had first to assign, if possible, the *idea* on which it depended;—whether it was regulated for instance, by *space*, or by *time;* whether it was determined by the positions of other stars at each moment, or went on progressively with the lapse of ages. And when there was found reason to select *time* as the regulative *idea* of this change, it was then to be determined how the change went on with the time;—whether uniformly, or in some other manner: the *conception*, or the rule of the progression, was to be rightly constructed. Finally, it being ascertained that the change did go on uniformly, the question then occurred what was its *amount:*—whether exactly a degree in a century, or more, or less, and how much: and thus the determination of the *magnitude* completed the discovery of the law of phenomena respecting this star. (pp. 187–88)

He observes rather acutely that these three steps correspond to three steps in every mathematical investigation, the determination of the *variable,* of the *formula,* and of the *coefficients*.

There is another opinion of this eminent thinker which must be taken into account before we can thoroughly enter into the mental atmosphere through which he contemplates the logic of science. It is that the loftiest results of natural science are universal truths, in the strictest sense. It follows that though as clear conceptions they arise only after long study of nature and much colligation of facts, yet that they are, in reality, derived from within. Every universal proposition is derived from within. All results of induction have a partial universality and that shows that they contain an element or a principle derived from within. As science goes on to more and more general propositions, this element makes up more and more of its widest results and when it attains a proposition which is strictly universal, in which there is no limitation as to what objects it applies to, that is to say when all the matter of cognition is displaced from it completely, then that proposition is purely *à priori* or derived exclusively from within. Some very strict Kantians, among others the author of the *Limits of Religious Thought*, strenuously oppose this view. Their objection seems to be that a necessary truth must be also apodictic; that is, that if these results of science are derived from within they must always have been in the mind and however unconscious we may have been of them however obscure they may have remained they must still have had their necessary force and that consequently any supposition contrary to them must have been rejected at once although we may not have been conscious of the ground of rejection. But suppositions contrary to all sorts of inductive results have been made and consequently these cannot be strictly universal. This reply to Whewell seems to me quite unsound. In the first place because the absolute universality of these representations which result from induction is a simple question of fact which no indirect argument can settle. In the second place Whewell's view seems to me compatible with Kantism because Kant himself though he might hesitate to admit that a conception in the strict sense could be obscure yet speaks himself of that kind of indistinctness of concepts even of simple ones which arises from a weakness of consciousness. Now if a representation be weak, no matter if it be a representation of a necessary relation, it will not have the force to prevent our thinking contrary to it. If any proposition can be shown to be universal, I will admit that it is derived from within. But I do not thereby admit that it is certain; and even if it be proved to be true, it will not necessarily be a primary belief but may be derived from others.

Turning now to those points with which we are more immediately concerned, I find in the first place that Whewell recognizes two distinct subjects under the name of logic.

The *Logic of Induction* consists in stating the Facts and the Inference in such a manner, that the Evidence of the Inference is manifest; just as the Logic of Deduction consists in stating the Premises and the Conclusion in such a manner that the Evidence of the Conclusion is manifest. (p. 97, Aphorism XVII)

The relation of the successive Steps of Induction may be exhibited by means of an *Inductive Table*, in which the several Facts are indicated, and tied together by a Bracket, and the Inductive Inference placed on the other side of the Bracket; and this arrangement repeated, so as to form a genealogical Table of each Induction, from the lowest to the highest. (p. 98, Aphorism XXI)

The form which he uses for induction is exhibited in two tables, one of Gravitation and the other of Optics. The small bit of one of them which I have copied on to the board will suffice as an example. [Pass round the book]

Now I wish to call your attention to the most important aphorism of all. He says, "The *inductive act of thought* by which several Facts are colligated into one Proposition, may be expressed by saying: The several Facts are exactly expressed as one Fact, if, and only if, we adopt the conceptions and the Assertion of the Proposition." [Repeat.]

The first thing to be noted about this is that there is here at least the possible germ of a strictly logical doctrine of induction; for we may conceive that the question of deciding whether or not certain propositions may be collected into any narrower proposition than a certain given one, we may I say at least conceive that the solution of this question should be reduced to a purely formal problem. In the second place, it is to be observed that the generalization is here made to take place according to Kantian principles; that is to say, he has not made the form of the proposition to be evolved out of its matter at all but to be imposed by the mind so that we can readily see how each step would eliminate the arbitrary element more and more untill at last a pure form of the understanding alone remains. Thirdly it is clear that if this is the law of induction, a transcendental principle must lie at the bottom of the process. "The several facts are expressed as one fact, if, and only if we adopt the Conceptions and the Assertion of the Proposition." The sceptic might not admit that they can be expressed as one fact; and so he would nip the induction in the bud; unless the philosopher could get some *deduction* of this right to assume that they could. In the fourth place, we can see at once that if this is the law of induction then the logic of induction must afford a sure rule for ascertaining that this law has been complied with. Now does his table afford any such criterium whatever? Can it fairly be compared to the syllogism, which is not merely three propositions in a row but is furnished with such a machinery and such rules that it becomes a simple act of understanding without any exercise of talent, experience, sound sense, to tell whether anything be a syllogism or not? It seems to me evident at a glance that there is nothing of this kind here. Take the case written on the board.

Is there any other conception besides that adopted which would have colligated these facts? How am I to know? I do not possess all possible conceptions; there may be; there may not. The form says Whewell makes the Inference manifest. It does not make it manifest to me, especially in view of Dr. Whewell's suggestion that some conceptions which are quite fundamental may never have dawned upon my consciousness so that there may be such a conception though none is possible to my mind at present.

Whewell has never noticed this difficulty. There is, indeed, another which is urged by Mr. Mill which seems at first to be something like it, namely that one set of facts is "often fulfilled equally well by two conflicting hypotheses." This objection Whewell at once demolished by a reference to the well-known axiom which it contradicts; namely that from a false hypothesis a false conclusion must follow. But no similar axiom is admitted in the case of conceptions. Different coëxtensive conceptions are admitted by all logicians I believe. It is true, of course, that every conception is true to the facts which it colligates and hence that between two coextensive conceptions there is no preference in point of truth. Nevertheless if there be two concepts whose intension is different but whose extension is the same, there will always be a difficulty in induction for the following reason. In induction we do not know all the facts but only some; hence we cannot say *this* conception colligates actual facts, but only that a conception which nearly coincides with this one colligates actual facts. But if there be two conceptions of the same extent; then we are only warranted in saying that a conception which partially coincides with one of them colligates the truth. And if we are unaware of all the coëxtensive concepts we may miss the truth completely. This is a difficulty which no considerations of formal logic can possibly remove. For example, suppose that everything which had had any admixture of yellow in its color had happened to be round. And suppose we were to notice a number of such coincidences in some blue-green objects; then we might overlook the yellow element and say that everything blue is round and so be utterly mistaken. Now you may say, it is no great thing to prove that we can be mistaken in an induction. But it is perfectly essential to a logic of induction that it should give us rules to prevent our making a *complete* mistake. For if there may be one completely wrong conception which we may hit upon, there may be a million such, and in that case it's a million to one that we get the wrong one. Or there may be an infinite number and in that case it's certain we get the wrong one. In any case we are utterly ignorant how many there may be, and therefore we are utterly ignorant of the truth of our induction.

Other parts of Dr. Whewell's books seem to show that if this difficulty were urged against his theory he would support it by another which if proved would bring him out triumphantly. To Mr. Mill's objection that the condition of a hypothesis accounting for all the known phenomena is "often fulfilled equally well by two conflicting hypotheses," Whewell replies, "I know of no such case in the history of Science, where the phenomena are at all complicated; and if such a case were to occur, one of the hypotheses might always be resolved into the other." This seems to mean that there is only one conception which will colligate one set of facts. That consequently if there are two conceptions which will colligate nearly the same facts, they must be species of one general conception which will colligate the sum of the facts colligated by both the others. Consequently, that when any hypothesis is broached which will colligate among others some of the facts required to be colligated, that hypothesis if not true comprehends the true hypothesis with an admixture perhaps of some error; which error is likely to be less, the greater the variety of the facts observed and satisfied. Whewell does not seem to me to have proved this theory or even to have explicitly enunciated it. But I believe he has had it in his mind and that if it were proved it would solve the grand problem of the logic of science.

I regret that we cannot consider any of the rest of the philosophy of this man of science; he is the most profound writer upon our subject and had he had the luck to be a German his fame would have been spread far and wide.

The Positive Philosophy of Auguste Compte resembles the Baconian system in one respect, in that it is founded entirely upon a particular notion of the object of science. In everything else it is the antipodes of Bacon's theory, inasmuch as this notion is that causes and especially quiddities can never be discovered. Hence it is that the classificatory sciences appear in Compte's scheme only as a branch of Biology and are very meagrely treated in his *Course*. He admits of imperfect inductions; that is he admits we may go beyond what is given by sense, but he denies all principles which could possibly carry us beyond sense.

When I assert that this opinion—which is as weak since Kant as it was weighty before his researches—is the real origin and basis of the positive philosophy, I am well aware that Compte himself imagines that it is founded principally upon an argument drawn from the apparent law of the course of history. But every philosophy that can have any adherents, not only appears to be but actually is a result of the historic evolution of human thought. Only, time brings forth more than one at a birth. Hegelianism is as truly and legitimately a product of the age as positivism. So may be Frothinghamism. Once take up the standpoint of any one of these systems and all the heavens and all the earth seems to centre round you. It is odd enough to find a skeptic, a man who professes a wisdom and prudence above that of his fellow mortals and who can't believe in causality because it is of subjective origin, caught by such a simple illusion as this; which deceives no one else. The historical argument is obviously incompetent to prove any system. When Compte tells us that his system is founded on the law of progress from the theological age, through the metaphysical age, to the scientific age; his very terms show that his attention is occupied with the object of science; for theology, metaphysics, and physics (which is his science) are distinguished by their different objects. It is true that these studies begin to receive attention in the order which he has indicated; if that proves anything it is that theological science is the condition of metaphysical science and metaphysical science of physical science. But Compte holds that Theology and Metaphysics are nearly died out—he utters this opinion in the year 1830, three years after the publication of Hegel's great encyclopaedia. And it proves conclusively enough that he is helplessly restricted to a single intellectual point of view.

The disciples of this 'philosophe', have extolled his greatness in several branches of science. But all such pretensions are now exploded. His great specialty is mathematics. He was terribly incensed that the illustrious geometer Sturm was appointed professor of Analysis in the Polytechnic School when *he* was a candidate for the same office. And yet mathematicians refuse to this day to acknowledge his right to a place among them whether high or low. In the second place he has offered himself as a theoretical astronomer; and he professes to have demonstrated the nebular hypothesis so as to leave no hypothesis in it. But Sir John Herschel showed that his demonstration was nothing but hypothesis. In the third place, he is set up as an authority in zoölogy. Mr. Mill quotes his objection to Cuvier's system that one has to cut open an animal to determine his class according to this, with admiration. He, also, praises him for having risen to the sublime conception that all animals have their rank in one chain of classes without more complicated arrangements. As for his sociology—whether including or not his pantheon of heroes *I* do not know—this is thought to be truly sublime. But I am told that specialists do not admire Compte at all.

To return, however, to the *philosophie* itself. Its essence is that we cannot have any principle which would give us a right to go beyond present perceptions of sense. Yet we may in fact go beyond these provided we follow certain rules given by M. Compte without any deduction whatever. There is one of these to which great prominence is given and which is still heard of now and then. Let us examine it. It is the only part of Compte's big book which directly bears on our subject. It concerns hypothesis and is as follows.

The method of approximation employed by geometers first suggested the idea; and without it all discovery of natural laws would be impossible in cases of any degree of complexity; and in all, very slow. But the employment of this instrument must always be subjected to one condition, the neglect of which would impede the development of real knowledge. This condition is to imagine such hypotheses only as admit, by their nature, of a positive and inevitable verification at some future time,—the precision of this verification being proportioned to what we can learn of the corresponding phenomena. In other words, philosophical hypotheses must always have the character of simple anticipations of what we might know at once, by experiment and reasoning, if the circumstances of the problem had been more favourable than they are. Provided this rule be scrupulously observed, hypotheses may evidently be employed without danger, as often as they are needed, or rationally desired. It is only substituting an indirect for a direct investigation, when the latter is impossible or too difficult. But if the two are not employed on the same general subject, and if we try to reach by hypothesis what is inaccessible to observation and reasoning, the fundamental condition is violated, and hypothesis, wandering out of the field of science, merely leads us astray.

He thus divides all judgments into two classes, 1st such as experience and reasoning might display to us, in other words such as are given empirically and 2nd Gratuitous hypotheses. Now it is clear that there is no distinction as to validity between those hypotheses which are deliberately made and those which slip in without our notice. But how are we to distinguish between a hypothesis when it is not consciously made and an empirical datum? Not by an Interior or Common Sense according to the positive philosopher any more than to the Kantian. "The pretended direct observation of the mind by itself is," he says very incautiously, "a pure illusion." He must resort then to some logical test such as that of universality and necessity. But this would remove space and time from the class of empirical representations and so his rule of hypotheses would reject them altogether. He cannot escape from this paradox by saying that what he means by experience is what Kant means, namely the phenomenon after active thought, for this kind of experience involves causality. He cannot escape any better by saying that he means Kant's appearance or the phenomenon before active thought. For all verification of a hypothesis supposes the truth of recollection as well as of sense. This is a distinctly separable hypothesis, and it is one which cannot receive direct verification. Suppose, for instance, we make some hypothesis now. We have now to do two things; 1st to look at the object 2nd to compare the observation with the hypothesis. These must be done separately in time and in this order; but the comparison is of no value unless we make the hypothesis that our memory served us right. And so we shall be supporting one gratuitous hypothesis by another gratuitous hypothesis, according to Compte's rule. I almost hear the positivist exclaim that this is miserable trifling. I accept that word. It *is* miserable trifling to doubt the testimony of memory in such a case, notwithstanding its being an unverifiable hypothesis. I have heard it said that the rule is worded badly; it is not worded badly but thought badly. There is a germ of truth in it; that hypothesis is a dangerous kind of inference, but it required no *philosophe* to tell us that. It is the *correct analysis* of which Compte boasts very demonstratively and this is truly as good a specimen of analytic power as there is in his book.

Finally, I will suppose that Compte by his verifiable hypothesis means a hypothesis of a fact and by an unverifiable hypothesis a formal one merely. How do we begin an algebraical solution? We *suppose x =* the answer. That is not a hypothesis of fact; and on that very account we can suppose it, if convenient. And now what if we set out to think about this table; we begin (do we not?) with supposing a substance. *It* is hard; *it* is red. This *it* which is here the x is not a hypothesis of fact, for fact has reference to the world of phenomena and this is a thing-in-itself. Then why not admit it; at least, as within our thought of the *phenomena*. If we do, it can lead to no error for it introduces no fact. If we don't we must stop thinking. Now this *substance* was one of the very hypotheses the rule was framed to exclude. If you can, imagine Compte, with his well known hatred for algebra (an odd trait by the way in a great mathematician) exaggerated in some superpositive moment and rubbing out $x =$ the answer which his pupil has written on the board, with the exclamation "away with these metaphysical entities," and you have a more obvious but not a more radical absurdity than his denunciations of the *symbolic conceptions* of logic and metaphysics.

We come now to the *System of Logic* of Mr. John Stuart Mill. The worst thing to be said of this thinker is that he is an admirer of Auguste Compte. But in fact Mr. Mill has but a limited acquaintance with natural science and was thus easily taken in by Compte's pretension;—the more so, from sympathizing with his philosophic opinions. Mill's *System of Logic* is the most extensive and one of the most instructive works on the Logic of science which has ever been written. The first edition the only one I have seen is disfigured by several grave mistakes —such I mean as can be shown to be so beyond a doubt—but I understand that some of these have been corrected in later editions. It is not my purpose however to make an impartial criticism of Mr. Mill but only to examine those points which bear directly on the subject we have in hand, which happen to include most of those parts of the book to which as it seems to me there is much to object.

The source of much of the divergence between the opinions of Mill and those which I maintain, lies in the different definitions of inference. "To infer," says Sir William Hamilton, "is to recognize that two notions stand to each other in the relation of a whole and its parts, through a recognition, that these notions severally stand in the same relation to a third," and again, "Inference indicates the carrying out into the last proposition what was virtually contained in the antecedent judgments." According to this definition, neither a philosophical presumption that is a product of Scientific Induction or Analogy nor a hypothesis are inferred. I agree with Mr. Mill in extending the signification of the word so as to include both of these. But he defines inference as a progress from the known to the unknown, and this seems to me to give the word a wider sphere than logic can properly cover. It seems to me that if it is desired to define logic (as he does) as the science of inference and of subsidiary matters; that it is necessary to include in the word *inference* the conception that the proposition concluded is determined by the premises according to *formal* and not merely *psychological* laws. If one conception only *suggests* another, there may be a passage from the known to the unknown. But logic does not treat of the laws of suggestion; nor can it be made to do so without confounding what it is essential to keep distinct.

However unimportant this error may seem and however incredible it may appear that Mill does not really recognize the element of determination, it is certain that he is led into paradoxical statements about inferences which are only to be reconciled with the truth by a sense of the word in which no determination is involved; and it is also certain that Mill has devoted a great deal of space to refuting opinions by means of arguments which if they involve a determinating inference are clearly invalid and yet unless they do, fail completely of their aim.

The first of these arguments is as follows. Let us take the syllogism

All Men are mortal
Lincoln is a man
∴ Lincoln is mortal.

Of course the major premiss of this syllogism was derived from induction; we will say, for instance, thus

Socrates &c. were mortal
Socrates &c. were men
∴ All men are mortal.

Now says Mill, we may conclude from the data of the induction and from the minor premiss of the syllogism that Lincoln is mortal without once clearly comprehending that all men are mortal; thus,

Socrates &c. were mortal
Socrates &c. were men
Lincoln is a man
∴ Lincoln is mortal.

And this inference will be just as valid as though we had clearly comprehended that all men are mortal. All this is perfectly true. But what does he conclude from it? Why that the conclusion of a syllogism is not inferred from its major premiss but from the particulars from which that major premiss was induced; and that the syllogistic form is theoretically faulty and only of practical value. Now if by inference we mean merely the passage from the known to the unknown it is true that we can sometimes infer particulars from particulars in the way he has described. But suppose an inference is determined according to formal laws by its premisses. To determine is to make a thing different from what it would have been otherwise, hence that which determines a thing is its *conditio sine qua non*. But it is clear that in the example (No. 3) the conclusion is not valid unless it be valid to say that all men are mortal and *vice versa* if the general proposition is valid the other is. Hence the validity of the proposition that All men are mortal is the *conditio sine qua non* of the validity of the conclusion that Lincoln is mortal and hence the latter is inferred from the former. Logic is an analysis of forms not a study of the mind. It tells *why* an inference follows not *how* it arises in the mind. It is the business therefore of the logician to break up complicated inferences from numerous premisses into the simplest possible parts and not to leave them as they are.

There is another argument of Mr. Mill's in which the same error is still more striking. He proves at great length that Axioms are Inductions from experience. But what does he mean by induction? The inference from particulars. All then that he shows is that axioms are the result of a progress from particular experiences. There is nothing new about that. All experience is particular. And the very first words of Kant's *Kritik* are as follows: "That all our knowledge begins with experience there is no doubt whatever." And yet Mr. Mill evidently thinks that he has refuted Kant. What he has failed to see and what would prove their derivation *à priori*, is that the axioms find exemplifications in *every* appearance. Take for example the axiom that a straight line is the shortest path between two points or what comes to the same thing, that that line which points straight in any direction, reaches further in that direction than any other. Now give me any geometric figure you please. Take the circle.　○　Is it not plain in the appearance that any one point is further from any other along the circumference than it is more to the right or the left. This is an instance of the axiom. And the circle thus affords just as much inductive inference of the axiom as you please to require, and so does any other appearance. Now to determine is to make a thing different from what it would have been otherwise. Hence since there is the same amount of evidence namely an indefinitely great amount whatever appearance be cogitated, it follows that no appearance determines the axiom and that it is a representation *à priori*.

It may be thought bold to charge a man who has so many admirers with an *ignoratio elenchi* but this depends entirely on whether the charge has been substantiated. Mr. Mill says the reason for the axioms of geometry is to be found in experience. And how does he support it? Merely by showing that experience is the antecedent of such axioms. But no one denies that these axioms appear in experience meaning by that, that they appear in empirical cognition. It is admitted that if the validity of empirical cognition be granted, the truth of axioms will follow. In that sense, doubtless, we may say that experience is *a* reason for them. The question is what is *the* reason—is it internal or external? *The* reason for a proposition is its logical condition. Now the logical condition of an axiom is not this or that experience, but any experience. A human soul awakened by a presentation is all that is required. And this is all we mean when we say that space is the mode in which the sense is affected.

The Kantian, then, says that axioms are involved in the conditions of experience—or more strictly speaking of *appearance*. Mr. Mill does not invalidate this position by showing that they *might* follow inductively from some appearances; unless he can show that they *could* not follow from *any* appearance. The very nature of an inductive inference consists in a presumption of the conditions of a limited experience. For example, suppose I go over to the Zoölogical Museum and Mr. Agassiz selects for me 200 specimens of a single *genus*. I examine them and I find that they all have a certain peculiarity. Upon that, I make an induction. And what does my inference consist in? Why, in presuming that this general peculiarity of my experience was involved in the condition of my experience. I go to Mr. Agassiz and ask what the condition of my experience was—what the principle of his selection was. He gives me the name of the genus; whereupon I say that genus has this peculiarity. Here is a scientific induction and you perceive that it is nothing more than a presumption that a universal peculiarity is a condition of experience. And notice this, too. It is said that inductions are not certain. But where does the uncertainty come in, in this example? Not surely when I said that the peculiarity of the experience was involved in the condition of the experience; for this is an analytic proposition; but when I attempted to state what the condition of the experience was. When I supposed that the only condition I had any knowledge of was the only condition that existed.

Accordingly we may grant to Mr. Mill that axioms *might* be inferred inductively from some appearance; provided he will grant that they might be induced from any appearance. For it will follow that they are as Kant says, involved in the condition of all appearance. The condition of all appearance is that our sense should be affected. Hence they are involved in our sense being affected. In other words, they are part of the manner in which objects affect us. And this is the transcendental conclusion.

Book the Third of Mill's *Logic,* which treats of Induction, centres about two chapters, "On the Ground of Induction," and "Of the Evidence of the Law of Universal Causation." The former chapter, begins with the observation that there is "an assumption involved in every case of induction." This assumption relates to the order of nature. It is hard to express it precisely but it is to the effect that the course of nature is uniform. It seems to me that all must assent at least to this much that there is a transcendental principle or what a transcendentalist ought to call a transcendental principle involved in every case of induction.

Mill goes further than this. He says that this principle has the same relation to the inductive conclusion, which the major premiss of a syllogism has to its conclusion. This point may be waived. It is worth while, however, to notice the opinion because it is connected with a curiosity of philosophy; namely, that a sturdy English matter of fact logician should seriously attempt to show that a *petitio principii* is not a fallacy.

The next question is what is the ground for accepting this principle. Eighteen chapters intervene between this question and its solution. These though interesting and important concern us very slightly. It is held that induction by simple enumeration is not valid.

Before we can be at liberty to conclude that something is universally true because we have never known an instance to the contrary, it must be proved to us that if there were in nature any instances to the contrary, we should have known of them. . . . No such assurance, however, can be had, on any of the ordinary subjects of scientific inquiry. (p. 187)

This thought is made the basis of an extended discussion of scientific methods, but it has no logical value, for the assurance that we should know of objections will always rest on induction and thus we must rest on mere accumulations of arguments each of the same logical character as the simple enumeration. Mill, however, has 4 methods of Scientific Discovery. One of these the Method of Residues is merely a means of observation of facts not of explaining them. The other three methods those of Agreement, of Difference, and of Concomitant Variations, correspond with Bacon's three tables of Instances.

The law of Causation is discussed at length and is decided to be though not the complete expression of the law of the uniformity of nature yet the most important part of it. The question therefore of the grounds of the former may be solved by a consideration of the grounds for the latter. The other points touched upon in these intermediate chapters, it is unnecessary even to refer to. We come then to the evidence of Universal Causation. Mill says the law is obtained by Induction; in other words the necessary condition of its validity is the major premiss which is itself. This is a *petitio principii* no doubt, but it is logical nevertheless according to Mill. This law is he says (p. 184) "an assumption involved in every case of induction." It is proved therefore by being assumed. And this proof of a law by assuming it, goes by the name of induction in Mill's system. This is too ridiculous, to be as obviously false as it seems; for of course such difficulties are patent to all minds. He does not hint at Kant's argument for causality and no one in reading his chapter would imagine that such a view existed. Only the doctrine of the Scotch receives notice. We may pass at once therefore to his positive arguments. But first let us ask what a professed skeptic can mean by causation.

It is necessary to our using the word cause, that we should believe not only that the antecedent always *has* been followed by the consequent, but that, as long as the present constitution of things endures, it always *will* be so. . . . This is what writers mean when they say that the notion of cause involves the idea of necessity. If there be any meaning which confessedly belongs to the term necessity, it is *unconditionalness*. . . .

Invariable sequence, therefore, is not synonymous with causation, unless the sequence, besides being invariable, is unconditional. (p. 203)

This is a complete definition of what is technically known as the remote efficient. That we do not know particular efficients in the narrow sense that is to say particular proximate efficients, is no news at all but was admitted at once by all the earliest opponents of Hume; though some still hold that we know them within the mind. I cannot see but this is all the cause we ask for; here it is with the element of *necessity*. For condition implies necessity. Now for the evidence.

The truth is, as M. Comte has well pointed out, that (although the generalizing propensity must have prompted mankind from almost the beginning of their experience to ascribe all events to some cause more or less mysterious) the conviction that phenomena have invariable laws, and follow with regularity certain antecedent *phenomena,* was only acquired gradually; and extended itself, as knowledge advanced, from one order of phenomena to another, beginning with those whose laws were most accessible to observation. This progress has not yet attained its ultimate point; there being still, as before observed, one class of phenomena, the subjection of which to invariable laws is not yet universally recognized. So long as any doubt hung over this fundamental principle, the various Methods of Induction which took that principle for granted could only afford results which were admissible conditionally; as showing what law the phenomenon under investigation must follow if it followed any fixed law at all. As, however, when the rules of correct induction had been conformed to, the result obtained never failed to be verified by all subsequent experience; every such inductive operation had the effect of extending the acknowledged dominion of general laws, and bringing an additional portion of the experience of mankind to strengthen the evidence of the universality of the law of causation: until now at length we are fully warranted in considering that law, as applied to all phenomena within the range of human observation, to stand on an equal footing in respect to evidence with the axioms of geometry itself. (p. 341)

What can Mr. Mill a follower of Hume mean by this? Do we know a *condition—*a *necessary condition?* Pray how is this shown? Here is the whole matter assumed at the outset. A *petitio principii* again. But even this may be waived. Suppose the necessity to constitute no difficulty. Still is it true that we know it to be true of by far the greatest number of phenomena? First observe that the uniformity of succession does not apply to *phenomena per se* at all but to the relations of phenomena—to *facts.* Now do we know it to be true of by far the greatest number of relations of phenomena? By no means; in the first place it is only an infinitesimal proportion of the relations of phenomena which we ever notice. [Rap at blue] How many of the successions of events which take place in an hour do we notice? For the purpose of illustrating this point I rapped on the table after every s in the last sentence. You all heard it but how many took note of that relation of succession? How countless must be the number of such relations which no one notices. The successions we notice are the striking ones and they are those in which there is an obvious rule in which the law of uniformity is seen to hold. The rest are not taken account of.

I apprehend that the considerations which give, at the present day, to the proof of the law of uniformity of succession as true of all phenomena without exception, this character of completeness and conclusiveness, are the following:—First; that we now know it directly to be true of far the greatest number of phenomena; that there are none of which we know it not to be true, the utmost that can be said being that of some we cannot positively from direct evidence affirm its truth; while phenomenon after phenomenon, as they become better known to us, are constantly passing from the latter class into the former; and in all cases in which that transition has not yet taken place, the absence of direct proof is accounted for by the rarity or the obscurity of the phenomena, our deficient means of observing them, or the logical difficulties arising from the complication of the circumstances in which they occur; insomuch that, notwithstanding as rigid a dependence upon given conditions as exists in the case of any other phenomenon, it was not likely that we should be better acquainted with those conditions than we are. (p. 341)

What are complications? Phenomena are only complicated in reference to the mind. Those are complicated in which no uniformity is discernible. What he says then amounts to this that we may suppose that there is a uniformity because none is discernible.

Besides this first class of considerations there is a second, which still further corroborates the conclusion, and from the recognition of which the complete establishment of the universal law may reasonably be dated. Although there are phenomena, the production and changes of which elude all our attempts to reduce them universally to any ascertained law; yet in every such case, the phenomenon, or the objects concerned in it, are found in some instances to obey the known laws of nature. . . . I do not believe that there is now one object or event in all our experience of nature, within the bounds of the solar system at least, which has not either been ascertained by direct observation to follow laws of its own, or been proved to be exactly similar to objects and events which, in more familiar manifestations, or on a more limited scale, follow strict laws: our inability to trace the same laws on the larger scale and in the more recondite instances being accounted for by the number and complication of the modifying causes, or by their inaccessibility to observation. (pp. 341–42)

To all this I may reply that no hypothesis of a fact can stand strong which has received *no test*. But causality evades verification. It cannot be brought to a conclusive test. *There is no case whatever supposable which if it occurred could be said to show that the hypothesis failed.* I have no time to dwell upon this, but a little reflection will show that it is true. Accordingly all thought of proving the law by experience is preposterous.

The progress of experience, therefore, has dissipated the doubt which must have rested upon the universality of the law of causation while there were phenomena which seemed to be *sui generis,* not subject to the same laws with any other class of phenomena; and not as yet ascertained to have peculiar laws of their own. This great generalization, however, might reasonably have been, as it in fact was by all great thinkers, acted upon as a probability of the highest order, before there were sufficient grounds for receiving it as a certainty. For, whatever has been found true in innumerable instances, and never found to be false after due examination in any, we are safe in acting upon as universal provisionally, until an undoubted exception appears; provided the nature of the case be such that a real exception could scarcely have escaped our notice. When every phenomenon that we ever knew sufficiently well to be able to answer the question, had a cause on which it was invariably consequent, it was more rational to suppose that our inability to assign the causes of other phenomena arose from our ignorance, than that there were phenomena which were uncaused, and which happened accidentally to be exactly those which we had hitherto had no sufficient opportunity of studying. (p. 342)

Here is the question begged again. We ask Mr. Mill what is the ground of Induction. The law of Causality. And what is the ground of causality? Induction. But how could the law be acted upon before induction established it; in other words what ground had men for making inductions before induction was proved valid by induction? He answers they had the ground of Induction.

It is all the reason he can yield. It seems to me to amount to *none.*

The next lecture is to be on Waddington, De Remusat, Gratry, and Apelt.

Lecture VI: Boole's Calculus of Logic

MS 100: March–April 1865

Perhaps the most extraordinary view of logic which has ever been developed with success is that of the late Professor Boole of Dublin. His book is entitled *An Investigation of the Laws of Thought, on which are founded the Mathematical Theories of Logic and Probabilities.* It is destined to mark a great epoch in logic; for it contains a conception which in point of fruitfulness will rival that of Aristotle's *Organon*.

For two centuries many schemes have been proposed for representing logical processes in some other *set of symbols* than those *two* which are commonly in use;—I mean *words* and *thoughts*. These different systems are divisible into two classes. The first class embraces such symbols as have in their original nature something corresponding to logical laws. An example of this class is Euler's circles. Upon this system—the subordination of one term t[o] another is represented by ⊙ one circle within another. Thus the larger term may represent animals and the smaller one vertebrates. Logical intersection is represented by intersecting circles ⦰ . Thus, one might be *marine animals* and the other *mammals*. Exclusion—the relation between such terms as *men* and *ships* is represented by circles side by side. It is clear that these circles may be made to represent all the principal kinds of demonstration—which depend entirely upon relations containing and contained. These circles are merely concrete representations of the action of the very same laws. For this reason, they are most useful in enabling us to think rapidly and easily about logic; but for the same reason they cannot explain the laws of logic, at all.

The other class of logical symbols, is more algebraical. It consists of arbitrary signs upon which the laws of logic so far as they are understood, are arbitrarily imposed; but since the symbols are not naturally subject to any such laws the application of the laws scarcely reaches any further than has been explicitly supposed. This is the case with Hamilton's system of notation. He has one mark to signify the subject, another to signify the predicate, another for affirmation, another for negation, another for distribution or universality of a term, another for non-distribution. But as these marks have no connection with each other except such as is explicitly laid down; the system is of no practical value whatever. A very similar instance is the Notation of Ploucquet, of which I will give an example. Take the propositions

> Every man is a creature
> Some man is not an Ethiopian.

Ploucquet would write the first sentence thus, *Mc. M* stands for man and *c* for creature. Writing them together without anything between them, shows that they are affirmatively connected. Writing the M first shows that it is the subject. Writing the M in capital shows that it is distributed and writing the c in small letter shows that it is undistributed. In every respect, therefore, except the mere outward marks, this is like Hamilton's notation $M:$ ▬▬ , C. 'Some man is not an Ethiopian' would be written by Ploucquet thus, $m > E$. The crooked line makes negation. Hamilton would write it $M,$ ━┿━ :ϵ. Now Ploucquet can write his two propositions together taking care to make every letter small which occurring in both propositions is not a capital in both. Thus Mc and $m > E$ become $mc > E$. In the same way Hamilton may write $\epsilon:$ ━┥◄ , M ▬▬ , C. Next Ploucquet can drop the m and the conclusion is $c > E$ or Some creature is not an Ethiopian. So Hamilton can drop the M and have either $\epsilon:$ ━┿━ , C or $\epsilon:$ ━┥◄ , C which amount to the same thing.

Such a notation as this has one point of superiority over the geometrical systems; in that it involves some analysis of the laws of logic. But as it will do nothing with these laws except what we have decided beforehand that it ought to do, it is utterly useless both in practice and as the basis of a conception of the science.

The notation which Boole invented combines the excellencies of both these classes of symbols. For like the literal notations it is abstract and deals with the laws of logic themselves and like the geometrical notations it brings out a harmony between logic and mathematics, so as to render the former easier to think about. In addition to this, it has a peculiar excellence of its own for it reflects upon mathematics a new light from logic and immensely facilitates the solution of difficult questions of probabilities. I am very far from saying that the system is a perfect representation of logic, on the contrary I shall point out immense gulfs in its notation which were entirely overlooked by its author and shall show that but a very small fraction of all judgments can be expressed in this way. But then it must be remembered that the method is in its infancy yet, while even now it throws a light upon many points which is invaluable.

I will briefly describe it. The sign of equality, which in algebra signifies agreement in number; in other branches of mathematics denotes some other kind of agreement. In logic, then, it should signify logical agreement, or *identity*. Accordingly,

$$a + b + c = d$$

will mean not merely that a and b and c taken together are as many as d but that taken together they make up d. Thus a might be animals, b vegetables, c minerals, and d natural objects. Then the equation would signify that animals, vegetables, and minerals constitute natural objects, or *what is the same thing*, that every natural object is either an animal, or a vegetable, or a mineral. The sign *plus*, then, makes an extensive sum of two classes; $x + y$ denotes a class which has the extension of x and that of y also or which has the comprehension which is common to x and y. The rule of transposition is nothing but the definition of the sign *minus*. It must therefore hold good in every system. We may therefore assume that it holds and then inquire what the sign *minus* must mean in order that it should hold. Transposing c then in the last equation, we get,

$$a + b = d - c$$

Now what are animals and vegetables in terms of natural objects and minerals? They are all natural objects except minerals. The sign *minus* then signifies extensive subtraction; that is, $x - y$ denotes a class which has the extension of x not shared by y and the comprehension of x and that of non-y together. Observe, however, that in addition to this something is implied in the expression $x - y$ in regard to the relation of y to x, namely that y is subordinate to x in extension, for otherwise $x - y$ would be an absurdity and incapable of interpretation. It is important to remember what is implied in this inverse process.

The Rule of Transposition not only defines the sign *minus* it also defines *zero* for by transposition $a - a = 0$. *Zero* then denotes that class whose extension is nothing and whose comprehension is non-existence.

The idea of multiplication in all branches of mathematics is combination into one. It is supposed that the two factors are two completely independent measures of the quantity and that their product is that which is measured by both. Now the measure of a symbol is its comprehension. It is the comprehension which measures the extension not *vice versa*. Accordingly if R means Roman and C means christian, rc would mean that which has the comprehension Roman and that of Christian at once. Or in other words it would be a Roman Christian. xy, then, has the comprehension of x and of y both and the extension which is common to x and y. Just as $x + y$ has the extension of both, and the comprehension which is common to the two.

The rule for clearing from fractions is the definition of division. Let $x = \frac{b}{a}$. Then the question we have now to ask is what is the meaning of x in terms of b and a. The answer is $ax = b$. That is x is a class which when determined by the comprehension of a gives b. In other words $\frac{b}{a}$ is a class which includes b and nothing but b that is at the same time a; that is, it comprises all b and some, all, or none of what is not a beside. At the same time just as the inverse process of subtraction implies in itself that the extension of the subtrahend includes the extension of the minuend; so the inverse process of division implies that the comprehension of the dividend includes the comprehension of the divisor. Thus take $\frac{x}{y}$. Now unless x contains in itself y as a factor the division cannot be performed and the expression is incapable of interpretation.

Just as the rule of transposition serves to define not only subtraction but also the *zero;* so the rule of clearing from fractions defines not only division but also the *unity.* For by this rule $b = b \times 1$. Now what is that class whose comprehension makes a part of that of every other class and whose extension includes that of every other class. It is the *existent.* All existent includes everything. Existence is implied in every class. Hence if a class $=$ *zero* or is non-existent, there is thereby an absurdity in it.

We thus see that addition in this system means union in extension and that multiplication means union in intension or comprehension.

Exponentials, Logarithms, Signs and other functions can be interpreted upon Boole's system only by developing them into algebraic forms.

Let us now endeavor to express upon Boole's system the three fundamental laws of logic—those, namely, of Identity, Contradiction, and Excluded Third.

In order to express the law of Identity or All A is A; let us first express All X is Y and then substitute A for both X and Y. To say All X is Y is the same as to say that the class X is identical with the class which has the comprehension of X and Y together or $X = XY$. Now substituting A for X and Y we have $A = A^2$. Now does this express the law of identity? Unless the formula A is A means that A is B that is that A *is* something or in other words that every logical term is capable of an affirmative predicate or that it is *real;* I say unless the law of identity means this then *John is John* does not represent the law at all. For *John is John* means absolutely nothing more than that *John is X*, or *John is*. What the law may be taken to mean is this:—that all the individuals composing a class have the class-character.

> Let *A* denote a certain class
> Let *a* denote the individuals in it
> Let *α* denote whatever has the class-character.

Then the proposition that a class is composed of individuals having a certain character will be

$$A = a_\alpha$$

but *A a α* are all identical; hence we may write

$$a = a^2$$

as the symbol of the law.

But if the law be considered to mean merely that every logical term is capable of an affirmative predicate in so far as it obeys logical laws, then Boole's system will not express this law at all. The reason that it will not, I will explain shortly.

The law of excluded third is that *A* is either *B* or not-*B*. Here again if this law be taken as it usually is to mean *A vel est B vel est* non-*B* then the law cannot be expressed upon Boole's system, because the existence of *A* is here implied. I mean that kind of existence which is implied in an affirmative copula, and in Logical Identity in general. But if the law mean *A vel est B vel non est B*, then the law may be expressed. For this will mean that *A* is something or is not or in other words that *A* either is or is not. In other words that *a* has two roots *unity* or the existent and *zero* or the non-existent. In algebra if *x* has two roots x_0 and x_1 this fact is expressed in the following equation

$$(x - x_0)(x - x_1) = 0$$

for this equation can only be true when $x - x_0 = 0$ and when consequently $x = x_0$ or else when $x - x_1 = 0$ and when consequently $x = x_1$. Expressing then in this way that *a* equals either 1 or 0 we have

$$(a - 1)(a - 0) = 0$$

The law of contradiction, the third of the triad of fundamental laws may undoubtedly be expressed upon Boole's system. For it is merely that A is not-not-A or what comes to the same thing, A which is not-A is non-existent. The class not-A is that one which with A makes up the existent or in other words it is all the existent except a. That is $1 - a$. A which is not-A is then $a(1 - a)$ and this equals *zero* or $a(1 - a) = 0$.

These three fundamental laws as thus expressed are algebraically one and the same. And they amount to this, that in the calculus of logic every letter has one of two values *unity* or *zero*.

It is now incumbent upon me to exhibit the capacities of the system for expressing different kinds of propositions. I regret that we must come to the examination of this point now, because it will be sure to leave you with much too low an opinion of the method. I warn you therefore not to infer from the enormous deficiencies that the utility of the system is small nor need we give up the hope that they may be hereafter supplied.

Ordinary language is capable of distinguishing judgments in Modality, Relation, Quality, and Quantity. In modality judgments are either Problematic, Assertory, or Apodeictic. Apodeictic judgments can certainly not be distinguished from the Assertory upon Boole's system. It may be doubted whether problematic judgments can be expressed or not. xy may be taken to mean 'x may be y'; and perhaps it does. In Relation, judgments are Categorical, Hypothetical, and Disjunctive. Hypotheticals and Disjunctives cannot be expressed upon Boole's system. The author endeavored to express them in the following way. Take the judgment "If there is an east wind, the barometer will rise." He would say Let a express There is an east wind; and let b express The barometer will rise. Then $a = ab$ will mean If there is an east wind the barometer will rise. But in the first place, this alters the meaning of the sign of equality; and belongs therefore to a system inconsistent with that upon which Boole expresses Categoricals. In the second place it entirely destroys the possibility of expressing problematic propositions, except by single letters. In quality, ordinary language expresses the difference between affirmatives and negatives. An affirmative I define to be a proposition which implies the reality of its terms. Logicians might call this statement in question. The word *reality* which is the correct one here, is certainly liable to be misunderstood. In an analytical proposition, in which an identity of concepts merely is asserted, it is merely implied that the concepts are real. But that this is implied is evident from the fact that there is no contradiction between any two propositions if affirmatives admit the case of the nothingness of both terms. Thus if griffins do not exist it is true to affirm anything whatever of griffins. If anything can be affirmed of a four-sided triangle it is that it is foursided, but this may certainly be denied of it, for otherwise we could not show it an absurdity. Of course, in the case of a problematic proposition this reality is only problematic. In the case of an analytic proposition it merely concerns concepts. But in all synthetic assertory affirmatives, there is a reality asserted in the ordinary sense. As a further illustration of the implication of Entity in Affirmatives, take the following reasoning which follows strictly unless either affirmatives or particulars imply the Entity of their subject.

> No black is white
> No non-smooth black is white
> If any black is not smooth it is not white
> If any black is white it is smooth
> All White black is smooth
> Some smooth is white black
> Some smooth black is white black
> Some smooth black is white
> Some black is white

The fallacy here consists I believe in the inference from No black white is non-smooth to All black-white is smooth. Taking then this definition of affirmatives, we find that affirmatives cannot be expressed upon Boole's system. In this respect, the system of Leibniz from which Boole may have derived the hint for his own, is superior to the latter one. If he wishes to say all men are mortal letting h be *men* and m mortal, he writes $h = hm$. The men are identical with the mortal men; but yet there may be *non*-men. In fact, *man* may be an absurdity. $h = hm$ therefore means No man is immortal but not All men are mortal.

In Quantity, ordinary language expresses the difference of Universal and Particular. Professor Boole gave as the expression for the particular negative Some X is not Y

$$vx = v(1 - y)$$

where v denotes the indefinite class *some*. But the absurdity of this is evident from the fact that by transposing we get

$$vy = v(1 - x)$$

or Some Y is not X. But it does not follow from Some X is not Y that Some Y is not X. This expression is therefore wrong. The cause of the defect of it is evident. He has represented *some* as being merely an indefinite class. As though we were to say instead of Some animals are not men

Four-legged animals are not men.

Now it does follow that if Four-legged animals are not men, Four-legged men are not animals. Boole's system then as he has left it can only express assertory, categorical, negative universals. But it is possible that all its defects might be remedied. In fact, the particular quantity can be easily supplied. When we say Some animals are not men *some* is not a wholly indefinite class for it is understood to be a class of animals; in other words there are none of the whole class *some* who are non-animals. Now this is expressed by the equation

$$vxy + v(1 - x)y + v(1 - x)(1 - y) = 0$$

Or by $\quad v = vx(1 - y) \quad$ Or $\quad v[1 - x(1 - y)] = 0$

While Boole's system is insufficient to express most of the kinds of judgment expressed in speech, it is capable of noting some points which common forms of language cannot. Thus the difference between an analytic and synthetic judgment, is easily noted.
$\frac{x}{y}$ shows that x in itself implies that it is not y, while $xy = 0$ leaves it doubtful.

Language has no way of distinguishing disjunctives from divisives. Boole's system can express the latter unequivocally. Definitions can hardly be expressed precisely elegantly in language; we can say All A is all B but it is an awkward and unnatural phrase. Boole simply writes $a = b$ that is there is no A which is not B and no B which is not A.

It is curious that extensive combination should be represented by addition; and comprehensive combination by multiplication when the extensive and intensive quantities stand in reciprocal relation. It is not obvious at first glance how multiplication can undo the work of addition and *vice versa*. An example, however, will make this plain.

Let a and b be two distinct classes and to represent the fact that they are distinct we may write them $a(1-b)$, $b(1-a)$. Now let us add them $a(1-b) + b(1-a)$. Next let us multiply by a. $a \times a(1-b)$ is $a(1-b)$ for $a^2 = a$, $a \times b(1-a) = 0$ for $a(1-a) = 0$. The multiplication therefore separates this term $a(1-b)$ which the addition combined with another. We might have begun with the multiplication. Let x and y be two terms. Multiply them, we have xy. Add x, $xy + x$. This $x = xy + x(1-y)$. We have then $2xy + x(1-y)$ but the coefficient means nothing. It may be struck off. We have then $xy + x(1-y)$ or x.

The application of Boole's calculus to ordinary reasoning depends upon two very simple theorems which I proceed to give.

The use of the first is to enable us to interpret complex expressions. For example $\frac{(a-b)^2}{1-(a-b)^2}$ could hardly be interpreted as it stands. In general, it is required then to simplify fx. Now x has one of two values. Calling these x_0 and x_1, we have the algebraical law

$$(x_1 - x_0)fx = (x - x_0)fx_1 + (x_1 - x)fx_0$$

This equation is always true for $x =$ either x_1 or x_0. When it $= x_0$ the equation becomes

$$(x_1 - x_0)fx_0 = (x_0 - x_0)fx_1 + (x_1 - x_0)fx_0$$

where the first term of the second member disappears; and when $x = x_1$ it becomes

$$(x_1 - x_0)fx_1 = (x_1 - x_0)fx_1.$$

This equation then being true let us substitute for x_1 and x_0 the values which they have in logic namely unity and zero and we have

$$fx = xf1 + (1-x)f0$$

Now I will show how to use this formula by developing the expression $\frac{1-(a-b)^2}{a}$. This has to be developed in terms of a and b. We have to complicate the formula a little

$$f(a,b) = af(1,b) + (1-a)f(0,b)$$

Developing this again according to b we have

$$f(a,b) = abf(1,1) + a(1-b)f(1,0)$$
$$+ (1-a)bf(0,1) + (1-a)(1-b)f(0,0)$$

Now to apply it.

When $a = 1$ and $b = 1$ $\frac{1-(a-b)^2}{a} = 1$
The first term then is ab

When $a = 1$ and $b = 0$ $\frac{1-(a-b)^2}{a} = 0$
The second term disappears

When $a = 0$ and $b = 1$ $\frac{1-(a-b)^2}{a} = \frac{0}{0}$
The third term then is $\frac{0}{0}(1-a)b$

When $a = 0$ and $b = 0$ $\frac{1-(a-b)^2}{a} = \frac{1}{0}$
The fourth term then is $\frac{(1-a)(1-b)}{0}$

We have then

$$\frac{1-(a-b)^2}{a} = ab + \frac{0}{0}(1-a)b + \frac{(1-a)(1-b)}{0}$$

We have here two coefficients $\frac{0}{0}$ and $\frac{1}{0}$ which we have not yet interpreted. To find what $\frac{0}{0}$ means put it equal to x, $\frac{0}{0} = x$; multiply by *zero* and we have $0 \times x = 0$. Now this is true whatever be the value of x. $\frac{0}{0}$ therefore is a wholly indeterminate class and means *all, some,* or *none.* $\frac{0}{0}(1-a)b$ means *some, all,* or *none* of b which is not a.

To find what $\frac{(1-a)(1-b)}{0}$ means we must remember that when one letter is divided by another, as $\frac{x}{y}$, it must be that the dividend contains the divisor as a factor. Now to say that $(1-a)(1-b)$ contains *zero* as a factor is to say, not merely that $(1-a)(1-b)$ does not enter into the meaning of $\frac{1-(a-b)^2}{a}$ but that it enters into the meaning of nothing and does not exist. This same result may also be obtained thus. Let $\frac{(1-a)(1-b)}{0} = y$; then multiplying by zero $(1-a)(1-b) = 0$, while the value of y is wholly indeterminate.

Such being the meanings of $\frac{0}{0}$ and $\frac{1}{0}$, I pass to the second fundamental theorem which enables us to suppress a letter from an equation. Let $fx = 0$ be an equation from which we wish to eliminate x. As x is either $= 1$ or $= 0$ we have either $f(1) = 0$ or $f(0) = 0$. In any case $f(1)f(0) = 0$.

Take for example the equation $ab + (1 - b)c = 0$. Required to eliminate b. When $b = 1$ this becomes $a = 0$. When $b = 0$ it becomes $c = 0$. In any case then $ac = 0$.

I will now show you how to perform a reasoning process in this calculus. We shall always have two equations which are to be combined. We must develope each of them fully. Then we shall have it in the form

$$Ma + N(1 - a) = 0$$

M or N may either or both be negative but if the equation is squared we have

$$M^2a + N^2(1 - a) = 0$$

and each term is then positive.

Each term therefore is separately equal to zero. The two equations may then be added together and the superfluous expressions eliminated. Take this example.

> No animals are vegetables
> All men are animals

The first is $av = 0$. The second is $m(1 - a) = 0$.

$$m(1 - a) + av = 0$$

Eliminating a we have $vm = 0$, No men are vegetables. I would give a more complex instance but have hardly time.

Since x is equal either to *one* or *zero*, either $f(1) = 0$ or $f(0) = 0$; in either case $f(1)f(0) = 0$, which is the equation with x left out.

We now come to the property of these symbols which enables us to draw logical conclusions. This property is that in this calculus any number of different equations can be combined into one equation which shall express all the facts contained in the several equations. I will show you how this can be done. Let us take two equations $a = b$ and $c = d$ to combine into one. We have first $a - b = 0$ and $c - d = 0$. Square these equations $a^2 - 2ab + b^2 = 0$ and $c^2 - 2cd + d^2 = 0$; but as $a = a^2$ for either *one* or *zero*, this is the same as $a - 2ab + b = 0$ and $c - 2cd + d = 0$, which may be written $a(1 - b) + b(1 - a) = 0$ and $c(1 - d) + d(1 - c) = 0$. Now as the value of a letter never exceeds *unity* all these terms are positive and consequently if they are all added together into one equation $a(1-b) + b(1-a) + c(1-d) + d(1-c) = 0$; this equation itself implies that the terms are separately equal to zero and consequently that $a(1-b) = b(1-a)$. That is $a - ab = b - ab$ or $a = b$ and in the same way it is implied that $c = d$; so that this one equation contains now all that was contained in the original two. The practical value of this method can only be illustrated by very complicated cases; but in order to show how it is used I will take a very simple case. From these two premises what follows?

> The ancestors of Negroes had no tails
> Monkeys have tails

Let m be monkeys, n ancestors of Negroes, t whatever has a tail. Then the premises are $0 = nt$ or There are no tailed ancestors of Negroes and $m = tm$ or Monkeys are all tailed monkeys. The second equation gives $m - mt = 0$ or $m(1-t) = 0$. Add the two equations and we have $nt + m(1-t) = 0$. We wish now to get rid of t. Now t must equal either *one* or *zero*. In the former case we have $n = 0$, in the latter case $m = 0$; in either case $mn = 0$ or None of the ancestors of Negroes were monkeys.

The application of this calculus to questions of probabilities is very beautiful. I wish to call particular attention to this application because it shows conclusively that we can draw no argument for the validity of induction from the doctrine of chances. It was for the sake of showing this that I brought Boole's method to your notice. The theory of its application to probabilities is exceedingly simple and is best exhibited in an example.

Given the probability that one or both of two events happen; and let it equal p. Given also the probability that one or both of them fail to happen; let it equal q. What is the probability that one only will happen?

Let the two events be x and y. Let the case that one or both happen be s; that is $s = xy$ (that they both happen) $+ x(1-y)$ (or x happens without y) $+ (1-x)y$ (or y happens without x). Let the case that one or both fail be t; that is $t = x(1-y)$ (that x happens without y) $+ (1-x)y$ (or y happens without x) $+ (1-x)(1-y)$ (or neither happens). Let the case that only one happens be w; that is $w = x(1-y)$ (that x happens without y) $+ (1-x)y$ (that y happens without x).

We must first reduce these three equations to one. Taking the first one and transposing the second member we have

$$s - xy - x(1-y) - (1-x)y = 0$$

Apply to this the formula $fs = sf(1) + (1-s)f(0)$. When $s = 1$ the equation becomes $(1-x)(1-y) = 0$. When $s = 0$ it becomes $xy + x(1-y) + (1-x)y = 0$. In general then it is $(1-s)xy + (1-s)x(1-y) + (1-s)(1-x)y + s(1-x)(1-y) = 0$. By the same developement the other two equations become

$$txy + (1-t)x(1-y) + (1-t)(1-x)y + (1-t)(1-x)(1-y) = 0$$

$$wxy + (1-w)x(1-y) + (1-w)(1-x)y + w(1-x)(1-y) = 0$$

We may now take the sum of these three equations *equal to zero*. The next thing to be done is to get rid of x and y because there is nothing said about the simple events in the problem. For this purpose if we find what our equation becomes

1st when $x = 1$ $y = 1$	2nd when $x = 1$ $y = 0$	3rd when $x = 0$ $y = 1$	4th when $x = 0$ $y = 0$

we shall have four expressions all equated to *zero*, one or other of which is really equal to *zero;* and therefore the product of them is certainly equal to *zero*.

When $x = 1$ and $y = 1$ everything except the coefficients of xy will disappear and we shall have

$$(1-s) + t + w = 0$$

When $x = 1$ and $y = 0$ everything except the coëfficients of $x(1-y)$ will disappear and we shall have

$$(1-s) + (1-t) + (1-w) = 0$$

When $x = 0$ and $y = 1$ everything except the coefficients of $(1-x)y$ will disappear and we shall have

$$(1-s) + (1-t) + (1-w) = 0$$

When $x = 0$ and $y = 0$, everything except the coefficients of $(1-x)$ $(1-y)$ will disappear and we shall have

$$s + (1-t) + w = 0$$

We must now multiply these four equations together. I will not stop to perform this process but will merely give the result which is

$$st(1-w) + s(1-t)w + (1-s)t(1-w)$$
$$+ (1-s)(1-t)w + (1-s)(1-t)(1-w) = 0$$

And this by a very simple reduction gives

$$w = \frac{st + (1-s)t + (1-s)(1-t)}{st + (1-s)t - s(1-t)}$$

Let us now develope this fraction by a formula made on the same principle as the one I have just used; namely

$$f(s,t) = stf(1,1) + s(1-t)f(1,0)$$
$$+ (1-s)tf(0,1) + (1-s)(1-t)f(0,0)$$

When	$s = 1$	$t = 1$	$w = 1$
When	$s = 1$	$t = 0$	$w = 0$
When	$s = 0$	$t = 1$	$w = 0$
When	$s = 0$	$t = 0$	$w = \frac{1}{0}$

Hence in general

$$w = st + 0s(1-t) + 0(1-s)t + \tfrac{1}{0}(1-s)(1-t)$$

We have now completed the logical solution of the problem. We must next apply the theory of probabilities. For this purpose instead of insisting any longer upon allowing s and t only the two values *zero* and *unity*, we must allow them values proportionate to the number of cases in which they will occur. Then the probability of s will be represented by a fraction whose numerator is s and whose denominator is the sum of all the possible cases. Now the cases which are impossible are those represented by $(1-s)(1-t)$ as is shown by the coefficient $\frac{1}{0}$. Hence, the probability of s or

$$p = \frac{s}{st + s(1-t) + (1-s)t}$$

In the same way
$$q = \frac{t}{st + s(1-t) + (1-s)t}$$

And in the same way the probability of w which is sought, is since by the equation st represents all the cases in its favor

$$X = \frac{st}{st + s(1-t) + (1-s)t}$$

From these three equations we must now eliminate s and t. For this purpose we have $\frac{p}{s} = \frac{q}{t} = \frac{X}{st}$. $s = \frac{X}{q}, t = \frac{X}{p}$.
Substituting these values in that of X we have

$$X = \frac{\frac{X^2}{pq}}{\frac{X}{p} + \frac{X}{q} - \frac{X^2}{pq}} = \frac{X}{q+p-X}$$

$$1 = \frac{1}{q+p-X}$$

$$X = q + p - 1$$

which is the probability required.

I will now take a case where an attempt is made to work inductively.

Let the probability that it *thunders* on a given day be p. Let the probability that it *thunders and hails* be q. Required the probability that it *hails* or X.

Let x be It hails. Let y be It thunders. Let u be It thunders and hails. Then $u = xy$ and $x = \frac{u}{y}$. Developing this we have $x = uy + \frac{1}{0}u(1-y) + 0(1-u)y + \frac{0}{0}(1-u)(1-y)$. This solves the logical question; proceeding with probabilities we have

$$p = \frac{y}{y + (1-u)(1-y)}$$

$$q = \frac{uy}{y + (1-u)(1-y)}$$

$$X = \frac{uy + \frac{0}{0}(1-u)(1-y)}{y + (1-u)(1-y)}$$

Elimination of u and y results in the following value of X

$$X = q + \frac{0}{0}(1-p)$$

which is as you perceive an indeterminate result; showing merely that the data were insufficient.

Let z be some complicated system of phenomena; let y be the concomitant circumstances under which these phenomena are observed. Let x be a physical hypothesis which perfectly accounts for them. Required X large or the unknown probability of this hypothesis. In this case we have the equation $xy = xyz$ which expresses that if the hypothesis holds, then under these circumstances the actual phenomena are sure to appear or are accounted for. Observe that there cannot be a stronger case for the hypothesis, than that. The value of x from this

$$x = \tfrac{0}{0}yz + 0y(1 - z) + \tfrac{0}{0}(1 - y)z + \tfrac{0}{0}(1 - y)(1 - z)$$

These indeterminate coefficients will necessarily appear in the solution; which is in fact completely indeterminate.

I shall conclude by reading some remarks of Boole's upon this subject:

These problems are all of a similar character. A certain hypothesis is framed, of the various possible consequences of which we are able to assign the probabilities with perfect rigour. Now some actual result of observation being found among those consequences, and its *hypothetical* probability being therefore known, it is required thence to determine the probability of the hypothesis assumed, or its contrary. . . .

The general problem, in whatsoever form it may be presented, admits only of an *indefinite* solution. Let x represent the proposed hypothesis, y a phænomenon which might occur as one of its possible consequences, and whose calculated probability, on the assumption of the truth of the hypothesis, is p, and let it be required to determine the probability that if the phænomenon y is observed, the hypothesis x is true. The very data of this problem cannot be expressed without the introduction of an arbitrary element. We can only write

$$\text{Prob. } x = a, \qquad \text{Prob. } xy = ap;$$

a being perfectly arbitrary, except that it must fall within the limits 0 and 1 inclusive. (p. 365)

Lecture on Kant

MS 101: March–April 1865

There is a very intimate relation between the question of the logic of science, namely how can material inference be valid, and one of the fundamental questions of metaphysics, how can the conceptions of cause, substance, necessity, *et cetera* be valid. How this connection comes about we shall be able to see as soon as we have distinct notions of the comprehension of these two questions. Suffice it for the present to assert that they are as transcendental problems so bound together that we cannot intelligently criticise the various opinions which are held about one without having some elementary notions of the other of these questions. Locke undertook to say that the principle of causality is learnt from experience, like everything else. This opinion was received for a time and then Hume showed conclusively and beyond long dispute that this was impossible, and inferred that the whole notion of *cause* is illusory. Reid disputed Hume's inference on the ground that causation is revealed by consciousness, while *Kant* disputed Hume from certain considerations of the logic of science. Other opinions besides those of Hume, Reid, and Kant are still extant; but these are the most widely influential. They are the philosophies of positivism, common-sense, and transcendentalism. And with every desire to avoid entanglement in metaphysics, I cannot escape saying something of Kant's philosophy. A technical discussion of logical forms would have very little interest for you. Were I addressing Kantians I should not hesitate to devote the whole course to that matter, because for Kantians logical forms are of the very highest importance and everything rests on them; but as you probably care next to nothing for them, I am driven to another point of view from which to present the subject and this is the question what is the ground of scientific presumption and hypothesis. But this question is a transcendental one and I must treat it from the standpoint of transcendentalism and so I am forced back again to Kant and find myself unable to take a single step until I have defined somewhat the principles upon which his philosophy is founded.

It is specially necessary to have some understanding of the Transcendental Philosophy. Carlyle says:

Among a certain class of thinkers, does a frantic exaggeration in sentiment, a crude fever-dream in opinion, anywhere break forth, it is directly labeled as Kantism; and the moon-struck speculator is for the time silenced and put to shame by the epithet. For often, in such circles, Kant's Philosophy is not only an absurdity but a wickedness and a horror; the pious and peaceful sage of Königsberg passes for a sort of Necromancer and Blackartist in Metaphysics; his doctrine is a region of boundless baleful gloom, too cunningly broken here and there by splendors of unholy fire; spectres and tempting demons people it; and, hovering over fathomless abysses, hang gay and gorgeous aircastles into which the hapless traveller is seduced to enter, and so sinks to rise no more.

Such impressions as these have passed away forever. Kant is now acknowledged everywhere as the master of philosophy. The most opposite schools of thought appeal to him. But his preëminence has attracted a class of parasites, who live by tearing him to pieces. It is a fine thing now-a-days, to pick a flaw in the great *Critic's* reasoning. Every new man who wishes to vindicate his pretensions to philosophic power must display it by the discovery of an error in Kant. In this way he has come to be reputed the great erratic thinker. Ten men read his works to find where his mistake lies for one who is on the search for truth. Such, at least, is the inference to be drawn from the character of published criticisms of his works. Most of them prove conclusively that their authors neither had a distinct conception of Kant's meaning nor the faintest glimmer of insight into the sources of his power. The evidences of this are many. In the first place, the definitions usually given of Kantian terms are vague in the extreme. For instance, Kant applies to primary beliefs the terms *universal, necessary, pure, à priori, synthetic, conditions of experience, forms,* &c. Of course, all these expressions mean different things. Yet an eminent French writer, undertaking to define the Kantian *form* writes as follows:—"the particular, variable, accidental elements of cognition constitute its *matter;* and the general and fundamental element constitutes its *form.*" This is true enough as a statement of what objects the words are applied to, but it does not in the least tell what characters they refer to or what they mean. In the old metaphysics from which these words are borrowed *matter* is not necessarily an accident, far less synonymous with it, and *form* may be accidental as well as essential. The question therefore which arises and which any expositor of Kant is bound to answer is how he came to apply these words in this connection? In fact, exposition of the Kantian phrases will consist in the plainness with which the rationale of their transcendental acceptation is made out. Now I will read you the very words with which this Frenchman answers this question. "Kant in his passion for strictness and exactitude both of thought and of expression has marked the distinction between the accidental and fundamental elements by two bizarre but energetic words revived from the peripatetic and scholastic philosophies." Is not this beautiful? Kant has such a passion for exactitude that he uses words in wrong senses. Yet this is from a work of high reputation written by a popular idol. You may often catch one of these critics *guessing* that Kant thought one thing when he himself has said the direct contrary but they avoid attack on that score by saying that in fact Kant did not know what he meant. Sometimes an objection will be raised with the remark that it had never occurred to Kant when he has devoted pages to the consideration of it. An instance of this sort occurs in an essay on "The Philosophy of Space and Time" in a late number of the *North American Review*. The author says:

We draw or conceive a particular triangle for the sake of demonstrating that the sum of the three angles is equal to two right angles; having gone through a series of successive intuitions, we arrive at last at the demonstrated truth of the theorem *in this particular instance*. This is the utmost that experience will warrant us in concluding. But this conclusion is instantaneously and irresistibly extended to all possible triangles, although such an extension is objectively inadmissible without being fully accounted for.

He then shows that Kant's theory of *intuition* will not account for this extension; and concludes by observing that "In reality, Kant did not foresee this difficulty and makes no provision against it." Now let us see whether it is true that Kant did not foresee this difficulty in reality. Note this statement which I read from the *Critik der reinen Vernunft* (p. 125). "No image whatever could possibly be adequate to the conception of a triangle in general. For it would not attain the generality of a conception which is valid for all triangles right and oblique, but would be limited to one part of this sphere." There is the reviewer's difficulty. Hence Kant asks in almost the same words (p. 122): "How is the subsumption of an intuition under a conception possible? This natural and important question is the sole motive for investigating the transcendental doctrine of the Judgment." Accordingly he does inquire into the Judgment at length and 117 pages of octavo are devoted to the exposition of his results; a large part of which bears directly upon this question. It follows that in reality, Kant did foresee the difficulty and that, in reality the reviewer has overlooked one of the broadest features of Kantianism. You will find sometimes oracular personages; setting down some distinction of Kant's as a new-fangled absurdity when it is in fact a bequest of antiquity. In this way someone objects that there is no difference between Kant's categories of Realität and Daseyn or reality and actuality; as though Thomas Aquinas, who held that substantial forms did not exist *in actu*, was any the less a consistent *Realist*. I might instance many more cases of these absurdities and also of a critic's referring for Kant's opinion upon some point to a place where the subject is barely referred to and overlooking entirely the most remarkable passage bearing on it in his works, or quoting some sentence from Kant which he himself had noted in the same work as loose and misleading. Sometimes indeed no accurate acquaintance with the works of the great master is needed to detect the flippant and petty character of the strictures made upon his views. If a reviewer urges a gross inconsistency in Kantism either with itself or with obvious truth, but supports it only by alledging a sentence or two from the *Critic of the Pure Reason*, who cannot see that just as "no prophecy is of private interpretation" so here—whether the citations are garbled or not—the question is not whether the individual Kant be inconsistent but whether Transcendentalism his great bequest to the race be so or not? Again, if a writer is in the habit of speaking of Kant as a Don Quixote, a foolish head, a philosophic eunuch, an exquisitely fuddled adept, and of his philosophy as endless imbecility, desperate and maudled cant, dapper little pedantry, bewildered gabble, is it not plain that that man cannot understand the source of Kant's power? A philosopher cannot have been the power in the world that Kant has been and be a foolish head. Indeed we may say of him what he himself said of Hume.

The unlucky fate was in store for his metaphysics that none should understand it. It is impossible to see without a certain feeling of pain, how totally his adversaries Reid, Oswald, Beattie and finally Priestly also, missed the point of his problem; and how by taking for granted just what he doubted and again proving with vehemence and with great indecency too, what he never thought of doubting in sense, they so misconstrued his hint for improvement that everything remained in the old state as though nothing had happened.

The *Critic of the Pure Reason* has a two-fold object; first to show that such conceptions as cause *et cetera* are valid up to a certain point and second to show that they are not valid beyond that point. The constructive part is opposed to Hume and so to Compte and Mill, his modern followers; the destructive part is opposed to Wolff and all such metaphysicians as seek to prove or think they know the truth of doctrines of God, Freedom, and Immortality; which are according to Kant, part of man's *credo* not of his *scio*. It is this latter argument for which the great *Critic* is most celebrated. Thus De Quincey speaks of "The world-shattering Kant! He was the Gog and he was Magog of Hunnish desolation to the existing schemes of philosophy. He probed them; he showed the vanity of vanities which besieged their foundations; the rottenness below, the hollowness above." And it must be added that it was this anti-dogmatical feature of his philosophy, which Kant himself looked upon as likely to exert the most powerfully beneficial effect upon science. But whatever advantages were to accrue from this distinction of speculative and practical philosophy are by this time already enjoyed. Dogmatism hardly is heard of now among men of science. Nay an irrepressible conflict has sprung up between Science and Dogmatism under the name of Religion. But in these days, the doctrine of *Hume* has acquired a great ascendency; and if the destructive part of the *Critic* has done its work, the constructive part has doubled in importance and needfulness. Here is to be found the most powerful argument against positivism which has ever been produced,—and, as many think, an irrefragable one. Accordingly, no man can hold the position of a positivist with dignity who has not studied and digested and thoroughly mastered and carefully weighed this remarkable argument. Yet I should be at a loss to mention the positivist who has given evidence of having done this.

I need not say how a comparison between Kant and Compte in point of analytic power would turn out. The apostle of positivism is a man who considers logic as the last relic of theology and the calculus of probabilities as unfounded because its conclusions when intelligible are simply those of good sense. With Kant, on the contrary, Logic is not merely the method but the foundation of all metaphysics. The very divisions of his book correspond with those of logic. Like that, it has its stoicheiology and Methodology; and the great body of the work is entitled "Transcendental Logic." This again is separated into "Analytic" and "Dialectic" and the "Analytic" itself into the "Analytic of Concepts" and the "Analytic of Judgments."

It is only the constructive portion or proof of the validity and applicability of causality &c. for possible objects of sense which concerns us at all and this is all contained in the Transcendental Analytic with the Preliminary Treatise on Transcendental Esthetic and the Introduction.

The introduction to the book is devoted to establishing two logical distinctions; the first is between thought *à priori* and *à posteriori;* the second is between explicative and ampliative judgments.

The terms *à priori* and *à posteriori* in their ancient sense denote respectively reasoning from an antecedent to a consequent and from a consequent to an antecedent. Thus suppose we know that //an/every// incompetent general will meet with defeat. Then if we reason that because a given general is incompetent that he must meet with a defeat, we reason *à priori;* but if we reason that because a general is defeated he was a bad one, we reason *à posteriori.* Kant however uses these terms in another and derived sense. He did not entirely originate their modern use, for his contemporaries were already beginning to apply them in the same way, but he fixed their *meaning* in the new application and made them household words in subsequent philosophy. If one judges that a house falls down on the testimony of his eyesight then it is clear that he reasons *à posteriori* because he infers the fact from an effect of it on his eyes. If he judges that a house falls because he knows that the props have been removed he reasons *à priori;* yet not purely *à priori* for his premisses were obtained from experience. But if he infers it from axioms innate in the constitution of the mind, he may be said to reason purely *à priori.* All this had been said previously to Kant. I will now state how he modified the meaning of the terms while preserving this application of them. What is known from experience must be known *à posteriori,* because the thought is determined from without. To determine means to make a circumstance different from what it might have been otherwise. For example, a drop of rain falling on a stone determines it to be wet, provided the stone may have been dry before. But if the fact of a whole shower half an hour previous is given, then one drop does not determine the stone to be wet; for it would be wet, at any rate. Now //I say/, it is said,// that the results of experience are inferred *à posteriori*, for this reason that they are determined from without the mind by something not previously present to it; being so determined their determinants or //causes/reasons// are not present to the mind and of course could not be reasoned from. Hence a thought determined from without by something not in consciousness even implicity is inferred *à posteriori*. Kant, accordingly, uses the term *à posteriori* as meaning what is determined from without. The term *a priori* he uses to mean determined from within or involved implicitly in the whole of what is present to consciousness (or in a conception which is the logical condition of what is in consciousness). The twist given to the words is so slight that their application remains almost exactly the same. If there is any change it is this. A primary belief is *à priori* according to Kant; for it is determined from within. But it is not *inferred* at all and therefore neither of the terms is applicable in their ancient sense. And yet as an explicit judgment it is inferred and inferred *à priori*.

Is there any knowledge *à priori*? All our thought begins with experience, the mind furnishes no material for thought whatever. This is acknowledged by all the philosophers with whom we need concern ourselves at all. The mind only works over the materials furnished by sense; no dream is so strange but that all its elementary parts are reminiscences of appearance, the collocation of these alone are we capable of originating. In one sense, therefore, everything may be said to be inferred from experience; everything that we know, or think or guess or make up may be said to be inferred by some process valid or fallacious from the impressions of sense. But though everything in this loose sense is inferred from experience, yet everything does not require experience to be as it is in order to afford data for the inference. Give me the relations of *any* geometrical intuition you please and you give me the data for proving all the propositions of geometry. In other words, everything is not determined by experience. And this admits of proof. For suppose there may be universal and necessary judgements; as for example the moon must be made of green cheese. But there is no element of necessity in an impression of sense for necessity implies that things would be the same as they are were certain accidental circumstances different from what they are. I may here note that it is very common to misstate this point, as though the necessity here intended were a necessity of thinking. But it is not meant to say that what we feel compelled to think we are absolutely compelled to think, as this would imply; but that if we think a fact *must be* we cannot have observed that it *must be*. The principle is thus reduced to an analytical one. In the same way universality implies that the event would be the same were the things within certain limits different from what they are. Hence universal and necessary elements of experience are not determined from without. But are they, therefore, determined from within? Are they determined at all? Does not this very conception of determination imply causality and thus beg the whole question of causality at the outset? Not at all. The determination here meant is not real determination but logical determination. A cognition *à priori* is one which any experience contains reason for and therefore which no experience determines but which contains elements such as the mind introduces in working up the materials of sense, or rather as they are not new materials, they are the working up.

It is not to be supposed that Kant intends to say that the total content of consciousness at any one instant is either wholly *à priori* or wholly *à posteriori*. It is only abstracted elements thereof which are determined from within or from without. For example when Kant speaks of the pure intuition from within of space; he does not mean that that intuition can exist without also some empirical representations such as color being present. The word *pure* is used not to show that such representations are not present to the mind but to signify that the intuition intended is that from which these impurities have been eliminated by abstraction. I mention this, because the mistake, unaccountable as it is after Kant had expressly said that the mind only works up the raw material of sense, has not only been made but recently published.

Let us now pass to the second preliminary distinction set up by Kant. This is between analytic or explicatory and synthetic or amplificative judgments. An analytic judgment is one whose predicate is implied in its subject. As, all bodies are extended. This is an analytical judgment because *body* implies extension. If the subject not merely implies but expresses the predicate, as all red cows are red, an identical proposition arises; here no analysis is performed and no judgment is really made. A synthetic judgment is one whose subject does not imply its predicate; as all bodies are heavy. Kant says that the question of the *Critic* is How are synthetical judgments from within possible. The question of this whole course of lectures is how are synthetical judgments in general possible.

We must now undertake a preliminary study of the transcendental doctrine of esthetic or the inquiry into the objective validity of the representations of space and time. The term *objective validity* requires some explanation. Validity is legal tender. Greenbacks are not true cash but they will buy proportionally to cash because they are valid. In the same way colour is not true of objects because it is an affection of the mind and cannot be in matter but its modifications are true because they correspond to modifications of things. That therefore is valid whose modifications are true. A representation is subjectively valid which is consistent, whose modifications are true of a mere representation. A representation is objectively valid whose modifications are true of objects; or synthetically consistent.

With reference to the representations of space and time, we have two data. The first is that they are both necessary and universal. Whenever we think of an object as having geometric relations, that very predication of geometric relations for this object involves as its condition that all objects whatever have spatial relations to this one; for such is the nature of space; it is in this sense that the representation of space is said to be universal. In the same way if a mode of being is thought to have temporal relations, all such modes must be thought to have dates relatively to this one; and this is expressed by saying that the representation of time is universal. Again if an object has relations to any part of space, that is has any place, it has relations to every part of space and therefore could not have been so situated as not to have a spatial relation to its present place; in other words the representation of space is necessary. In the same way, if a mode of being has any temporal relations it has relations to all parts of time and could not have so existed as not to have a date relatively to its actual time; that is to say, the representation of time is necessary. So then the representations of time and space are universal and necessary. That is our first premiss.

The second premiss is that there is but *one* space and *one* time. If I say A is three and B is three, those two threes are different threes not parts of the same three. But if I say A is extended and B is extended; these two extensions are part of one and the same space. We may express this by saying that A and B contain their threeness but are contained in space.

These then are two data. From the first it follows that space and time are as representations determined from within. For to determine means to make anything otherwise than it might have been. But space and time are necessary, which means that they represent that bodies would have been in them however other circumstances had been. Again what is determined from without is given implicitly in the impressions of sense but space and time are universal that is relate to all bodies whether affecting our senses or not. This is perhaps clearer in a concrete example. Our memory of the time which has elapsed since the beginning of the lecture, does in itself involve time, in general. Hence is it, that we are perfectly sure that there was time before we remember and also that there will be time hereafter. We have certainly not felt this future time; yet this future time is inseparably involved with the supposition of any time; hence every representation of time is derived from within not from without. The same argument applies to space. And I might give a still more striking example of the same thing from the mode of apprehension of time and space; but I prefer to keep clear from all physio-psychological considerations and shall therefore postpone that to another occasion.

From the other premiss that there is but one time and one space we may infer that extension and protension differ altogether from class-concepts; such as the understanding produces. Take for instance *horse;* if this has any general totality it is one which is merely rendered possible by the separate cases of horses but it is not the several spaces and several times which render the universal space and time possible, but only the universal space and time which render the limited spaces and times possible.

Now there are but the fundamental faculties of the soul: Sensibility, Understanding, and Feeling. Feeling is not a faculty of knowledge, at all. Understanding produces only class-concepts. Hence space and time are products of Sensibility.

But we can carry our conclusions from our two data further than we have hitherto done by combining them with transcendental principles.

In the first place then since the representations of space and time are determined from within they cannot be said to represent properties of things; since a representation is determined by that which it represents. But at the same time this is very far from saying that space and time are illusory representations for their empirical modifications or determinations may represent things. Just, in the same way, color is not itself a representation of things and yet its modifications correspond to modifications of things. In fact, space and time if valid at all have an objective validity not possessed by color; for from given modifications of space and time other modifications may be inferred by means of the general representations of space and time, which inferred modifications are also true. But this is not the case with color. And whether the modifications of space and time are true of things-in-themselves or not, they are certainly true of things so far as they are related to us, that is to objects.

Finally from the other datum we may further infer that space and time are forms of intuition. The word *form* in its old sense was fully discussed in the last lecture. We saw that in so far as things are considered as determined by their own nature and circumstances, they are determined by *form* and *matter*. *Matter* is that which makes things exist. *Form* is that which makes them *as* they are. But in a transcendental inquiry all conception of cause must be eliminated. Accordingly Kant in his first essay on this subject, which was published 12 years before the *Critic*, uses matter and form for the effect of the material and formal causes. That which the world is (abstracted from how it is) is its elementary parts. How the world is (abstracted from its existence) is the coördination of those parts or their relation to each other as parts; potential or actual. Thus hardness is a potential relation of one part to those adjacent. But in the *Critic* he again modified the meaning of the terms. Instead of making the parts and coördination merely subjective he regards them as belonging to the immediate object of perception antecedent to thought, which he calls the appearance. This approximates to the original meaning again. For as originally *matter* and *form* were the real determinants or causes of the *that* and *how;* so with Kant they become the logical determinants or reasons of the *that* and *how.* The Matter is that in the appearance which corresponds to the impression upon the sense; for without sense no mental representation could exist. The Form is the condition of the possibility of the relations of the elementary parts of the representation. Now it is held that space and time are forms of intuition; meaning by intuition not the faculty of that name but its product. In other words they are what render possible the arrangement seen in our representations antecedently to active thought. We have already seen that they are antecedent to active thought, because they are not class-conceptions. We have seen also that they are units so that they cannot be part of the matter of appearance, for that resides in the parts; third they are not themselves appearance but the conditions of appearance, hence they are clearly the conditions *sine qua non* of the coördination of the parts.

To sum up and combine the two parts of the argument; to say that space and time are forms of intuition and are not properties of objects is as much as to say that they are merely the manner in which objects affect us; they are the products of those receptive faculties by which we are enabled to know the relations of the parts of objects with each other. But they are of such a nature that they enable us to infer relations which are not logically contained in any data of sense by means of their *formal* character. Hence, they are not only valid but objectively valid.

They do not hold good for things-in-themselves because they are introduced by the mind. But does it follow from that, that Kant's theory is opposed to common sense; by no means, for common sense has nothing to do with things-in-themselves. If you ask Kant are things-in-themselves in space and time? he will not reply Yes or No, but will repel the question as nonsensical for since all that we can know or think are objects relatively to thought—phenomena, therefore, not things-in-themselves—he holds that not only nothing can be said of the latter but that nothing can even be asked of them consistently.

We may occupy the remainder of the hour with the consideration of certain logical distinctions between different judgments, which play an important part in the main body of the *Critic*. None of these distinctions are original with Kant; he either copied them out of the logics of the day or revived them from older systems. He holds that judgments may be distinguished logically in four different ways according to their quantity, their quality, their relation, and their modality.

> In quantity, they may be either universal,
>   particular, or singular
> In quality, they may be either affirmative,
>   negative, or infinite
> In relation, they may be either categorical,
>   hypothetical, or disjunctive
> and   In modality, they may be either assertoric,
>   problematic, or apodictic.

All four of these divisions are objected to by modern logicians. No general accord has been come to on the subject but Sir William Hamilton for example would write them thus

Quantity of subject	universal or particular
Quantity of predicate	universal or particular
Quality	Affirmative or negative
Relation	Categorical, Hypothetical, Disjunctive, or Hypothetico-disjunctive

Modality does not belong to logic, according to him.

Kant's divisions of quantity and quality must certainly be given up. In the first place there is no logical distinction between universal judgments such as *all men are mortal* and singular judgments such as *George Washington was a great man.*

Kant himself admits this to a certain extent. He says:—

Logicians are justified in saying that, in the employment of judgments in syllogisms, singular judgments can be treated like those that are universal. For, since they have no extension at all, the predicate cannot relate to part only of that which is contained in the concept of the subject, and be excluded from the rest. The predicate is valid of that concept, without any such exception, just as if it were a general concept and had an extension to the whole of which the predicate applied. If, on the other hand, we compare a singular with a universal judgment, merely as knowledge, in respect of quantity, the singular stands to the universal as unity to infinity, and is therefore in itself essentially different from the universal. If, therefore, we estimate a singular judgment (*judicium singulare*), not only according to its own inner validity, but as knowledge in general, according to its quantity in comparison with other knowledge, it is certainly different from general judgments (*judicia communia*), and in a complete table of the moments of thought in general deserves a separate place—though not, indeed, in a logic limited to the use of judgments in references to each other. (p. 72)

There appears to be a confusion here between logical quantity and number. For 1st suppose this quantity here spoken of means number then there is no such distinction between Universal and Singular judgments. All the blackboards in this room coincide in point of number with this one. 2nd Suppose it be logical extension which is referred to. This kind of quantity has reference to the sub-classes a class can be broken up into. Thus All men are animals may be broken up into All mortal men are animals and All immortal men are animals or into All good men are animals and All bad men are animals. A particular subject cannot be so broken up; Some men are Negroes cannot be broken up into Some good men are Negroes and Some bad men are Negroes, for the logical *some* excludes *none* but Some men are Negroes does not exclude No good men are Negroes or No bad men are Negroes, only it excludes the supposition of both at once. Now let us take a singular proposition. George Washington is mortal may be broken up into Young George Washington is mortal and Old George Washington is mortal and therefore stands in the same predicament as a universal. Accordingly, Kant's remark on this point is unsound and it is generally considered so by logicians.

In respect to quality, Kant makes judgments either affirmative, negative, or infinite. An infinite judgment differs from a negative one by having the *not* applied to the predicate instead of to the copula thus

$$[\text{REPEAT.}] \begin{cases} \textit{homo non est quadrupes} \text{ is negative} \\ \textit{homo est non quadrupes} \text{ is infinite} \end{cases}$$

But such an infinite judgment has the sense of an affirmative and Kant is wrong in distinguishing them in logic. I will read his defence on this point, also. Before reading it I will remark that according to Hamilton the name *infinite* is merely a mistranslation of Aristotle's term ἀόριστος, indefinite. Kant says:—

> In like manner *infinite judgments* must, in transcendental logic, be distinguished from those that are *affirmative,* although in general logic they are rightly classed with them, and do not constitute a separate member of the division. General logic abstracts from all content of the predicate (even though it be negative); it enquires only whether the predicate be ascribed to the subject or opposed to it. But transcendental logic also considers what may be the worth or content of a logical affirmation that is thus made by means of a merely negative predicate, and what is thereby achieved in the way of addition to our total knowledge. (p. 72)

The answer to this is much the same as to the other passage. In point of number or in point of logical quantity, the predicate of an affirmative is exactly as infinite as that of an infinite judgment. By this argument one would suppose Kant were endeavoring to establish Thomson's and Spalding's division of Affirmatives, Negatives, and Substitutives, their substitutives being total affirmatives such as definitions where there is really a definite limitation of the sphere of the predicate. If Kant had been arguing for this, his argument would have proved more convincing than it has.

To the categorical, hypothetical, and disjunctive judgments, has been added a fourth the hypothetico-disjunctive. An example of this class would be "If an action be prohibited, it is prohibited either by natural or by positive law." But this may be fairly objected to; it should be recognized that grammatical forms and logical forms are entirely different. The grammatical form depends on the expression; the logical form depends on the sense. In another lecture, I shall argue this point in full; at present, I can only take it for granted. Now it is required to divide propositions into disjunct classes according to their relation. It will be obvious that, under this condition, and with the prolepsis I have just stated, that the following proposition

> If any man is good, he will go to heaven

though grammatically hypothetical is logically categorical for it means merely, All good men go to heaven. A hypothetical then must have a different subject for its antecedent and consequent.

Disjunctives in order to be a distinct class must be so understood that the different alternatives exclude each other; for the only possible difference between

> Either the earth or the moon is heavy

> If the earth is not heavy, the moon is heavy

is that the latter class does not exclude the case that both are heavy.

It might seem as though the disjunction might be put into either the subject or predicate. But this is not true.

Let me call your attention to the difference in the meaning of *or* in subject and predicate. Even the word *and* has a different effect in subject and predicate. For example, if I say

> This is eatable and This is a berry

or what is the same

> This is eatable and a berry

I place *this* in a smaller class than if I only say it is a *berry*. On the other hand if I say

> Berries are organized products and Eatables are organized products

or what is the same

Berries and eatables are organized products

the subject is a *larger* class than in Berries are organized products. Now if the effect of the word merely differed like this when in subject and predicate; I should not say that it has two senses and that only one is disjunctive. But in fact what do we find?

This person is either a man or woman

This is no more than to place the person in a class composed of the extensive sum of the classes men and women. It is therefore a mere categorical whose predicate is defined imperfectly by two differences instead of one. Now take a disjunction in the subject.

Either Northerners or Southerners are in the wrong

If *or* behaved like *and;* we should expect that the subject here would be some class smaller than either Northerners or Southerners. But this is not the case. The subject is no class at all; it is the whole of one of two classes. Here then is a form of assertion which cannot possibly be reduced to the Categorical or Hypothetical either and this I take to be a true type of Disjunctives.

We can now see that the so called hypothetico-disjunctives do not form a separate class at all. For take the judgment

If you are right, I am either mad or a fool

This is precisely the same as to say

If I am sane and sensible, you are wrong

Or take this case

If we contradict, either I or you are wrong

This is the same as

If I and you are right, we do not contradict.

Kant's momenta of Relation, therefore, seem to me to be correctly enumerated.

Finally, *modality* has been objected to *in toto* as having nothing to do with logic. This is an ill-considered objection. The premisses of a syllogism are assertoric, the conclusion is apodictic; of course logic must consider the difference between them. The difference between a possible, an actual, and a necessary fact has nothing whatever to do with logic. But an apodictic judgment is one which is taken on some ground considered to determine it. An assertoric judgment is one which is taken for granted. A problematic judgment is one which is considered as a concept and indeed is a concept rather than a judgment. No one can think of denying that *thus* defined these are logical distinctions.

Lecture VIII: Forms of Induction and Hypothesis

MS 105: April–May 1865

In the last lecture, we inquired into the definition of logic. All the progress that has been made in the subject by the moderns may be traced to their more perfect conception of its nature. And in large measure to abstraction of their attention from insignificant but often exceedingly perplexing questions which at once arise when logic is contaminated with anthropology and psychology. Kant's definition, which is the best yet given, is nearly freed from all such admixture. And perhaps the strongest point of Hegelianism is the purely impersonal character which it attributes to the unity of apperception. In this respect, I follow Hegel; but I do so without budging from the critical standpoint. Though I talk of forms as something independent of the mind, I only mean that the mind so conceives them and that that conception is valid. I thus say that all the qualities we know are determinations of the pure idea. But that we have any further knowledge of the idea or that this is to know it in itself I entirely deny.

The first distinction we found it necessary to draw—the first set of conceptions we have to signalize—forms a triad

Thing   Representation   Form.

Kant you remember distinguishes in all mental representations the matter and the form. The distinction here is slightly different. In the first place, I do not use the word *Representation* as a translation of the German *Vorstellung* which is the general term for any product of the cognitive power. Representation, indeed, is not a perfect translation of that term, because it seems necessarily to imply a mediate reference to its object, which *Vorstellung* does not. I however would limit the term neither to that which is mediate nor to that which is mental, but would use it in its broad, usual, and etymological sense for anything which is supposed to stand for another and which might express that other to a mind which truly could understand it. Thus our whole world—that which we can comprehend—is a world of representations. No one can deny that there are representations for every thought is one. But with *things* and *forms* scepticism, though still unfounded, is at first possible. The *thing* is that for which a representation might stand prescinded from all that would constitute a relation with any representation. The *form* is the respect in which a representation might stand for a thing, prescinded from both thing and representation. We thus see that *things* and *forms* stand very differently with us from *representations*. Not in being prescinded elements for representations also are prescinded from other representations. But because we know representations absolutely, while we only know *forms* and *things* through representations. Thus scepticism is possible concerning *them*. But for the very reason that they are known only relatively and therefore do not belong to our world; the hypothesis of *things* and *forms* introduces nothing false. For truth and falsity only apply to an object as far as it can be known. If indeed we could know things and forms in themselves, then perhaps our representations of them might contradict this knowledge. But since all that we know of them we know through representations, if our representations be consistent they have all the truth that the case admits of.

We found representations to be of three kinds

Signs   Copies   Symbols.

By a *copy*, I mean a representation whose agreement with its object depends merely upon a sameness of predicates. By a *sign*, I mean a representation whose reference to its object is fixed by convention. By a symbol I mean one which upon being presented to the mind—without any resemblance to its object and without any reference to a previous convention—calls up a concept. I consider concepts, themselves, as a species of symbols.

A symbol is subject to three conditions. 1st it must represent an object or informed and representable thing. Second it must be a manifestation of a *logos,* or represented and realizable form. Third it must be translatable into another language or system of symbols.

The science of the general laws of relations of symbols to logoi is general grammar. The science of the general laws of their relations to objects is logic. And the science of the general laws of their relations to other systems of symbols is general rhetoric.

To give a new conception of a science is necessarily to alter its limits, but as a hundred different conceptions of it have already been given a new one may be excused provided it offers any special advantages. Now logic in its present state contains a mixture of various inquiries; most of these are of a purely formal character and admit of absolutely certain answers, but others are of a psychological character and the answers given are but little better than guess-work. The definition now offered will leave all those of the former class and weed out the others entirely so as to reduce the whole science to mathematical exactitude.

We come now to the question of scientific inferences. And here we have two things to do. First we require to class scientific inferences, to show their precise relation to the syllogism and if they are of different kinds, their relation also to each other. Second, we have to inquire upon what principles do these inferences rest and how are these principles shown to be valid. The question of classification must come first and is to form the subject of the present lecture.

I must begin by recalling to your minds the *precise* definitions of some logical terms denoting different parts of the syllogism. And I must give some new terms also.

> No men are stones
> Some animals are men
> ∴ Some animals are not stones

The symbol of a class is called a *term.* Thus here there are three terms: *men, stones,* and *animals.* The symbol of the least extensive or narrowest class of the three spoken of in a syllogism is called the *minor extreme.* In the present case *animals* is the *minor extreme;* for though *animals* is *in fact* a wider class than *men,* yet the inference is only valid so far as *some animals* are contained under *men.* The symbol of the widest class is called the *major extreme;* thus here *stones* is the major extreme for though in fact it is not by itself so wide as *animals* yet the syllogism only holds by *men* being contained under *not stones.* The term intermediate in extension here *men,* is called the *middle term.* In every syllogism there is one term which is the subject of two propositions, one which is predicate of two, and one which is predicate of one and subject of another. I will distinguish these as the twice-subject, the twice-predicate, and the subject-predicate. In the present case *animals* is twice-subject. *Stones* is twice-predicate and *man* is subject-predicate. The term which forms the subject of the inferred proposition I will call the *final subject,* the term which forms its predicate the *final predicate,* and the term which does not appear in the inferred proposition, I will call the *eliminated term.* Of the propositions: those two which are given are called the *premisses;* of these that which contains the final predicate is called the *thesis* and that which contains the final subject the *condition;* the proposition which is inferred is called the conclusion. The proposition which contains the major extreme and middle term is called the major proposition; the proposition which contains the middle term and minor extreme is called the minor proposition. The proposition which contains both extremes I will call the *colligant* or *syllogizing* proposition. The proposition which contains the twice-subject and predicate-subject may be called the *subjecting proposition;* that which contains the twice-predicate and predicate-subject may be called the *predicating proposition* and that one which contains the twice-subject and twice-predicate the *copulating proposition.*

Syllogisms are of three figures. In order to understand this you should first observe that a syllogism has reference to the result of a subsumption under a rule. Hence one of its three propositions affirms or denies a rule. Another affirms or denies a subsumption under the rule. And the third affirms or denies a result of such subsumption. Now if the conclusion of the syllogism contains the *result,* the syllogism is of the 1st Figure. If the conclusion contains the *subsumption* the syllogism is of the 2nd figure. And if the conclusion contains the *rule* the syllogism is of the 3rd figure. In order that this conclusion should follow necessarily, the *result* must be affirmed if it is concluded and otherwise be denied; while the rule and the antecedent respectively must be denied when they are in the conclusion and otherwise affirmed. Hence we have (denoting affirmation by + and negation by −)

1st Figure		2nd Figure		3rd Figure	
Rule	+	Rule	+	Result	−
Subsumption	+	Result	−	Subsumption	+
Result	+	Subsumption	−	Rule	−

The predicate of the subsumption is the subject of the rule. The predicate of the result is the predicate of the rule, and the subject of the result is the subject of the subsumption. Hence denoting the Rule by AB, A being the subject and B the predicate, and denoting the subject of the subsumption by L we have

1st Fig.	2nd Fig.	3rd Fig.
AB	AB	LB
LA	LB	LA
LB	LA	AB

Every rule is universal and no subsumption can be negative. The result has the quantity of the subsumption and the quality of the rule. Hence, if we take the following system of propositions

A   Universal Affirmative
E   Universal Negative
I   Particular Affirmative
O   Particular Negative

we shall have the moods represented in the following table

1st Fig.   2nd Fig.   3rd Fig.

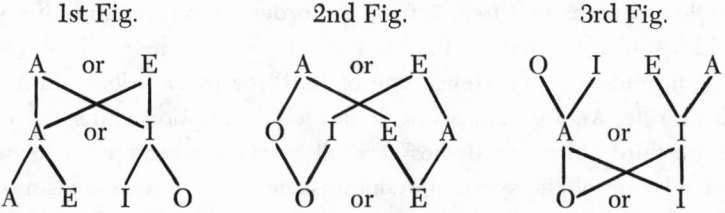

There are two moods usually assigned to the third figure called *Darapti* and *Felapton,* which the rules I have just given permit but which I have not given in the figure. The reason is that I do not regard these inferences as being syllogisms at all, although from their data the premisses of a syllogism can at once be inferred.
Thus

All men are mortals

and   All men are animals

are the data of *Darapti*, if from either of these universals we immediately infer a particular we shall have the premisses of a syllogism of the third figure.

A fourth figure has been proposed, the type of which is given here

Fig. 4

XY

YZ

ZX

I reject this figure and all its moods not as being invalid but as being indirect, and unsyllogistic. It will be replied to me that many moods that I have admitted are indirect. But the only indirectness which I recognize is this. We set out to analyze inferences. We find them of various kinds with two, three, four, or more premisse[s.] All these inferences are equally direct and simple in themselves; but all are not equally intelligible. Hence, we reduce the hard ones to compounds of easy ones. The easy ones are so because they have direct reference to well-established conceptions; the hard ones are so because their reference to such conceptions is indirect. Whether therefore an inference be direct or indirect depends entirely upon the primary conceptions adopted. I have adopted as my primary conceptions those of the relations of a *rule, subsumption,* and *result;* hence the first three figures are with me direct the fourth indirect because its moods can only be reduced to these conceptions by means of immediate inferences.

The premisses of all or almost all the moods of the second and third figures will give by immediate inference the premisses of a syllogism of the first figure whose conclusion is the same as that of the first syllogism. This is called reduction of syllogisms. The principles of it which are two may be formulated thus: 1st The denial of a result stands in the same relation, under the converse of a rule, to the denial of the subsumption, that the subsumption does under the rule itself to the result and 2nd that the converse of the subsumption stands in this same relation also to the denial of the rule under the denial of the result.

The same principles are the principles of the two kinds of *reductio ad absurdum.* Thus take the example

No men are black
Some Negroes are men
Some Negroes are not black

We may say the result is false; therefore since

and   Nothing black is man
       All Negroes are black
       No Negroes are men

Or we may say the result is false, therefore

       All Negroes are black
But as   Some men are Negroes
∴ Some men are black

We thus see that

Rule +	Rule +	Result −
• •	• •	• •
Subsumption + ∴	∴ Result −	∴ Subsumption +
• •	• •	• •
Result +	Subsumption −	Rule −

We are now prepared to consider the forms of induction. The example upon this diagram is given by Aristotle.

Man, horse, and mule are long-lived
Man, horse, and mule are without gall
∴ Every animal without gall is long-lived

This you perceive is truly an induction because it gathers particulars under a general principle. The first two propositions are its premisses. The third is its conclusion. But the conclusion does not follow necessarily from the other two. There is however a conclusion which follows from the other two as appears in the left-hand form, for it follows from

and   Every animal without gall is long-lived
that   Man, horse, mule are animals without gall
       ∴ Man, horse, mule are long-lived.

From this it appears that an induction is a syllogism of which the major proposition forms the conclusion.

To show that this is Aristotle's doctrine, I read the following passage from the *Prior Analytics*.

"Induction (he says) and the syllogism from induction is the conclusion of one extreme as a predicate to the middle term by arguing from the other extreme." This you perceive is the case in the example *long-lived* which is the widest class or major extreme, has been inferred of *animals without gall* which is the middle term, by argument from *man horse mule* which is the narrowest class or minor extreme. I must remark that Aristotle denotes the major extreme by A, the middle term by B, and the minor extreme by C. Here he continues "Let A be long-lived, B without gall and C everything long-lived as man horse mule." He does not state what inference he intends to draw but as he uses the same argument materially in another place, there can be no mistake about it. He next adverts to the right-hand arrangement and says "A then belongs to the whole of C; for everything without gall is long-lived [major premiss] but B also, or what is without gall inheres in the whole of C [minor premiss.]" Finally he undertakes to state the condition of the validity of the inductive inference thus: "Now if C and B reciprocate and each is all the other, it follows necessarily that A inheres in all B. But we *must* regard C as made up of all the individuals; for induction has its inference from all."

That induction is only through complete enumeration; or, at least, that there is such an induction, is the doctrine of all logicians. I object to it *in toto*, nevertheless. Aristotle evidently supposes that a general term is equal to a sum of singulars and that we can say this man, that man, that man, and that man are all men. But the extension of a universal term consists in the total of all *possible* things to which it is applicable and not merely of those which are found to occur. Thus all men means strictly man in general. And even supposing all men now in existence were enumerated, how could I enumerate all the men who have been, far less the men who are to be? No matter how limited the expression may be, if it has definite generality it is incapable of enumeration. 'All the words on this page' for instance, does not mean all that are here according to any one inspection or plural of inspections. If this *were* the meaning it would have no generality. But it is not; what is meant is all the words there at any possible inspection within certain limits of time; and this total of possibles is not capable of enumeration. When we count the words, we infer inductively that our one or several countings represent all countings; hence to explain induction by enumeration is only explaining one induction by another.

The error of making generals composed of singulars was long ago noticed; and though individuals are still sometimes called *infimæ species*, it is customary now to speak of the enumeration of the particulars instead of the enumeration of the singulars composing a whole of extension. This enumeration of particulars amounts to the division of a logical genus into its species. It must be accomplished either 1st by scientific inference, or 2nd by the implication of the species themselves. Neither of these however will answer to account for the premiss of the formula of induction. For as to enumeration by a scientific or material inference; this bare supposition cannot account for induction the whole difficulty of which consists in its being such an inference. Division of a genus by the implication of the species leads to a sort of syllogism which has been called induction but there is really no more enumeration about it than there is in a dilemma which is a reasoning of the same character. Enumeration supposes that its terms are taken into account successively one by one from first to last; whereas in dilemma and the false induction when all but one have been represented the last one is already implicitly represented or the reasoning does not hold good. Dilemma has never been supposed to explain true induction; why then should this so-called complete induction which is merely a categorical dilemma? This complete datum of induction, which has been taken for granted, is not among logical possibilities although there is something entirely different which seems to have borrowed the same name.

We are here led to a fundamental proposition; namely, that the problem how we can make a scientific or material inference is one and the same with the problem how we can make any universal statement, with reason; for there is no way left in which such a statement can originate except from scientific inference or pure fiction. Hereby we strike down at once all such attempts at solving the problem as involve the supposition of a major premiss as a datum. Such explanations merely show that we can arrive at one universal statement by deduction from another, while they leave the real question, untouched. The peculiar merit of Aristotle's theory consists in this, that after the objectionable portion of it is swept away and after it is thus left utterly powerless to account for any certainty or even the smallest excess of probability in favor of the inference from induction, it still presents these *forms* which show what the *actual relation of the process to deduction is*.

What has been the process in Aristotle's example? We first selected a number of objects upon the principle that all were animals without gall. This is expressed by the minor proposition 'Man horse mule are without gall'. Upon examining these objects we light upon a most remarkable fact namely that they are all of them long-lived. That of a number of animals not selected in reference to this point all should be long-lived is so improbable, that when it is found to occur it demands an explanation; that is to say it demands the existence of some less improbable fact from which it should follow. Now we know that a universal predicate of any experience must be involved in the conditions of that experience; and as we know of but one condition of this particular experience namely the principle of our selection, we take it for granted that this universal predicate is a result of that. Now that "all animals without gall should be long-lived" is not improbable. Hence as we must believe that man horse mule are long-lived because it is a fact, as this is a great marvel in itself, we must believe in a great marvel unless we adopt the belief that "all animals without gall are long-lived"—in which case we believe in no marvel although we have been forced to assume something without apodictic warrant (to avoid a marvel) and have therefore assumed the only proposition we knew of which would answer the purpose.

This being the proper form of induction in the syllogistic system, it is clear that Aristotle has left a great gap in his account of the matter. For according to this form an induction is clearly nothing more than a syllogism in which the major proposition is the conclusion. But Aristotle says that it is a syllogism in the conclusion of which the major extreme is predicated of the middle term; now in the second figure the major extreme is not predicated of the middle term at all. It is clear therefore that Aristotle conceives of no other induction than that which is derived from the major premiss of the first figure. Now there is only one kind of induction which can be thrown into this form; and this is no other than induction by *simple enumeration*. Bacon therefore was right when he said that Aristotle gave the rules for this form only.

Let us now put a Baconian induction into form. Suppose the problem be to investigate the characters of cloven-hoofed animals. We first form a Table of Existence and Presence.

Table of Existence and Presence

1 Neat
2 Swine
3 Sheep
4 Deer

We find that all these are herbivora. From this we draw the induction exhibited here

All cloven-hoofed are herbivora
Neat &c. are cloven-hoofed
Neat &c. are herbivora

Having thus examined all the cloven-hoofed we can in order to confirm ourselves, we form a

Table of Declination

1 Rats are not herbivora
2 Dogs ”   ”   ”
3 Apes ”   ”   ”

We find that none of these are cloven-hoofed. This finds a ready explanation on the principle that All cloven-hoofed are herbivora. Thus we have an induction derived from the second figure of deductive syllogism; thus

All cloven-hoofed are herbivora
No rats, dogs, apes are herbivora
∴ No rats, dogs, apes are cloven-hoofed.

The only further confirmation we can have is an indirect one. We may proceed to make a

Table of Comparison

1 Some cloven-hoofed are ruminants

Now we may be able to ascertain that some ruminants are herbivora without knowing whether they are cloven-hoofed ruminants or not but even that is a confirmation; thus

All cloven-hoofed animals are herbivora
Some   ”   ”   are ruminants
Some ruminants are herbivora

which is an induction in the third figure.

Hypothesis is to be explained in a similar manner to induction. Hypothesis is quite a different thing from induction and is usually so considered although I have not found any definition given of it which brings out the difference distinctly. But it will be acknowledged that a hypothesis is a categorical assertion of something we have not experienced. Now in an induction there is nothing of this sort. We infer that because *neat swine sheep and deer* are herbivora that *all* cloven-hoofed animals are so. But for all there is in the *induction* to the contrary *neat swine sheep and deer* may be all the cloven-hoofed animals that are possible. There is therefore no categorical assertion of what has not come under our observation in induction. In the case of induction the predicate is known to be true of something not of the subject. In hypothesis *something* must have been known of the subject but not what is predicated. Hypothesis is in fact the inference of a minor proposition as in the following examples respecting light.

We find that light gives certain peculiar fringes. Required an explanation of the fact. We reflect that ether waves would give the same fringes. We have therefore only to suppose that light is ether waves and the marvel is explained.

Pursuing our researches we find that Light is not retarded in a denser medium. How is this explained? Why nothing retarded in a denser medium can be ether-waves. Hence we have only to suppose again that light is ether-waves.

But mathematics shows that Ether waves under some circumstances give effects of conical polarization. How does our theory get over this circumstance. It does it by simply trying whether light ever gives the same effects. As it does; the theory is confirmed.

We have then three different kinds of inference. Deduction or inference *à priori*, Induction or inference *à particularis*, and Hypothesis or inference *a posteriori*. It is necessary now to examine this classification critically.

And first let me specify what I claim for my invention. I do not claim that it is a natural classification, in the sense of being right while all others are wrong. I do not know that such a thing as a natural classification is possible in the nature of the case. The science which most resembles logic is mathematics. Now among mathematical forms there does not seem to be any natural classification. It is true that in the solutions of quadratic equations, there are generally two solutions from the positive and negative values of the root with an impossible gulf between them. But this classing is owing to the forms being restricted by the conditions of the problem; and I believe that all natural classes arise from some problem—something which was to be accomplished and which could be accomplished only in certain ways. Required to make a musical instrument; you must set either a plate or a string in vibration. Required to make an animal; it must be either a vertebrate, an articulate, a mollusk, or a radiate. However this may be, in Geometry we find ourselves free to make several different classifications of curves, either of which shall be equally good. In fact, in order to make any classification of them whatever we must introduce the purely arbitrary element of a system of coördinates or something of the kind which constitutes the point of view from which we regard the curves and which determines their classification completely. Now it may be said that one system of coördinates is more *natural* than another; and it is obvious that the conditions of binocular vision limit us in our use of our eyes to the use of particular coördinates. But this fact that one such system is more natural to us has clearly nothing to do with pure mathematics but is merely introducing a problem; given two eyes, required to form geometrical judgements, how can we do it? In the same way, I conceive that the syllogism is nothing but the system of coördinates or method of analysis which we adopt in logic. There is no reason why arguments should not be analyzed just as correctly in some other way. It is a great mistake to suppose that arguments as they are thought are often syllogisms, but even if this were the case it would have no bearing upon pure logic as a formal science. It is the principal business of the logician to analyze arguments into their elements just as it is part of the business of the geometer to analyze curves; but the one is no more bound to follow the natural process of the intellect in his analysis, than the other is bound to follow the natural process of perception. I mean to say, then, that every argument may be formally considered as a combination of syllogisms the rules of which shall fully determine the weight of that argument; provided that the major premiss, the minor premiss, or the conclusion be regarded as containing the inference. And I further say, that in every syllogism it is a certain one of these propositions which contains the inference; and not either of the others.

The first point, then, is to show that every argument may be resolved into *à priori, à posteriori,* and inductive elements. The second point will be to show that these three classes do not run into each other.

And first in reference to immediate inferences. Of deductive immediate inferences there are three kinds; namely,

1st   Simple Conversion
2nd   Inference from a universal to a particular
3rd   Inference from *A est* non-*B* to *A non est B*.

Of other immediate inferences there are only two kinds

1st   From a particular to a Universal

This evidently corresponds to Induction.

Some *A* is *B* is our premiss
All *A* is *B* is our conclusion

Here *B* is obviously the major term, All *A* the middle, and Some *A* the minor. Our conclusion therefore contains the major and middle and is a major proposition.

The other kind of immediate inference not deductive is from

A non est B   Premiss
A est non-*B*   Conclusion

In this case *A* is the minor extreme. Which is the major? The conclusion implies the premiss. Hence the comprehension of the predicate of the latter is less and its extension is greater. *B* therefore is the major and non-*B* the middle. We have then inferred a minor proposition and have consequently made a hypothesis.

Immediate inferences then can all be reduced to one of our three kinds of reasoning. If an argument involves more than two propositions as premisses, it may always be resolved into elements which have only two or one. We have only then to inquire whether all arguments from two premisses can be thrown into one of these forms, with or without the aid of an immediate inference. Every couple of premisses must either have a common term or must be reducible by immediate inference to such as have. Thus the two premisses

No *A* is non-*B*
No *B* is *C*

have no middle term although we may conclude from them that

No *A* is *C*

But the first premiss gives by immediate inference

All *A* is *B* or No *A* is

or   All *A* is *B* or No *A* is *C*

whence as   No *B* is *C*

No *A* is *C*

Every couple of premisses which has a common term belongs to one of the three figures of syllogism. The question is therefore whether all possible inferences in the three figures of syllogism can be thrown into these forms. Now these three tables represent all the direct inferences which can be drawn in either figure. The deductive syllogisms are in yellow, the inductive are in red, and the hypothetic are in blue. The rule is entered at the top (in the middle if asserted, at the sides if denied), the subsumption is entered at the side (in the middle if asserted, at the outside if denied), the result is found in the middle. To make the construction a little more intelligible, I will run over the Deductive moods pointing to the major premiss, minor premiss, and conclusion as I name each one.

Barbara &c.

Now as the whole table is filled up except the corners, which would be filled up also were indirect inferences admitted, it is clear that these forms admit inferences from every possible set of premisses and therefore every possible inference can be thrown into these forms, and there are no inferences except Deductions, Inductions, and Hypotheses, or such as are reducible to combinations of these.

We come now to the second question whether these classes do not run into each other. This is in reality answered by the tables now before us, for all the inferences of each kind are here displayed and upon no square are there letters of two colors.

It is true that a complex inference can generally be analyzed differently into elements of different logical character. Thus take the argument

The earth is a planet

Venus is a planet

The earth is inhabited

∴ Venus is inhabited

This may be reduced either to an induction and deduction or to a hypothesis and deduction; thus, I may say &c. [Tables of Venus.]

Again a simple induction or hypothesis can often *but not always* be reduced to a compound of the other two kinds of inference. Thus I may infer *à particularis* or inductively that

No carnivora are cloven-footed

because   Neat &c.

But I may also arrive at the same conclusion from the same premisses in another way. For from the fact that No neat swine sheep or deer are carnivora, I may infer deductively that No carnivora are neat swine sheep or deer. And then as Neat &c. are cloven-footed I may infer that no carnivora are cloven-footed hypothetically. This therefore is a case where a compound of deduction and hypothesis is equivalent to induction. It is like three perpendicular quadrants on a sphere. Their directions are as unlike as they can be and yet two of them reach together the same point as the third. This fact therefore is no argument that these classes of inference overlap each other. Nor I may add can any one of them be dispensed with and its place supplied by the others. When induction and hypothesis are looked upon in the proper point of view they are the very opposites of each other. Induction is an increase of the extension of a subject. Hypothesis is the increase of the comprehension of a predicate. Thus the law which induction discovers is a *prohibition;* while that which hypothesis discovers is an *imposition.* The following examples illustrate this

[*Juppiter*]

The induction restricts *Juppiter* to the ellipse, without opposing his being on a part of it merely. The hypothesis extends his motion over the ellipse without opposing his taking some additional flight.

The next lecture will treat of the DOMAIN OF LOGIC.

Lecture X: Grounds of Induction

MS 106: April–May 1865

We are already familiar with the distinction between the extension and comprehension of terms. A term has comprehension in virtue of having a meaning and has extension in virtue of being applicable to objects. The meaning of a term is called its *connotation;* its applicability to things its *denotation*. Every symbol *denotes* by *connoting*. A representation which *denotes* without connoting is a mere *sign*. If it *connotes* without thereby *denoting*, it is a mere copy. It is universally held that extension and comprehension are in reciprocal relation; thus if *horse* be divided into *black horse* and *non-black horse*, *black horse* has more intension and therefore less extension than *horse*.

It behooves me to say what the distinction between extension and comprehension is upon my view of logic. Before doing so, however, I must remark that the distinction extends to propositions; there are extensive and intensive propositions. An extensive proposition is defined to be one which states the relation between the extension of two terms. An intensive proposition is one which states the relation between the intension or comprehension of two terms. Subordination in extension is expressed by the term *contained under*. Subordination in intension is expressed by the term *contained in*. Hence in the case of affirmatives; an extensive judgment is expressed by the formula

A is contained under B

an equivalent intensive proposition by the formula

B is contained in A.

Thus black horse is contained under horse and horse [. . .]
What we have to distinguish, therefore, is not so much the quantity of

extension from the quantity of intension as it is the object of connotation from the object of denotation. In analytical judgments there is no denotation at all. In a synthetical judgment the subject is an object of denotation.

Analytic	Subject—O of C. Predicate—O of C	2nd Fig.	XY ZY
Synthetic Intensive	Subject O of D Predicate O of C	1st Fig.	YX ZY
Extensive	Subject O of D Predicate O of D	3rd Fig.	YX ZX

There cannot be a judgment whose subject is an object of connotation and whose predicate is an object of denotation. For a symbol *denotes* by virtue of *connoting* and not *vice versa,* hence the object of connotation determines the object of denotation and not *vice versa,* in the sense in which the subject of a proposition is the term determined and the predicate is the determining term. Whence if one of the terms is an object of connotation and the other an object of denotation, the latter is the subject and not the former.

In the other two cases, there is no difference between subject and predicate; except that one may be regarded as taken first.

Thus these cases in which both terms are of the same kind are two kinds of twists of the first kind, just as the 2nd and 3rd Figures of Syllogism are right-handed and left-handed twists of the 1st. This is expressed in the above table.

A Proposition would usually be called intensive if its predicate were an object of connotation; hence we have three kinds of propositions given by these two; namely,

> Analytic.
> Synthetic Intensive.
> Extensive.

There is no such thing as an analytic extensive proposition. For an analytic proposition containing no object of denotation is merely the expression of a relation of comprehension. Of course from an analytic proposition a synthetic one may be immediately inferred. From

> Man is mortal

we may infer

All men are mortals

but the predicate *mortals* is not a mere result of the analysis of *men*. I have here slightly narrowed Kant's definition of the analytic judgment so as to make it not merely needless but impossible to test one by experience.

We come now to an objection to the division of propositions which I have just given which will require us to examine the matter somewhat more deeply. It may be said: the copula in all cases establishes an identity between two terms. Hence as in one of the propositions the object of denotation is the subject and the object of connotation the predicate, these two objects are identical and hence the division into three kinds is a distinction without a difference.

In order to answer this objection we must revert to that distinction between *thing, image,* and *form* established in the lecture upon the definition of logic. A representation is anything which may be regarded as standing for something else. Matter or thing is that for which a representation might stand prescinded from all that could constitute a relation with any representation. A form is the relation between a representation and thing prescinded from both representation and thing. An image is a representation prescinded from thing and form.

Derived directly from this abstractest triad was another less abstract. This is Object–Equivalent Representation–Logos. The *object* is a thing corresponding to a representation regarded as actual. The equivalent representation is a representation in any language equivalent to a representation regarded as actual. A Logos is a form constituting the relation between an object and a representation regarded as actual.

Every symbol may be said in three different senses to be determined by its *object,* its *equivalent representation,* and its *logos.* It stands for its *object,* it translates its *equivalent representation,* it realizes its logos.

As every symbol is determined in these three ways, Symbols, as such, are subject to three laws one of which is the *conditio sine qua non* of its standing for anything, the second of its translating anything, and the third of its realizing anything. The first law is Logic, the second Universal Rhetoric, the third Universal Grammar.

But an object is a thing informed and represented. An equivalent representation is an image which is itself represented and realized and a logos is a form, embodied in an object and representation.

Hence the object of a symbol implies in itself both thing, form, and image. And hence regarded as containing one or other of these three elements it may be distinguished as *material object, formal object,* and *representative object.* Now so far as the object of a symbol contains the *thing,* so far the symbol stands for something and so far it denotes. So far as its object embodies a form, so far the symbol has a meaning and so far it connotes. Thus we see that the *denotative object* and the *connotative object* are in fact identical; and therefore an analytic, an intensive synthetic, and an extensive proposition may all represent the same fact and yet the mode in which they are obtained and the relation of the proposition to that fact are necessarily very different.

But since the object contains three elements thing, image, form, we ought to have another kind of object besides the denotative and connotative. What is this?

If we suppose ourselves to know no more of man than what is contained in the definition Man is the rational animal, then we might divide man into *man risible* and *man non-risible.*

man

man risible   man non-risible

And then the connotation of man would be less than that of either *man risible* or *man non-risible.* And conversely *man risible* and *man non-risible* would have a less extension than *man.* But we afterwards find that the class *man non-risible* does not exist and is impossible. Henceforward the idea of man and that of risible man are changed. The *extension* of risible man has become equal to that of *men* and the comprehension of *man* has become equal to that of *risible man.* And how has this change in the relations of the terms been effected? Before the information we knew (let us say) that there were certain risible men whom we may denote by A and there were other men who might or might not be risible whom we will denote by BB'. We have now found that BB' are also risible. When we said all men before we meant A + B + B'; when we say all men now we mean the same. The extension of *man* then has not changed. When we said risible men before we denoted A + B? that is to say the whole of A but none of B for certain;

but now when we say risible men we denote $A + B + B'$. Hence the extension of risible men has *increased,* so as to become equal to that of *men.* On the other hand the intension of *risible man* is now as it was before composed of *risible, rational,* and *animal;* while the comprehension of *man* which before contained only *rational* and *animal,* now contains *risible* also.

Thus the process of information disturbs the relations of extension and comprehension for a moment and the class which results from the equivalence of two others has a greater intension than one and a greater extension than the other. Hence, we may conveniently alter the formula for the relations of extension and comprehension; thus, instead of saying that one is the reciprocal of the other or

$$\text{comprehension} \times \text{extension} = \text{constant}$$

we may say

$$\text{comprehension} \times \text{extension} = \text{information.}$$

We see then that all symbols besides their denotative and connotative objects have another; their informative object. The denotative object is the total of possible things denoted. The connotative object is the total of symbols translated or implied. The informative object is the total of forms manifested and is measured by the amount of intension the term has, over and above what is necessary for limiting its extension. For example the denotative object of *man* is such collections of matter the word knows while it knows them i.e. while they are organized. The connotative object of *man* is the total form which the word expresses. The informative object of man is the total fact which it embodies; or the value of the conception which is its equivalent symbol.

Abstract words such as *truth, honor,* by the way, are somewhat difficult to understand. It seems to me that they are simply fictions. Every word must denote some *thing;* these are names for certain fictitious things which are supposed for the purpose of indicating that the object of a concrete term is meant as it would be did it contain either no information or a certain amount of information. Thus "charity is a virtue," means "What is charitable is virtuous—by the definition of charity and not by reason of what is known about it." Hence, only analytical propositions are possible of abstract terms; and on this account they are peculiarly useful in metaphysics where the question is what can we know without any information.

Coming back now to propositions, we should first remark that just as the framing of a term is a process of symbolization so also is the framing of a proposition. No proposition is supposed to leave its terms as it finds them. Some symbol is determined by every proposition. Hence, since symbols are determined by their objects; and there are three objects of symbols the connotative, denotative, informative; it follows that there will be three kinds of propositions, such as alter the denotation, the information, and the connotation of their terms respectively. But when information is determined both connotation and information are determined; hence the three kinds will be 1st Such as determine connotation, 2nd Such as determine denotation, 3rd Such as determine both denotation and connotation.

The subject of a proposition is usually said to be that term which is determined; but that this is an entirely inadequate definition is apparent from the circumstance that in every proposition which affords any positive information both terms are determined. Thus if I say No Britons are slaves, I hereby make non-slave to be an additional mark of Britons and also exclude slaves from those objects which are Britons. I would therefore limit the definition thus. The subject is the term which is determined by the proposition, if at all, in connotation. The predicate is the term which is determined by the proposition if at all in denotation.

Applying these definitions to our three classes of propositions we have

      1 Propositions determining only the subject
      2 Propositions   ”   ” ” predicate
      3   ”   ”   subject and predicate.

But we can now see that the connotative object cannot be subject nor the denotative predicate because a connotative term cannot determine another in denotation nor a denotative term another in connotation. In the analytical proposition *Logic is science* the idea conveyed is that the conception or translation of *logic* embodies the *form* of science. Here *logic* is immediately determined as to connotation and science is *mediately* determined in denotation.

If one of the terms of a proposition is an object of connotation and the other an object of denotation, it has already been seen that the former must be the predicate and the latter the subject. In this case the subject is determined in connotation and the predicate in denotation by the proposition, both immediately. Thus if I say unripe fruit is green, unripe fruit is determined to be green and green things to include unripe fruit.

If the subject be an object of denotation and the predicate of information; the former is determined mediately the latter immediately. Thus I describe the Russian Plague by giving an example of it; I determine the example mediately. That is when I find out the connotation of Russian Plague I shall know more about this case but immediately I only determine the Russian Plague and that only in denotation.

When both terms are objects of information as when I say *homo* is man, the phrase is only of grammatical import and is not to be considered here.

We have, then,

1st Analytical Propositions which are immediately determinative only of connotation and may be called connotative

2nd Extensive Propositions which are immediately determinative only of denotation and may be called denotative

3rd Synthetic Intensive Propositions which are immediately determinative both of denotation and connotation therefore also of information and may be called informative propositions.

The difference between connotation, denotation, and information supplies the basis for another division of terms and propositions; a division which is related to the one we have just considered in precisely the same way as the division of syllogism into 3 figures is related to the division into Deduction, Induction, and Hypothesis. Every symbol which has connotation and denotation has also information. For by the denotative character of a symbol, I understand application to objects implied in the symbol itself. The existence therefore of objects of a certain kind is implied in every connotative denotative symbol; and this is information. Now there are certain imperfect or false symbols produced by the combination of true symbols which have lost either their denotation or their connotation. When symbols are combined together in extension as for example in the compound term "cats and dogs," their sum possesses denotation but no connotation or at least no connotation which determines their denotation. Hence, such terms, which I prefer to call *enumerative* terms, have no information and it remains unknown whether there be any real kind corresponding to cats and dogs taken together. On the other hand when symbols are combined together in comprehension as for example in the compound "tailed men" the product possesses connotation but no denotation, it not being therein implied that there may be any 'tailed men'. Such conjunctive terms have therefore no information. Thirdly there are names purporting to be of real kinds as *men;* and these are perfect symbols. Enumerative terms are not truly symbols but only signs; and Conjunctive terms are copies; but these copies and signs must be considered in symbolistic because they are composed of symbols. When an enumerative term forms the subject of a grammatical proposition, as when we say 'cats and dogs have tails' there is no logical unity in the proposition at all. Logically, therefore, it is two propositions and not one. The same is the case when a conjunctive proposition forms the predicate of a sentence; for to say that 'hens are feathered bipeds' is simply to predicate two unconnected marks of them. When an enumerative term as such is the predicate of a proposition, that proposition cannot be a denotative one for a denotative proposition is one which merely analyzes the denotation of its predicate but the denotation of an enumerative term is analyzed in the term itself; hence if an enumerative term as such were the predicate of a proposition that proposition would be equivalent in meaning to its own predicate. On the other hand, if a conjunctive term as such is the subject of a proposition, that proposition cannot be connotative, for the connotation of a conjunctive term is already analyzed in the term itself, and a connotative proposition does no more than analyze the connotation of its subject. Thus we have

Conjunctive   Simple   Enumerative

propositions so related to

Denotative   Informative   Connotative

propositions that what is on the left hand of one line cannot be on the right hand of the other.

We are now in a condition to discuss the question of the grounds of scientific inference. This problem naturally divides itself into parts:

1st To state and prove the principles upon which the possibility in general of each kind of inference depends, 2nd To state and prove the rules for making inferences in particular cases.

The first point I shall discuss in the remainder of this lecture; the second I shall scarcely be able to touch upon in these lectures.

Inference in general obviously supposes symbolization; and all symbolization is inference. For every symbol as we have seen contains information. And in the last lecture we saw that all kinds of information involve inference. Inference, then, is symbolization. They are the same notions. Now we have already analyzed the notion of a *symbol,* and we have found that it depends upon the possibility of representations acquiring a nature, that is to say an immediate representative power. This principle is therefore the ground of inference in general.

But there are three distinct kinds of inference; inconvertible and different in their conception. There must, therefore, be three different principles to serve for their grounds. These three principles must also be indemonstrable; that is to say, each of them so far as it can be proved must be proved by means of that kind of inference of which it is the ground. For if the principle of either kind of inference were proved by another kind of inference, the former kind of inference would be reduced to the latter; and since the different kinds of inference are in all respects different this cannot be. You will say that it is no proof of these principles at all to support them by that which they themselves support. But I take it for granted at the outset, as I said at the beginning of my first lecture, that induction and hypothesis have their own validity. The question before us is *why* they are valid. The principles, therefore, of which we are in search, are not to be used to prove that the three kinds of inference are valid, but only to show how they come to be valid, and the proof of them consists in showing that they determine the validity of the three kinds of inference.

But these three principles must have this in common that they refer to *symbolization* for they are principles of inference which is symbolization. As grounds of the possibility of inference they must refer to the possibility of symbolization or symbolizability. And as logical principles they must relate to the reference of symbols to objects; for logic has been defined as the science of the general conditions of the relations of symbols to objects. But as three different principles they must state three different relations of symbols to objects. Now we have already found that a symbol has three different relations to objects; namely connotation, denotation, and information which are its relations to the object considered as a thing, a form, and an equivalent representation. Hence, it is obvious that these three principles must relate to the symbolizability of things, of forms, and of symbols.

Our next business is to find which is which. For this purpose we must consider that each principle is to be proved by the kind of inference which it supports. The ground of deductive inference then must be established deductively; that is by reasoning from determinant to determinate, or in other words by reasoning from definition. But this kind of reasoning can only be applied to an object whose character depends upon its definition. Now of most objects it is the definition which depends upon the character; and so the definition must therefore itself rest on induction or hypothesis. But the principle of deduction must rest on nothing but deduction, and therefore it must relate to something whose character depends upon its definition. Now the only objects of which this is true are symbols; they indeed are created by their definition; while neither forms nor things are. Hence, the principle of deduction must relate to the symbolizability of things. The principle of hypothetic inference must be established hypothetically, that is by reasoning from determinate to determinant. Now it is clear that this kind of reasoning is applicable only to that which is determined by what it determines; or that which is only subject to truth and falsehood so far as its determinate is, and is thus of itself pure *zero*. Now this is the case with nothing whatever except the pure forms; they indeed are what they are only in so far as they determine some symbol or object. Hence the principle of hypothetic inference must relate to the symbolizability of forms. The principle of inductive inference must be established inductively, that is by reasoning from parts to whole. This kind of reasoning can apply only to those objects whose parts collectively are their whole. Now of symbols this is not true. If I write *man* here and *dog* here that does not constitute the symbol of *man and dog,* for symbols have to be reduced to the unity of symbolization which Kant calls the unity of apperception and unless this be indicated by some special mark they do not constitute a whole. In the same way forms have to determine the same matter before they are added; if the curtains are green and the wainscot yellow that does not make a *yellow-green*. But with things it is altogether different; wrench the blade and handle of a knife apart and the form of the knife has disappeared but they are the same thing—the same matter—that they were before.

Hence, the principle of induction must relate to the symbolizability of things.

All these principles must as principles be universal. Hence they are as follows:—

All things, forms, symbols are symbolizable.

The next step is to prove each of these principles. 1st then, to prove deductively that all symbols are symbolizable. In every syllogism there is a term which is predicate and subject. But a predicate is a symbol of its subject. Hence, in every deduction a symbol is symbolized. Now deduction is valid independently of the matter of the judgment. Hence all symbols are symbolizable.

Next; to prove inductively that all things are symbolizable. For this purpose we must take all the collocations of things we can and judge by them. Now all these collocations of things have been selected upon some principle; this principle of selection is a predicate of them and a *concept*. Being a concept it is a symbol. And it partakes of that peculiarity of symbols that it must have information. We have no concepts which do not denote some things as well as connoting; because all our thought begins with experience. But a symbol which has connotation and denotation contains information. Whatever symbol contains information contains more connotation than is necessary to limit its possible denotation to those things which it may denote. That is every symbol contains more than is sufficient for a principle of selection. Hence every selected collocation of things must have something more than a mere principle of selection, it must have another common quality. Now by induction this common quality may be predicated of the whole possible denotation of the concept which serves as principle of selection. And thus every collocation of things we can select is symbolized by its principle of selection. Now by induction we pass from this statement that all things we can take are symbolizable to the principle that all things are symbolizable. Q.E.D. This argument though inductive in form is of the highest possible validity, for no case can possibly arise to contradict it.

Thirdly, we have to prove hypothetically that all forms are symbolizable. For this purpose we must consider that *forms* are nothing unless they are embodied, and then they constitute the synthesis of the matter. Hence the knowledge of them cannot be directly given but must be obtained by hypothesis. Now we have to explain this fact, that all forms are to be regarded as subjects for hypotheses, by a hypothesis. For this purpose, we should reflect that whatever is symbolizable is symbolized by terms and their combinations. Now we saw at the last lecture that the process of obtaining a new term is a hypothetic inference. So that everything which is symbolizable is to be regarded as a subject for hypothesis. This accounts for the same thing being true of forms, if we make the hypothesis that all forms are symbolizable. Q.E.D. This argument though only an hypothesis could not have been stronger for the conclusion involves no matter of fact at all.

Thus the three grounds of inference are proved. All have been made certain. But the manner in which they have attained to certainty indicates a very different general strength of the three kinds of inference. The hypothetic argument became certain only by speaking of that which has no sense except when this principle is true. The inductive argument became certain only by taking into account all that could possibly be known. The deductive argument alone was strictly demonstrative. Thus we have in order of strength Deduction, Induction, Hypothesis. Deduction, in fact, is the only demonstration; yet no one thinks of questioning a good induction, while hypothesis is proverbially dangerous. *Hypotheses non fingo*, said Newton, striving to place his theory on a basis of strict induction. Yet it is hypotheses with which we must start; the baby when he lies turning his fingers before his eyes is making a hypothesis as to the connection of what he sees and what he feels. Hypotheses give us our facts. Induction extends our knowledge. Deduction makes it distinct.

It now only remains to show how the three principles we have obtained and tested give rise to the various kinds of inference.

The three figures of deduction are as follows:—

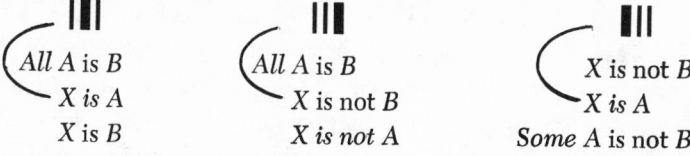

All A is *B*	*All A* is *B*	*X* is not *B*
X is A	*X* is not *B*	*X is A*
X is *B*	*X is not A*	*Some A* is not *B*

Now as I have said every predicate is a symbol of its subject. The first figure consists in taking as predicate, a predicate of a predicate. This clearly depends on the fact that every symbol of a symbol is itself a symbol. The second figure abolishes as predicate that of which the predicate cannot be predicate. Its rule is therefore, the symbol of that which is not a symbol of X is not a symbol of X. The third figure denies as universal predicate of A that which is not a predicate of what A is predicate of. Its rule is That is not a symbol of a symbol which is not a symbol of the object.

Now these three rules are but expressions of the nature of a symbol; namely that a mediate symbolization is possible. But that a mediate symbolization is possible is summed up in the formula Every symbol is symbolizable.

The two figures of induction are

X is A

X is B

All A is B

X is A

Some A is not B

X is not B

The two figures of hypothesis are—

X *is* B

All A is B

X *is* A

X *is not* A

All A is B

X is not B.

In order to understand these, it is necessary to premise that a Rule cannot be a mere denotative proposition the essence of which is to indicate a class by an example, merely. Hence, every rule must have a connotative object as its predicate. In the same way a Subsumption cannot be a Connotative proposition which merely analyzes its subject and does not subsume it to anything. Hence every subsumption must have an object of denotation as its subject. Now in these *schemes,* ☞ B is the predicate of a Rule and X the subject of a subsumption. Hence B is a *form* and X is a *thing.* While A, which may occupy any position except these, may be taken as a symbol in general. Now you observe that it is impossible to form an induction without saying X *is* A that is a thing has a symbol and thus the principle of the universal symbolizability of things is the condition of Induction. In the same way, every hypothesis must say *All* A *is* B that is to say a form is embodied in a symbol and thus the principle of the universal symbolizability of forms gives rise to hypothesis.

In every induction we have given some remarkable fact or piece of information

$$S \text{ is } B$$

where B is an object of connotation. We infer that something else

$$\Sigma \text{ is } B$$

Let us suppose that Σ contains more *information* than S. Then, if Σ is no more extensive than S, Σ is B is a better judgment than S is B because it contains more information without predicating B of anything doubtful. Thus, it is better to say 'All men are mortal' than 'all rational animals are mortal' for the former implies the latter and contains no more possibility of error and is more *distinct*. But in every case of induction Σ is also more extensive than S. Then in case S is a true symbol and S is B is a single true judgment, this judgment or proposition must be the result of induction, as we saw in the last lecture that all propositions are. The question is, therefore, which is the preferable theory, S is B or Σ is B. The greater information of Σ causes the latter theory to contain more truth but its greater extension renders it liable to more error. If in Σ the extension of S is increased more than the information is, the connotation will be diminished and *vice versa*. Accordingly the greater the connotation of Σ relatively to that of S, the better is the theory proposed, Σ is B. Which of the two theories to select in any case will depend upon the motives which influence us. In a desperate practical case, if one's life depends upon taking the right one, he ought to select the one whose subject has the greatest connotation. In a cool speculation where safety is the essential; the least extensive should be taken. So much for the preference between two theories. But in proceeding from fact to theory—in such a case as that about *neat, swine, sheep,* and *deer*—S is a mere enumerative term and has no connotation at all. In this case therefore Σ increases the connotation of S absolutely and Σ is B ought therefore to be absolutely preferred to S is B and be accepted assertorically; as long as there is no question between this theory and some other and as long as it is not opposed by some other induction.

In the case of hypothesis we have given some remarkable state of things

$$X \text{ is } P$$

where X is an object of denotation; we explain this by supposing that

$$X \text{ is } \Pi$$

and Π always contains more information than P. If Π, therefore, has no more comprehension than P, it is better to say X is Π than X is P. It is *clearer* to say that Every man is mortal than to say that Every man is either a good mortal or a bad mortal. But in the case of hypothesis, Π always comprehends more than P. To decide then between the two; we have to consider whether Π has more denotation than P for if it has, the information of P is increased more in Π than its comprehension is and *vice versa;* and we must be decided which to take by our motives. This is the case of a preference between hypotheses. But in the first proceedure from facts P is a mere conjunctive term, destitute of any denotation before this proposition. Hence in this case the information is increased absolutely, the connotation only relatively, and the hypothesis is absolutely needed and must be taken as a *pis aller* unless opposed by some other argument and until a better one presents itself. Polarization for instance is a series of phenomena which it is impossible to name or define without the use of a hypothesis.

The next lecture will be devoted to the consideration of the *quantity* and *quality* of propositions.

Lecture XI

MS 107: April–May 1865

The last lecture was devoted to the fundamental inquiry of the whole course, that of the grounds of inference.

We first distinguished three kinds of reference which every true symbol has to its object. In the first place, every true symbol is applicable to some real thing. Hence, every symbol whether true or not asserts itself to be applicable to some real thing. This is the *denotation* of the symbol. All that we know of things is as denotative objects of symbols. And thus all denotation is comparative, merely. One symbol has more denotation than another or is more extensive when it asserts itself to be applicable to all the things of which the first asserts itself to be applicable and also to others. In the second place, every genuine symbol relates or purports to relate to some form embodied in its object. This is its *connotation*. It is, in fact, only by means of this reference to a form that a symbol acquires its applicability to the thing. The more form a symbol relates to, the greater its intension, comprehension, or connotation. Other things being equal, the greater the comprehension of a symbol the less its extension. For since its denotation is created by its connotation, the more the latter is determined, the more the former is limited. But this rule does not always hold good. For just as there are real kinds in nature, that is to say classes which differ from all others in more respects than one, so there are symbols which imply that their collected objects are real kinds and thus they connote more forms than one either of which would be sufficient to limit their extension to the extent to which it is limited. Hence if a symbol changes in information it may change either its extension or comprehension without changing both and thus the reciprocal relation of extension and comprehension only holds good when the information is not changed. Information then may be defined as the amount of comprehension a symbol has over and above what limits its extension. A symbol not only may have information but it must have it. For every symbol must have denotation that is must imply the existence of some thing to which it is applicable. It may be a mere fiction; we may know it to be fiction; it may be intended to be a fiction and the very form of the word may hint that intention as in the case of abstract terms such as *whiteness, nonentity,* and the like. In these cases, we pretend that we hold *realistic* opinions for the sake of indicating that our propositions are meant to be explicatory or analytic. But the symbol itself always pretends to be a true symbol and hence implies a reference to real things. Thus, no matter how general a symbol may be, it must have some connotation limiting its denotation; it must refer to some determinate form; but it must also connote *reality* in order to denote at all; but *all* that has any determinate form has reality and thus this reality is a part of the connotation which does not limit the extension of the symbol. And so every symbol has information. To say that a symbol has information is as much as to say that it implies that it is equivalent to another symbol different in connotation.

There are certain pseudo-symbols which are formed by combinations of symbols, and which must therefore be considered in logic, which lack either denotation or connotation. Thus, *cats and stoves* is a symbol wanting in connotation because it does not purport to relate to any definite quality. *Tailed men* wants denotation; for though it implies that there are men and that there are tailed things, it does not deny that these classes are mutually exclusive. All such terms are totally wanting in *information*.

In short the formula

$$\text{Connotation} \times \text{Denotation} = \text{Information}$$

holds good thoroughly.

The difference between subject and predicate was also considered in the last lecture. The subject is usually defined as the term determined by the proposition, but as the predicates of A, E, and I are also determined, this definition is inadequate. We were led to substitute for it the following:—The subject is the term determined in connotation and determining denotation; the predicate is the term determined in denotation and determining in connotation. We found that a term may be subject by virtue of being either denotative or by virtue of being informative and that a term may be predicate by virtue either of being connotative or informative. But the reference of both subject and predicate cannot be informative. Thus we have three kinds of judgments.

IC
DC
DI

In the first case the subject is informative, the predicate connotative; that is to say, the connotation of the symbol which forms the subject is explicated in the predicate. Such judgments usually called explicatory or analytic, I call connotative.

In the second case the subject is denotative, the predicate connotative; that is to say, the thing which is denoted by the subject is said to embody the form connoted by the predicate. I call these judgments *informative*.

In the third case the subject is denotative, the predicate is informative. That is the thing which the subject denotes is offered as an example of the application of the symbol which forms the predicate. I call such judgments denotative.

Having thus far established

1st The distinction of thing, form, and representation; together with the subsidiary one of object, logos, and image

2nd The distinction of sign, symbol, copy

3rd The definition of logic as the general condition of the reference of symbols to objects

4th The difference between deduction, induction, and hypothesis

5th The fact that every mental representation is a symbol in a loose sense and that every conception is so strictly

6th The fact that hypothesis gives terms or problematic propositions; inductions propositions strictly speaking—assertory propositions; and deduction apodictic propositions or syllogisms proper. That thus every elementary conception implies hypothesis and every judgment induction

7th The relations of denotation, connotation, and information and

8th The peculiarities of simple, enumerative, and conjunctive terms

we found ourselves in a condition to solve the question of the grounds of inference by putting together these materials.

In the first place with reference to the nature of the problem itself. It is not required to prove that deduction, induction, or hypothesis are valid. On the contrary, they are to be accepted as conditions of thought. It had been shown in previous lectures that they are so. Nor was a mode of calculating the probability of an induction or hypothesis now demanded; this being a merely subsidiary problem at best and one which may for ought we could yet see, be absurd. What we now wanted was an articulate statement and a satisfactory demonstration of those transcendental laws which give rise to the possibility of each kind of inference.

Those grounds of possibility we found to be that All things, forms, symbols are symbolizable. For these laws must refer to symbolization because symbolization and inference are the same. As grounds of possibility they must refer to the possibility of symbolization. As logical laws they must consider the reference of symbols in general to objects. Now symbols in general have three relations to objects; namely so far as the latter contain things, forms, symbols. Finally as general principles they must be universal.

Each ground-principle must be proved entirely by that same kind of inference which it supports. But we cannot arrive at any conclusion by mere deduction except about symbols. We cannot arrive at any conclusion by mere induction except about things. And we cannot arrive at any conclusion by mere hypothesis except about forms.

Hence the ground of deduction relates to symbols; that of induction to things; that of hypothesis to forms.

The three principles were proved by the several kinds of inference with certainty. The inductive proof attained certainty by considering all the instances that could be taken. And the hypothetic inference attained certainty by having only a subjective character.

The influence of the three principles was shown in the case of deduction by the rule of *Nota notae* without which there could be no deduction. In the case of Induction by the affirmative denotative proposition which must always be the first premiss. And in the case of Hypothesis by the Universal connotative proposition which must always be the second premiss.

Finally we found a test for deciding whether an inductive or hypothetic conclusion is to be accepted or not. In the case of deduction we infer in all cases from S is C to Σ is C. In case S is a simple term or real symbol; S is C must itself be an inductive conclusion or an inference from such a conclusion. We are therefore to regard this case as presenting a question of preference between two inductions. We found that the answer depends partly upon our motives and partly upon the relative comprehension of S and Σ the more comprehensive subject being preferable. For example, we select a number of West Point officers, let us say the Engineers. We find that the Engineers have generally military genius. Can we infer that *All* West Point officers have military genius? To answer this we should consider whether Engineers or West Point officers has the most comprehension. It is clear that Engineers has the most, for a man *cannot be* an engineer without being a West Point officer. So the induction would not be valid. But suppose that instead of selecting from West Point officers; we had made a selection from great masters of fortification and had taken the engineers as being generally such. Then can we infer that because all the engineers are good field officers that all great masters of fortification are so? In this case great master of fortification implies much more than engineer (it being an extraordinary fact that all our engineers are great masters of fortification)—has much more connotation so that the induction satisfies this condition. But it is still a question of prudence whether we should adopt the inference. I need not say that I have not in this instance sought for *true* premisses; I wished merely to give a conceivable case. If the induction is in the other figure this rule will be reversed.

We infer from S is C to Σ is C. Now if S is not a simple but an enumerative term—as neat, swine, sheep, deer—it has no connotation and hence Σ is C presents an absolute preference over S is C in the one figure and the reverse is the case in the other. But it is to be remembered in applying this that all arguments and all that is known must be taken into account.

Hypothesis presents similar conditions. We here infer from D is P to D is Π and the validity of the inference depends upon the relative denotation of P and Π. This is nothing else than the well-known rule that the hypothesis must have unity, that subsidiary hypotheses are to be suspected. But it also includes what is usually given as a separate rule that the supposition must be possible. Take for example the question whether Mercury moves round the sun or the earth, the question between Tycho's hypothesis and Ptolemy's. The fact that the elongation of Mercury from the sun has a maximum is accounted for upon both views. Geocentrically, by a subsidiary hypothesis that the times of revolution are the same or nearly so. Heliocentrically, by the hypothesis itself by means of the acknowledged fact that Mercury passes between the sun and the earth. The subsidiary hypothesis necessary upon the geocentric view is a limitation of the extension of the predicate of the geocentric hypothesis, because it is a limitative addition to the connotation. For the symbol 'revolving about the earth within the earth and the sun in the same time as the sun' is not applicable necessarily to 'all that revolves about the earth within the earth and the sun'. But in the predicate of heliocentric hypothesis the corresponding part of the connotation is not limitative of extension, for the symbol 'revolving round the sun and passing between the earth and the sun and having a limited elongation' is necessarily applicable to all that revolves round the sun and passes between the earth and the sun. Thus we see that the two rules of the Possibility and Unity of the hypothesis are reducible to one namely that its predicate should in one figure increase and in the other diminish the denotation of the other predicate of the same subject.

In the case when P in one figure or Π in the other is a conjunctive term; the other predicate absolutely increases its denotation. Hence the hypothetic inference in such a case is absolutely preferable.

So far we went at the last lecture. The first point which naturally presents itself to-day is this. The rules just given for hypothetic and inductive inference are mere rules of preference. Now a hypothetic or inductive conclusion may be the best way of combining together the facts. And yet the matter which it adds to the facts may be false. Is not the principal question, then, whether or not the hypothetic matter of a hypothesis and the inductive matter of an induction have any certainty or even any weight of probability and if so how this can be proved or estimated in any case? The question which seems so fundamental is, in fact, subsidiary; and its solution follows as a corollary from what has already been established. In the first place we have found that all forms and all things are symbolizable; this followed from the admission of the validity of a certain induction and hypothesis. But from this it follows that in all cases some true induction and some true hypothesis are possible. Hence to ask what is the probability that an induction or hypothesis is true is the same as to ask what is the probability that two inductions or two hypotheses will agree. That contrary inductions and contrary hypotheses are possible is notorious. Let us see how this contrariety can arise. In the first place the predicate of a hypothesis may contain superfluous comprehension; comprehension that is to say which is limitative of the extension and which being taken away, the fact is still explained; in the same way the subject of an inductive conclusion may have superfluous extension that is to say extension limitative of comprehension and which being cut off the fact would still be explained. Of course all such superfluity is unwarrantable and I may add that it is also a violation of the logical rules already laid down. After the induction or hypothesis has been corrected by the retrenchment of such superfluity, some writers on the subject contend that there is no longer any possibility of disagreement. But it seems to me that they do not face the difficulty, and that all their arguments beg the question. We may represent the matter thus:—

Let D is C be the fact to be explained by hypothesis and suppose we know both All I is C and All J is C as we obviously may. Then we may infer hypothetically either D *is* I or D *is* J. Thus there are two hypotheses possible. Again let D is C be the fact to be explained by induction. Then D may have been selected as being either I or J. We have then either D *is* I or D *is* J whence by induction

$$\text{All } I \text{ is } C \qquad \text{or} \qquad \text{All } J \text{ is } C.$$

It is commonly said that if all possible consequences of an induction or hypothesis were taken into account, contrary explanations would be impossible. It seems certainly to be so when real kinds are neglected, but when they are taken into account, it is by no means obvious.

A better way of looking at the matter is this. If we examine the two hypotheses we see that they are founded on the two principles *All I* is *C* and *All J* is *C*, in which, of course, both *I* and *J* possess denotation or they are false hypotheses. Having denotation they symbolize *things*. Hence we have All *I* and *J* are *C*, where the subject may not be a true symbol. But since all things are symbols a true induction is necessarily possible which includes *I* and *J*; we may call it *K* is *C*. Hence a third hypothesis is possible

$$D \text{ is } C$$
$$\text{All } K \text{ is } C$$
$$D \text{ is } K$$

This hypothesis is more general than either of the others. It includes them both, hence it is preferable to either of them. It follows that neither of the others can be the true one. Hence when two hypotheses explain the same finite series of facts, one of them can either be reduced to the other by proper retrenchment by means of inductions or else both can be so reduced to the truth.

It is precisely the same with induction. The two inductions depend on the two facts *D* is *I* and *D* is *J* but hypothesis may always explain the fact *D* is *I* and *J* by showing that *D* is *L* and then the induction All *L* is *C* is preferable to either of the others. Hence as before the retrenchment of every induction by means of deduction and hypothesis will give the truth.

Every induction, then, and every hypothesis yields a certain amount of truth.

I might also show that no induction or hypothesis is completely true except such as we call cognitions *à priori*. For the chance against it is infinite. Hence, the question what is the *probability* of an induction or hypothesis is senseless and the true question is how much truth does an induction contain. For the same reasons by how much truth should not be meant what proportion of inferences therefrom are true but simply of how much value are certain premises in giving us truth by induction or hypothesis.

We must distinguish therefore the truth which an inductive or hypothetic conclusion may have by accident from that which it must have from the nature of the facts explained. The former cannot properly be estimated. The latter can. For to consider first induction; if the same conclusion result inductively as the least truthful explanation possible of two different sets of facts, it is plain that a certain amount of truth it is obliged to have on account of each instance, that is on account of the extension of the subject of the fact. And each instance determines a certain amount of truth independently of the others. So that the number of different kinds of instances measures the least amount of truth the induction can have. In the same way with hypothesis the number of different properties explained measures the least possible truth of the hypothesis.

In this way truth is measured upon a scale of numbers from *one* to *infinity*. And thus we cannot measure the ratio of the truth to the falsehood but only the ratio between the pregnancy of two sets of facts. Of any particular conclusion therefore we can only judge by ascertaining by further experience whether it can be improved. But the comparative usefulness of the facts upon which it proceeds may be estimated with an approach to precision.

We may sum up then by the rule that the value of facts is in proportion to their number; and that from given facts the best inference when all possible retrenchment has been made, is the one which being inductive has the most comprehensive subject and which being hypothetic has the most extensive predicate.

This seems to complete the logical theory of inference; our doctrine is capable of an infinite variety of illustration but as I desire to make this lecture the conclusion of the course, I must pass at once to the criticism of the popular system of logic which as it stands is opposed to this whole theory of induction and hypothesis.

I mean the theory of Sir William Hamilton; the fundamental principle of which is the definition of the proposition as the statement of the relation of quantity between two concepts, thus annihilating all distinction of subject and predicate. I shall not think of denying that such a definition may be arbitrarily assumed and a consistent system of logic deduced from it, much simpler it may be than that which I have employed. I do not imitate Hamilton in considering every mode of analysis but my own as false. I consider that this is as though the mathematician Hamilton—*the* Hamilton—when he had brought forward his Calculus of Quaternions had considered the old doctrine that two sides of a triangle exceed the third as false because it conflicts with his views. I shall aim simply to show 1st that Hamilton's system has not been consistently developed and 2nd that when consistently developed it does not conflict with my doctrine of induction and hypothesis.

Hamilton is of opinion that logic is rightly based upon a series of *postulates* of which the most important is that we be allowed to state in language all that is contained in thought. He then undertakes to show that we often assign *some* and *all* to the predicates of our judgments; as for example when we say "God alone is good," that is, God is all that is good. Accordingly he applies this quantification, as he calls it, uniformly so as to have instead of the old

All *A* is *B*   Some *A* is *B*   No *A* is *B*   Some *A* is not *B*

the following eight propositions:—

1. All *A* is all *B*   i.e. All *A* is *B* and All *B* is *A*
2. All *A* is some *B*   i.e. All *A* is *B*
3. Some *A* is all *B*   i.e. All *B* is *A*
4. Some *A* is some *B*   i.e. Some *A* is *B*
5. Any *A* is not any *B*   i.e. No *A* is *B*
6. Any *A* is not some *B*   i.e. Some *B* is not *A*
7. Some *A* is not any *B*   i.e. Some *A* is not *B*
8. Some *A* is not some *B*   i.e. All *A* and all *B* are not one individual.

Now the idea that logic rests on series of postulates shows a radically false notion of logic. For what is a postulate? Simply the condition of solving some problem. But a problem belongs only to applied science, pure science being composed of theorems. Hamilton conceives, therefore, only an applied logic and the matter of his postulates especially of the one I just stated, shows that he conceives of logic only as applied to thought—of mere Psychological Logic. And, yet, there is scarcely a point of view from which his peculiar system can be regarded from which it appears more unsatisfactory than as a statement of how we really think. As a question of the theory of logic, the doctrine of the quantification of the predicate is to be discussed not by means of a postulate or permission to do something but by means of a criterion of logical relevancy. By means of the postulates of geometry we are allowed to represent all the properties of extension. But it does not follow from this that because there can be no lines except as edges of solids that therefore plane geometry which neglects this circumstance is false. For the fact is simply irrelevant. In the same way when we say *Every rose is a flower,* we may perhaps be forced to think also of flowers and make a judgment of them at the same time. The proposition *every rose is a flower* does not in that case represent the whole thought but only that element of it which determines the connotation of rose to the exclusion of that element which determines the connotation of flower. We may be obliged to think of flower as having some limits of denotation, but all consideration of these limits is irrelevant to the proposition of which *roses* is the subject. He may if he pleases take it into account, but we may also neglect it without any error. Only upon Hamilton's view all logical distinction between the two terms of a proposition except so far as they stand in different quantitative relations to each other—that is except so far as one may be subordinate to the other and not superordinate—is annihilated and cannot be consistently introduced again.

Hamilton adds four new forms of judgment to the old A E I O. Of these the first, All *A* is all *B*, cannot be objected to upon his principles; although it may be said that being equivalent to All *A* is *B* and All *B* is *A*, it is a symbol having the same reference to its object as these two propositions taken together and therefore, according to our definition of logic, it is logically the same as these two.

The *second* and *third* of Hamilton's innovations, Some *A* is all *B* and Any *A* is not some *B*, are merely results of the conversion of All *A* is *B* and Some *A* is not *B*. He lays it down as an axiom that every proposition ought to be capable of conversion; and this is his justification of these forms. Now if the distinction between subject and predicate be maintained the axiom is manifestly false. For the subject is the term which is determined or which is determined in connotation. Thus, if we say

Some kings are not Assyrians

kings is determined. But Assyrians is not determined in the same sense, at least. To show this replace the indefinite class *some* by the definite class *virtuous.* Thus we have

Virtuous kings are not Assyrians

This is the same as to say of Assyrians that

> Every Assyrian is either not a king or is not virtuous

Now restore the word *some* or still better its definition in place of *virtuous* and we have

> Every Assyrian is either not a king or else is not a member
> of an indeterminate class compatible with kings.

And this is the true converse of Some kings are not Assyrians. But it is clear that it does not determine Assyrians at all, and is a senseless proposition.

The axiom therefore that all propositions are convertible fails if the distinction of subject and predicate be kept up. Now suppose that the distinction is abrogated. Then it follows immediately that a proposition and its converse are logically identical. True; it will be necessary in considering syllogisms to distinguish All *A* is some *B* from Some *A* is all *B* but this is a subsidiary distinction altogether dependent merely upon the transposition of the matter of the terms; the two being All *A* is some *B* and All *B* is some *A*. Distinct forms of propositions they are not. Hence these two forms should be struck out.

The *fourth* and last innovation is Some *A* is not some *B*. This means merely that the sum of all the different individuals to which *A* and *B* separately are applicable is greater than *one*. It is astonishing that a logician should deceive himself so far as to admit this as a separate form of judgment. I take it to be incontrovertible that every proposition may be contradicted,—I will not say by some one proposition but by some combination of them. Now how is

> Some *A* is not some *B*

to be contradicted? Only by saying All *A* and *B* are the same individual, that is by introducing the individual as a part of the *matter* of the judgment. Now if it is part of the matter in one of the two contradictories it is part of the matter of the other. And it is not too severe to say that Hamilton has committed an absurdity in making it part of the form in one case.

Hamilton's eight propositions are thus reduced to *five*. Applying this result, as well as the principle by which we rejected *Darapti* and

Felapton, to his 108 moods of syllogism, these also are reduced to 7 which I give in his own notation.

$$\begin{array}{llll}
: & \overline{} \;:M:\; \underline{} & : \\
: & \overline{} \;,M:\; \underline{} & , & \text{Barbara} \\
, & \overline{} \;,M:\; \underline{} & , & \text{Darii Disamis Datisi} \\
: & \overline{} \;,M:\; \underline{} & : & \text{Celarent Cesare Camestres} \\
: & \overline{} \;,M:\; \underline{} & , & \text{Baroko} \\
: & \overline{} \;,M:\; \underline{} & , & \text{Bokardo} \\
: & \overline{} \;:M,\; \underline{} & , & \text{Festino Feriso Ferio}
\end{array}$$

This is a capital classification of syllogisms. All these moods except the first will give inferences containing M of two kinds; namely, those in which M is distributed in the conclusion and those in which it is not. And thus Induction and Hypothesis will be distinguished though by a somewhat different boundary. The first mood is of a more elementary character and yields no distinction between Deduction, Induction, or Hypothesis because none of the three terms are distinguished at all. It is the only mood which contains the Form of Judgment All A is all B and should be called simply Unmodified Inference, and that form of Judgment should be called Unmodified Judgment.

Hamilton's System then consistently developed abolishes Figure and Conversion and gives Unmodified forms of Judgment and Inference; but leaves all that is requisite for the outlines of the theory of Induction and Hypothesis. His list of propositions undoubtedly had its origin in a desire to form a symmetrical scheme in which the formula of definition All A is all B should have a place. But being led away by the superficial notion of the distribution of a term, he fell into error everywhere. The way in which he ought to have proceeded to form such a scheme is this. He should first have regarded the conception of quality as the distinction of clear, distinct, and adequate and noticed how that is applicable to the copula. When our knowledge of any proposed subject is the most imperfect possible which can enable us to predicate anything of it, it cannot be absolutely obscure. We must, at least, distinguish it from something. And then we can deny something of it. Thus the negative judgment implies no more than some clearness of cognition. The moment our conception attains the least distinctness—

the moment we recognize any part of it we can affirm that part. Thus affirmation implies some distinctness of cognition. When we have an adequate notion of the subject, then we can predicate that of it whose extension could not be made less relatively to the narrowest sense of the subject; in this case, we know that this predicate is applicable to the subject in its narrowest sense exclusively and we have

All *A* is the only *B*
Some *A* is the only *B*

The first form is the same as All *A* is all *B*. But the second is not equivalent to 'some *A* is all *B*' because it excludes All *A* is all *B*. For if I have an adequate notion of the subject, then I know to how much its predicate applies and therefore whether it applies to all *A* or not. We must not be led away by the words *some* and *all;* but stick to our logical conceptions.

The very same distinction applies to the quantity of the subject. When we say *All A* we denote the real subject by an adequate symbol. When we say *Some A* the symbol is inadequate but has some distinctness since it distinguishes *A* as one of the marks of the real subject. Now to complete the scheme we ought to have an *indistinct* form of the subject. Such a form we shall obtain if we suppose the real subject to be denoted by a term which either intersects or is subordinate to it in extension, for thus we shall know no mark of the real subject whatever. Thus we shall have

Some *A* &c. is not *B*
   i.e. Some *A* is not *B* and Some *B* is not *A*
Some *A* &c. is *B*
   i.e. Some *A* is *B* and Some *B* is not *A*
Some *A* &c. is the only *B*
   i.e. Some *A* is *B*, Some *A* is not *B*, and Some *B* is not *A*

Thus we should have a uniform set of propositions by the application of the three degrees of quality—adequate, distinct, indistinct—to both subject and predicate. There is, however, a different method of investigation which we might pursue to attain a complete set of propositions. There are four possible relations in which two terms can stand to each other: 1st Coëxtension, 2nd Subordination, 3rd Intersection, 4th Exclusion. Our propositions ought to indicate each of these and all modes of indeterminateness of knowledge between them in which direct experience can possibly leave us.

But if we know by direct experience that two terms do not intersect, we must know whether or not they exclude each other. For to know that they do not intersect, we must have found either that they nowhere coincide or that one is in the other throughout. The former case determines exclusion, the latter excludes it. It follows that if a proposition is true of D and B or A and D it is true also of C.

In the case of subordination the terms are not in convertible relation; hence we must here distinguish one term from the other.

Now if we know by direct experience that one particular term is not subordinate to the other, then we must either know that they are not coëxtensive or must know that they neither intersect nor exclude each other. For in order to have found that x is not subordinate to y, we must have found either that x is somewhere without y which excludes coextension, or that y is nowhere without x which excludes both Intersection and Exclusion. It follows that if a proposition is true of A and C or A and D it is true of both B and β (or of both Subordination and superordination).

Further if we do not know whether either term is subordinate to the other or not, then we cannot have found that they are not in relation either of intersection or coëxtension. For to know that they are not coextensive we must have found one extending beyond the other and must know therefore that it is not subordinate to the other. And to know that they do not intersect, we must either have found that they nowhere coincide when there can be no subordination or must have found one which does not go beyond the other and which therefore is not superordinate to the other. It follows that a proposition not true of A and C *both* is not true of B and β both.

These three rules limit our propositions to such as shall indicate the following cases

A		B		C	D
A or B			B or C	C or D	
	A or B or β or C			β or C or D	

Now these nine cases are precisely those of the nine propositions which we just obtained by the other method of investigation

A is	All *A* is the only *B*
B is	Some *A* is the only *B*
C is	Some *A* &c. is the only *B*
D is	No *A* is *B*
A or *B* is	All *A* is *B*
B or *C* is	Some *A* &c. is *B*
C or *D* is	Some *A* &c. is not *B*
A or *B* or *β* or *C* is	Some *A* is *B*
β or *C* or *D* is	Some *A* is not *B*

I have described this scheme of the thorough-going qualification of the subject in order to show how easy it is to produce a system quite as thorough-going and far more rational than Hamilton's. There is no definite quantification of the predicate in either affirmatives or negatives. Definite quantification is such as determines limits of extension. Now no affirmation or negation has anything to do with the limits of the predicate.

The scheme of thorough-going qualification is a consistent solution of the problem set before us namely to produce a uniform system of propositions introducing the formula of definition. But in reality the question itself is irrelevant. Of these 9 propositions several are formed by combinations of the others. The combination of two subalternates of one proposition will always give that proposition. Hence *B*, *C*, and *BC* are to be struck out as having two subalternates. When *B* without *β* occurs in a proposition, its combination with its converse will eliminate *B* hence *CD* should be struck out on account of *βCD* and *A* on account of *AB* and thus we are left with the old A E I O as a perfect logical system of propositions. In reference, however to these four propositions it is to be observed that there is *one*—the particular negative—which stands in a totally different relation from either of the others. For if we take account of the difference between negatives and infinites, Some *A* is not *B* or *Non omnis A est B* can never express all that we know of *A* in reference to *B*. For to know this much we must either know of some *A* which is not *B*, in which case we know not merely *Non omnis A est B* but also *Aliquis A est* non-*B* which is in reality a particular affirmative or else we know that there is no *B* which is *A* in which case we also know that no *A* is *B*. The particular negative therefore really exists only as the contradictory of the universal affirmative and is enunciated always with reference to contradicting, never as a statement of fact. This leads us to make an arrangement of the propositions to express their logical relations; thus

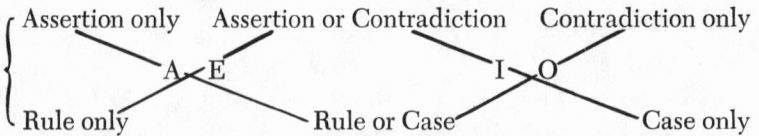

A exists as assertion only, O as contradiction only. E and I as either. E is a Rule only. I is a Case only. A and O are neither particularly. Unite the middle of either line with either extremity of the other and you have the four forms of proposition.

I fear I have wearied you in these lectures by dwelling so much upon merely logical forms. But to the pupil of Kant as to the pupil of Aristotle the Analytic of Logic is the foundation of Metaphysics. We find ourselves in all our discourse taking certain points for granted which we cannot have observed. The question therefore is what may we take for granted independent of all experience. The answer to this is metaphysics. But it is plain that we can thus take for granted only what is involved in logical forms. Hence, the necessity of studying these forms. In these lectures, one set of Logical forms has been pretty thoroughly studied; that of Hypothesis, Deduction, Induction. Another set has been partly studied, that of Denotation, Information, Connotation.

Corresponding to these there are evidently certain conceptions of objects in general. To denotation corresponds the conception of an *object*, to information the conception of a real kind, and to connotation the conception of a logos or quality. So to Induction corresponds the conception of a Law, to Hypothesis the conception of a Case under a Law, and to Deduction the conception of a Result.

There are also principles of the Judgment corresponding to these conceptions of which we have instances in the laws that all things, forms, symbols are symbolizable.

All the principles that can be so derived from the forms of logic must be valid for all experience. For experience has used logic. Everything else admits of speculative doubt.

I thank you, gentlemen, for your kind attention.

Teleological Logic

MS 108

Begun 1865 May 14

Chapter I

Definition

Logic is objective symbolistic.

Symbolistic is the semiotic of symbols.

Objective symbolistic is that branch of symbolistic which considers relations to objects.

Semiotic is the science of representations.

Representation is anything which is or is represented to stand for another and by which that other may be stood for by something which may stand for the representation.

Thing is that for which a representation stands prescinded from all that can serve to establish a relation with any possible relation.

Form is that respect in which a representation stands for a thing prescinded from all that can serve as the basis of a representation and therefore from its connection with the thing.

Thus Science is divided into

1 Positive Science. Or the science of things.
2 Semiotic. Or the science of representations.
3 Formal Science. Or the science of forms.

Representations

are of three kinds according to their truth or coincidence with their objects. These are

1. *Signs.* Representations by virtue of a convention.
2. *Symbols.* Representations by virtue of original
   or acquired nature.
3. *Copies.* Representations by virtue of a sameness
   of predicates.

By a symbol is meant such a representation as is regarded as a representation in another system of representations. A word for instance upon being presented to the mind, immediately calls up a conception of the object without resembling it and without any reference to the convention, which has however existed. Concepts are a species of symbols.

A symbol is created by a *logos,* equivalent to another symbol in the system in which it is regarded as a symbol, and stands for an object.

A *Logos* is an embodied form.

An *object* is an informed thing.

The science of the general conditions to which every symbol is subjected in so far as it is related

to
$\begin{cases}
\text{a logos is } \textit{General Grammar} \\
\text{a language is } \textit{General Rhetoric} \\
\text{an Object is } \textit{General Logic.}
\end{cases}$

Hence we have

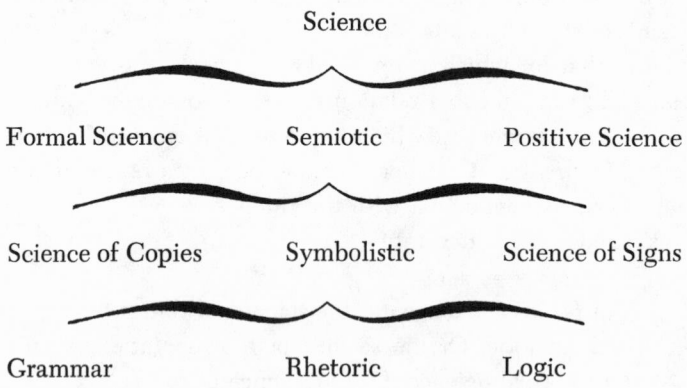

	Science	
Formal Science	Semiotic	Positive Science
Science of Copies	Symbolistic	Science of Signs
Grammar	Rhetoric	Logic

An Unpsychological View of Logic to which are appended some applications of the theory to Psychology and other subjects

MS 109: May–Fall 1865

Chapter I. Definition of Logic

Of the numerous definitions which have been given of Logic—amounting to a hundred, at least,—those which are at all rigid may be divided into four classes; first such as regard logic as an art of wrangling; second such as regard it as an organon of inquiry; third such as regard it as a science of the laws of the mind; and fourth such as regard it as a science of the laws of words considered as the products of the mind's action.

As many different views of the subject are included under each of these heads they are necessarily loose descriptions. But in a general way it may be said that the conception entertained by the body of logicians of their science has gradually been progressing from the first to the last of these.

The definition of Kant upon which most of those prevalent at present are founded is as follows. Logic is the science of the laws of the mind's action or what is the same thing of the forms of thought in general. The latter branch of this definition is less psychological than the first. For a Kantian form is less an affair of the mind than is commonly supposed or than he himself would have admitted. When the form is considered apart from the mind Geometry and Algebra show that an enquiry is liable to no entanglements in psychological questions. Moreover *thought in general* is a very different affair from *thought*. Thought in general prescinded not only from intuition—and so reduced to an *ens imaginarium* which is one of Kant's four species of *nothing*—but also from all connection with the individual mind, is nothing but a fiction which expresses merely the possibilities of discourse. I propose to adhere to the essence of this definition but to regard it from such a point of view that it may not seem to have any more relation to psychology than it really has.

Suppose that in an undecipherable inscription of a long-extinct people an argument is written. Is that any the less logically correct or fallacious because no one can read it and so no one can think it? I believe the reader will agree that it is not. It seems to me to be in exactly the same condition as a flower in the desert. This is said to have colour, though colour is nothing but in the eye; and no one can see this flower. This colour is nothing actual—nothing physically possible—but it is a fiction from which all the fictitious element has been eliminated by a device of language. Such fictions freed from fiction are common in mathematics, where they are exceedingly useful; and they can evidently do no harm, so long as they are understood. I may say that this page has a red spot upon it, although it has none provided I add that the spot has no size or that it is *in potentia*, or that the color is devoid of all intensity, or that it is neutralized by anti-redness. By such a fiction as this I propose to hold that meaning resides in words and other material representations whether these representations be understood or not and whether they be actually written or fashioned or not.

There are three aspects under which every phenomenon may be considered and which may be regarded also as three elements of the phenomenon. Every phenomenon is in the first place an image; so that it may be considered to be or to contain a representation. In the second place, the phenomenon may be objectified, or looked upon as a reality; in this way it is said to be or (more usually) to contain *matter*. For matter is that by virtue of which anything is. In the third place, the differences of its parts and its qualities may be considered, and in this point of view, it is said to be or (more usually) to contain *form*. For form is that by virtue of which anything is such as it is. Corresponding to these three elements of actual cognitions or phenomena; there are three corresponding elements of those possibilities of cognition or substrata of phenomena which are supposed for the purpose of explaining the regularities of cognition. These hypotheses amount to this; that every phenomenon is matched by some noumenon, or that to every actual cognition there corresponds a possible cognition. If I see John Jones, I suppose that there will be and has been a possibility of seeing John Jones. Corresponding, then, to internal representation we have a representation, in general, internal or external; which is a supposed thing standing for something else. Corresponding to the matter of phenomena we have the supposition of external realities or *things;* and corresponding to the form of phenomena we have *qualities*. Of these, representation is not altogether hypothetical since we have at least something precisely similar in consciousness. *Things* are legitimate hypotheses, as we shall see when we have developed the logic of hypothesis. *Qualities* are fictions; for though it is true that roses are red, yet redness is nothing, but a fiction framed for the purpose of philosophizing; yet harmless so long as we remember that the scholastic realism it implies is false. When the element of quality is eliminated from *things* by abstraction; we have noumenal matter. When the connection with things is eliminated from qualities, we have Pure Forms. When the material and mental element is eliminated from representations we have Concepts or, as I prefer to say in order to avoid the apparent connection with the mind, Logoi. The three prescinded elements are fictions. The embodiment of a pure form in noumenal matter makes a thing with qualities. The realization of a pure form in the mind makes a mental representation. The embodiment of a pure form in a *logos* united with noumenal matter gives an outward representation. The use of these phrases is to formulate the analysis of a thing, a thought, and a representation into three several elements on the one side and one common element on the other.

The relevancy of this analysis consists in this, that if logic deals with the form of thought, it can be studied just as well in external as in internal representations, while by so doing we shall avoid all possible entanglement in the meshes of psychological controversy. Logic then deals with representations. But not with all kinds of representations. Representations are of three sorts.

1st *Marks,* by which I mean such representations as denote without connoting. If the applicability of a representation to a thing depends upon a convention which established precisely what it should denote, it would be a *mark.* A proper name is an instance.

2nd *Analogues,* by which I mean such representations as connote without denoting. A picture for instance which is a representation (whether intentional or not) of whatever it looks like, really resembles everything more or less, and so denotes nothing; although we may infer what was intended.

3rd *Symbols,* by which I mean such representations as denote by connoting. [See lecture]

Of these three kinds of representations logic evidently refers only to the last, taking account of signs and analogues only when their laws happen to coincide with those of symbols or when combinations of symbols produce non-denotative or non-connotative representations.

There are three points of view from which symbols may be studied which correspond to the three elements or aspects of phenomena. For a symbol is a kind of thing which typifies exactly a mind thinking. Its connotation may be said to be a thought embodied in it. Its denotation is that which it perceives. More precisely, corresponding to the matter of phenomenon is the object or thing which the symbol represents. Corresponding to the form of the phenomenon, we have in the symbol the quality which it embodies. And, finally, corresponding to the phenomenon considered subjectively, is the reference of the symbol to other possible modes of representing the same thing. In which of these relations does logic deal with symbols? In the first place the reference of symbols to equivalent symbols is clearly not the study of logic. For logical purposes all equivalent symbols are one and the same; because their relation to inference is one and the same. The reference of symbols, in general, to qualities seems to be the same as their connotation, which is a subject for logic; but it seems to me that the connotation of a word is the reference to the quality only so far as the latter is embodied in a thing, because all connotation effects denotation. Under the reference of symbols to qualities in general I should rather place distinctions between such words as *creative, creation, create;* in other words I should say that this was the subject of general Grammar. Logic seems to be the science of the relations of symbols in general to their objects. A logical inference is true if its premisses are true. In other words, that inference is logical which conforms to the general conditions of passing from premisses which have a real object to a conclusion which has a real object.

Again take this proposition. "This very proposition is true." Why is this absurd? Because its subject being the proposition itself it has no subject except itself and since by its predicate it only refers to the reference of itself to its object, it has no object but a reference to an object, which object being in turn a reference to an object and so on *ad infinitum* it has no object. This shows that if a symbol can have no object it is absurd—which is the same as illogical—so that logic is concerned with the reference of symbols in general to objects.

An Unpsychological View of Logic
to which are appended some applications
of the theory herein contained to
Psychology and other subjects

Chapter I. Definition of Logic

A certain growth may be traced in the conception of logic held by the body of philosophers of different times. At first, it was a mere art of wrangling. Then it was an organum of discovery. Then it was a science of the mind. Now it is the law which rules the products of the mind without showing the mental processes themselves. The human elements of the conception have thus been gradually eliminated; first the selfish element, then the personal element, finally the psychological element. It is surprising how little the definition now usually given namely that it is the science of the forms of thought in general, has to do with the mind. The instances of Geometry and Algebra suffice to show how little a science of Kantian Forms need have to do with any introspection. *Thought in general* too is a very different thing from a thought in the mind. In the first place, it does not exist in the individual mind but is common to you and me. In the second place it is prescinded from intuition and so reduced to an *ens rationis* which is one of Kant's four species of nothing.

All advanced logicians would probably agree that the greatest stumbling-blocks in the way of logical research always have been and are now psychological difficulties. Thus the question of the thorough-going quantification of the predicate depends upon *how we think*. The doubtful matter of reasoning in two quantities, and all the questions of the day, have the same character. Finally it is from certain doctrines of psychology that one school of logicians has been led to deny explicitly and another implicitly the fundamental principle of contradiction. If therefore it could be shown that the conditions of valid argument have no more to do with how we think than geometry has with how we intuite, so that logic should be extricated once and forever from all the entanglements of introspection, we might hope that its future progress however slow would be as free from the impediments of controvertible doctrine as that of mathematics itself.

Is this, after all, ridiculous? Suppose that in an undecipherable inscription of a long-extinct people a syllogism be contained. Is this syllogism, this argument any the less correct or fallacious because, nobody being able to read it, nobody can think it? Such an inscription is like a flower in a desert. Has this not colour because nobody can see its colour? It is true that to call that a colour which cannot be seen is a sort of fiction; but it is a fiction which is purified from its fictitious element completely as soon as we add that it cannot be seen. Without this kind of fiction, not only modern mathematics would be impossible; but philosophy, itself, would be deprived of all its terms. What are such words as *blueness, hardness, loudness,* but fictions of this kind? It has been said that these "abstract names" denote qualities and connote nothing. But it seems to me the phrase "denoted object" is nothing but a roundabout expression for a thing. What else is a thing but that which a *perception* or *sign* stands for? To say that a quality is denoted is to say that it is a thing. And this gives a hint of the veritable nature of such terms. They were framed at a time when all men were realists in the scholastic sense and consequently things were meant by them, entities which had no quality but that expressed by the word. They, therefore, must denote these things and connote the qualities they relate to. To use them, now, then (and no philosophical doctrine is possible without their use) is to make use of a fiction, but one which is corrected by a steady avoidance of all realistic inferences. Nor is this a peculiarity of abstract sciences. To express any fact, we must make use of some fiction. The word *it*, which may be said for our present purpose to be implied in the third person of all verbs, is a fiction. It means, as Mr. Mill would say, a possibility of feeling; but possibility is itself a fiction, for it is the mode in which that is which is only more or less expected. Now to say that that which is expected is, is either to make a hypothesis or to invent a fiction; but in the case of the word *possibility* no hypothesis is intended, so that it is a fiction. It is difficult to demonstrate that a fiction can lead to no error so long as its peculiar character is properly taken into account; because, it is difficult to find any premiss more evident. Let A be an adjective incompatible with B, then AB will be a type of such fictions. It means in reality what B would be were it changed so as to become A but changed in no other respect. Provided this be understood what harm can there be in such an expression?

By a logically valid argument which no one can read, is meant one which, if it could be read and if it has any ultimate premisses whatever which given in experience or analyzable out of experience, would yield a belief such as would never be contradicted by any experience. If it follows from the fact that somebody must be supposed to read an argument in order to define the meaning of the word, that the science of arguments involves introspection; then it follows from the fact that an animal cannot be fully defined except as that which upon being perceived, discriminated, and recognized presents certain characters, that the science of animals demands introspection.

Logic is nothing but a generalized expression (however obtained) for those inferences which any man makes coolly and carefully. To say then that if any man writes down premisses and the conclusions he draws from them, that he has here the facts themselves which form the data of logic and not merely representations of the facts, is an inaccuracy; but only in the sense in which it is an inaccuracy to say that this volume is present to the reader's sense instead of a nervous excitation. In this sense, it is equally an inaccuracy to speak of a remembered inference as one of the particular facts of which logic purports to be a generalization whereas it is really a representation of such a fact; and in the same sense it is an inaccuracy to speak of the first recognition of an inference as being one of these facts whereas it is really a representation of that process of the mind which is recognized and which is the veritable fact. The exact relation of a written word, proposition, or syllogism to logic may be stated as follows.

Every phenomenon has three aspects which may be called its elements. In the first place it may be differentiated from other phenomena and considered in its qualities; the phenomenon considered as having qualities may be called the phenomenal form. In the second place the phenomenal form may be objectified that is thought of—reproduced in the imagination; untill this is done we do not make it the subject of a thought, we do not say *it is*. Considered as a subject of thought the phenomenon may be called the phenomenal matter. Finally, as the phenomenon in the first aspect is regarded subjectively and so as within us, and in the second aspect objectively and so as without us, these aspects give rise to a third, that in which the phenomenon is regarded as a representation of something not present,—the noumenon. It is the regularities of the form which induce the objectification of the phenomenon, as will be explained in the appendix to this book. The notion of the noumenon is nothing more than the expectation of a recurrence of these regularities—a hypothesis that everything seen is matched by something not seen. It results from this similarity between phenomenon and noumenon that the latter is analyzable into the same elements as the former. Corresponding to the phenomenon considered as a representation we have the *accidents* of the noumenon; for they are external and therefore noumenal and yet representative of the substance or the thing itself.

Corresponding to the matter of the phenomenon we have the substantial matter of the noumenon and corresponding to the form of the phenomenon we have the substantial form of the noumenon. These terms imply elements; the *accidents* are regarded as prescinded from all substance whether form or matter, the matter as prescinded from form substantial or accidental, and the substantial form as prescinded from matter and accidents. In order to indicate these elements as aspects of one and the same noumenon, that is as elements to which the other elements are attached, the following terms may be used: instead of *accidents, object;* instead of *matter, thing;* instead of *form, qualities.* Having steeped ourselves now in these mysteries, shall we make a transcendental orgy? It is not to our taste. Let us rather turn towards the concrete again. It is obvious that an external representation of a thing cannot be perfect without being the thing itself; for no words can within finite limits say all that can be said of a thing, so that a perfect representation must be a copy and as it must represent the thing in its place it would be indistinguishable from the thing and the only difference between them would be in name. Now so far as a representation is true to the thing it represents—that is, so far as it is a representation— it is perfect and therefore for all such purposes as depend upon this attribute of it exclusively, it is the same thing. Take for example the word *white* and the color *white.* I do not know that anybody has succeeded in stating precisely what the notion is that the word calls up in our minds, but it can hardly be disputed that it is only so far as it calls up the same notion as the color that it is a representation of it or means it, at all. So with the word *locomotive* and the thing. The difference between them is that if one is attached to a car it will move it, and the other will not; and yet this is the very circumstance which the word expresses with reference to the locomotive. And yet what is the *thing* locomotive but a noumenon which excites a mental representation identical with that which the word excites, except in distinctness? A thing then and an external representation of it stand to each other in the very relation of matter and its accidents or rather of a thing and an object. Furthermore, the mental representation may be said to be identical with the thing for all purposes which depend exclusively upon those attributes which constitute it a representation. The mental representation so far as it is a representation is the *qualities* of the thing. Thus the thing represented, the external and the internal representations are, so far as their truth of the representation reaches, respectively *thing, object,* and *qualities.* Let us now see how each of these partakes of the three elements *matter, form,* and *accidents.*

Chapter II. The Syllogism

From the assertion of a rule and of a case under a rule, the affirmation of a result would follow necessarily. Such a conclusion would belong to the first figure of syllogisms. The terms *rule, case, result* are here employed to express facts in reference to the character of the propositions which express them and the relations of these propositions to each other. A rule is a fact expressed in a universal proposition whose predicate is the predicate of some fact included under it called a *result*. A case is a fact expressed in an affirmative proposition whose predicate is the subject of a rule. A *result* is a fact whose subject is the subject of a *case* and which has the quality of the rule and the quantity of the case. Thus the above definition of a syllogism of the first figure amounts to this; that from a universal premiss whose subject is Y and whose predicate is X and an affirmative premiss whose subject is Z and whose predicate is Y, a conclusion may be drawn whose subject is Z and whose predicate is X and which is affirmative or negative according as the premiss is affirmative or negative and universal or particular as the second premiss is universal or particular.

From the theorem that from the existence of a rule and the existence of a case, the existence of a result follows, two corollaries may be drawn; the first is that from the existence of a rule and the non-existence of a result the non-existence of a case follows and the second is that from the non-existence of a result and the existence of a case the non-existence of a rule follows. These corollaries are the statements of the cogency of the second and third figures. The three are represented in the diagrams on p. 316.

Explanation of Diagram. The three lines under each figure refer to the three Propositions of the Syllogism. The first column distinguishes these propositions. The second states the reference of each to rule, case, or result. The third and fourth denote the terms of each proposition so that a glance shows where any term of either proposition reappears in one of the others. The letters in circles show the *moods* or variations under the figures arising from differences in the quantity and quality of the proposition. A stands for a Universal Affirmative Proposition, E for a Universal Negative, I for a Particular Affirmative, O for a Particular Negative. The circles representing the two premisses and the conclusion of any mood are always in a straight line; thus in the first figure E as the major premiss, A as the minor, and E as the conclusion are in a straight line.

This diagram may be objected to as omitting 1° the Fourth figure and 2° two moods of the third figure A A I and E A O. The principle upon which these omissions are to be defended is this. Logical forms being merely devices for expressing arguments; all that can be required of

First Figure

	Subject	Predi-cate		Different possible propositions
Rule asserted	I	C	First Premiss	(A) or (E)
Case asserted	D	I	2nd Premiss	(A) or (I)
Result asserted	D	C	Conclusion	(E) or (A) or (O) or (I)

2nd Figure

	Subject	Predicate		
Rule asserted	I	C		(A) or
Result denied	D	C		(O) or (E) or (I) or (A)
Case denied	D	I		(O) or (E)

3rd Figure

	Subject	Predicate		
Result denied	D	C		(I) or (O) or (A) or (E)
Case asserted	D	I		(A) or (I)
Rule denied	I	C		(O) or (I)

them is that they should be capable of expressing every argument and their relations to each other, and should be developed from a plain conception. Now taking the notion of a rule, case, and result as our fundamental conception, we find no such moods in the third figure as A A I and E A O; and examining these moods themselves we find more is asserted in the premisses than is required to necessitate the conclusion, for a particular premiss may be substituted for either of the universal ones in both these moods. Now this is the case in no other instance in the first three figures. It would, therefore, be wrong to put these moods in the same class as those we have admitted, as though their premisses stood in the usual relation to their conclusions. The fourth figure, as it is called, depends upon the principle that a rule, a case under it which is itself a rule, and a case under this secondary rule which is contradictory of a result inferable from the primary rule and its case, cannot coëxist. Hence if any two of them are asserted the other must be denied. Now the primary rule must be negative because its result is contradictory of a case, and a result has the quality of its rule, while a case is always affirmative; while the contradictory case must be particular, because it contradicts a result of a case which is itself a rule, and all rules are universal and the result has the quantity of the case. For contradictories differ in quantity and quality.

Hence the primary rule, the secondary rule, and the contradictory case have each but one form; namely,

Primary Rule	No Y is X
Secondary Rule	All Z is Y
Contradictory Case	Some X is Z

There are obviously three different varieties of this so-called figure which in their turn are called moods. They are as follows:—

1st

Secondary Rule Asserted	All Z is Y
Primary Rule Asserted	No Y is X
∴ Contradictory Case Denied	No X is Z

2nd

Primary Rule Asserted	No Y is X
Contradictory Case Asserted	Some X is Z
∴ Secondary Rule Denied	Some Z is not Y

3rd

Contradictory Case Asserted	Some X is Z
Secondary Rule Asserted	All Z is Y
∴ Primary Rule Denied	Some Y is X

Two other moods are usually enumerated as belonging to this figure, namely A A I and E A O, but they are to be rejected upon the same principle that two moods were rejected in the third figure since they are included in I A I and E I O. From the premisses of A A I, however, more may be inferred than from those of I A I, although not in this figure. The kind of argument here described, ought to be taken into account as much as the second and third figures; but it differs from the other forms of syllogism so entirely in its structure, that it should not be called a figure but a different *class* of syllogism. Moreover its moods, as they are called, are not properly such but rather figures, since they are variations caused by interchanging a premiss with the conclusion and taking the contradictory of both, and not by making all allowable variations of each premiss independent of the other and combining them by permutation, for no premiss of this kind of argument admits of variations independently of the other premiss. We may call this fourth figure, then, triangular syllogism in allusion to the fact that it has three terms each of which is subject once and predicate once; while reasoning in the other figures may be called linear syllogism because it has extremes, one of the terms being never subject and another never predicate. The figures of triangular syllogism should be numbered as in the scheme just given.

The second, third, and fourth figures may be converted into the first; the second by converting the first premiss, the third by converting the second premiss, the fourth by converting the conclusion. Thus the fourth figure differs from the second and third as the conclusion differs from a premiss. The following are examples of Conversion.

1
All I is C
Some D is not C
∴ Some D is not I

As All I is C, I equals C which is I. As Some D is not C, Some D is not C which is I. Hence we have

All C which is I is I
Some D is not C which is I
∴ Some D is not I.

2
Some D is not C
All D is I
∴ Some I is not C

As Some D is not C, All D not C is I. Hence we have

> No D not C is C
> Some I is D not C
> ∴ Some I is not C

3

> No Y is X
> Some X is Z
> ∴ Some Z is not Y

This gives

> All X which is Z is Z
> Some not-Y is X which is Z
> ∴ Some not-Y is Z

There is no difficulty in converting the other moods.

As logic is the conditions of the relation of symbols in general to objects, two propositions which are expressive of the same fact are logically speaking one. Hence, as the second, third, and fourth figures differ from the first only by the difference of propositions expressive of the same fact—as is proved by conversion—this difference is extra-logical. But certain grammatical differences are to be taken into account in logic for the purpose of finding the means of expressing the necessary logical distinctions, and among these is the grammatical difference of the figures.

All the moods of syllogism are given in this table.

	I	A	E	O
E	o	E	A	i
A	I	**A**	**E**	O
I	A	I	**O**	E
o	e	O	I	a

In this table, as far as linear syllogism is concerned the proposition concerning the rule is entered at the top, that concerning the case at the side, and that concerning the result in the middle. **A E I O** denote moods of the first figure, A E I O those of the second, and A E I O those of the third. Triangular reasoning is entered in a different way. The contradictories of the premisses are entered at the top and sides, the primary rule being never at the side nor the contradictory case at the top. In the middle is found the converse of the conclusion when the first premiss is entered at the side, and the conclusion itself when the first premiss is entered at the top.

There are three relations between the propositions of a syllogism. The first is that between the proposition which follows apodictically from the others and that from which it follows. This is logical distinction in the strictest sense. The second is between the propositions as relating to a rule, a case, and a result. Since this distinction leads to that between the figures, it must be considered to be grammatical. The third is between the conclusion or proposition which is inferred, that is which is believed in on account of a belief in the others, and these others are the premisses. This is a rhetorical distinction. The proposition which follows apodictically, the proposition affirming or denying a result, and the conclusion will be called medial propositions. The proposition containing the subject of a medial proposition will be called a sinister proposition and the proposition containing the predicate of a medial proposition will be called a dexter proposition. The terms *grammatically, logically,* and *rhetorically, medial, sinister,* and *dexter* will then express all the distinctions between propositions. Thus

	sinister	medial	dexter
grammatically	affirmation or denial of case	affirmation or denial of result	affirmation or denial of rule
logically	proposition containing subject of apodictic conclusion	proposition following apodictically	proposition containing predicate of logically medial proposition
rhetorically	premiss containing subject of conclusion	conclusion	premiss containing predicate of conclusion

The subject of a medial proposition will be called the sinister term; the predicate the dexter term. The term not contained in the medial proposition the medial term.

	sinister	medial	dexter
grammatically	subject of case and result	predicate of case subject of rule	predicate of rule and result
logically	subject of proposition logically medial	subject of logically dexter predicate of logically sinister	predicate of logically medial and dexter
rhetorically	subject of conclusion	eliminated term	predicate of conclusion

In applying these terms to triangular syllogism for rule, case, result; substitute primary rule, secondary rule, and contradictory case respectively.

Logic of the Sciences

MS 113: Fall–Winter 1865

§1. *Conception of Logic*

Against the common conception of logic, I shall urge a sweeping objection. Almost every definition of the science that has ever been propounded has made it refer exclusively to thought or cognition. Now, if by thought is meant thought as it is, I object that thought is concrete and limited in time and otherwise, while the relations of logic have no such limitation. Suppose a syllogism to be written down; then every time that it is read it produces conviction; and this shows that it has a permanent convincing power or relevancy in itself, as much as the repeatedly observed blackness of the letters shows that they have a quality of blackness in themselves. But if by thought be meant thought in general from which everything that is particular has been eliminated, I then reply that such thought cannot really be thought; it is too pure and abstract; and that consequently logic does not deal with psychological laws as is now commonly supposed. In fact, thought may be illogical; it is only correct thought which is logical. What is this correct thought? It is thought which represents the intuition. Logic therefore deals with thought only in so far as the latter is a representation. And as I said every representation has its logical relations whether it is actually thought or not. So that it is more correct to say that logic is the science of the forms of representation than that it is the science of the forms of thought.

It is clear, however, that not all representations are subjects of logic. There are three kinds of representation; which I denominate

Signification
Imitation
Verity

A *sign* is a representation which accords with its object without any real and essential correspondence.

A *copy* is a representation which really and in its self refers to its object by resembling it.

A //*type/symbol*// is a representation whose correspondence with its object is of the same immaterial kind as a *sign* but is founded nevertheless in its very nature and is not merely supposed and fictitious.

Chapter I

The term *representation* denotes with Hamilton a mediate cognition, with Hegel a mental image, and with Kant a cognition in the widest sense. Its original and ordinary meaning, is that it is something which stands for another thing. In the present work instead of being restricted to something within the mind, it will be extended to things which do not even address the mind. We are capable of understanding representations only by having conceptions or mental representations, which represent the given representation as a representation. Then, why is not every representation which translates another or otherwise represents it in its representative character, addressed by it? A conceptualist might reply, that the conception actually realizes the abstraction which the word only indicates; but it does not realize what is in the thing, and so it stands on the same footing as the word. Man has sensation or receptivity, but so has a looking-glass. Man has the power of testing the truth of representations by comparison; but so has a syllogism on paper. Man elaborates knowledge by abstraction; but so does a proposition. Man first made words not words man; but the mind itself has been made by natural representations. It would be false to say, that man makes use of words, any more than words employ man. A word may be written down over and over again, and every inscription of it is necessarily the same in sense; while man is in one place and in one time,—that is, has identity. But it is not the man himself but his conceptions, which are representations; and these have no more individuality in their representative character than words have. Conceptions comprehend themselves, while words require conceptions to understand them. It is true; but if conceptions require nothing else to translate them into conceptions, no more do words require anything to translate them into words. Thus we are forced to say that a representation which represents another representation as a representation is the *subject* of that representation,—in the same sense in which the human conception is. We must thence also admit that a thing in its attributes is a representation of the same thing in itself.

We can, now, apply induction to *all that is,* in the widest sense; and so find the character of the *summum genus.* Whatever is immediately present to us, will be instances of *what is.* These instances, have then two characters

1 They are representations

and   2 They are addressed to *us.*

That they are addressed to *us,* is only the limitation of our selection, and therefore must be abstracted from. That they are representations, arises from their being *taken* as instances. They are not merely representations of instances, but are representations *as* instances. Hence, we presume that *whatever is* is a representation. This is confirmed by an indirect form of argument.[1] If there were something which were not a representation it would not be represented, for an object represented is a representation of the same object in itself. But the supposition of anything unrepresented, is self-contradictory since that which is supposed is thereby represented. Hence *all is representative.*

It would be impossible to analyze representation into its inward constituent characters since any elements into which it might seem to be separated would be, themselves, representations. Representation implies contrast; hence it has an inward character only so far as that can be contrasted with something. Now, as all things are representations alike, they can only be contrasted in their relations. Hence, the only inward character of representation is the relation of anything to itself,—*identity.* But the different essential external relations of representation can be distinguished very well, because all things do not stand in essential relation to any one representation. It is true, that these relations are themselves representations and so involve each other. But though they cannot be separated in the nature of things, they can in representation.

To understand representation as a mark, we must consider the different orders of marks. By a mark of the 1st, 2nd, 3rd order is meant one which indicates a state of things which essentially supposes one

---

1. I say *form* of argument for I do not pretend that these arguments contain any matter.

thing, two things, or three things. A mark of the second order determines the subject in two ways, viz.: 1st to relate to a certain object and
2nd to relate to it in a certain respect. Hence it consists of two marks of
the first order which are essential to each other; viz.: 1st a mark which
the subject has in common with the correlate and 2nd the distinction
which the subject has from the correlate. For example; "on my right
hand" consists 1st of being relatively to *me* and 2nd of being at the
right hand.

A mark of the third order, implies two things beside the subject; it
therefore 1st determines the subject to stand in a certain relation to the
first thing, 2nd to stand in a certain relation to the second thing, 3rd to
stand in such relations to the two that these relations shall involve each
other, for otherwise we should have merely two marks of the second
order and not any of a different order. Hence, a mark of the third order
consists of three mutually involved marks of the 2nd order. Each of
these marks of the second order must consist of two marks of the 1st
order. Accordingly the mark of the third order consists of

1 Being relatively to A
2 Being of a kind a
3 Being relatively to B
4 Being of a kind b.

Chaper I. Definition of Logic

It is requisite first to define logic; and to indicate not merely its
genus and difference, but also the genus and difference of its *proximum
genus* up to the *genus summum*.

What is the *genus summum?* *Being,* an ambiguous word—in one of
its senses is the name for it. But we wish, not its name, but its character.

We wish to find the character of the *summum genus*. That is, to
make the widest possible induction. To find the character of a class by
induction we must take instances of that class. Now therefore we must
take instances in general. Now, instances taken by us, are 1st in virtue
of being taken by us feelings, and 2nd in virtue of being instances they
are representations (that is, are considered as representations). The
first character belongs to them by virtue of the limitation of our selection. Taking, therefore, the other character alone we by induction at-

tribute this to the class of which they are instances. Hence we infer that *all is representation.*

There seems to be a fallacy here. For, it may be said, whenever we take instances of a class in order to make an induction we must take representations but we do not conclude that the character of those representations as images belongs to the class. Thus we do not say all horses have representations of manes but all horses have manes. But this objection will not hold, because in other cases we are making inductions about what is supposed and not about what is given. Hence the representations are not themselves instances but representations of instances; although the instances may be themselves representations. An image of a horse is not a horse; an image of a horse has an image of a mane; hence we *suppose* that a horse has a mane; and hence we make the induction that all horses have manes. But in the present case, the representations are the very instances themselves. So that this objection does not hold.

Another objection may be made. It may be admitted that the induction is legitimate but its probability may be held to be small owing to the probability that the character of representation is peculiar to the mind. Any one who attempts to *prove,* that representation is peculiar to the mind is either attempting to prove a theory of idealism, upon which I do not commit myself at present, and is therefore arguing beside the question; or else he does not understand fully what representation is. An Aztec inscription which no one can read, a natural face upon a rock which no one has seen or shall see, is still a representation. The color of a flower upon the flower is the representation of the flower in itself. To suppose, therefore, that there are things which are not representations is to suppose that there are things which are wrapped up in themselves and have no attributes. Now what is the probability of such a supposition? It is unwarrantable not only for us, not only for every mind, it not only has no mentally representable facts to go upon, but it has no representable facts at all to go upon. No proposition can be expressed in any way whether as readable or not which would warrant it, for that proposition would be a representation of the thing in some respect, and this respect would be an attribute of the thing. Hence it is an *absolutely* unwarrantable supposition and hence the probability of our induction amounts to absolute certainty.

The *Summum Genus,* or What is, is representation, then. Now what are its proximate differences? To ascertain these we must first consider what it implies. Certain points are implied in representation, because they result from the induction by which it was prescinded. Representation implies first an *object* represented; 2nd a mind or rather abstracting from the personal element, a representation (itself or other) to which it addresses itself. I call this the *subject*. 3rd a *Ground* or Reason which determines it to represent that object to that subject. We have nothing else implied in the representation as representation. Hence representation has three marks only namely—

1 Reference to an Object
2 Reference to a Ground
3 Reference to a Subject.

Accordingly, the differences of representation are differences of one or more of these marks. As these marks are references they are determined first by the object of reference, 2nd by the subject of reference, and 3rd by the Ground of reference. Hence, their differences (the subject of reference or representation being already determinate) are either differences of the object of reference—i.e. Object, Ground, or Subject of the Representation—or of the Ground of Reference. Now the ground of reference of each of these references is the Ground of the representation. Hence, a difference in the ground of representation is the only difference which necessarily implies a difference in all three of the marks of representation.

Now proximate or highest differences are such as affect the greatest number of marks. This can be shown by example. Being male is not a proximate difference of animal because it affects but few marks; but having a backbone is, because it affects almost all the marks. Hence as differences in the Ground are the only ones which affect all the marks of representation, they must constitute the proximate differences of representation. Now the ground of a representation has three marks

1st It determines a certain representation
to refer to a certain Object
2nd It determines that representation
to refer to it
3rd It determines that representation
to refer to a certain subject

These marks are all marks of determination. Now a determination is in reference to another determination either mediate or immediate; that is, it either results from the latter or not. The second of the above determinations is absolutely immediate and the others are mediate in reference to it. They are either mediate or immediate in reference to each other. Such differences will affect both of these marks and so the ground and so its second mark by affecting the object of it. Hence they are proximate differences of the ground and hence they are proximate differences of representation. So the species of representation are three; to wit,

1. Representations whose object is determined by its subject; that is to say whose Ground is a character of the Subject. If this subject is plural, of course the character must be common. Thus, if two men *agree* to have a certain sign denote certain things, that sign is a representation of this kind. Accordingly, I call this species of representation *Sign*.

2. Representations whose subject and object depend immediately upon the ground and not upon any character of either. But the ground in any case must be a character of the representation which connects it with subject and object. Hence such representations are those which agree immediately with both subject and object in some characters. It is this sort of representation which an individual is of itself; and also which a sensation is. For a sensation agrees immediately with the thing in affecting the sense and with the mind in being affected by the thing. It is this sort of representation also which a picture is. Accordingly I call this species of representation *copy*.

3. Representations whose subject depends upon its object. That is which are intelligible to those who can comprehend a certain character of the object—if there are several objects, a common character. It is this sort of representation which a *conception* is; and which a word is, after it has once been acquired as a *sign*. I call this species of representation *Symbol*.

Now it is to be observed that the Ground of either kind of Representation is a common character and therefore may be prescinded. And any common character not only may but does serve as the Ground of some representation. Hence, Ground and Prescindible are coëxtensive terms, and we may more concisely define as follows:—

Representations are either

    1. Signs; whose prescindible is from the subject

    2. Copies; whose prescindible is from Subject and Object

    3. Symbols; whose prescindible is from the object.

We are now ready to assign logic its definition. For this purpose, it must be granted that logic is a symbol

whose essential end is

to test

$\Big\{$ truth,

$\Big($ by reasons.

Now firstly since its object then is a representation which has a reason for its truth; it cannot be a sign for a sign has no ground in the object and hence is arbitrary or irrational. And secondly since the object of logic has truth—that is determinate reference to an object and that by reason—it cannot be a copy, for copies are true only in so far as they are like their objects, but nothing is totally unlike anything since all things are representations at least, and nothing is exactly like anything except that which is identical with it; that is, itself. Hence copies have no determinate or exclusive reference to any objects but themselves. Now the truth of a thing of itself is self-grounded and has no reason for reasonable truth is mediate truth. Hence no copies have reasonable truth and are not objects of logic.

Hence only symbols are objects of logic and as their reference to their object is always owing to a common character or reason within the objects, they all have reasonable truth and logic must refer to them universally.

Logic tests its object. But tests are the result of classification, are but the utilization of classification. Hence logic classifies symbols.

Now we have seen that logic comes under the genus symbol. To define it we must state the difference of this genus. But this would necessitate the classification of symbols which is the implication of logic. Now a definition relates only to essence and does not enter into implication. Hence since we can go no further without entering into the implication of logic we must already have defined logic in saying that it is the symbol which classifies symbols in general in reference to the reason of their reference to their objects.

Chapter II

As Logic is a classificatory science, the study of it should be preceded by the study of the pure laws of classification; but as these have never been developed, we must study them as we go along. The science of classification regards matters as explained when the class under which they come is stated. Thus, that neat, swine, sheep, and deer are herbivora is explained by the fact that all cloven-footed animals are herbivora. Hence, since that which is explained is a result of that which explains it, it is proper in classificatory science to regard every species as a product of the union of the abstractions which are embodied in it. Then the character of any genus is an abstraction which is realized in its species by means of its differences; and all the differences are all the ways in which it is realized. Hence, if we are considering as we always should in pure science, not what is but what is possible, the division of a genus into its species, is the solution of the problem "how can the abstraction which is the character of this genus be realized?" The character of the genus is the Datum and the difference is the Requisitum. But in general there will not be sufficient connection between these taken alone, and it will be necessary to add certain Conditions and as these vary so will the system of classification vary.

We may take as an example the division of representations made in the last chapter. Representation is the character of standing to a subject for an object upon some ground. The character which must belong to that character was the quaesitum. The condition was that the division should concern representation as representation that is that the character required should be a relation between the essential elements of representation. Now the Ground is the only element of representation which is a relation; it is an agreement and may lie in the subject, in the object, or between them. This gives our three species.

In the case, which now comes before us, which is the highest logical division of symbols, the conditions are different. They are two; first that symbols should be considered in regard to their reference to objects and second that this reference should be considered in respect to its ground. Since the object is mediately or immediately symbolized by every subject of its symbol; and since also the ground of the symbol is a character of the object, every symbol refers to its subject and ground not only immediately but also mediately through its object. It thus has an objective reference, not merely to its object in itself, but also to its subject and ground.

We may then call the object in itself prescinded from subject and ground the *matter*, the ground considered as in the object the *form*, and the subject considered as referring to the object, the *entelechy*.

Now the function of a symbol is to stand for its object to its subject. Hence its function in respect to the subject is to stand for its object.

But a function in respect to a subject is a use; so the use of a symbol is to stand for its object.

[More on the Categories (A)]

The universal hypothesis which we are forced always to make is of a substance, that there is something which *is*. This necessity is the first law of the understanding and its product is the first category.

Next we find by induction that whatever is, is of some kind; whence we say that were it not of some kind there would be no necessity of supposing that it is. Thus we attain the notion of Quality, which is the second Category and the First order of mark. What is, must have a *ground* for being.

Next we find also by induction, that of whatever kind any thing is, it is in regard to something else; whence we say Quality is the outward of a thing and could not be were there nothing without. Thus we attain the notion of Relation, which is the third category and the second order of mark. What is, must not only have a ground for being, but an *object*. Is anything blue, there must be something which is not so, so that it is blue relatively to that. A mark of the second order, such as "patriotic" is one wherein this *object* is explicit. It consists of a mark of the first order, as *loving*, and of a mode of a mark, as having reference to country. And these are taken in synthesis. A mark of the second order applied to one substance, supposes another, which other shall have an other mark of the same order which supposes the first. But the two *grounds* may be identical and so may the two objects. Either of two correlative qualities may be taken as the ground of either of the two interdependent relations, and thus there are two kinds of marks of the second order, the positive and the negative. Thus, that A is great in comparison to B is a positive relation of A to B, but that B is that in comparison to which A is great is a negative relation of B to A. A relation considered objectively is a *fact;* objectively positive relation is *action;* objectively negative relation is *passion* (suffering).

Next we find by induction that whatever is of a certain kind in comparison to another, is so for somebody; hence we say that comparison supposes that someone makes a comparison. Thus we get the notion of Representation which is the third order of mark, and the fourth Category. What is, must not only have a ground and an object, but also a subject. Blueness, supposes not merely something not blue, but also, the word which expresses—or as we may say perceives—the distinction. A mark of the third order such as "Madonna" is one wherein this *subject* is explicit. It supposes a mark of the second order, such as resemblance to a holy woman, and also a mode of that mark, as addressing the eye. And these are taken in synthesis. A mark of the third order applied to one substance supposes two others, each of which shall have a mark of the same order which supposes the other two, but with perhaps different grounds. The three grounds may, however, coincide as also may the three substances. Thus *portrait* supposes sitter and painter, and the ground is a certain form and color. But the *sitter* also represents the portrait to the painter; the ground in this case as it happens being the same. The painter also represents

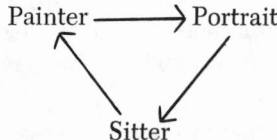

Portrait represents sitter to Beholder
Sitter represents beholder to Portrait
Beholder represents Portrait to Sitter

Eglise represents Church to Frenchman
Church   ”   Frenchman ” Eglise
Frenchman ”   Eglise   ” Church

because churches all have that character.

[More on the Categories (B)]

The general explanation which is usually given of all things is that there is some substratum, of which they are only phenomena. The hypothesis is only that there is that which *is*.

Everything has some character. This should be the first grand Induction of abstract science. Had anything no character, what would be the necessity of supposing it to be? If none, the truth of this induction is the condition of the validity of our first hypothesis, although it is only in the light of that result that this can be attained. To explain this relation, we say that whatever is must have a *ground* for being; that is, it must have qualities or marks and it is only in virtue of them that it is.

Everything stands in relation to something. This is the second grand induction. Were anything not in comparison with something, what character would it have? If none, the truth of our second induction is the condition of the validity of the first; although it can only be made after the first. To explain this we say that, whatever has a *ground* must have an *object*.

Everything may be comprehended or more strictly translated by something; that is has something which is capable of such a determination as to stand for something through this thing; somewhat as the pollen-grain of a flower stands to the ovule which it penetrates for plant from which it came since it transmits the peculiarities of the latter. In somewhat the same sense, though not to the same degree, everything is a medium between something and something. Everything has a relation to something which relation has a character which corresponds in some degree to the relation of the first thing to something. This is the third grand Induction. That to which a thing stands for something is that which brings the thing into comparison with that for which it stands. Now, were a thing not brought into comparison with anything, how would it be in comparison with anything? If not at all, then the truth of this third Induction is the condition of the validity of the second, though its enunciation supposes the latter. Hence we infer, that whatever is in relation to an *object* must have a *subject*, which is that which it determines in respect to its object.

From what has been said, it appears that marks may be regarded from three points of view according to their greater or less determination. A mark which is determined in reference to the ground alone, may be called a mark of the first order; if it is determined also in reference to the object, a mark of the second order; and if it is determined in reference to the subject also, a mark of the third order.

The mark of the first order does not seem to have any salient points. The mark of the second order implies a relation. A relation finds place between two things one of which is determined in itself relatively to the other. If each is determined relatively to the other and it is not denied that in what were called real relations or events this is always the case; but if so there are two relations, not one. One relation then determines one object in itself and not the other. Thus if a needle points to a pole, the needle is determined to point in a certain direction but not so the pole. True the pole is determined to be situated in a certain line but this owing to the fact that the above relation implies another. Now both correlates have marks of the second order, but these two marks are of different kinds since in one case the *ground* inheres in that to which the mark belongs and in the other case in the *subject*. So that there are two classes of relations of which the former may be termed *positive*, and the latter *negative*.

The mark of the third order is the mark of *representation*. Representation takes place between three things one of which is related to the other two, one of which is therefore related mediately to the other. The ground of the representation, then, may inhere in the mediating thing or in one of the extreme things. In the former case there can be no distinction between the extremes. In the latter case, one extreme contains the ground and the other does not. Hence there will be three kinds of marks of the third order

> 1st those whose ground inheres in the subject
> 2nd those whose ground goes with the mark itself
> 3rd those whose ground inheres in the object.

Let us have a clear notion of this division:—

In the first place, then, if the ground determines the subject in itself, there will be no relation of the representation to its object in itself but only in the subject. No quality of the object will be implied by the representation, therefore, since that would be a ground of agreement in the object. The representation will therefore be unsusceptible of truth. An imperfect example of such a representation is a *proper name* the ground of which is a convention between the persons who use it. Such a representation may be called an index. But the only adequate example of an index is the representation to one's self of one's own identity by one's relation to anything. Thus only can a generalization be excluded; and generalization refers to the quality of the object. Such a representation is therefore in reality nothing but relation considered as representation; that is, there is no subject, other than the object.

In the second place, if the ground of the representation determines the representation in itself.

[More on the Categories (C)]

The first conception of all is that of substance or that which *is*.

Whatever is is of some kind; were it not of some sort there would be no necessity for supposing it to be. This conception, therefore, of

Internal Mark—or Quality (which is the same, objectified)—is the generalization of that which receives its physical explanation by the hypothesis that it is, though it is a generalization which can only be made in the light of the theory of *substance*. It is therefore a new law; namely, that whatever is must have a *ground* or general essence. This ground, to which being such and such is reference to, when prescinded from this reference is a pure form or idea.

Of whatever kind anything is, it is in comparison with something else; Quality is only the outside of substance and implies therefore something without. This notion which appears as Relation or Act—according as it is viewed subjectively or objectively, is a second generalization which that of Quality enables us to make. What is must not only have a *ground* but also and therefore, an *object*. This *object*, regarded abstractly, is matter.

In whatever relation anything is, it is for some purpose, effect, or actuality; if nobody should make a comparison the comparison would not be made. This notion of representation or purpose—according as it is taken as logical or real—is a third generalization which succeeds to that of Relativity. What is, and has a *ground*, since it has also an *object*, has in the third place a *subject*. This *subject*, which must not be supposed to be a mind though it may be a human representation, and which is only that which is determined by the representation to agree with it in its reference to the object on that ground,—this subject is an abstraction which philosophers have left too much out of account.

There is no fourth generalization which can be made in this line.

Each of these three general conceptions, reference to the ground, reference to the object, and reference to the subject, has three phases: the Grammatical, Logical, and Real or as I prefer to say the Rhetorical. The grammatical phase comes first. The first element of grammar is the noun or rather the pronoun *This*. Then the reference of this to the ground is the application of the verb; the reference to the object is the suffering object; and the reference to the subject is the personal object. Grammarians enumerate two other completing objects viz.:—the genitive and the factitive. But a genitive object is only a suffering object which is considered particularly in its reaction; while the factitive object is philosophically a part of the verb for if I make a man a barbarian (or barbarize him) what particular barbarian I make him is only the barbarian which *that* man would be. Application of the verb, of the suffering object, and of the personal object, appear in logic as three kinds of marks; 1st the internal mark or the character of a term considered in itself; second the relation to a particular term; and third representation as a character of a term. The internal mark, relation, and representation; in their transcendental (or rhetorical) transformation, appear as quality, event, and purposeful act.

But the purport of the above generalizations is that whatever is has a ground and then an object, and then a subject. That every noun has a verb applicable is obvious. But every verb does not appear to have a suffering object. Thus, the sentence, this is blue, is complete, in itself. But, if we retrace our steps, we observe that we said, everything is such as it is in comparison with something else. This is an old and established axiom. Now, we may have used suffering object in too wide a sense, but in such sense as we have used it, it is evident that anything *not blue* might be added as the suffering object of the above sentence. In fact, the effect of this ancient maxim is that '*blue*' MEANS 'blue in comparison to' and therefore requires a suffering object. The transitive verb supplies this comparison. If a man kills a deer, that in comparison to which he is a killer is the deer. No other comparison is *needed*. Even if we say "sorghum resembles broom corn," though there is no such contrast that broom corn does not in its turn also resemble sorghum, yet there is the form of a contrast, that is to say there is a contrast if we abstract from the peculiar meaning of the verb. But we shall examine this matter of resemblance further on. There is undoubtedly a philosophical distinction between a transitive and an intransitive verb; but the latter is nothing but that species of the former which allows its object most readily to be dropped—which amounts to supplying its place by an indefinite pronoun. He murders something and he is a murderer are the same. In the third place every sentence is said to require a personal object. That is; if A kills B he kills him to or for someone. This point is best illustrated in its other phases.

Let us take up now the logical phase. That every term has an internal [. . .]

/The Logic Notebook/

MSS 114 and 117:
12 November 1865–8 December 1866

Miscellaneous Observations

12 Nov. 1865

What is a real definition? A definition of a word whose essence lies in its denotation.

12 Nov. 1865

There are three forms of question.
1. Are quadrupeds animals?
2. Are there quadruped animals?
3. Are quadruped animals either quadruped or animal?
The affirmative answers will be
To 1. Universal Affirmative. Yes. Quadrupeds are animals.
To 2. Particular Affirmative. Yes. Quadruped animals exist.
To 3. Universal Negative. Yes. There is no animal quadruped.

Nov. 14

There is no difference logically between hypotheticals and categoricals. The subject is a sign of the predicate, the antecedent of the consequent; and this is the only point that concerns logic.

Nov. 14

Admit that there are no coëxtensive notions (and there never are *known* to be) and the system of propositions is reduced to great simplicity, thus

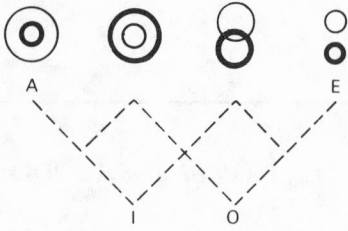

If we have four simple relations *abcd* and join them thus

  a   *b*   *c*   *d*

    ab   *bc*   *cd*   to make nine judgments of a simple character,

      abc   *bcd*

five others remain: *ac ad bd abd acd.*

Nov. 14

Deduction may be reduced to the inference of A (informative)
Induction   "   "   "   to the inference of E (connotative)
Hypothesis   "   "   "   to the inference of I (denotative)

and thus the whole of logic is developable from the distinction of Substantial Form, Matter, and Accident.

Nov. 14

The doctrine of Immortality which makes man last forever is not so ennobling as its contrary which must make man's interest outrun himself, in time as well as space.

Do you say that man lives in all time? I will match all your arguments by others to show that he lives in all space.

Nov. 15

A fallacy is a miracle. I cannot admit its existence as a violation of logical law. A fallacy is a reasoning from mistaken data. That is 1st from insufficient data or from a fallacious inference or 2nd from using as data something different from what appears to be used. Thus for example if I say for fun

> It either rains or it doesn't rain
> It doesn't rain
> ∴ It rains

This conclusion is not reached directly from the premisses written here but from certain emotional premisses relating to fun.

Nov. 15

The common-sense doctrine is to be held as far as this goes,—that there are no fallacies. Prove that a given belief really arises from certain data universal to all mankind and it must be admitted. Doubt that (as Hume did) and what has common-sense to say? Scepticism may doubt everything in particular; it must not lay down any rule of doubt for therein it ceases to be scepticism.

Dec. 13

It is necessary to reduce all our actions to logical processes so that to do anything is but to take another step in the chain of inference. Thus only can we effect that complete reciprocity between Thought and its Object which it was Kant's Copernican step to announce.

Dec. 13

The Scotch philosophers used to tell us that the burden of proof is in favor of the results of Common Sense. The burden of proof is a phrase of the court-room where questions *must be decided* one way or the other and has no place in speculative science where indefinite suspension of judgment is permissible. However, since several of the important questions of philosophy are matters of practical interest, it may be allowed to speak of a burden of proof in their practical reference. In general, it will lie with a metaphysical theory. But common sense is itself a congeries of metaphysical theories. And moreover the history of modern philosophy may be stated in epitome as the awakening of the mind to the unsatisfactoriness of that theory that *man feels*. It cannot indeed be denied that there is some truth in this; at any rate it is a hypothesis which accounts very prettily for many facts. In particular it accounts for the partial and only partial confirmation which opinions receive from the opinions of others. How natural it is to infer from this that they are *our* opinions, and so to get an idea that *we are* and that *we think*. Perhaps we cannot even yet devise any more satisfactory explanation of this fact. But the theory puts an *I* and a *not-I* over against each other in absolute separation and yet so that one determines the other. Now immediately upon this, Scepticism arises as to the validity of this conception of the determination of a thing by another without it, of *causality*, that is to say. To resolve this problem we have been forced first to consider the object as also determined by the subject. And this is to encroach already upon the absolute boundary of *I* and *not-I.* But even thus the object itself does not determine the subject, a false object does it.

* * * * * *

What shall we finally say then? The theory that man is is incomprehensible and self-contradictory.

But is it not justified? Yes.

Shall we then attempt to satisfy our intellects with an incomprehensible and self-contradictory hypothesis? Certainly not. Nay, such a hypothesis is not intellectual by the very definition of the intellect. It cannot be held in a comprehensible form but it may be held.

The intellect did not make this hypothesis. The intellect makes no hypotheses which are incomprehensible. The intellect is not therefore alone concerned in any proposition.

But we make it. All that the words convey is something incapable of being made distinct. Hence it is emotional, in its own nature. And as an emotion it is justified.

Dec. 14

Hegel makes a great boast of the fact that his Logic developes its own method. Mine pursues a rational method of which the logic itself is but the deduction and proof. Moreover I am not forced to make my book unintelligible in order to follow mine, but on the contrary it is the very proceedure which perspicuity demands. Another thing; Hegel never deduces the necessity of considering what he considers before considering it; but I never introduce a distinction without having deduced the necessity for it.

Dec. 15

When the implication is constant, if two symbols are equal in extension or intension they are equal in both. Neither can be increased relatively to the other in either respect without diminishing it in the other respect. Accordingly,

1. If A and B are coëxtensive, they are cointensive.

2. Increase the extension of A; you diminish its intension. Hence if A is superordinate to B in extension, it is subordinate in intension. If we had increased the intension of B, we should have produced the same result.

3. Next add to *B* an extension which *A* has not. You diminish its intension. You cannot however leave it subordinate, superordinate, or cointensive with *A*. And *supposing that there is a symbol which denotes any sum of symbols,* there will be a symbol *C* to which both *A* and *B* are subordinate in extension. Hence, they will both be superordinate to it in intension and will have in common the intension of *C*. Hence they will intersect in intension.

If on the other hand we had added to *A* an intension excluded from *B*, we should have diminished the extension of *A* without leaving it subordinate, superordinate, or coextensive with *B*. And *supposing that any sum of intensions has some symbol to connote it,* there will be a symbol *C′* to which both *A* and *B* are subordinate in intension. Hence they will both be superordinate to it in extension and will intersect in extension.

4. Next suppose that from the extensions of both *A* and *B* we take away that part which they have in common. This will only add to the intension of both and as they cannot be subordinate, superordinate, or cointensive, they will still intersect in intension.

Or suppose they are made to exclude each other in intension; then by the same reasoning, they would intersect in extension.

Hence since intersection in either quantity by (3) implies intersection in both it follows that upon the suppositions of (3) there can be no exclusion either in extension or intension. But if there is no exclusion, there is no coincidence or subordination since these imply exclusion (?) and hence nothing but intersection.

But the intension of *C* may be only *being* which is the *Summum Genus,* and the extension of *C′* may be only *nothing* which is the *Infima Species.*

In the former case therefore they may be said to exclude each other in intension and in the latter case to exclude each other in extension.

Then we have when information is constant—

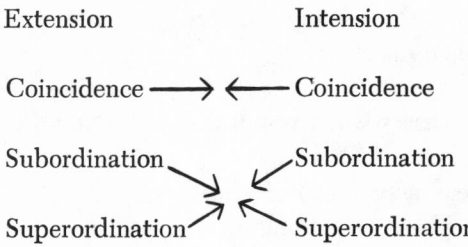

Extension	Intension
Coincidence ⟶ ⟵ Coincidence	
Subordination	Subordination
Superordination	Superordination

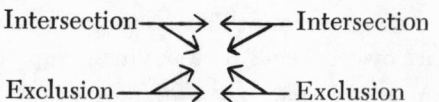

If *A* and *B* exclude each other both in extension and intension, their common extension is *nothing* and their common intension *being*.

Let us now change our implication. If we have no implication we shall have no relations of extension and intension but intersection. Hence we shall have no nothing nor being. All connotation will be self-contradictory and all denotation will be obscure.

When implication is at a maximum intersection in extension and intension will be abolished. Consequently subordination will be abolished. Consequently all classes will exclude each other and their common extension will be *nothing* and their common intension *being*.

In the formula
$$\text{Extension} \times \text{Intension} = \text{Implication}$$
we may have the values

$$
\begin{aligned}
&(1) & 0 &\times 0 = 0 \\
&(2) & 0 &\times n = 0 \\
&(3) & 0 &\times \infty = 0 \\
&(4) & 0 &\times \infty = n \\
&(5) & 0 &\times \infty = \infty \\
&(6) & n &\times 0 = 0 \\
&(7) & n &\times n = n \\
&(8) & n &\times \infty = \infty \\
&(9) & \infty &\times 0 = 0 \\
&(10) & \infty &\times 0 = n \\
&(11) & \infty &\times 0 = \infty \\
&(12) & \infty &\times n = \infty \\
&(13) & \infty &\times \infty = \infty
\end{aligned}
$$

(7)   will be the case with any ordinary symbol.

(4)   is the ordinary *nothing*.

(10) the ordinary *being*.

These are the cases when Implication is n. Now for those where it is 0.

(6)   is the case of a *sign*, (2) of a *copy*.

(1)   would be a sign of nothing or a copy of being which are undetermined to be representations.

(9)   would be *being* supposing it were not known to be, or *being* considered abstractly of the fact that it is.

(3)   would be *nothing* abstracting from the fact that there is anything so that its opposition is taken away.

A being which isn't, would be a nothing which is unopposed to anything; hence *being* abstracted from the fact that it is is abstracted from all that makes it differ from nothing abstracted from its opposition and *vice versa.*

We will now take up the cases where the implication = ∞.

(12) is *being* of which some determinate quality is supposed to be known.

(8)   is a contradiction it being implied that it exists.

(13) is *being* which is supposed to have all attributes.

(11) would purport to be a complete list of all beings.

(5)   would purport to be a complete conjunction of all attributes.

What has just been said and the perfect balance of extension and comprehension here made manifest, calls to our mind that the forms E I O of propositions are modifications of the primary form A in extension only, but A is contradicted not only by I or

"A class subordinate to A in extension is denoted by a symbol exclusive of B in extension"

but also by

"A class exclusive of A in comprehension is denoted by a symbol subordinate to B in comprehension."

Let a class exclusive of A in comprehension be called a reverse of A. And Let a symbol subordinate to B in comprehension be called somewhat B.

Then we have

A   All A is B   No reverse of A is at all B
I   Some A is B
W   A reverse of A is B   Some A is not in any given respect B
E   No A is B
O   Some A is not B
U   A reverse of A is not B
H   All A is somewhat B   No reverse of A is B
Ω   Some A is somewhat B
Y   A reverse of A is somewhat B   Some A is not B

A is contradicted by O and Y
I   ”   ”   ” E
W is   ”   ” H
E ”   ”   ” I
O ”   ”   ” A
U
H is contradicted by W
Ω
Y ”   ”   ” A.

Proof of the above relations

S is P

1. If we take A and O both Informatively it will appear that both may be true if P has no intension and both false if S has no extension. But taking the five cases of extension we see that A has 2 and O the other three.

In the same way if we take A and Y informatively both may be false if P has no intension and both true if S has no extension. But of the 5 relations of intension A admits 2 and Y the other 3.

Dec. 20

I find that a good deal of the above is wrong. Propositions have relations of Intension corresponding to

Subalternation
and   Contradictory

which are relations of Extension. Two forms of Propositions are contradictory when taking any symbol as predicate term all terms are divisible into such which may be put as subject term of one and of the other.

Corresponding to this will be a relation between two forms such that any symbol being taken as subject term of both, all symbols are divisible into such as may be put into predicate term of one or the other.

Thus   All A is B   and
        Some A is not B   are contradictory.

Because if the whole extension of A is in that of B then it is not true that some of it is excluded from A. And *vice versa.*

Now take   All A is B
and   The reverse of A is somewhat B

Now if the whole intension of B is in the intension of A, no part of it is excluded from the intension of A; hence no part of it is in that which is entirely excluded from A; and hence no part of it is in that from which the intension of A is entirely excluded. On the other hand take any intension you please it is either wholly in A or else some part of it is out of A, if it is out of A it is in what is excluded from A, and hence is in that from which the intension of A is entirely excluded.

For example let B be taken as *quadruped* and A as *sentient.* Now since quadruped is not in sentient, part of it out of sentient, part of it therefore is in that in which no part of sentient is. The reverse of A has all the qualities which A has not hence it has that part of B which A has not.

The propositions   Some A is not B
and   The reverse of A resembles B

will coincide when the former is denotative and the latter connotative.
The same intensive relation subsists between

{ A is somewhat B
{ The reverse of A is B

And the following are contradictory

{ The reverse of A is B
{ The reverse of A is not B

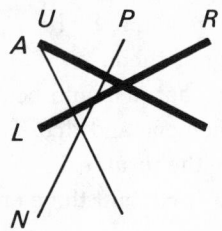

The following is important.

Since the reverse of A connotes all that A does not connote; A must be determined in every respect (that is must be an individual) or else the reverse will connote contradictory attributes and so have no extent. And, therefore, there is no reverse of a particular since there is no particular of an individual. Consequently reverses are *singular* judgments.

Since the negative of B denotes all that B does not denote; B must have a definite sphere (that is must be a simple attribute) or else its negative will denote heterogeneous classes and so have no intent. And therefore there is no negative of a limitative since there is no limitative of a simple attribute. Consequently negatives are simple statements.

A reverse however when connotative need not be singular, nor need a negative when denotative be simple.

If the reverse negative is a singular simple proposition, then from All A is B it follows that The reverse of A is not B and conversely. So that they coincide.

The difference between *being* and a heterogeneous sum of classes is that *being* not only has no intent but has all extent.

The difference between *nothing* and a self-contradiction is that *nothing* not only has no extent but has no intent.

We have therefore
{
Being
Sum of Classes
Nothing
Self-Contradictions
All self-contradictions at once.
}

Remarks on Passages in Kant

In the *Critic of the Pure Reason* ("Transcendental Stoicheiology," 2nd Part, 1st Division, Book I, Ch. 2, Section 2, No. 2, second paragraph) occurs the sentence:—

"There must therefore be something which makes this very Reproduction of the appearances possible, by being the Ground *a priori* of a necessary synthetical Unity of them."

This is not quite evident; but it should be considered first that there must be a Rule in the phenomena and that it must be a necessary rule, otherwise they will not give the result except by chance. And hence but seldom. And as the rule must contain the element of necessity, it must be *a priori*.

Liberty and Necessity

Suppose a man is in a room locked in and does not want to go out, so that his staying is *voluntary;* is he at liberty? No. But suppose that if he had wished to go out the doors would be unlocked, was he then at liberty? Yes. Now this is the situation of every man upon the theory of necessity. He prefers to do a certain thing and he cannot do otherwise, but yet if he should prefer to do otherwise he could do so. So that liberty and necessity do not conflict.

March

Two kinds of disquiparants

1st   Those which would be of the same internal character as they are, even without reference to the correlate as *greater*.

2nd   Such whose internal character is affected by the reference to a correlate as *killed*.

This division seems to correspond to that of symbols into *terms*, *propositions, arguments*.

For a *term* would have the same character even if its object should be destroyed.

A *proposition* would remain the same even if its interpretant should cease. Though not if its object were destroyed.

An *argument* would not be the same if either object or interpretant were destroyed.

1. A term is a symbol which in itself is not held as representing an object. No matter how great its information may be, if it is not *asserted*, it is not held to represent any object. Thus *dragon.*

2. A proposition stores knowledge, does not produce it.

3. An argument produces knowledge.

---

1. A term is a part of a symbol, which may be itself a symbol but is considered as that element of the symbol which gives reference to a ground.

2. A proposition is part of a symbol which though possibly itself a symbol is such by giving reference to the object.

3. An argument is a total symbol considered as such.

---

1. Disquiparants of the 1st kind, effect their correlates only as equiparants.
2. Disquiparants of the 2nd kind, effect their correlates as disquiparants.

1866 October 25

Boole in his method of probabilities, introduces rightly the symbol $\frac{0}{0}$. But he does not sufficiently consider cases where this would become very small. It would be interesting to discuss those cases and thus perhaps justify the Method of Least Squares.

Nov. 20

Boole's multiplication is finding the least common multiple.

Nov. 20

What is not a question of what can possibly be known is not a question of fact.

Nov. 23

All murder is wicked
All abortion is murder
∴ All abortion is wicked

This begs the question because *wicked* is part of the essence of murder and therefore no one need admit abortion to be murder until it is otherwise shown to be wicked. This shows that the rule must be an *accidental* not an *essential* proposition.

1866 Dec. 6

Remarks on Berkeley's *Principles of Human Knowledge*

The design of this book is to introduce a further distinction between being and knowing.

Our ideas *exist* only in the mind; whether they are *thought* as being there or not. But our ideas are all that we immediately know. Hence we immediately know only what is in the mind. I do not see therefore that Reid's criticism was irrelevant.

The question next is what evidence we have of the absolute existence of matter, of external qualities, and of spirit. Berkeley maintains that *matter* has no meaning, or is inconceivable. It is totally invalid as an hypothesis inasmuch as the *facts*, the *ideas*, do not apodeictically follow from it. It is the same with external qualities. On the other hand *spirit* is a good hypothesis because it does explain the facts. Only it is admitted it does not explain the influencing of one mind by another. That is inexplicable.

The doctrine is good against an absolute matter. But an equally strong argument could be brought against an absolutely existing spirit.

1866 Dec. 8

In order to prove the greater simplicity of my Rules of Syllogism, I propose to show how 1st the old rules are proved by mine and 2nd how mine are proved by the old rules.

1st   That no term can be distributed in the conclusion which is not distributed in one of the premisses.

Proof. The rule and case can only appear in the conclusion when denied. Hence as their common term is undistributed in but one, its distribution must be the same in both propositions when it appears in the conclusion. As but one proposition can be conclusion and as the result can be out of the conclusion only when denied, no term of the result can be in the conclusion unless both the propositions in which it occurs are affirmed or both denied. And hence as the result agrees in quantity and quality with the case and rule respectively, in which its subject and predicate respectively occur, these terms must agree in distribution.

2nd   That the middle term must be distributed at least once.

If the subject-predicate is the middle term it must be distributed in the rule of which it is subject and which is universal. Any other term must be of different distributions if occurring twice in the premisses, because the subject and predicate of the result are subject and predicate respectively again and the result if in the premiss must be denied, but the result agrees in quantity and quality with the propositions in which its subject and predicate respectively occur.

3rd   From two affirmatives a negative cannot be concluded.

As rule and result agree in quality, the propositions containing them must agree in quality if one is conclusion, since then both or neither are denied, and hence in that case the conclusion cannot be negative without a premiss being negative. But if both are in the premisses they must disagree in quality and hence both cannot be negative.

4th   One premiss must be universal.

Either the rule is a premiss in which case it is universal, or the result is denied in one premiss and the case affirmed in the other, whence as result and case agree in quantity, the premisses must disagree in quantity and hence both cannot be particular.

5th   One premiss must be affirmative.

Proved in the same way.

6th   The conclusion follows the worse part.

If the result is conclusion it agrees in quantity and quality with certain premisses, the others having the best modification. If it is premiss it agrees with the conclusion in the same way and the terms not appearing in the result must have the best modifications in the premisses and hence the worst in the conclusion.

Proof of my rules from the old ones

1st   The rule must be universal.

If the particular rule be a premiss of the other propositions one must be affirmative and the other negative and hence the case and result must differ in quantity. If it be conclusion the premisses must both be universal and hence again result and case must differ in quantity. The rest of the proof is below.

2nd   The case must be affirmative.

Otherwise, as before, the rule and result must differ in quality.

3rd   The result must agree with the case in quantity.

If both are in the premisses this is allowable provided the result is particular; otherwise not, for then there would be two particular premisses. If one is in the conclusion the propositions which contain them will disagree in quantity and hence the conclusion must be particular; otherwise there will be an illicit process of the minor. If the conclusion is particular and the minor universal the major must be particular; otherwise the worse part would not be followed. Then the subject of the major is either major or middle term. If the former, the minor must be negative; otherwise the middle would be undistributed and then the conclusion must be negative to follow the worse part and then the major must be affirmative which will give an illicit process or negative which will give two negative premisses. If the subject of the major is major term then since the subject of the minor is minor term, the middle term is predicate twice. Hence one premiss must be negative or there would be an undistributed middle. Then the conclusion is either affirmative and does not follow the worse part or negative and makes an illicit process.

4th   The result agrees with the rule in quality.

Proved like the last.

Logic Chapter I

MS 115: Winter–Spring 1866

No study seems so trivial as that of formal logic, not only at first sight but until after long research. It is far too indeterminate to be of much use in actual reasoning, and it is too simple to interest like Mathematics by involutions and resolutions of forms. It has, however, a deep significance, one which was perceived most clearly by Aristotle and Kant and the recognition of which gave their two philosophies such preëminent vitality. It is the circumstance that the commonest and most indispensible conceptions are nothing but objectifications of logical forms. The categories of Kant are derived from the logical analysis of judgments, and those of Aristotle (framed before the accurate separation of syntax and logic) are derived from a half-logical half-grammatical analysis of propositions. Now upon the table of the categories philosophy is erected,—not merely metaphysic but the philosophy of religion, of morals, of law, and of every science. To form a table of the categories is, therefore, the great end of logic.

Kant first formed a table of the various logical divisions of judgments, and then deduced his categories directly from these. For example, corresponding to a categorical form of judgment is the relation of substance and accident, and corresponding to the hypothetical form is the relation of cause and effect. The correspondences between the functions of judgment and the categories are obvious and certain. So far the method is perfect. Its defect is that it affords no warrant for the correctness of the preliminary table, and does not display that direct reference to the unity of consistency which alone gives validity to the categories.

Partly in order to remedy this defect, Hegel produced his logic. He begins at the unity of being and runs through the categories guided by the homogeneousness of their internal relationships, and ends with the functions of judgment. He brought to the task such a surpassing genius for this kind of thought, that by the result of his labor, this inverted method must be finally judged. Now his procedure does not seem to give determinate solutions; but the results seem to be arbitrary; for whereas he has finally arrived at the same divisions of the judgment as were made by Kant and currently received at Hegel's day, the more recent researches of logic have essentially modified these and have shown them to be wrong.

The method which ought to be adopted is one which derives the categories from the functions of judgment but which has its starting-point in pure being. The first step of such a process may be described beforehand. Sensation presents a manifold and this manifold must be conjoined under the unity of consistency. Now to combine the manifold of the immediately present, in general, requires the introduction of a conception not given, precisely as the manifold of optical phenomena can only be reduced to harmony by the foreign conception of a luminiferous ether. But perhaps this introduced conception in order to be combined with the immediately present requires the introduction of another conception. And so on, until the conception of being, which *is* the unity of consistency, can be directly applied. If, therefore, we begin with the conception of being and ask what it is that it conjoins to that which is present, we shall have the first conception under it. Then if we ask what *this* conception conjoins to that which is present we shall have the second conception. And we can proceed in this way until we finally arrive at the conception which directly combines together the immediately present, in general. This proceedure seems to be absolutely determinative and to give no room for anything arbitrary. Now let us put it in practice.

The final unity of consistency is given by the conception of being, which is the force of the copula of a proposition. It is a conception without content, that is, to say that A is, is to say nothing of it. On this account its introduction requires no justification but its own possibility. Its function is to conjoin the subject presented with the predicate, and it is therefore possible whenever there is a predicate. Predication, therefore, or abstracting from reference to a mind, possession of character, is the first conception with content. Character is the ground of being; whatever is, is by being *somehow;* at least, so we must conceive the matter. Character is then always a ground, and as ground is also always a character; the two terms are coëxtensive. Reference to a ground i.e. possession of a character is not a conception given in the impressions of sense but is the result of generalization. Now, generalization is from related things; so that the immediate function of reference to a ground is to unite relate and correlate, and hence its introduction is justified by the fact that without it reference to a correlate is unintelligible. Accordingly, reference to a correlate is the second conception with content. This conception is itself not given in sensation, but is the result of comparison. Now comparison is the determination of a representation by the medium of that which is present, in contradistinction to its determination simply by that which is present. For example, I put A into relation to B, when in contemplating A, I as it were see B through it. The representation determined by the medium of A, may be called its *correspondent*. Then the immediate function of reference to a correlate is to conjoin that which is presented with its correspondent, and the introduction of the former conception is justified by the fact that only by it is the latter made representable. Accordingly reference to a correspondent is the third conception with content. This conception is itself not in what is immediately present in its elements. But it is directly applied to the immediately present in general; for the bringing of the elementary sensations together into a notion of the immediately present, in general, requires the introduction of the conception that this general represents its particulars, and in the conception of representation that of an image determined as correspondent is contained.

We have, then, a uniform chain of conceptions stretching from pure being to the intuition in general. Now the three links composing this chain, namely, reference to a ground, to a correlate, and to a correspondent afford the elements for a complete system of logic.

Abstraction or precision is of two kinds; by obscuration and by position. Thus, *two* may be prescinded from *units* by neglecting to make distinct the fact that it is always even in conception composed of units. On the other hand an elastic incompressible medium may be considered abstractedly of any phenomena of light or heat, by neglecting to take account of the circumstances which alone could give rise to such a conception.[1] Now, it is clear from what has been said, that the refer-

___

1. Neither kind of precision is at all the same as *partition* or separation by the imagination. The distinction between imagining and conceiving is a part of the very alphabet of philosophy. To imagine is to reproduce in the mind elementary sensible intuitions and to take them up in some order so as to make an image. To conceive is to collect under a supposition, to make a hypothesis, and therefore cannot dispense with the use of words. Thus, we comprehend the phenomena of polarization by the conception of a perfectly elastic incompressible solid. No one can imagine such a solid, because nothing like it is met with in experience except surfaces. But we can conceive it very well inasmuch as we can consistently state its deduced properties.

ence to a ground may be prescinded by position from the reference to a correlate, and the latter in the same way from reference to a correspondent. Whereas, the reference to a correspondent cannot be prescinded by position from reference to a correlate, nor this from reference to a ground. This fact, affords the basis for a division of *attributes* into three kinds. First, such as contain only reference to a ground; or simple *Qualities*. Second, such as contain references to a ground and a correlate necessarily connected together; or real *Relations*. Third, such as involve references to a ground, a correlate, and a correspondent necessarily connected together; or *Representations*.

Relations on account of their double reference, will be separable again into two kinds; and representations on account of their triple reference, will be separable into three kinds. To begin with relation.

Every relate has both a reference to a correlate and also necessarily connected with that a reference to a ground. If no reference to an interpretant is involved, the reference to a ground may be prescindible from reference to the correlate, that is, it may be in itself a simple quality, or it may require the introduction of reference to a correlate in order to be represented and then it may be termed a relative quality. Let it be remembered that we speak here only of real relations, that is to such as can be prescinded by position from all reference to a comparer or *correspondent*. We have already seen that the correlate to which a simple quality refers, is such a one as makes a generalization possible; that is to say it is a correlate of *agreement*. A reference to a ground which implies a reference to a correlate is such as killing, approaching, &c. It is, thus, a ground of difference *in actu*. Difference in predicates merely, as *larger* &c., can only be considered as an ideal relation, because the two terms cannot be represented as having any connection thereby except to a *correspondent*. It thus stands on a different footing from agreement, which can be prescinded by position from all such reference, and still be a relation. Agreement, then, and difference *in actu* are the two kinds of real relations. We may here note a few of their peculiarities. If A agrees with B, B also agrees with A upon the same ground; but if A differs from B, B differs from A upon the contrary ground. This is true of all relations, real or ideal.[2] Agreement in-

2. Contrariety has proved difficult to define. The essence of it seems to be the relation between a pair of relative qualities which are the grounds of the two reciprocal differences of two differing things. Thus if A is light relatively to B, B is heavy in comparison with A; and hence *heavy* and *light* are termed contraries.

volves a setti[ng o]ver against, which is possible when there is a difference, real or ideal, between the agreeing terms. At the same time, if no
real diversity between the two terms is supposed, agreement may be
prescinded by position from difference. But the converse proposition
does not hold. For, in the first place, total exclusion in comprehension,
that is absolute unlikeness is an absurdity, since things so unrelated
could not be brought under one conception, whereas it is the only possible justification of a hypothesis that it makes the manifold comprehensible. Now we may take for granted, for argument's sake, what only *may*
be justified; but we cannot suppose that our own supposition is unjustifiable, and still continue to make the supposition. In order, therefore, to
suppose or conceive an exclusion in comprehension, we must neglect
what nevertheless is contained in the conception, namely that it is
unjustifiable; that is to say we can only conceive of real difference without agreement by confusion but not by position. Since then real difference involves agreement, but not conversely, we must understand
agreement, first, in order to understand real difference.

As relations separate into two kinds on account of the double reference they contain, so representations from containing a triple reference
separate into three kinds. For the relation of a repraesentamen to its
object (correlate) may be a real relation and, then, either an agreement
or a difference, or it may be an ideal r[elati]on or one from which the
reference to a correspondent (subject of representation) cannot be prescinded by position. In the first case, that is where the repraesentamen
has a real agreement with its object, the representation consists in the
likeness; a simple quality of the object is shown but the object itself is
not said to exist. In the second case, there is a real difference of the
repraesentamen from its object, that is to say not a mere difference in
quality but also a bringing of them together in nature; in this case the
representative character of the one will consist in constant accompani-
ment by the other, so that it *indicates* the existence of the latter without
noting any characters of it. Such a representation may be termed an
index. In the third case, where the relation of the repraesentamen to its
object is ideal, the ground of this relation is an attribute of the correlate
attributed to the relate, and then the relate or repraesentamen represents the object or correlate on account of the quality attributed to it.
This gives a *general sign,* a word or conception, for the repraesentamen
will necessarily apply to everything which contains its attributed quality. In order to find a fit term for this kind of representation we shall

do well to recall the following celebrated passage of Leibniz. "For the most part," says he, "especially in //longer/more remote// analysis, we do not intuite at once the whole nature of the thing, but in place of the things use signs, whose explication in any present cognition we are accustomed to pretermit, knowing or believing that we have it in our power; so when I think a chiliogon or polygon of a thousand equal sides, I do not always consider [. . .]

THE LOGIC OF SCIENCE;
OR,
INDUCTION AND HYPOTHESIS

[Lowell Lectures of 1866]

Lecture I

MS 122: September–October 1866

Ladies and Gentlemen

I address you upon an exceedingly dry subject which I cannot hope to make entertaining; but the great importance of which to everyone who is to use his mind at all ought to render it interesting. I shall be obliged to call upon you for an exertion of intellect which is unnecessary in a popular lecture upon any subject which presents less unity or depends less upon long trains of thought; but I think that for the sake of the object to be gained you will be willing to make the effort, and I refuse to believe that a people as subtile as any under the sun and who promise to eclipse every nation since the Greeks in their genius for abstract studies should be generally unable to follow the necessarily complicated arguments of the Logician.

Logic is a much abused science. Like Medicine, Law, and in short any branch of knowledge which has important practical bearings, it is brought by its applications to an ordeal which is sure to make its shortcomings manifest. It is no more perfect than any other product of humanity and we have the same right to be dissatisfied with its present state that we have with everything else that *we are in a condition to improve*. But many persons not resting here, go so far as to say that it is utterly useless,—and since they do so while unacquainted with the present state of the science—they ought consistently to maintain that it never can be improved so as to be of any use.

This is one of those slashing judgments, so common with men who have not had the benefit of logical discipline. What is Logic? It is the science by which we are enabled to test reasons. Now to test anything there is a particular sort of facts which it is necessary to know. You can see for yourselves that this is so. There is a particular kind of knowledge which the man who examines flour to brand it with its value, and the man who examines a piece of paper money to tell whether it is good, and the man who makes a chemical analysis of an unknown substance, all require. What kind of knowledge is this? There are many curious and important facts about flour which are of no consequence at all to the inspector of flour. What proportions of the chemical elements enter into the composition of the best flour, whether Nitrogen or Phosphorus ought to be present in large quantities, is of no practical moment to him. To the physician, these facts are of vast practical consequence, but of none at all to the inspector of flour. Because it is his business simply to discriminate and say what sort of flour it is that he has offered for his examination. It is the same with the bank-teller and the analytical chemist. The methods of making a good engraving and the precautions which have to be taken in printing from it are of little account to the former, nor do theories of the constitution of chemical bodies trouble the head of the latter. What each wishes to know with reference to that general class of objects which it is his business to test is, what are the different kinds of these things and what are the characteristic properties of each kind. The bank-note detector contains the science by which we test bank-notes and that consists in a classification of all bank-notes with an accurate description of each species. So with analytical chemistry; it is nothing but a system of classification of bodies; and the whole subject of chemical physics—the reason *why* in chemistry—is totally out of the analyst's line. And so you will find that it is a universal rule that to have a *testing art* we need no other knowledge than a *classifying science*. And accordingly, if we wish to be able to test arguments, what we have to do, is to take all the arguments we can find, scrutinize them and put those which are alike in a class by themselves and then examine all these different kinds and learn their properties. Now the classificatory science of reasons so produced is the science of Logic. And it is so obvious, that the research I have described, however difficult presents nothing transcending human power altogether; and that the possession of the resulting knowledge—so long as men are constantly erring in reasoning and so long as the scientific world is divided upon a question which it must call in logic to solve— would be very useful, that those who sneer not merely at this or that antiquated yet once valuable logic but at all logical studies whatever display an ignorance not only of what logicians have already accomplished but also of the very nature of the science itself.

But, indeed, few persons who have not had some special interest in the subject are at all aware of the immense progress which has been made in the science during the present century. School-books are usually antiquated; and those who know nothing later than Whately, might as well judge Chemistry by the Shaw's Boërhaave or Lemery's chemistry which they find in their grandfathers' libraries as judge modern logic by that. And even the more recent works in our language, generally reflect the system of a learned but insular logician, who seems to have been impressed with no one later than the immediate disciples of Kant and who certainly ignored the now well-nigh universal views as well as those which these have displaced.

Logic is a very ancient science; it is 2300 years of age. It has been more constantly studied than any except Law, Medicine, and Divinity. It has always been pursued by men of learning principally. And it found its Newton, almost at its birth. In consequence of this the logic of one generation has been religiously handed down to the next, in almost every age, but since at the same time each age has taken its peculiar view of the subject, involving some necessary distinctions of its own, these being preserved after the conception of the whole subject which was their life has disappeared, and so the subject has gradually become encumbered with a great mass of useless subtileties; and those who have undertaken to dispense with them have not always been judicious in the selection of those they were to retain. This has been one cause of the contempt into which logic had fallen when the Kantian revival at the end of the last century took place.

Another thing which brought logic into disrepute was the fierce dispute of the nominalists and realists. No definite notion of the nature of the disagreement can be afforded by a brief statement. Suffice it to say that the Realists believed that there is really humanity in man, animality in animals, and so forth; while the Nominalists held that humanity, animality, and such terms, are merely words indicating the applicability to men, animals, *et cetera*, of their class appellations. The controversy seems to go back to the earliest times; in the middle ages it was begun in the 11th century and soon began to excite universal attention. At this time the dispute was a fourteen-sided battle; that being the number of different opinions enumerated by Prantl the historian of Logic, as having been held by different philosophers of that century. Afterwards, nominalism seems to have died out for a while, long enough to allow the hatching of a quarrel almost as bitter between the realists among the Dominican and Franciscan orders of monks. But in the fourteenth century, William of Ockham, the greatest of the Nominalists appeared and the old controversy was excited again and raged with tenfold fury. The discussions of the learned doctors sometimes ended with black eyes and bloody noses; and even monarchs patronized one party or the other and protected it by the power of the state. All this has long ago passed away. It cannot be denied that differences still exist among logicians, and that the ingenious may trace in them a resemblance to those which divided the Doctors of the middle ages; but it is a most unwarrantable inference that these differences will never be reconciled, or that logic has not advanced even in reference to the points which these differences concern. No one can deny that great advances were made from century to century in the understanding of these points even during the middle ages; and at the present time a full understanding appears to be approaching us apace.

We have, at present, Formal logicians and Anthropological logicians. Anthropological logicians think that Logic must be founded upon a knowledge of human nature and requires a constant reference to the facts of human nature. Formal logicians believe that logic can be learned merely by the comparison of the products of thinking. For my part, while admitting that the greater array of talent is upon the side of anthropologists, I agree myself with the formal logicians.

We have seen that logic is a classificatory science by which we are enabled to test reasoning; and we have seen that all information as to the forces which produce things of any kind is quite irrelevant to the business of classifying those things. The inspector of flour does not care to know by what agencies wheat grows; nor does the analytical chemist need to find by what processes the substances which he examines are manufactured. No more, then, does it concern the logician by what mental process arguments are produced. This is the simple but decisive argument which my reason approves and which all that bears upon the subject in my experience as a student of logic confirms.

Let us suppose, for example, that the opinion of James Mill be adopted that all inference arises merely from the association of ideas. Here is one of those psychological facts which Stuart Mill thinks has a great bearing upon logic. But would such a fact make any argument good which we had hitherto supposed to be bad? Not at all. Does it make any argument bad which we had hitherto supposed to be good? Not at all. Does it alter the degree or character of the belief we ought to repose in any inference, when certain premisses have been admitted? Not at all. Does it afford any new characteristic by which we can distinguish good reasoning from bad or what we should believe in one mode from what we should believe in another? It does not. Then I say that however true and important the discovery may be, it has nothing to do with logic whatsoever.

I shall add but two remarks upon this subject. 1st That I admit some anthropological facts have a great bearing upon logic; but unfortunately they are facts which are supported only by the science of logic itself and cannot therefore constitute its foundation, and 2nd that it seems to me the anthropological theory has gained support principally from a belief that formal logic cannot give an account of the most important reasonings of any; those, I mean, by which we advance in science. I hope to show you in subsequent lectures that this is quite a mistake. That kind of inference, namely Induction and Hypothesis, or judging of the whole by a part, and of the cause from its effect, will be the special subject of this course.

We must begin, however, with the simplest kind of argumentation—that which is called Deductive reasoning—or as we may call it reasoning from preconceived ideas—that which traces out what is implicitly involved in what we already admitted. Few errors are made by any but the most careless reasoners in this kind of argument; and it may seem, therefore, not worth studying but the more difficult kinds of inference cannot possibly be understood without a thorough knowledge of Deduction.

Here is the simplest sort of argument there is:—

> All men are free agents
> All rational creatures are men
> ∴ All rational creatures are free agents.

Let us study this argument a little. Remember, it is *this* argument only which we have to consider. We do not estimate the arguments by which the premisses are established. Let those be good or bad; we consider only the inference from these premisses when admitted of this conclusion. Of course this argument is good. It consists of two propositions besides the conclusion. The first proposition All men are free agents is a *general rule*. The second All rational beings are men, puts a case under that rule; in logical language, it is the subsumption of a case under a rule. I shall use this term *subsumption* often; it means the statement considered as stating that something belongs to a certain class. But you must learn the exact shade of meaning by practice. When we said that all men are free we actually stated that men belong to the class of free beings but it was not necessary to consider that rule in that way; we might regard it as attributing a certain quality to men. When, however, we say that all rational beings are men, it is necessary —in order to draw the inference—to observe that rational beings are said to be denoted by that word—or what is the same thing, put under that class—which forms the subject of the general rule. The first proposition, then, is a *rule*, the second the subsumption of a *case;* the conclusion is the assertion of the action of that rule in that case, in other words of the result of that rule.

I now propose to study the conditions of the validity of this argument by comparing it with others which differ from it in a single respect and yet are bad reasonings. In the first place, suppose that instead of saying that All rational creatures are men we say that they are women; so that the argument reads

> All *men* are free agents
> and   All rational beings are *women*

Here we have no argument at all, nothing follows from those premisses. It is essential therefore that the *subject* of the rule should be the *predicate* of the case. These must be identical not merely in external aspect but in their meaning; otherwise we shall fall into the greatest absurdities. We could prove a miser to be poor by saying

> Whoever has not enough is poor
> A miser has not enough
> ∴ A miser is poor.

But here he who has not enough has two different meanings in the two premisses; in the first it means he who has not enough to satisfy his needs, in the second he who has not enough to satisfy his wishes. So the subject of the rule and the predicate of the case must really be the same.

Let us replace *men* instead of women, then, in the subsumption of the case and suppose that we say *Some* men are free agents; All rational creatures are men; here again nothing follows. If we do not assert the rule of *all* it is not a rule. *Some* need not deny all; it means some at least; but still if the rule is not asserted of all, no conclusion follows. A servant who was carrying up a roasted stork to his master for dinner, was prevailed upon to take off the leg and give it to his sweetheart. The master unfortunately noticed the deficiency and asked him what had become of the other leg. O, said he, storks have but one leg. The master was so astonished at the impudence of this, that he said nothing at the time but took the servant out to walk the next day to find a stork. Presently they saw one, standing on one leg as storks always do with the other drawn up. There, said the servant, I told you they only had one leg. Hereupon the master flung a stone at the stork who immediately put down the other leg and flew away. Yes, said the servant, but master you didn't fling a stone at that stork Yesterday. The servant thought the master's argument a bad one. He understood him to reason thus:—[Slow]

Storks who have stones thrown at them have two legs by nature
The bird at dinner yesterday was a stork
∴ The bird at dinner yesterday had two legs by nature.

Now, he says, storks who have a stone thrown at them are not *all* storks but only some storks:—and it does not follow because

	Some storks are two-legged
and	That bird was a stork
That	that bird was two-legged.

The man did not apprehend the full nature of the master's argument; his objection was unsound but ingenious and based on a truth of logic. The rule then must assert of *all* not of *some*. In logical language it must be *universal*, not *particular*. Universal means predicating of all; particular, predicating of some.

We can say:—

All men are free agents
Some rational beings are men

From these premisses it will not follow, that All rational beings are free agents but it will follow that Some rational beings are free agents. The *case*, or subsumption of the case, then, may be particular as well as universal, only if it is particular the result will be particular. As we express it, the result agrees in *quantity* with the case; that is, agrees with it in being universal or particular.

On the other hand, suppose we leave the case universal, but make it negative; thus

> All men are free agents
> No rational creatures are men

Here nothing follows. The case, then, must be *affirmative*, not *negative*. It is different with the rule; we may say

> No men are free agents
> All rational creatures are men

and this will be a good argument; only the result will be *negative* when the rule is negative. As we say, the result agrees in quality with the rule; that is agrees with it in being affirmative or negative.

The rule then is *universal;* the case, *affirmative;* the result agrees in quality with the rule and in quantity with the case. We can formulate that in this manner.

Let A stand for a Universal Affirmative proposition as All *X* is *Y*. I for a Particular Affirmative, E for a Universal Negative, O for a Particular Negative. These abbreviations have been used, thus, for 800 years; and their usefulness is incontestable. They are supposed by some to be derived from the vowels of πᾶς τὶς οὐδέν and οὐ πᾶς; words used by the Greek logicians to denote the four kinds of propositions. Others think they are the first two vowels of *affirmo* and *nego*. I shall ask you to remember the meaning of the four vowels, whatever may be the origin of it.

Now then; as the rule is universal it is either A or E. As the case is affirmative it is either A or I; and as the result agrees with rule in quality and the case in quantity it is A E I O as the lines indicate. So that the three propositions are either A A A, A I I, E A E, or E I O. These have been made the vowels of four words.

Barbara, Celarent, Darii, Ferio.

These words are constructed by merely throwing consonants in with the three significant vowels so as to make a euphonious combination. Just as we could treat the notorious sophism of the French minister

Lavilette in his recent circular, thus. The argument is *All* Europe is at peace, A; *Some* time must elapse without war, I; hence *No* expense should be spared to raise an army, E. And filling it up we have LAVI-LETTE. So that we might call an argument of that *peculiar* form a *Lavilette*.

I shall now take up another syllogism, quite different from those we have considered:—

> All men are free agents
> Some rational creatures are not free agents
> ∴ Some rational creatures are not men.

This is, plainly, a good argument. It begins as the first did with asserting a rule. But, then, instead of going on to subsume a case under that rule, it denies the operation of a rule in a particular case; the consequence is that it must be denied—as it is in the conclusion here—that that case comes under the rule.

This is called the *second figure* of syllogism. Here as in the *first figure* the rule is universal, the case affirmative, and the result agrees with the rule in quality and with the case in quantity. Only as we proceed from the

> Assertion of Rule
> and   Denial of Result
> to   Denial of Case

the first proposition is universal. As for the third, since a case is affirmative, the denial of a case is negative, therefore this conclusion must be negative, as it is in the example on the board. And as the result agrees with the rule in quality, the denial of the result must disagree with the rule in quality; that is the 2nd proposition must be negative if the first is affirmative and *vice versa*. And as the result agrees with the case in quantity, the denial of the result must agree with the denial of the case in quantity; that is the second proposition must be universal if the conclusion is universal. These principles will be plainer, if we take each

$$A$$

mood of the first figure separately. First, then, we have A. Correspond-

$$A$$

ing to this is a mood of the second figure. The rule asserted is the first proposition in both first and second figures; the first A therefore will be repeated as the first proposition in the second figure. The second proposition in the first figure is the assertion of the case; while in the second figure the denial of the case is the third proposition. And the result which is the third proposition of the first figure, being denied becomes the second proposition of the second figure. So that to get the second figure from the first we transpose the second and third propositions and deny them both. I call that *contraposing* those propositions A–A

A✕ . Now if we deny A—if we deny All X is Y—we say Some X is not
A

Y—which is O. The denial of A then is O. So we have $\begin{smallmatrix} A & A \\ A & O \end{smallmatrix}$✕. In the

same way from I we have $\begin{smallmatrix} A & A & A \\ I & I \end{smallmatrix}$✕ ; the denial of I—or Some X is Y—is No

X is Y—that is E. So we get E. From A, $\begin{smallmatrix} A & E & E–E & E & E \\ E & E & E & O & O & E \end{smallmatrix}$ A✕I and from I, A. Those therefore are the moods of the second figure.

Now we will take up another figure.

> Some rational beings are not free agents
> All rational beings are men
> ∴ Some men are not free agents.

This is the third and last figure. Here we begin by denying the result of the rule in the case in hand; but we assert that the case comes under the rule. It follows that the rule is not true. That is we reason from the

	Denial of result
and	Assertion of case
to	Denial of rule

So that we have contraposed the conclusion with the other premiss— not contraposed in the second figure. In this figure as before the rule is universal, and therefore the denial of the rule is particular. The case is affirmative. And the denial of the result agrees with the denial of the rule in quality and disagrees with the case in quantity. So we get

Now we may make a table of all the moods. At the top we will enter the proposition asserting or denying the rule. At the side the proposition asserting or denying the case. We will put the 2nd Figure in in *red* and the 3rd in blue chalk. We get

	I	A	E	O
E		E	A	
A	I	A	E	O
I	A	I	O	E
O		O	I	

In this case the A's E's I's and O's will run in lines, symmetrically.

Those who know something of logic may perhaps think they catch me tripping in enumerating only 12 moods of the three figures instead of fourteen which is the number given in the books. I give four moods

I A O E

of this figure A I A I derived by contraposition from the four

I I O O

$$\begin{matrix} & \text{A} & & \text{E} \end{matrix}$$

moods of the first figure. Logicians, generally, add A and A, which

$$\begin{matrix} & \text{I} & & \text{O} \end{matrix}$$

$$\begin{matrix} \text{E} & & \text{A} \end{matrix}$$

would correspond to A and A in the second figure. I will give an ex-

$$\begin{matrix} \text{O} & & \text{I} \end{matrix}$$

ample in words:—A A I is like this

> All whales are mammals
> All whales live in the sea
> ∴ Some mammals live in the sea.

This corresponds to the following syllogism in the first figure

> No mammals live in the Sea
> All whales are mammals
> ∴ Some whales do not live in the sea.

There can be no question that these syllogisms correspond. Neverthe-less, although logicians reckon the additional two in the third figure they do not recognize the additional two in the first figure. This incon-sistency has already been exposed by De Morgan. Both must be ad-mitted or both rejected. Now it is plain that in saying All X is Y we actually say that Some X is Y. Hence the syllogism

$$\left. \begin{matrix} \text{All } Z \text{ is } Y \\ \text{All } X \text{ is } Z \\ \therefore \text{ All } X \text{ is } Y \end{matrix} \right\} \text{ includes } \left\{ \begin{matrix} \text{All } Z \text{ is } Y \\ \text{All } X \text{ is } Z \\ \therefore \text{ Some } X \text{ is } Y \end{matrix} \right.$$

$$\begin{matrix} & \text{I} & & \text{A} \end{matrix}$$

and upon the same principle, since the mood A differs from A by one

$$\begin{matrix} & \text{I} & & \text{I} \end{matrix}$$

of the premisses of the latter expressing more, it is plain that this *more* which it expresses, does not help the argument, and therefore is irrele-

$$\begin{matrix} \text{A} & & & \text{I} \end{matrix}$$

vant. And as A plainly expresses A since A expresses I, the former mood

$$\begin{matrix} \text{I} & & & \text{I} \end{matrix}$$

is not distinct from the latter but is a case under it. And it is the same

E

with A. These are the reasons which lead me to apparently omit these

O

two moods, which I maintain that other logicians count twice over.

Logicians like dictionary-makers copy one another's blunders. Knowing how easy it is to avoid an error they believe their predecessors have escaped errors; thus they fall into the technical fallacy of an ambiguous middle.

I now come to a question, the precise force of which it is difficult to convey. We have seen that it is the business of logic to classify arguments. It must, then, be important to ascertain how much difference there is between arguments. Now the question arises, are syllogisms in the three figures arguments of different kinds—is the manner of inference different and following different Leading Principles—or is there one principle applied to different premisses? No one will hesitate to admit that the differences between the four moods of each figure, differences resulting from affirmative and negative rules and universal and particular cases, are differences which affect the matter to which the principle of inference is applied and not that principle itself. It is true we usually speak of the moods as different forms of syllogism; but this is but a figure of speech, for I believe we intend to maintain only that the forms of their parts are different, not that the essential form of inference is different.

But when we ask the same question respecting the figures there is a difference of opinion among logicians; the greater body considering them as essentially different, while many of the best modern authors consider them the same.

In order to answer this question, I must call your attention to the orders of the *terms* subjects and predicates in the three figures. We have seen that the subject of the rule is the predicate of the case; that the subject of the result is the subject of the case; and that the predicate of the result is the predicate of the case. Accordingly if we just write the subject and predicate of each proposition without the *is, is not, all,*

or *some*, we have in the first figure $\left. \begin{array}{l} MP \\ SM \\ SP \end{array} \right\}$. This may represent any mood.

All M is P		No M is P
All S is M	or	Some S is M
$\therefore$ All S is P		$\therefore$ Some S is not P

In the second figure the case and result are contraposed and we

have $\frac{MP}{SP}$. In the third figure the rule and result are contraposed and

we have $\frac{SM}{SP}$. Now you perceive that in the first figure the *term* which

$\frac{SP}{SM}$

we have. Now you perceive that in the first figure the *term* which

$\frac{MP}{}$

is contained in the two first propositions is the subject of the first and the predicate of the second, and of the other two terms one is subject twice and the other predicate twice. It is different with the second and third figures; in the second the term which is in the two first propositions is predicate of both; in the third figure the term which is in the two first propositions is subject of both. Now I shall show you that there are three ways in which the terms of the second figure and three ways in which the terms of the third figure can be transposed so as to give them the same arrangement which is found among the terms of the first figure.

Firstly, if the second and third propositions of the second figure are transposed we get the arrangement of the 1st figure and in the same way if the first and third propositions of the third figure are transposed we get the arrangement of the first figure. Now we know that these transpositions can be made if we deny both propositions, without destroying the logical sequence of the conclusion from the premisses.

Secondly, if the terms of the first proposition of the second figure

are transposed we get $\frac{PM}{SP}$ where the subject of the first proposition is

$\frac{SM}{}$

the predicate of the second and the other two terms are twice subject and twice predicate. The same result will be got in the third figure by transposing the terms of the second proposition from SM to MS. Now if we have any proposition MP we can always find another PM which means the same thing. And therefore syllogisms of the 2nd and 3rd figures can always be reduced to the first in this second way also.

Thirdly, if in the second figure, we transpose the terms of both the 2nd and third propositions so as to make them PS and MS and at the

same time transpose the first and second propositions we have $\frac{PS}{MP}$

$\frac{MS}{}$

which has the form of arrangement peculiar to the first figure. And in the same way, if we transpose the terms of the first and third propositions of the third figure and at the same time transpose the two first

$$SM$$

propositions we have PS which again is in the first figure. These trans-

$$PM$$

positions also can always be performed.

I must apologize for taxing your attention so heavily but this sub-ject is of greater importance than it seems. You perceive that there are three syllogisms in the first figure which are tantamount to any syllo-gism in either of the other figures. Now in order not to enter any further into technical details, which however curious are difficult to follow, I will state to you that in every case the equivalence of a syllogism in the second figure with a syllogism in the first figure depends upon the equivalence of

$$\text{No } X \text{ is } Y \quad \text{and} \quad \text{No } Y \text{ is } X$$

and the equivalence of any syllogism of the third figure with one in the first depends upon the equivalence of

$$\text{Some } X \text{ is } Y \quad \text{is} \quad \text{Some } Y \text{ is } X.$$

What sort of an inference then is it, from No X is Y to No Y is X? This can be thrown into a syllogistic form by means of the premiss All Y is Y; thus

$$\text{No } X \text{ is } Y$$
$$\text{All } Y \text{ is } Y$$
$$\therefore \text{No } Y \text{ is } X$$

This is the only way of putting this into syllogistic form and this is an inference in the second figure. Thus it appears that if every syllogism in the second figure is tantamount to one in the first, it is so only by virtue of an inference in the second figure. So that the syllogism in the second figure is not strictly equivalent to a syllogism in the first figure, but only to a syllogism in the first combined with one in the second figure. And in the same way the inference from Some X is Y to Some Y is X can be thrown into a syllogism only thus:

All X is X
Some X is Y
∴ Some Y is X

which is a syllogism in the third figure. So that a syllogism in the first figure cannot by itself replace a syllogism in either second or third figures, but can do so only when combined with another syllogism in the same figure as that of the syllogism which is replaced. This tends strongly to show that the three figures are essentially different forms of inference, although they certainly have this in common, that they all depend upon the possibility of inferring a result of a rule, from the rule itself, and the subsumption of a case under it.

The sort of syllogism which we have thus far studied may be called Aristotelean. We now come to a different kind which I shall denominate Theophrastean syllogism. An instance is this:—

　　　No body heated by fire retains a constant temperature
　　　　　without consumption of fuel
but　　　Some things which retain a constant temperature
　　　　　without consumption of fuel are red hot
Hence,　Some red hot things are not heated by fire

It is very difficult to class such syllogisms. Theophrastus made them moods of the first figure; Galen is believed to have made them constitute a fourth figure. I should treat them as follows.

☞ Suppose we have 1st a Rule, 2nd a case under that rule which is itself a rule, and 3rd a case under that second rule. From the first rule and case under it one result will follow, while from the second rule and case a second result will follow: thus

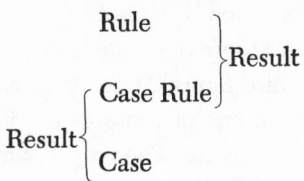

Or writing subject and predicate

$$\left.\begin{array}{l} YZ \\ \\ XY \end{array}\right\} XZ$$

$$ZY\left\{\begin{array}{l} \\ ZX \end{array}\right.$$

You perceive that the first result contains the same terms X and Z as the second case; and the second result the same terms Y and Z as the first rule. Suppose now that the first result and second case are incompatible, as well as the second result and first rule. It is plain then that of the three original propositions all cannot be true. Consequently if either two are asserted the third must be denied. Now the proposition which is both a Rule and a Case must be Universal Affirmative; Universal because a Rule, Affirmative because a Case. The 1st Rule is universal negative; universal because a rule, negative because a result from it which agrees with it in quality is inconsistent with a case. The 2nd Case must be Particular Affirmative; affirmative because a case, particular because a result from it which agrees with it in quantity is incompatible with a rule. Hence the three propositions are

No Y is Z

All X is Y

Some Z is X

Now if any two of these propositions are maintained, the third must be controverted. Suppose first that a rule and its case are maintained. Then the syllogism will belong to the first figure. This rule and case will be either the first and second or second and third propositions. So we have the two moods, as shown in the diagram on the next page.

If a rule is asserted and its case denied, there is a syllogism of the second figure. These two moods, one of which is identical with one of those of the 1st figure are these. If a rule is denied and its case asserted, the syllogism is of the third figure. Here again we have two moods, one of which is identical with one of those of the first and the other with one of those of the second figure. The reason why Theophrastean syllogisms of different figures can be identical is that they all involve those inferences from No X is Y to No Y is X and from Some X is Y to Some Y is X which make the essential difference between figures.

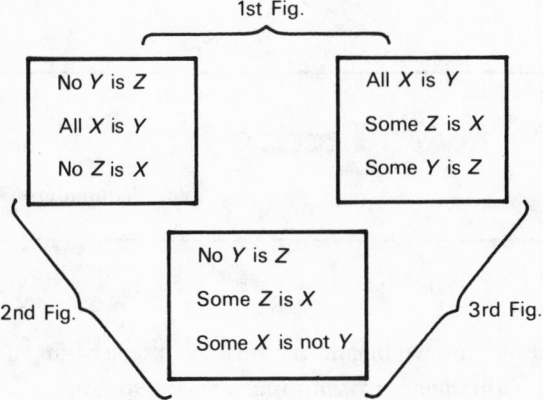

So much for the categorical syllogism. I have been forced to condense a vast field of study into this lecture and have therefore been as dry as any digest must be; I trust the succeeding lectures will be less difficult to follow.

Two Examples.

Some statues are life-like
Some statues are uncolored
∴ Some uncoloured things are lifelike.

He who is most hungry eats most
He who eats least is most hungry
∴ He who eats least eats most.

Lecture II

MS 123: September–October 1866

At the last lecture, we began the business of classifying all the forms of reasoning *deductively* or from preconceived opinions.

The syllogisms which we then took up divided themselves in Aristotelean and Theophrastean. I hope, however, I did not emphasize this division too strongly. Those Theophrastean moods have been the great puzzle of logicians. The manner of regarding them which I suggested satisfies me better than any other; but still it does not satisfy me. I shall, therefore, say no more about these very unusual forms of argument; only two or three instances of the use of which can be found in all literature.

The Aristotelean syllogisms are of three figures. The first proceeds from

the Assertion of a Rule
and　the Assertion of a Case
to　the Assertion of a Result

The 2nd from

the Assertion of a Rule
and　the Denial of a Result
to　the Denial of a Case

The 3rd from

the Denial of a Result
and　the Assertion of a Case
to　the Denial of a Rule

In order to test a given syllogism we must first reduce it to three propositions containing three terms. In order to do this, we may be obliged to change the phraseology; and perhaps to add a proposition which is intended without being expressed. For example, we read that "With some of them God was not well pleased; for they were overthrown in the wilderness." Here it seems to be implied that "no one overthrown in the wilderness pleases God." Hence we write the syllogism thus:—

> No one overthrown &c. is pleasing to God
> Some Jews were overthrown &c.
> Some Jews were not pleasing to God.

You observe that a term need not consist of one word only; thus person overthrown in the wilderness makes but one term inasmuch as it is collectively the subject of one proposition and predicate of another. So person pleasing to God makes but one term.

So it is said: "He that is of God heareth my words; ye therefore hear them not, because ye are not of God." The syllogism is

> All men of God are hearers of me
> Some of you are not hearers of me
> ∴ Some of you are not men of God.

Here "men of God" and "Hearers of my words" are each one term. Having first then arranged the syllogism in three propositions and having accurately observed that there are but three terms, not apparently only but in meaning, the next step is to find that term which is *subject* of one proposition and *predicate* of another. There will either be three such terms or only one. If there are three the syllogism is *Theophrastean;* if there is but one, it is *Aristotelean.* It is very seldom that you will meet with a Theophrastean syllogism; if you do you will find that it contains two propositions which are Universal Negative or Particular Affirmative. By transposing the terms of either of these you will turn it into an Aristotelean syllogism. There are therefore two Aristotelean syllogisms into which you can thus convert it. If these are good, the Theophrastean is good; if not, not. And it belongs to the same two figures as the two Aristotelean syllogisms into which it is converted. It is not likely, however, that such a syllogism would ever be brought to your notice. If the syllogism is Aristotelean, that is, if it has but one term which is subject of one proposition and predicate of the other, you will know that the proposition of which it is the subject—in the case on the board All men of God are hearers of my words—is the assertion or denial of the Rule; while the proposition of which it is the predicate— here Some of you are not men of God—is the assertion or denial of the case. And the remaining proposition is the assertion or denial of the Result. Now we can mark

> The assertion or denial of the rule by ①
>
> „   „   „   „   „   „   case   ②
>
> „   „   „   „   „   „   result   ③

The next step is to find the assertion of rule, case, and result. For this purpose if the assertion or denial of either rule or case is the conclusion of the syllogism it is a *denial*, otherwise it is an *assertion*. While it is just the other way with the assertion or denial of the result; if it is the conclusion it is the assertion, otherwise it is the denial.

We may mark

> *assertion* +
> *Denial*   −

So that in the case before us we have

> ① +
>
> ③ −
>
> ② −

Then if we take the contradictory of the denials we have the corresponding assertions. In this case

> ② + All of you are men of God
>
> ③ + All of you are hearers of me.

Having arrived at this point we have only to notice whether the *Rule* is universal, the case *affirmative*, the *Result* of the same quality as the Rule and the same quantity as the case. In this case the rule is

All men of God are hearers of me. This is universal. The case is All of
you are men of God. This is affirmative. The result is All of you are
hearers of me. This is affirmative like the rule and universal like the
case. Hence the syllogism is good. And it does follow since All that are
of God hear my words and Ye hear them not, that Ye are not of God.

The art of putting arguments into the form of syllogism was studied
with great minuteness by the scholastics, and their rules for doing this—
the *parva logicalia*—are the most intricate and perplexing part of logic.
In our age, which with all its superiority is immeasurably inferior to
the XIIIth and XIVth centuries in logical exactitude, the *parva logicalia* are thoroughly mastered by very few. We cannot enter into the
subject, at large; but we must learn how to put the commonest arguments into regular syllogistic form.

Take this argument:—

> If any man is good, he will go to heaven
> This man is good
> ∴ This man will go to heaven.

This is easily brought into syllogistic form by writing the first proposition thus:—

> Every good man is going to heaven

Indeed it is plain that

> If A is B, A is D

is equivalent to

> All A which is B is D

But if the proposition be

> If A is B, C is D

it cannot be reduced in that way. This is equivalent to writing Every
BA makes C, D. For example, to say that If the wind is east the barometer rises, is equivalent to saying Every east wind makes the barometer
rise. But such a transformation will not enable us to throw arguments
into syllogistic form.

If the wind is east the barometer rises
The wind is east
∴ The barometer rises.

That is one of the commonest modes of argument; but it is astonishing what a difficulty has been experienced classifying it. To begin with it is doubted whether it be a syllogism at all. This is altering the natural boundary of the genus merely to evade the difficulty. As Mr. De Morgan says, such a fallacy is like the proceeding of a landlord who unroofs a house to get rid of a tenant. "If the wind is east the barometer falls" lays down a rule; "The wind is east" puts a case under that rule. "The barometer falls" states the result. Plainly, then, we have here the essence of a syllogism in the first figure. It may be put thus:—

Every occasion of the wind being east is
an occasion of the barometer's rising
The present occasion is an occasion of the
wind being east.
∴ The present occasion is an occasion of the
barometer's rising.

It is true that we talk here of *occasions* instead of *things* as in ordinary propositions; and the objects which our terms denote are *bounded* by dates not by *positions*. But this difference is logically speaking an exceedingly minute one, smaller than a difference of mood. These conditional propositions may be Universal Affirmative, as If M, then N; Universal Negative, as If M, not N; Particular Affirmative as If M, sometimes N (that is, some occasions of M are occasions of N); or Particular Negative as If M, sometimes not N. Hence we have every mood

A	If M, N
E	If M, not N
I	If M, sometimes N
O	If M, sometimes not N

If M, N	If M, N	If M, not N	If M not N
M	sometimes M	M	sometimes M
∴ N	sometimes N	Not N	∴ Sometimes not N

These propositions which do not state expressly upon what occasion
M occurs are supposed to mean on the present occasion. When we say
The barometer rises, we mean the same as if we should say If things are
in their present state, the barometer rises. But the occasion may be a
different one, and therefore the full forms are

If *M, N*	If *M, N*	If *M*, not *N*	If *M*, not *N*
If *L, M*	If *L*, sometimes *M*	If *L, M*	If *L*, sometimes *M*
∴ If *L, N*	∴ If *L*, sometimes *N*	∴ If *L*, not *N*	∴ If *L*, sometimes not *N*

In the second figure we have

If *M, N*	If *M, N*	If *M* not *N*	If *M*, not *N*
If *L*, sometimes not *N*	If *L*, not *N*	If *L*, sometimes *N*	If *L, N*
If *L*, sometimes not *M*	∴ If *L*, not *M*	∴ If *L*, sometimes not *M*	If *L*, not *M*

In the third figure, we have

If *L*, sometimes not *N*	If *L*, not *N*	If *L*, sometimes *N*	If *L, N*
If *L, M*	If *L*, sometimes *M*	If *L, M*	If *L*, sometimes *M*
If *M*, sometimes not *N*	If *M*, sometimes not *N*	∴ If *M*, sometimes *N*	∴ If *M* sometimes *N*

It seems unnecessary to remark that *L, M*, and *N* here represent propositions which may be either Universal or Particular, Affirmative or Negative–or themselves conditional. We might have for example such a syllogism as this:—

> If it is the case that when some matches
>   are scraped, fire sometimes results,
>   then it is never the case that if all
>   manufacturers of matches are careless,
>   some of their establishments are safe.
> But if we speak of a time subsequent to
>   the invention of Lucifers it is the
>   case that when some matches are
>   scraped, fire sometimes results
> Therefore if we speak of a time subsequent
>   to the invention of Lucifers it is never
>   the case that if all manufacturers of
>   matches are careless, some of their
>   establishments are safe.

And in short *there is no end* to the complications which might be introduced; showing the hopeless task which those old logicians under-

took who attempted to enumerate all minutest species of conditional syllogisms.

Another way of putting an Argument is this:—

> Either homeopathy or allopathy is false
> But homeopathy is false
> ∴ Allopathy is not false.

This is the same as saying If homeopathy is false, allopathy is not. But homeopathy is; therefore allopathy is not.

Then there is the dilemma, which is another form of conditional syllogism.

> If either *A* or *B*, then *C*
> But either *A* or *B*
> ∴ *C*

This is one of the countless forms which I just referred to.

I am now going to take up a syllogism which differs considerably from any of those which I have mentioned. It is this:—

> Everyone loves him whom he treats kindly
> James treats John kindly
> ∴ James loves John.

Here we have plainly a *rule:* Everyone loves him whom he treats kindly. A *case:* James treats John kindly. And an inferred *result:* James loves John. We have therefore a syllogism in the first figure. But, yet there is a peculiarity about it; inasmuch as there is a substitution not of a new subject for that of the rule but of a new subject and accusative both. It seems to me we cannot make the two substitutions by two successive syllogisms such as we have hitherto studied owing to the peculiar force of *he* in the first proposition. You observe that no noun can be substituted for this pronoun; we do express the same idea by saying Everyone loves him whom everyone treats kindly; we may say Every benefactor loves him whom *the* benefactor benefits. But here the him whom *the* benefactor benefits has the force of a pronoun still. Now observe how this pronoun stands in the way of bringing the argument to any of the forms we have thus far considered. We may say

[Diagram] {
　　Every benefactor loves him whom the
　　　benefactor benefits
　　Every benefactor of John is a benefactor
　∴ Every benefactor of John loves him whom
　　　the benefactor benefits
　　James is a benefactor of John
　∴ James loves him whom the benefactor benefits
　= The benefactor benefits no one not loved by
　　　James
　　James is *the* benefactor
　∴ James benefits no one not loved by James
　= Everyone benefitted by James is loved by
　　　James
　　John is benefitted by James
　∴ John is loved by James.
　= James loves John.
}

This long process is the simplest way in which this apparently in-complex argument can be reduced to any of those sorts of syllogism which we have considered, hitherto.

In making this reduction we have been obliged to introduce two peculiar premisses

　　1st That, Every benefactor of John is a benefactor
　　2nd That, James is *the* benefactor.

It seems to me that the necessity of introducing these betrays the pecul-iar nature of the inference. The first is plainly a logical fact, one of which logic should take cognizance. When we go to consult a logic, to apply its rules; we are expected to furnish the *premisses* proper,—but we are not expected to furnish the principles of logic, we expect the logic to furnish those. If, then, this argument [POINT] can only be reduced to our forms, if we inform those forms with a logical fact, it is plain that they do not comprehend all the logical facts required to make them cover this inference, and therefore this inference is of a different form. As to the other premiss introduced, that James is *the* benefactor, it is not implied in saying that James is *a* benefactor of John, for *the* bene-factor is not then mentioned; nor is it implied in saying that Every benefactor loves him whom *the* benefactor benefits for no *James* is then mentioned. It is only implied in the combination of the two. Now it is *our* business in using logical forms, to say what each single proposition implies; but it is the business of the logic to tell us what is implied in their combination; and as the forms hitherto studied fail to do this, it is plain that they are inadequate to this kind of syllogism.

We are forced, therefore, to make a special kind of syllogism to include such cases of a double subsumption of the case under the rule. And here we find ourselves forced to recognize the difference of active and passive propositions, of the difference between

$$[Diagram] \begin{cases} P \text{ is } Q \text{ relatively to } R\text{—Active} \\ P \text{ is that relatively to which } R \text{ is } Q\text{—Passive} \end{cases}$$

as well as the broader difference between propositions composed of a subject and predicate; and those composed of subject, relative predicate, and correlate.

We are also forced to recognize as a special kind of proposition—what may be termed a *relative rule*—that is a proposition in which whatever things have a certain relation the one to the other are said to be or not to be in a certain other relation the one to the other.

Syllogisms like this one about James and John, depending upon a complex subsumption, obviously admit of every variety of figure and mood. I think it will be unnecessary to give examples to show this. They, also, have some special variations of their own, arising from substitutions of propositions in the passive voice for propositions in the active voice. All these things, however, are of minor importance. But it is necessary to note how complicated the subject and correlate may be; and that there may be any number of simultaneous substitutions resulting from the subsumption of the case. Thus we may have such a syllogism as this

Whoever tells another person that one
thing resembles another thing leads
that person to think that the first
thing is not the same as the second
John tells James that Wien is like Vienna
∴ John leads James to think that Wien is not
the same as Vienna.

[diagram]

Here there is a four-fold substitution of *John, James, Wien,* and *Vienna.* And I might have made a four-hundred-fold substitution just as well.

But in all cases the principle of the derivation of the result remains the same; namely, that when the subject of the rule is "whatever thing has a certain relation," which is the same which the case implies that something has, then the entire determination of that relation, as given by the case, is to be applied to every part of the rule.

This kind of syllogism is of great importance inasmuch as all mathematical demonstration is of this kind. Take for example the inference from

$$3 \times 4 = 12$$
$$\text{to} \quad 4 \times 3 = 12$$

The rule here is "Whatever number results from the multiplication of one by another results also from the multiplication by that one of that other." The case is "12 is a number which results from the multiplication of 4 by 3." The result is "12 results from the multiplication by 4 of 3."

So with this

$$1 + 2 = 3$$
$$3 + 1 = 4$$
$$\therefore 2 + 1 + 1 = 4$$

Some persons think this a syllogism. It plainly is not since there is no rule and case under it. It is compound of two syllogistic inferences; thus:—

The sum of two numbers is the sum of the first with those numbers of which the second is the sum. That is the first rule.

The case under it is 4 is the sum of 1 and 3.

The result is 4 is the sum of 1 and those numbers of which 3 is the sum. This is taken as a new rule, under which we have the case 3 is the sum of 1 and 2. Hence the final result 4 is the sum of 1 and 1 and 2.

Now in order to show the importance of a study of logic, even of the despised syllogism, I will mention that logicians have found such extreme difficulty in reducing mathematical demonstrations to syllogistic form, that some have boldly pronounced it impossible, and on that impossibility have founded a peculiar philosophy of mathematics, and of space and time with which it deals. But a further study of syllogism has led to the discovery of these new forms, by which mathematical demonstrations *can* be reduced to syllogism, and thus not only is a false theory of mathematics and of space and time overthrown but a careful analysis of demonstrations by means of these forms has led to the discovery of the great principles of mathematics, and the essential nature of space and time upon which they are based. It seems to me that such things should lead us to attach a greater importance to logical studies.

I must now mention another kind of argument which was brought forward by Mr. De Morgan about twenty years ago as a new kind of syllogism. He calls it the numerically definite syllogism and gives this example:—

> At least three-fourths of a company wear hats
> At least three-fourths wear low shoes
> ∴ At least two-thirds of those of the company
> who wear low shoes wear hats.

This certainly looks like a syllogism in the third figure refuting—and corresponding to—the following in the first:—

> Not two-thirds of those who wear low shoes
> wear hats
> At least $\frac{3}{4}$ of the company wear low shoes
> ∴ Not $\frac{3}{4}$ of the company wear hats

Or what is the same

> At least $\frac{1}{3}$ of those of the company who
> wear low shoes do not wear hats
> At least $\frac{3}{4}$ of the company wear low shoes
> ∴ At least $\frac{1}{4}$ of the company do not wear hats.

If we substitute the Letters *A B C* for the terms:—being of the company, wearing low shoes, and not wearing hats, and also *m* for $\frac{1}{3}$ and *n* for $\frac{3}{4}$, we have the syllogism brought to the form

Some m of A who are B are C
Some n of A are B
Some $m \times n$ of A are C

This is quite different from any of the syllogisms which we have thus far studied. Indeed it is not properly a syllogism at all; and unless we propose to import the whole of mathematics into logic it is no peculiar form of inference. It can be reduced to one of the forms we have already considered. For this purpose the two propositions are to be expressed in this way

> All of the company who wear shoes and hats
> are among a third of the company who wear
> shoes

and   All of the company who wear shoes are among
> $\frac{3}{4}$ of the company.

Now we must introduce this mathematical premiss.

> Every class bearing a certain proportion
> to one class which is in another is
> in the same proportion of that other.

Whence it follows from this as the relative rule and the 2nd Proposition as its case that

> Every third of the company who wear shoes
> are among a third of three-fourths of
> the company

And from this as a rule and the first proposition as a case it follows that

> All of the company who wear shoes and hats
> are among $\frac{3}{4}$ of $\frac{1}{3}$ of the company.

It is unnecessary, therefore, to reckon the numerically definite syllogism as a special kind of syllogism.

We have now examined all the forms of Deductive reasoning; and I propose to pass the remainder of the hour in examining some of those celebrated and subtile sophisms which the ancient Greeks were so fond of. Most of these quibbles are not in syllogistic form; and many of them were invented before the syllogism. One very well-known case is said to have come up practically. A young man had been to a rhetorician to learn the art of eloquence, and the agreement had been made that the master was to receive no pay for the instruction unless the young man gained his first suit in the courts. After the young man had gained his education, he never went to law and the rhetorician brought a suit against him to recover his pay. The young man argued that he did not owe the money, for if he did he must lose this cause. But this cause was his first cause and consequently if he lost it, by the terms of the agreement he did not owe the money. The Judge is said to have been so perplexed that he postponed the case for a hundred years. This was practically deciding in favor of the young man, who was the party common-sense would favor, in as much as he could not be expected to get into a quarrel with someone merely for the sake of settling his account with the rhetorician, who in making the bargain he did ran the risk of the young man's never having a law-suit. The suit brought by the rhetorician was therefore a vexatious one; and the decision of the judge worked practical justice. But what the rhetorician hoped for was that the judge would have decided in favor of the young man, as I must say I think he should have done; in that case, he would have immediately brought another suit against him and the records of the court would have shown that the young man had gained his first cause, and so the rhetorician would have got his money. If the judge had come to any decision either way the rhetorician would get his money; but by not deciding, he practically decided in favor of the young man, at the same time giving himself the opportunity if the young man were to gain his next cause, to decide this earliest one, one way or the other, and so force the young man to pay his just due to the rhetorician. So, I think, the court behaved with an astuteness worthy of Solomon.

A simpler case of the same kind is that of the Crocodile. The crocodile stole a child, and his mother went and begged him to give it back. The crocodile replied:—If you answer this question truly, I will; otherwise I will not. Am I going to give back your child? It was plain that if the mother were to say he was going to give it back, the crocodile would have eaten it, and said, So you have answered wrong. So she said, No you are not. This fastened the crocodile upon a dilemma; if he did not return the child, the mother had answered correctly, and he would break his oath; on the other hand if he returned the child, the mother had not answered correctly and again he had broken his oath. After considering a moment, "well," said he, "if I am not going to return your child, what are you waiting here for." This was crawling out of the difficulty as such a scaly reptile might be expected to do. He was forced to break his oath because he had foolishly allowed himself to be led into swearing to a contradiction; but he might have expiated that sin by breaking it in the generous way.

Trifles of this sort, were constantly invented by the Athenian idlers. The specimens I have given are at least, ingenious and amusing; but most of them are simply inane. It is difficult to imagine men of culture pluming themselves upon such catches as this:—

Dionysodorus asks:—

Is this dog yours? Yes. But this dog is a father; therefore, this dog is your father.

Then there is the celebrated proof: that the weight of a single hair will break a camel's back. Because you can keep adding them singly until he has any number of tons on his back when the last hair will break it. Chrysippus originated this.

Then there is the question Do you know who that is coming at a great distance? No. That is your father; so you don't know your own father. The honor of this noble invention is disputed by Eubulides and Diodorus.

Then there is this:—

> What you once had and now have not you have lost.
> You once had ten dollars and now have not but nine
> ∴ You have lost ten dollars.

The authorship of this is also doubtful.

Marvellous that a people who could produce such poets and artists, and philosophers, should so carefully cherish the names of men whose claim to wisdom rested upon getting up these "*sells*." As there is but a step from the sublime to the ridiculous; there is but a step from the profound to the absurd. There certainly is truth in that. The absurdities of some of the forms of law are intimately connected with the justice of law in general; and if the English had been less patient in preserving useless but logical consequences of certain great principles, the principles themselves must have been lost sight of. In a somewhat similar way, if it had not been for the Sophists and Megarics who were always trying to make the rules of argument lead to falsehood, these rules would not have received the developement they did. The contempt which Aristotle expresses towards these perverters of logic, did not prevent his diligently applying himself to find the precise point of their fallacies: and the thought bestowed upon this, might have led him to the discovery of the syllogism. An error is never a thing to avert our eyes from; but something in which is reflected the inverted image of the truth.

Of a much more profound character, are some of the Paradoxes of Zeno; who we are repeatedly informed was considered by Aristotle as the originator of Logic. If so it was the mere germ of the science which he originated: our gratitude is chiefly due to Aristotle himself. In order to understand Zeno's curious arguments we should observe his historic standpoint. For three hundred years after the Homeric poems, the Greeks were satisfied with such an account of the *all* of things as their mythology afforded. Then first appeared the Ionian wise men who thought that all the world was made out of *water* or some other element. The necessity for a unity in all things had begun to be recognized and at first they sought it in its crudest form as the one material of the universe. A century later, the Eleatic philosophers seized upon this unity in all its abstractness. "All that is, is one," said Xenophanes; and herein he enunciated the first postulate of Philosophy. To explain is to show the unity at the heart of the manifold. To explain the conduct of Hamlet is to show how one character gave rise to his most contradictory actions. To explain the polarization of light is to show how all the varied phenomena arise from a single property. In the same way, to explain the totality of things, which is the business of philosophy, we must show that one essence is at the bottom of it all. What we call the Absolute, is what the Greeks more philosophically termed the *One*. In saying then that all things are one, Xenophanes laid the corner-stone of Metaphysics. But Parmenides added: The *Many* is a mere illusion, he carried out the conception one-sidedly. However such came to be the opinion of the only school of real philosophers at that time; that the *one* alone was real, the *many* false and illusive. Zeno was the pupil and defender of Parmenides; and Protagoras, the greatest of the Sophists, was his contemporary. These two men, Zeno and Protagoras, were antipodes, for they rested their several philosophies upon two contrary propositions. In this way, they are a commentary upon one another. Protagoras said, there is no absolute, every man is the measure of things, of what is that it is, and of what is not that it is not. Both phillosophers, therefore, identified *being* and *thinking*, but in different ways. Zeno made the unity of thought the real being. Protagoras made the manifold of experience the only reality. He adopted from Heraclitus the opinion that all things are in a state of flow—never are but only are *becoming*—and so his central conception was that of CONTINUITY. On the other hand, it was an axiom with Zeno that continuity is incomprehensible, and therefore false. And it is upon that axiom that his four famous arguments against the possibility of motion, or rather against the reality of space owing to certain characters of motion, were founded.

It is for the sake of these arguments, which have been handed down from logician to logician, as the most subtile of fallacies, that I have mentioned Zeno at all.

The first proof runs thus: Any body which moves over any distance, as the point of this piece of chalk ∫ , before it can pass through the whole of any distance, must pass through the half of that distance. That is his first premiss: that a body which passes through any distance must first pass through the first half of that distance and then through the second half. His second premiss is that the half of any finite distance is itself a finite distance. Now what is the consequence? Having passed through the half of the distance, it still has a finite distance to go; it must there first pass over the half of it; it then has still a finite distance to go; and must pass over a half of it. And so it must pass over an infinite number of these distances before it reaches its terminus; for $\frac{1}{2}$ raised to that power which is indicated by the number of distances it has already gone over, is the ratio of this distance which it has to go at any time to the whole distance which was to have been passed over. Now this ratio has a finite value whenever the number of distances gone over is finite and therefore as I said it must go over an infinite number of these partial distances. But an infinite number of these partial distances are finite, for the first one is finite and therefore if there is not an infinite number, there must be a last one of those which are finite. But the half of this one has to be gone over, and a half of a finite distance is finite; and therefore an infinite number of finite distances has to be passed over. Now an infinite number of finite distances must make an infinite distance. And therefore if motion is possible everything which moves must go an infinite distance in passing over the smallest finite distance. And therefore anything which moves over a finite distance *only* does not move at all.

This is Zeno's first argument against the *many*. I ought to mention that as all the arguments are stated with extreme brevity by their reporter, I take the liberty of expanding them so as to make them as strong as possible.

The second proof is similar to the first. It is designed to show that Achilles would never overtake a tortoise. For the tortoise having a certain start over Achilles, before the hero had reached the spot where the tortoise was at first, the tortoise would have got on to a second point and before Achilles reached that point the tortoise would have reached a third point. And so on *ad infinitum*.

The entire irrelevancy of most of the replies made to these two arguments, sufficiently shows the greatness of the difficulties they present. Diogenes replied by walking about; upon this Mr. Mansel happily remarks:—"The solution of Diogenes proves nothing. Zeno contends that reason contradicts the evidence of the senses. Diogenes replies that the evidence of the sense contradicts that of reason. Who denied that?" The real error is assuming a sum of an infinite number of finites is necessarily infinite. Any finite taken an infinite number of times is infinite. But an infinite decreasing geometrical series, is infinitely smaller than the number of terms multiplied by any one term, on account of its having no term than which it has not an infinitely greater number smaller than larger.

Zeno's third argument is that a moving body at *each instant* is in a *certain place;* in which place there is no motion since the place is no larger than the body and so does not give it room to move. But if there is no motion at any point in time, there is no motion in all time.

The answer to this is that though there is no motion *in* an instant, it does not follow that there is not motion *at* that instant. This reply is furnished by Aristotle. Motion he says is the difference of the positions of a body at different dates. More than one date, therefore, is required for *motion;* though one date is sufficient for *velocity*.

The fourth argument as well as I can make it out is like this:—

If a man takes 5 steps towards the East of 3 feet each; he goes 15 feet to the East. But if he is upon a vessel which is sailing rapidly to the West, he moves toward the West; but if he is not very near the pole the motion of the Earth carries him much more swiftly to the East again. And thus all motion is relative, to something else. And therefore a body may appear to move and yet in reality be stationary.

I have reserved for the last the King of Sophisms, which goes by a name worthy of its exalted rank—the *Liar*.

Lecture III

MS 124: September–October 1866

I have here a bag of balls. I shake them up well; and draw out one. It is red. I draw out another. It is red. I draw out another. It is red. I shake them up again and draw out another. It is red, again. Another: red. Another: red. One more: still red.

Now I suppose you have no doubt that almost all the balls in that bag are red. **Why?** Upon the correct answer to that question much depends. Our fate hangs upon it. All difficult questions require an understanding of the reason of our faith in experience as a witness to the future and unexperienced. Yet, already, I am put upon my defence, for some persons think there is no sense in this question; no need of it and no answer to it. They also decry the question as an unnatural one. Without stopping to reflect upon the odd objection that the question is unnatural, I shall go on to consider whether it means anything, whether it is of any use, and whether it admits of any answer.

It is urged that the question *why* the future generally resembles the past, and *why* what we come to know resembles what we have hitherto known, means nothing, because the question *why* asks only for a rational account, an account in accordance with the principles of inference, but the fact we now consider is a principle of inference and therefore it is itself an answer to *why*, and this question cannot be applied to it.

It is also urged that the question is meaningless because the question *why*, seeks only for a general statement of the facts, but the fact here presented is a general one and therefore *why* cannot be asked of it.

It is urged that the question is needless. Because we only need an explanation of things which surprize us, but nothing so common as that the future should resemble the past can surprize us, and therefore needs no explanation.

It is urged that the question is unanswerable, because the answer to it would be a fact, but there is no way of arriving at such a fact except by means of the very principle to be explained.

In reply to all this, I shall not go about to prove that the question may have a meaning, a use, and an answer. It will be quite sufficient, if I state its meaning, then answer it, and finally give some practical applications of the answer.

We admit that we do not know anything of the colours of balls except by our eyesight; we also admit that the sight is evidence only of the balls that are seen. Nevertheless, we here look at seven balls and immediately are able to state with probable truth the colours of those which remain in the bag; and in general by means of a sample we are able to judge of the whole, with truth. This is also admitted. Now there seems to be something paradoxical here; something contradictory between the first principles I have mentioned and this last one. Deductive reasoning simply explicates our knowledge; that is a faculty that we are ready to attribute to intellect—to elaborate knowledge. But induction leads us to some new belief—as dreaming does—and yet it is found generally to accord with the fact. Here, then, the intellect seizes the premisses afforded by sense, and not merely explicates them, but discovers new facts, such as sense would seem to be needed to have found out, and yet those facts are generally true. The question is whether our familiar conception of the processes of thought—of the logical processes such as take place when the eyes are shut—as merely elaborative or twisting into new forms without trenching upon the province of sense which is to provide us with the matter of fact. The question, I say, is whether this view is capable of explaining the fact of induction; that is to say, whether induction is capable of being classed in any way under syllogism or deduction; and if not, if this view must be given up what new classification of induction giving it what relation to syllogism, and involving what new conception of the process of thought in general, must be adopted. This is what is meant by the question before us: it is a question of classification. It asks what sort of an argument this is about the balls. Whether it is nothing but a rearrangement of knowledge—which is the only function we are accustomed to attribute to speculation. And if so, how that is made out, what species of rearrangement it is; or whether it is a process of acquiring knowledge, if so what are its relations to syllogism and what are then to be considered the common characters of argument in general.

Hm! This is all you mean! is it—some professed omniscient will say; why I can answer you that in a jiffy. They have an admirable readiness in answering questions,—these born encyclopaedias. They think any one a fool who can hesitate for an instant over problems upon which the greatest intellects have exhausted themselves, in vain. But since we cannot help hesitating—even over the replies which they pronounce—we can only admit our ignorance and plod along in the old way of study and research. There are several common answers to the question, and the first which I shall consider is that it is mathematically more probable that most of the balls in the bag are red. This is the answer given by Laplace and the mathematicians. In order to test its accuracy it is necessary that we should inquire a little into the theory of probabilities.

By a probability in Mathematics we must not understand a likelihood but only a numerical ratio; namely, the ratio of the number of occurrences of a specific event to the whole number of occurrences of a supposed *certainly* known generic event of which the first event is a special kind. [*Repeat.*] For example: since we know that when a *die* is cast very often; the side numbered *six* will turn up about $\frac{1}{6}$ of the whole number of times, we say that the probability of throwing a six is $\frac{1}{6}$.

If I put into this bag an equal number of black and white balls, then since I know that in the long run white balls will be drawn half the time, we say that the probability of drawing a white ball is one-half.

Thus probability is the ratio of the frequency of the occurrence of the event in question to the frequency of the occurrence of the event we know happens.

Suppose I take three bags; in the first, I place only blue balls; and mark it with chalk below. In the others I put three yellow balls for every blue ball. And I put the three bags in a basket. Now if I draw out balls at random from that basket; experience will show that I shall draw out blue balls half the time. I take one of the bags at random then and am going to take out one of the balls at random, the probability of my drawing a blue ball is $\frac{1}{2}$. But now I look to see whether it is the bag which had the chalk mark upon it. I find that it is not that bag. And as I know that in the others, there were three yellow balls for every blue one, and that consequently in the long run red balls would be drawn only a *fourth* of the time, the probability of drawing a blue ball is *reduced* from $\frac{1}{2}$ to $\frac{1}{4}$.

This shows that the generic event whose frequency we take as the denominator of our fraction, must be as specific and determinate as any relatively to which we know the frequency of the event whose probability we are considering.

It cannot escape your attention that mathematical probability expresses an *outward fact*—the relative frequency of an event—and therefore *not* the degree of expectation with which the event ought to be looked for. It is, indeed, supposed to *correspond to* the intensity of a proper feeling of expectation, and it is on that account that it is called probability, but that correspondence is not a fact which it belonged to the mathematician to discover; and all that he has a right to decide is the relative frequency of an event.

Suppose I take two bags and fill them with blue balls and fill one bag with three blue balls for every white one, and then put these bags together into a basket. What is the probability of the first ball drawn being white? I should in the long run draw out a ball from the right bag $\frac{1}{3}$ of the time, as there are three bags and only one contains white balls. And I should draw out a white ball from that bag a fourth of the time that I drew from that bag, because only a fourth of the balls in this bag are white. Since therefore, I get a white ball a fourth of the time that I draw from the right bag, and draw from the right bag a third of the time that I draw; it follows that I draw a white ball a *third of a fourth* of the time that I draw. And, therefore, a third of a fourth is the probability of my drawing a white ball.

Let us take another somewhat similar case. What is the probability of throwing *sixes* with two dice, at the first throw. One die turns up *six* one-sixth of the times because it has six equal sides and is of the same specific gravity throughout, and the 2nd die turns up *six* one-sixth of those times that the first turns up six, for it turns up *six* one-sixth of all the times and no oftener or less often when the other turns up six, and therefore turns up six one-sixth of the times that the first comes six. The two sixes come up therefore $\frac{1}{6}$ of $\frac{1}{6}$ of the times. Hence $\frac{1}{6}$ of $\frac{1}{6}$ is the probability of throwing sixes at any one throw.

In general then the probability of the concurrence of two events is equal to the probability of one of them, multiplied by the probability of the *other, if the first one occurs.* [Repeat]

Suppose I take the bag of balls which contains three blue ones for every white, and draw one out and put it back, shake up the bag, and draw out another. What is the probability that one of these will be white and the other blue? There are two ways in which this can happen: either the 1st may be blue and the 2nd white or the 1st may be white and the 2nd blue. The probability that the first will be blue, since $\frac{3}{4}$ of the balls are blue, is $\frac{3}{4}$. The probability that if the first is blue the second will be white, since in that case $\frac{1}{4}$ of the balls will be white is $\frac{1}{4}$ and therefore $\frac{1}{4}$ of $\frac{3}{4}$ is the probability that the 1st will be blue and the 2nd white. The probability that the 1st will be white is $\frac{1}{4}$ and the probability that if the 1st is white the second will be blue is $\frac{3}{4}$. Hence the probability that the 1st will be white and the 2nd blue is $\frac{3}{4}$ of $\frac{1}{4}$, or $\frac{3}{16}$. In the long run then one ball will be blue and the other white, in the first way, $\frac{3}{16}$ of the time, and in the second way $\frac{3}{16}$ of the time, and as it cannot happen in both ways at the same time, it will happen in one way or the other $\frac{3}{16}$ and $\frac{3}{16}$ or $\frac{6}{16}$ of the time. Therefore the probability of drawing first a ball of one colour and then one of the other in one trial is $\frac{6}{16}$ or $\frac{3}{8}$. Again let us put into a bag nine yellow balls, six white ones, and twelve black ones. What is the probability of drawing a light colored ball? A light coloured ball is either yellow or white. There are nine yellow balls and 27 balls in all. Hence, the probability of drawing a yellow ball is $\frac{9}{27}$ or $\frac{1}{3}$. There are six out of twenty-seven white balls; hence the probability of drawing a white ball is $\frac{6}{27}$ or $\frac{2}{9}$. Hence the probability of drawing either a yellow or white ball is $\frac{1}{3}$ added to $\frac{2}{9}$.

In general, then, the probability of an event which can happen in two ways, but not in both at once is the sum of the probabilities of its happening in each way. [*Repeat*]

We now know what the signification of the *sum* of two probabilities is, and what the signification of the *product* of two probabilities is.

The sum of the probabilities of two events is the probability of one or other happening supposing both cannot happen, at once. [Repeat] The product of the probabilities of two events is the probability of both happening at once, supposing that they are quite independent that is that one happens no oftener or less often when the other happens than when it does not. [Repeat]

As we now understand the addition and multiplication of probabilities, we can easily find what the meaning of subtraction and division is.

If we know that the probability of drawing out a light ball from this bag is $\frac{3}{4}$ and the chance of drawing out a *white* ball is $\frac{1}{4}$ we know that the probability of drawing out any light ball except a white one is $\frac{2}{4}$. Thus the remainder of one probability subtracted from another is the probability of the first happening in any other way than by the other, supposing that whenever the second happens the first happens.

Suppose that in the case of my having 3 bags in a basket, I know that the probability of drawing out a white ball is $\frac{1}{4}$ and that the probability of drawing from the only bag which contains white ones is $\frac{1}{3}$. Then I know that the probability if I do draw from the right bag of getting a white one is $\frac{1}{4}$ divided by $\frac{1}{3}$ or $\frac{3}{4}$. So that the quotient of one probability divided by another is the probability of the first happening if the second does supposing that the first cannot happen unless the second does.

We have now the fundamental principles of probabilities.

Let us now turn our attention to the connection between probability and weight of evidence. If there are ten balls in a bag and all are black, then the probability of the first ball drawn being black is by the definition of probability the ratio between the number of times a black ball will be drawn to the total number of balls drawn. This ratio is $\frac{10}{10}$ or 1. But in this Case we are certain to draw a black ball the first time. And you can easily see that the probability of anything else which is certain is 1. On the other hand the probability of drawing a white ball is nothing, because a white ball would never be drawn; now it is impossible that a white ball should be drawn the first time, and therefore the probability *zero* corresponds to impossibility.

Moreover the oftener an event happens, the more apt it is to occur in the long run, the more apt it is to occur in the special case, the more evidence we have that it will occur in the special case.

Let us ask ourselves why is this:—Suppose there are 2 blue balls for every yellow one in this bag. Then we say,

All the yellow balls are in $\frac{1}{3}$ of the balls
The balls of the color drawn are not in $\frac{1}{3}$ of the balls
∴ The balls of the color drawn are not yellow

The two last propositions are only *likely*, not *certain*. But what does this word *likely* mean? That is *likely*, I should say, which is got at by a method which will yield truth oftener than falsehood. Is not this the meaning of *likely*? I say it is *likely* a yellow ball will not be drawn; that is, I acknowledge a yellow ball *might* be drawn, but the opinion that the first ball is not yellow, is obtained by a sort of inference which will not *often* deceive me.

Some, I know, will deny that this *is* the meaning of the term *likely*; they will say that *likely* is a simple and unanalyzable conception. This is a favorite mode of getting over a difficulty with some philosophers. They present some hypothesis of things, of the antecedent probability of which we know nothing. The only possible objection, then, which can be made to such a theory is that there are facts which it will not explain. But the moment you urge one of these facts in the way of objection, the philosopher replies, O *that fact* is inexplicable. You know what would be said to such a plea in a court of law. If a party were to say, this fact is inexplicable, the judge would say you *must* have your theory, or you will lose your case. The facts which these philosophers call inexplicable, are so upon their theory, but they are not so upon another theory. Inexplicable, with them, means inexplicable to me. But suppose, neither party could explain the facts; the question in a court of law would in that case be decided by a legal presumption, that is to say, by a rule by which unproved cases are decided, a rule which would conform to general experience if there be any such experience, but at any rate is framed so as to dispose of the case somehow. These rules are necessary in the law, because it is for the well-being and peace of the community that every quarrel should be decided, and it is better to have it decided wrongly than not at all; but it is entirely different in speculative philosophy; here it is our interest to get at the truth if centuries are required to reach it, and it is better not to decide than to decide without reason. If, therefore, neither party can explain the facts, they cannot continue to hold their respective opinions, they must both give up and wait till the explanation comes. But, it is said, there must be something ultimate, something inexplicable. Undoubtedly;—in one sense. That is to say, there must be a point where each system fails; man never can attain to absolute insight. But this is not to admit that there is a point which no system can explain. Man can advance indefinitely; he cannot go to infinity, but he may be able to pass beyond any assignable point. Every system must fail; but when it has failed, it must be given up. Let me point out with reference to this mode of doing away with a difficulty that it is so very *easy* and so generally applicable instead of a logical analysis, that we should be on our guard against it and should be careful that we do not admit any conception to be simple without a positive test. Everything must be presumed to be explicable till proved inexplicable, otherwise we fall back everywhere into mental stagnation. But allow that the term *likely* is itself simple; then I ask what is the immediate justification of its employment. Do we know by intuition that something is likely? If so, it implies we know not what that is objective, it has no definition, it is a mere peculiar feeling, and there is no use and no need of any search for a justification of it.

Others perhaps will admit that likelihood may be defined, but will not admit that I have given the true definition. They may say that it is an approximation to certainty. All will admit this; but wherein does this approximation to certainty consist if not in what I have said? In a preponderance of evidence for over evidence against? Certainly not; because the preponderance of evidence supposes that each piece of evidence by itself yields some approximation to certainty which is far from complete. "Such evidence," says Dr. Reid, "may be compared to a rope made up of many slender filaments twisted together. The rope has strength more than sufficient to bear the stress laid upon it, though no one of the filaments of which it is composed would be sufficient for that purpose." But as each filament of the rope must have some strength, so each piece of evidence must give some likelihood to the conclusion. Probability cannot therefore arise from a preponderance of evidence, since there can be no such preponderance unless there is some probability without opposition of evidence. What, then, is meant by the approximation to certainty afforded by each portion of evidence?

A piece of evidence which yields a likelihood always yields that likelihood by a process which would more often yield truth than the reverse; and every process which is known to yield truth more often than the reverse gives likelihood. This is the only property of likelihood we know of, but the meaning of the word must be some constant and peculiar character of that to which it is applied and must be one which we know; hence this must be what we mean by *likely*, if we mean anything.

To this argument, I can add the authority of a great analyst. Locke in his *Essay Concerning Human Understanding* says:—

As demonstration is the showing the agreement or disagreement of two *ideas*, by the intervention of one or more proofs, which have a constant, immutable, and visible connection one with another; so *probability* is nothing but the appearance of such an agreement or disagreement, by the intervention of proofs, whose connection is not constant and immutable, or at least is not perceived to be so, but is, or appears for the most part to be so, and is enough to induce the mind to *judge* the proposition to be true or false, rather than the contrary. (Vol. 3, Book 4, Ch. 15, §1, p. 149)

This then being what we mean by *likely;* it is plain that that which is mathematically the more *probable* of two events is also the more likely. For example, when we conclude that a yellow ball will not be drawn the first time from this bag because only a third of the balls it contains are yellow, the frequency with which a conclusion drawn from this sort of argument is true is just equal to the frequency with which non-yellow balls will be drawn from the bag. So that the mathematical probability is just equal to the probability in the sense of likelihood. And so it will evidently always be.

If the probability of an event is equal to $\frac{1}{2}$, if for example the number of yellow balls in a bag be just equal to the number of black and white ones together, then there is no more reason to think that this event will occur than that it will not; for instance, the reasons for believing a yellow ball will be drawn are just balanced by the reasons for thinking that another one will be drawn, inasmuch as it is just as likely that the ball drawn will be yellow as that it will be of another colour.

Let us compare this with a state of complete ignorance upon the contents of the bag. Here is a bag whose contents we do not know, except that it is balls. We have no reason to think that the first ball will be blue, and no reason to think that it will not be blue except our general knowledge that blue balls are not so common as balls of all other colours put together; but suppose that we did not know even this. Then as we should have no reason to think either one way or the other, our reasons would be balanced because *zero* balances *zero*. Thus our state of mind would be in some respects the same as though we knew that half the balls were blue.

If a bet were to be made as to the ball being blue, in both cases it would be just that the bets upon both sides should be equal. It would not be imprudent for a person who was in the habit of betting to bet a small sum, if he knew that half the balls were blue, because he would know that in the long run he would not lose much by such bets, the probability of $\frac{1}{2}$ implies that. It might not be imprudent for him to bet in the other case, because he may know that in the long run he would not lose much by such bets either; but this is supposing that he has some further knowledge upon the subject. In a state of complete ignorance it would be imprudent for him to bet.

But whether the proper state of mind in the two cases would be exactly the same or somewhat different; there would be a great difference in the fraction which expresses the mathematical probability. In one case, that namely in which $\frac{1}{2}$ of the balls are known to be blue, the fraction is $\frac{1}{2}$; in the other case where nothing is known upon the subject, it would be totally unknown.

Some mathematicians have sought to represent absolute ignorance by the probability of $\frac{1}{2}$. But the principle by which alone such a proceeding could be justified is self-contradictory. Since we do not know what proportion of blue balls there are in this bag, the probability of the first ball being blue is $\frac{1}{2}$ according to that principle; and since we do not know how many non-blue balls there are, the probability of the first ball not being blue is $\frac{1}{2}$. But blue balls are either light blue or dark blue balls and hence the probability of the blue ball if drawn being dark blue is $\frac{1}{2}$ and of its being light blue is $\frac{1}{2}$. But since all the balls are either light blue, dark blue, or not blue, and we do not know any reason for thinking either will predominate, the probability of each is $\frac{1}{3}$ and consequently the probability of the first ball not being blue is $\frac{1}{3}$ only and yet is $\frac{1}{2}$ which is self-contradictory.

I will put this argument in another form. The doctrine that, absolute ignorance is represented by $\frac{1}{2}$, can only be justified by the principle that possible events of which nothing more is known are equally probable. But suppose A and Z are the only possible events and suppose A may be of two kinds b and c.

$$A \left\{ \begin{array}{l} b \\ \\ c \end{array} \right.$$
$$Z$$

Then A and Z are equally probable upon this principle and yet b, c, and Z are also equally probable, which is impossible. There are only two modes of escaping this contradiction, 1st to forbid the division of any event into its kinds and second to insist upon the division of every event into all its possible kinds. But 1st if no event is to be divided into its kinds, what is the probability of the event b upon this principle? Answer: $\frac{1}{2}$. What is the probability of the event A? Answer: $\frac{1}{2}$. Thus we are landed in a new contradiction. If on the other hand each event is to be divided into all its possible kinds, since every event has an infinite number of kinds, the probability of any event is infinity divided by infinity—the value of which we do not know. For instance there are any infinite number of shades of colours; so the probability of drawing a ball which is blue is equal by that principle, to the number of shades of blue, divided by the number of all shades. And as both these numbers are infinite, the probability is infinity divided by infinity which is we know not what.

The notion, therefore, that absolute ignorance can be represented by a probability of one-half—or an even chance—must be entirely given up. Is it an even chance, asks Mr. Mill in the first edition of his *Logic*, that the inhabitants of Saturn have red hair? In subsequent editions he seems to answer that it is; but we have seen that this is wrong.

Let us now return to our original question. We draw a few balls from this bag as samples of its contents; and as we find that these are all red we infer that all the balls in the bags are red. *Why?* Almost all the mathematicians who treat of probabilities tell us that their science can afford the solution of this question; although the principles upon which different mathematicians solve it are widely different. Let us then undertake the examination of the competency of mathematics to answer this logical question.

We will suppose for the sake of convenience that three red balls have been drawn and replaced. We do not know how many balls there are in the bag. But suppose first that there is *one*. In that case it is certain that that one is red. Suppose there are two; then if only one were red the probability of drawing that one successively three times would be $\frac{1}{2} \times \frac{1}{2} \times \frac{1}{2}$ or $\frac{1}{8}$. If both balls were red the probability of what has occurred would be 1. If there are 3 balls, they are either all red or 2 red or 1 red. If all red the probability of what has occurred would be 1. If two are red, the probability would be $\frac{2}{3} \times \frac{2}{3} \times \frac{2}{3} = \frac{8}{27}$. If one were red $\frac{1}{3} \times \frac{1}{3} \times \frac{1}{3} = \frac{1}{27}$.

If 4.

4 red	$\frac{4}{4} \times \frac{4}{4} \times \frac{4}{4} \ldots$	1
3 red	$\frac{3}{4} \times \frac{3}{4} \times \frac{3}{4}$	$\frac{27}{64}$
2 red	$\frac{2}{4} \times \frac{2}{4} \times \frac{2}{4}$	$\frac{1}{8}$
1 red	$\frac{1}{4} \times \frac{1}{4} \times \frac{1}{4}$	$\frac{1}{64}$

Now in order not to complicate the subject any further, we will suppose that we know there are not 5 balls in the bag.

The question, then, is: how frequently when seven balls successively have been drawn from a bag and all are found to be red, will it prove that all the balls in the bag are red; or that any large proportion are red. Now this plainly depends upon the frequency with which a large proportion of the balls in a bag are red, because if it were very very rarely that this happened, it might be a more common occurrence to draw out the same ball seven times successively extraordinary as that is, than to find a bag of which all the balls were red.

Suppose I were to open a book and look at seven pages, and were to find that the first letter upon each of these pages was a vowel. I should not conclude that every page of the book began with a vowel; because that would be even more extraordinary than that the first 7 pages that I lit upon began with vowels.

It is the same with the red balls; unless we know how frequently any proportion of balls in bags in general are red we cannot say how frequently that proportion will be found to be red after we have found the first seven drawn were red; unless the frequency of the latter has been made a matter of observation.

If the mathematicians are allowed to assume, as they usually do, that any one proportion of red balls is as probable as any other, they certainly can solve the problem; but they cannot do this upon the basis of absolute ignorance, and it is supposed no observations have been made as to frequency of the occurrence of red balls.

I will yield to no one in my admiration for the genius of great mathematicians; in this very matter, it is wonderful how well they have made up for a want of the logic of induction; but I am bound as a student of logic to say that the premisses upon which they have proceeded, are logically invalid and that consequently their results do not apply to those problems to which they have applied them.

Mathematical transformations, it is admitted, are deductive; that is, they can only infer what was implicitly given in the premisses. But a probability is a matter of fact; namely, a frequency of a species of events relatively to its genus. Hence, no correct cyphering can begin with ignorance and land us in a knowledge of a probability.

And, hence, mathematics cannot explain why we are justified in believing that all or nearly all of the balls in this bag are red, when we have drawn out only *seven*.

The argument to prove this which I have presented to you in a general way will be found given with mathematical precision in the great work of Professor George Boole—a man who united a genius for mathematics with a high originality as a logician. His book is Logic put into Algebra. Every proposition makes an equation and the process of inference is an algebraical process performed upon equations. The system is a marvellous piece of ingenuity, and as sound as it is ingenious. And the result which I have presented to you, so imperfectly, will be found

capable of the exactest proof by his method. I would recommend anyone who desires to know an easy and certain method of solving questions of probabilities to study Boole's *Laws of Thought.*

The inference which we have made with reference to all the balls
in this bag from only seeing a sample of them, is what we call an Inductive inference. It is very similar in its nature to hypothesis and may
be taken as the type of scientific reasoning in general. Those capitalists
who layed out so many millions in laying the Atlantic telegraph—not
because they were improvident and overweening madcaps for they
were solid Englishmen, intrepid, unflinching, and cool; upon what did
they rest their hopes of success? Why, upon just such an argument as
this about the balls. If a telegraph can work across the Channel, they
said, it can work across the Atlantic. Every argument by which we get
to any new truth is also of such a kind as this. The faculty for this sort
of reasoning makes up shrewdness, and is the essence of genius. The
alliance of man with the divinity is more plainly seen here than anywhere. He observes the regularities of the animal kingdom now, and
he knows from that how it was in some geological era—a million ages
ago. He observes that a thousand, or a million or a billion men have
died, and he leaps to the fact that all men *will* die;—he has not *observed*
it of those who now live but he *knows* it of them and all other men who
ever shall be, though they be so numerous that a billion will be to them
but as the number of grains of sand in ten thousand cartloads to all that
lie upon the sea-shore. In short, he observes the finite and he seems to
know the possible infinite.

How is it possible that this should be; how can we comprehend such
a proceeding? We call such inference, resting upon observation; but
when we have drawn seven balls from this bag, we have not observed
a single one of the remainder which we infer are all red. So astounding
does such a faculty seem; that some logicians have said—it is inspiration
and nothing less. This you may be sure is said not by any sneerer by
trade who is bound to see nothing wonderful in the totality of things,
and who means that Inspiration is only Shrewdness; but by pious and
spiritual minds who can see that even Shrewdness is essentially Inspiration. For my part, I could not imagine a more sublime manifestation of
the Deity, than that which thus appears in the nature of inference itself. Nor can I conceive of a function so appropriate to Infinite Power
as that of regulating not the universe merely but the very consistencies
upon which the possibility of a universe depends. And it seems to me

that the power of judging the unseen by the seen,—even if it be applied to the most sordid and wicked objects—affiliates man to the Creator of all things.

Nevertheless I must say that these theological conclusions, do not explain Induction; they are no part of *Logic*. Man requires to comprehend his own arguments; and unless he can comprehend them he is dashed from this lofty pinnacle to the level of an irrational machine. If he is impelled, he knows not upon what principle, without any conscious principle from one belief to another, he has no more reason than the pen with which he writes. But the very faculty of judging the whole from the parts, of classifying objects presented to him, enables him to classify arguments, to state what they all have in common, and thus to enounce the principle upon which they proceed. The lofty speculations of the theological logicians are therefore not needed in logic, for the mere faculty of colligating facts and drawing general conclusions from them—a faculty however which appears to be as divine as any other—is quite sufficient to show the rational nature of induction.

The same logicians who take this view of scientific presumption, also sometimes tell us that induction rests upon the goodness of God. There is one sense in which this would be true, but irrelevant; namely if it were intended to say that the faculty of making inductions is evidently given by the goodness of God and so testifies to that goodness. That would be true; but would not explain upon what principle our knowledge of the truth of induction rests. But that is not what is meant by the logicians I refer to. They mean that our knowledge of the goodness of God is our evidence of the truth of induction. I think they forget that if the logic rests on Theology, theology cannot in its turn rest upon logic. One or the other must be known otherwise than on the testimony of the other. Theologians drive their arguments more recklessly than any other class of thinkers in the world. They have such confidence in their ultimate conclusion, that they care not what risks they make their premises run. Some Divines of every stripe, from him who thinks he could not go to heaven if it were not for his total depravity, to him who thinks that the infallible accuracy of the account of creation in Genesis is indispensible to our faith; will tell you that their whole religion hangs on this or that extremely doubtful proposition. But of all logical improvidence, it seems to me that the greatest is that of those men who would deprive themselves of the advantage of using Induction and Scientific reasoning generally, as an evidence of the goodness of God.

If this most goodly frame the earth, and this most excellent canopy the air, look you, this brave o'erhanging firmament, this majestical roof fretted with golden fire, will not prove that God is good, think you that any syllogism which is at best but a barren turning about of what we know already is going to do it? Fie! There is no sense in such a thought. And yet this is the logical consequence of resting Induction upon Theology.

At the next lecture I shall consider another common answer to our question.

Lecture IV

MS 125: October 1866

Gentlemen and Ladies

At the last lecture we asked ourselves an important question. Having taken a bag of balls, we drew seven from it and found them all red; whereupon we judged that nearly all the balls in the bag were red. The question then arose *why* we know those balls we have not seen to be red?

Before entering upon this question; we examined it to ascertain whether it had any meaning and if so what. We found it to mean, does this argument come under the general head of syllogistic arguments such as we have examined hitherto, and if so what is its specific difference from other syllogisms which only explicate knowledge and do not add to it; or does it differ from syllogistic argument, and if so what are the relations of the two modes of inference, and what are the common characters of inferences in general?

I then mentioned that various answers are commonly given to this question; and we began to scrutinize some of the most widely spread views of the subject.

The first answer that we examined was that of certain mathematicians which being interpreted into logical language is as much as to say, that the inference is a syllogistic or demonstrative one—but one which deals with probable premisses instead of certain ones. We found however that this solution was made out by those mathematicians by means of a principle which formally taken is inconsistent with the fundamental propositions of probability and materially taken is untrue. So that this answer is a mistake. And I referred you to the work of a mathematician who proves that it is so.

We next took up the answer of certain theologians, who say that our knowledge that the future is like the past and the unseen like the seen, is a syllogistic inference from the goodness of God, because it would be inconsistent with His goodness to make the world so that we could not understand it. In treating of this argument, I did not stop to reflect upon the perfect comprehension it supposes us to possess of the Divine Character that we should be able to deduce so remote a consequence from it with such confidence—that it is supposing in fact that we know the Almighty better than almost any of his creatures—whereas in reality our notions of him are so imperfect and crude that they are unfit to draw any deductions from whatever. Without urging this, which rests upon a premiss which would not be admitted; I proceeded to show how such a view must imperil religion, inasmuch as we cannot know God by induction, if we know the truth of induction only by the light of Theology. Indeed, I could not believe that the *existence* of God can be shown without any aid from scientific reasoning whatsoever. This explanation was therefore set down as insufficient.

We come now this evening to take up another answer to the question; namely, that we know the future is like the past and the unseen like the seen, because we have always found it to be so hitherto. This is the answer given by Mr. Mill in his *Logic*. I shall give some reasons for believing that Mill does hold to this view. You must not suppose, however, that the passages which I am about to quote are the only ones which support my opinion of Mill's doctrine or that I rest wholly upon any number of isolated passages; for I am also supported in part by the general tenor of the work and the tendencies of the philosophy of which Mill is a representative.

We must notice in the beginning that Mill uses the term *inference* in a sense peculiar to himself. He defines it in his Introduction as the "process of advancing from known truths to unknown."[1] And, though it must be admitted that this expression might have inadvertently slipped from the pen of any logician, yet the peculiar views of Mill are so well explained by supposing this to be *exactly* his meaning of the word, and it is at the same time so consonant with his father's philosophy to lay the principal stress on that which is here implied, that I believe it is to be regarded as the precise definition of the term as used by Stuart Mill. There are two respects in which the use of the term *inference* to denote "the process of advancing from known truths to unknown" differs from that of other logicians. In the first place, syllogism does not advance from known truths to unknown. When we have said that Andrew Johnson is a man, and that all men are mortal we have already said indirectly that is have implied that Andrew Johnson is mortal. Here then the inference is no advance to unknown truths; it is only a clearing up of what we already obscurely admit. I do not believe the logician lives who would deny this. And yet there has been a tendency from the very beginning rather to restrict the term *inference* and its equivalent *illation* to this process alone. The first time the term is met with it is defined as that which is **collected** from what is admitted. And Sir William Hamilton says—it is "the carrying out into the last proposition what was *virtually* admitted in the antecedent judgments." Mr. Mill, therefore, restricts the term in an unusual manner. It is owing to this restriction that he denies that a syllogism is an inference. He says:—"Logicians have persisted in representing the syllogism as a process of inference," and goes on to say that they are wrong. It is to be observed that the meaning of terms is not a mere matter of convenience in logic. Logic, like Botany and Comparative Zoölogy, is a Classificatory science. And in all such sciences, to alter the meaning of a word is to alter the classification. And classification is not a purely arbitrary and subjective affair. It deals with facts; with real kinds, and their resemblances. To change the meaning of a logical term is therefore to alter the doctrine of logic. I do not mean to inquire, now, whether Mr. Mill is right or wrong in the change he has made; I only wish to call attention to the fact of the change.

There is another peculiarity in Mr. Mill's use of the term *inference;* fully as great as the other. Logicians generally would not admit that all

1. The References to Mill are to the 6th Ed. of his *Logic.* I have added in pencil the references to Book, Chapter, and Section.

advance from known truths to unknown is inferential. We may, for example, *dream* something; and that dream is derived by an association of images from the facts which have come to our notice the previous day. At the same time, the dream may accidentally be true. And like all truths it will be believed in, in the sense of not being doubted. Here, therefore, would be an advance from known truths to an unknown one, and yet logicians generally would not admit that there was an inference. Mr. Mill has not expressed himself upon such a case, as far as I remember; but he has left us to presume that he would draw no line between an association of ideas which leads to truth, from some recondite cause, and that which does so upon a principle which we are aware of.

Having carefully noted this peculiar use of the term *inference* and its equivalents, a use which I may observe that Mr. Mill himself does not signalize as unusual, we must next take into consideration his peculiar conception of the syllogism.

I have already said that Mill does not regard a syllogism as an inference. Of course, he admits that the conclusions of many syllogisms are inferred; but his doctrine is that when the premisses of the syllogism have been obtained all the inference requisite for reaching the conclusion has been made. In short, he holds that the conclusion of the syllogism is inferred from premisses which do not coincide with what are called the premisses of the syllogism. All this follows from his use of the term *inference;* but we now come to a special peculiarity. It is that in the first figure—where as you remember we reason (as *we* have said for he would not allow it to be reasoning) from a general rule and the putting of a case under that rule, as from All men are mortal and Andrew Johnson is a man, to the action of that rule in that case, as Andrew Johnson is mortal—Mr. Mill would admit the subsumption of the case to be one of the premisses from which the conclusion is inferred but would deny that the Rule is one of the premisses; in place of it he would put those particular instances from which the rule was inferred. Thus he would say and does say that

In the argument which proves that Socrates [or as we say Andrew Johnson] is mortal, one indispensible part of the premisses will be as follows: "My father, and my father's father, A, B, C, and an indefinite number of other persons, were mortal"; which is only an expression in different words of the observed fact that they have died. This is the major premise divested of the *petitio principii,* and cut down to as much as is really known by direct evidence. (Vol. 1, Bk. 2, Ch. 3, § 6, p. 227)

It seems strange to me that he should not put the Rule and Case upon a par, and deny that either help the conclusion. For if to say "All men are mortal" says already that Socrates is mortal because he *is* a man whether known to be so or not; equally I should think that to say "Socrates has the attributes of man" (which I adopt from Mr. Mill as an equivalent of Socrates is a man) implies that Socrates has mortality which is one of the attributes of man whether known to be so or not. I pass over this, however, as not necessary to be fully argued now; nor is it of much consequence to say that in such a syllogism as this:—

> Socrates is a man
> Socrates is mortal
> ∴ Some man is mortal

both premisses would appear to be on the same footing although Mr. Mill's language would make one a real premiss and deny that the other is so.

It is plain that Mill's denial that the rule is a premiss, is to be taken in a peculiar sense, corresponding to his meaning of "infer." In the first edition of his *Logic* there is, I believe, no indication that he was aware of using this word in a different sense from others. In his last edition, on the other hand, he seems to make his view of the syllogism a mere matter of phraseology (Vol. 1, Bk. 2, Ch. 3, §8, p. 232 note). In fact, the difference is owing to a difference of classification.

Now, does Mr. Mill admit that the Rule is a premiss in the ordinary sense? It appears to me that he means to do so when he says, "I quite admit that the rule is an affirmation of the sufficiency of the evidence on which the conclusion rests." Only, he does not quite apprehend the ordinary sense. The common meaning of the word *premiss* is this:—A *material* fact, which either by itself or in connection with others, being subjected to a certain process, gives a proposition which is likely, if the premisses were true. By a *material* fact is meant any proposition other than the general principle of the inferential process so far as it is the principle of the process. In this sense, everyone *must* admit that the rule is a premiss. If all men are mortal and all kings are men it certainly follows that all kings are mortal; and that all men are mortal is not a fact that logic itself ought to take cognizance of but is one which we must supply directly or indirectly in using any general rules of inference.

It is of the utmost importance that we should not err in saying that the Rule is a premiss in the usual sense; and for that purpose we must be sure that we can really distinguish between the principle of a process of inference and a premiss. We might have a logic which took account of a great many facts not generally taken account of; that would be what Kant calls a particular logic. We should not have to supply so many premisses to such a logic. Suppose on the other hand, we try to have as few logical principles as we can, and yet have enough to perform every inference; that is, enough to arrive at every likely conclusion which could anyhow be obtained and from the same aggregate of premisses and leading principles,—only by such leading principles as would enable us to get along with the fewest possible. It is plain, that since we should then have to have some processes of inference, we should be obliged to have some principles of logic. Now these fewest facts which logic must in any case take cognizance of, is what I mean by the principles of logic. It is plain, that All men are mortal is not one of these. It is also plain that the fact that Socrates is a man gives the certain proposition Socrates is mortal, when it is taken in connection with certain logical facts and also with All men are mortal. Hence it is plain that in this usual sense the Rule All men are mortal is a premiss of the syllogism

> All men are mortal,
> Socrates is a man;
> ∴ Socrates is mortal.

So much for Deduction.

Mr. Mill's doctrine of Induction is exceedingly intricate. He believes that it is essentially an inference from one instance to others like it. Here is a peculiarity. Let me illustrate it by our example of the bag of balls. I should say that after having drawn 7 balls at random from the bag and finding them all red, we believe the others to be red, only because it is necessary to suppose that *all* or *most* are red in order to *explain* these seven being red, and that we think so not owing to any *similarity* between the balls drawn and those that remain, but owing to these having been taken at random from *among those*. True, the having been in the same bag constitutes a slight similarity but it is not necessary to take that fact into account to draw the inference. But Mr. Mill would *entirely deny* this view. The mind he would say, naturally associates those balls drawn with the others owing to their having been in the same bag and so believes that each of those in the bag are red like these. We infer of all in inferring of each, he would say; but do not infer of each *because* we infer of all. I merely wish to state this view of Mill's; I do not wish to argue it at present. I ought to add that this is merely his account of the essential process of induction; he holds it necessary to make this secure by manifold devices.

Observe, now, how this view of induction applies to Mill's conception of the syllogism. When we say All men are mortal; Andrew Johnson is a man; therefore Andrew Johnson is mortal:—we infer in reality from the fact that Charlemagne, Napoleon 1st, Louis XIV, &c., were mortal. And we simultaneously and by the same act infer that All men are mortal and that Andrew Johnson is a mortal. It is very important to notice this opinion that the rule and the result are inferred at once and by the same inference from the same particular premisses.

Suppose, now, that we ask Mr. Mill this question which we have put to ourselves with reference to these balls. What is the Ground of the Induction? His answer will be, it is the Uniformity of Nature. It is to the examination of this reply that I propose to devote the remainder of the hour this evening.

As to the *meaning* of this uniformity of nature I shall inquire later; I merely wish now to advert to the opinion which I have heard expressed that by the uniformity of nature, Mr. Mill means an *unknown* constitution of things only definable as that which makes inductions come out true; so that when he says that nature is uniform he means nothing more—nothing else, than that inductions come out true. I cannot believe this; first, because I think Mill expressly says the contrary, and second, because I cannot see any appearance of sense in saying that our warrant for the truth of induction is the truth of induction. Such an answer would be still more obviously open to the objections I am about to urge to Mr. Mill's real answer.

It is of more importance first of all to inquire in what sense this principle is a warrant for all inductions? Mill answers:—"In the only sense in which the general propositions which we place at the head of our reasonings when we throw them into syllogisms, ever really contribute to their validity."

We have seen how he looks upon *a rule* in a syllogism. He regards it as something inferred together with the result from certain particular facts by induction. That is to say, he does not regard the result as inferred from the rule in *his* sense; in our sense, he must admit it to be inferred, from the rule. Now he considers this uniformity of nature as just such a rule, obtained by induction from particular uniformities (so he expressly states); as therefore not a proof (*in his sense*) of the truth of the special inductions but as inferred as a syllogistic rule along with those as results. At the same time, observe that whether he is aware of it or not, in asserting that the uniformity of nature is the rule of a syllogism of which every particular induction is a result, he really asserts that *in our sense*, it is a premiss from which these inductions are inferred.

Now, in common with most modern logicians, I maintain that to make our *warrant* for induction (that is his phrase) itself *proved by* induction (again his phrase) he falls into that common fallacy called "begging the question." I suppose that there never was a reader of Mill's *Logic*, who did not ask himself whether this were not the case; and indeed Mr. Mill puts the question himself. The first thing to ask, therefore, is how *he* thinks that he has escaped this fallacy. He says, that he does not advance from the knowledge of the uniformity of nature to that of the truth of induction, because there is no advance from a *rule* to a *result*, and therefore though he advances from the truth of induction to the knowledge of the uniformity of nature a link is absent to constituting the vicious circle with which he is charged.

Now it seems to me that this reply of Mill shows a misapprehension of the difficulty. Precisely what this is will be understood more readily by a little examination of deductive reasoning. The principle by which we obtain the conclusion that Napoleon III is mortal, is that if a Rule and Case are true, the Result is true. Suppose now that we use this principle as a premiss; we shall have this doubly substitutive syllogism:—

[Diagram]

Rule　If a rule and case are true, their result is true

Case　That All men are mortal and that Napoleon III is a man are a rule and case, whose result is that Napoleon III is mortal

Result　If it is true that all men are mortal and that Napoleon III is a man, it is true that Napoleon III is mortal

and by using this result as a new Rule, with the Case that it is true
that All men are mortal and Napoleon III is a man, we reach as our
final result that Napoleon III is mortal. But now we have here two *new*
proceedures from Rule and Case to Result; and these are only Valid
from that same principle that if a Rule and Case are true the result
from them is True. If, therefore, that principle ought to have been accounted as a premiss to the simple syllogism and *that* therefore to be
reduced to a very complex argument, in like manner that complex argument ought to be resolved into a still more complicated one by the rein-
troduction of the same principle as its premiss and so on to infinity.
Why? Because, if this principle was a premiss of the first argument, it
is *in the same way* a premiss of the second argument; and must be
added to the second just as it was added to the first. To omit its statement, therefore, would be in a certain sense begging the question for
if it required to be granted in one case it requires to be explicitly admitted in the other. In order, therefore, to avoid this absurd carrying to
infinity of every syllogism, which would be equivalent to ignoring all
logic of the syllogism; we consider this proposition that if a Rule and
its Case are true the Result is true, as a *logical* principle,—something
of which logic itself shall take cognizance and which *we* have not to
supply in applying the rules of inference.

Now, Mr. Mill tells us that the principle of the uniformity of nature
is the principle of induction; and he further tells us that it is a premiss
of induction in *our* sense; that is, that it occupies the same relation to
the conclusion that the rule of any syllogism whatever occupies to the
result. But he also tells us that the rule of any syllogism and this one
in particular is derived from induction also, and, therefore, it follows
that unless there is to be the same sort of begging the question that
there would be in deduction were we to place the principle of it as a
premiss once and not every time, there must be a *regressus ad infinitum*
as in the other case. And the conclusion which we thus reach is that
Mr. Mill is in error in making this principle occupy the same relation to
the inductive conclusion which any rule does to its result.

This cannot be evaded by saying that the kind of induction by
which this principle of the uniformity of nature is reached is of a very
elementary and rude sort; for it is this sort of induction according to
Mill upon which all induction rests, and the principle of the uniformity
of nature in general should apply primarily therefore to just this induction. It is true that Mr. Mill holds that there is an induction which does
not consciously recognize this principle and this would be an answer

were the difficulty such as he suggests; but it does not at all apply to the real difficulty.

Having, thus, shown that this principle is not as Mr. Mill supposes a rule by which we deduce inductions; let us next inquire a little more narrowly into the question whether it is an inductive fact such as he supposes.

This doctrine is as follows:—Every thing in the world belongs to some natural class or real kind. The difference between an artificial class and a natural class or real kind lies in this: that the things which belong to an artificial class have but a few points of resemblance, whereas the things that compose a natural class resemble one another in innumerable respects. I may, here, remark that to consider the existence of real kinds, which have been almost forgotten by logicians since the ascendency of nominalism, is indispensible to discovering the logic of induction; at the same time, I cannot agree to Mill's definition of a real kind. *Horse* is a natural class; *red horse* is not. Yet the members of the latter class resemble each other in one more respect than do the members of the former class. The true difference seems to be this: *Red horses* have nothing whatever in common except what all horses have in common together with what all red things have in common; whereas it would be impossible so to define horses, that the definition itself should imply all that horses have in common. Passing over this, however, you perceive that Mr. Mill holds, very rightly, that everything there is belongs to some real kind; and it seems to me likely that when he defines the uniformity of nature as the fact that whatever is true of one case is true in all cases of a certain description, he means to identify it with the fact that everything belongs to a real kind.

Before entering upon this question, we ought, in a strictly formal discussion, to decide what is *meant* by the uniformity of nature. But, I think, it will give us really clearer ideas to try a number of different interpretations and see whether observation proves that nature is uniform in each sense.

But, first, in order to show that I am not discussing entirely with a man of straw, I shall read a paragraph from Mr. Mill to show that it is his opinion that in some sense, the uniformity of nature is proved by experience.

The latter supposition might have been an admissible one in a very early period of our study of nature. But we have been able to perceive that in the stage which mankind have now reached, the generalization which gives the Law of Universal Causation has grown into a stronger and better induction, one deserving of greater reliance, than any of the subordinate generalizations. We may even, I think, go a step further than this, and regard the certainty of that great induction as not merely comparative, but, for all practical purposes, absolute. (Vol. 2, Bk. 3, Ch. 21, §4, p. 105)

Now in opposition to this I would first observe, that there are obviously many more relations in nature which are totally irregular than of those which are uniform. Indeed, the proportion of the latter to the former seems to be infinitesimal. Take any individual object you please and for every circumstance which you can mention about it which presents any uniformity, I can mention a hundred, a thousand, or any number which are totally irregular and accidental. Take any pear. It is sweet and all pears are sweet. There is a uniformity. But it is *mine;* and all pears are not mine. It is next to a bunch of grapes and all pears are not next to a bunch of grapes. It is ripe and all pears are not ripe. It grew on a grafted tree, and all pears do not grow on grafted trees. It grew 5 miles from a certain apple-tree and all pears do not grow 5 miles from that apple-tree. And so I might go on indefinitely. Indeed when it is remembered that everything in the world is related to every other in countless ways; it is plain that there is no end to the excess of accidental relations over those which present any regularity.

It is true that the number of extraordinary regularities in the world is very great; but if the world had resulted from chance, it would have been in the highest degree extraordinary if innumerable conjunctures of any degree of improbability had not happened. Chance brings many strange things to pass, and among an infinite number of relations an infinite number of strange coincidences were to be expected.

Without pursuing this train of thought any further, let us observe that although the number of accidental relations is so great in this case of any individual object, it is much less in the case of any natural class. If we consider all the characters which belong in common to all horses, it will be seen that there is a larger proportion of those which are uniformly related. The reason is that all horses are not related to everything in the same way—in more than a few respects. Compare *horses* with *locomotives*. All horses can do work for man and so do all locomotives. All horses are swift and so are locomotives. In point of *color* however horses differ and therefore have no common relation to locomotives in that respect. And so in reference to relative strength, ownership, age, &c.

Yet even with respect to classes the number of irregularities greatly exceeds the regularities. Horses are all swift and all strong, but all strong things are not swift. They all have backbones and are timid. But all timid things have not backbones. They are all herbivorous and have long heads, but all things which are herbivorous have not long heads. So that even in this respect nature is not very uniform.

That which gives the approximation to uniformity in this case is plainly the existence of natural classes. What if we say, then, that the uniformity of nature consists in the existence of natural classes? What *is* a natural class? Mr. Mill gives the following account of the matter:

It is a fundamental principle in logic, that the power of framing classes is unlimited, as long as there is any (even the smallest) difference to found a distinction upon. Take any attribute whatever, and if some things have it, and others have not, we may ground on the attribute a division of all things into two classes; and we actually do so, the moment we create a name which connotes the attribute. The number of possible classes, therefore, is boundless; and there are as many actual classes (either of real or of imaginary things) as there are general names, positive and negative together. (Vol. 1, Book 1, Ch. 7, §4, p. 135)

The difference then between a natural class like *horses* and an artificial class like *red horses,* is this: Though *Red horses* have one more character in common than horses have, yet they have no characters excepting such as belong to all horses, together with such as belong to all red things; whereas it would be impossible (at least, at present) for us to define a horse by a substantive and adjective, which would severally denote two classes of things the sum of whose common characters would make up all the characters of horses. In other words horses have more common characters than it is requisite to state in order to distinguish them from all other things or which can be deduced (at present, at least) from those which would suffice so to distinguish them.

Now if there were no natural classes, no universal propositions would be true except such as Kant calls explicative or analytic judgments and Aristotle propositions *per se* of the first mode. These are propositions which assert something already contained in the definition of their subject. Thus if we define Man as a rational animal, then to say that Man is rational is a proposition *per se* of the first mode. Such a proposition states no matter of fact; it only states the meaning of a word or analyzes a confused conception. But if there were no natural classes, such propositions would be the only universal propositions which would be true. For to state something else of a whole class would be to state that that class has other properties than those which are implied in its definition and these other characters would make it a natural class.

This is equally true, whether the proposition is the result of induction or of intuition. And as such universal propositions seem to express uniformities, it may seem that the uniformity of nature consists in *everything's belonging to a natural class.*

Let us inquire into this:—to say that All men are mortal is the same as to say that of the four classes into which we might imagine all things symmetrically divided in respect to humanity and mortality; namely, mortal men, immortal men, mortals not men, and immortals not men— I say that of these four classes, to say that All men are mortal is to say that one, namely immortal men, does not exist. Such a proposition therefore establishes a dissymmetry, in nature. Suppose, then, that the proposition were *not* true and we suppose a symmetry—which is a sort of regularity. Suppose the furthest remove from any universality—that is that just $\frac{1}{2}$ of men be mortal and we have a striking symmetry.

Look at the matter from another point of view. To say that Every man is mortal is to say that every man will come to an end. Now this is true not of men alone but of everything in the world. Nothing *endless* exists; it is even unimaginable. Now to say that some things not known to be self-contradictory are unimaginable, is rather to say that some words denote no objects, than to predicate any uniformity of nature. On the other hand, if we take a universal proposition which we can imagine to be false, as that No man has two heads, you will *generally* find that now and then an exception to it occurs. It must be admitted that there are exceptions, to almost every rule. Thus many of the characters which seem to belong to a class universally only belong to a part of it. We do not know how far this limitation extends; it seems probable that there really are natural classes and that nearly everything belongs to one. But does this bare circumstance constitute any uniformity?

Suppose this black board were dotted all over with chalk; and let these dots represent the individuals in the world. Then let us draw a circle around those which have any common character. Let this circle for example include all the animals and this other all the rational beings. Then what they both include would be rational animals. And this will be represented as a natural class if it be entirely or nearly enclosed by another circle. That will be all that is required to make it a natural class for then it will have a universal character besides the rational and animal which compose its definition. Now imagine the board to be all covered over with circles, of every size, and in the most irregular manner. Do you not see that the utter irregularity itself oc-

casions every part of the board to be included in some segment sur-
rounded by many circles—that is to be in a natural class. Here is no
uniformity; yet there is natural classification. Natural classes then cannot constitute a uniformity in nature.

Mill tells us that the uniformity of nature consists in this that the
universe, "is so constituted, that whatever is true in one case, is true
in all cases of a certain description." (Vol. 1, Book 3, Ch. 3, §1, p. 343).

Here would certainly be a uniformity. But is this statement warranted by experience? Every student of physics knows that a law which
is exactly conformed to in nature without interference from other laws,
is almost if not quite unknown. Every law that is discovered therefore
is found after a few years not to be exact. What do we say? Why that
it is true in all cases of a certain description; but that we haven't found
of what description. All bodies gravitate we say; well, it is found that
comets' tails do just the reverse, they fly away from the sun. There must
be some reason we think. Undoubtedly they are electrified. Very likely,
but if we ever come to measure their electricity, who believes that this
will be found *exactly* to explain the facts? No astronomer. Since the
days of Hipparchus, he has found too uniformly that there were some
residual phenomena which each successive modification of his theory
fails to explain. In short, he and every accurate observer, is perpetually
approximating towards the discovery of a rule true in all cases and
perpetually evading the confession that none has been found by a
promise to himself that the discrepancies shall be accounted for.

Now all these devices would be entirely inadmissible did the fact
that what happens in one case always happens in cases of a certain
description, rest upon observation alone.

There is still another sense in which we might speak of the uniformity of nature. If we select a good many objects on the principle
that they shall belong to a certain class and then find that they all have
some common character, pretty much the whole class will generally be
found to have that character. Or if we take a good many of the characters of a thing at random, and afterwards find a thing which has all
these characters, we shall generally find that the second thing is pretty
near the same as the first.

It seems to me that it is this pair of facts rather than any others
which are properly expressed by saying that nature is uniform. We shall
see that it is they which are the leading principles of scientific inference.

Let us ask, then, whether these facts are statements of a particular constitution of the world so as to be properly speaking matters of fact or whether they are purely formal propositions, laws of logic, having no more application to one state of things than they would have to any other.

In the first place, I would call your attention to the quantitative indeterminateness of both propositions. The first speaks of a *good many* samples being selected, and of *pretty much* all the things in the class from which they are taken being like them, and of this occurring *almost* always. The second speaks of a *good many* characters of a thing being taken, and of any thing found to have them being *pretty near* the same thing, and of this happening *almost always*. We have no means whatsoever of defining the propositions in either of the three respects in which they are thus seen to be so utterly vague.

Now you know how a malicious person who wishes to say something ill of another, prefers *insinuation;* that is, he speaks so vaguely that he suggests a great deal while he expressly says nothing at all. In this way he avoids being confronted by fact. It is the same way with these principles of scientific inference. They are so vague that you cannot bring them to any touchstone of experience. They rather insinuate a uniformity in nature than state it. And as insinuation always expresses the state of feeling of the person who uses it rather than anything concerning its object, so we may suppose these principles express rather the scientific attitude than a scientific result.

But what if we were in a world of chance? How would it be with these principles then or, to simplify the matter, with the first principle? In that case, it would be extremely seldom that, having selected a number of objects as having certain characters, we should find that they had any other common character; and thus there would be very little applicability for this principle. But, we have seen that the proportion of cases where this principle applies is indefinitely small in our present world. Cases might occur, doubtless would in a world of chance and when they did occur the principle doubtless would hold true.

It is a mistake to suppose that there would be no laws in a world of chance. At least, so I should think. Suppose we were to throw a die any number of times and set down the numbers thrown in a column. I could show you that there would be some very curious laws in reference to those numbers. They would appear quite surprizing. So that *chance* is not the abrogation of all laws.

But there is a peculiarity about those laws that chance does not abrogate. Suppose that in throwing the die other numbers had turned up from those which actually turned up, so that the row of numbers would have been somewhat different; still the laws would have held; they would hold with one set of numbers as well as with another. Whereas if we were to give a whale legs or a woman wings, the laws of the animal kingdom would be interfered with. So that there are two kinds of laws, those which in a different state of things would continue to hold good and those which in a different state of things would not hold good. The former we call *formal* laws, the latter *material* laws. The formal laws do not depend on any particular state of things, and hence we say we have not derived them from experience; that is to say, any other experience would have furnished the premises for them as well as that which we have experienced; while to discover the material laws we require to have known just such facts as we did. But as the laws which we have mentioned, that as is the sample so is the whole and that the sameness of a number of characters manifests identity, are laws which would hold so long as there were *any* laws, though only formal ones, it is plain that no alteration in the constitution of the world would abrogate them, so that they are themselves formal laws, and therefore not laws of *nature* but of the conditions of knowledge in general.

Two classes of thinkers wish to make the difference between formal and material laws merely relative; namely, those who would reduce all formal laws to material laws, and those who would reduce all material laws to formal laws. But neither can deny that there is a great difference between what we must consider formal and what we must consider material laws. Those who would reduce all material laws to formal laws, have indeed shown that what we call material laws are only those which *we cannot discover* to be formal, and thus that all material laws may be formal; and in so doing they have cut anyone off from saying that there is a peculiar uniformity of nature consisting in its material laws. On the other hand, those who would reduce formal laws to material laws, among whom is Mr. Mill, have shown that laws may be thought to be formal, that is to be such that a violation of them is unimaginable, owing to a want of imaginative power in us arising from a defective experience, and they infer from that that *all* formal laws may be material. But so long as there are any laws whatsoever, *these* laws that the whole is as the sample and that identity goes with similarity in respects not chosen to make out the similarity, *these* laws I say must exist. For these are but as much as to say that there *is* law. That we shall see in future lectures. Now all law may, in one sense, be contingent. But that there should be knowledge without the existence of law, that there should be intelligence without anything intelligible, all admit to be impossible. These laws therefore cannot be abrogated without abrogating knowledge; and thus are the formal conditions of all knowledge.

Mr. Mill says,

I am convinced that any one accustomed to abstraction and analysis, who will fairly exert his faculties for the purpose, will, when his imagination has once learnt to entertain the notion, find no difficulty in conceiving that in some one for instance of the many firmaments into which sidereal astronomy now divides the universe, events may succeed one another at random, without any fixed law; nor can anything in our experience, or in our mental nature, constitute a sufficient, or indeed any, reason for believing that this is nowhere the case. (Vol. 2, p. 97)

Let us inquire into this matter a little. If we count the number of suicides in Massachusetts for ten years and calculate the ratio of that number to the population, it is well known that we can predict with certainty about how many suicides will take place the next year. This is induction and corresponds to a special uniformity in the world. It is the type of all uniformity and all induction. *Statistics;* that is induction. When we drew these balls out of the bag, if a few had been green, we should have inferred that a small proportion of what remained *[. . .]*

Lecture V

MS 126: October 1866

Thus far we have learned nothing of the logic of scientific inference except its difficulty. We have found that syllogisms arrange themselves in a symmetrical and compact system which, as far as concerns the Aristotelian syllogisms, is represented by this table

	E	A	
I	A	E	O
A	I	O	E
	O	I	

There seems to be no room in this systematic whole for any addition and scientific inference has no place in it. Some logicians attempt to show that scientific inference is syllogism; but we have seen by strict analysis that such inferences have no probability which syllogisms can take account of. Finally we have seen to use the expression of Plato that syllogism never moves a step beyond its starting point—the conclusion is implicitly contained in the premisses—while scientific inference transcends the limits of the finite, and passes not a little but infinitely beyond the premisses. If from these considerations you are fully convinced of the impossibility of reducing scientific inference to syllogism and of the consequent necessity for erecting a distinct class of arguments to cover all inferences which increase our knowledge, we are in a fit condition to begin the direct study of them this evening.

Let me call your attention to two examples of scientific inference. The first is this:—Suppose that we take at random a number of instances of cloven-hoofed animals, as neat swine sheep and deer; now we find that all these animals live exclusively upon vegetables in their natural state; hence we shall do right to presume from these samples that all cloven-hoofed animals or, at least, by far the larger part of them are herbivora. We may briefly state the argument thus

> Neat swine sheep and deer are cloven-hoofed
> Neat swine sheep and deer are herbivora
> ∴ All cloven-hoofed animals are herbivora.

Another case of scientific inference is this:—Light manifests some peculiar phenomena of an exceedingly complicated character, termed phenomena of polarization. Now if light were ether-waves, it would necessarily exhibit exactly these phenomena. This affords rational ground for thinking that light is ether-waves. In other words

Light is polarizable
Ether waves are polarizable
∴ Light is ether waves.

Now if we compare these two inferences with each other, we shall notice in the first place that there are two important characters which they have in common. The first is that they both enlarge our knowledge, because their conclusions are not contained in their premises even implicitly. When we infer that all cloven-hoofed animals or that the major part or any other ratio of all cloven-hoofed animals are herbivora we speak of more than we have ever seen, and more than we can ever be sure of ever having seen. We never can know that we have come across all the individuals of any class whatever. We can never be sure that those which we have not seen are not infinitely more numerous than those which we have seen. In like manner when we say that light is ether waves, we assert something we have not seen, and something which we can at no time know is *precisely* correct. These inferences then extend our knowledge beyond the limits of our experience,—beyond our possible experience. This is the first character which they have in common. The second is that both *explain* certain facts. One explains the fact that of a large number of animals selected without explicit reference to their being herbivora every one has turned out to be herbivorous. The other explains the fact that light exhibits a certain series of very complicated phenomena. We say that a fact is *explained* when a proposition—possibly true— is brought forward, from which that fact follows syllogistically. For instance if we admit that

	All cloven-hoofed animals are herbivora
then since	Neat swine sheep and deer are cloven-hoofed
it follows that	Neat swine sheep and deer are herbivora.

And in the same way since

	Ether waves are polarizable
If we admit that	Light is ether waves
it follows that	Light is polarizable.

Thus to explain a fact is to bring forward another from which it follows syllogistically; and the second common character of these two inferences is that they explain one of their premises; that is that from the conclusion and one premiss the other premiss follows syllogistically.

There are also several general respects in which the two examples I have chosen differ from each other. In the first place, from the premisses of the argument about cloven-footed animals or as I shall call it the Inductive inference or induction—from the premisses of this argument a certain syllogistic conclusion could be drawn; from the facts that

Neat swine sheep and deer are cloven-hooved
and   Neat swine sheep and deer are herbivora

it certainly does not follow syllogistically that all or any particular proportion of cloven-hoofed animals are herbivora but it does follow syllogistically that *some* cloven-hoofed animals are. On the other hand from the premisses of the argument about light, or as I shall henceforward term it the hypothetic inference, that is from

Light is polarizable
and   Ether-waves are polarizable

nothing follows syllogistically. This is the first difference between the induction and the hypothesis; the former merely stretches—though to an infinite degree—a valid syllogistic conclusion; the other is inferred from premisses from which no syllogistic conclusion is valid. The induction is thus a little stronger argument than the hypothesis.

In the second place, though both the inductive and the hypothetic inference explain facts, they do so in very different ways. The induction explains certain things having a certain character in common by the presumption that it is a character which pertains to the class to which they belong. But why this character should pertain to that class it does not inform us. That all cloven-hoofed animals are herbivora explains, in one sense, the fact that neat swine sheep and deer are so. But still we do not see *why* all cloven-hoofed animals should be herbivora. Thus inductions only enable us to discover all the general characters of classes and so to distinguish between those characters which are merely individual and those which are essential and form the basis of a classification. In short, the result of a number of inductive inferences is a natural classification, because natural classification consists in arranging things according to those characters which are invariably accompanied by many others, and induction discloses to us what characters those are. The question *why* a certain class should have a certain general character, why all light for instance should be polarizable, is the question which the hypothetic explanation solves. But as induction does not afford hypothetic explanation, neither does hypothesis afford inductive explanation. The hypothesis of ether waves explains the polarization of light but we may still ask upon what principle it is that light is ether waves. Thus induction informs us upon what principle it is that certain things have a common character; hypothesis enables us to see why a certain thing should possess peculiar properties.

The difference between our inductive and hypothetic argument is this. The syllogism by which the fact is explained, in the case of induction has the inference which we draw as its rule, but in the case of hypothesis has that inference as its case. Thus our induction was

> Neat swine sheep and deer are cloven-hoofed
> Neat swine sheep and deer are herbivora
> ∴ All cloven-hoofed animals are herbivora

and the syllogism by which the fact that neat swine sheep and deer though selected merely as being cloven-hoofed turn out to be herbivora is this:

> All cloven-hoofed animals are herbivora
> Neat swine sheep and deer are cloven-hoofed
> ∴ Neat swine sheep and deer are herbivora

Here you perceive that the inductive conclusion appears as the rule in the explaining syllogism. On the other hand our hypothetic argument is

> Light is polarizable
> Ether waves are polarizable
> ∴ Light is Ether waves

The fact explained here is that light is polarizable and the syllogism by which it is explained is this—

Ether waves are polarizable
Light is ether waves
∴ Light is polarizable.

Here the rule is Ether waves are polarizable; Light is ether waves, which is the Hypothetic conclusion, is the case.

These differences between these two scientific inferences are so great that it seems to me essential to a right understanding of the subject that we should recognize two kinds of scientific reasoning, Induction and Hypothesis. Induction is the process by which we find the general characters of classes and establish natural classifications. It is the logic of zoölogy, botany, and chemistry as well as of statistics, of logic, and of many other sciences. Hypothesis alone affords us any knowledge of causes and forces, and enables us to see the *why* of things. It is employed in two classes of sciences, first in Pure Physics such as Optics, Acoustics, &c., and second in mixed sciences such as History, Physiology, Geology, &c. It will be found that the further we progress in the study of logic, the deeper will appear the line of separation between these two kinds of scientific reasoning. And we shall find eventually that they differ as much from each other as either does from syllogistic or deductive reasoning. So that we have

Deduction
Induction
and   Hypothesis

as three coördinate classes of reasoning.

All that we have established, at present, however is that there are two distinct kinds of scientific inference, induction and hypothesis.

The next question which we have to ask is how many different forms of induction and hypothesis there are. Beginning, then, with induction and recurring to our old example, which I will now write only as it appears when applied as an explaining syllogism we have

☞ All cloven-hoofed animals are herbivora
Neat swine sheep and deer are cloven-hoofed
Neat swine sheep and deer are herbivora

I put an index against the inductive conclusion. The first proposition is the rule, the second is the case, and the third is the result of the explaining syllogism.

Now let us see how this might be varied. The conclusion might be made particular, that is we might say Some cloven-hoofed animals are herbivora; and then the argument would be a valid syllogism. But considered as an induction it would be invalid because it would cease to explain the fact since nothing follows from a particular rule; and it is the essence of induction to explain. In short, then, no modification can be admitted which shall falsify or destroy the explaining syllogism. The rule may, however, be made negative if we take the result negative; for we may clearly substitute not carnivorous for herbivorous and reason that because Neat swine sheep and deer are a sample of cloven-hoofed animals and none of them are carnivorous, that no cloven-hoofed animals are carnivorous; and this would be as valid an induction as the affirmative one. Whether the case and result may be made particular—to make the case negative would destroy the explaining syllogism—is a delicate question. Suppose I enter a room and find a boy taking beans out of a bag and dealing them out into boxes. I see him put one into each box. The natural supposition is that he has dealt out more; perhaps all the beans in the boxes have been taken from the bag, perhaps there were some in the boxes before. I put my hand into the boxes and take out a single bean from each; all these beans are black. This is a feeble but valid argument that all the beans in the bag are black. Now what is our conclusion?

> All the beans in the bag were black

and our premisses are

> Some of the beans in each box had been in the bag
> Some of the beans in each box are black

Thus it is plain that any inference is competent from a particular case and result. And so it appears that the explaining syllogism of an induction may belong to any of the four moods of the first figure. That is it may be either

   A A E E
   A I A I
   A I E O

and the first premiss or rule of the explaining syllogism is the conclusion of the inductive argument.

Now the question is whether the explaining syllogism of an induction may belong to the 2nd or 3rd figures. Now if we bear in mind the fact that the 2nd figure is obtained from the 1st by transposing the case and the result and denying both, and that the 3rd figure is obtained by interchanging the rule and the result and denying both, so that the three figures are

1st	2nd	3rd
Rule asserted	Rule asserted	Result denied
Case asserted	Result denied	Case asserted
Result asserted	Case denied	Rule denied

and if we further remember that it is the assertion of the rule which is the inductive conclusion, we perceive, at once, that to say that inductions are valid whose explaining syllogism is in the 3rd figure is merely to say that if any inference would be justly drawn from certain premisses, then if that inference is false we may justly infer that the premisses are not both true. Now let us see how this principle holds. If we say, certain beans have been taken out of a bag and these beans are black, accordingly all the beans in the bag were probably black, we make an induction whose explaining syllogism is

   All in the bag were black
   These were in the bag
  ∴ These were black

Now the corresponding syllogism of the third figure would be

   These are not all black
   These are taken from the bag
  ∴ Not all in the bag were black.

Can we make the induction corresponding to this? Plainly we can. If we were to pick out some beans out of a bag which we know contains some white beans, we may infer by induction that some of those we pick out will also be white. This obviously depends upon the same principle that guides induction, namely that as is the sample so is the whole. This figure of induction results from the first by transposing the conclusion of the explaining syllogism with one of the premisses and denying both. But it also results from transposing the conclusion of the inductive argument with one of the premisses and denying both. The question suggests itself, therefore, whether the conclusion of the induction may not be transposed with the other premiss and both denied.

Suppose for example we know that

	Some of the beans in a bag are not black
and that	All of a certain large number of beans are black
then we presume that	These beans were not taken at haphazard from that bag.

Every cautious man is familiar enough with that reasoning. But a suggestion occurs to us which throws the first glimmer of light upon the logic of induction. We have seen that induction and hypothesis are two different kinds of reasoning. They are both explanatory, however; that is, from the inductive or hypothetic conclusion and one of the premisses the other premiss follows syllogistically so that, in fact, the grand distinction between these modes of inference and syllogism is that in induction and hypothesis we infer one of the premisses of a syllogism from the conclusion and the other premiss. At least we have seen that there must be such an explaining syllogism; that is a syllogism one of whose premisses is inferred from the other two propositions in hypothesis and induction. The question next arose of what figures and moods can this explaining syllogism be? We have seen that in the case of induction it can be of any mood of the first figure. We saw also that it might be of the third figure when this consideration struck us:—The first figure of syllogism is

Rule asserted		Result asserted
Case asserted	and the corresponding	Case asserted
Result asserted	induction is	Rule asserted

The third figure of syllogism is obtained by transposing the conclusion and first premiss or denying both.

Result denied		Rule denied
Case asserted	and the corresponding	Case asserted
Rule denied	induction is	Result denied

We have seen that this new form of induction is a valid one. But this form might be obtained in two ways; either in the way in which we have obtained it by taking the first explaining syllogism and contraposing the propositions and then transposing them. Now if we regard this second form of induction as obtained in this way, symmetry demands that there should be another form obtained by transposing not the conclusion and first premiss of the first explaining syllogism and denying both but by doing the same thing with the conclusion and second premiss. In that way we should get for our new syllogism of explanation

Rule asserted		Result denied
Result denied	and for the corre-	Case denied
Case denied	sponding induction	Rule asserted

But our second form of induction may be regarded as produced in another way; that is simply by the transposition of the conclusion and first premiss of the first induction with the denial of both. In this case symmetry demands that there should be another form, derived by transposing the conclusion and *second* premiss of the first induction and denying both. This would give

> Result asserted
> Rule denied
> Case denied

Now to ascertain whether this is a good induction or not we constructed an example. Suppose we know that some of the beans in a bag are not black. This is the denial of a Rule. Suppose we know also that certain beans purporting to be taken from that bag are all black. That is the assertion of a result of the rule which has just been denied. We certainly can infer that these beans have not been taken out of that bag at random. We certainly cannot infer that they have not been taken out of the bag but it will be observed that in the other form of induction whose explaining syllogism is of the first figure we add the words "at random." Thus we say, neat swine sheep and deer are animals taken, at random, from among those that are cloven-hoofed. For were they not taken at random, were they for instance taken as being herbivorous cloven-footed animals, their being herbivorous would not go a step to prove that all cloven-hoofed animals are herbivorous. When therefore we infer that these beans have not been taken out of the bag at random, we seem to be inferring the contradictory of what we should have to assume if we wished to reason from the character of these beans to that of those in the bag. And so we seem to have made a new form of inductive argument by transposing the conclusion of the first form with the second premiss and denying both. But let us be sure that the ambiguous expression 'at random' does not mislead us. When we say that neat swine sheep and deer are a sample taken at random of cloven-hoofed animals, we do not mean to say that the choice depended upon no other condition than that all should be cloven-hoofed; we can not know *that* and the presumption is the other way since there is a certain limitation of that class indicated by our having taken so few instances. What we mean, then, in saying that neat swine sheep and deer are taken at random from among cloven-hoofed animals, is that being cloven-hoofed was the only condition that consciously guided us in the selection of these animals. But now take the argument from Some of the beans in a bag being not black and All of a certain selection of beans being black. Can we infer from this that if these beans were taken from the bag the person who took them was conscious of being influenced by another condition? Hardly I should say. I should suppose the inference to be that he was influenced by another condition. In short, I should say that although 'tis a fair presumption when we are conscious of no disturbing condition to suppose that there is none, yet it is hardly fair when there is one to suppose we are conscious of it. It may seem that in both cases the same assumption is made, but it is not so and there is a preference of the first for the second if it is more usual to have no disturbing condition than to be conscious of one. Induction, however, would be valid if it should at first lead us into a hundred errors for one truth for even then truth would prevail in the long run. But this inference which we are now considering can only become valid by a knowledge of what cannot be known—the ratio between the disturbing conditions of which we are and those of which we are not conscious. There is also another particular in which such an inference would differ altogether from induction, namely that it is not explanatory; it shows that a circumstance is not explained by another but affords no explanation at all.

Thus we find that of the two modes which offered themselves for completing a symmetrical whole of inductive forms of argument, the most promising has entirely failed. Let us then try the other method.

According to this other method if we take any induction whose explaining syllogism is of the first figure, and deny both premisses, we have a form for the true induction of the same conclusion as before. This certainly seems incredible, that when both the premisses of an induction are denied the conclusion follows the same as though the premisses had been admitted. But let us examine the matter. Let us deny the two premisses Neat swine sheep and deer are cloven-hoofed and Neat swine sheep and deer are herbivora; only to avoid falsity let us take other animals which are not herbivora, as lions, cats, dogs, wolves. Then we have

> Lions cats dogs wolves have been selected
> as not being herbivorous
> They have not cloven hoofs

Such are our premisses. Now it certainly follows that Everything not herbivorous is not cloven-hoofed or in other terms that Every cloven-hoofed animal is herbivorous. Thus we find that the same conclusion follows as if we had taken the contradictory of both premisses.

We find then that as all Aristotelean syllogisms are of these three Figures

1st	2nd	3rd
Rule asserted	Rule asserted	Result denied
Case asserted	Result denied	Case asserted
Result asserted	Case denied	Rule denied

so these same forms represent forms of induction if we only consider the first line as indicating the conclusion, instead of the third.

Let us now take up hypothetic reasoning and see whether in a similar manner that infers the second line in all the moods of all the figures.

To begin with then it is obvious that the case may be particular if the result is particular. Thus if instead of light we had said something which affects the senses is polarizable, we should still have had ground for thinking that something which affects the senses is ether waves. It is also very plain that the rule and result, the two premisses of hypothetic argument, might both be negative. Thus it would make no difference whether we spoke of light being polarizable or not unpolarizable. All the moods therefore are represented, if all the figures are. The question is then in reference to the 2nd and 3rd Figures. When the explaining syllogism of a hypothesis is in the 2nd Figure the hypothetic inference is from the denial of the case and the assertion of the rule to the denial of the result. We can show by an example that such a hypothesis is fair. It is a curious fact that St. Paul is not in heaven,—that is, if we believe Swedenborg; how is this to be accounted for, what keeps him out? If we examine the persons who are in heaven, we find that they none of them oppose Swedenborg's theology. Now is not this a ground for supposing that St. Paul does not gibe entirely with Swedenborg?

Hypothesis whose explaining syllogism is in the third figure reasons from the denial of rule and result to the assertion of a case. How do we account for the circumstance that some apostles are not in heaven? We remember that no opposers of Swedenborg's theology are in heaven; hence we may suppose that some opposers of Swedenborg are apostles.

We thus see that the explaining syllogism of either induction or hypothesis—that is that syllogism by which the fact upon which the induction or hypothesis rests—is shown to follow syllogistically from the other hypothetic or inductive premiss and from the conclusion. This explaining syllogism thus produced by a mere transposition of the propositions making up an inductive or hypothetic argument, may be in any figure and any mood of Aristotelean syllogism. The three figures of Aristotelean syllogism are

Rule asserted	Rule asserted	Result denied
Case asserted	Result denied	Case asserted
Result asserted	Case denied	Rule denied

If the proposition indicated by the third line is inferred, we have deduction. If the 1st line is inferred by the other two we have induction; if the second line is inferred we have hypothesis.

Whether or not the explaining syllogism may be Theophrastean, we are not yet able to determine; owing to a deficient understanding of that kind of reasoning. We shall at another lecture be able to solve the question, which is however of very little consequence.

The explaining syllogism may be composed of propositions of three terms. Thus, if we select a number of women as being mothers, and find that each of them loves her child; we may infer by induction that all mothers love their children. And here the explaining syllogism is

> All mothers love those of whom they are mothers
> A is mother of B
> A loves B.

In the same way if we observe that a woman has an extravagant love for a child we may infer with Solomon, that she is its mother; and the explaining syllogism is the same as before.

It is needless for me to show that the second and third figures of this kind of syllogism may also afford forms for explanations, for they are formed from the first exactly as in categorical syllogism and therefore the possibility of the matter has already been sufficiently illustrated.

Thus, every species of syllogism, except perhaps the Theophrastean, may comprize syllogisms of explanation; and corresponding to each form of syllogism we have a form of induction and another of hypothesis.

But we have not yet sufficiently defined these forms to be able to discriminate between a valid induction or hypothesis and one which is not valid. Thus take the first mood of the first figure of syllogism. It is

> All I is C
> All D is I
> $\therefore$ All D is C

and the induction which this explains is

> All D is C
> All D is I
> $\therefore$ All I is C

Now we have already seen that a valid induction may be of such a form as this, but it is plain that every argument in this form is not valid. If for instance I say

> All these beans were in this bag
> All these beans were black

it is totally irrational to conclude that

> All black things were in this bag.

And if we were to take the trouble to examine all the forms of induction and hypothesis which I have given, we should find that while there might be valid arguments in these forms, there might also be invalid arguments having the same forms, so that it is apparent that we must take into account some distinctions between propositions which we have hitherto overlooked. Allow me to call your attention to this irresistible conclusion. We have hitherto divided categorical propositions into Universal and Particular; and Affirmative and Negative. By means of these distinctions we have been enabled to separate arguments into various groups. And in the case of deductive or syllogistic argument, we seem to have been pretty successful in making these groups sufficiently small to distinguish valid arguments from paralogisms. But in the case of induction and hypothesis, we find that each of these groups of arguments, comprizes some which are good and others which are bad. It is absolutely indispensible, therefore, to a classificatory or testing science of reasonings, to subdivide these groups and make them smaller. Now this can only be done by another division of propositions,—and you perceive that without searching for subtileties we find ourselves absolutely compelled to inquire for some distinctions between propositions which we have hitherto overlooked.

These distinctions must be sufficient to carry our division of arguments down to that point that each group comprizes only valid or only invalid arguments. Then corresponding to each group of valid inductive and hypothetic arguments, there must be a group of syllogisms, to serve as their explanations. And if the rule still holds, as it probably will, that any kind of syllogism may be an explaining syllogism, there will be no form of syllogism to which forms of valid induction and hypothesis do not correspond. So that the difference between deduction, induction, and hypothesis, will be this: that of three propositions

A

B   C

deduction infers A from B and C, induction infers B from A and C, and hypothesis infers C from A and B.

It is true that there must always be a difference of strength between a deduction, an induction, and a hypothesis. But this is a matter which we cannot profitably consider as yet; it is sufficient to observe that the question whether an argument can have any strength, that is whether it is valid, is quite distinct from the question how strong it happens to be. This latter question we shall consider hereafter.

At present we must concentrate the powers of our mind upon the problem which is presented to us by the curious triangular relation between deduction, induction, and hypothesis. We have here a hint for a method of discovering the true conditions of valid induction and hypothesis.

The distinctions between propositions which it is necessary for us to take account of, must by the introduction of them, make our inductive and hypothetic forms stronger than they now are. That is the premisses of valid inductions and hypotheses *say more* in proportion to what their conclusions say, than is the case with the forms that we are now in possession of. For example, the syllogism

All I is C		All D is C
All D is I	affords the induction	All D is I
$\therefore$ All D is C		$\therefore$ All I is C

but to make this a form which shall belong exclusively to valid inductions, something must be added to the premisses or something must be taken from the conclusion. And the same must be the case with the forms of hypothesis. The premisses must be made stronger or must say more relatively to the conclusion. But the premiss which induction and hypothesis have in common is the conclusion of syllogism and the conclusions of induction and hypothesis are the premisses of syllogism and, therefore, if the premisses of induction and hypothesis are made strong relatively to their conclusion, the premisses of syllo-gism will be made weak relatively to their conclusion. If, therefore, our forms make inductions and hypotheses invalid they must make syllogisms needlessly strong. Hence two modes suggest themselves whereby we may discover the true conditions of valid induction and hypothesis; first, to find what needs to be added to our forms of in-duction and hypothesis; and, second, to find wherein our syllogistic forms are stronger than they need be. We shall discover hereafter that it is the latter method upon which we must principally rely.

The following out of this inquiry must be left for the next lecture. Meantime I may remark that although the syllogistic forms we now have err generally by being so strong, nothing prevents their also giving rise to fallacious arguments. And this is a point which I pro-pose to close this lecture by illustrating.

All logicians agree that the word *is* in the logical form of propo-sition does not imply that the subject exists; for instance we can say all fictitious animals are non-existent, without any contradiction be-tween the *are* and *non-existent*. Accordingly it is true that

<blockquote>
All griffins have wings
and that   All griffins are quadrupeds;
</blockquote>

both these points are part of the definition of griffins. But from these premisses, if our syllogistic forms are right, it follows that

<blockquote>
Some quadrupeds have wings.
</blockquote>

Now this is false. Even if we allow it not to say that any quadrupeds exist, it does say that if any exist, some of them have wings.

We shall have in the first and second figures the corresponding fallacies—

No quadrupeds have wings	No quadrupeds have wings
All griffins are quadrupeds	All griffins have wings
∴ No griffins have wings	∴ No griffins are quadrupeds.

In all these cases the premisses are correct and yet the conclusions are wrong.

By taking advantage of the same error in the ordinary system of logic I can prove that some black is white.

We start with

> No black is white
> ∴ No hard black nor no soft black is white
> ∴ There is no hard black white
> ∴ No black white is hard
> ∴ No black white is hard non-black

In the same way

> ∴ No black white is non-hard non-black
> ∴ No black white is non-black
> ∴ All black white is black

In the same way

> All black white is white
> ∴ Some black is white.

/Lecture VI/

MS 128: October–November 1866

Practical Maxims of Logic

1. Beware of a syllogism.

2. Remember that a *hypothesis* must have more antecedent probability than the facts which it explains. Extent of predicate greatest possible.

3. In reasoning from individuals to a whole class, the class should be

the one, including those individuals whose content is the greatest possible.

4. There is no valid inference from parts to whole if the parts have not been taken at random.

5. Everything can be explained.

I begin this evening with a brief *resumé* of the Logic of Science. The two elements of scientific inference, Induction and Hypothesis, are explanatory in their nature—that is to say, they infer something from which as a premiss the facts observed necessarily follow. They cannot therefore, be understood, without a full understanding of the Syllogism or Deductive Process, according to which the facts do follow from the Inductive or Hypothetic Inference.

We began therefore, by studying the Syllogism, we analyzed all its varieties, and showed that in every case it involves the principle, that if a Rule is true—and a Case comes under it, the Predicate of the Rule is true of the Subject of that Case. All deductive inference, however complicated, involves nothing more than this principle, together with the principles by which the meaning of propositions is determined. It will therefore be sufficient, if we confine ourselves in this *resumé* for the sake of simplicity to *direct* syllogistic inference where the rule and the case are the premisses, and the result the conclusion, and to the Inductions and Hypotheses which depend directly upon these syllogisms. In this direct syllogism, then, the rule and the case are premisses and the result is the conclusion. Now we have seen that Induction and Hypothesis being explanatory, there is always a syllogism by which one of their premisses follows from, or is explained by, the inference which is inductively or hypothetically drawn. The inductive or hypothetic conclusion, therefore, stands to one of its premisses in the relation of a deductive or syllogistic premiss to its conclusion, the second premiss of the induction or hypothesis remaining a premiss in this explaining syllogism. It is in fact a sufficient definition of a scientific inference to say that it is the inference of one of the premisses of a syllogism from the other premiss and from the conclusion. In fact, every such inference is valid, that is to say, lends an additional probability to the proposition inferred, altho' the fact indicated by this proposition may still remain entirely unknown or even grossly improbable.

In another point of view however, it is perfectly correct to say that an induction from a single instance or a hypothesis from a simple phenomenon, is no induction or hypothesis at all, inasmuch as the occurrence of a single instance or a simple phenomenon requires no explanation, since it presents no manifold to be reduced to unity. This circumstance, however, would follow from our first view of the matter—inasmuch as we found that the case must be *subsumptive* and the rule *necessary*. The case must be subsumptive—that is to say, its subject must have been taken out of the collection of things indicated by its predicate, and if it be taken out of a smaller collection of things, out of a collection which forms but a part of that collection indicated by the predicate—then, in the case of deduction, it is not the genuine premiss, but only a deduction from the premiss—and in the case of *induction*, it does not in any way go to establishing the conclusion. If only one instance is taken we cannot state from what class the subject of the case has been drawn—we can only say, that it has been drawn from the proximate species of this individual. In such circumstances, therefore the genuine premiss in deduction it is difficult to state at all, and the proposition laid down is of no use in induction whatever. My time does not permit me to illustrate this by an example—this has been already done in one of the previous lectures. The Hypothesis from a simple phenomenon is excluded in a similar manner by the condition that the "rule is necessary." In the weakest cases of valid induction and hypothesis then, we have a combination of several inductive or hypothetic arguments, each of which has a certain small and not measurable weight independent of the others, although were it not *for* the others, it could not be known to have even *that* weight. The strength of an induction or a hypothesis therefore, is a very different thing from its validity, and is owing entirely to massing together of arguments so as to make them bear upon one point.

Passing over the second study which we made of the subject from the point of view of general principles and the union of the two in one by means of primary conceptions as well as the psychological applications of the theory, I shall take up tonight some practical views.

I shall take up this evening without any order some maxims for practical application in testing reasonings. I shall illustrate these maxims by instances of bad reasoning such as we actually meet with.

I must offer some apology for doing this in as much as it will necessitate entering upon questions of a practical kind—questions of good sense in politics, religion, and the daily conduct of life; which are matters which we have not come here to discuss, and the full discussion of which would be quite aside from the purpose of these lectures. But it is obvious that I cannot illustrate the real value of a logical maxim, by a merely fictitious example. Unless I take such fallacies as men actually will fall into sometimes, you would doubt whether men actually would require to apply maxims so obvious as to seem to be mere truisms. I must therefore oppose actual arguments—such as men really employ—such as some of you very likely employ. I must ask you therefore to reflect that when I oppose a particular argument, I do not necessarily oppose the conclusion to which it leads. I only oppose that conclusion so far as it rests upon that argument alone. The best opinions are often defended by the most absurd arguments. For example, we often hear this argument employed

> All murder is wicked,
> This or that act is murder;
> ∴ This or that act is wicked.

Now the act may in fact be wicked or innocent; but this argument is a silly begging of the question. What is meant by murder? The killing of a man with malice prepense. And what is meant by malice? A wicked intention. All that is meant by murder then is a *wicked* and deliberate killing of a man. Of course, then, no one need admit an act to be murder until it is proved in some other way to be wicked.

This illustrates how bad an argument may be made to support an excellent conclusion. So that when we oppose an argument we may very well applaud the conclusion provided we do so upon other grounds.

I may have occasion to attack arguments which are favorites of some of you. I may very likely be unjust in some of my criticisms. In that case, I shall ask you having examined what I say patiently, to reject it without passion.

The first maxim is—Beware of a syllogism. *Syllogism* is deductive reasoning. Now we have seen that deductive reasoning concludes nothing not implied in the premisses. It does not therefore advance our knowledge in the least; but its only use is to render our notions more distinct. This is a very great use certainly. All geometry is implicitly involved in its Definitions, Postulates, and Axioms. These definitions, postulates, and axioms constitute a confused knowledge of space. But we all know that much reasoning is required to see that, in consequence, the sum of the squares of a right triangle is equal to the square of the hypothenuse. The importance of deductive reasoning must on no account be denied, and we should not regard every syllogism with distrust. But it should be remembered that very many syllogisms are required in order to pass from the premisses of geometry to such a conclusion as the Pythagorean theorem. No one single syllogism can do more than a very little. No combination of them can do much except in subjects of which we have a pretty advanced though confused knowledge. If therefore we find a single syllogism which seems to be of great avail we should scrutinize it carefully to see whether it is not false. We often hear it said

>All men are equal in their political rights
>Negroes are men;
>∴ Negroes are equal in political rights to whites.

Far be it from me to say anything which could hinder justice from being done to that people whose guardianship the people of the North have assumed. By altering their social condition we have made ourselves responsible for their welfare, to some extent. But this argument which seems to carry us so far, becomes suspicious from the very fact that it does carry us so far while it is only a syllogism. The Declaration of Independence declares that it is "self-evident that all men are created equal." Now men are created babies and therefore, in this case, *men* is used in a sense that includes babies and therefore nothing can follow from the argument relatively to the rights of Negroes which does not apply to babies, as well. The argument, therefore, can amount to very little.

It is not my business to expound the real doctrine of the Declaration, but I would advise those who wish to understand it to read Locke's Essay on Government.

A syllogism which seems to give us an advance in knowledge and not merely to render our notions more distinct will generally be found to have one of two faults. It either begs the question or else the subject of the rule is different from the predicate of the case.

The fallacy of begging the question is so common a one that it ought to be thoroughly understood and yet it has never been satisfactorily described or analyzed. If a man adopts as a premiss something which another will not accept, he simply fails to convince that man but he does not commit any fallacy. But if he adopts what no man can accept and doubt the conclusion for an instant, he *begs the question*. The commonest way of begging the question is improperly to assume the case as a premiss. If the rule were a statement of a part of what is implied in the very meaning of a word the *case* would be assumed improperly. For instance. Suppose it were desired to prove that a certain figure had three sides. It would necessarily beg the question to say this Figure is a triangle, for to ask anyone to admit that it is a triangle is to ask him to admit that it has three sides since that is a part of what the word *triangle* means. The rule cannot therefore be a definition or a part of a definition without the case being improperly assumed as a premiss.

Many arguments are rightly enough said to beg the question when one of the premisses contains a fact indeed but one which everyone but an idiot would be pretty sure to have taken into account. Thus if anyone were to reason thus:—

> Whatever is in the Bible is true
> The Mosaic account of creation is in the Bible
> ∴ The Mosaic account of creation is true.

This would be called begging the question because probably no sane man would admit the first premiss and be in doubt about the conclusion even for a moment.

Some have said that every valid syllogism begs the question. As a practical rule this comes pretty near to being true.

Begging the question is the weakness of prejudiced persons. A man who cannot conceive of anyone's doubting an opinion, when asked to prove it will be very likely to lay down as a premiss something which no man who doubts the conclusion would admit, because never having put himself in that man's position, he does not understand what he would and what he would not admit about the matter in hand. A doubt which a man has never entertained startles and confounds him; he gropes about in the dark for something to say in reply, and as he has never gone so far in his inquiries before he is unable now to do anything more than reiterate his opinion in another form.

If a syllogism which seems to advance our knowledge does not beg the question it is usually because it has four terms. That is to say one of its terms is taken in two different senses in the 2 propositions in which it occurs. It often requires great great subtilty to avoid such fallacies. And the great practical use of the study of the old logic is the exercise it gives in detecting these ambiguities. It is now just eight hundred years since Anselm put forth his celebrated proof of the existence of a God. It runs thus, God is that than which nothing greater can be thought. What really exists is greater than what does not exist. Hence, it is impossible to think that God does not exist because it is possible to think that he does exist. And therefore something greater than anything which is thought not to exist, can be thought. But God is not thought unless he be thought to be that than which nothing greater can be thought. Hence it is impossible consistently to think that God does not exist. As this argument is extremely subtile I will repeat it. We believe God to be something than which nothing greater can be thought. The question is whether there is any such nature. The fool has said in his heart that there is no God. But certainly that fool, when he hears what I say "something than which nothing greater can be thought" understands what he hears, and what he understands is in his understanding even if he does not understand it to *be*. It is one thing for a thing to be in the understanding and another to understand it to be. But that than which nothing greater can be thought, cannot be in the understanding alone, for it can be thought to be in fact, which is *more*. Therefore it exists.

As soon as this argument appeared a book was written against it called "A book in favor of the fool," in which it was stamped as a fallacy. In this book a parallel instance is brought forward. We are told, says the author, of an island in the ocean, which is called the Lost Island on account of the difficulty or rather the impossibility of finding what does not exist. And they tell greater stories about the richness and luxury of this island, than they do of the fortunate islands, and in short they say that nothing can be finer. Now then the Lost Island is by definition one than which none can be finer. But unless it exists something can be finer. Therefore, by Anselm's reasoning, this island must exist.

Anselm wrote a book in reply to this book in favor of the fool. And this is what he says in reference to this island. Something can certainly be finer than this island, because it is *lost*. God is an island that cannot be lost; he is the only *best*. And to admit that there is any parallel instance to the one I have given would be at once to admit the falsity of my argument.

In subsequent ages this argument has attracted much attention sometimes being attacked and sometimes defended. I will endeavor to present to you the strong points against and for. Against it, it may be said: This argument seeks to make out that *existence* is a *property* and not merely an *accident* of *deity;* that is, it undertakes to prove that existence follows syllogistically from or what is the same thing is implicitly contained in the definition. Now all that may be admitted and yet it will not follow that God exists. For example, we may define the word *Buz* [write it] as a flaming dragon which has the singular property of appearing to the sight as soon as *B–u–z* is written down. That being a mere definition must be admitted. Well, *B–u–z* is written down. Does it follow that such a flaming dragon has appeared to us? Not at all. Now Anselm's proof is precisely similar to this. *God* is a word which means implicitly that if any such thing can be thought it actually exists. Grant that it can be thought: it does not follow that it actually exists. Why not, if we admit the truth of the definition and definitions cannot be disputed? Because all that a definition says or as a definition can say is not how a thing exists but of what sort it would be if it were to exist. A griffin breathes fire by definition. That is, he would do so were he to exist. The definition of *God*, then, is not peculiar in implying the existence of its object. Every definition does so. Anything would exist if it did exist. And what a thing would be if it did exist is all that a definition can assert. The argument, therefore, rests upon a confusion between *would be* and *is,* between *being thought* and *being.*

In defence of the argument, it may be said that the distinction of *being thought* and *really being* does not exist in the case of deity. What is meant by truth? What do we mean for instance when we say that it is *true* that there is a statue of Daniel Webster in front of the State-house? We mean that if we were to go there we might see it and feel it. That is what we mean and yet to say that we should see it and feel it, that is should have such sensations, is not to say that it is there so much as to say that *evidence* of its being there would be afforded. We mean then by saying that a fact is true, that an indefinitely great amount of evidence upon the point, not *ex parte*, would be overwhelmingly in favor of the fact, not against it.

If, therefore, a hypothesis is required—an indefinitely large number of facts or as many as you please being taken into account—that constitutes the truth of the hypothesis.

Now if we take up that sophism about a flaming dragon we see at once that that *name* Buz was required only in an ideal state of things and therefore has no actual validity. In the theological argument it is quite different. That an ideal of a God is required to bring our general conceptions to unity is admitted on all hands. And that ideal God would not be such unless it were regarded as having existence and therefore it constitutes a hypothesis of a real God and as this hypothesis is required in every state of Cognition, its truth is constituted thereby.

I have entered into this discussion in order to illustrate how much subtilty is required both for attack and defence in inquiring whether an argument rests on an ambiguity. Mr. Mill remarks

Few people (I have said in another place) have reflected how great a knowledge of Things is required to enable a man to affirm that any given argument turns wholly upon words. There is, perhaps, not one of the leading terms of philosophy which is not used in almost innumerable shades of meaning, to express ideas more or less widely different from one another. Between two of these ideas a sagacious and penetrating mind will discern, as it were intuitively, an unobvious link of connexion, upon which, though perhaps unable to give a logical account of it, he will found a perfectly valid argument, which his critic, not having so keen an insight into the Things, will mistake for a fallacy turning on the double meaning of a term. And the greater the genius of him who thus safely leaps over the chasm, the greater will probably be the crowing and vain-glory of the mere logician, who, hobbling after him, evinces his own superior wisdom by pausing on its brink, and giving up as desperate his proper business of bridging it over. (Vol. 1, Book 1, Ch. 8, §7, p. 172 note)

This is very true, but prudence requires that we should not without necessity take those leaps which may be very glorious but whose glory is measured by their hazardousness.

So much then for our first maxim to beware of syllogisms.

The second maxim relates to induction. Do not take as a sample a picked specimen nor a small one.

It is by violating this maxim that figures are made to lie. Medical statistics in particular are usually contemptibly small, as well as open to the suspicion of being picked. I am speaking now of the statistics of reputable physicians. It is extremely difficult to collect numerous facts relating to any obscure point in medicine, and it is still more difficult to make it evident that those facts are a fair representation of the general run of events. This accounts for the slow progress of medical science notwithstanding the immense study which has been bestowed upon it and for the great errors which will often be received for centuries by physicians. Probably there is no branch of science which is so difficult in every point of view. It requires a really great mind to make a medical induction. This is too obvious to require proof. There are so many disturbing influences—personal idiosyncrasies, mixture of treatment, accidental and unknown influences, peculiarities of climate, race, and season,—that it is particularly essential that the facts should be very numerous and should be scrutinized with the eye of a lynx to detect deceptions. And yet it is peculiarly difficult to collect facts in medicine. One man's experience can seldom be of decisive weight, and no man can judge of matters beyond his personal knowledge in medicine, he must trust to the judgment of others. So that while a sample requires to be more extensive and more carefully taken in this science than in any other, in this more than in any other these requisites are difficult to fulfill.

Nothing, therefore, more pitiably manifests the looseness with which people in general reason than the readiness of nine persons out of ten to pronounce upon the merits of a medicine upon the most limited, the most inexact, and the most prejudiced experience which it is possible to call experience at all. Any old woman who has seen any amelioration of symptoms follow after the administration of a medicine in a dozen cases at all resembling one another, will not hesitate to pronounce it an infallible cure for any case resembling at all any one of the dozen. This is shocking. But what is worse still, treatment will be recommended even upon a hearsay acquaintance with one or two cases.

Observe, I pray you, the combination of fallacies involved in such a proceeding. In the first place, no induction can, with propriety, be drawn unless a sample has been taken of some definite class. But these foolish creatures—who think that merely spending time in a sickroom has made Galens of them—are utterly unable to define the disease in question. Suppose it to be *diphtheria* for instance. How do they know diphtheria from sore-throat? Their samples are in reality samples of no definite class at all.

In the second place, the number of their instances is scarcely sufficient for the simplest induction. In the third place the instances are very likely derived from hearsay. Now in addition to the inaccuracy which attaches to this kind of evidence; we are more likely to hear of extraordinary things relatively to their frequency than we are of ordinary ones. So that to take into account such instances is to take picked samples. In the fourth place, the predicate which belongs to all the instances in common is usually utterly vague. In the fifth place, a deduction is usually made respecting a case in hand without carefully considering whether it really comes under the class from which the sample was drawn. In the sixth place more is apt to be predicated of the case in hand than has been found of the previous instances. All these fallacies are combined in a sort of argument which one can scarcely go a week without hearing an instance of.

The most difficult science next to medicine is, perhaps, meteorology. Here, again, the phenomena are so complicated and the *content* of the observations so meagre that very little is known of the matter. And still less would be known were it not for the happy circumstance that several minds well disciplined in less difficult sciences have turned their attention to it. Here, also, you find people ready to advance from particulars to generals at the slightest provocation. How often you will hear people predict that the next Sunday will be rainy because there has been a succession of rainy Sundays lately. There are several fatal defects in such an argument. In the first place, the instances are picked. We are more apt to remember rainy days than pleasant ones. Ask yourself what proportion of days during the last year have been rainy and then compare your guess with a meteorological journal and you will find you have stated too high a ratio. I have often, most often, found that people who predicted a rainy Sunday on such grounds had forgotten several pleasant ones within six weeks. In the second place, LATELY is altogether too indefinite a sample to be at all a fair one. In the third place, LATELY is so small a sample that no induction can be drawn from it. And in the fourth place, any meteorological journal will show that the weather has no cycle of seven days, at all. Thus the argument betrays extreme indolence in investigation. No one who broaches it ever undertook to test his theory by comparison with recorded observations.

In regard to hypotheses, I shall read you a passage from Kant—the greatest philosopher of modern times; both on account of the important practical remarks it contains and because it largely supports what has been said in previous lectures of this manner of Inference.

A hypothesis is a holding-to-be-true of a judgment of the truth of a ground, for the sake of its sufficiency for consequences; or, in short: The holding-to-be-true of a presupposition as a ground.

All holding-to-be-true in hypotheses is based on a presupposition which, as a ground, is sufficient to explain other cognitions as consequences. For here we conclude from the truth of the consequence to the truth of the ground. But since this manner of conclusion, as noted above, gives a sufficient criterion of the truth and can lead to apodeictic certainty only when *all possible* consequences of an assumed ground are true, and since all possible consequences can never be determined by us, it becomes clear that hypotheses always remain hypotheses, that is, presuppositions whose complete certainty we can never attain. The probability of a hypothesis nevertheless can increase and rise to an *analogon* of certainty, if, namely, all consequences *that have occurred to us* can be explained out of the presupposed ground. For in such a case there is no reason why we should not assume that all possible consequences will be susceptible of being explained by it. We thus commit ourselves to the hypothesis as if it were perfectly certain, although it is so only *through induction.*

And yet, something must be apodeictically certain in every hypothesis, namely:

1) The *possibility of the presupposition itself.* For instance, when we assume a subterranean fire for the explanation of earthquakes and volcanoes, such a fire must be possible, if not as a flaming, yet as a heated body. But for the sake of certain other appearances, to make the earth an animal in which the circulation of inner fluids causes heat, is to put forward a mere piece of fiction and not a hypothesis. For actualities may be imagined, but not possibilities; these must be certain.

2) The *consequence.* From the assumed ground the consequences must follow correctly, otherwise the hypothesis becomes a mere chimera.

3) *Unity.* It is an essential requirement of a hypothesis that it be only one and need no subsidiary hypotheses for its support. If in the case of a hypothesis we have to adopt several others in support of it, it thereby loses much of its probability. For the more consequences can be derived from a hypothesis, the more probable it is; the fewer, the more improbable. Tycho de Brahe's hypothesis, for example, was not sufficient to explain a number of appearances; he therefore assumed several new hypotheses to supplement it. Here we may already guess that the adopted hypothesis is not the true ground. The Copernican system, on the contrary, is a hypothesis from which everything to be explained by it—*so far as it has yet occurred to us*—can be explained. Here we need no *subsidiary hypotheses.*

There are sciences that do not permit of hypotheses, e.g., mathematics and metaphysics. But in physics they are useful and indispensable. (Vol. 3, p. 262)

These maxims are exceedingly valuable. I shall reduce the 1st and 3rd to one which is a little more axiomatic and no less practical. It is this:—*Facts cannot be explained by a hypothesis more extraordinary than those facts themselves; and of various hypotheses the least extraordinary must be adopted.*

This maxim is rather too vague to make a part of a logical theory, but it is sufficiently precise to be readily applied in practice.

Take for example, homeopathy. What are the facts upon which homeopathy goes. That patients carefully nursed and without any appreciable medicine will get well, as soon and as certainly or even more so, than if largely drugged and carelessly nursed.

Let me say two words to show that these are the facts. That homeopathists pay greater attention than others to diet and nursing is well known. By saying that they give no appreciable medicine, I mean that there is absolutely no other reason to think that they give *any* except the fact that patients who have taken their doses get well. That nobody ever has found any other mode of detecting the existence of such small amounts of bodies is a plain fact. Nor can any analogy warrant our thinking them there. It is the prevalent opinion among scientific men that matter is not infinitely divisible but that there are *molecules* which cannot be divided without a chemical decomposition of the substance. What the size of these molecules may be we do not know except that they are smaller than light vibrations; when we get down to bodies smaller than those vibrations we may expect to meet them at any time. Now even if a homeopathic dose of the 30th dilution contains but a single molecule—the ratio of the size of that molecule to the length of a wave of light would be less than the ratio of the smallest thing which can be seen under a microscope to the distance of the earth from the sun. Analogy certainly does not warrant our carrying the divisibility of matter to such a point, if there are any molecules at all. Nor do we gain much by giving up molecules. We know that the smaller a body is the greater is its strength compared with its weight. The more force therefore in the way of a shake is required to break it. There is likely therefore to be a practical limit to the divisibility of matter even if there are no molecules. And analogy will not justify us in supposing that *any* of the medicine is contained in a homeopathic dose.

The *facts* then to be explained are simply that very careful nursing without appreciable medicine has been followed by as speedy or speedier a recovery in some cases than ordinary treatment has in others. These facts are noticeable and important. I cannot say they are very extraordinary. Now what is the hypothesis proposed for their explanation?

1st   That there is some simple drug which produces a disease almost identical with any disease.

2nd   That the disease produced by the drug cures the other disease.

3rd   That this curative effect of the drug-disease is almost independent of its intensity.

4th   That the effect of a medicine (they do not say which effect) is inversely proportional to the logarithm of the reciprocal of the weight dose, one grain being taken as the dose. And that this measure is *exact*.

5th   That the effect of a medicine is largely increased by diluting it. And that this has no limit.

This is the hypothesis. Now I ask what *facts could* be more extraordinary than such a bundle of hypotheses? It condemns the whole system at once.

Spiritualism affords another instance of a hypothesis wildly improbable and without analogy to explain facts which find their counterpart in the hall of every juggler. A book by Mr. J. Stanley Grimes illustrates this very well. Some of his stories are quite instructive,[1] but I prefer to read to you some excellent remarks upon the logic of Spiritualists:—

The spiritualists are in the constant habit of boasting, that the human testimony in favor of their physical manifestations, is of the same nature as that upon which the Holy Bible is received; and, that any facts or arguments which will overturn the one, will, necessarily, endanger the other. (p. 393)

In order not to offer any more of these maxims than can easily be remembered I shall propound but one more which is however

---

1. For example he tells of a girl whom he went to see move a table; the table was always moved away from her, she was near one of the legs and the motion always stopped if anyone looked under the table. Moreover whenever the table was *moved* forward the upper part of her body moved back. In reference to this last circumstance the lady of the house remarked. " 'See,' said she, 'how it draws upon her shoulders—this proves, that the influence reaches the table *through* the medium' " (p. 388). This surely was a very extraordinary hypothesis compared with that of supposing she shoved the table with her foot.

worth more than all the others put together: It is this—Always stand ready to accept the truth whatever it may be.

Bad reasoning is almost as bad as bad morals. A fallacy committed ought to be taken to heart and repented of, with the resolve to do better in future. But in general men are as proud and unwilling to confess their errors in logic as they are in morals. The greater part of the fallacies in the world *are* sins—mere lies.

Certainly there be [says Lord Bacon] that delight in giddiness; and count it a bondage to fix a belief; affecting free-will in thinking, as well as in acting. And though the sects of philosophers of that kind be gone, yet there remain certain discoursing wits, which are of the same veins, though there be not so much blood in them as was in those of the ancients. But it is not only the difficulty and labour which men take in finding out of truth; nor again, that when it is found, it imposeth upon men's thoughts; that doth bring lies in favour: but a natural though corrupt love of the lie itself. . . . But it is not the lie that passeth through the mind, but the lie that sinketh in, and settleth in it, that doth the hurt, such as we spake of before. But howsoever these things are thus in men's depraved judgments and affections, yet truth, which only doth judge itself, teacheth, that the inquiry of truth, which is the love-making, or wooing of it; the knowledge of truth, which is the presence of it; and the belief of truth, which is the enjoying of it; is the sovereign good of human nature.

Lecture VII

MS 129: October–November 1866

Ladies and Gentlemen

In entering upon the second half of the course, I cannot refrain from expressing my appreciation of the attentive hearing which you have accorded to me thus far. The subject, though of supreme importance, is altogether shunned by unreflecting minds; it is of a kind which requires a real exertion for a trained mind to follow, and when delivered orally this difficulty is much increased. That a hundred gentlemen and ladies, engrossed in their daily business or avocations, should be found to listen to six lectures upon the forms of syllogism was something which, I confess, was not to be anticipated, and which it seems to me puts in a very clear light the superior cultivation and greater intellectual taste of the people of this city. I am confident that such a dry course of lectures would have been impossible anywhere else in the country than in the hall of this celebrated and extraordinary institution. I said in my first lecture that it seemed to me the New Englanders had a peculiar genius for philosophy; it is not only because they have Edwards, Channing, Parker, Bushnell, Emerson, James, Bowen, Abbot, and many other philosophical writers, although we have here a list of names very creditable both individually and for the variety of mind they show. But what more than this makes me hope that New England will shed a light upon these subjects is the subtlety and ideality of the Yankee mind as seen in its uncultivated state. The Scotch and the Germans are the peoples with whom the New Englanders ought to be compared, as they are THE metaphysical nations. The Scotchman is extremely hard-headed and shrewd, much more so than the Yankee I should say; but there is a certain perversity or obstinacy in his shrewdness,—which while it has excited him to glorious deeds performed in the strangest, the oddest, and yet the most admirable manner, is perhaps better calculated to make him a redoubtable champion of truth than an humble enquirer after it. The German speaks the most philosophical of the modern languages and has a philosophical activity and fertility to which the Scotchman can never attain; he is accused of neglecting the material world, and we have all heard the story of the Frenchman, the Englishman, and the German, each of whom undertook to write a work upon the Camel. The Frenchman went to the *Jardin des Plantes,* measured the camel there with metres and weighed him with grammes, and then went home and wrote a book of which each sentence formed a paragraph, containing the minutest and yet the most *spiritual* account of the animal he had seen. I suppose it was something like Victor Hugo's description of the cuttlefish. The Englishman spent a fortune in fitting out an expedition to Arabia where he spent 25 years and produced a work in three volumes octavo full of undigested and inconsiderable facts. The German retired into his chamber and evolved the pure

idea of a camel from the depths of his *Ichheit*. Now this is most unjust to the German. Do German travellers, then, I should be glad to
know, rank so far behind those of other countries? Did Humboldt
learn physical geography, or Dr. Kohl national characteristics in their
chambers? Did Rothschild evolve his wealth, and Bismarck the Prus-
sian army from the depths of their moral consciousness? No; the German is as devoted an observer as anyone when the question in hand
is one of observation. The weakness of the German, as it seems to
me, is that he sometimes becomes confused. In several of their greatest
systems of philosophy, absurdities are met with which an unclouded
mind detects, at once. And I should say that a confusion is evident,
even admitted, in the present state of German philosophy especially.
Now I think the Yankee will never fall into either the fault of the
German or that of the Scotchman. He will be content to be shallow
sooner than to be confused and he is always open to conviction and
recognizes a plain fact and accepts it. There are many special points
in the Yankee character which I think fit him for philosophy. His
love of research and especially of history,—so manifest in the great
number of historians in New England, notwithstanding our distance
from the documents—is one. It has been truly said that history is the
metropolis or capital city of philosophy; when we have once mastered
it we may easily extend our conquests everywhere. Scotland and
Germany are both celebrated for their historians. Another essential
element of a philosophic people which we possess is a capacity for
being elevated by an idea. But it is the Yankee's ingenuity which I
believe will prove his strong point in philosophy, because he possesses
it in a higher degree even than the Germans and because it seems to
me that to make a good invention requires just the same combination
of persistency in following out one idea and readiness to abandon
it when it has failed, the same mixture of enthusiasm and patience,
which are required to originate a philosophic theory. But though the
Yankee is thus fitted to do so much good service in philosophy, let
us by no means forget that he has not done it hitherto. Let us not
mistake *promise* for *performance*. No American Philosophy has as yet
been produced; and we may perhaps never live to see our country take
the place which she ought to do before the world in this particular.
Since our country has been independent, Germany has produced the
whole developement of the Transcendental Philosophy, Scotland the
whole Philosophy of Common Sense, France her Eclectic Philosophy

and Positive Philosophy, England the Association Philosophy. And what has America produced? Hickok has made a not very creditable modification of German Philosophy and Frothingham has supposed two Absolutes which is a contradiction in terms. That is all.

I, for one, as an humble student of the works of philosophers am ready to stand by the first Yankee who can do something better. I do not mean to say that I am ready to adopt his philosophy, but I am ready to do what little I can to encourage the developement and presentation of his thoughts.

We have, now, studied syllogistic forms pretty thoroughly and have learned from them nearly all that they can teach us. That there is something very peculiar about the method of investigation which we have thus far pursued, something in these syllogisms very different indeed from the modes of laying down general principles and gradually extending them, now adopted by writers on abstract subjects, must I think have attracted your notice. Not a single abstract principle have we laid down so far. How amazingly unlike the common methods of thinkers is this! I think that modern logicians have hardly considered sufficiently this peculiar character of the syllogism considered as a mode of investigation. They have added to the *Analytics* of Aristotle a number of abstract principles under the name of higher laws of logic and which they conceive to make a great improvement upon the Aristotelean system. They yield the honor of having announced many of these laws to Aristotle; but though he may casually have given them expression you will not find that where he treats of the forms of syllogism he lays any of them down as fundamental laws of logic. In fact, whatever merit there may be in the generalizations by which the higher laws of logic are recognized—it is a merit which is quite foreign to a syllogistic system. Syllogism, as the analysis we have made illustrates, stands in need of no general abstract principles. What is the use of an abstract principle? It is to give our knowledge *unity*. As Epicurus says—it is a synthesis which resumes in itself, in a few words, all the particular facts which have previously been studied. But syllogism has a unity of its own. Like geometry—it has a certain unity of intuition expressed in the symmetry of the syllogistic doctrine more philosophically and more precisely than it could be in any abstract principle whatever. These higher laws, then, do but mar the doctrine of syllogism. The philosophy of employing *forms* instead of *laws*, is one which some logicians do not seem to appreciate. It should be their business, therefore, to develope the laws and to leave syllogisms out of their logics altogether. Is it imagined that logic stands in absolute need of syllogisms? If men would rely a little more upon their own strength and less upon the dead past, they would see that this is not so. School after school of thinkers has arisen in the history of this ancient science, each with a conception which if consistently and independently developed would have yielded an instructive and true system; but reverence for what has been established has prevented *that*, and nothing has been produced but an abortive excrescence,—destroying the symmetry there had been before and in its turn standing in the way of the erection of a new system. From each perfected system much may be learned; from the hodge-podge of all, very little. Having, thus far, considered logic in the light of syllogism, which for a reason I shall give you further on, I consider the most philosophical view of all; I propose in this lecture especially and more or less in all the rest to take up one of the numerous modes in which it may be formulated in general principles—that one which I think by far the most beautiful and instructive.

It is obvious that all deductive reasoning has a common property unshared by the other kinds—in being purely *explicatory*. Buffier mentions a definition of logic as the art of confessing in the conclusion what we have avowed in the premises. This bit of satire translated into the language of sobriety—amounts to charging that the logicians confine their attention exclusively to deductive reasoning. A charge which against the logicians of other days, was quite just.

All deductive reasoning is merely explicatory. That is to say, that which appears in the conclusion explicitly was contained in the premises implicitly. All explication is of one of two kinds—direct or indirect.

Explication direct consists in simply substituting for a word what is implied in that word. A statement therefore in order to imply something not expressed must either say that a word denotes something or else that something is meant by a word. Then the direct explication consists in saying that that what a word denotes is what is meant by the word.

Indirect explication consists in saying that what is not what is meant by the word is not denoted by the word or else in saying that which what a word denotes is not is not meant by the word.

Explication in general, then, may be said to be the application of the maxim that what a word denotes is what is meant by the word.

It is important to distinguish between the two functions of a word: 1st to denote something—to stand for something and 2nd to mean something—or as Mr. Mill phrases it—to *connote* something.

What it denotes is called its *Sphere*. What it connotes is called its *Content*. Thus the *sphere* of the word *man* is for me every man I know; and for each of you it is every man you know. The *content* of *man* is all that we know of all men, as being two-legged, having souls, having language, &c., &c. It is plain that both the *sphere* and the *content* admit of more and less. Thus the *sphere* of Negro is less than the *sphere* of man; while the *content* of Negro is greater than the *content* of man, because it contains *being black* which the latter does not. Now the sphere considered as a quantity is called the Extension; and the content considered as quantity is called the Comprehension. Extension and Comprehension are also termed Breadth and Depth. So that a wider term is one which has a greater extension; a narrower one is one which has a less extension. A higher term is one which has a less Comprehension and a *lower* one has more.

The narrower term is said to be contained under the wider one; and the higher term to be contained in the lower one.

We have then

What is *denoted*	What is *connoted*
Sphere	Content
Extension	Comprehension
Breadth $\begin{cases} \text{wider} \\ \text{narrower} \end{cases}$	Depth $\begin{cases} \text{lower} \\ \text{higher} \end{cases}$
What is contained *under*	What is contained *in*.

The principle of explicatory or deductive reasoning then is that

> Every part of a word's Content belongs to
> every part of its Sphere

or

> Whatever is contained *in* a word belongs to
> whatever is contained under it.

Now this maxim would not be true if the Extension and Comprehension were directly proportional to one another; this is to say if the Greater the one the greater the other. For in that case, though the whole Content would belong to the whole Sphere; yet only a particular part of it would belong to a part of that Sphere and not every part to every part. On the other hand if the Comprehension and Extension were not in some way proportional to one another, that is if terms of different spheres could have the same content or terms of the same content different spheres; then there would be no such fact as a content's *belonging* to a sphere and hence again the maxim would fail. For the maxim to be true, then, it is absolutely necessary that the comprehension and extension should be inversely proportional to one another. That is that the greater the sphere, the less the content.

Now this is evidently true. If we take the term *man* and increase its *comprehension* by the addition of *black*, we have *black man* and this has less *extension* than man. So if we take *black man* and add *non-black man* to its sphere, we have *man* again, and so have decreased the comprehension. So that whenever the extension is increased the comprehension is diminished and *vice versa*.

The highest terms are therefore broadest and the lowest terms the narrowest. We can take a term so broad that it contains all other spheres under it. Then it will have no content whatever. There is but one such term—with its synonyms—it is *Being*. We can also take a term so low that it contains all other content within it. Then it will have no sphere whatever. There is but one such term—it is *Nothing*.

Being	Nothing
All breadth	All depth
No depth	No breadth

We can conceive of terms so narrow that they are next to nothing, that is have an absolutely individual sphere. Such terms would be innumerable in number. We can also conceive of terms so high that they are next to *being*, that is have an entirely simple content. Such terms would also be innumerable.

Simple terms	Individual terms

But such terms though conceivable in one sense—that is intelligible in their conditions—are yet impossible. You never can narrow down to an individual. Do you say Daniel Webster is an individual? He is so in common parlance, but in logical strictness he is not. We think of certain images in our memory—a platform and a noble form uttering convincing and patriotic words—a statue—certain printed matter—and we say that which that speaker and the man whom that statue was taken for and the writer of this speech—that which these are in common is Daniel Webster. Thus, even the proper name of a man is a general term or the name of a class, for it names a class of sensations and thoughts. The true individual term the absolutely singular *this* and *that* cannot be reached. Whatever has comprehension must be general.

In like manner, it is impossible to find any simple term. This is obvious from this consideration. If there is any simple term, simple terms are innumerable for in that case all attributes which are not simple are made up of simple attributes. Now none of these attributes can be affirmed or denied universally of whatever has any one. For let A be one simple term and B be another. Now suppose we can say All A is B; then B is contained in A. If, therefore, A contains anything but B it is a compound term, but A is different from B, and is simple; hence it cannot be that All A is B. Suppose No A is B, then not-B is contained in A; if therefore A contains anything besides not-B it is not a simple term; but if it is the same as not-B, it is not a simple term but is a term relative to B. Now it is a simple term and therefore Some A is B. Hence if we take any two simple terms and call one A and the other B we have

Some A is B
and   Some A is not B

or in other words the universe will contain every possible kind of thing afforded by the permutation of simple qualities. Now the universe does not contain all these things; it contains no *well-known green horse*. Hence the consequence of supposing a simple term to exist is an error of fact. There are several other ways of showing this besides the one that I have adopted. They all concur to show that whatever has extension must be composite.

The moment, then, that we pass from nothing and the vacuity of being to any content or sphere, we come at once to a composite content and sphere. In fact, extension and comprehension—like space and time—are quantities which are not composed of ultimate elements; but every part however small is divisible.

The consequence of this fact is that when we wish to enumerate the sphere of a term—a process termed *division*—or when we wish to run over the content of a term—a process called *definition*—since we cannot take the elements of our enumeration singly but must take them in groups, there is danger that we shall take some element twice over, or that we shall omit some. Hence the extension and comprehension which we know will be somewhat indeterminate. But we must distinguish two kinds of these quantities. If we were to subtilize we might make other distinctions but I shall be content with two. They are the extension and comprehension relatively to our actual knowledge, and what these would be were our knowledge perfect.

Logicians have hitherto left the doctrine of extension and comprehension in a very imperfect state owing to the blinding influence of a psychological treatment of the matter. They have, therefore, not made this distinction and have reduced the comprehension of a term to what it would be if we had no knowledge of fact at all. I mention this because if you should come across the matter I am now discussing in any book, you would find the matter left in quite a different state.

With me—the *Sphere* of a term is all the things we know that it applies to or the disjunctive sum of the subjects to which it can be predicate in an affirmative subsumptive proposition. The *content* of a term is all the attributes it tells us or the conjunctive sum of the predicates to which it can be made subject in a universal necessary proposition.

The maxim then which rules explicatory reasoning is that any part of the content of a term can be predicated of any part of its sphere.

We come next to consider inductions. In inferences of this kind we proceed as if upon the principle that as is a sample of a class so is the whole class. The word *class* in this connection means nothing more than what is denoted by one term,— or in other words the sphere of a term. Whatever characters belong to the whole sphere of a term constitute the content of that term. Hence the principle of induction is that whatever can be predicated of a specimen of the sphere of a term is part of the content of that term. And what is a specimen? It is something taken from a class or the sphere of a term, at random—that is, not upon any further principle, not selected from a part of that sphere; in other words it is something taken from the sphere of a term and not taken as belonging to a narrower sphere. Hence the principle of induction is that whatever can be predicated of something taken as belonging to the sphere of a term is part of the content of that term. But this principle is not axiomatic by any means. Why then do we adopt it?

To explain this, we must remember that the process of induction is a process of adding to our knowledge; it differs therein from deduction—which merely explicates what we know—and is on this very account called scientific inference. Now deduction rests as we have seen upon the inverse proportionality of the extension and comprehension of every term; and this principle makes it impossible apparently to proceed in the direction of ascent to universals. But a little reflection will show that when our knowledge receives an addition this principle does not hold.

Thus suppose a blind man to be told that no red things are blue. He has previously known only that red is a color; and that certain things *A*, *B*, and *C* are red.

The comprehension of red then has been for him   *color.*
Its extension has been   *A*, *B*, and *C*

But when he learns that no red thing is blue, *non-blue* is added to the comprehension of red, without the least diminution of its extension.

Its comprehension becomes   *non-blue colour*
Its extension remains   *A*, *B*, *C*

Suppose afterwards he learns that a fourth thing *D* is red. Then, the comprehension of *red* remains unchanged, *non-blue colour;* while its extension becomes *A*, *B*, *C*, and *D*. Thus, the rule that the greater the extension of a term the less its comprehension and *vice versa*, holds good only so long as our knowledge is not added to; but as soon as our knowledge is increased, either the comprehension or extension of that term which the new information concerns is increased without a corresponding decrease of the other quantity. The reason why this takes place is worthy of notice. Every addition to the information which is incased in a term, results in making some term equivalent to that term. Thus when the blind man learns that *red* is not-blue, *red not-blue* becomes for him equivalent to *red*. Before that, he might have thought that *red not-blue* was a little more restricted term than *red,* and therefore it was so to him, but the new information makes it the exact equivalent of red. In the same way, when he learns that *D* is red, the term *D-like red* becomes equivalent to *red.* Thus, every addition to our information about a term, is an addition to the number of equivalents which that term has. Now, in whatever way a term gets to have a new equivalent, whether by an increase in our knowledge, or by a change in the things it denotes, this always results in an increase either of extension or comprehension without a corresponding decrease in the other quantity. For example we have here a number of circles dotted and undotted, crossed and uncrossed

Here it is evident that the greater the extension the less the comprehension

dotted	4 circles
dotted and crossed	2 "

Now suppose we make these two terms *dotted circle* and *crossed and dotted circle* equivalent. This we can do by crossing our uncrossed dotted circles. In that way, we increase the comprehension of *dotted circle* and at the same time increase the extension of *crossed and dotted circle* since we now make it denote *all dotted circles.*

Thus every increase in the number of equivalents of any term increases either its extension or comprehension and *conversely.* It may be said that there are no equivalent terms in logic, since the only difference between such terms would be merely external and grammatical, while in logic terms which have the same meaning are identical. I fully admit that. Indeed, the process of getting an equivalent for a term, is an identification of two terms previously diverse. It is, in fact, the process of nutrition of terms by which they get all their life and vigor and by which they put forth an energy almost creative—

since it has the effect of reducing the chaos of ignorance to the cosmos of science. Each of these equivalents is the explication of what there is wrapt up in the primary—they are the surrogates, the interpreters of the original term. They are new bodies, animated by that same soul. I call them the *interpretants* of the term. And the quantity of these *interpretants*, I term the *information* or *implication* of the term.

We must therefore modify the law of the inverse proportionality of extension and comprehension and instead of writing

$$\text{Extension} \times \text{Comprehension} = \text{Constant}$$

which crudely expresses the fact that the greater the extension the less the comprehension, we must write

$$\text{Extension} \times \text{Comprehension} = \text{Information}$$

which means that when the information is increased there is an increase of either Extension or comprehension without any diminution of the other of these quantities.

Now, ladies and gentlemen, as it is true that every increase of our knowledge is an increase in the information of a term—that is, is an addition to the number of terms equivalent to that term—so it is also true that the first step in the knowledge of a thing, the first framing of a term, is also the origin of the information of that term because it gives the first term equivalent to that term. I here announce the great and fundamental secret of the logic of science. There is no term, properly so called, which is entirely destitute of information, of equivalent terms. The moment an expression acquires sufficient comprehension to determine its extension, it already has more than enough to do so. We all know how deceptive a *word* or *phrase* may be. That is why there are so many syllogisms afloat. The middle term serves to lead our minds to conclusions, by its false *implication*. All careful reasoners know what dangers lie in such syllogisms as these: The Negro is a man and Every man should vote therefore The Negro should vote. Observe, I do not criticise the conclusion. That may be very very true. I only say that the question would arise whether the Negro is not merely a man for the purpose of zoölogy, for the purpose of religion, but whether he is also a man for the purpose of politics. In short the question is whether every man is a man. Not that the word *man* has two meanings but that it has very much implication and that the truth of all that implication is not agreed to by both parties. This is a type of the commonest of all fallacies—and I have selected this particular argument as an example of it both because it is one which all of you must have heard urged and also because it turns on the word *man* which has of all words the most implication because of all things in the universe this is the one of which we all know the most.

We are all, then, sufficiently familiar with the fact that many words have much implication; but I think we need to reflect upon the circumstance that every word implies some proposition or, what is the same thing, every word, concept, symbol has an equivalent term— or one which has become identified with it,—in short, has an *interpretant*.

Consider, what a word or symbol is; it is a sort of representation. Now a representation is something which stands for something. I will not undertake to analyze, this evening, this conception of *standing for* something—but, it is sufficiently plain that it involves the standing *to* something *for* something. A thing cannot stand for something without standing *to* something *for* that something. Now, what is this that a word stands *to*? Is it a person? We usually say that the word *homme* stands to a Frenchman for *man*. It would be a little more precise to say that it stands *to* the Frenchman's mind—to his memory. It is still more accurate to say that it addresses a particular remembrance or image in that memory. And what *image,* what remembrance? Plainly, the one which is the mental equivalent of the word *homme*—in short, its interpretant. Whatever a word addresses then or *stands to,* is its interpretant or identified symbol. Conversely, every interpretant is addressed by the word; for were it not so, did it not as it were overhear what the word says, how could it interpret what it says. There are doubtless some who cannot understand this metaphorical argument. I wish to show that the relation of a word to that which it addresses is the same as its relation to its equivalent or identified terms. For that purpose, I first show that whatever a word addresses is an equivalent term,—its mental equivalent. I next show that, since the intelligent reception of a term is the being addressed by that term, and since the explication of a term's implication is the intelligent reception of that term, that the interpretant or equivalent of a term which as we have already seen explicates the implication of a term is addressed by the term. The interpretant of a term, then, and that which it stands to are identical. Hence, since it is of the very essence of a symbol that it should stand *to* something, every symbol—every word and every *conception*—must have an interpretant—or what is the same thing, must have information or implication.

Let us now return to the information. The information of a term is the measure of its superfluous comprehension. That is to say that the proper office of the comprehension is to determine the extension of the term. For instance, you and I are men because we possess those attributes—having two legs, being rational, &c.—which make up the comprehension of *man*. Every addition to the comprehension of a term, lessens its extension up to a certain point, after that further additions increase the information instead. Thus, let us commence with the term *colour;* add to the comprehension of this term, that of *red*. *Red colour* has considerably less extension than *colour;* add to this the comprehension of *dark;* dark red colour has still less comprehension. Add to this the comprehension of *non-blue*—*non-blue dark red colour* has the same extension as *dark red colour* so that the *non-blue* here performs a work of supererogation; it tells us that no *dark red colour* is blue, but does none of the proper business of connotation, that of diminishing the extension at all. Thus information measures the superfluous comprehension. And therefore as every term must have information, every term has superfluous comprehension. And, hence, whenever we make a symbol to express any thing or any attribute we cannot make it so empty that it shall have no superfluous comprehension. I am going, next, to show that inference is symbolization and that the puzzle of the validity of scientific inference lies merely in this superfluous comprehension and is therefore entirely removed by a consideration of the laws of *information*.

For this purpose, I must call your attention to the differences there are in the manner in which different representations stand for their objects. In the first place there are likenesses or copies—such as *statues, pictures, emblems, hieroglyphics,* and the like. Such representations stand for their objects only so far as they have an actual resemblance to them—that is agree with them in some characters. The peculiarity of such representations is that they do not determine their objects—they stand for anything more or less; for they stand for whatever they resemble and they resemble everything more or less. The second kind of representations are such as are set up by a convention of men or a decree of God. Such are *tallies, Proper names,* &c. The peculiarity of these *conventional signs* is that they represent no character of their objects. Likenesses denote nothing in particular; *conventional signs* connote nothing in particular. The third and last kind of representations are *symbols* or general representations. They connote attributes and so connote them as to determine what they denote. To this class, belong all *words* and all *conceptions.* Most combinations of words are also symbols. A proposition, an argument, even a whole book may be, and should be, a single symbol. Yet there are combinations of words and combinations of conceptions which are not strictly speaking symbols. These are of two kinds of which I will give you instances. We have first cases like

man and horse and kangaroo and whale

and secondly, cases like

spherical bright fragrant juicy tropical fruit.

The first of these terms has no comprehension which is adequate to the limitation of the extension. In fact, men, horses, kangaroos, and whales have no attributes in common which are not possessed by the entire class of mammals. For this reason, this disjunctive term, man and horse and kangaroo and whale, is of no use whatever. For suppose it is the subject of a sentence; suppose we know that men and horses and kangaroos and whales have some common character. Since they have no common character which does not belong to the whole class of mammals, it is plain that mammals may be substituted for this term. Suppose it is the predicate of a sentence, and that we know that something is either a man or a horse or a kangaroo or a whale; then, the person who has found out this, knows more about this thing than that it is a mammal; he therefore knows which of these four it is for these four have nothing in common except what belongs to all other mammals. Hence in this case the particular one may be substituted for the disjunctive term. A disjunctive term, then,—one which aggregates the extension of several symbols,—may always be replaced by a simple term. Hence if we find out that neat are herbivorous, swine are herbivorous, sheep are herbivorous, and deer are herbivorous; we may be sure that there is some class of animals which covers all these, all the members of which are herbivorous. Now a disjunctive term—such as neat swine sheep and deer, or man, horse, kangaroo, and whale—is not a true symbol. It does not denote what it does in consequence of its connotation, as a symbol does; on the contrary, no part of its connotation goes at all to determine what it denotes—it is in that respect a mere accident if it denote anything. Its *sphere* is determined by the concurrence of the four members, man, horse, kangaroo, and whale, or neat swine sheep and deer as the case may be. Now those who are not accustomed to the homologies of the conceptions of men and words, will think it very fanciful if I say that this concurrence of four terms to determine the sphere of a disjunctive term resembles the arbitrary convention by which men agree that a certain sign shall stand for a certain thing. And yet how is such a convention made? The men all look upon or think of the thing and each gets a certain conception and then they agree that whatever calls up or becomes an object of that conception in either of them shall be denoted by the sign. In the one case, then, we have several different words and the disjunctive term denotes whatever is the object of either of them. In the other case, we have several different conceptions —the conceptions of different men—and the conventional sign stands for whatever is an object of either of them. It is plain the two cases are essentially the same, and that a disjunctive term is to be regarded as a conventional sign or index. And we find both agree in having a determinate extension but an inadequate comprehension.

Accordingly, if we are engaged in symbolizing and we come to such a proposition as "Neat, swine, sheep, and deer are herbivorous," we know firstly that the disjunctive term may be replaced by a true symbol. But suppose we know of no symbol for neat, swine, sheep, and deer except cloven-hoofed animals. There is but one objection to substituting this for the disjunctive term; it is that we should, then, say more than we have observed. In short, it has a superfluous information. But we have already seen that this is an objection which must always stand in the way of taking symbols. If therefore we are to use symbols at all we must use them notwithstanding that. Now all thinking is a process of symbolization, for the conceptions of the understanding are symbols in the strict sense. Unless, therefore, we are to give up thinking altogether we must admit the validity of induction. But even to doubt is to think. So we cannot give up thinking and the validity of induction must be admitted.

A similar line of thought may be gone through in reference to hypothesis. In this case we must start with the consideration of the term

spherical, bright, fragrant, juicy, tropical fruit

Such a term, formed by the sum of the comprehensions of several terms, is called a conjunctive term. A conjunctive term has no extension adequate to its comprehension. Thus the only spherical bright fragrant juicy tropical fruit we know is the orange and that has many other characters besides these. Hence, such a term is of no use whatever. If it occurs in the predicate and something is said to be a spherical bright fragrant juicy tropical fruit, since there is nothing which is all this which is not an orange, we may say that this is an orange at once. On the other hand, if the conjunctive term is subject and we know that every spherical bright fragrant juicy tropical fruit necessarily has certain properties, it must be that we know more than that and can simplify the subject. Thus a conjunctive term may always be replaced by a simple one. So if we find that light is capable of producing certain phenomena which could only be enumerated by a long conjunction of terms, we may be sure that this compound predicate may be replaced by a simple one. And if only one simple one is known in which the conjunctive term is contained, this must be provisionally adopted.

We have now seen how the mind is forced by the very nature of inference itself to make use of induction and hypothesis.

But the question arises how these conclusions come to receive their justification by the event. Why are most inductions and hypotheses true? I reply that they are not true. On the contrary, experience shows that of the most rigid and careful inductions and hypotheses only an infinitesimal proportion are never found to be in any respect false.

And yet it is a fact that all careful inductions are nearly true and all well-grounded hypotheses resemble the truth; why is that? If we put our hand in a bag of beans the sample we take out has perhaps not quite but about the same proportion of the different colours as the whole bag. Why is that?

The answer is that which I gave a week ago. Namely, that there is a certain vague tendency for the whole to be like any of its parts taken at random because it is composed of its parts. And, therefore, there must be some slight preponderance of true over false scientific inferences. Now the falsity in conclusions is eliminated and neutralized by opposing falsity while the slight tendency to the truth is always one way and is accumulated by experience. The same principle of balancing of errors holds alike in observation and in reasoning.

Lecture IX

MS 130: November 1866

Ladies and gentlemen:—

At the last lecture, we made some reflections upon the proper mode of conceiving the progress of truth from the outward things to the full understanding. We found that the first impressions upon our senses are not representations of certain unknown things in themselves but are themselves those very unknown things in themselves. Our first impressions are entirely unknown in themselves and the matter of cognition is the matter of fact and what is not a question of a possible experience is not a question of fact. These impressions are grasped into the unity which the mind requires, the unity of the *I think*—the unity of consistency, by conceptions and sensations. These are nothing else than predicates which the mind affixes by virtue of a hypothetical inference in order to understand the data presented to it. A hypothetical predicate is one which is affixed to a thing which has not been experienced as possessing it in order to bring the manifold in the experienced thing to unity. Now this is just the character of a conception or sensation. Take the sense of beauty as an example; when we hear a sonata of Beethoven's the predicate of beautiful is affixed to it as a single representation of the complicated phenomena presented to the ear. The beauty does not belong to each note or chord but to the whole. We have not there-

fore *heard* the beauty for we have heard only the single chords successively. What we have heard is therefore only the *occasion* of the feeling
that it is beautiful, only the data to reduce which to unity the sense of
beauty serves. *Beautiful* is therefore a hypothetically adjoined predicate. This illustrates how the logical function of *sensations* is that of a
hypothetical predicate. The same thing is still more obvious in the case
of a conception. I make five dots on the board ⋅ ⋅ ⋅ ⋅ ⋅ . Now, a person in
a drowsy state might see those dots and not reflect that they were *five*.
The conception of *five* is, therefore, not in the eye, is not seen, since
that drowsy person would see all that we do, but is introduced by the
mind in order to comprehend (or reduce to a consistent whole) what
is seen. Thus both sensations and conceptions are hypothetic predicates. They are, however, hypotheses of widely different kinds. A sensation is a sort of mental name. To assign a name to a thing is to make
a hypothesis. It is plainly a predicate which is not in the *data*. But it is
given on account of a logical necessity; namely the necessity of reducing the manifold of the predicates given to unity. We give the name *man*
because it is needed to convey at once rationality, animality, being two-
legged, being mortal, &c. To give a name is therefore to make a hypothesis. Such a hypothesis, however, differs from what we usually comprehend under that term in a very important respect; namely, that while
the data require *some* name they do not require any name in particular.
Chou is as good a word as *cabbage* except for the sailor who thought
the French inconsistent in using it. It is the same with a sensation; if
all that is painful to me had been pleasurable and *vice versa*, I should
have derived as correct a knowledge of things from these sensations as
I now do, because all the knowledge these sensations give us now is
only that there is a difference between pleasurable and painful circumstances without telling us anything of the nature of the difference. It is
the same with any other sensation. The sensation of *redness* corresponds only to a particular rate of vibration in the luminiferous ether,
which the sensation itself tells us nothing of. All that the sensation is
good for therefore is to tell us that *red* things are alike and differ from
other things. This sensation might have been of some other kind therefore without being any the less true. So that a sensation is like a name—
the data demand it but do not demand that it shall be of any particular
sort so long as it is consistent. In the next lecture we shall go a little
deeper into the logical nature of sensations, but this is all we require
for our present purpose.

Sensation is, as it were, the writing on the page of consciousness. Conception is the meaning of the sensation. A conception, therefore, is not in the mind in the sense in which a sensation is; it requires to be embodied in a sensation, as much as it requires to be embodied in matter in order to be carried out into the external world.

Of the numerous conceptions of the mind, some apply only to certain special collections of impressions and are called *particular*. Others apply to all collections of impressions and are called *universal*. Of universal conceptions, the most outward, the first that is reached as truth enters the mind, is *Substance*—or the *very thing*—that is the conception of the immediately present in general. In another point of view it is that which can only be subject never predicate. The last conception, the most inward, which lies at the centre of consciousness and completes the act of understanding is *being*—or that which whatever is intelligible possesses in itself.

Between *substance* and *being* we found that there intervene three universal conceptions:—

> Reference to a Ground.
>   "   " " Correlate.
>   "   " " Interpretant.

The manner in which we made sure that these three conceptions and these only intervene between the manifold of substance and the unity of being is sufficiently simple when you once take it in. To avoid all confusion, we began by distinguishing three different kinds of mental separation: 1st *dissociation,* 2nd *abstraction* or *precision,* and 3rd *discrimination*. We dissociate one object from another when we think of it without thinking of that other at the same time. We can for example dissociate a *colour* from a *sound;* but we cannot dissociate space from colour. We *prescind* one object from another, when we suppose it to be without that other. For example, we can *prescind* space from colour because we can suppose a space to be uncoloured. We discriminate one thing from another when we can recognize that they are not the same—thus we can discriminate colour from space though we cannot prescind colour from space.

This distinction seems to be sufficiently plain and it is perfectly indispensible. It is *precision* with which we have to deal in our present investigation.

We saw that the data which justify an unanalyzed conception cannot be prescinded from it. If a certain piece of music is judged beautiful we cannot suppose it to sound as it does and not be beautiful. We saw also that the occasion of the introduction of a simple conception justifies its introduction.

The function of universal conceptions in general is to bring the manifold of substance to the unity of *being*. Each one therefore connects the manifold of substance itself or else connects a necessary conception with substance.

Now we have only to notice as a fact what is the occasion of the introduction of a conception and we shall find it is the occurrence of the substance in connection with a certain conception, and this conception is the one which next precedes the given conception in the progress of truth from substance to being.

We found, for example, that *being* is what is implied in the copula. Now the copula conjoins predicate to subject. The subject denotes the substance, the predicate its Quality. Quality therefore or reference to a *Ground* is the 1st conception before *being*. By a *ground*, you remember, I meant the pure form or abstraction which is the original of the thing and of which the concrete thing is only the incarnation. Reference to such a *ground* or *respect* of likeness is implied in every attribution.

To find the next conception in order we asked upon what *occasion* the conception of quality is introduced. We found it to be when generalization and contrast takes place, that is when things are put into comparison. Hence, *relation* or reference to a correlate is the next conception in order. *Relate* and *correlate*, you remember, are terms employed to signify merely the thing related and the thing related *to*.

To find what is the next conception in order we inquired what is the *occasion* of the introduction of reference to a correlate. It appeared that it is the reference of things to a mediating representation or *interpretant*. Reference to an interpretant is therefore the next conception in order; and by an interpretant wᵢ mean a representation which represents that something is a representation of something else of which it is itself a representation.

We then asked what is the next conception and for that purpose inquired what is the occasion of the reference of things to a mediating representation. We found it was the presentation of a manifold; and hence substance, which is the conception of this presented manifold in general, is the next conception in order.

We have then between the Unity of being and the manifold of substance these three and only these three universal conceptions

Reference to a Ground
Reference to a Correlate
and Reference to an Interpretant

Reference to a ground is the possession of Quality. Double Reference to Correlate and Ground is Relation. Triple reference to Interpretant, Correlate, and Ground—is Representation. Relation is of two kinds —Equiparance and Disquiparance. Representation is of three kinds— Likeness, Indication or Correspondence in fact, and Symbolization. Equiparance is agreement in a determinate respect; Disquiparance is a disagreement or an agreement in a respect which does not determine the internal quality of the related thing. Thus, an equiparant is a relate whose reference to a ground may be prescinded from its reference to a correlate; in other words the ground of equiparance is an internal character. A disquiparant is a relate whose reference to a ground necessarily supposes a reference to a correlate; in other words the ground of disquiparance is an external or relative character—as greater, less, or equal. A Representation is either a Likeness, an Index, or a Symbol. A likeness represents its object by agreeing with it in some particular. An index represents its object by a real correspondence with it—as a tally does quarts of milk, and a vane the wind. A symbol is a general representation like a word or conception. Scientifically speaking, a likeness is a representation grounded on an internal character—that is whose reference to a ground is prescindible. An index is a representation whose relation to its object is prescindible and is a Disquiparance, so that its peculiar Quality is not prescindible but is relative. A symbol is a representation whose essential Quality and Relation are both unprescindible—the Quality being Imputed and the Relation ideal. Thus there are three kinds of Quality

Internal Quality (Quality proper)—
   the Quality of an Equiparant and Likeness
External Quality—
   the Quality of a Disquiparant and Index
Imputed Quality—
   the Quality of a Symbol

and two kinds of Relation

Real Relation (Relation proper)—
  the Relation of Likeness and Index
Ideal Relation—
  the Relation of a Symbol

Or we may write the scheme thus

Quality $\left\{\begin{array}{l} \textit{proper} \text{ or Internal} \\ \text{External} \\ \text{Imputed} \end{array}\right.$

Relation $\left\{\begin{array}{l} \textit{Proper} \text{ or Real} \\ \text{Ideal} \end{array}\right.$ $\left\{\begin{array}{l} \text{Equiparance} \\ \text{Disquiparance} \end{array}\right.$

Representation . . . . . $\left\{\begin{array}{l} \text{Likeness} \\ \text{Indication} \\ \text{Symbolization} \end{array}\right.$

We may also make the following scheme. Let

1 stand for Reference to a Ground
2   ”   for Reference to a Correlate
3   ”   for Reference to an Interpretant

The 1 is Quality, $\frac{1}{2}$ is relation, $\genfrac{}{}{0pt}{}{1}{\genfrac{}{}{0pt}{}{2}{3}}$ is representation. In relation, the refer-

ences are separable in Equiparance which we may write $\frac{1}{2}$ and insepa-

rable in Disquiparance which we may write c_2^1. In representation: in

Likeness the references are all separable $\genfrac{}{}{0pt}{}{1}{\genfrac{}{}{0pt}{}{2}{3}}$; in Indication, reference to

a ground is not separable but the two first references are separable to-

gether $\genfrac{}{}{0pt}{}{c_2^1}{3}$; in Symbolization all are inseparable $\genfrac{}{}{0pt}{}{c^1}{\genfrac{}{}{0pt}{}{c 2.}{c 3}}$.

Having thus made a complete catalogue of the objects of formal
thought, we come down to consider symbols, with which alone Logic
is concerned—and symbols in a special aspect; namely, as determined
by their reference to their objects or correlates.

The first division which we are to attempt to make between different kinds of symbols ought to depend upon their intention, what they are specially meant to express—whether their peculiar function is to lie in their reference to their ground, in their reference to their object, or their reference to their interpretant. A symbol whose intended function is its reference to its ground,—although as a symbol it must refer also to an object and an interpretant, and although the nature of its reference to its object is alone the study of the logician—is nevertheless *intended* to be nothing more than something which has *meaning* and to which a certain character has been imputed; in other words it is a symbol only because the imputation of a certain character has made it one —the imputation of the character is the same as putting it for a thing or things—so that it is merely considered as expressing a thing or things in their internal characters—as standing in place of a thing and as being, like that thing, an incarnation of a certain ground, though only by imputation and not internally. If we write "White"—this word standing by itself, means nothing; it stands there merely in place of a white thing so that we have by imputation put a white thing on the board. So if we write "Aristotle" this means nothing except so far as it embodies certain characters of mind, of nationality, and of position in space and time, which belonged internally and not by Imputation to the real Aristotle. Thus a *term* is a symbol which is intended only to refer to a Ground or what is the same thing, to stand instead of a Quale or what is again the same, to have *meaning* without *truth*.

Next suppose a Symbol whose intended function is the reference to an object or correlate. The reference of a Symbol to its object is its *truth*. This kind of symbol is therefore one which is intended merely to Embody a truth. So that it is a *proposition*. But as reference to a correlate cannot be intended or even supposed without reference to a ground, as truth *supposes* meaning, to intend that a symbol should refer to a correlate is to intend that it should refer to correlate and ground, that is be a relate, by imputation; or in other words stand instead of a relate—or represent a relate. So that to say that a proposition is a symbol which is intended to refer to a correlate is the same as to say that it is one which represents a relate as such.

In the third place, a symbol may be intended to refer to an interpretant or to have *force*. It is, then, intended also to contain a statement, since reference to an interpretant cannot be prescinded from the other references. It is intended therefore to inculcate this statement into the interpretant; that is to produce the equivalent statement with the interpretant—not merely the statement that this symbol makes the statement, but a restatement. For an interpretant is something which represents a representation to represent that which it does itself represent. Now that which, thus, appeals to an interpretant—that is is constructed and intended so as to develope a restatement on the part of another or assent —is an argument, a syllogism *minus* the conclusion, for the Conclusion of a syllogism is no part of the argument but is the assent to it, the interpretant. An argument, therefore, is a symbol intended to refer to an interpretant and I could show very easily that this is the same as a symbol which from its form, represents a representation.

Thus we have

Symbol
{
Term intended to refer to a ground—
whose object is formally a Quale
Proposition intended to refer to a correlate—
whose object is formally a Relate
Argument intended to refer to an interpretant—
whose object is formally a Representation

Having, thus, made the first grand division of symbols—a division which is properly logical since as the second series of definitions shows it concerns the reference of the symbol to its object—we must take up each kind of symbol and study it by itself.

We begin then with the term whose object is formally a Quale. A quale is to be regarded as the incarnation of the ground of its quality. Moreover it necessarily is represented by something, for all impressions require logically to be represented and they are the matter of fact—so that an absolutely and at all times unrepresented thing is nothing. A quale, therefore, has a direct reference both to the ground and the interpretant of the *term* which represents it. That term, therefore, in referring to its object, thereby refers in another way to its own ground and interpretant. Now the direct reference of a *term* to its object is what we have called the *denotation* of the term—the object itself being its *sphere*—and the sum of that object reckoned by other terms its ||*extension/extent*||. The indirect reference which a term has to its ground through its reference to its object is the qualities which its object universally has—that is, is its *connotation*, the sum of the qualities reckoned by other terms being its //*comprehension*/*content*//. The indirect reference which a term has to its interpretant through its reference to its object is its *implication*—or considered as a quantity, its *information*. Thus

Reference to ground through object   is *Connotation*
Direct reference to object   " *Denotation*
Reference to interpretant through object   " *Implication*

The reason why

$$\text{Extension} \times \text{Comprehension} = \text{Information}$$

is that Extension and Comprehension can only be reckoned by the interpretants, each interpretant measuring either the one or the other.

Let us next consider the different kinds of terms. A term may in the first place represent its object directly as a quale; or second as a quale but without determining it except as the correlate of a certain relate; or third still as a quale but defined only as the object of a certain representation.

In the first case we have a simple term—like *man* or *white*.

The second case where the object is determined merely as the correlate of the object of another term on the ground of the ground of that term,—this case divides into two according as the relation is an equiparance or a disquiparance. Now for the sake of fixing our imagination let us suppose that the term whose object is the relate whose correlate is the object of the required term is the term *white*. Then suppose the relation is an equiparance; then the object of the given term is something which agrees with the *white* in whiteness. What is this? A particular white thing or things. *Some white*. Suppose on the other hand, the relation is a disquiparance. Then the question arises how can *whiteness*, which is an internal character, be the ground of a disquiparance. The answer is that every quality may be considered as relative, if you please; those characters upon which whiteness depends are possessed more or less down to nothing by all things—so that what we call white are only things which are whiter than anything not-white. Hence white is *whiter* and this is a ground of disquiparance—and if what we call *white* be taken as the relate, something not-white is the correlate. Hence, terms whose object is defined only as a correlate of the object of a certain term on the ground of the ground of that term are either

<table>
<tr><td>Subalternate terms</td><td rowspan="2">or</td><td>Negative terms</td></tr>
<tr><td>as Some-white</td><td>as Not-white</td></tr>
</table>

according as the relation is one of Equiparance or Disquiparance. We may here remark that as *negation* is thus a notion which depends upon that of disquiparance and therefore upon relation to a correlate; it is plain why it does not apply to being, into which the notion of reference to a correlate does not enter. So that Hegel is wrong in making Negation enter so early as he does into Logic.

Finally let us suppose that the object of a term is defined only as the object of a representation. This representation may be either a Likeness, an Index, or a Symbol. Suppose first that the representation is a likeness —then this likeness must be described, since its representation lies wholly in its description; this description will be a conjunctive term or sum of characters. And so any conjunctive term, as red fiery ball falling from the Moon, has merely the object of a likeness as its object. 2nd suppose, the mediating representation be an index. Then the things which correspond to it must be summed up, as in them is the essence of the representation of an index. This will give a disjunctive term, as man, horse, and whale. Finally, when the mediating representation is a Symbol we have the simple term again, since the interpretant of a simple term is a mediating symbol. Terms are therefore divided into

Simple
A

Subalternate   Negative
Some *A*   not-*A*

Conjunctive   Disjunctive
ABC $A + B + C$

Of course, we should get a countless number of other varieties by supposing the *A* here to be not a simple term. For instance, we might have such a term as this

Horses not swift together with Some men and non-dogs and
Everything not a tree nor some English things.

Other divisions of terms might be obtained by twining together the
three references; but I have mentioned only those which we have already found necessary in order to explain induction and hypothesis.

We come next to *propositions*. These we have seen represent their
objects as relates. These must be either equiparants or disquiparants. As
the relate and correlate of an equiparance are related to one another
in the same way and upon the same ground, the proposition which represents a relate of equiparance as such will necessarily also represent
its correlate as a relate at the same time; in short relate and correlate
cannot be distinguished in an equiparance. They may therefore be
thrown into one term. Another term however will be needed to express
the ground of equiparance. Thus propositions of equiparance have two
terms, subject and predicate; the subject expresses the relate and correlate or agreeing things, the predicate expresses the ground of the relation
—provided the *not* of a negative proposition is considered as part of the
predicate. Thus No elephants are red—means elephants agree in being
not red. On the other hand, if a disquiparant is represented by the
proposition—since its correlate will generally be related to it upon a
different ground from that upon which it is related to that correlate,
three terms will be required: subject, predicate, and object; the first
expressing the relate, the second the ground, and the third the correlate.
As an instance, take the proposition

Every man loves those who love him

Every man is the subject, loves is the predicate, those who love him
is the object.

Propositions thus being divisible into propositions of equiparance
and propositions of disquiparance, let us next consider the sub-divisions
of each kind.

Every proposition has, like a term, its //extension/extent// and
//Comprehension/content//. This will be obvious if we only reflect that
many terms are synonymous with propositions. What does the term
Jehovah mean? It means the supreme being, who is at the same time
the God of the Hebrews—who appeared on Sinai. To use this word,

therefore, *unless a disqualifying clause is attached,* is to say that the supreme being appeared on Sinai. We can attach a disqualifying clause to this proposition as well as to the term—so that the two are near enough *identical* in logical meaning although their grammatical relations are different.

What is the extension of *Jehovah?* The supreme being that is the extension of that term which forms the subject of the proposition. [quote] Thus, the extension of a proposition is the extension of its subject. And in like manner, I could show that the comprehension of a proposition is the comprehension of its predicate.

Since a proposition, like a term, has these two references—extension and comprehension—upon which the division of terms is based, it would seem to follow that propositions can be divided just as terms are; and indeed they may be so, only such division always leaves one kind of propositions not included.

For instance, terms are divided into simple terms, subalternate terms, and negative terms. Corresponding to simple terms we have simple propositions such as *A* is *B*—which we have previously called

Universal Affirmative Contingent Attributive

propositions. A subalternate term is one which refers to its object as something which agrees with the object of a stated term upon the ground of the comprehension of that term. So a subalternate proposition will be one which denotes a state of things resembling that denoted by a given proposition upon the ground of the comprehension of that proposition. Thus Some *A* is *B* denotes something which resembles All *A* (which is *B*) upon the ground of the comprehension of that term—*A* (which is *B*). A negative term is defined to be one whose object differs from that of a given term in respect to the comprehension of that term. So a negative proposition is one whose object differs from a given proposition in respect to the comprehension of that proposition. Thus, *A* is not *B* differs from *A* is *B* in respect to being *B*.

We can have Subalternate Negative terms—as some not-*A*—but we do not find any advantage in enumerating them. In the case of Propositions we enumerate all the species

All *A* is *B*	No *A* is *B*
Some *A* is *B*	Some *A* is not *B*.

And thus we have Affirmative and Negative, Universal and Particular Propositions.

Thus the subject of a proposition may be either a simple term or a subalternate term; while the predicate may be either a simple term or a negative term. It may be asked why a subalternate term may not be made predicate or a negative term subject. A negative term *may* be made subject: we may say Nothing but men obtain salvation. That is All not-men are unsaved. But in the syllogism such a proposition has the same effect as an ordinary Universal—that is it may be made a rule and therefore there is no need of analyzing *not-men* but we may consider it as a simple term. Mr. De Morgan in his logic has taken account of such propositions and has stated their properties in a masterly manner. I do not enumerate them as I think it would only encumber the subject, not elucidate it. Subalternate terms may also be made predicates but in the predicate they have the same effect as simple terms. To say that *A* is *B*—that is, is among or has the common properties of all *B*'s—is the same as to say that *A* is some *B*—that is, is among or has the properties of some *B*'s *at least*. A division of propositions on this ground is therefore unnecessary. It is true that many logicians, among whom I may mention as recent and original writers Hamilton, De Morgan, Thomson, and Spalding, make a distinction between All *A*'s are all *B*'s and All *A*'s are some *B*'s; because they make the former mean that All *A*'s are *B* and All *B*'s are *A*. They regard the copula *is* as a sign of equality—whereas I follow the great body of logicians in making it a sign of predication, that is of attribution or subsumption. *All B* is the same as *B*, and therefore All *A*'s are all *B*'s would be a woefully awkward way of saying All *A*'s are among or have the common characters of all *B*'s—that is All *A*'s are *B*'s. I think, however, that the words would suggest a different meaning, namely that Every *A* is every *B*, or *A* and *B* are the same individual.

While I am upon this subject, I will mention certain other forms of proposition suggested by Sir William Hamilton, about which his admirers have made such a to-do. He proposes the forms Any *A* is not some *B* and Some *A* is not some *B*. Any *A* is not some *B*, naturally means that if you take any *A* whatever you will find that there is some *B* which it is not;—Hamilton, however, makes it mean that there is some *B* which is not to be found among all *A*'s: that is it means the same as Some *B* is not *A*. The meaning of Any *A* is not some *B*, is according to Hamilton precisely the same as that of Some *B* is not *A*. There is he thinks a difference in the attitude or subjective state of the mind in the two cases. But that is not proved and if it were, it is not at all probable that he has begun to enumerate all the attitudes of the mind which bear the same meaning. But even admitting that he had done that, a distinction based merely on a difference of subjective states of mind is of no relevancy in logic, for Logic is the science of the reference of symbols in general to their objects—or as the great German metaphysician Herbart expresses it:

Unsre sämmtlichen Gedanken lassen sich von zwei Seiten betrachten; theils als Thätigkeiten unseres Geistes, theils in Hinsicht dessen, *was* durch sie gedacht wird. In letzerer Beziehung heissen sie *Begriffe*, welches Wort, indem es das *Begriffene* bezeichnet, zu abstrahiren gebietet von der Art und Weise, wie wir den Gedanken empfangen, produciren, oder reproduciren mögen.

Now if we consider Sir William Hamilton's other form of proposition, Some A is not some B, we shall find it still more objectionable. What do you suppose he makes this proposition Some A is not some B mean? Why that A and B are not the same individual. They may be the same class, but then the proposition is not false; it is false only when A and B are the same *individual*. Now if a special form of proposition is required to say *that*, of course a special form must be required to deny it and to say that A and B are the same individual—but he admits no such form as *this* is necessary, and therefore his form contradicting this is unnecessary.

Hamilton insists that his system is *true* and all others *false*. In fact, truth and falsity refer to the correspondence of a representation with its object while a *system* is not a representation but only an arrangement whose virtues are *unity* and *comprehensiveness* but not *truth*. Hamilton also pronounces forms of arguments illogical because they will not come into his system while admitting that they necessarily yield true conclusions from true premisses; now this is the most that *logical* ever means.

So much for the division of propositions into A E I O.

Terms are further divided into Likeness-terms, Index-terms, and Simple-Terms. An Index term is one which has no adequate extension; a proposition will have the same character when its subject is an index term. A likeness term is one which has no known extension; this can hardly be the case with a proposition, for the predicate of a proposition is determined in extension by the proposition itself. It may, however, be the case that the predicate in itself independently of the proposition should be wanting in extension. This will be the case if it is a Likeness-term. Finally the Subject may be an Index term and the predicate a likeness-term, at the same time. Thus we have

Subject	Predicate		
Simple	Simple	Necessary	Subsumptive
Index	Simple	Contingent	Subsumptive
Simple	Likeness	Necessary	Attributive
Index	Likeness	Contingent	Attributive.

We come finally to the third kind of symbol; namely, the argument. This we have defined as a symbol which owing to its very form represents a representation. It will therefore be divided into three species according as this representation is a likeness, index, or symbol.

These three species are the same as Hypothesis, Induction, and Deduction. Hypothesis brings up to the mind an image of the true qualities of a thing—it therefore informs us as to comprehension but not as to Extension, that is it represents a representation which has Comprehension without Extension; in other words it represents a likeness. Induction informs us of the whole extent of those things which have certain characters—for example, it infers that all cloven-hoofed animals are herbivora,—it therefore informs us as to extension but not as to comprehension, that is it represents a representation which has extension without comprehension, which is an Index. Deduction does not strictly speaking afford any information; it only explicates the notion which is in both premises and shows that it involves bringing two other terms together as subject and predicate,—and it thus equally affords extension to the one and comprehension to the other, so that it represents a symbol.

The divisions of arguments into figures and moods obviously arise from the divisions of propositions; so that we have as a general scheme of the division of Formal Objects 1st

Quales Relates and Representations

or those which refer only to a ground, those which refer doubly to ground and correlate, and those which refer triply to ground, correlate, and interpretant.

Then the relates are divided into equiparants and disquiparants or those whose fundamental quality is prescindible and those in which it is not. While representations are divided into likenesses, indices, and symbols, or those whose fundamental relation and quality are both prescindible, those whose fundamental relation only is prescindible, and those in which neither is prescindible.

Passing to the division of symbols we find that they are either terms, propositions, or arguments. Terms from their form represent quales, propositions relates, arguments representations. Hence propositions are either propositions of equiparance or propositions of disquiparance, and arguments are either hypotheses, inductions, or deductions.

These are the most important logical distinctions and you perceive that they flow directly from the three references which were found to intervene between the Unity of Being and the Manifold of Substance. The other divisions which we have found ourselves forced to make are in my opinion all more or less arbitrary;—nevertheless they are plainly derived from these three references though not in so direct a manner.

It is important to ask of a theory of logic whether it presents a systematic and homogeneous whole, for though it may do this and still be faulty from omissions or positive errors, yet as the whole end of logic is to make reasonings intelligible, that is to reduce them to a unity of classification, no system can be true where this unity is wanting and its presence is a strong argument in favor of the value of the system. Now such a unity is found in great perfection in the system to which we have been led. We have a division of objects into three classes. The first of these has one subdivision, the second two, the third three. The first of the subdivisions of any class has one further subdivision, the second two, the third three, and so on throughout. Moreover each of these divisions springs directly from the three references to ground, correlate, and interpretant which are little if anything more than the notions of 1st, 2nd, and 3rd.

We have now taken a slight survey of the science of Logic itself and I propose to occupy the three remaining lectures of the course with some illustrations of the application of the theory which we have studied in the previous lectures. And I will call your attention in the first place to the classification of the sciences which follows from the division of arguments into hypotheses, inductions, and deductions. Most of the classifications of the sciences which have been proposed rest upon a classification of the things of which they treat. This method is objectionable for two reasons: first that many sciences treat of everything, as the science of mechanics, that of geometry, that of chemistry, and so forth; second because the classification of things needs to rest upon a classification of sciences. The first great division of things is according to their functions and hence it is that the homologies or likenesses which pervade a whole kingdom of nature as mouths, stomachs, and locomotive apparatus among animals are *functional* homologies. Now the function of a thing in itself considered cannot be determined; whatever it does or is it is its function to do or be. Hence any division of the functions of things is only a division of different sciences which ask different questions about things, and thus the classification of things rests finally on the classification of sciences.

There have been various schemes of the classification of sciences which have been based upon their logical proceedure, but with these there has been a total want of any exact consideration of that proceedure. Among inductive sciences are commonly placed optics and other branches of physics. Now this is totally wrong; for induction only discovers natural classification—only from neat goats sheep and deer finds that all ruminants are cloven-hoofed—that is erects ruminants into a natural kind or one which possesses universal characters over and above those which serve to define it. Now classification is no part of *physics*. Optics and such sciences discover causes—remote efficients—and this can only be done by hypothesis. On the other hand, sciences are commonly excluded from the inductive class without any reason—Logic is one of these, for as we saw at the first lecture logic is purely a classifying science and therefore purely inductive; and yet it has usually been placed among the deductive sciences merely on account of its great exactitude.

For my part, I should place under the head of deductive science, mathematics, Law, and political economy alone. It seems to me that these are the only sciences whose sole object is to trace out consequences. And I am not sure that even mathematics should not be regarded as an inductive science, because it makes classifications.

Among inductive or classificatory sciences we have Natural History (or Zoölogy, Botany, and Mineralogy), Morphology, Descriptive Astronomy, Chemistry, Logic, Philosophy, Physiognomy, a portion of Physical Geography.

Among hypothetic or causal sciences we have two orders. First those the unity of which is the unity of the hypothesis they make—as

Gravitation, Mechanics, Acoustics, Optics, Heat, Electricity, &c. And second those whose unity is the unity of their object—History, Geology, Physiology.

A further division of the sciences is exceedingly necessary. Yet the rude scheme here sketched out will be found to furnish much food for reflection. In the first place, it is a fact that students of classificatory and students of hypothetic science have but little appreciation of each other's labors. The physiologist has too often been found to slight the discoveries of the morphologist. The Physicist scarce attaches sufficient importance to the works of the classifying mathematician. The great disputes of science have usually been between those who ask for causes and those who ask for classification; and the Darwinian controversy is an instance in point.

Another thing to which I would call your attention is that hypothetic science is generally founded upon some classificatory knowledge. Thus Gravitation is founded on Kepler's laws which are inductions in the proper sense. Classificatory science is founded upon some deductive knowledge but the matter does not rest here for every deductive science requires a knowledge of the general principles whose consequences it searches out and these are derived from induction and every induction requires the knowledge of a hypothetic conclusion. The next lecture will treat of the logical character of mental modifications.

Lecture X

MS 131: November 1866

We have seen that all cognition whatever is inferred from some other cognition. Every premiss is a conclusion and there is no first premiss or intuition.

I can illustrate this by a diagram. Let this line represent a certain cognition and let the clearness of it—the intensity or liveliness of consciousness in it—be indicated by the length of the line.

Under it I put a dot. Let this dot represent the fact of which this line is the cognition. The dot is placed under the line to show that the cognition is based on that fact. And it is made a *dot* without length to show that it is something without the consciousness of which we have no immediate consciousness at all.

The cognition represented by that line is inferred from another which I will place below it—to show that they are related as premiss to conclusion, and at a finite distance to show that they are not identical; and this premiss I will draw shorter to show that we have not so lively a feeling of it.

This cognition is based on another [draw it]. This on another less lively. This on another less lively and so on *ad infinitum*. Thus every premiss is based on a conclusion different from itself and in consciousness although the consciousness of this latter is less lively. And the only ultimate premiss is the matter of fact itself which is not in the consciousness.

I have already stated the reasons for adopting this opinion. They are 1st That the reasons for supposing ultimate sensations are futile, 2nd That all the sensations now supposed to be ultimate, are more probably inferences, 3rd That no sensation can possibly be known to be an ultimate premise and that consequently no error of *fact* is involved in saying that there is no ultimate premise, since *fact* refers to a possible experience only.

The result of adopting this view is that we are neither forced into *idealism,* nor yet into *ontological ignorance,* nor yet into a senseless fastening ourselves up in a stronghold of natural prejudice. In short, all the difficulties of a theory of cognition are got over at once.

The question is, what reason is there to think that we really know things external to us.

Philosophers have generally been forced to say either first that we do not know the real things in themselves, or second that the only realities are *feelings,* or third to say that the only ground for believing that we really know things is natural prejudice.

But upon this view, there is a reality out of consciousness, which is represented by the dot which has no length. We really know this thing inasmuch as it is the real premiss of this series of cognitions, as much and in the same sense as any one of these is of those which follow after. And third that we have as much reason for saying that we know those real things as we have for any other inference whatever.

In short we have reduced the paradox of cognition to the paradox of Achilles and the tortoise which I explained and showed how it was identical with that of the Liar by means of that moving boundary between a red and a blue space.

Lecture XI

MS 132: November 1866

Gentlemen and Ladies—

Philosophy is the attempt—for as the word itself implies it is and must be imperfect—is the attempt to form a general informed conception of the *All*. All men philosophize; and as Aristotle says we must do so if only to prove the futility of philosophy. Those who neglect philosophy have metaphysical theories as much as others—only they are rude, false, and wordy theories. Some think to avoid the influence of metaphysical errors, by paying no attention to metaphysics; but experience shows that these men beyond all others are held in an iron vise of metaphysical theory, because by theories that they have never called in question. No man is so enthralled by metaphysics as the totally uneducated; no man is so free from its dominion as the metaphysician himself. Since, then, everyone must have conceptions of things in general, it is most important that they should be carefully constructed.

I shall enter into no criticism of the different methods of metaphysical research, but shall merely say that in the opinion of several great thinkers, the only successful mode yet lighted upon is that of adopting our logic as our metaphysics. In the last lecture, I endeavored to show how logic furnishes us with a classification of the elements of con-

sciousness. We found that all modifications of consciousness, are inferences and that all inferences are valid inferences. At the same time we
found that there were 3 kinds of inference: 1st Intellectual inference
with its three varieties—Hypothesis, Induction, and Deduction; 2nd
Judgments of sensation, emotions, and instinctive motions which are hypotheses whose predicates are unanalyzed in comprehension; and 3rd
Habits which are Inductions whose subjects are unanalyzed in extension. This division leads us to three elements of consciousness: 1st *Feelings* or Elements of comprehension, 2nd *Efforts* or Elements of extension, and 3rd *Notions* or Elements of Information, which is the union
of extension and comprehension. I regret that the time does not permit
me to dwell further upon this theory but I wish to pass to a loftier and
more practical question of metaphysics in order to put in a still stronger
light the advantages of the study of logic. The question which I shall
select is "what is man?" I think I may state the prevalent conception
thus: Man is essentially a soul, that is, a thing occupying a mathematical point of space, not thought itself but the subject of inhesion of
thought, without parts, and exerting a certain material force called volition. I presume that most people consider this belief as *intuitive*, or, at
least, as planted in man's nature and more or less distinctly held by all
men, always and everywhere.

> Most ignorant of what he's most assured
> His glassy essence

On the contrary, the doctrine is a very modern one. All the ancients and
many of the scholastics, held that man is compact of several souls; three
was the usual number assigned, sometimes two, four, or five. Every attentive reader of St. Paul is aware that according to him, man has a
three-fold being. We derive the notion of the soul's being single from
Descartes. But with him, thought itself makes the man; whereas with
us consciousness *is* not the man but is in man. Descartes, also, does not
admit that the will of man exerts any force upon matter; as we mostly
believe. In fact, the prevalent view of the present day is a heterogeneous hodge-podge of the most contradictory theories; its doctrines are
borrowed from different philosophers while the premisses by which
alone those philosophers were able to support their doctrines are
denied; the theory thus finds itself totally unsupported by facts and in
several particulars at war with itself; and this is admitted by most of

those who have subjected it to rigid criticism. Upon the diversities of theories of the soul there are some pretty lines by Sir John Davies in his poem on Psychology.

> For her [the soul's] true form how can my spark discern,
>   Which, dim by nature, art did never clear?
> When the great wits, of whom all skill we learn,
>   Are ignorant both what she is, and where.
>
> One thinks the soul is air; another, fire;
>   Another, blood, diffus'd about the heart;
> Another saith, the elements conspire,
>   And to her essence each doth lend a part.
>
> Musicians think our souls are harmonies;
>   Physicians hold that they complexions be;
> Epicures make them swarms of atomies,
>   Which do by chance into our bodies flee.
>
> Some think one gen'ral soul fills every brain,
>   As the bright sun sheds light in every star;
> While others think the name of soul is vain,
>   And that we only well-mixt bodies are.
>
> In judgment of her substance as they vary,
>   So vary they in judgment of her seat;
> For some her chair up to the brain do carry,
>   Some thrust it down into the stomach's heat.
>
> Some place it in the root of life, the heart;
>   Some in the liver fountain of the veins;
> Some say, she's all in all, and all in ev'ry part;
>   Some that she's not contain'd, but all contains.
>
> Thus these great clerks but little wisdom shew,
>   While with their doctrines they at hazard play;
> Tossing their light opinions to and fro,
>   To mock the lewd, as learn'd in this as they.
>
> For no craz'd brain could ever yet propound,
>   Touching the soul, so vain and fond a thought,
> But some among these masters have been found,
>   Which, in their schools, the self-same thing have taught.

One source of all this diversity of opinion, has been the want of an accurate discrimination between an inductive and a hypothetic explanation of the facts of human life. We have seen that every fact requires two kinds of explanation; the one proceeds by induction to replace its subject by a wider one, the other proceeds by hypothesis to replace its predicate by a deeper one. We have seen that these two explanations never coincide, that both are indispensible, and that quarrels have sprung up even in physical science where there are so few disagreements in consequence of trying to make one theory perform both functions. Let us take care that we do not confound these two separate inquiries in reference to the soul. The hypothetic explanation will inform us of the causes or necessary antecedents of the phenomena of human life. These phenomena may be regarded internally or externally. Regarded internally they require an internal explanation by internal necessary antecedents, that is by *premisses;* and this explanation was given in the last lecture. If they are regarded externally or physically, they require a physical explanation by physical antecedents, and this inquiry must be turned over unreservedly to the physiologists. They will find the truth of the matter, and we may rest satisfied that no explanation which is based squarely upon legitimate hypothesis from the facts of nature, can possibly conflict with a purely inductive explanation of man. It is true that the question for the physiologist is what are the physical antecedents of man's actions, that is what sort of an automaton is man; so that it is assumed as the condition of the problem that man is an automaton. For, automatism in this connection, consciousness being of course admitted, means nothing but regular physical antecedence—implies only that nature is uniform; and this as we have seen is not a mere law of nature or fact of observation, but is a postulate of all thought, which no man consistently or persistently denies. Yet this automatism seems, no doubt, to many to conflict with the notion of man as a RESPONSIBLE and IMMORTAL soul. But, then, we should remember that in our minds, the essential conceptions of responsibility and immortality are covered over with a mass of parasitical reflection derived from every philosophy and every religion of past time; so that if *we* cannot reconcile the doctrines of responsibility and immortality with the postulates of thought or with themselves, this is sufficiently accounted for by the obscurity and confusion of our notions on this subject, and we are by no means forced to adopt that which is the only other alternative and say that these doctrines are essentially false. These doctrines are a part of our religion; and one of them—if not both —are among its most precious consolations, which it would be difficult indeed to wring from the breast of a people which has entertained them for a thousand years. Talk as they please, of the weariness of unceasing day, of the balm of an eternal sleep, of the nobility lent to humanity by regarding it as capable of struggling and suffering for that which transcends its own responsibility and life-time; we still cling by nature original or acquired, to the dear hopes of our ancient religion. But while I have thought it proper to dwell for a moment upon the possibility of our being unable to reconcile responsibility and immortality with physical necessity, I must add that in fact we are not driven to that point, at all. On the contrary the philosophers of the Brownist school have shown uncontrovertibly that they are capable of being reconciled, and their arguments are very forcibly stated in an American work called *Liberty and Necessity,* written by Judge Carleton of Louisiana and published in Philadelphia in 1857. There may be other modes of reconciling these conceptions besides that which they have pointed out but still they have shown that a rational reconciliation is possible.

Thus, the hypothetic explanation of human nature stands by itself and will present no contradiction to the inductive explanation, which is what we desire when we ask what is man? To what real kind does the thinking, feeling, and willing being belong? We know that externally considered man belongs to the animal kingdom, to the branch of vertebrates, and the class of mammals; but what we seek is his place when considered internally; disregarding his muscles, glands, and nerves and considering only his feelings, efforts, and conceptions.

We have already seen that every state of consciousness is an inference; so that life is but a sequence of inferences or a train of thought. At any instant then man is a thought, and as thought is a species of symbol, the general answer to the question What is man? is that he is a symbol. To find a more specific answer we should compare man with some other symbol.

I write here the word *six.* Now let us ask ourselves in what respects a *man* differs from that word. In the first place, the body of a man is a wonderful mechanism, that of the word nothing but a line of chalk. In the second place, the meaning of the word is very simple, the meaning of a man is a very Sphynx's question. These two differences are very obvious,—they lie upon the surface. But what other difference is there?

A man has consciousness; a word has not. What do we mean by consciousness, for it is rather an ambiguous term. There is that emotion which accompanies the reflection that we have animal life. A consciousness which is dimmed when animal life is at its ebb, in age or sleep, but which is not dimmed when the spiritual life is at its ebb; which is more lively the better animal a man is, but is not so the better man he is. You can all distinguish this sensation I am sure; we attribute it to all animals but not to words, because we have reason to believe that it depends upon the possession of an animal body. And, therefore, this difference is included under the first that we mentioned and is not an additional one. In the second place, consciousness is used to mean the knowledge which we have of what is in our minds; the fact that our thought is an index for itself of itself on the ground of a complete identity with itself. But so is any word or indeed any thing, so that this constitutes no difference between the word and the man. In the third place, consciousness is used to denote the *I think,* the unity of thought; but the unity of thought is nothing but the unity of symbolization—consistency, in a word (the implication of *being*) and belongs to every word whatever. It is very easy to think we have a *clear* notion of what we mean by consciousness, and yet it may be that the word excites no thought but only a sensation, a mental word within us; and then because we are not accustomed to allow the word written on the board to excite that sensation, we may think we distinguish between the man and the word when we do not.

> Most ignorant of what we're most assured
> Our glassy essence!

Consciousness is, also, used to denote what I call *feeling;* as by Mr. Bain whom I mention in order to say that he recognizes the unity of sensation and emotion under this term although he has not carried out the conception consistently. Has that word feeling? Man, say the sensationalists, is a series of feelings; at any one moment, then, *is a feeling.* How is it with the word? Feelings, we all know, depend upon the bodily organism. The blind man from birth has no such feelings as red, blue, or any other colour; and without any body at all, it is probable we should have no feelings at all; and the word which has no animal body probably therefore has no *animal* feelings, and of course if we restrict the word *feeling* to meaning animal feeling the word has no feelings. But has it not something corresponding to feeling? Every feeling is cognitive—is a sensation, and a sensation is a mental sign or word. Now the word has a word; it has itself; and so if man is an animal feeling, the word is just as much a written feeling.

But is there not this difference. Man's feelings are perceptions, he is affected by objects. He sees, hears, &c. A word does not. Yes, that is true;

but perception, plainly, depends upon having an animal organism and therefore there is here no further difference beyond the obvious two mentioned at first. Yet even here there is a correspondence between the word and the man. Perception is the possibility of acquiring information of meaning more; now a word may learn. How much more the word *electricity* means now than it did in the days of Franklin; how much more the term *planet* means now than it did in the time of Hipparchus. These words have acquired information; just as a man's thought does by further perception. But is there not a difference—since a man makes the word, and the word means nothing which some man has not made it mean, and that only to that man? This is true; but since man can think only by means of words or other external symbols, words might turn round and say, you mean nothing which we have not taught you and then only so far as you address some word as the interpretant of your thought. In fact, therefore, men and words reciprocally educate each other; each increase of a man's information is at the same time the increase of a word's information and *vice versa*. So that there is no difference even here.

You see that remote and dissimilar as the word and the man appear, it is exceedingly difficult to state any essential difference between them except a physiological one. A man has a moral nature, a word apparently has none. Yet morals relate primarily to what we ought to do; and therefore as words are physiologically incapacitated to act we should not consider this as a separate point of distinction. But if we consider morality as the conformity to a law of fitness of things,—a principle of what is suitable in thought not in order to make it true but as a prerequisite to make it spiritual, to make it rational, to make it more truly thought at all—we have something extremely analogous in the good grammar of a word or sentence. Good grammar is that excellence of a word by which it comes to have a good conscience, to be satisfactory, not merely reference being had to the actual state of things which it denotes, not merely to the consequences of the act, but to it in its own internal determination. Beauty and truth belong to the mind and word alike. The third excellence is morality on the one hand, Grammar on the other.

Man has the power of effort or attention; but as we have seen that this is nothing but the power of denotation, it is possessed by the word also.

Perhaps the most marvellous faculty of humanity is one which it possesses in common with all animals and in one sense with all plants, I mean that of procreation. I do not allude to the physiological wonders, which are great enough, but to the fact of the production of a new human soul. Has the word any such relation as that of father and son? If I write "Let *Kax* denote a gas furnace," this sentence is a symbol which is creating another within itself. Here we have a certain analogy with paternity; just as much and no more as when an author speaks of his writings as his offspring,—an expression which should be regarded not as metaphorical but merely as general. Cuvier said that Metaphysics is nothing but Metaphor—an identity which is prettily typified in those acted charades, in the first of which two doctors come in at opposite sides of the stage, shake hands, and go out for the first scene, then repeat the same thing for the second scene and again for the whole word; and then do the same thing three times for the three scenes of the second word. The two words are of course *metaphysician* and *metaphor;* and their identity suggests that the charades must have been the invention of some one who thought with Cuvier that Metaphysics is another term for Metaphor. If metaphor be taken literally to mean an expression of a similitude when the sign of predication is employed instead of the sign of likeness—as when we say this man *is* a fox instead of this man is like a fox—I deny entirely that metaphysicians are given to metaphor; on the contrary, no other writers can compare with them for precision of language. But if Cuvier was only using a metaphor himself, and meant by metaphor broad comparison on the ground of characters of a formal and highly abstract kind,—then, indeed, metaphysics professes to be metaphor. That is just its merit—as it was Cuvier's own merit in Zoölogy.

To return. This sentence on the board has a real but slight resemblance to a father, more to an author. But suppose we write a syllogism

$$X \text{ is thus}$$
$$\text{This is } X.$$

Springing out of the union of these two symbols, which play essentially different parts, is another. It may be our knowledge of the relation of parentage is not sufficient to say positively, but it may be that here there is a great analogy to the parental relation. If it be so, then as one of these symbols affords the content and the other the sphere of the new symbol, one parent ought to give the *feelings*, the other the *energies* of the child. This has never been observed, I believe; although that power of concentration, which depends on effort, belongs more to one sex and capacity for feeling to the other is notorious.

Enough has now been said, I think, to show a true analogy between a man and a word. I dare say this seems very paradoxical to you; I remember it did to me, at first. But having thought it over repeatedly, it has come to seem the merest truism. A man denotes whatever is the object of his attention at the moment; he connotes whatever he knows or feels of this object, and is the incarnation of this form or intelligible species; his interpretant is the future memory of this cognition, his future self, or the other person he addresses, or a sentence he writes, or a child he gets. In what does the identity of man consist and where is the seat of the soul? It seems to me that these questions usually receive a very narrow answer. Why, we used to read that the soul resides in a little organ of the brain no bigger than a pin's head. Most anthropologists now more rationally say that the soul is either spread over the whole body or is all in all and all in every part. But are we shut up in a box of flesh and blood? When I communicate my thoughts and my sentiments to a friend with whom I am in full sympathy, so that my feelings pass into him and I am conscious of what he feels, do I not live in his brain as well as in my own—most literally? True, my animal life is not there; but my soul, my feeling, thought, attention are. If this be not so, a man is not a word, it is true, but is something much poorer. There is a miserable material and barbarian notion according to which a man cannot be in two places at once; as though he were a *thing!* A word may be in several places at once, *six six,* because its essence is spiritual; and I believe that a man is no whit inferior to the word in this respect. Each man has an identity which far transcends the mere animal;—an essence, a *meaning* subtile as it may be. He cannot know his own essential significance; of his eye it is eyebeam. But that he truly has this outreaching identity—such as a word has—is the true and exact expression of the fact of sympathy, fellow feeling—together with all unselfish interests,—and all that makes us feel that he has an absolute worth. Someone will ask me for *proof* of this. It seems to me that I have already given both the proof and the confirmation. The whole proof was very long but its principal *lemmas* were these. 1st What is man is an inductive question in its present sense. 2nd The inductive explanation is only the general expression of the phenomena, and makes no hypothesis. 3rd Whatever man is he is at each instant. 4th At each instant the only internal phenomena he presents are feeling, thought, attention. 5th Feelings, thought, attention are all cognitive. 6th All cognition is general, there is no intuition. 7th A general representation is a symbol. 8th Every symbol has an essential comprehension which determines its identity. The confirmation I offered was the fact that man is conscious of his interpretant, his own thought in another mind—I do not say immediately conscious—is happy in it, feels himself in some degree to be there. So that I believe that nothing but an undue ascendency of the animal life can prevent the perception of this truth.

This essence of which I speak is not the whole soul of man; it is only his core which carries with it all the information which constitutes the developement of the man, his total feelings, intentions, thoughts. When I, that is my thoughts, enter into another man, I do not necessarily carry my whole self; but what I do carry is the seed of the part that I do not carry—and if I carry the seed of my whole essence, then of my whole self actual and potential. I may write upon paper and thus impress a part of my being there; that part of my being may involve only what I have in common with all men, and then I should have carried the soul of the race, but not my individual soul, into the word there written. Thus every man's soul is a special determination of the generic soul of the family, the class, the nation, the race to which he belongs. Among the lower animals the generic soul is the greater part of their being—*bees* are more alike than men. Among inferior races, there is less individuality than in the higher race. Among the laboring men there is less true individuality,—though more perverse individuality perhaps—than among artisans; among artisans less than among educated persons. These last differences are owing to differences in information or experience; but there are also among men differences in native depth. There is no reason to suppose that any wretched old woman picking rags out of a dust heap could by any amount of experience become greater than Dante, Newton, and Napoleon rolled into one. She would always be a subordinate character; the exponent of a class, with the class-soul, and little more. Isabella is wrong in saying that "the poor beetle that we tread upon, in corporal sufferance finds a pang as great as when a giant dies." The old woman's whole sense of individuality is less than that of the philanthropist who, judging others by himself, performs such sacrifices in her behalf. Not that I would accuse most philanthropists of this error; on the contrary, I think, they are particularly clear-sighted on this point; hence they rightly direct their efforts to classes more than to individuals. In fact it is the very foundation of charity that a man should be respected as an embodiment of the race, however worthless he may be as an individual.

The principle that the essence of a symbol is formal not material has one or two important consequences. Suppose I rub out this word (*six*) and write *six*. Here is not a second word but the first over again; they are identical. Now can identity be interrupted or ought we to say that the word existed although it was unwritten? This word *six* implies that *twice three* is *five and one*. This is eternal truth; a truth which always is and must be; which would be though there were not six things in the universe to number, since it would still remain true that *five and one* would have been *twice three*. Now this *truth* is the word, *six;* if by *six* we mean not this chalk line, but that wherein *six, sex,* ἕξ, *sechs, zes, seis, sei* agree. Truth, it is said, is never without a witness; and, indeed, the fact itself—the state of things—is a symbol of the general fact through the principles of induction; so that the true symbol has an interpretant so long as it is true. And as it is identical with its interpretant, it always exists. Thus, the necessary and true symbol is immortal. And man must also be so, provided he is vivified by the truth. This is an immortality very different indeed from what most people hope for, although it does not conflict with the latter. I do not *know* that the Mohammedan paradise is not true, only I have no evidence that it is. Animal existence is certainly a pleasure, though some speak of being weary of it; but I think it is confessed by the most cultivated peoples that it is not immortal, otherwise they would consider the brutes as immortal. Spiritual existence, such as a man has in him whom he carries along with him in his opinions and sentiments—sympathy, love—this is what serves as evidence of man's absolute worth, and this is the existence which logic finds to be certainly immortal. It is not an impersonal existence; for personality lies in the unity of the *I think*—which is the unity of symbolization, the unity of consistency—and belongs to every symbol. It is not an existence, cut off from the external world, for feeling and attention are essential elements of the symbol itself. It is, however, a changed existence; one in which there are no longer any of the glories of *vision* for colors require an animal eye; and in the same way all the feelings will be different.

This immortality is one which depends upon the man's being a true symbol. If instead of *six,* we had written *Jove,* we should have had a

symbol which has but a contingent existence; it has no everlasting witness in the nature of things and will pass away or remain only in men's
memories without exciting any response in their hearts. It is, indeed,
true so far as it means a *supreme being;* its generic soul is true and eternal, but its specific and individual soul is but a shadow.

Each man has his own peculiar character. It enters into all he does.
It is in his consciousness and not a mere mechanical trick, and therefore it is by the principles of the last lecture a cognition; but as it enters
into all his cognition, it is a cognition of *things in general.* It is therefore
the man's philosophy, his way of regarding things; not a philosophy of
the head alone—but one which pervades the whole man. This idiosyncrasy is the idea of the man, and if this idea is true he lives forever; if
false, his individual soul has but a contingent existence.

That the idiosyncrasy of a man—his peculiar character—is his peculiar philosophy, is best seen in the earliest stages of its formation before
those complications have been developed which render it difficult to
seize upon it. The cunning speeches of children just as they begin to
talk often startle one by their philosophical nature. The drawer of
Harper's Magazine has been filled for years with the sayings of "our
three year old"—who seems blessed with perennial three-year-old-ness
—but if all these stories are true, they are very valuable as showing the
character of the childish mind in general, and particularly the philosophical tendencies of children. I shall not trouble you with the recita-
tion of any of these funny stories—they are stale and therefore flat; but
I will mention a case, which has nothing laughable in it—but which
illustrates remarkably well how the peculiar differences of men are differences of philosophian method. A certain child who is rather backward in learning to speak,—not from dullness, but from a want of apti-
tude in imitating the words which it hears,—has got to use three words
only; and what are these? *Name, story,* and *matter.* He says *name* when
he wishes to know the name of a person or thing; *story* when he wishes
to hear a narration or description; and *matter*—a highly abstract and
philosophical term—when he wishes to be acquainted with the cause of
anything. *Name, story,* and *matter,* therefore, make the foundation of
this child's philosophy. What a wonderful thing that his individuality
should have been shown so strongly, at that age, in selecting those three
words out of all the equally common ones which he heard about him.
Already he has made his list of categories, which is the principal part
of any philosophy. Constantly, in using these words, this philosophy
becomes more and more impressed upon him until, when he arrives at

maturity of intellect, he may be able to show that it is a profound and legitimate classification. Tell me a man's *name,* his *story,* and his *matter* or character; and I know about all there is to know of him. Aristotle says there are two questions to be asked concerning anything: the ὅτι and the διότι, the *what* and the *why*—the account of premises and the rational account or explanation; or as this child would say the *story* and the *matter;* but Aristotle has not noticed that previous to either of these questions must come the fixing of the attention upon the object—the determination of the mind to it as an object—and the demand for this determination is asking for its *name.* Here we have therefore in this child, a philosophy which furnishes an emendation upon the mighty Aristotle—the leader of the thought of ages, the prince of philosophers. But why should I presume to expound that soul's philosophy; could I enter fully into it he would have no private personality—he would not be the mysterious Island that every soul is to every other. No, I dare not attempt to fathom the awful depths of that child's possibilities; when he grows up, in some way and to some degree he will manifest his character, his philosophy; then we can judge as much of it as we can see, but its intrinsic worth we never can judge; it is hid forever in the bosom of its God.

Gentlemen and ladies, I announce to you this theory of immortality for the first time. It is poorly said, poorly thought; but its foundation is the rock of truth. And at least it will serve to illustrate what use might be made by mightier hands of this reviled science, logic, *nec ad melius vivendum, nec ad commodius disserendum.*

There is another important corollary which may be drawn from the law of symbols. As each thing has its symbol, so every thing has its symbol. I do not mean the empty conception of *being,* the interpretant of absolutely undetermined feeling whose comprehension is *naught;* nor the blind conception of *substance,* the interpretant of absolutely undetermined attention. But that symbol whose information is all-embracing; which signifies every fact about everything, not contingently but necessarily. As every soul of man is a relative philosophy so this symbol is the absolute unattainable philosophy. This is the Creator of the World since all is necessarily conformed thereto. A personal being for the same reason that all symbols are personal, but also further the well-spring of all personality since only by virtue of this Law does the unity of consistency become part of the finite symbol. This infinite Symbol being necessary denotes not the contingent facts of the universe but the absolute law in all its detail and unity to which the universe is subjected, but this law is essentially identical with the Symbol since it is, like every fact, the symbol of itself. The interpretant of the symbol like every interpretant is also essentially identical with the symbol; and finally the ground of the symbolization or the comprehension of the symbol, since it completely determines the symbol in all respects, is also essentially identical with it. Here, therefore, we have a divine trinity of the object, interpretant, and ground. Each fully constitutes the symbol and yet all are essential to it. Nor are they the same thing under different points of view but three things which attain identity when the symbol attains infinite information. In many respects, this trinity agrees with the Christian trinity; indeed I am not aware that there are any points of disagreement. The interpretant is evidently the Divine *Logos* or word; and if our former guess that a Reference to an interpretant is Paternity be right, this would be also the *Son of God*. The *ground*, being that partaking of which is requisite to any communication with the Symbol, corresponds in its function to the Holy Spirit. I will not, however, carry this speculation any further, as it may be offensive to the prejudices of some who are present. I will only say that if anyone wishes to use this as an argument for the Holy Trinity he must remember that the System of logic must first be accepted upon which it rests. This may conflict with something else he desires to find true.

With reference to this conception of the deity it may be asked whether such a God would be a God of Prayer. Here it is necessary to make a distinction between what I shall call spiritual and mechanical prayer. I may illustrate this distinction by a comparison with the prayer of a child to its earthly father. Suppose a child to get up on its father's knee and ask to be loved. That would be an instinctive motion connected with an emotion and would certainly find a response in the father's breast. Suppose, again, that a child were to come and make a long harangue to its father, requesting that he would not neglect his paternal duties but would exercise a proper superintendence over its discipline and education, would see that its masters were proper persons, and in particular were to take it away from a certain school which the father must already know perfectly well to be an unfit place. In an earthly father, this would scarcely meet with a respectful hearing. With reference to a prayer of the first kind, there can be no doubt that it would find its interpretant in the divine symbol, being an emotion full of truth. An answer it would also receive through the proper chain of material necessary antecedents. On the other hand, the question of the efficacy of the second kind of prayer is altogether a question of fact. It admits of a rigid solution, by observation—and ought to be submitted to methodical examination. The prophets of old, if we are to believe what is written, had faith enough to submit their praying to the test of experiment—and miracles were wrought with no other object. Now, of course, the answering any such prayer as a prayer for rain, is a miracle. No one can deny that. The question is whether in the long run there is any more tendency to rain when it has been prayed for than when it has not. Statistics must answer that. If one prayer out of a hundred is heard, the statistics would show it. These statistics are undoubtedly at hand. I take it all meteorologists note upon their journals whenever rain is prayed for; for it would plainly prevent any discovery of the regular laws of the weather if their action is continually interfered with by miracles which are not taken account of. We have only, therefore, to ask the meteorologists what is the effect of prayer upon the weather and they can tell us at once.

Having now sufficiently illustrated the manner in which the distinctions of logic may be applied to metaphysics, I shall conclude the lecture with a little sketch of the history of this method of metaphysical research.

Memoranda Concerning the
Aristotelean Syllogism

(*P 18: Privately printed and*)
Distributed at the Lowell Institute,
November 1866

The QUANTITY of Propositions is the respect in which *Universal* and *Particular* Propositions differ. The QUALITY of Propositions is the respect in which *Affirmative* and *Negative* Propositions differ.

NAMES AND SIGNS FOR PROPOSITIONS

Universal Affirmative: **A:** Any S is P.
Particular Affirmative: **I:** Some S is P.
Universal Negative: **E:** Any S is not P.
Particular Negative: **O:** Some S is not P.

Terms occupying the places of S and P in the above, are called the logical *Subject* and *Predicate*.

RELATIONS OF PROPOSITIONS

In the following diagram, the different propositions are supposed to have the same logical Subject and Predicate. The lines connecting A with O, and E with I, are meant to indicate that these connected propositions contradict one another. The sign ⊳ has its broad end towards a proposition which implies another, and its point toward the proposition implied.

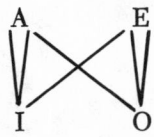

RULE, CASE, AND RESULT

A syllogism in the first figure argues from a *Rule*, and the subsumption of a *Case*, to the *Result* of that rule in that case.

> *Rule:* Any man is mortal,
> *Case:* Napoleon III is a man;
> *Result:* Napoleon III is mortal.

The Rule must be universal; and the Case affirmative. And the subject of the Rule must be the predicate of the Case. The Result has the quality of the rule and the quantity of the case; and has for its subject the subject of the case, and for its predicate the predicate of the rule.

The letters A, E, I, O, in the following diagram are so arranged that inferences can be made along the straight lines.

It is important to observe that the second and third figures are *apagogical,* that is, infer a thing to be false in order to avoid a false result which would follow from it. That which is thus reduced to an absurdity is a Case in the second figure, and a Rule in the third.

THE THREE FIGURES

Figure 1

Assertion of Rule,

Assertion of Case;

Assertion of Result.

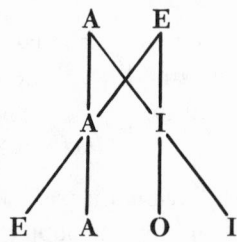

Figure 2

Assertion of Rule,

Denial of Result;

Denial of Case.

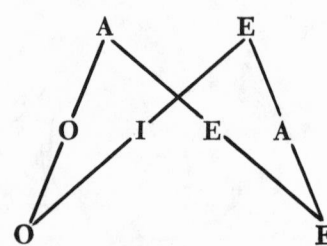

Figure 3

Denial of Result,

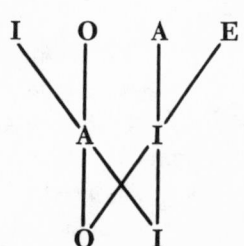

Assertion of Case;

Denial of Rule.

To *contrapose* two terms or propositions is to transpose them, and at the same time substitute for each its contradictory. The second figure is derived from the first by the contraposition of the Case and Result, the third by the contraposition of the Rule and Result. The Rule and Case of the first figure cannot be contraposed, because they already occupy the same logical position, namely, that of a *premiss;* their contraposition in either of the other figures converts these figures into one another.

Let F, S, T, denote syllogisms of the first, second, and third figures, respectively. And let s, t, f, denote the processes of contraposition of the case and result, rule and result, and rule and case, respectively. Then

$$sF = S \qquad sS = F$$
$$tF = T \qquad tT = F$$
$$fS = T \qquad fT = S$$
$$s^2 = t^2 = f^2 = 1$$
$$f = st = ts \quad s = ft = tf \quad t = fs = sf$$

The following table exhibits all the moods of Aristotelean syllogism (varieties resulting from variations of the Quantity and Quality of the

	I	A	E	O
E		E	A	
A	I	A	E	O
I	A	*I*	*O*	E
O		*O*	I	

propositions). Enter at the top, the proposition asserting or denying the rule; enter at the side, the proposition asserting or denying the case; find in the body of the table the proposition asserting or denying the result. In the body of the table, propositions indicated by Italics belong to the first figure, those by Light Roman to the second figure, and those by Medium Roman to the third figure.

Two moods of the third figure, namely, A A I and E A O, are omitted, for two reasons. The first is that they correspond by contraposition to two moods in the first figure, A A I and E A O, never given by logicians, who, therefore, act inconsistently in admitting these. The second reason is, that, like those moods in the first figure, they are virtually enumerated already, if the change of a proposition from universal to particular be not an inference; but if it be, then, again like those moods of the first figure, the argument they embody may be analyzed into a syllogism and an inference from universal to particular.

The celebrated lines of William of Shyreswood(?) are here given. The vowels of the first three syllables of each word indicate the three propositions of the syllogisms. He enumerates, along with the moods of the first figure, the Theophrastean moods (two of which we omit for the same reason that we do those two in the third figure).

> *Barbara: Celarent: Darii: Ferio: Baralipton:*
> *Celantes: Dabitis: Fapesmo: Frisesomorum.*
> *Cesare: Camestres: Festino: Baroco. Darapti:*
> *Felapton: Disamis: Datisi: Bocardo: Ferison.*

The diagram upon the opposite page shows the relations in which the second and third figures stand to the first. In order to understand the seven syllogistic formulas there set down, it is necessary to notice that propositions may be divided into four parts: 1st the *Any* or *Some,* 2d the Subject, 3d the *is* or *is not,* and 4th the predicate. When a proposition admits of varieties in either of these parts, they are shown in the diagram by two words or letters, one above the other, as $\frac{is}{is\ not}$ in the rule of the first figure. Two independent variations may occur in one formula, and the variations of different parts are independent, but in the same part either the upper or lower line must always be read, in any one syllogism.

For example, the result in the first figure has four forms; Any *or* some S is *or* is not P; but if *Some* has been read in the case, *some* must also be read in the result. So in the second figure, where a variation is possible in the quality of either premiss; but the same line of the third part of both propositions must be taken.

Fig. 1   Fig. 2   Fig. 3

Any M $^{is}_{is\,not}$ P   Any M $^{is}_{is\,not}$ P $^{Some}_{Any}$ S $^{is\,not}_{is}$ P

$^{Any}_{Some}$ S is M $^{Some}_{Any}$ S $^{is\,not}_{is}$ P $^{Any}_{Some}$ S is M

$^{Any}_{Some}$ S $^{is}_{is\,not}$ P $^{Some}_{Any}$ S is not M   Some M $^{is\,not}_{is}$ P

Any $^{not\,P}_{P}$ is not M   Any $^{some\ S}_{S}$ S $^{is\,not}_{is}$ P

$^{Some}_{Any}$ S is $^{not\,P}_{P}$ Some M is $^{some\ S}_{S}$

$^{Some}_{Any}$ S is not M   Some M $^{is\,not}_{is}$ P

Any $_{not\,P}^{P}$ is not $^{some\ S}_{S}$ Any $_{some\ s}^{S}$ s is M

Any M is $_{not\,P}^{P}$ Some $_{P}^{not\,P}$ is $^{S}_{some\ s}$

Any M is not $^{some\ S}_{S}$ Some $_{P}^{not\,P}$ is M

At the top of the diagram are given the formulas of the first figure, and of the second and third, as derived from that of the first by contraposition of the propositions. Under the second and third figures, respectively, are given forms expressing the same arguments in the first figure. It is necessary to study carefully the manner in which this reduction to the first figure is effected.

It will be perceived that the arrangements of the terms in the three figures, as determined by the rules given on pages 506–7, are as follows: where the first letter of each pair indicates the subject of a proposition of the syllogism and the second its predicate.

	Fig. 1	*Fig. 2*	*Fig. 3*
1st.	B A	N M	Σ Π
2d.	Γ B	Ξ M	Σ P
3d.	Γ A	Ξ N	P Π

It is plain that there are two ways of transposing the arrangements of the terms of the second and third figures without removing a term from the conclusion, so as to give the term the same arrangement as that of the first figure. This is shown in the following table, where the

columns headed s show the propositions whose terms are to be transposed, while those headed m show the propositions to be transposed.[1]

	Fig. 2		Fig. 3	
	s	m	s	m
Short Reduction	1st		2d	
Long Reduction	2d 3d	2d 1st	1st 3d	1st 2d

The effect of these transpositions is here shown.

SECOND FIGURE

	Short Red.	Long Red.
N M	M N	M ≡
≡ M	≡ M	N M
≡ N	≡ N	N ≡

THIRD FIGURE

	Short Red.	Long Red.
Σ Π	Σ Π	Σ P
Σ P	P Σ	Π Σ
P Π	P Π	Π P

It must next be shown how these transpositions may be made, in
syllogisms themselves.

The short reduction of the second figure is shown in the second syllogism of that column of the large diagram headed Fig. 2. The term
not-P is introduced. This we define as that class to which some or any
S belongs, when it is not P. Accordingly, for 'some or any S is not P',
we can substitute 'some or any S is not-P', and this substitution is made
in the reduction. But we cannot, on that account, substitute 'any M is
not-P' for 'any M is not P'. For 'any M is not P', is substituted, in the

---

1. "Ubicunque ponitur *s* significatur quod propositio . . . debet converti sim-
pliciter . . . et ubicunque ponitur *m* debet fieri transpositio in præmissis."—*Petrus
Hispanus*

reduction, 'any P is not M'; and for 'any M is P' is substituted 'any not-P is not M'. The only syllogisms by which these substitutions can be justified are these: —

Any M is not P,   Any M is   P,
Any P is   P;   Any not-P is not P;
∴ Any P is not M.   ∴ Any not-P is not M.

Both these are syllogisms in the second figure.

The short reduction of the third figure is shown in the second syllogism of the column headed Fig. 3. The term *some-S* is introduced. The definition of this term is that it is that part of S which is or is not P when some S is or is not P. Hence, we can and do substitute 'Any some-S is or is not P' for 'Some S is or is not P', though we could not substitute 'Any some-S is M' for 'Some S is M'. For 'Some S is M' we substitute 'Some M is S'; and for 'Any S is M' we substitute 'Some M is some-S'; and these substitutions are justified by inferences which can be expressed syllogistically, only thus:—

Any S is S,   Some S is some-S,
Some S is M;   Any S is   M;
∴ Some M is S.   ∴ Some M is some-S.

These are both syllogisms in the third figure.

The long reduction of the second syllogism is shown in the third syllogism of the column headed Fig. 2. Here not-P is defined as that class to which any M belongs which is not P. Hence we can substitute 'Any M is not-P' for 'Any M is not P'. Some-S is defined as in the short reduction of the third figure. Hence, for 'Some S is or is not P', we can say 'Any some-S is or is not P'. Then, we use the inferences which are expressed syllogistically, thus:—

Any $^{some}_{S}$ S is not P,   Any $^{some}_{S}$ S is   P,
Any P   is   P;   Any not P is not P;
∴ Any P is not $^{some S.}_{S.}$ ∴ Any not P is not $^{some S.}_{S.}$

These are both syllogisms of the second figure. Substituting their conclusions for the second premiss of the second figure and transposing the premisses we obtain the premisses of the reduction. The conclusion of the reduction justifies that of the second figure, by inferences which are expressed syllogistically, as follows:—

Any   M is not some-S,   Any M is not S,
Some S is   some-S;   Any S is   S;
∴ Some S is not   M.   ∴ Any S is not M.

Both these are syllogisms of the second figure.

The long reduction of the third figure is shown in the third syllogism of the column headed Fig. 3. Some S is here defined as that part of S which is M when some S is M. Hence, for 'Some S is M', we can substitute 'Any some-S is M'. Not-P is defined as in the short reduction of the second figure. Hence, in place of 'Some or any S is not P', we can put 'Some or any S is not-P'. In place of 'Some S is P or not-P' we again substitute 'Some P or not-P is S', and in place of 'Any S is P or not-P' we substitute 'Some P or not-P is some-S', in virtue of inferences which are expressed syllogistically thus:—

Any   S is S,   Some S is some-S,
Some S is $^{\text{not P}}_{\text{P}}$;   Any S is $^{\text{not P}}_{\text{P}}$;
∴ Some $^{\text{not P}}_{\text{P}}$ is S.   ∴ Some $^{\text{not P}}_{\text{P}}$ is some S.

These are syllogisms of the third figure.

Then, the premisses being transposed, we have the premisses of the reduction. The conclusion of the reduction justifies that of the third figure by inferences which are expressed syllogistically, thus:—

Any   not-P is   P,   Any   P is P,
Some not-P is   M;   Some P is M;
∴ Some   M is not-P.   ∴ Some M is P.

These are syllogisms of the third figure.

The reduction called *reductio per impossibile,* is nothing more than the repetition or inverse repetition of that contraposition by which the second and third figures have been obtained. It is not *ostensive* (that is, does not yield an argument with essentially the same premisses and conclusion as that of the argument thus to be reduced), but apagogical, that is, shows by the first figure that the contradiction of the conclusion of the second or third leads to the contradiction of one of the premisses.

Contradiction arises from a difference in both quantity and quality. But it is to be observed that in the contraposition which gives the second figure, a change of the *quality* alone, and in that which gives the third figure, a change of the *quantity* alone of the contraposed propositions is sufficient. This shows that the two contrapositions are of essentially different kinds. The reductions *per impossibile* of the second and third figures respectively involve, therefore, these inferences:—

Fig. 2

The Result follows from the Case;
∴ The negative of the Case follows from the negative of the Result.

Fig. 3

The Result follows from the Rule;
∴ The Rule changed in Quantity follows from the result changed in Quantity.

These inferences may also be expressed thus:—

Fig. 2

Whatever (S) is M is $\genfrac{}{}{0pt}{}{\text{P};}{\text{not P}}$;
∴ Whatever (S) is $\genfrac{}{}{0pt}{}{\text{not P}}{\text{P}}$ is not M.

Fig. 3

Any $\genfrac{}{}{0pt}{}{\text{S}}{\text{some s}}$ is whatever (P or not-P) M is;
∴ Some M is whatever (P or not P) $\genfrac{}{}{0pt}{}{\text{some S}}{\text{S}}$ is.

And if we omit the limitations in parentheses, which do not alter the essential nature of the inferences, we have

Fig. 2

Any M is $\genfrac{}{}{0pt}{}{\text{P};}{\text{not P}}$;
∴ Any $\genfrac{}{}{0pt}{}{\text{not P}}{\text{P}}$ is not M.

Fig. 3

Any $\genfrac{}{}{0pt}{}{\text{S}}{\text{some s}}$ is M;
∴ Some M is $\genfrac{}{}{0pt}{}{\text{some S}}{\text{S}}$.

We have seen above that the former of these can only be reduced to a syllogism in the second figure, and the latter only to one in the third figure.

The ostensive reductions of each figure are also apagogical reductions of the other. There are also the following:—

Any not-M is $\genfrac{}{}{0pt}{}{\text{not S,}}{\text{not some S,}}$ Any some-M is $\genfrac{}{}{0pt}{}{\text{some S,}}{\text{S,}}$

Any $\genfrac{}{}{0pt}{}{\text{not P}}{\text{P}}$ is not-M;   Any $\genfrac{}{}{0pt}{}{\text{some P}}{\text{some not P}}$ is some-M;

Any $\genfrac{}{}{0pt}{}{\text{not P}}{\text{P}}$ is $\genfrac{}{}{0pt}{}{\text{not S.}}{\text{not some S.}}$ Any $\genfrac{}{}{0pt}{}{\text{some P}}{\text{some not P}}$ is $\genfrac{}{}{0pt}{}{\text{some S.}}{\text{S.}}$

But all these reductions involve the peculiar inferences we have found in those which have been examined, inasmuch as they are but complications of the latter.

Hence, it appears that no syllogism of the second or third figure can be reduced to the first, without taking for granted an inference which can only be expressed syllogistically in that figure from which it has been reduced. These inferences are not strictly syllogistic, because one of the propositions taken as a premiss in the syllogistic expression is a logical fact. But the fact that each can only be expressed in the second or third figure of syllogism, as the case may be, shows that those figures alone involve the respective principles of those inferences. Hence, it is proved that every figure involves the principle of the first figure, but the second and third figures contain other principles, besides.

/On a Method of Searching for the Categories/

MS 133: November–December 1866

INTRODUCTION
§1. Impressions

Intuition is a term, which by the consent of philosophers stands for *immediate cognition;* but what *immediate cognition* stands for is not quite so well settled. In its most approved sense, however, it means any mental representation which does not represent its object by representing another conscious representation of the latter; in other words, it is that knowledge between which and the thing no other representation in consciousness, intervenes. Unfortunately, this definition turns on the word *consciousness,*—a sadly equivocal expression, itself. Still, the widest acceptation of this term, to include the presentative character of all that is within us, is to be preferred both on the ground of usage and because it is the only way we have of expressing that most important conception. Thus interpreted, *immediate cognition* is the same as what is otherwise termed an ultimate fact; that is, a premiss not itself a conclusion, an empirical constituent of knowledge not itself containing non-empirical parts, in short, an *impression*.

Whether there be any such ultimate premisses is a difficult question. It amounts, however, merely to this; whether the boundary of consciousness is in consciousness or out of it. In whichever way it be decided, the employment of a word to denote that boundary is legitimate.

No one can know what an impression is like, in itself; for a recognized difference between two impressions would be a difference between them *as compared,* that is as mediately known, and not between them *in themselves.* An impression in itself is an uncomprehended impression, and hence, an undifferentiated sensation, like the feeling of our heart's motion. Colour is sometimes given as an example of an impression. It is a bad one; because the simplest colour is almost as complicated as a piece of music. Colour depends upon the *relations* between different parts of the impression; and, therefore, the differences between colours are differences between harmonies; and to see this difference we must have the elementary impressions whose relation makes the harmony. So that colour is not an impression, but an inference.

Whatever part impressions play in our knowledge, they need to be reduced by the understanding to the unity of consistency and therefore to be combined, and that not by chaotic aggregation but in a determinate form. This form or way of combining impressions is an element of cognition not given in the impressions combined, but added to them in order to reduce them to the requisite unity. It is, therefore, a *hypothetically* adjoined element; for a hypothesis is something assumed in order to reduce an otherwise incomprehensible *datum* to unity. This element of cognition is termed *conception*.

We have, then, first an infinite manifold of points of impression upon the circumference of consciousness. Second, these are embraced into different groups by conceptions, and these conceptions by others until one conception is universal and embraces all. Third, if this conception has any manifoldness, it is itself subjected to another; and so on untill Fourthly, all are subjected to the unity of consistency or *I think* which is the centre of consciousness.

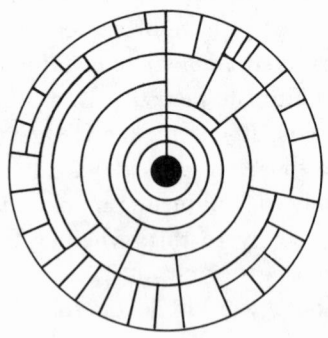

§2. Substance

Impression in general or as such, is itself by virtue of its generality not an impression but a conception. An impression does not so much as conceive itself to be an impression. It is an undifferentiated feeling whose vagueness is feebly shadowed forth by that sense of dyspepsia which tinges a man's sentiments with melancholy without being directly noticed. Any reflection upon an impression, since it is a step towards bringing it to the unity of consistency, is a conception. To say, therefore, that this or that is an ultimate fact or even that it is present or is a fact, begins to go beyond the immediate fact itself and to be a hypothesis. Hence the predicate of such a statement, or *what is present in general,* is a hypothetic conception; that is, it cannot be applied to a subject without hypothesis. The hypothetic character of that predicate, however, consists merely in the impression's being viewed subjectively or reflected upon as being present. Now this reflection does nothing more than enable us to //differentiate/discriminate// the character of the fact from the fact itself; and therefore to say that "A is immediately present" is merely to say that A can have attached to it a predicate, real or verbal. But as this predicate is left entirely indeterminate, what has been said of A is an empty form. It has, therefore, the form of hypothesis without its matter; it is the starting-goal of all hypothetic thought. This conception of the immediately present as such, since it implies merely that A is the subject of a proposition, but not a predicate (since predicates are mediate cognitions), is properly indicated by the term *substance.*

§3. Being

When we can make a proposition, we *understand* the subject of it so far as the predicate indicates. Thus, when we say "man is intelligent," we have an understanding of *man* in respect to his mind. It is undoubtedly very confused in this instance, but the fact that it can only be made more distinct by predicating still more of man, shows that the unity to which the understanding reduces impressions is the unity of a proposition. This unity consists in the connection of the predicate with the subject; and introduces the conception of *being,* or that which is implied in the copula. The copula has two meanings, *actually is* and *would be,* as in the two expressions "There *is* no griffin" and "A griffin *is* a winged quadruped." But as both these propositions afford understanding of their subjects, the meanings of the copulas should be comprehended under *being.*

Being introduces nothing into the thought; for "A griffin is or would be" means nothing. Hence, this conception is not materially hypothetical. It is rather the end of all hypothesis—the accomplishment of that unity for which hypotheses are instituted. If we say, "The ink is black," the ink is the *substance,* from which its blackness has not been differentiated; and the *is* while it leaves the substance just as it was seen, explains its confusedness by the application of blackness to it, as a hypothetical predicate.

Though *being* does not affect the subject, it implies an indefinite determinability of the predicate. For, if one could know the copula and predicate of a proposition; as "——— is a tailed man," he would know that the predicate applied to something supposable, at least. Accordingly, we have propositions whose subjects are entirely indefinite as "There is a beautiful ellipse," where the subject is *something* merely. But we have no propositions whose predicate is entirely indeterminate for it would be quite senseless to say "A has the common characters of all things," since there is no such character. Hence, to say that a *quality* has being or finds being, means something; but to say that *substance* has being is absurd for it must cease to be substance before being or non-being, in the present sense, are applicable to it.

Thus substance and being are the two poles of thought. Substance is the beginning, being the *end* of all conception. Substance is inapplicable to a predicate, *being* is equally so to a subject.

§4. Precision, Discrimination, and Dissociation

Precision and abstraction are two terms for the same process; and are now limited not merely to separation by the mind, but even to a particular kind of mental separation, namely, that by *attention* to one point and *neglect* of another. That which is *attended* to is said to be *prescinded;* and that which is neglected is said to be *abstracted from.* This definition should be strictly adhered to, however narrowly it may limit the application of the terms. Attention is a definite conception or *supposition* of one element of consciousness, without any positive *supposition* of the other.

Abstraction, therefore, supposes a greater distinction between its members than *discrimination* which is the mere recognition of the difference between the presence or absence of an element of cognition; but it supposes less distinction than *dissociation* which is the consciousness of one thing without the necessary simultaneous consciousness of the other. Thus, I can discriminate red from blue, space from colour, and colour from space; but not red from colour. I can prescind red from blue, and space from colour (as is manifest from the fact that I actually believe that there is an uncoloured space between my face and the page), but I cannot prescind colour from space, nor red from colour. I can dissociate red from blue, but I cannot dissociate space from colour, colour from space, nor red from colour. In the following table O shows what I can hold and X what I cannot hold.

	blue without red	space without colour	colour without space	red without colour
By discrimination	O	O	O	X
By precision	O	O	X	X
By dissociation	O	X	X	X

If A can be discriminated or dissociated from B, B can also be separated from A, in the same mode. But precision is not thus reciprocal; but on the contrary it is frequently the case that though A cannot be prescinded from B, B can be prescinded from A. This circumstance is easily accounted for. Elementary conceptions only arise upon the occasion of experience; that is they are produced for the first time according to a general law the condition of which is the existence of certain impressions. Now if a conception does not reduce the impressions which it accompanies to unity, it would be a mere arbitrary addition to the latter, for there is no other condition for the production of a conception except that it shall make impressions comprehensible. Now if the impressions could be definitely conceived without the conception, the conception would not reduce them to unity. But attention is definite conception; therefore impressions (or more immediate conceptions) cannot be attended to, to the neglect of an elementary conception which reduces them to unity. On the other hand, when such a conception has once been obtained, there is no reason in general why the premises which have occasioned it should not be neglected, and therefore the explaining conception may abstract from the more immediate ones and from the impressions.

§5. Method of Searching for the Categories

Every conception is introduced for the purpose of bringing the manifold to unity; and in the case of an elementary conception this function is a condition of the possibility of the conception's arising. A universal conception is one which is applicable to every aggregate of impressions. The end of such a conception is either to unite the manifold of substance in general or to conjoin to the latter some conception necessary to its being brought to unity.

These facts afford the basis for a mode of discovering all the conceptions which reduce the manifold substance to the unity of being. For if we begin with being and ask what it conjoins to substance, the answer will be easily obtained by observing the occasion of the introduction of being. Then the application to substance of this conception, which being joins to it, is the immediate justification and condition of the introduction of being, and is, therefore, the first conception in order in passing from being to substance. Now we may treat this conception in the same way in which we have treated being. That is, we may ask 1st what is the occasion of the introduction of this conception, 2nd What conception besides substance is required in such a state of cognition, which is joined to substance by the given conception. Then this second conception is the next conception in order in passing from being to substance. And we may repeat this process until we get to a conception which does not unite anything to substance but only brings the manifold of substance itself together, and this will be the last conception.

These conceptions between *being* and *substance* are termed *accidents;* and universal conceptions are termed *categories.*

$$\text{CATEGORIES} \begin{cases} \text{BEING} \\ \text{ACCIDENTS} \begin{cases} \text{Quality} \\ \text{Relation} \\ \text{Representation.} \end{cases} \\ \text{SUBSTANCE} \end{cases}$$

It should be noticed that throughout this process of finding the categories as well as throughout the book, *introspection* is never resorted to. Nothing is assumed respecting what is thought which cannot be securely inferred from admissions which the thinker will make concerning external facts.

§6. The Ground

The conception of *being* arises upon the formation of a proposition. A proposition, besides a term to express the substance, always has another to express the quality of that substance; and the function of the conception of being is to unite the quality to the substance. Quality, therefore, is the first conception in order in passing from being to substance.

Quality, at first sight, like every other elementary conception, seems to be given in the impression. Such results of introspection are untrustworthy.

A proposition asserts the applicability of a mediate conception to a more immediate one,—asserts, that is, that the former affords a means of reducing the latter to unity. Since this is *asserted,* the more mediate conception is clearly regarded independently of this circumstance, for otherwise the two conceptions would not be distinguished, but one would be thought through the other, without this latter being an object of thought, at all. The mediate conception, then, in order to be *asserted* to be applied to the other must be considered first without regard to this circumstance, and taken immediately. But, taken immediately it transcends what is given, the more immediate conception, and its applicability to the latter becomes hypothetical. Take, for example, the proposition "Ink is black." Here, the conception *ink* is the more immediate; that of *black* is the more mediate, which to be predicated of the former must be discriminated from it and considered *in itself,* not as applied to an object but simply as embodying a quality, *blackness.* Now this *blackness,* is a pure *species* or abstraction, and its application is entirely hypothetical.

In the words of a philosopher of the 12th Century "cum dicitur 'Socrates est rationalis' hic est sensus 'Socrates est unus de subjectis huic formae quae est rationalitas'."[1] *Embodying rationality* defines *rational.* We mean the same thing when we say "the ink is black" as when we say "there is blackness in the ink"; *embodying blackness* defines *black.* The proof is that these conceptions are applied indifferently to precisely the same facts. If, therefore, they were different, the one which was first applied would fulfill every function of the other; so that one of them would be superfluous. But now a superfluous elementary conception is

1. *De Generibus et speciebus,* p. 528.

impossible; for a superfluous conception would be an arbitrary fiction, whereas elementary conceptions arise only upon the requirement of experience. Moreover, the conception of a *pure abstraction* is indispensible, because we cannot comprehend an agreement of two things except as an agreement in some *respect*, and this respect is such a pure abstraction as *blackness*.

The pure abstraction reference to which constitutes a *quality* may be called a *ground,* of the character of the substance which has the quality. Reference to a ground, then, is the first accident. It cannot be prescinded from *being*, but being can be prescinded from it.

§7. The Correlate[2]

All students of philosophy know that we can become aware of any quality only through the relation of its subject of inhesion to something else; and it is an equally familiar fact that no relation can have place without a quality or reference to a *ground*. The occasion of the introduction of reference to a ground, therefore, is generalization or contrast.

In generalization and contrast, the primary substance has annexed to it a correlate. Reference to a correlate, then, is the next conception in order after reference to a ground. This conception is so easy to seize that no elucidation of it is needed. It cannot be prescinded from reference to a ground, although this latter can be prescinded from it.

§8. The Interpretant

Reference to a correlate is clearly justified and made possible solely by comparison. Let us inquire, then, in what comparison consists. Suppose we wish to compare L and Γ; we shall imagine one of these letters to be turned over upon the line on which it is written as an axis; we shall then imagine that it is laid upon the other letter and that it is transparent so that we can see that the two coincide. In this way, we shall form a new image which mediates between the two letters, in as much as it represents one when turned over to be an exact likeness of the other. Suppose, we think of a murderer as being in relation to a murdered person; in this case we conceive the act of the murder, and in this conception it is represented that corresponding to every mur-

2. This section should be enlarged and rewritten.

derer (as well as to every murder) there is a murdered person; and
thus we resort again to a mediating representation which represents
the relate as standing for a correlate with which the mediating representation is itself in relation. Suppose, we look out the word *homme* in
a French dictionary; we shall find opposite to it the word *man,* which,
so placed, represents *homme* as representing the same two-legged creature which *man* itself represents. In a similar way, it will be found
that every comparison requires, besides the related thing, the ground
and the correlate, also a *mediating representation which represents the
relate to be a representation of the same correlate which this mediating
representation itself represents.* Such a mediating representation, I call
an *interpretant,* because it fulfills the office of an interpreter who says
that a foreigner says the same thing which he himself says.

Every reference to a correlate, then, unites to the substance a reference to an interpretant; which is, therefore, the next conception in
the order we have adopted.

It must not be supposed that in giving a definition of interpretant,
we admit at all that reference to an interpretant is a compounded conception. This definition is only a verbal one; for the conception of representation which it introduces itself contains that of reference to an
interpretant. Reference to an interpretant, is simply the *addressing* of
an impression to a conception. To *address* or *appeal to,* is an act we, in
fact, suppose everything to perform, whether we attend to the circumstance or not. It is unanalyzable, I think; though it may be expressed
more perspicuously by a periphrasis, as above.

It may perhaps be objected, that since an interpretant is necessarily
a correlate, reference to an interpretant is merely a particular determination of the conception of reference to a correlate, and should not be
coördinated with the latter. But an interpretant is not referred to as
establishing a relation to a correlate, in so far as it is a correlate; it is
not therefore *quatenus ipsum* a correlate.

Reference to an interpretant is rendered possible and justified by
that which renders possible and justifies comparison. But this is clearly
the diversity of impressions. It is plain, that if we had but one impression, this impression would not require to be reduced to unity, and
would, therefore, not need to be thought of as referred to an interpretant and the conception of reference to an interpretant would not arise.
But the moment there are several impressions, that is a manifoldness
of impression, we have a feeling of complication or confusion, which

leads us to differentiate this impression from that, and they require to be brought to unity. Now they are not brought to unity until we conceive them together as being *ours*, that is, until we refer them to a conception as their interpretant. Thus the reference to an interpretant arises upon the holding together of diverse impressions, and therefore it does not join a conception to the substance, as the other two references do, but unites directly the manifold of the substance, itself. It is therefore the last conception in order, in passing from *being* to *substance*.

§9. Formal Objects

We have found between the unity of being and the manifold of substance, three universal and necessary (//*de omni*/κατὰ παντός//) conceptions; namely

> Reference to a ground
> Reference to a correlate
> Reference to an interpretant.

A ground is that pure abstraction, the embodiment of which makes a quality. A correlate is a second substance with which the first is in comparison. An interpretant, is a representation which represents that that which is referred to it is a representation of the same object which it does itself represent.

These three conceptions are all we require to erect the edifice of logic. Why they should be three is unknown; although a reason can be given for every other logical division. But this number may indicate an anthropological fact.

In the section on precision, it was shown that more immediate conceptions cannot be prescinded from elementary conceptions which explain them; while there is no such impossibility of prescinding the more mediate from the less mediate. Hence, as the order in which we have taken the three references proceeds from the more mediate to the less mediate, it follows that no reference to an interpretant can abstract from reference to a correlate; nor any reference to a correlate from reference to a ground; whereas reference to a ground may be of such a kind that it can be prescinded from reference to a correlate; and reference to a correlate may be such that it can be prescinded from reference to an interpretant. Thus the three references give three prescindible objects; namely,

   1 Single reference to a ground,
   2 Double reference to ground and correlate,
   3 Triple reference to ground, correlate, and interpretant.

These may be termed Quality, Relation, and Representation and the objects to which they belong as characters, may be called Quale, Relate, and Representamen.

The quale, the relate, and the representamen may be termed formal objects because the prescinded conceptions of them contain no reference to variously determinable impressions.

§10. Subdivision of Formal Objects

§12. Division of Formal Science

A conception which is prescindible is unconditional. Every reference which is unprescindible from another, is subject to certain conditions in consequence, because conceptions are not combined without some form of combination. This will be illustrated presently.

Now the unprescindible references are

1 The reference of the equiparant to its correlate
2 The reference of the disquiparant to its ground
3 The reference of the disquiparant to its correlate
4 The reference of the likeness to its interpretant
5 The reference of the index to its object
6 The reference of the index to its interpretant
7 The reference of the symbol to its ground
8 The reference of the symbol to its object
9 The reference of the symbol to its interpretant.

The conditions of these nine references afford nine formal sciences, by which we mean not a very extensive doctrine but one which forms a system by itself. The possibility of each of these must now be briefly illustrated.

1 Reference of equiparants to their correlates. The correlate of equiparance is related to its relate upon the same ground and in the same manner as the relate to the correlate. Accordingly, in equiparance there is no distinction of relate and correlate; for any distinction would at once constitute a disquiparance. The conception of a correlate, in its narrower sense, does not therefore belong to equiparance and it is perhaps preferable to speak of the reference of the relates of equiparance to each other, than of "the reference of equiparants to their correlates." Equiparance is in fact the constitution of a *class,* and a correlate of equiparance is nothing more than another member of the same class. By a *class* is meant a number of agreeing things.

The ground of equiparance admits of quantity; it is greater or less, according as it is more or less determinate. This quantity is termed the comprehension, intension, or depth of the equiparant. Thus, "birds and lobsters agree in being animals" and "birds and fishes agree in being vertebrate animals"; but the latter equiparance is more intensive than the former. The object of equiparance admits of quantity also; being greater the greater number of individuals are comprehended under it. This quantity is the extension or breadth of the equiparance. Those things which agree in being animals are more numerous than those which agree in being vertebrate animals.

The greater the extension of a class the less its intension and *vice versa.* For, if we add to all the individuals which agree in a certain respect another individual, it is clear that the new sum of individuals do not agree in so many respects as the old; and if we substitute for one class another whose members agree in the same respects, and more respects besides, it is clear that the former class must include the latter and another class besides.

This law of the reciprocal ratio of extension and intension forms by itself a science of *classes* or the reference of equiparants to their correlates. It may be called ———.

2 *Reference of the disquiparant to its ground.* The ground of a disquiparance has an intimate connection with a ground of equiparance. Thus *bluer* is connected with *blue.* This connection is such, that the ground of disquiparance includes the ground of equiparance and has besides a special determination which the latter has not. This is not evident in the case of a disquiparance which is merely an equiparance undetermined as to its ground, as when we say the elephant is as strong as the hippopotamus, corresponding to which relation is an equiparance of the elephant and the hippopotamus whose ground is a certain degree of

strength. But the ground of equiparance implied in this disquiparance is one less determinate than that of this equiparance, it is "strength of a hippopotamus"; for "the elephant is as strong as the hippopotamus" implies that "the elephant and the hippopotamus agree in hippopotamus-like strength." But the disquiparance implies that they are also diverse and therefore have some further determination besides that in which they agree.

The correlate of a disquiparant has a relation of disquiparance to its relate, upon a ground which may be different from the relation of the relate to the correlate. But these two grounds determine each other. Thus if A exceeds B, B is exceeded by A. This mutual determination of the two grounds is expressed by saying that one is the *inverse* of the other. A disquiparance upon its own ground is called *active;* a disquiparance upon the inverse ground is called *passive.* Thus "A is greater than B" is an active disquiparance; "A is something than which B is less," is a passive disquiparance. Sometimes the inverse grounds are the same; thus, that A equals B is the same as that A is equaled by B. The inverse of the inverse of a ground is always the ground itself; thus that A is something by which B is exceeded is the same as that A exceeds B.

[Kind of Ground]

If B is disquiparant to C, upon the same ground on which A is disquiparant to B, then A is disquiparant to C upon the same ground also. But if the grounds of the two first disquiparances are different this does not follow. If the ground of the disquiparance of B to C is the inverse of that of A to B, then the disquiparance of A to C has either one ground or the other or else rests upon some different ground altogether or does not exist at all; and, in any case, there is no ground of disquiparance between A and B which there was not between A and C or B and C. The relations give rise to a peculiar quantity of grounds of disquiparance; depending upon the number of repetitions of a given inverse disquiparance which shall just neutralize a direct disquiparance. Thus, let the ground of disquiparance of A to B be the inverse of that of B to C and suppose that they are such that there is no disquiparance between A and C. Now suppose that the ground of the disquiparance of B to C be simply inverted, that is suppose it to change from active to passive without altering in any other respect whatever. Then we have a disquiparance between A and C which is just *twice* that between

A and *B*. And thus we introduce the conception of *measure*. No other kind of quantity except the amount of the ground of a disquiparance can be measured.

The science of the reference of disquiparants to their grounds, that is the science of measurable quantity, is called *mathematics*. When only inversions are taken into account it is *algebra*. When differences in the kind of ground are taken into account, it affords (for example) *geometry*.

3 Reference of the disquiparant to its correlate. The terms, *exclusion in extension* and *opposition,* indicate the reference of a disquiparant to its correlate. The ground of a correlate besides that quantity which is measurable, and of which we have just treated and which may be termed its immediate quantity has another also which is similar to the quantity of the ground of equiparance, which may be called its intension, comprehension, or, since it is the quantity of the ground considered as embodied inversely in the correlate, it may be termed the mediate quantity. This quantity is the number of respects in which there is disquiparance. The number of individual and disquiparant correlates may be termed the extension of the disquiparance. The extension and intension of disquiparance are in inverse ratio to each other. But there is this remarkable difference between the law of equiparance and that of disquiparance; namely, that equiparance entirely undetermined in intension is no relation at all; and equiparance of one total intension is a relation, that of *identity;* whereas disquiparance of entirely undetermined intension is a most important relation, that of *contradiction* as between man and non-man; and disquiparance in the whole intension is impossible. These remarks are sufficient to show that the science of opposition usually made a part of logic, is the science of the reference of disquiparants to their correlates.

4 Reference of the likeness to its interpretant.

APPENDIX

/Diagram of the IT/

MS 52

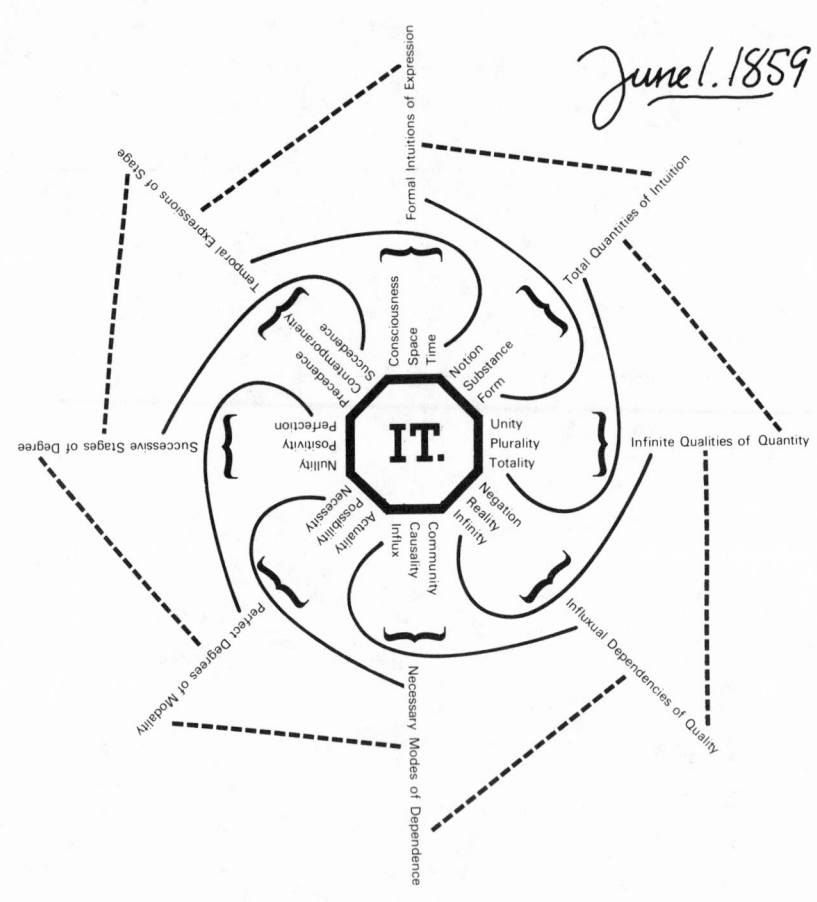

June 1. 1859

Editorial Notes

These notes serve various functions which are, generally, self-explanatory. But there are three kinds of notes that require brief explanation.

The first of these is the initial note to each selection which serves as a headnote and provides brief descriptions of the manuscript or published article and, when possible, reasons for its composition.

The second type of note identifies names, that is those not found in the *Dictionary of American Biography*, the *Dictionary of National Biography*, the 15th edition of the *Encyclopædia Britannica*, *The Encyclopedia of Philosophy*, or the *New Century Cyclopedia of Names*.

The third type of note identifies the sources of quotations. Scarcely anything in the present volume that was not published by Peirce was intended for publication in anything like the form in which he left it. He was not consistent in his use of source material. He rarely cited his source fully and often omitted documentation altogether. Sometimes he used quotation marks when he was merely paraphrasing, at other times he omitted quotation marks when transcribing verbatim. Our original policy was to identify only those passages quoted verbatim, but it was soon clear that Peirce paraphrased and interpreted the work of others extensively in these early formative years and that knowing the sources for these materials would be of help to the reader. We therefore changed our policy.

Material in quotation marks which was found to be verbatim copy or a very close paraphrase of a specific passage is identified. When Peirce put in quotation marks what is not a quotation but his own interpretation of the author to whom he is referring, we provide a reference to the passage in which the author comes nearest to saying what Peirce reported. When without using quotation marks Peirce offered a summary statement in his own words of the general view of an author on a certain point, we supply no reference, lest we do both Peirce and the author a disservice by referring to what may not be the nearest approach to the view that Peirce ascribes to that author. In the case of a rhetorical flourish in quotation marks we of course supply no note.

Every effort has been made to cite the editions that Peirce owned or that we know he used. When such information was lacking or when the edition he used was not available, we cite one that was accessible to Peirce. In many cases we have added in brackets a reference to an edition more readily available to the modern reader.

Citations are generally given in shortened form; full bibliographic information is provided in the bibliography following the editorial notes. Books we know Peirce owned are identified by the degree symbol (°).

My Life

Two forms of this survive. One, headed "Peirce," was inscribed by Peirce shortly before graduation in the Harvard College Class-Book of 1859, preserved in the Harvard Archives. (A copy of the Class-Book entry is in MS 51.) The other, headed "My Life written for the Class-Book," is in MS 63, a notebook begun 10 September 1860 and entitled "Book of Characters." The notebook further contains references to "my remarks on character in general," that is to Items 31, 36, and 37 in MS 55, as well as lists of expenses for March through September 1863. Class-Book entries printed by permission of Harvard University Archives.

2.6 C. H. Mills] Charles Henry Mills (1812–1872) was a brother of Peirce's mother.

2.7 T. R. Sullivan] A Unitarian minister, Thomas Russell Sullivan (1799–1862) taught in Boston from 1825 until his death.

3.7–8 "Vanity . . . !"] Eccles. 1:2, 12:8.

Private Thoughts

These selections are taken from MS 55, a notebook begun 7 June 1860. Thoughts I–LVII were inscribed during the last seven months of 1860, although some thirty had been written earlier (one survives in MS 6); Thoughts LVIII–LXXIV during 1861 to 1869; and Thought LXXV on 17 March 1888. An earlier version of the Thought XIX diagram is on a separate sheet at the end of the manuscript.

5.3   Cicero *Philippics*, 12.2, 5. The exact quote is "Cujusvis hominis est errare."

7.13–14   When a child . . . prudence.] In the margin of the manuscript Peirce wrote "St. A." Several possible sources fitting this abbreviation have been examined but none contains this quotation. However, the example of a child who burns his finger occurs in Reid, *Works*, vol. 2, p. 549 [*On the Active Powers of Man*, essay 3, pt. 1, chap. 2]; also in Mill, *Logic* (1846), p. 125 [bk. 2, chap. 3, sec. 3]; Hume, *An Enquiry Concerning Human Understanding* [sec. 4, pt. 2].

9.6–8   Just as Science . . . Void.] Kant, *Werke*, vol. 2, p. 56 [*Critique*, A51, B75].

Sense of Beauty

Members of the Harvard Class of 1859 were required to write thirty-six compositions: nine during the sophomore, fourteen during the junior, and thirteen during the senior year. Peirce was ill the last few months of 1858 and consequently missed the first six senior compositions. The other thirty are preserved in MSS 7–9, 12–19, 21–26, 30–35, 38–39, 41–42, and 47–49. "Sense of Beauty," the fourth sophomore composition, was due 26 March 1857. The margins of the manuscript contain a few marks and notes by an instructor, as well as Peirce's responses to them. For two rewritten passages, see the notes below.

10.5–6   "Schiller, ..."] Ruskin, *Modern Painters*, vol. 2, p. 136 [pt. 3, sec. 1, chap. 15] with minor changes in wording.

10.12–13   "Beauty. . . ."] Twenty-second Letter, *Sämmtliche Werke*, vol. 10, p. 221. The translation in the text is apparently Peirce's own, although he did own a copy of Weiss's translation (see p. 102).

10.20–11.3   Twentieth Letter, *Sämmtliche Werke*, vol. 10, pp. 217–18; Weiss, pp. 96–97. The instructor corrected Peirce's omission of the auxiliary (l. 22) by inserting "may"; following Weiss's translation and Peirce's probable intention, "can" has been inserted.

11.12–31   Man consists . . . freedom.] These two paragraphs summarize Letters 11 to 14 of Schiller's *Esthetic Letters*. In the margin the instructor wrote, "Cannot this be put into less technical language?" Although Peirce responded, "I don't see how," he rewrote the two paragraphs as follows:

> This may seem contradictory. The two impulses *do not conflict in the same objects*, because although the formal impulse would reduce every object to the "I", the necessary synthetical unity of self-consciousness, to unity as respects form, it would not thereby reduce the manifoldness of the matter of that object; and the sensuous impulse although it would multiply objects, as regards their matter and appearance, yet it would not multiply the "I" which is the ground of the unity of their form.

On the other hand, the two impulses can, and must be, *balanced*, because, since the function of the formal impulse (and, as it seems to me, the peculiar business of mortals is to reduce to form matter which is furnished by the sensuous impulse for no other purpose, the preponderance of either would give a surplus of faculty which would be either unemployable or of no ultimate advantage.

11.37–12.3   On the other hand . . . morality.] A symbol in the margin seems to indicate that the instructor did not understand this sentence. In response Peirce wrote, "In the preceding sentence, I have said that beauty puts the mind into a state of 'infinite indeterminateness'. It will be seen that this renders it possible to put it in a state in which anything would give the mind an exclusive and single direction. Such a state would be one of 'infinite determinableness'."

12.14   splendid language] The instructor underlined the words "splendid language" and wrote in the margin, "I would rather hear yours," to which Peirce responded as follows: "I should say that these were the I impulse [and] faculty, and the IT impulse and faculty; and also the THOU impulse and faculty which (it seems to me) is what Schiller regards as that of beauty."

Raphael and Michael Angelo

This is the third junior composition, due 23 October 1857. There are a few notes and marks by an instructor in the margins, and the third footnote is inscribed separately at the end. An earlier, much shorter variant of the composition, written on a Thursday, either 22 or 15 October, contains no marks or notes; perhaps the instructor rejected it as too short.

Scientific Book of Synonyms

The Preface represents the only consecutive text in MS 20. Two earlier title pages, which are followed by rough and sketchy lists of words, especially synonyms and antonyms, indicate that this Book was begun 13 October 1857. The Preface was composed a month or two later.

17.22–28   Graham, *Synonymes*, p. 150. Though it is against editorial policy to emend Peirce's errors in transcribing direct quotations, "condition, we mean" (l. 26) has been inserted because the sentence is otherwise nonsensical; the spelling of "imaginary" (l. 28) has been corrected. Peirce's "supposititious" (l. 27) is "suppositious" in the original.

18.13–18   Whately, *Synonyms*, p. 52.

Think Again!

Peirce wrote this letter to the editor in response to "Taming of the Shrew" (*Harvard Magazine* 4 [March 1858], 58–67). This "utterly heretical" article, which is attributed to Francis Custis Hopkinson, had accused Shakespeare of irreconcilable and artless inconsistency in the characterization of Katharina, the heroine of Shakespeare's play. MS 26, one of Peirce's Harvard compositions, also contains a reference to Hopkinson's article.

20.4–5 Shakespeare, *The Taming of the Shrew*, 4.1.14–15.
20.7 A writer . . . *Magazine*] "The Taming of the Shrew," *Harvard Magazine* 4 (1858): 58–67. Attributed to Francis Custis Hopkinson, Harvard '59, in the two sets of *Harvard Magazine* in The Harvard University Archives.
20.25–30 Shakespeare, *Plays* (Johnson), vol. 7, p. 403.
21.30–33 "We shall find, ..."] "The Taming of the Shrew," *Harvard Magazine*, 60–61.
21.34–37 "Violent . . . ,"] *Ibid.*, 61.
21.38–22.2 "It is the true, . . . ,"] *Ibid.*, 60–61.
23.10–11 "ventures to say . . . ,"] *Ibid.*, 64.

Analysis of Genius

This is the tenth senior composition, due 19 March 1859. There are a few minor internal revisions, but no notes or marks by an instructor. A separate folded sheet at the end of the manuscript contains two two-page sections, one of which discusses Johnson's concept of genius; the other is an expanded recapitulation of Peirce's whole argument. For that earlier recapitulation, see the note below.

25.7–8 "large general powers. . . . "] Johnson, *Works*, vol. 9, p. 2 ["Cowley," in *Lives of the Poets*].
25.25–26 "A mind of . . . ."] *Ibid.*
26.4–5 blue ink] Where Peirce wrote "faculties" in blue ink, boldface type is used.
30.5–8 I will now . . . other men.] On a separate sheet at the end of the manuscript Peirce repeats these two paragraphs and continues with what follows:

I now wished to prove that man has faculties. I undertook this two ways. 1st because he has innate ideas & whoever has innate ideas has faculties. I began with the major premiss.

I assumed in the first place that all our conceptions are produced by experience. I reasond from that that innate ideas if there are any are produced by ex. but that since they are not produced by the object they arise from the very act of thought. And that consequently they are a plurality of effects produced by a single cause. & Therefore the mind in which they are supposed to be produced must have an oranism & therefore must have faculties

I then undertook to show thinking that we have innate ideas by the argument from un. nec. & the relativity of knowledge.

I then advanced another argument for the existence of faculties. Namely that people are often deficient in special mental powers. Which ended all I had to say.

Axioms of Intuition

This six-page manuscript, which has a single minor revision, is contained in a folded yellow cover-sheet entitled "Quantity."

31.4–7   All Intuitions . . . whole.] Kant, *Werke*, vol. 2, p. 142 [*Critique*, A162–63, B202–3].

Three Essays on Infinity and God

These three essays, or three variants on the same topic, are part of the many writings in Peirce's first metaphysical period, 1859–1862. All three variants are printed to give an indication of Peirce's method of working. The second variant is untitled, and only the third bears a date: 25 October 1859. The first two were composed a month or two earlier, probably in August. All three variants contain a few, mostly minor revisions.

Proof of the Infinite Nature of the Creator

This one-page manuscript was written, very probably, during the summer of 1860. The word "INFLUX" is inscribed in the upper left-hand corner.

I, IT, and THOU

This is one of many manuscripts in which Peirce attempts to work out a viable system of the formal categories (the later Firstness, Secondness, Thirdness). Only the first two pages of the manuscript, parts of which may have been composed as much as a year earlier than the date assigned, have consecutive text. The remaining thirteen pages, not printed here, contain rough sketches of the categories, as well as doodles and scribbles.

The Modus of the IT

This manuscript was written, very probably, on the same day as the first two pages of MS 65, and it too contains numerous revisions. The upper left-hand corner of the last three pages of this four-page manuscript bears the mark "IT" followed by the page number.

Views of Chemistry

There are seven home-made notebooks, each in brownish-yellow wrappers and each entitled separately, in this manuscript; several other notebooks are missing. Most of these were written in the summer and early fall of 1861. There are three variants of the first notebook, the earliest entitled "Salts" and the other two "Kinds of Matter," and one version each of "No 2. Chemical Method," "No 5. Part 3 of The Elements. Qualitative Analysis," "No 8. Equivalence of Force; Concluded. States of Aggregation," and a concluding "Tables illustrating the Equations of Chemical Force." Peirce may have written these notebooks for the chemistry course he taught at the Ellen M. Hight School for Girls in the fall of 1861 in Cambridge, or for the young ladies of the Fay family in Vermont. (One of these ladies, Zina Fay, became Peirce's first wife in 1862.) The two notebooks printed here represent the most finished and interesting efforts in the manuscript.

50.10–12 when a child . . . prudence.] See editorial note, 7.13–14.
51.9–12 Worcester, *Dictionary*, p. 1268.
51.18ff. 1. GLAUBER . . .] Peirce's terminology is as follows:

Chemical Compound	Peirce's term	Peirce's symbolism
$NaCl$	common salt or sea salt	Na^+Cl^-
KCl	culinary salt or sal	K^+Cl^-
Na_2SO_4	Glauber's salt or *sal admirabile*	Na^+V^-
Na_2CO_3	mineral alkali	Na^+ [the metal only]
H_2SO_4	oil of Vitriol	V^- [the sulfate only]
HCl	spirit of sea salt	Cl^- [for as much of the acid as reacts]
K_2SO_4	Tartarus Vitriolatus	K^+V^-
K_2CO_3	vegetable alkali	K^+ [the metal only]

55.21 Byron, *Works*, vol. 10, p. 75. "She walks in beauty, like the night."

Treatise on Metaphysics

This manuscript represents the culmination of Peirce's early metaphysical period. The Preface and Contents are on two torn half sheets; the former is dated 21 August 1861. Some parts of the manuscript may have been written before that date. Whereas most of the manuscript seems to be in nearly finished form, the last section—"Metaphysical. Chapter II. Nature of the Perfect"—is merely a rough outline of the second chapter of Book I. A separate sheet at the end, which Peirce probably included when he sent part of the manuscript to Zina Fay, reads as follows: "Metaphysical.—I have had so much to say and so little time to put the words together, that I have been fearfully concise in some places. Worst in S 3.C.—The most unfinished part is S 2.—The representations of Kant and Hume I have been very careful with. I feel sure they are right unless perhaps I give H. credit for one syllogism too much.—Don't lose it, please." For earlier variants of parts of the treatise, see MSS 74, 67, 57, and 52.

58.6–7 "which is desirable . . . ,"] Aristotle, *Metaphysics*, 982ª14–19. Peirce owned a copy of M'Mahon's translation (see p. 7).

58.15–16 "Definition, ..."] Hamilton, *Logic*, pp. 104–5 [lect. 8, par. 26] has "*Definition* and *Division* are severally the resolution of the Comprehension and of the Extension of notions, into their parts."

58.30–31 "a definition . . ."] Aristotle, *Topics*, 101ᵇ39. Peirce owned a copy of Owen's translation of the *Organon* (see vol. 2, p. 363).

58.33–34 [The best . . . Sect. 1.]] Kant, *Werke*, vol. 2, p. 565 [*Critique*, A731, B759].

59.32–38 That is a thing, . . . word.] *Ibid.*

61n.1–2 Plato, *Phaedrus*, 345C.

62.25–26 Job 28:14.

63.1–3 The efficacy . . . we pray.] These two sentences appear, with slight differences, in MS 55, entry LVI, which is headed "The Thought of the Year 1860."

70.25–28 is one out of twenty . . . vigintillions.] Peirce's number works out to $(20)(10^{1002})$; the correct number is 10^{1000}.

71.1–6 from a chain of . . . bet on!] Fifteen syllogisms, each having two premises and a conclusion, contain at most 45 different propositions; but in a chain of syllogisms, every conclusion but the last is used also as a premiss, so that in Peirce's example there are at most $30 - 14 = 16$ premises which are not conclusions. If the probability of each premiss and the probability of the validity of each inference is 0.9, the probability of the final conclusion is $(0.9)^{31} = 0.038$ which is 1 out of 26. For a 0.5 to 1.0 probability scale, take $(0.38)/2 = 0.019$; then $0.500 + 0.019 = 0.519$.

If the probability of the premisses only is increased to 0.99, the calculations are $(0.99)^{16} \times (0.9)^{15} = 0.175$; half of this added to 0.5 yields 0.588.

71.7–10 Moreover, . . . proved it.] $0.588 - 0.519 = 0.069$ which rounds up to 0.07; add this to 0.5 to obtain 0.570. Translating back to the 0 to 1 probability scale, $0.07 \times 2 = 0.14$ which is roughly 1 out of 7. The assumption that a probability of 0.5 is appropriate for a "mere unsupported hypothesis" is open to question. The *a priori* probability that a proposition is true (say) is 0.5, but it is very seldom that a hypothesis is advanced relative to no other more-or-less-probable knowledge.

Analysis of Creation

In addition to the first nine pages of the manuscript that are printed here, there are fourteen pages of different starts and incomplete attempts at the various sections. They all represent earlier and unfinished variants of different parts of the nine-page section at the beginning of the manuscript.

S P Q R

Unfinished and brittle in several places, this manuscript is nonetheless an interesting attempt at working out a system of the material categories. The manuscript consists of two distinctly different parts, on different kinds of paper, whose order of composition cannot be determined. The first part ends with an incomplete paragraph, not printed here, that seems to be superseded by the first paragraph of the second part, beginning at 93.14. Three separate sheets at the end, not printed here, seem to be variants of sections of the first part. The title of the manuscript is explained in MS 52, in a section called "New Names and Symbols for Kant's Categories": "Thing Quality Dependence Fact I will represent by letters which shall not stand for any particular names, nor interfere with logical letters but which yet shall be easy to remember viz: SPQR. . . . Those persons who consider the letters SPQR as fanciful and foolish, can pretend they stand for Subjectum, Predicatum, Quo, and Realitas." (According to *The Century Dictionary*, they stand for "*Senatus Populusque Romanus*, the senate and the people of Rome.")

Chemical Theory of Interpenetration

The occasion for this article, Peirce's first important professional publication, is not known. Peirce entered the Lawrence Scientic

School in the spring of 1861, and two years later he graduated *summa cum laude* with a degree in chemistry. The article may have been a requirement for the degree, or it may have been inspired by a requirement from one of his instructors.

96.25   Diehl] Not located.
96.29   Svanberg] Lars Fredrik Svanberg (1805–1878), Swedish chemist and physicist.
96.29   Norlin] Not located.
96.30   Peirce's criterion] See Raymond Clare Archibald: *Benjamin Peirce 1809–1880* (Oberlin, Ohio: The Mathematical Association of America, 1925), p. 13.
96.31   Maumené] Edme Jules Maumené, French chemist, was born in 1818. His major works are on wine and sugar.
97.13–18 K is . . . is. 782.] The paragraph following the table is difficult to understand. Peirce seems to think there are thirteen, rather than eleven, elements in the table. Contemporary thinkers would evaluate the probability that only one difference exceeds a given quantity using a multinomial distribution, but it is not known if Peirce arrived at .0000087 in this fashion. Nor is it clear why he selected .25/4 as the given quantity; the contemporary probabilist will specify any quantity suitable for his purposes. Finally, the *sum* of the differences being a small quantity, +.001, it is not considered significant when taken independently of the actual differences (or the sum of their squares).
97.33–98.2   II. I shall now . . . constituents.] Kant, *Werke*, vol. 5, p. 388 [AK 530–31].
98.32–99.2   Let us call . . . elasticity.] Not located.

The Place of Our Age

The reason for Peirce's invitation to deliver the oration is not known; having left Cambridge High School under somewhat inauspicious circumstances in July 1854, he graduated from Dixwell Preparatory School in June 1855. As there is no manuscript of the oration, we must assume that the account in the *Chronicle* represents the largest part of what Peirce actually delivered. But see the note below for an error in printing.

102.2–5   "all the kings . . ."] Rev. 6:15.
102.8   "heavens depart . . ."] Rev. 6:14.
102.16–19   "the sun becomes . . . ."] Rev. 6:12–13.
103.24–34   The human mind . . . produced.] In MS 75, which contains a copy of the *Chronicle*, Peirce drew a bracket around this paragraph and in the left margin wrote, "Printed wrong."

104.1–2 "How do we know . . . ?"] Hume, *Philosophical Works*, vol. 1, pp. 106–11 [*Treatise*, bk. 1, pt. 3, sec. 3].

104.14–15 "We say . . . ?"] This almost certainly is not a quotation from Hume or from Kant but is Peirce's interpretation of Kant's intent (as expressed, for example, in the *Critique* A758–69, B786–97).

107.21–22 "All things . . . ."] 1 Cor. 15:25–28.

107.23 "His service . . . ."] "A Collect for Peace" from The Order for Daily Morning Prayer in *The Book of Common Prayer* has "God . . . whose service is perfect freedom."

113.1–7 Emerson, "Ode inscribed to Wm. H. Channing," *Poems*, p. 119.

113.11–12 the *end* . . . man.] Bacon, *Works* (Spedding) vol. 2, p. 142 [*Of the Advancement of Learning*, first bk.].

Peirce to Chase

This letter, an interesting treatment of "how we ought to investigate the categories," is unfinished and unsigned, and apparently it was never sent. If Peirce sent another version, he probably received no response; for there are no letters from Chase in the Peirce Papers.

115.26–27 "which is desirable . . . ,"] Aristotle, *Metaphysics*, 982ª14–19; M'Mahon, p. 7.

Shakespearian Pronunciation

Peirce's interest in orthoepy and Shakespearian pronunciation probably began while he was a member of the Harvard Orthoepy Klub during his senior year. Shortly thereafter, in the second half of 1859, he and John B. Noyes began work toward this highly important, albeit neglected, review article. (James Russell Lowell saw its beginnings in 1860, and in 1863 recommended it to the editor of *The Atlantic Monthly*.) Peirce later said that he was "the first to undertake a systematic study of all the evidences" and that Alexander J. Ellis's monumental *Early English Pronunciation* did not disprove his and Noyes's findings. Their different methods, however, led to some different findings. The seven major parts of Peirce's method are described at some length in "The Editor's Manual," a manuscript (Robin 1181) written in 1900: (1) John Wallis's scientific and unmistakable descriptions of English sounds are taken as the *point d'appui*; (2) a revolution in the pronunciation of a language does not take place without something like a social upheaval, and no such upheaval occurred in England between the beginning of Elizabeth's reign and the Great Rebellion; (3) every printed account of the pronunciation of a language refers to the pronunciation as it was twenty or thirty years earlier; (4) the best evidence concerning pronunciation is found in the statements of orthoepists; (5) every spelling must be explained; (6) rhymes afford useful information, provided they are used cautiously; (7) the ear of any people for the sound of their language is of the nature of a specialized instinct, so that they will draw with ease excessively fine distinctions in some directions, while in others they will confound sounds somewhat widely unlike. For earlier attempts at the review article, see MS 62, written between early 1860 and 3 January 1863. The majority of pages is in Noyes's hand, and at the end of the manuscript there are a few pages of "Notes," almost certainly in the hand of Peirce's brother James Mills Peirce.

118n.1–3   The "old writer" is Gil and the quote is found in the preface to his *Logonomia*. Wade has not been identified.

119.21–22   1619 . . . . London. 4°.] Although the 1619 edition is cited in the text, the authors used the second edition, 1621, in making references.

120.12   Mr. Jennison,] James Jennison was instructor in elocution at Harvard from 1851 to 1860, and tutor in history, philosophy, and other subjects from 1851 to 1872.

120.21–28   Peirce and Noyes translated into English all passages quoted from Gil, as well as those from De la Touche, Pomey, Sewel, Smith, and Wallis.

121.13   I thinke] The original reads "methinke."

121n.1   The quotation itself is found in vol. 12, p. 430; vol. 2, p. 320 contains a paraphrase.

123n.7   Nat Strong] Nathaniel Strong, a seventeenth-century English grammarian.

124.6   De la Touche] A French grammarian who was born in the second half of the seventeenth century, De la Touche (the more common form of his name is La Touche, Nicolas de) died about 1730 in England, where he had settled after the revocation of the Edict of Nantes. *L'Art de bien parler françois*, dedicated to the Duke of Gloucester, is the only work attributed to him.

124.19–27   Wallis, *Grammatica*, pp. 23–25.

127.33–34   Pope, *Essay on Criticism, Works*, vol. 1, p. 206.

128.2–3   "in *lose*, ..."] Sharp, *Short Treatise*, p. 17.

129.1   The correct reference for this line has not been located.

129.2 Shakespeare, *Julius Caesar*, 1.1.39.

129.3–4 "In the last . . . ."] Jonson, "The English Grammar," *Works*, vol. 9, p. 267.

130.5 abused] The original reads "misused."

130.21–22 "the barbarous speech . . . ."] Coote, *Schoole-master*, p. 27.

130.28 "entermedle . . ."] Mulcaster, *Elementarie*, p. 133.

131.7–9 1633. Ben Jonson . . . .] Jonson, "The English Grammar," *Works*, vol. 9, p. 261.

131.13 Festeau] Paul Festeau was a seventeenth-century French grammarian. This quotation is from his *French Grammar*. There is no 1673 edition; the mistake seems to be the authors' according to evidence contained in MS 62.

131.15 Berault] A French grammarian who wrote in English as well as in French, Pierre Berault also wrote on religious subjects. This quotation is from his *French and English Grammar*. There is, however, no 1698 edition; the mistake seems to be the authors' according to evidence contained in MS 62.

131.16 *Fat,*] The original publication has the nonsensical *Fal.*

131.29 Taudon] Not located.

132.18–20 1623. "A is . . . ."] Percivale, *Grammar*, first page.

132.22–25 1650. "A in . . . ."] Cotgrave, *Dictionary*, first page of section titled "The French Grammar."

132.33–35 1660. "*Of the* . . . ."] Hexham, *Dictionary*, first page of grammar section.

133.10–12 1690. "A is . . . ."] Pomey, *Dictionaire*, first page of section 1.

133.12 Pomey] François-Antoine Pomey (1619–1673) was a French Jesuit who taught humanities and rhetoric for many years in a variety of colleges. He authored several books on mythological, religious, and rhetorical and grammatical subjects.

134.2 Saxon] Samuel Saxon, English grammarian.

134.14 Giles Du Guez,] There has been confusion concerning the correct spelling of the name of this sixteenth-century French grammarian. "Dewez" is the French spelling and "Du Wes" is its Anglicized form. "De Guez," as Peirce and Noyes spelled it, arose because there is no name on the title page of the *Introductory* but there is an acrostic which reveals the name as "Du Guez."

134.16–17 Dewez, *Introductory*, p. 899. This work is bound together with Palsgrave's *L'Eclaircissement* in the edition Peirce and Noyes used.

136n.2–3 "Not on thy soale: . . . ,"] White's reference eludes verification but he apparently quoted from the First Folio.

136n.6–9 Hood, *Works*, vol. 4, p. 39.

142.10–12 Gil, *Logonomia*, p. 15. The extra "or" that appears in the original publication is apparently a printer's error.

142.19–20   Wallis, *Grammatica*, pp. 63–64.
143.1   *niwter,*] The original publication has the nonsensical *niwty*.

Analysis of the Ego

This interesting treatment of existents and subjectivity is carefully written at the beginning; but toward the end it becomes hurried and a mere outline.

145.33–34   it is something . . . itself,] Plato, *Phaedrus*, 245C.
149.37–39   "that which moving . . . ."] *Ibid.*

Major Premisses of Natural Science

This manuscript contains three variants, the first two dated 5 August 1864; the third, the one printed here, was probably written the same day. The first variant has the title "A Treatise of the Major Premisses of the Science of Finite Subjects" (or the superscribed "Nature" for the last two words). The second variant is untitled. The chronological order of the three variants is properly indicated by roman numerals, though not in Peirce's hand.

152.16   "mistress of the sciences"] Aristotle, *Posterior Analytics*, 76^{a}18; Owen, vol. 1, p. 265.

Immediate Perception

This carefully written six-page manuscript is contained in a folded cover-sheet with the short title "Immediate Perception."

153.7–10   "the complement. . . ."] Hamilton in Reid, *Works*, vol. 2, pp. 756–57 [note A, "On the Philosophy of Common Sense"].

Peirce to Abbot

This fourteen-page letter, preserved in the Abbot Papers in the Harvard Archives, was prompted by Abbot's "The Philosophy of Space and Time," *North American Review* 99(1864):64–116. Abbot's response, which does not survive, was according to Peirce's letter of 2 March 1865 "by no means satisfactory as an explanation." (Copies of this and several other letters from the Abbot Papers, including the one of 5 February, have been added to L 1.) It cannot be determined which of the two postscripts of 5 February was written first: the short one is inscribed in the top margin of the first page of Peirce's letter. Printed by permission of Harvard University Archives and Katharine Abbot Wells.

156.18–22   "The mere Form. . . ."] Kant, *Werke*, vol. 2, pp. 236–37 [*Critique*, A291, B347].
156.29   *Kritik* (p. 93)] [A98–99].
157.1   (p. 753)] [B160–61].
157.13   (pp. 122–130)] [A137–47, B176–87].
157.19   (p. 761)] [B202–3].
157.27   (p. 85)] [A87–88, B119–21].
157.37–158.6   Kant, *Werke*, vol. 3, p. 44 [*Prolegomena*, sec. 13, remark 1].
158.37–38   (*Werke* vii. p. 16 et seq.).] [*Anthropology*, sec. 3].
160.26   (*Kritik* p. 258)] [A320, B376].

Harvard Lecture I

This is the first of a series of twelve Harvard University Lectures, entitled "On the Logic of Science," that Peirce was scheduled to deliver on Friday afternoons at 5, beginning 17 March 1865. Peirce had no audience for the first meeting—due, perhaps, to inclement weather —but he gave eleven lectures during the following weeks. Only nine manuscripts survive. They all consist of folded sheets originally bound together into gatherings, and they are numbered consecutively. Though MS 94 seems finished, the penultimate verso has the pencil inscription "An hour all but 19 minutes 3 more sheets"; these sheets have not been found. Some of the quotations in the printed text appear as bibliographic references in the manuscript. Sheets are marked "Lecture 1" in the upper left-hand corner.

163.22   Logic is . . . Demonstration.] Such a definition might be read into *Posterior Analytics*, 71[b].
163.23–24   "theory of inference"] Spalding, "Logic," *Britannica*, vol. 13, p. 567.
163.27   the science of truth.] Not located.
163.33–34   "Ratiocination. . . ."] Hobbes, *Works*, vol. 1, p. 3 [*Elements of Philosophy*, chap. 1, sec. 2].
163.37–38   "Dialectica. . . ."] Cicero, *De oratore*, 2.38, 157.
164.2   "Ars et via docendi"] Not located.
164.3   ars dirigendi. . . .] Not located.

164.7-9   the science of the necessary laws. . . .] Kant, *Werke*, vol. 3, p. 171 [*Logic*, intro.].

164.14-15   the science of . . . cognition.] Ueberweg, *System of Logic*, p. 1 [intro., sec. 1].

164.15-16   the science of . . . Conceptions.] Not located.

164.16-17   the science of . . . thinking.] Mansel, *Logica*, p. 1 [chap. 1].

164.18-20   "Logic is the science of. . . ."] Mill, *Logic* (1846), p. 7 [intro., sec. 7].

164.20   Duval-Jouve] Joseph Duval-Jouve (1810-1883) was a French natural scientist and academician who spent his early career in Grasse where he first taught rhetoric and then philosophy. He married the daughter of the principal of the college, M. Jouve, and added her name to his. In 1846 he replaced his father-in-law as principal and began publishing articles and books on natural science, geology, and logic.

164.20-22   it is the science of . . . .] Duval-Jouve, *Logique*, p. viii [preface].

164.22-23   it treats of . . . .] Krause, *Grundriss*, p. 3.

164.23-24   "branch of inquiry. . . ."] De Morgan, *Logic*, p. 26 [chap. 2].

166.17-19   "It is the science of . . . ."] Mill, *Logic* (1846), p. 7 [intro., sec. 7].

169.10   logic is . . . .] Hegel, *Encyklopädie*, pt. 1, p. 25 [*Logic*, sec. 19].

170.36-172.3   Locke, *Essay*, pp. 134-35. [The five quotations that follow in the next paragraph (pp. 172-73) are from sections 4, 4, 5, 6, and 7, respectively.]

Harvard Lecture II

This manuscript contains a variant two-page beginning of the lecture, with following page or pages missing. It is unclear whether this variant post- or ante-dates the printed text. Sheets are marked "Lecture 2" in the upper left-hand corner.

176.8-10   "Induction and . . . ."] Aristotle, *Prior Analytics*, 68^{b}15-17; Owen, vol. 1, p. 230.

177.12-17   Aristotle, *Prior Analytics*, 68^{b}17-22; Owen, vol. 1, pp. 230-31.

177.18-29   "Let A be long-lived, ..."] The quotations that follow in this paragraph are all from *Prior Analytics*, 68^{b}17-29; Owen, vol. 1, pp. 230-31. A "Physiological discussion" may refer to *On the Parts of Animals*, 677^{a}30-35.

180.21   [Give it.]] No table is given in the manuscript, but Peirce may have had something like this in mind:

a priori reasoning	*induction*	*a posteriori reasoning*
Major premiss	Conclusion	Major premiss
Minor premiss	Minor premiss	Conclusion
Conclusion	Major premiss	Minor premiss

181.36   In the centre of this table,] The table that Peirce constructs is composed of two parts, a right-angled figure whose sides bulge out slightly, and a cross containing 12 squares:

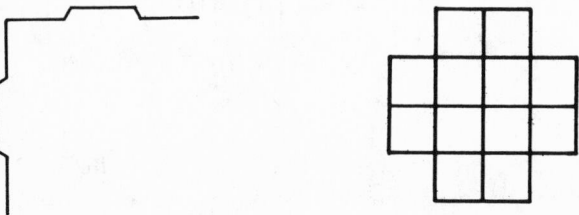

When put together in the way Peirce intended, with the right-angled figure covering or framing the cross, three areas are distinguished: center, top, and side.

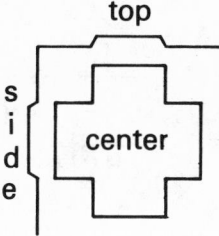

His instructions for filling in the table depend on the arrangement of terms in the first three figures of the syllogism. Let S, P, and M represent the minor, major, and middle terms respectively:

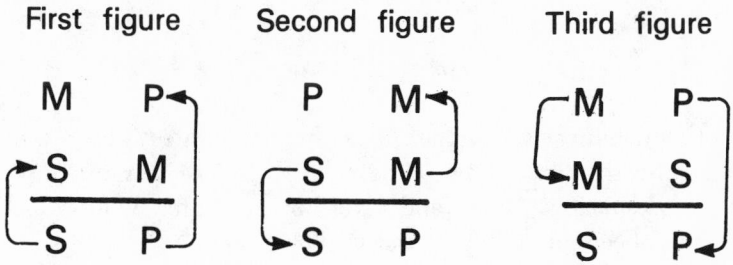

The arrows connect "like" terms. In the center of the table Peirce entered the conclusion of first figure syllogisms, the minor premiss of second figure syllogisms, and the major premiss of third figure syllogisms. At the top he entered the proposition whose predicate is like the predicate of the proposition in the center; at the side, the proposition whose subject is like the subject of the proposition in the center. The eliminated term in each case is the middle term. The completed table looks like this:

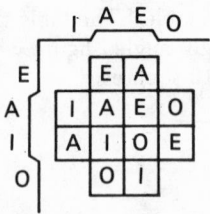

Following Peirce's instructions we can read out the valid moods, major premiss first, minor premiss second, and conclusion last. This may be clarified by the following diagrams which reproduce only what pertains to a single figure:

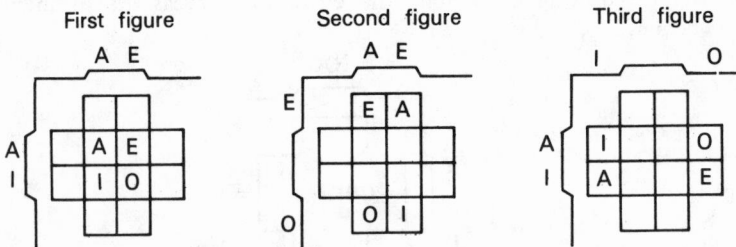

To obtain the valid moods of the second figure, for instance, we read first from the top (for the major premiss), then from the middle (for the minor premiss), and finally from the side (for the conclusion). This gives us the four moods AEE, EAE, AOO, and EIO.

186.15   *Hypotheses non fingo,*] Newton, *Principia,* "General Scholium."

Harvard Lecture III

This manuscript is neither marked nor paginated, but in the latter part Peirce has written two time notations in the margin: "6:00" and "6:7," presumably 6 p.m. and seven minutes after. One crossed out page has been reinstated for the sake of continuity.

199.17–22   They are useful . . . false arguments.] Aristotle, *On Sophistical Refutations,* 175ª5–12.

199.30–32   it is not conclusive . . . beginning.] Aristotle, *On Sophistical Refutations,* 167ᵇ13–20. Peirce discussed this same passage years later in his article "Non sequitur" for Baldwin's *Dictionary,* vol. 2, p. 181 (1902).

200.9–13   that the unintellectual man . . . forms.] See Aristotle, *On Sophistical Refutations,* chap. 16.

Harvard Lecture on Whewell, Mill, Compte

This is, almost certainly, the fourth lecture in the series; the next lecture, announced at the end, has not been found. Some of the quotations in the printed text appear as bibliographic references in the manuscript. The mark "Whewell" precedes sheet numbers.

205.8   Waddington] Charles Tzaunt Waddington (1819–1914), French Protestant philosopher (of English Protestant extraction), was a prolific writer on the history of philosophy. A few of his more relevant writings include: *De l'utilité des études logiques; De la méthode déductive; Pierre de la Ramée, sa vie, ses ecrits et ses opinions;* and *Essais de logique.*

205.29–206.2   "the two processes. . . ."] Whewell, *Novum Organon*, aph. 1, p. 27.

206.7–9   "Induction, ..."] *Ibid.*, aph. 12, p. 70.

207.1–7   "We have given. . . ."] *Ibid.*, pp. 30–31.

208.5   the author] Henry Longueville Mansel.

209.9–12   "The inductive act. . . ."] Whewell, *Novum Organon*, aph. 19, p. 97.

209.26–27   "The several facts. . . ."] *Ibid.*, aph. 19, p. 97. The quotation as given in the preceding paragraph with "exactly expressed" is correct.

210.11–12 and 211.8–9   "often fulfilled. . . ."] Mill, *Logic* (1846), p. 296 [bk. 3, chap. 14, sec. 6].

211.9–12   "I know of no such case. . . ."] Whewell, *Discovery*, p. 271. Where Peirce has "all complicated," Whewell has "all numerous and complicated."

212.14–16   is founded on . . . age] Comte, *Positive Philosophy*, vol. 1, pp. 1–2.

212.38–213.3   one has to cut . . . arrangements.] Mill, *Logic* (1846), p. 435 [bk. 4, chap. 7, sec. 2].

213.13   follows.] At this point Peirce referred to "vol. ii, p. 434" of the original French edition of Comte's *Positive Philosophy;* he apparently did his own impromptu translation. The text supplied (l. 14–31) is from Harriet Martineau's translation of Comte's work, vol. 1, p. 225.

213.40–214.1   "The pretended direct observation. . . ."] Not located.

215.23–26   "To infer, . . . ,"] Hamilton, *Logic*, p. 193 [lect. 15, par. 53]. Peirce begins "To infer," but Hamilton has "To reason."

215.26–27   "Inference indicates. . . ."] *Ibid.*, p. 196 [lect. 15, par. 53]. Where Peirce has "Inference indicates," Hamilton has "*Inference or illation* (from *infero*), indicates."

215.31–32   a progress from . . . unknown,] Mill, *Logic* (1846), p. 7 [intro. sec. 7].

215.34–35   as the science of . . . matters;] *Ibid.*

216.29–32   the conclusion of a syllogism . . . value.] *Ibid.*, p. 131 [bk. 2,

chap. 3, sec. 5]. The preceding arguments are modeled on those given
by Mill in bk. 2, chap. 3, sec. 2–5.

217.17–18   The inference from particulars.] See Mill's *Logic,* bk. 2, chap.
6, sec. 1.

217.21–22   "That all our knowledge. . . ."] Kant, *Werke,* vol. 2, p. 695
[*Critique,* A1, B1].

218.1–2   the reason for . . . experience.] Mill, *Logic* (1846), pp. 152f.
[bk. 2, chap. 6, sec. 4].

219.9–10   "an assumption. . . ."] *Ibid.,* p. 184 [bk. 3, chap. 3, sec. 1].

219.16–18   this principle . . . conclusion.] *Ibid.,* pp. 184–85 [bk. 3, chap. 3,
sec. 1].

219.27ff.   Peirce does not quote but gives page references only for this and
the following five extracts. The passages he read may have been more or
less extensive than those supplied.

221.31   [Rap at blue]] Peirce is referring to the *s*'s overlined in blue in the
manuscript, here indicated by boldface type.

Harvard Lecture VI

Peirce seems to have expanded this lecture in the latter part, for
some of the sheet numbers, which are preceded by the mark "Boole,"
have been crossed out and replaced by higher numbers. Some of the
quotations in the printed text appear as bibliographic references in the
manuscript. At the very end of the manuscript Peirce has written in
pencil, "Next lecture."

229.27–30   "If there is an east wind, ..."] This way of expressing the
conditional proposition follows quickly from formula (36) on page 54
of Boole's *The Mathematical Analysis of Logic.* Boole altered his approach to such "secondary" propositions in his *Laws of Thought* (see
p. 170).

230.11–14   As a further illustration . . . subject.] The inference seems to be
invalid unless the entity/existence of subject and predicate is assumed.

230.15–23   The following Boolean formulas were added by Peirce in pencil:

$$bw = 0$$
$$vbw + (1 - v)bw = 0$$
$$vbw = 0 \quad bw = bw(1 - v)$$
$$x(1 - v) = (1 - v)bw$$
$$xb(1 - v) = (1 - v)bw$$
$$xb(1 - v) = (1 - v)wM$$
$$Lb = wM$$

Not all of them correspond to the propositions on the same line (see
lines 16 and 18, for instance), but if *x* and *M* and *L* are taken as signs

of an indefinite class, every proposition seems to be expressed by some formula or other.

230.24–25 No black white . . . smooth.] On the contrary, the two propositions "No black white is non-smooth" and "All black white is smooth" are equivalent.

230.36–231.5 $vx = v(1 - y)$ . . . not X.] Opposite these lines, on the verso of the preceding page, an otherwise blank page, Peirce gives the following Boolean formulas in pencil:

$$bw = 0$$
$$vbw + (1 - v)bw = 0$$
$$vbw = 0$$
$$bw = \frac{0}{v} = \frac{0}{0}(1 - v) = bw(1 - v)$$
$$b = wb(1 - v) + \frac{0}{0}(1 - w)b(1 - v)$$

The sequence of formulas does seem to constitute a proof of the last one in the sequence, but it is not a proof of the inference attempted on 230.15–23.

238.13 I will now take a case . . .] This problem is taken from Boole's *Laws of Thought*, pp. 276–77.

239.14ff. remarks of Boole's] Peirce gives only the page number (365) of Boole's *Laws of Thought* in the manuscript, but it is likely that he read at least as much as we have inserted into the text. He may also have read the conclusion to this line of reasoning, which Boole stated as a theorem on page 366:

> The calculated probability of any phænomenon y, upon an assumed physical hypothesis x, being p, the à posteriori probability P of the physical hypothesis, when the phænomenon has been observed, is expressed by the equation
>
> $$P = \frac{ap}{ap + c(1 - a)},$$
>
> where a and c are arbitrary constants, the former representing the à priori probability of the hypothesis, the latter the probability that if the hypothesis were false, the event y would present itself.

Harvard Lecture on Kant

This is, almost certainly, the seventh lecture, with which Peirce began the second half of the series. Eight pages from the end of the manuscript Peirce has written in pencil, "Nearly ten minutes more." The mark "Kant" precedes sheet numbers.

241.6–16   Carlyle, *Essays*, vol. 1, p. 80.

241.35–37   "the particular, ..."] Cousin, *Philosophie moderne*, vol. 5, p. 44 [intro.].

242.8–12   "Kant in his passion for strictness. . . ."] *Ibid.*

242.23–29   Abbot, "The Philosophy of Space and Time," *North American Review* 99(1864):105, with changes. Peirce rearranged the quotation but did not change its meaning. The original reads: "For an illustration let the following theorem be taken: 'The sum of the three angles of any triangle is equal to two right angles.' We draw or conceive a particular triangle for the sake of the demonstration; and having . . . accounted for."

242.31–32   "In reality, ..."] *Ibid.* Abbot has "makes no provision in his theory against it."

242.35–38   "no image whatever. . . ."] [A141, B180].

243.1–4   "How is the subsumption. . . ."] [A137–38, B176–77].

243.25–26   "no prophecy . . . interpretation"] 2 Pet. 1:20 reads "no prophecy of scripture is of private interpretation."

243.36–244.5   Kant, *Werke*, vol. 3, p. 7 [*Prolegomena*, intro.].

244.14–18   "The world-shattering Kant! . . . ."] De Quincey, *Literary Reminiscences*, vol. 1, p. 171 [chap. 6, the first of four chapters titled "Samuel Taylor Coleridge"]. De Quincey has "the world-shattering Kant. He could destroy—his intellect was essentially destructive. He was the Gog and he was the Magog. . . ."

247.32–38   An analytic judgment . . . heavy.] Kant, *Werke*, vol. 2, p. 21 [*Critique*, A6–7, B10–11].

247.38–248.1   the question of . . . possible.] *Ibid.*, p. 705 [*Critique*, B19].

250.18   his first essay] *De Mundi Sensibilis atque Intelligibilis Forma et Principiis Dissertatio.* (Kant's Inaugural Dissertation) Königsberg, 1770.

251.29–36   Kant, *Werke*, vol. 2, p. 71 [*Critique*, A70, B95].

252.12   He says:—] At this point Peirce refers to p. 72 of the Rosenkranz and Schubert edition; he apparently did his own impromptu translation. The text supplied (l. 13–28) is that of Norman Kemp Smith, *Immanuel Kant's Critique of Pure Reason* (London: Macmillan and Co., 1953), p. 107 [A171, B96–97].

253.20–28   Again, the translation supplied is Smith's, p. 108 [A71–72, B97].

Harvard Lecture VIII

Besides the fourteen consecutive and complete sheets of the lecture, the manuscript contains two sheets marked "Aristotle," followed by numbers 9 and 10. Peirce saved the two sheets—which are either from a different lecture or, what is more likely, from an earlier attempt at the present lecture—because they are to be inserted between sheets 12 and 13. The mark "Forms" precedes sheet numbers.

262.18–20 Aristotle, *Prior Analytics*, 68ᵇ17–23; Owen, vol. 1, p. 231.

262.25 left-hand form,] In the text of this manuscript, no "left-hand form" or "right-hand arrangement" (263.14) is displayed. However, the arrangement is given, and with the same explanation, in another lecture; see page 177.

263.3–21 "Induction (he says) . . . inference from all."] The quotations in this paragraph are all from *Prior Analytics*, 68ᵇ15–19; Owen, vol. 1, pp. 230–31.

271.25 The "Juppiter" example is given in Harvard Lecture II, p. 181.

Harvard Lecture X

Though numbered X, this lecture almost certainly followed the one numbered VIII. Sheet 2 of the lecture is missing. The manuscript also contains a variant two-page beginning, entitled "Lecture on the Grounds of Inference," and a two-page variant marked "Grounds 8." It is not clear whether these two originally belonged together and whether they post- or ante-date the complete variant printed here. The mark "Grounds" precedes sheet numbers.

283.21 *Hypotheses non fingo*,] Newton, *Principia*, "General Scholium."

Harvard Lecture XI

Twelve lectures in twelve weeks had been scheduled for the series "On the Logic of Science." As the first lecture was canceled, this is almost certainly the last lecture that Peirce delivered. The mark "XI" precedes sheet numbers.

294.39–295.1 *the* Hamilton] Sir William Rowan Hamilton.

295.6–8 Hamilton . . . thought.] See Hamilton's *Logic*, pp. 524–25 [app. 5, sec. 3].

295.15–22 See Hamilton's *Logic*, pp. 529–30 [app. 5, sec. 4].

296.26–28 every proposition . . . forms.] See Hamilton's *Logic*, p. 524 [app. 5, sec. 3].

298.3–9 See Hamilton's *Logic*, pp. 676–79 [app. 11, sec. 3].

Teleological Logic

Torn from a notebook, this four-page manuscript was written in a single day, 14 May 1865—notwithstanding the fact that Peirce wrote "Begun" before the date.

Unpsychological View of Logic

In addition to Chapter II and the two variants of Chapter I printed here, MS 109 contains the following: an incomplete two-page beginning of "Chapter III: Forms of Induction and Hypothesis"; two variants, of nine and four pages, of "Chapter II: Extension, Comprehension, Implication"; three variants, of fifteen, seven, and four pages (of which only the last is complete), of "Chapter II: Connotation, Denotation, Information"; and eight pages, sketchy and not fully consecutive, entitled "Extension Intension etc."

306.10–12   Logic is . . . in general.] Kant, *Werke*, vol. 3, p. 175 [*Logic*, intro., sec. 1].
306.17–21   Thought in general . . . discourse.] *Ibid.*, vol. 2, p. 237 [*Critique*, A292, B348].
308.21   [See lecture]] The reference is to Harvard Lecture X; 273.12–16.
311.10–11   *ens rationis* . . . nothing.] Kant, *Werke*, vol. 2, p. 237 [*Critique*, A292, B348].
313.23   appendix] No appendix has been found.
320.5   at the top.] At this point in the manuscript occur two paragraphs which Peirce intended to delete; their replacements are given in the text, but the deleted paragraphs are given here because they present an interesting alternative account:

> In the ordinary logic, each proposition & term of the syllogism has one name. In the present system each must have three names in order to connote different attributes. Here follows their definitions
> The conclusion is the proposition inferred. The first premiss is that one which contains the subject of the conclusion. The second premiss is that one which contains the predicate of the conclusion. The copulant is the proposition which follows apodictically from the other two. The subjiciant is the other proposition which contains the subject of the copulant, the predicant contains the predicate of the conclusion. The thesis is the assertion or denial of a rule. The subsumption is the assertion or denial of the case. The colligant is the assertion or denial of a result. The final subject & final predicate are the subject & predicate of the conclusion. The eliminate is the term not contained in the conclusion. The consequent subject is the subject of the copulant, the consequent predicate is the predicate of the copulant & the consequent copula is the term which does not occur in the copulant. The twice subject is the subject of the colligant. The twice predicate is the predicate of the colligant. And the subject predicate is the term which does not occur in the colligant.

Logic of the Sciences

This manuscript contains a number of different sections, some of which are incomplete, and several scattered and fragmentary pages;

numerous others are missing. As it is not possible to establish a firm order for what is contained in the manuscript, what we have printed is in fact an array of miscellaneous fragments. In addition to these, MS 113 contains a three-page "Chapter I. Elementary Moments"; a two-page "Chapter 2: First Division of Symbols in Logic"; a one-page earlier variant of the first Chapter 1 printed here; a two-page earlier variant of the last section printed here, entitled "Chapter I"; an unfinished page entitled "Definition of Logic"; and several unrelated, fragmentary pages. It is possible that some of the pages or sections were written earlier than the date indicated, perhaps as early as the spring of 1865.

323.9–10   mediate cognition,] Hamilton, *Logic*, vol. 1, p. 90 [lect. 7, par. 20].
323.10   mental image.] Hegel, *Encyklopädie*, pt. 3, pp. 404–5 [*Philosophy of Mind*, sec. 451].
323.10–11   a cognition] Kant, *Werke*, vol. 2, p. 258 [*Critique*, A320, B376].

Logic Notebook

Peirce's "private notebook of logical studies," now known as the Logic Notebook, is the single most fruitful of all his unpublished manuscripts. Though originally a bound book, it became separated and for years lay scattered among several boxes of the Peirce Papers. Don D. Roberts gathered all the leaves in 1961–62 and arranged them chronologically. There are now 271 leaves, or 542 pages, of which 202 are blank. The first leaf bears the simple inscription "LOGIC." It is not known how many leaves, in addition to the covers, are missing. Peirce began the notebook 12 November 1865, and he made the last entry 1 November 1909—or rather, that is the last entry found in the Peirce Papers. Nineteen years are represented: 1865–69, 1880, 1891, 1894, 1896–1906, 1908–9. For the sake of chronological convenience, the notebook has been divided into nineteen separate manuscripts. The entries for 1865 and 1866 are printed in their entirety.

338.diagram   Four of the circles—the ones represented by the thicker lines —were drawn in the manuscript in blue pencil, the others in red.
339.11–12   complete reciprocity . . . Object] See Kant, *Critique*, Bxvi and Bxxii note.
343.29, 31, 35, 37   The sentences to the right of these lines were added by Peirce in pencil.
345.diagram   The diagram is drawn in red and blue, with the help of nine dots arranged in a square:

1 2 3
4 5 6
7 8 9

The cross formed by the lines connecting points 1 and 6, and 4 and 3, are blue and are represented in the text in heavier lines; the other cross is red.

346.30–32   "There must therefore . . . ."] Kant, *Werke*, vol. 2, p. 95 [*Critique*, A101].

349.9   old rules] No specific source for what Peirce calls the "old" rules has been located, though they are common enough. But Peirce's rules can be obtained from Hamilton's if Hamilton's term "sumption" is replaced by Peirce's term "rule," and Hamilton's "subsumption" by Peirce's "case." See Hamilton, *Logic*, pp. 215–16.

Logic Chapter I

This carefully written manuscript may have been composed several months earlier than the date indicated, perhaps as early as the fall of 1865. It is not known how many pages are missing at the end.

356.1–7   "For the most part, . . .] Leibniz, *Opera*, vol. 1, pp. 79–80 [*Thoughts on Knowledge, Truth, and Ideas*].

Lowell Lecture I

This is the first of a series of twelve Lowell Institute lectures, entitled "The Logic of Science; or, Induction and Hypothesis," that Peirce delivered in Boston on Wednesday and Saturday evenings at 7:30, from 24 October to 1 December 1866. Only ten lectures, in eleven manuscripts, survive. MS 121 is an earlier, longer, and more technical and rambling variant of MS 122, the first lecture actually delivered by Peirce. Like most of the other manuscripts in the series, MS 122 consists of folded sheets originally bound together into gatherings, and it contains time numbers or notations in the margins: Peirce wanted to make sure to use his allotted time fully and accurately. The tables and drawings for the first lecture have been taken from the earlier variant, because they appear in mere outline in MS 122, the one printed here.

366.1   Lavilette] The specific French minister Peirce had in mind has not been identified.

368.2ff.   So we get] The diagrams at this point in the manuscript are carelessly done. They have been replaced by diagrams from MS 121, the earlier variant.

368.6   a table] The table and its use are explained in the note to 181.36.

369.11–14   Nevertheless, . . . De Morgan] De Morgan, *Formal Logic*, p. 15.

Lowell Lecture II

This is a continuation of the first lecture given in the series. Zeno's fourth argument, which appears on a separate sheet at the end of the manuscript, has been inserted in the appropriate place.

377.4–6   "With some of them. . . ."] 1 Cor. 10:5.

377.15–16   "He that is . . . ."] John 8:47.

380.8–9   such a fallacy . . . tenant.] De Morgan, *Formal Logic*, p. 245 [chap. 13].

386.12ff.   De Morgan's fullest exposition of the numerically definite syllogism is given in his *Formal Logic* (1847), chap. 8.

387.7–388.1   to one of the forms . . . the ancient Greeks were] In the top margin of this page in the manuscript Peirce has written "Diagram for this page"—perhaps as a reminder to himself to provide one on the blackboard. It is not possible to determine either the nature or the placement of this diagram.

389.14–15   Is this dog . . . your father.] Plato, *Euthydemus*, 298D.

389.16–19   that the weight . . . break it.] Not located.

389.20–22   Do you know . . . father.] Not located.

390.22   "All that is, is one,"] Plato, *Sophist*, 242D.

390.32   The *Many* . . . illusion,] This is not a literal translation of anything in Parmenides. It uses language characteristic of Zeno to paraphrase Parmenides. The nearest approaches in quotations from Parmenides are in Simplicius's commentary on Aristotle's *Physics*.

390.40–391.1   there is . . . it is not.] Plato, *Cratylus*, 386A; Plato, *Theaetetus*, 152A.

391.9   four famous arguments] One account of Zeno's four arguments is in Aristotle's *Physics*, 239^b–240^a.

392.14–16   "The solution of Diogenes. . . ?"] Aldrich, *Rudimenta* (Mansel), p. 144n.

392.23–26   a moving body . . . in all time.] Aristotle, *Physics*, 239^b.

392.29–31   Motion . . . *velocity*.] Aristotle, *Physics*, bk. 6, chap. 3, especially pp. 234^{a}24–29. See also chap. 6, 237^{a}14; chap. 8, 239^{b}1–4;

chap. 10, 241ᵃ23–26. Aristotle neither says nor implies that "it does not follow that there is not motion *at* that instant" or that "one date is sufficient for velocity." Of Zeno's arrow Aristotle says at 239ᵇ1–2 that in an indivisible instant it is neither in motion *nor at rest,* and at 239ᵇ 8–9 that "time is not made up of indivisible 'nows'."

Lowell Lecture III

Two separate sections at the end of the manuscript—one of one and two-thirds pages labeled A, the other of four pages labeled B—have been inserted at the places indicated by Peirce. Two separate pencil inscriptions, "Lecture Tuesday 5 PM," indicate that the lecture, or parts thereof, was used again in the later series of "Lectures on British Logicians," delivered at Harvard University between 14 December 1869 and 18 January 1870. Nine lectures were originally planned in that series; fifteen were actually given.

400.10–14   "Such evidence, ..."] Reid, *Works,* vol. 1, p. 482 [*Essays on the Intellectual Powers of Man,* essay 7, chap. 3].
403.3–4   Is it . . . hair?] Mill, *Logic* (1846), p. 322. [Dropped from subsequent editions.]

Lowell Lecture IV

Like the preceding lecture, this one was also used again in the series of "Lectures on British Logicians": delivered 28 December 1869 as the seventh lecture. The first nine sheets of the manuscript bear the pencil inscription "Lecture Tuesday 5 PM." The fact that there are two sets of time notations in the margins of the manuscript is probably due to the insertion of an extra page. One or more pages missing at the end have not been found.

408.8   the work] The reference is to Boole's *Laws of Thought.*
409.1 and 409.9–10   "process. . . ."] Mill, *Logic* (1865), vol. 1, p. 11 [intro. sec. 7].
409.20–22   "the carrying out. . . ."] Hamilton, *Logic,* p. 196 [lect. 15,

par. 53]. The italics are Peirce's, and where he has "admitted," Hamilton has "contained."

409.24–25 "Logicians. . . ,"] Mill, *Logic* (1865), vol. 1, p. 206 [bk. 2, chap. 3, sec. 2].

411.26–28 "I quite admit. . . ."] *Ibid.*, p. 230 [bk. 2, chap. 3, sec. 8]. Peirce has "rule" where Mill has "major."

413.35–38 "in the only sense. . . ."] *Ibid.*, p. 345 [bk. 3, chap. 3, sec. 1].

414.19–21 does not . . . *result.*] *Ibid.*, pp. 345ff. [bk. 3, chap. 3, sec. 1].

416.6 supposes.] At this point in the manuscript Peirce crossed out a passage which is of some interest since he speaks warmly of Mill's doctrine of real kinds. In his words "This doctrine is one to which I warmly assent, and think the enunciation [of] it one of Mill's greatest claims to our gratitude."

423.9–16 [bk. 3, chap. 21, sec. 1].

Lowell Lecture V

This very important lecture was formerly thought to belong to the Harvard lecture series of 1865. There are no marginal time notations in this manuscript—probably because this is a carefully rewritten version of a manuscript, no longer extant, in which Peirce had already timed himself.

440.1–15 Similar inferences were attempted on page 230. The propositions "No black white is black" and "All black which is white" are trivially true. Nevertheless, the proposition "Some black is white" does not follow even by the traditional logic, unless the existence of some "black white" is granted. But to grant this is to grant the conclusion.

Lowell Lecture VI

Though this manuscript has no marginal time notations, and contains three separate sections, it almost certainly served as the sixth lecture delivered 10 November 1866. The three sections are (1) a single sheet containing a brief outline of practical maxims; (2) four and one-quarter pages, the first four in the hand of Peirce's first wife, with "Memoranda" written at the top of the first page—probably as a reminder to distribute P 18 ("Aristotelean Syllogism") at the beginning of this lecture; and (3) twenty-one pages in Peirce's hand that represent a nearly complete lecture. Two additional pages have been inserted at the place indicated by Peirce, after the first sentence of the third section.

446.11–28   It runs thus, . . . exists.] See chap. 3 of *Monologium et proslogion.*

446.30   "A book . . . ,"] This is the *Liber pro insipiente* by Gaunilo, an eleventh-century monk of Marmoutier, which is included in vol. 1 of Anselm's *Opuscula philosophico-theologica.*

446.31–39   We are told, . . . must exist.] See sec. 6 of Gaunilo's *Liber.*

447.1   a book] This is the *Liber apologeticus contra Gaunilonem respondentem pro insipiente.*

447.2–6   Something can . . . of my argument.] See chap. 3 of Anselm's *Liber.*

448.19–33   Mill, *Logic* (1865).

452.2–3   (Vol. 3, p. 262)] Peirce is referring to the *Logik* in the Rosenkranz and Schubert edition. The text supplied (451.6–452.3) is from the translation by Robert S. Hartman and Wolfgang Schwarz, *Immanuel Kant: Logic* (Indianapolis: Bobbs-Merrill Co., Inc., 1974), pp. 92–93.

453.23   A book] *The Mysteries of Human Nature.*

454.8–22   *Works,* vol. 1, p. 261.

Lowell Lecture VII

This lecture, like the fifth, was formerly thought to belong to the Harvard lecture series of 1865. The first sentence is crossed out, and has been replaced by a new five-page introduction. The manuscript also contains a variant two-page beginning, as well as two separate sheets that may belong with the incomplete variant. One is about necessary propositions and the other, which Peirce marked "IMPORTANT," about truth as the reference of the symbol to its object. Lecture VIII has not been found.

456.20–21   history is . . . philosophy;] In the manuscript Peirce crossed out "Polybius says" and substituted "It has been said." The works of Polybius have been examined but the reference has not been found.

457.32–34   it is a synthesis . . . studied.] Diogenes Laertius, *Lives,* p. 437 [*Epicurus* 10.36].

458.22–23   the art of . . . premisses.] Not located.

Lowell Lecture IX

This manuscript contains a 28-page lecture and an eight-page variant beginning. Marginal time notations indicate that Peirce meant to substitute the variant beginning for the first one and two-thirds pages of the lecture. A separate page at the end of the manuscript, entitled "A Passage from Herbart," has been inserted at the place indicated by Peirce.

482.8 [quote]] It is not clear what quotation Peirce intended to use; Exod. 3:14 is one possibility.

484.9–14 Herbart, *Lehrbuch*, p. 77 [sec. 34].

> All our thoughts may be considered from two points of view; partly as activities of our mind, partly in relation to what is thought through them. In the latter respect they are called *concepts*, which term, by signifying *what is conceived*, requires us to abstract from the mode and manner in which we might receive, produce, or reproduce the thought. (Editors' translation)

Lowell Lecture X

This manuscript consists of only three pages, complete and self-contained. The marginal time notation at the beginning seems to indicate that Peirce read the three pages, but it is not known what followed.

Lowell Lecture XI

The content and marginal time notations seem to indicate that Peirce meant to insert the last three pages of this manuscript, which are unlabeled, at a place marked "A." It is not known if this was the last lecture in the Lowell series; a twelfth lecture has not been found.

491.22–23 Shakespeare, *Measure for Measure*, 2.2.119–20.

492.4–35 Reid, *Works* (Hamilton), p. 203.

492.8–20 Peirce identified the sources of Davies' theories of the soul—as expressed in stanzas 2, 3, and 4—in his *Century Dictionary* definition of "soul."

495.19–20   Shakespeare, *Measure for Measure*, 2.2.119–20, with minor changes. The quotation as it appears on 491.22–23 is correct.

497.10–11   Metaphysics . . . Metaphor] See *Les révolutions*, p. 49 and *Sciences naturelles*, pp. 328, 368f.

498.32   of his eye it is eyebeam.] From Emerson's "The Sphinx." More than by any other poetic phrases, Peirce was haunted throughout life by Shakespeare's "his glassy essence" and by Emerson's "Of thine eye I am eyebeam." It was primarily the latter line that he had in mind when, about 1890, he gave to one of his major unfinished books the title *A Guess at the Riddle*.

499.35–37   "the poor beetle. . . ."] Shakespeare, *Measure for Measure*, 3.1.79–81.

502.4–6   there are two . . . explanation;] Aristotle, *Posterior Analytics*, 78ª22.

Aristotelean Syllogism

Peirce distributed this privately printed brochure to the members of his audience at the Lowell Institute, probably at the beginning of his sixth lecture on 10 November 1866. There is an incomplete copy of the brochure in MS 127.

510n.1–3   Petrus Hispanus, *Summulae*, p. 250.

Searching for the Categories

The first several sections of this manuscript are very carefully written. Sections 10 and 11 were either never written or they have not been found. Section 12 is in an earlier, less finished stage of composition than the first nine sections.

521.28–30   "cum dicitur . . . ."] *Ouvrages inédits d'Abélard* (Cousin), p. 528. In his own copy of Cousin's edition, which is at The Johns Hopkins University, Peirce wrote on the title-page of *De generibus et speciebus:* "Not by Abelard."

524.2–4   Now they . . . interpretant.] Kant, *Werke*, vol. 2, pp. 733–34 [*Critique*, B134].

Diagram of the IT

This very carefully drawn diagram of material categories appears on a separate sheet in MS 52, where it follows a section entitled "Explanation of the Categories." It is an early attempt at one of Peirce's greatest concerns during his early metaphysical period, 1859–1862. For references to and discussions of these and similar categories, see MSS 12, 53, 57, 64, 65, 66, 67, 70, 71, 72. (All but the third, fourth, and seventh are printed in this volume.)

Bibliography of Peirce's References

Abbot, Francis Ellingwood. "The Philosophy of Space and Time." *North American Review* 99(1864):64–116.

Abelard, Peter. *Ouvrages inédits d'Abélard pour servir à l'histoire de la philosophie scolastique en France.* Edited by Victor Cousin. Paris: Imprimerie Royale, 1836.

Aesop. *Aesops Fables in true Ortography with Grammar Notz.* Translated by William Bullokar. London, 1585.

Aldrich, Henry. *Artis logicæ rudimenta.* Edited by H. L. Mansel. London: Rivingtons, 1862.

Anselm. *Monologium et proslogion nec non liber pro insipiente cum libro apologetico.* Vol. 1 of *Sancti Anselmi Contuariensis opuscula philosophico-theologica selecta.* Edited by Carolus Haas. Tübingen, 1863.

°Aristotle. *The Metaphysics of Aristotle.* Translated by John H. M'Mahon. London: Henry G. Bohn, 1857.

°———. *Organon.* 2 vols. Translated by O. F. Owen. London: Henry G. Bohn, 1853.

Bacon, Francis. *The Works of Lord Bacon.* Vol. 1. London: Henry G. Bohn, 1846.

°———. *The Works of Francis Bacon.* Collected and edited by James Spedding, Robert L. Ellis and Douglas Denon Heath. Vol. 2. Boston: Houghton, Mifflin and Co., [1857–74].

Bales, Peter. *The Writing Schoolemaster.* London, 1590.

Baret, John. *An Alvearie or Triple Dictionarie, in Englishe, Latin, and French.* London, 1573.

Berault, Pierre. *A new and compleat French & English grammar.* Translated by Roger L'Estrange. London, 1707.

Berkeley, George. *A Treatise Concerning the Principles of Human Knowledge.* Pt. 1. Dublin, 1710.

°Boole, George. *An Investigation of the Laws of Thought, on which are founded the Mathematical Theories of Logic and Probabilities.* London: Walton and Maberly, 1854.

———. *The Mathematical Analysis of Logic, being an Essay towards a Calculus of Deductive Reasoning.* Cambridge: Macmillan, Barclay and McMillan, 1847.

Bullokar, William. *Bullokars Booke at large, for the amendment of orthographie for English Speech.* London: Henrie Denham, 1580.

Butler, Charles. *The English Grammar, or The Institution of Letters, Syllables, and Woords, in the English tung.* Oxford, 1634.

———. *The Feminin' Monarchi', or the histori of bees.* Oxford, 1634.

Byron, George G. *The Works of Lord Byron.* Vol. 10. Edited by Thomas Moore. London: J. Murray, 1832.

°Carleton, Henry. *Liberty and Necessity.* Philadelphia: Parry and McMillan, 1857.

Carlyle, Thomas. *Critical and Miscellaneous Essays.* Vol. 1. Boston: James Munroe and Co., 1838.

Chase, Pliny Earle. "Intellectual Symbolism: A Basis for Science." *Transactions of the American Philosophical Society* 12(1862):463–594.

°Cicero. *Opera omnia.* Vol. 2. Edited by K. F. A. Nobbe. Leipzig: Tauchnitz, 1849.

Comte, Auguste. *Cours de philosophie positive.* 2 vols. Paris: Bachelier, Imprimeur-Librairie, 1835.

———. *The Positive Philosophy of Auguste Comte.* Translated and condensed by Harriet Martineau. Vol. 1. New York: D. Appleton and Co., 1854.

Coote, Edmund. *The English Schoole-Master.* 15th ed. London, 1624.

Cotgrave, Randle. *A French and English Dictionary.* With additions by James Howell. London, 1660.

Cousin, Victor. *Histoire de la philosophie morale au XVIIIe siècle, école de Kant.* Cours de l'histoire de la philosophie moderne, 1st ser., vol. 5, new ed. Paris: Ladrange and Didier, 1846.

°Craik, George L. *The English of Shakespeare: Illustrated in a Philological Commentary on his "Julius Caesar."* London: Chapman and Hall, 1857.

Cuvier, Georges. *Discours sur les révolutions de la surface du globe, et sur les changemens qu'elles ont produits dans le règne animal.* 3d ed. Paris: G. Dufour and Ed. d'Ocagne, 1825.

———. *Histoire des sciences naturelles, depuis leurs origine jusqu'à nos jours, chez tous les peuples connus.* Completed and edited by Magdeleine de Saint-Agy. Vol. 3. Paris: Fortin, Masson and Co., 1841.

D'Avenant, William. *The Works of Sir William D'Avenant.* London, 1673.

De Morgan, Augustus. *Formal Logic: or The Calculus of Inference, Necessary and Probable.* London: Taylor and Walton, 1847.

De Quincey, Thomas. *Literary Reminiscences; from The Autobiography of an English Opium-eater.* Vol. 1. Boston: Ticknor, Reed, and Fields, 1851.

De Wes, Giles. *An Introductory for to Learn to Read, to Pronounce, and to Speak French, 1532?* English Linguistics: 1500–1800, No. 327. Selected and edited by R. S. Alston. Menston, England: The Scolar Press Limited, 1972.

°Diogenes Laertius. *The Lives and Opinions of Eminent Philosophers.* Translated by C. D. Yonge. London: Henry G. Bohn, 1853.

Duval-Jouve, Joseph. *Traité de logique, ou essai sur la théorie de la science.* Paris: Librairie Philosophique de Ladrange, 1844.

°Emerson, Ralph Waldo. *Poems.* 7th ed. Boston: Phillips, Sampson and Co., 1858.

Festeau, Paul. *French Grammar*. 3d ed. London, 1675.

Gataker, Thomas. *De diphthongis, sive bivocalibus; dissertatio Philologica*. London, 1646.

Gil, Alexander. *Logonomia anglica*. London, 1621.

°Graham, G. F. *English Synonymes, Classified and Explained*. Edited by Henry Reed. New York: D. Appleton and Co., 1847.

Grimes, J. Stanley. *The Mysteries of Human Nature: Explained by a System of Nervous Physiology*. Boston: James Munroe and Co., 1860.

Hamilton, William. *Lectures on Metaphysics and Logic*. Edited by Henry L. Mansel and John Veitch. 2 vols. Boston: Gould and Lincoln, 1860.

Hamilton, William Rowan. *Lectures on Quaternions*. Dublin: Hodges and Smith, 1853.

Hart, John. *An Orthographie*. London: W. Serres, 1569.

Hegel, Georg Wilhelm Friedrich. *Encyklopädie der philosophischen Wissenschaften im Grundrisse*. 2d ed. Heidelberg: August Osswald, 1827.

°Herbart, Johann Friedrich. *Schriften zur Einleitung in die Philosophie*. Vol. 1 of *Sämmtliche Werke*. Edited by G. Hartenstein. Leipzig: Leopold Voss, 1850.

Hexham, Henry. *A Copious Englisg and Netherduytch Dictionarie, Composed out of our best English Authours*. Rotterdam, 1660.

Hillard, George Stillman. *A First Class Reader: Consisting of extracts, in prose and verse, with biographical and critical notices of the authors*. Boston: Hickling, Swan and Brown, 1856.

°Hobbes, Thomas. *The English Works of Thomas Hobbes*. Edited by Sir William Mosesworth. Vol. 1. London: John Bohn, 1839.

Hood, Thomas. *The Poetical Works of Thomas Hood*. Vol. 4. Boston: Little, Brown and Co., 1856.

[Hopkinson, Francis Custis]. "The Taming of the Shrew." *Harvard Magazine* 4(1858):58–67.

Hume, David. *The Philosophical Works of David Hume*. 4 vols. Boston: Little, Brown and Co., 1854.

Johnson, Samuel. *The Lives of the Poets*. Vol. 9 of *The Works of Samuel Johnson*. Edited by Arthur Murphy. London, 1806.

Jonson, Ben. *The Works of Ben Jonson*. Vol. 9. Edited by W. Gifford. London, 1816.

°Kant, Immanuel. *Anthropologie in pragmatischer Hinsicht*. Pt. 7:2 of *Sämmtliche Werke*. Edited by Karl Rosenkranz and Friedrich Wilhelm Schubert. Leipzig: Leopold Voss, 1838.

°————. *Critique of Pure Reason*. Edited by M. D. Meiklejohn. London: Henry G. Bohn, 1855.

°————. *Kritik der reinen Vernunft*. Pt. 2 of *Sämmtliche Werke*. Edited by Karl Rosenkranz and Friedrich Wilhelm Schubert. Leipzig: Leopold Voss, 1838.

°————. *Prolegomena zu einer jeden künftigen Metaphysik, die als Wissenschaft wird auftreten können und Logik*. Pt. 3 of *Sämmtliche Werke*. Edited by Karl Rosenkranz and Friedrich Wilhelm Schubert. Leipzig: Leopold Voss, 1838.

°————. *Schriften zur Philosophie der Natur.* Pt. 5 of *Sämmtliche Werke.* Edited by Karl Rosenkranz and Friedrich Wilhelm Schubert. Leipzig: Leopold Voss, 1839.

Krause, Karl Christian Friedrich. *Grundriss der historischen Logik für Vorlesungen.* Jena, 1803.

La Touche, Nicolas de. *L'Art de bien parler françois.* New ed. Vol. 1. Amsterdam: R. & G. Wetstein, 1710.

°Leibniz, Gottfried Wilhelm. *Opera philosophica.* Vol. 1. Edited by J. E. Erdmann. Berlin, 1840.

Liddell, Henry George, and Scott, Robert. *A Greek-English Lexicon, based on the German Work of Francis Passow.* New York: Harper and Bros., 1852.

°Locke, John. *An Essay Concerning Human Understanding.* 3 vols. London, 1795.

°Mansel, Henry Longueville. *The Limits of Religious Thought.* Boston: Gould and Lincoln, 1859.

————. *Prolegomena logica: An Inquiry into the Psychological Character of Logical Processes.* 2d ed. Oxford: Henry Hammans, 1860.

Marsh, George P. *Lectures on the English Language.* 1st ser. 4th ed. New York: Charles Scribner, 1862.

Mill, John Stuart. *A System of Logic, Ratiocinative and Inductive: Being a Connected View of the Principles of Evidence, and the Methods of Scientific Investigation.* New York: Harper and Bros., 1846.

°————. *A System of Logic, Ratiocinative and Inductive: Being a Connected View of the Principles of Evidence, and the Methods of Scientific Investigation.* 2 vols. 6th ed. London: Longmans, Green, and Co., 1865.

Mulcaster, Richard. *The First Part of the Elementarie which entreateth chefelie of the right writing of our English tung.* London, 1582.

Nares, Robert. *Elements of Orthoepy.* London, 1784.

Newton, Sir Isaac. *Philosophiæ naturalis principia mathematica.* London, 1687.

Palsgrave, Jean. *L'Eclaircissement de la langue française, suivi de la grammaire de Giles Du Guez.* Edited by F. Genin. Paris: Imprimerie Nationale, 1852.

Percivale, Richard. *A Spanish Grammar.* Edited by John Minsheu. London, 1623.

Petrus Hispanus. *Summulae logicales.* Venice, 1597.

°Plato. *The Works of Plato.* Vol. 1. Translated by Henry Cary. London: Henry G. Bohn, 1854.

————. *The Works of Plato.* Vol. 3. Translated by George Burges. London: Henry G. Bohn, 1859.

[Pomey] Pomai, François. *Le grand dictionaire royal.* 4th ed. Frankfurt, 1709.

Pope, Alexander. *Essay on Criticism.* In vol. 1 of *The Works of Alexander Pope.* Edited by William Warburton. London, 1751.

°Reid, Thomas. *Reid's Essays on the Intellectual Powers of Man.* Edited by William Hamilton. Edinburgh: Maclachlan and Stewart, 1853.

————. *The Works of Thomas Reid: Now Fully Collected, with Selections from his Unpublished Letters.* Edited by William Hamilton. 3d ed. Edinburgh: Maclachlan and Stewart, 1852.

°Roget, P. M. *Thesaurus of English Words.* Revised and edited by Barnas Sears. Boston: Gould and Lincoln, 1854.

Ruskin, John. *Modern Painters.* Pt. 3. Rev. ed. New York: John Wiley, 1848.

Saxon, Samuel. *The English schollar's assistant, or the rudiments of the English tongue.* 2d ed. Reading, 1737.

°Schiller, Friedrich. *The Aesthetic Letters, Essays, and the Philosophical Letters of Schiller.* Translated by J. Weiss. Boston: C. C. Little and J. Brown, 1845.

————. *Sämmtliche Werke.* Vol. 10. Stuttgart: J. G. Cotta'scher Verlag, 1844.

Sewel, William. *Korte Wegwyzer der Engelsche Taale.* Amsterdam, 1705.

Shakespeare, William. *The Plays of William Shakespeare.* Vol. 7. Edited by Samuel Johnson. London, 1768.

————. *The Works of William Shakespeare.* Edited by Richard Grant White. Boston, 1861.

Sharp, Granville. *A Short Treatise on the English Tongue.* London, 1767.

Sidney, Philip. *The Defence of Poesie.* London, 1595.

Smith, Thomas. *De recta et emendata linguae anglicae scriptione, dialogus.* Paris, 1568.

Spalding, William. "Logic." *The Encyclopædia Britannica or Dictionary of Arts, Sciences, and General Literature.* Vol. 13. 8th ed. Boston: Little, Brown and Co., 1857.

Steevens, George. *Six old plays.* London, 1779.

Strauss, David Friedrich. *The Life of Jesus, Critically Examined.* Translated from the 4th German ed. by Marian Evans. New York: C. Blanchard, 1855.

Strong, Nathaniel. *England's Perfect School-Master.* 2d ed. London, 1704.

Ueberweg, Friedrich. *System der Logik und Geschichte der logischen Lehren.* Bonn: Adolph Marcus, 1857.

Wallis, John. *Grammatica linguae anglicanae.* Oxford, 1653.

°Whately, Elizabeth Jane. *A Selection of English Synonyms.* Rev. and enl. ed. Boston: James Munroe and Co., 1852.

°Whewell, William. *Novum Organon Renovatum.* 3d ed. London: John W. Parker and Son, 1858.

————. *On the Philosophy of Discovery: Chapters Historical and Critical.* London: John W. Parker and Son, 1860.

Wilkins, John. *An Essay towards a Real Character, and a Philosophical Language.* London, 1668.

Worcester, Joseph E. *A Dictionary of the English Language.* Vol. 2. Boston: Hickling, Swan, and Brewer, 1860.

CHRONOLOGICAL LIST
1849-1866

Three kinds of materials are included here:

1. All of Peirce's known publications, identified by P followed by a number. For these numbers and for further bibliographical information, see *A Comprehensive Bibliography and Index of the Published Works of Charles Sanders Peirce with a Bibliography of Secondary Studies,* ed. Kenneth Laine Ketner et al. (Greenwich, CT: Johnson Associates, 1977).

2. All of Peirce's known manuscripts and annotated offprints, identified by MS followed by a number. These numbers reflect the Kloesel rearrangement and chronological ordering of the so-called Peirce Papers, the originals of which are in The Houghton Library of Harvard University, and of papers found in other collections. Parentheses after the MS number give either the name or location of those collections, or they identify the Robin manuscript number. See Richard S. Robin, *Annotated Catalogue of the Papers of Charles S. Peirce* (Amherst: University of Massachusetts Press, 1967), and "The Peirce Papers: A Supplementary Catalogue," *Transactions of the Charles S. Peirce Society* 7(1971):37–57.

3. Selected letters and letter drafts, identified by L followed by a (Robin) number. Parentheses give the location of letters not contained in the Peirce Papers.

Manuscripts and a few rarely republished items that have appeared in earlier editions are identified in brackets at the end of the entry. CP refers to the *Collected Papers,* NE to *The New Elements of Mathematics;* other references are given in full.

Dates of publication or composition appear to the right; if set in italics, they are Peirce's own. Descriptive or supplied titles appear in italic brackets. Journal titles are abbreviated. All items marked with an asterisk are included in the present volume.

MS 1 (1629, 1574)   fall 1849–July 1854
  [Cambridge High School Themes and Exercises].
MS 2 (1521)   1852, 1854, 1859
  Riddles, Conundrums, etc.
MS 3 (1521)   1854
  Alfred—a drama.
MS 4 (1629)   December 1854–June 1855
  [Dixwell Preparatory School Themes and Exercises].
MS 5 (1629)   February 1855, 1857–58
  [Valentines].
MS 6 (Sylvia Mitarachi)   1855
  Theories, of C. S. Peirce's, 1854.
MS 7 (1633)   2 September 1856
  Harvard Composition 1: When the people of Crete. . . .
MS 8 (1629, 1633)   23 October 1856
  Harvard Composition 2: The compatibility of Poetical Genius with
  Practical Talent, illustrated.
MS 9 (1633, 1629)   29 October 1856
  Harvard Composition 3: What is your favorite virtue?
MS 10 (S 65)   winter 1856–57
  Aphorismi Urbigerani.
MS 11 (1628)   *14 February 1857*
  The Warsaw Times.
°MS 12 (1633)   26 March 1857
  Harvard Composition 4: The Sense of Beauty never furthered the
  Performance of a single Act of Duty.
MS 13 (1633)   30 March 1857
  Harvard Composition 5: Historical Account of the Celebration of
  Christmas in New England.
MS 14 (1633)   2 April 1857
  Harvard Composition 6: The Death-Bed a Detector of the Heart.
MS 15 (1633)   26 April 1857
  Harvard Composition 7: The Immediate Effects of the Discovery
  of an Extensive Gold-Mine.
MS 16 (1633)   10 June 1857
  Harvard Composition 8: On the Character in which Vanity or
  Self-Conceit coexists with Kindness of Heart.
MS 17 (1633)   26 June 1857
  Harvard Composition 9: The Uses of Novels.
MS 18 (1633)   20 September 1857
  Harvard Composition 10: "A man has only himself to blame if at
  any time his life seem void of interest or amusement."

MS 19 (1633)   *11 October 1857*
Harvard Composition 11: There is no living with thee—nor without
thee. . . .

*MS 20 (1142, 1141, 1140)   *13 October 1857*
A Scientific Book of Synonyms.

*MS 21 (1633, 1629)   22 October 1857
Harvard Composition 12: Raphael and Michael Angelo compared
as men.

MS 22 (1633)   16 November 1857
Harvard Composition 13: The American Country Gentleman—The
Ideal and the Reality.

MS 23 (1633, 1629)   16 November 1857
Harvard Composition 14: The Strength and the Weakness of the
Present Dynasty in France.

MS 24 (1633)   8 December 1857
Harvard Composition 15: "Is it their soil . . . that the English have
the advantage of many other nations" (Goethe).

MS 25 (1633)   2 January 1858
Harvard Composition 16: It is melancholy to observe how much
private misery lies at the bottom of all great action.

MS 26 (1633)   6 January 1858
Harvard Composition 17: "In Shakespeare we discern no aim to
enforce a moral. . . ."

MS 27 (1635)   *4 February 1858–June 1859*
The Class of 1859 of Harvard.

MS 28 (1555)   *27 February 1858*
Catalogue of the Library of Charles S. Peirce.

MS 29 (1630)   March–July 1858
Notes to Lectures on Mathematics, 2nd Term Junior.

MS 30 (1633)   26 March 1858
Harvard Composition 18: Lazy and quiet men, who could not discern
consequences, and were unwilling to antedate their miseries.

MS 31 (1633)   31 March 1858
Harvard Composition 19: Describe some of the circumstances
which make men recluses.

MS 32 (1633)   22 April 1858
Harvard Composition 20: An Example of the Different Estimation
in which Great Men have been held in Different Times.

*P 1   April 1858
"Think Again!" *Harvard Mag* 4, 100–105.

MS 33 (1633)   2 May 1858
Harvard Composition 21: The Moral and Religious Character of
Coleridge.

MS 34 (1633)   27 May 1858
Harvard Composition 22: The Condition of Shakespeare in his
own Time.

MS 35 (1633)   3 June 1858
  Harvard Composition 23: So savage were the party quarrels. . . .
MS 36 (1005, 1006, 1007)   summer 1858–fall 1864
  [Translation of parts of Kant's *Critique*].
MS 37 (1631, 1629)   September 1858–May 1859
  Notes to the Lectures of Prof. Peirce on Mathematics, delivered
  in the year 1858–9 A.D.
MS 38 (1633)   3 January 1859
  Harvard Composition 24: "In time of peace prepare for war."
MS 39 (1633)   *7 January 1859*
  Harvard Composition 25: [Whether more good or evil has resulted
  to the world from the life and the religion of Mohammed].
MS 40 (1137)   *January 1859*
  The Natural History of Words.
MS 41 (1633)   12 March 1859
  Harvard Composition 26: Whether great talents are favorable to
  the happiness of their possessor.
°MS 42 (1633, 1118)   19 March 1859
  Harvard Composition 27: Analysis of Genius.
MS 43 (918)   March 1859
  On the Classification of the Human Faculties.
MS 44 (1636)   spring 1859
  Proposed New Constitution [for the Harvard O.K.].
MS 45 (1259)   spring 1859
  Rules for editing *Midsummer Night's Dream*.
MS 46 (1594, 1574)   spring 1859–1862
  [Index to Gil's *Logonomia anglica*].
MS 47 (1633)   1 April 1859
  Harvard Composition 28: Some Considerations which seem to show
  that despotic governments are not more essentially aggressive. . . .
MS 48 (1633)   18 April 1859
  Harvard Composition 29: The alleged intolerant and persecuting
  conduct of the Pilgrim Fathers.
MS 49 (1633)   28 April 1859
  Harvard Composition 30: Is wisdom best learned from books or
  from experience in the world?
°MS 50 (1003)   May 1859
  The Axioms of Intuition: After Kant.
°MS 51 (Harvard Archives)   May 1859
  Peirce [Harvard Class-Book entry].
MS 52 (921)   *21 May–25 October 1859*
  [Drafts of a treatise on metaphysics].
P 2–7   3–10 August 1859
  "The Thirteenth Annual Meeting of the American Association for
  the Advancement of Science." *Boston Daily Evening Traveller*.

°MS 53 (858, 921)   August–25 *October 1859*
  [Three Essays on Infinity and God].
MS 54 (988)   30 *May 1860*
  Metaphysical Axioms and Syllogisms (from Plato).
°MS 55 (891, S 66)   7 *June 1860–17 March 1888*
  Private Thoughts principally on the conduct of life.
MS 56 (743, 1571)   23 *June 1860*
  The Rules of Logic: Logically Deduced.
MS 57 (921)   30 *June–16 December 1860*
  [Drafts of a treatise on metaphysics].
MS 58 (822, S 66, 921)   June–July 1860
  Hamilton and Mansel.
MS 59 (S 83)   summer 1860
  [Notes on Human Character].
MS 60 (1555a)   summer *1860*
  List of all the Books in the House.
°MS 61 (859)   summer 1860
  Proof of the Infinite Nature of the Creator.
MS 62 (1222)   summer 1860–3 *January 1863*
  An Inquiry into the Pronunciation of Shakespearian English.
  [See P 13.]
MS 63 (1634)   10 *September 1860*–fall 1863
  Book of Characters.
MS 64 (922, 923)   10 *December 1860–8 June 1862*
  [Tables of Categories].
°MS 65 (917, 923, 919, 1571, 278, S 66)   spring 1861
  I, IT, and THOU: A Book giving Instruction in some of the
  Elements of Thought.
°MS 66 (916)   spring 1861
  The Modus of the IT.
MS 67 (921, S 64)   spring–fall 1861
  [Drafts of a treatise on metaphysics].
MS 68 (1048, 1348)   summer–fall 1861
  [Chemical Notes].
°MS 69 (1047)   summer–fall 1861
  Views of Chemistry: sketched for Young Ladies.
°MS 70 (920, 919)   21 *August 1861–30 March 1862*
  [A Treatise on Metaphysics].
°MS 71 (1105, 921, 919, 741)   fall–winter 1861
  Analysis of Creation.
°MS 72 (923, 921, 927)   winter 1861–62
  S P Q R.
MS 73 (1046, 1048)   winter–spring 1862
  Chemical Curves.
MS 74 (921, 922, 833, 919, S 64, S 66)   winter–spring 1862
  [Drafts of a treatise on metaphysics].

°P 11   January 1863
"The Chemical Theory of Interpenetration." *Am J of Science and Arts* 2d ser. 35, 78–82.

P 15   7 November 1863
"Reports of Professor Benjamin Peirce, of Harvard, upon the Occultations of the Pleiades, in 1841 and 1842." *Coast Survey Report 1863*, 146–54.

°P 12   21 November 1863
["The Place of Our Age in the History of Civilization"]. *Cambridge Chronicle* 18:47, 1. [MS 75 (1638) contains a copy with a note by Peirce. Published in parts in *Values in a Universe of Chance*, ed. Philip P. Wiener (Garden City, NY: Doubleday, 1958), pp. 3–14; rpt. as *Charles S. Peirce: Selected Writings* (New York: Dover, 1966).]

MS 76 (S 95)   winter 1863–64
Note on the meaning of the Innovations in Dress which the 3 brothers adopted.

MS 77 (1571)   March 1864
Chemical Classification.

°L 82a   *4 April 1864*
Letter Draft, Peirce to Chase.

°P 13   April 1864
["Shakespearian Pronunciation"]. *North Am R* 98, 342–69. [See MS 62.]

°MS 78 (1116, 919)   spring 1864
Analysis of the Ego.

MS 79 (1601)   *June 1864*
Family Record.

°MS 80 (926, 924, 925)   *5 August 1864*
A Treatise of the Major Premisses of Natural Science.

°MS 81 (1103)   August 1864
On the Doctrine of Immediate Perception.

MS 82 (741)   *September 1864*
Induction.

MS 83 (991)   September 1864
Categories.

MS 84 (S 8)   fall 1864
[Notes on Space and Time].

MS 85 (741)   fall 1864
Considerations of the Advantages of Sir W. H.'s Analytic.

MS 86 (194, 839, 1571, S 25, S 43)   fall 1864
[Notes on Boolian Algebra].

MS 87 (927, 1571)   fall 1864
Possible extensive relations of Subject and Predicate.

MS 88 (741, 744, 278, 839, 1571, 1574, S 64)   fall–winter 1864
On the Figures and Moods of Logic.

MS 89 (741, 1571)   fall–winter 1864
   Quality is the only Quantity.
MS 90 (741)   fall–winter 1864
   Further Arguments for a Quantified Predicate.
MS 91 (1156)   1864–1869
   [Philosophical Terms from A to Z].
MS 92 (1596)   1864–1869
   [Philosophical Notes].
MS 93 (1571)   winter 1864–65
   Definitions of Logic.
°L 1 (Abbot Papers)   5 February 1865
   Letter, Peirce to Abbot.
°MS 94 (340, 734)   February–March 1865
   Lecture I (Harvard 1865).
°MS 95 (341, 765)   February–March 1865
   Lecture II (Harvard 1865).
°MS 96 (342)   February–March 1865
   Lecture III (Harvard 1865). [Published in NE 3:1, pp. 298–312.]
MS 97 (348a)   March–April 1865
   [from a lecture on Bacon].
MS 98 (837)   March–April 1865
   [from a lecture on Comte and hypothesis].
°MS 99 (350)   March–April 1865
   Logic of Science. Lecture on the Theories of Whewell, Mill, and
   Compte (Harvard 1865).
°MS 100 (344)   March–April 1865
   Logic of Science. Lecture VI. Boole's Calculus of Logic (Harvard
   1865). [Published, with one paragraph omitted, in NE 3:1, pp.
   313–27.]
°MS 101 (349)   March–April 1865
   Logic of Science. Lecture on Kant (Harvard 1865).
MS 102 (727)   spring 1865
   [Definitions of Intension and Extension].
MS 103 (741)   spring 1865
   Notation.
MS 104 (741, S 64)   April–May 1865
   [Notes on Induction and Hypothesis].
°MS 105 (346, 758)   April–May 1865
   Logic of Science. Lecture VIII. Forms of Induction and Hypothe-
   sis (Harvard 1865).
°MS 106 (347)   April–May 1865
   Logic of Science. Lecture X. Grounds of Induction (Harvard 1865).
°MS 107 (348)   April–May 1865
   Logic of Science. Lecture XI (Harvard 1865).
°MS 108 (802)   14 May 1865
   Teleological Logic.

°MS 109 (726, 731, 741)   May–fall 1865
An Unpsychological View of Logic.
MS 110 (1556)   summer 1865
Classified List of my Books.
MS 111 (1534)   August 1865
Tricks.
MS 112 (724)   fall 1865
Logic. Chapter I. Terms.
°MS 113 (769, 734, 729, 921, 922, 728, S 66)   fall–winter 1865
Logic of the Sciences.
°MS 114 (339)   12 November–20 December 1865
[The Logic Notebook].
°MS 115 (720)   winter–spring 1866
Logic Chapter I.
MS 116 (733)   winter–spring 1866
Logic Chapter 1.
°MS 117 (339)   March–8 December 1866
[The Logic Notebook].
MS 118 (734, 741, 1571, 730)   spring–summer 1866
Logic. Chapter 2. Formal Logic.
MS 119 (1059)   12 July 1866–25 September 1869
[Star Observation Records].
MS 120 (1059)   31 July 1866–9 April 1870
[Star Observation List].
MS 121 (351)   September–October 1866
Lecture 1 (Lowell 1866).
°MS 122 (352)   September–October 1866
Lecture I (Lowell 1866).
°MS 123 (353)   September–October 1866
Lecture II (Lowell 1866).
°MS 124 (354)   September–October 1866
Lecture III (Lowell 1866). [Published in NE 3:1, pp. 218–29.]
°MS 125 (355)   October 1866
Lecture IV (Lowell 1866). [Last few pages published in CP
7.131–138.]
°MS 126 (343)   October 1866
Lecture V (Lowell 1866).
°P 18   October–November 1866
Memoranda Concerning the Aristotelean Syllogism. (Privately
printed and) Distributed at the Lowell Institute, November
1866. [Unmarked copy in MS 127 (S 63).]
°MS 128 (696)   October–November 1866
[Lecture VI]: Practical Maxims of Logic (Lowell 1866).
°MS 129 (356, 345, 919, 1571)   October–November 1866
Lecture VII (Lowell 1866).
°MS 130 (357)   November 1866
Lecture IX (Lowell 1866).

°MS 131 (358)   November 1866
    Lecture X (Lowell 1866).
°MS 132 (359)   November 1866
    Lecture XI (Lowell 1866). [Published, with two deletions and
    the omission of the last seven pages, in CP 7.579–596.]
°MS 133 (732, 809)   November–December 1866
    [On a Method of Searching for the Categories].
MS 134 (271)   winter 1866–67
    Pythagorean.
MS 135 (741, 278)   winter 1866–67
    On the Conversion of Quantity.
MS 136 (240, 241)   winter 1866–67
    A Mathematical Suggestion.
MS 137 (88, 741, 1575)   winter 1866–67
    Quaternions applied to Probabilities.
MS 138 (740, S 66)   winter 1866–67
    Appendix No. 2.
MS 139 (1571)   1866
    Plan of a Review article on the logic of Induction.

Essay on Editorial Method

The writings by Peirce contained in this volume are of two kinds: those published during his lifetime and those he left in manuscript form. Only five were published at the time, and four of those appeared in four different journals, printed according to four different house publication styles. The fifth, *Memoranda Concerning the Aristotelean Syllogism,* was a privately printed pamphlet to be used as a lecture handout and for private circulation; thus, Peirce probably had a good deal of control over what would ordinarily have been matters of house style.

Most of the Peirce texts in this volume exist in manuscripts never before published and never prepared for publication. The problems they pose derive chiefly from their physical state and from Peirce's working methods. Aside from the facts that numerous pages and runs of pages had become widely separated from the manuscripts to which they belonged, that there are no dates or running heads to assist in reassembling them, and that in four cases pages seem irretrievably lost, most of the manuscripts included in this volume are in good physical condition. In a few cases, portions of words are obliterated by frayed or torn edges, burns, or inkstains, but they are easily restored.

Peirce's working methods present an altogether different set of problems. Most of the manuscripts are unfinished or unpolished and, with few exceptions, they were never meant to be read by anyone other than himself. Hence, many are carelessly inscribed or hurriedly written, and some degenerate to mere outlines. Many contain what at first glance seem to be different "drafts" of the same piece. On closer scrutiny, it becomes apparent that this is not the case. Peirce seldom created "drafts" by copying out an earlier version. Rather, he was more likely to begin anew, repeating perhaps the same or a similar first sentence but then going in a different direction, and thus creating several versions of a single composition. More often than not, these several versions cannot be confidently dated as regards the order in which they were written, nor can they be collated; as a result, all become justifiable candidates for publication.[1]

Many of the manuscripts published here may fairly be called "working copies." They show much self-editing on Peirce's part, with many deletions, insertions, transpositions, false starts, incomplete revisions, notes to himself, and alternative words left undecided. Peirce was concerned with getting his early thoughts on paper, and he spent much time searching for the most appropriate and precise words in order to achieve a lucid expression of his ideas. But his search for lucid expression was at the expense of, or took precedence over, such matters as punctuation and spelling. His spelling is often phonetic, and many words display characteristic confusions of transposed ei and ie combinations, -ible and -able endings, or single and double consonants used with prefixes and suffixes. Furthermore, he often leaves out letters altogether and even drops complete syllables from the middle of words.[2]

His punctuation during this early period is haphazard, with only a few nineteenth-century patterns apparent, such as the use of dashes after other punctuation marks; and his placement of quotation marks when used in combination with a period, comma, colon, or semi-colon is rarely precise enough to make his intention clear. His hyphenation is capricious, his paragraphing curious and inconsistent. In the more hurriedly inscribed manuscripts, and in those that are mere outlines, he used many abbreviations and sprinkled ditto marks about liberally. At times, he omitted even the ditto marks.

The first, crucial step in preparing manuscripts for editing and subsequent publication lies in the transcription process. To assure the reader that he has before him what Peirce actually wrote, we have established certain transcription guidelines based on editorial theory and on the available working materials.

The Peirce Edition Project owns two sets of photocopies of the Peirce manuscripts deposited in The Houghton Library, Harvard University. These, unfortunately, were not made directly from the originals; they are third-generation copies, made from an electroprint copy, which, in turn, was printed from the negative microfilm copy at Har-

---

1. MS 53, for which we have supplied the title "Three Essays on Infinity and God," is a prime example of this working method.
2. Peirce to M. A. Sacksteder of the Open Court Publishing Company, 17 August 1892: "If I wrote Delbœuf's name Debœuf, it was the effect of an inveterate habit of leaving letters out of words." (Open Court Archives, Special Collections, Morris Library, Southern Illinois University.)

vard. The legibility of our photocopies is generally good, partly because Peirce used black ink as his basic writing medium. When he
used lead pencil or different colors of ink and pencil for revisions and
annotations, the legibility of our copies falls away sharply. For this
reason, the transcripts are read and checked several times prior to
emendation. After we have made the initial transcripts, they are read
at least two times, by two different editors, against our copies. During
these readings, the more difficult to read and questionable passages
are marked. One of the editors then takes the transcripts to The
Houghton Library and, with the help of a local person, re-reads them
a third time against the originals, paying careful attention to those
"questionable" or "difficult to read" passages. Also such features are
noted as holes, ink blots, or colored pencil contained in the originals
but not distinguishable on the copies. Upon return to the Project, the
transcripts are revised to coincide with the Harvard originals.

Certain points of editorial policy concerning these transcripts also
need to be stated. As mentioned above, Peirce made many internal
revisions in his manuscripts, usually during the process of composition. All such revisions are interpreted as Peirce's final intention and
are incorporated into the initial transcriptions. Material that Peirce
crossed out is omitted, including accompanying punctuation that he
failed to cross out; his careted-in revisions are inserted, passages he
marked for transposition are transposed, and his instructions for moving large blocks of material are followed.[3] For the most part, Peirce
clearly marked such revisions. Of the nearly 900 manuscript pages
published in this volume, however, there are sixteen instances in
which his intended revisions and marginal annotations are unclear.
In four cases we were able to insert the material into the text according to the context. In three other cases we placed Peirce's marginal
material into footnotes, because lacking his instructions, that is what
seemed best according to the context. Whether the material is incorporated into the text or placed as a footnote, all seven instances of
editorial intervention are listed as emendations, and an accompanying
textual note indicates the placement of the material on the manuscript
page. In the nine final cases, incorporating the marginal material or
placing it in a footnote would have created a nonsensical reading.

3. Peirce's alterations in the manuscripts are so numerous that a complete
record of them would greatly increase the size and cost of the volume. In view of
the accessibility of the microfilm edition and other photocopies of the original papers, we supply such information only in the few cases in which his final intentions
remain unclear.

Consequently, we have reproduced such material in the Editorial Notes, again with an explanation of its placement on the manuscript page. The only material on the manuscript page that the reader will not find reproduced are Peirce's page numbers and doodles, or later annotations by other persons. Peirce's incomplete revisions, misspellings, misplaced or omitted punctuation, etc., are transcribed exactly as they appear on the manuscript page. The underlinings (single, double, and even triple) that Peirce used for emphasis are included also, but are interpreted as modern copy-editing instructions and are printed in the volume as italic, small capital letters, and regular capital letters respectively.

One other point of editorial policy regarding the transcription of manuscripts and the interpretation of Peirce's intention must be noted. As Peirce's placement of quotation marks (both single and double) when used in combination with a period, comma, colon, or semi-colon is rarely precise enough to make his intention clear, we interpret all such combinations by modern standard punctuation practices.

Three sets of symbols have been adopted to reflect the physical limitations of the manuscripts. In the four cases where pages are lost, three ellipsis points within italic brackets mark the absence. Where manuscripts are partially destroyed and words or portions of them are editorially reconstructed, the reconstructions appear in italic brackets also; to give the reader some hint as to manuscript content, we have supplied titles within italic brackets to papers that Peirce left untitled. The third symbol combination incorporated into the text is that of double and single slashes used to alert the reader to cases where Peirce left choices of words or phrases undecided. The double slash signals the beginning and ending of the undecided choice, and the single slash divides the two alternatives. The reading to the left of the single slash is the original inscription, and that to the right the interlined alternative.

Choice of copy-text has not proved problematical, either for published papers or for unpublished manuscripts. Each published article in this volume went through only one printing, and no differences were found in collating three copies of each,[4] supplied by three different

---

4. The exceptions to this are *Memoranda Concerning the Aristotelean Syllogism* and *The Place of Our Age in the History of Civilization*. Only two copies of each could be located. Copies of the former were obtained from the Boston Public Library (2974.73) and from The Houghton Library (Phil. 2225.5.06). Peirce's own copy of the latter is MS 75 in the Peirce Papers; the other copy came from the Cambridge Public Library.

libraries.[5] Because Peirce's working method in his unpublished manuscripts created variant texts which cannot be collated, each variant text theoretically stands alone, as a separate item. Choice among these alternative texts was made with the advice of at least one of the contributing editors. That text was chosen for publication that seemed most carefully written and most fully developed and best argued. When a contributing editor thought more than one version worth publishing, more than one is published. Each version, then, serves as its own copy-text, and no other version of the same paper is considered as having any textual authority for that one, though we may refer to others for helpful information. In the very few cases where we do have successively written collatable drafts of a single paper, the latest is considered to reflect the closest approach to Peirce's final intention and is chosen as copy-text. All earlier drafts are considered to be pre-copy-text forms without any textual authority. With the single exception, then, of "My Life," each paper published in this volume has a single authoritative text, and all emendations are supplied by the editors.

Since our purpose in this volume is not to reproduce handwritten documents nor to represent the individual and sometimes antiquated printing styles of different publishing houses, but to offer readable texts that are reliable for the further study of Peirce's life and thought, the following guidelines are used in emending the texts.

Any spellings not accepted in the nineteenth and twentieth centuries are considered to be in error and are corrected. The *Oxford English Dictionary* is our standard reference for determining correctness of spelling, and no attempt is made to regularize Peirce's spelling when more forms than one were acceptable in his day. Similarly, alternative spellings of a given proper name are allowed to stand if they were once acceptable.

Closely related to the spelling problem is that of hyphenated words. As Peirce's intentions cannot be made out, the *Oxford English Dictionary* again serves as our guide, and hyphens are inserted or deleted accordingly.

Whatever Peirce marks as direct quotation is allowed to stand as

5. Our collation copies are as follows. For *Think Again!*: New York State Library; Widener Library, Harvard University (P 207.12); University of Iowa Libraries. For *The Chemical Theory of Interpenetration:* Indiana University Libraries, Bloomington (Q1/.A5/ser. 2); Duggan Library, Hanover College; Roy O. West Library, DePauw University. For *Shakespearian Pronunciation:* Indiana University Libraries, Bloomington (AP 2/.N8); Purdue University Libraries (GL/051/N81); and Indiana State Library.

he gives it, even if it differs from the original. In those cases where Peirce's oversight results in nonsensical readings, the text is emended, and the entry in the list of emendations includes a reference to the Editorial Notes, where all information on his quotations and their sources may be found.

Though no attempt is made to modernize or regularize his citations, they are corrected when unintelligible, and appropriate punctuation is added.

With few exceptions, such common abbreviations as Ch., Chap., Bk., etc., are retained, though missing periods are added. Uncommon abbreviations are expanded.

Peirce's ditto marks are retained except in cases where they might give rise to confusion of meaning because the line length of our printed text cannot accommodate the line length of his manuscript. In these few instances, the text is emended by replacing the ditto marks with the appropriate word(s) for which they stand. Ditto marks missing in Peirce's manuscripts are supplied by the editors.

Periods are added at the ends of sentences where Peirce's pen skipped or he inadvertently omitted them. Periods are deleted after the phrase "per cent" and after Roman numerals used as parts of titles. (Such periods are archaic printing practices to which Peirce does not adhere in his manuscripts.)

Except in special cases, commas are added to divide parts of a series, including a comma before the conjunction (which seems to be Peirce's more usual practice). A comma, dash, parenthesis, or quotation mark is added when it is the missing half of a pair, and apostrophes are inserted in possessives and contractions where Peirce carelessly omitted them.

Italics or quotation marks are added or changed to conform to modern usage in book, play, article, chapter, and other titles. Quotation marks are inserted around direct quotations where Peirce inadvertently omitted them; translated passages are left without quotation marks. Quotation marks are deleted where lengthy quotations are treated as extracts, and in cases of papers published by Peirce where the house style differs from our own.

Since Peirce is fairly consistent in capitalizing the first word of a syllogism in running text, we have done it for him when he neglected to do so.

Peirce uses several methods for the treatment of special terms and phrases. When his practice within a single paper can be established, we emend his oversights to accord with it. When his practice within a given paper cannot be established, we emend the text to conform to modern standards.

When Peirce is inconsistent in his use of paragraphing and hanging indentions, or when ragged margins make his intention unclear, we paragraph according to the context of Peirce's argument. All such questionable cases are listed as emendations.

Other changes are of course required from time to time, and in many cases the need for them arises from Peirce's heavy revising of his work. In the very process of revision, for example, he sometimes created grammatical errors. In other cases, he failed to complete his intended revision by crossing out a necessary word or phrase but not going back to replace it. In such instances we usually return to his original word or phrase, citing each occurrence of it in the Emendations. And we often find Peirce adding introductory clauses to already inscribed sentences but not going back to lowercase the first word of the original sentence. Again, we emend such misplaced capitalization for him.

The manuscripts for Peirce's Harvard University Lectures of 1865 and his Lowell Institute Lectures of 1866 present certain features and problems beyond those we have so far mentioned. They evolved into a final form, of sorts—the spoken and sometimes enacted word. It is in these manuscripts that we most often find Peirce deleting and inserting large blocks of material, writing notes and directions to himself, and combining the spoken word with physical activities such as placing explanatory diagrams on the blackboard. So far as possible, we treat these manuscripts like all others in the present volume. The chief exceptions are occasioned by the fact that in some of the lectures Peirce quoted heavily from earlier authors. He apparently carried the books to the lectures and read directly from them. At such points the manuscript usually contains only the instruction to himself to read a certain passage in a certain work of a certain author, often without specifying the edition, and without saying exactly where to begin and end the passage. In the case of books in English, we quote from an edition Peirce is known to have used. In the case of books in other languages, we quote from standard English translations. In including these passages for which the manuscripts supply only references, we trust we achieve the nearest approach to the lectures as Peirce actually gave them.

All emendations and editorial additions to the text discussed above are listed in the Emendations. The following modifications, however, are mainly concerned with the mechanical presentation of the printed material and are made silently.

All titles, heads, subheads, and dates used as subheads are printed here without periods. Such phrases as "By Charles Peirce," which may appear after the title of published papers or on the cover pages of manuscripts, are not reproduced.

The symbols or page-by-page numbering systems Peirce or his publishers used for footnotes are replaced by a single series of Arabic numerals for each paper.

Unless the material calls for other special treatment, all the papers begin with a paragraph indention.

In place of varying numbers of ellipsis points to mark omissions, modern standard form is followed.

For the convenience of the printer and our budget, superscribed portions of abbreviations such as M^r or 1st (Peirce's nineteenth-century practice) are placed on line. Raised decimal points which appear in *Chemical Theory of Interpenetration* are also lowered, and the pluses and minuses Peirce placed directly above the letters in chemical notations in "Views of Chemistry" are moved to the right of the letters in a superscript position.

Those points of punctuation which Peirce used with single and double quotation marks and which were modernized in transcribing his manuscripts, are modernized in the previously published papers as well, to achieve conformity between the two kinds of materials.

Except in the *Memoranda Concerning the Aristotelean Syllogism*, all variables appearing in the logic and mathematics are italicized. Peirce was aware of this practice but did not follow it with any consistency. The instances in which we perform this task for him are too numerous to enter as emendations.

Explanation of Symbols

Within the Text

Titles supplied by the editors appear in italic brackets.

Ellipsis points within italicized brackets indicate at least one full page of manuscript has not been found.

A set of italicized brackets surrounding only a few words or parts of words indicates an editorial reconstruction of a damaged portion of manuscript.

Sets of slashes are used to signal alternative readings given by Peirce. The double slashes indicate the beginning and ending of such a reading while the single slash divides the two alternatives.

Within the Apparatus

All page and line numbers refer to the present edition with each line of text, excluding running heads, counted. Footnotes at the bottom of text pages are lined separately from the text and are indicated by an *n* following the page number. Number(s) within parentheses following a line number indicate the first, second, or third appearance of the key word within that line. The use of *Also* following a complete entry indicates the same emendation occurs at the listed places within that selection.

Page and line numbers preceded by an asterisk (*) indicate a reference to a textual note in which that particular reading is discussed more fully.

A double dagger (‡) preceding a page and line number indicates a reference to an editorial note explaining an unavoidable change in a direct quotation.

All readings to the left of the square bracket ( ]) are from the present edition, and the source of these readings can be obtained in the headnote for each selection.

Stet immediately following the bracket signals the retention of a copy-text reading in cases where one would normally expect to find the copy-text emended.

The abbreviation *om.* is used to indicate the omission of a word, phrase, or passage in an authoritative text subsequent to the copy-text.

Not present signifies a word, phrase, or passage which does not appear in the copy-text or any other authoritative text prior to a later accepted emendation.

The use of the abbreviations *ital.* or *rom.* to the right of the square bracket indicates the listing to the left of the bracket was originally printed in italic (in the case of manuscripts, underlined) or roman (not underlined in the manuscripts) type.

The simple entry *extract* given with inclusive line numbers indicates the quotation which appears between those lines has been printed as an extract to conform to our own style, and quotation marks have been removed.

The term *reinstate* to the right of a bracket applies to manuscript material only and signifies that the reading to the left of the bracket had been deleted by Peirce in the original but reinstated by the editors.

Supplied is also a special convention for this volume used to signal those specific cases in the lectures in which Peirce read from volumes but did not include the quotation in the manuscript. The editors have supplied the quotation.

Two common conventions have been adopted here which pertain to punctuation and paragraphing changes only, the curved dash ($\sim$) and inferior caret ($\wedge$). The caret signals deletion or insertion of punctuation, and the curved dash is used to the right of the bracket to indicate the same word which appears to the left of the bracket. In this regard, all mathematical and logical symbols, with the exception of the prime, are treated as punctuation as well.

A vertical stroke ($|$) indicates a line change and is used in cases where it helps to clarify an emendation.

Textual Notes

10.11 This is an editorial footnote. Peirce interlined the sentence which appears here as footnote 1 in response to the instructor's underlining of the phrases "pretending to understand" and "yet presume to censure."

25.4 Ordinarily, "genius" would have been italicized. But Peirce italicized *word*. To retain the emphasis, genius was put in quotation marks.

26.33 Peirce was not consistent in inscribing the word *faculties* in blue ink. Here and at 26.36 and 27.1, he apparently forgot to switch pens. Instead, he underlined the words in blue.

38.30 The deleted passage is part of a revision the first half of which Peirce deleted; he failed to delete the second half which appears on the following manuscript page.

69.26 and 69.30 These emendations are taken from an earlier draft of section "B. As a Tendency" in MS 74. Peirce probably had the earlier draft before him as he carefully inscribed the manuscript printed here, but did not notice his inconsistency.

76.7 The punctuation would ordinarily have been removed. But the phrase "The Ideas of Reason." serves a double function here: as heading for the section that follows and as ending to the previous sentence.

176.16, 176.17, and 180.30–31 These carets do not represent deleted punctuation; rather, Peirce pencilled them in, intending to insert some interlined revision. There are no revisions here.

203.36 This emendation—and those at 204.12, 204.13, 204.14, 204.15—is due to Peirce's inconsistency in revising. In the first three instances of "blue" in this paragraph, Peirce had changed "green" to "blue"; the fourth "blue" appears in an interlined sentence added later. In the other instances, Peirce failed to change "green" to "blue."

220.30–34 This passage is written in pencil on the verso of the preceding page, without any indication where Peirce intended to insert it. It has been placed where it seems most appropriate in the context.

259.2 Again, Peirce failed to complete his revisions; in all other instances, he changed "pigs" to "stones."

267.29 Beginning with (267.30) "And first let me specify . . ." Peirce has inserted a little over two pages from the two separate sheets in this manuscript. Peirce often used the first few words from the beginning of an insert, as well as large carets to indicate its terminal point. The reading of the insert ends at 268.36 with " . . . do not run into each other." The rest of the lecture is continued from the consecutive text marked "Forms."

282.28 The caret removed here by the editors indicates an intended revision by Peirce which he did not carry out.

287.39–288.2 This final sentence of the paragraph is inscribed on the verso of the preceding page, without clear indication of its placement.

314.2–3 This editorially deleted partial sentence is actually an interlined revision that Peirce left incomplete. Rather than guess at Peirce's intended conclusion, the editors chose to delete the partial revision.

315.22 The diagrams of the three figures of syllogism which appear on page 316 originally followed this paragraph. The diagrams were moved as a convenience to the compositor of this volume.

320.5–6 The deleted paragraph is inscribed at the bottom of a page. Peirce deleted the following page and a half, but apparently forgot to go back to the preceding page.

332.9–10 The last portion of this sentence is taken from a deleted, but then revised, passage immediately preceding.

365.23 and 365.23 Boldface and italic types have been rearranged for the reader's convenience, because merely italic a, i, e, o (underlined in the manuscript) could not easily be discerned in the printed text.

368.15 This sentence is taken from MS 121 to replace an ambiguous phrase in the present lecture.

374.26 The diagram which appears at 375.1–7 appears in the manuscript following 374.26. It has been moved for the convenience of the compositor.

409.1 This is an editorially created footnote. It is written in pencil in the top margin of the first page of the lecture.

417.36–37 This emendation is due to Peirce's incomplete revising. Originally, he used "locomotive" and "steam engine" interchangeably, but then decided to use "locomotive" consistently. He missed this particular instance.

475.6 Here begins the portion of the text from the 28-page lecture. 471.9 through 475.5 is the variant beginning actually given by Peirce. There are no clear indications how much Peirce intended to replace except for marginal time notations (there are none at the beginning of the 28-page lecture) as well as the context.

500.37 and 500.37 Both of these editorial deletions are due to Peirce's incomplete and muddled revision. Rather than expand the phrase "an animal eye," it was thought better to delete "hearing" and "sounds &."

501.13 The superscript "A," deleted here, indicates that Peirce intended to insert something, namely the final three pages of the manuscript. Peirce forgot to mark these pages "A," but the "15" time notation on the second page obviously fits with the "10" and "20" notations before and after the superscript "A."

506.11   The diagrams of the three figures of syllogism which appear at 506.17–507.4 were printed in the original between 506.10 and 506.11. They have been moved for the convenience of the compositor.

506.19–507.4   The lines connecting the letters A, E, I, O in the three figures of syllogism are not printed in the original, though Peirce refers to them at 506.12. The omission is probably a printer's error.

508.5 and 508.6   In the diagram on page 507, the editors have replaced type styles which are no longer available. The diagram itself, which originally followed 508.6, has been moved for the convenience of the compositor.

509.21   Peirce's reference to "the second page" in the brochure has been emended to refer to the appropriate place in the present volume.

516.24, 517.21, and 518.20   The order of the original manuscript has been revised according to Peirce's notation. In the margin beside the diagram which appears after 516.23 Peirce wrote "[Note. §2 should come after §4.]." The original order was: §2. Precision, Discrimination, and Dissociation; §3. Substance; and §4. Being.

522.11   This is an editorial footnote. The content of the note was originally inscribed by Peirce as a small notation to himself directly following "The Correlate."

525.14   "But" has been deleted because originally Peirce inscribed the first two sentences in the reverse order in which they appear here. He then revised his original order with editorial transposition marks but failed to delete the now nonsensical "But."

526.27   The asterisk indicates that Peirce intended a footnote; none appears on this page.

Emendations

My Life

The two extant forms of "My Life," the second written more than a year after the first, are closely related, and internal evidence suggests both may stem from a single lost original. The earlier, MS 51, used here as copy-text was written for a public, albeit limited, audience, while the second, MS 63, Peirce kept for his own private interest and amusement. Consequently, of the thirty substantive changes Peirce introduced into MS 63, only three have been accepted as emendations: the title, because it is more accurate and descriptive; the entries for the last two and a half years which continue where MS 51 ends; and one other which is a correction of an error in information. With the exception of a correction of punctuation at 2.26, all other emendations (those labeled E) have been supplied by the editors. The following list then, serves as both an emendations list and a rejected substantive variants list. All emendations (or refusals to emend in the cases where the entry is marked *stet*) appear to the left of the bracket followed by the source and a semicolon. The readings to the right of the semicolon are rejected readings from the copy-text and/or MS 63.

1.1–2	My . . . Class-Book] 63; Peirce 51
1.6	September] *stet* 51; Sep. 63
1.6	Tuesday] *stet* 51; *om.* 63
1.8	Christened.] E; ~∧ 51,63
1.10	remember.] E; ~∧ 51,63
1.12	time.] E; ~∧ 51; ~. 63
1.14	marriage.] E; ~∧ 51,63
1.16	and] *stet* 51; & 63
1.16	education.] E; ~∧ 51; ~. 63
1.18	Quincy] E; Quincey 51,63

1.18	St.] *stet* 51; Street, and commenced my researches on the physiology of marriage. 63
1.20	going to] *stet* 51; going to school at 63
1.20	Ma'am] *stet* 51; Marm 63
1.20	and] *stet* 51; & 63
1.21	learnt much and fell violently in love] *stet* 51; at once fell in love 63
1.22	distinction's] E; distinctions 51,63
2.3	subject] *stet* 51; study 63
2.4	recommend] *stet* 51; reccommend 63
2.6	and] *stet* 51; & 63
2.7	the Rev.] *stet* 51; Rev. 63
2.7	T. R. Sullivan] 63; T. H. Sullivan 51
2.9	and] *stet* 51; & 63
2.9	laving] *stet* 51; *ital.* 63
2.10	and] *stet* 51; & 63
2.11	a] *stet* 51; as a 63
2.13	a "History] *stet* 51; "A History 63
2.17	debating ∧ society] *stet* 51; ~ - ~ 63
2.19	and] *stet* 51; & 63
2.19	schoolboy] E; school-boy 51,63
2.21	with honor] *stet* 51; finally 63
2.21	several] *stet* 51; numerious 63
2.22	and] *stet* 51; & 63
2.23	Mr.] *stet* 51; *om.* 63
2.25	and] *stet* 51; & 63
2.26	Schiller's] 63; Schillers 51
2.26	*Æsthetic Letters*] E; *rom.* 51; Esthetic Letters 63
2.26	and] E; & 51,63
3.2	and] *stet* 51; & 63
3.5	and] *stet* 51; & 63
3.7	and] *stet* 51; & 63
3.7	vanities!] *stet* 51; Vanities saith the Preacher, 63
3.8	vanity!"] *stet* 51; Vanity." 63
3.11–17	Appointed Aid . . . my object.] 63; *not present* 51
3.11	and] E; & 63
3.11–12	Louisiana.] E; ~∧ 63
3.14	Harvard.] E; ~∧ 63

Private Thoughts

Copy-text for "Private Thoughts" is MS 55. All readings to the left of the bracket are emendations supplied by the editors. All readings to the right of the bracket are rejected readings from MS 55.

4.6	desirable] desireable
4.27	¶The] ∧~
4.27	and] & *Also* 5.16, 5.20, 5.21, 5.22, 5.33, 7.19, 9.31
5.3	*Errare est hominis*] rom.
5.15	arise] arrise
5.23	may] make
5.24	phraseology] phaseology
6.4	he] He
6.17	important.] ~∧
6.29	exercising] excercising
6.30	repetition] repitition
7.8	¶Now] ∧~
7.8	done:] ~∧
7.9	active,] ~∧
7.9	3] 3r
8.5	ones] one's
8.22	system.] ~∧
8.23	one.] ~∧
8.29–30	infinitude.] ~∧
9.9	Philosophy] Pholosophy
9.29	Feb.] ~∧

Sense of Beauty

Copy-text for "Sense of Beauty" is MS 12. All readings to the left of the bracket are emendations supplied by the editors. All readings to the right of the bracket are rejected readings from MS 12.

10.6	(Ruskin).] ∧*Ruskin*∧.
°10.11	it.¹] it.
10.16	∧*Esthetic Letters,*∧] "Esthetic Letters,"
10.20–11.4	*extract*
‡10.22	can relate] relate
11.3	expression.] ~∧
11.5(1)	a] an
11.13(2)	from] From
11.28	play,] ~∧
11.29	and,] ~∧
12.1	a state] state
12.3	knowledge] knoledge
12.9	*Esthetic Letters*] rom.
12.13	is difficult] difficult

Raphael and Michael Angelo

Copy-text is MS 21. All readings to the left of the bracket are emendations supplied by the editors. All readings to the right of the bracket are rejected readings from MS 21.

13.1	and] &
13.6	it.] ~∧
13.9	approach] approch
13.10	OBSERVATION.] ~∧
13.12	Michael] Michel
13.13	DEFINITION.] ~∧
13.13	in.] ~∧
13.13–14	ARGUMENT.] ~∧
13.16	CONCLUSION.] ~∧
13.20	excellencies] exellencies
14.2	together] to-gether
14.4	¶Michael Angelo] ∧~ ~
14n.3	R.] ~∧
15.2	conceive] concieve
15.5	&c.] ~∧ Also 15.6
15.29	compel] compell
15n.6	face.] ~∧
16.9	truth,] ~∧
16.9	etc.,] ~.∧
16.9	justice,] ~∧
16.10	excel] excell
16.10	understanding,] ~∧
16.19	an] an an
16.21	believe] beleive

Scientific Book of Synonyms

Copy-text is MS 20. All readings to the left of the bracket are emendations supplied by the editors. All readings to the right of the bracket are rejected readings from MS 20.

17.5	seem] seems
17.9	sits] to sits
17.10	amiss] amis
17.21	*Synonymes*] Synonym's
17.22–28	*extract*

‡17.26   real condition, we mean the] real, the
‡17.28   imaginary] immaginary
18.4   this.] ~ₐ
18.5(1,2)   shadowiness] shadowyness
18.5   non-existence] nonexistence
18.6   and] & *Also* 19.8(1,2)
18.11   ₐWhately's] "Whateley's
18.12   *Synonyms.*ₐ] Synonymsₐ"
18.13–18   *extract*
18.20   reader] readers
18.22   *exist*] rom.
18.25   evidently] evidintly
18.25   suggested;] ~ₐ
18.26   preceded;] preceed,
18.28   preceded] preceeded
18.30   diversity] diversty
18.32   *Greek Lexicon*] rom.
18.33   meanings] meaning
18.34   disappearance–] dissappearanceₐ
19.1   two] too
19.4   this.] ~ₐ
19.6   terms,] ~ₐ
19.8   grammar,] ~ₐ
19.8   rhetoric,] ~ₐ
19.8   &c.] ~ₐ
19.10   conjunctions] conjunxions
19.10   prepositions,] prepopositionsₐ
19.11   got] a got
19.12   ₐ*Thesaurus*ₐ] "Thesaurus"
19.18   my] by

Think Again!

Copy-text is the only previous publication of the article in *Harvard Magazine* 4(1858):100–105. All readings to the left of the bracket are emendations supplied by the editors. All readings to the right of the bracket are rejected readings from the copy-text.

20.4–5   *extract*
20.7   *Magazine*] rom. *Also* 22.2–3
20.11   *Iliad*] rom. *Also* 21.1
20.11   *Odyssey*] rom.
20.24   *Cymbeline*] rom.
20.25–30   *extract*

21.23	*Taming of the Shrew*] rom. *Also* 23.38–24.1
23.12	∧*Taming of the Shrew,*∧] "Taming of the Shrew,"
24.1	Steevens] Stevens
24.2	∧*Six Old Plays*∧] "Six Old Plays"

Analysis of Genius

Copy-text for "Analysis of Genius" is MS 42. All readings to the left of the bracket are emendations supplied by the editors. All readings to the right of the bracket are rejected readings from MS 42.

°25.4	"genius"] ∧~∧ *Also* 25.6
25.7	"large] ∧~
25.8	direction."] ~∧∧
25.10	and] & *Also* 25.17, 25.19, 25.22, 25.24, 26.7, 26.8, 26.13, 26.14, 26.15, 26.18, 26.29, 26.31, 26.34, 27.1, 27.4, 27.6, 27.13, 27.21, 27.22, 27.24, 27.26, 27.37, 28.9, 28.18(1,2), 28.19, 28.26, 28.27, 28.38, 29.23, 29.25, 30.8
25.17	Dr.] ~∧
25.19	whole∧] ~,
25.25	"A] ∧~
25.26	directions."] ~∧∧
25.28	∧*The Lives of the Poets*∧] "The Lives of the Poets"
26.7	it,] ~∧
26.8(1)	them] the
26.16	result] resust
26.17	imminent] immanent
26.17	making,] ~∧
26.26	believe] beleive *Also* 26.35, 26.36, 27.36
26.32	disbelieves] disbeleives
°26.33	**faculties**] *faculties* *Also* 26.36, 27.1
26.37	said;] ~∧
27.16	argument] agument
27.16	noölogist.] ~∧
27.20	mind's] minds
27.21	(*blue*] ∧~
27.21	*degree*)] ~∧
28.1	being.] ~∧
28.2	determined] determened
28.3	experience.] ~∧
28.4	empirical,] ~∧
28.9	dimension,] ~∧
28.9	&c.,] ~∧∧
28.15	object,] ~∧

29.1	much,] ∼ᴧ
29.4	one's] ones
29.6	persons] person
29.8	perform] peform
29.21	that so] so
30.3	sense.] ∼ᴧ
30.6	Johnson] J.
30.7	was,] ∼ᴧ
30.8	doesn't] doesnt

Axioms of Intuition

Copy-text is MS 50. All readings to the left of the bracket are emendations supplied by the editors. All readings to the right of the bracket are rejected readings from the copy-text.

‡31.4	Quantities.] ∼ᴧ
31.18	and] & *Also* 31.19, 31.26, 32.3, 32.6, 32.16, 32.17, 32.29, 33.6, 33.9, 33.14, 33.22
31.27	occasions] occassions
32.6	thingsᴧ–] ∼.–
32.11	the degree to which any quality] " " " " " "
32.12	is realized in each unit of] " " " " " "
32.20	b] β
33.13	&c.] ∼ᴧ

Three Essays on Infinity and God

Copy-text for these three essays is MS 53. All readings to the left of the bracket are emendations supplied by the editors. All readings to the right of the bracket are rejected readings from MS 53.

Limits of Religious Thought

37.9	imagination?] ∼.
37.14	Suppose] Soppose
37.14	and] & *Also* 37.20, 38.6, 38.14, 38.20, 38.33(1), 39.2, 39.22, 39.27

37.23   this,] ~∧
38.3   *simple conception*] rom.
38.9   event.] ~∧
38.15   all,] ~.
38.23   Possibility;] ~∧
38.23   this is] this
38.24   exists∧] ~,
38.25   Actuality;] ~∧
°38.30   modality.] modality. is not susceptible of lesoning or increase.
38.32   successive] sucessive
38.37   expressions:] ~∧
38.37   Retrogression,] ~∧
39.1   expression:] ~∧
39.2   Space,] ~∧
39.3   intuition:] ~∧
39.5   quantity:] ~,
39.7   viz.] ~∧
40.2   of,] ~∧
40.3   noumenon,] ~∧
40.6   thought-of] ~∧~
40.13   influx—] ~∧

The Conception of Infinity

41.1   ideas] idea's
41.1   four-sided] foursided
41.2   and] &   *Also* 41.7, 42.18
41.8   in the third] the third
41.11   degrees.] ~∧
41.13   *good,*] ~∧
41.14   And] &
41.14   3rd] 3rdly
41.14   *good.*] ~∧
41.17   infinity;] ~∧
41.21   Twice] twice
41.22   depends] depend
41.23   small] smal
41.28   soul's] souls
42.2–3   four-sided∧triangle] foursided-triangle   *Also* 42.3
42.6   would] which
42.8   its] Its
42.10   consciousness∧] ~,
42.15   *noumenon*] neumenon
42.16   simply,] ~∧

42.17	of,] ~∧
42.17	thinking,] ~∧
42.17	thought,] ~∧

Why we can Reason on the Infinite

42.19	we] We
42.26	four-sided] ~∧~
43.4	synthesis] systhesis
43.4	that] than
43.5	and] & *Also* 43.21, 43.23
43.5	dependency] depency *Also* 43.16
43.6	good,] ~∧
43.7	good,] ~∧
43.9	therefore∧] ~,
43.14	"twice] ∧~
43.15	line"] ~∧
43.31	Pseudo-conceptions] ~∧~
43.35–36	stand precisely where negative conceptions stand;] stand precisely where negative conceptions stand precisely where negative conceptions stand;

Proof of the Infinite Nature of the Creator

Copy-text for this item is MS 61. The two emendations are supplied by the editors.

44.4	and] & *Also* 44.5

I, IT, and THOU

Copy-text for "I, IT, and THOU" is MS 65. The emendations have been supplied by the editors.

45.1	THOU∧] ~:
45.7	and] & *Also* 45.13(1,2), 45.14, 45.17

The Modus of the IT

Copy-text for "The Modus of the IT" is MS 66. The emendations appearing to the left of the bracket are supplied by the editors. All readings to the right of the bracket are rejected readings from the copy-text.

47.4	sense,] ~∧
47.5	consciousness,] ~∧
47.7	and] & *Also* 47.15, 47.27, 48.7, 48.15, 48.16, 48.18, 48.24, 48.27, 48.29, 48.34
47.12	world.] ~∧
47.17	spatial] spacious
47.17	dependence] depenendence
47.21	again.]] ~].
47.22	existence:] ~∧
47.24	feasibility;] feasability,
47.25	actuality;] ~∧
47.27	why] Why
47.28	feasibility] feasability *Also* 48.1
47.28	form∧of] ~-~
48.1	is not] is the same is not
48.1	feasible] feasable
48.9	why] which
48.10	not mere] not not me
48.13	¶But] ∧~
48.13	derivation.] ~∧
48.14	negation,] ~∧
48.15	reality,] ~∧
48.22	*unity*∧] ~,
48.30	whose] whose whose
48.39	elementariness.] ~∧
49.1	quality.] ~∧
49.6	Time.] ~∧
49.7	space. That] ~∧that

Views of Chemistry

Copy-text for "Views of Chemistry" is MS 69. All emendations are supplied by the editors and appear to the left of the square bracket. The rejected readings from the copy-text appear to the right of the bracket.

50.8	and] & *Also* 50.9, 50.17, 50.30, 51.3, 51.19(1,2), 51.22, 51.25, 52.4, 52.11(1,2), 52.15, 52.19, 52.28, 53.19, 53.24, 53.26(1), 53.29, 54.3(2), 54.12, 54.16, 54.33, 55.2, 55.10, 55.11(1,2), 55.16(1,2), 55.23, 55.27, 55.29, 55.33(1,2), 55.35, 55.36, 56.13(1,2), 56.14, 56.16, 56.18, 56.19, 56.25, 56.30(1,2)
50.11	disagreeable] disagreable
51.6	*New Dictionary*] rom.
51.7	*Salt*] rom.
51.9–12	*extract*
51.13	*salt*] rom. *Also* 51.15
51.23	*admirabile*ʌ] ~.
51.23	Salt).] ~)ʌ
51.28	¶3.] ʌ~.
52.2	culinary] culinery *Also* 52.3, 52.8, 52.19
52.2	*Silvii,*] ~ʌ
52.3	¶4.] ʌ~.
52.10	¶5.] ʌ~.
52.19	*Silvii*] *Sivii*
52.19	Exp. 3ʌ] ~ʌ ~.
52.20	Exp. 4ʌ] ~ʌ ~.
52.20	Cl⁻] CL⁻ *Also* 52.22, 52.24, 52.26, 53.2, 53.5, 53.9
52.21	water)ʌ] ~).
53.3	Alkali] Alcali
53.3–4	(regenerated Exp. 2)] ʌ~ ~ʌ ~ʌ
53.6	And] &
53.16	inquiries] inquires
53.19(2)	itself] it self
53.26	neutralizes] neutralize's
55.4	first] fist
55.6	*No. 2.*] ~ʌ ~ʌ
55.12	drowned ʌ] ~,
55.21	*extract*
55.25	beforehand] before hand
56.4	data.] ~ʌ
56.12	illustrate] illustratate
56.16	oxygen,] ~ʌ
56.16	brown,] ~ʌ
56.17	Copper,] ~ʌ
56.23–24	consequence ʌ] ~,
56.25	synthetical] sythethical

Treatise on Metaphysics

Copy-text for "Treatise on Metaphysics" is MS 70. All readings to the left of the bracket are emendations supplied by the editors. The readings to the right of the bracket are rejected readings from the copy-text.

57.11	and] & *Also* 59.27(1,2), 60.16, 60.31, 60.32, 61.23, 61.34, 62.4, 62.6, 62.8, 62.18, 62.29, 63.14, 64.8, 64.12, 64.21, 64.24(1,2), 67.14, 67.27, 68.4, 68.6, 68.11, 68.14, 69.10, 69.22, 69.30, 70.5, 70.18, 71.2, 71.21, 71.31, 71.34, 72.6(1,2), 72.20, 72.30, 74.10, 74.26, 76.5, 76.20, 77.5, 77.9, 78.7, 78.15, 78.19, 78.22, 80.31, 81.10, 82.30, 82.35, 83.11, 83.20, 84.3, 84.21, 84.22, 84.25, 84.32, 84.33, 84.37
57.17	2.] ~ʌ
57.17	Perfectʌ] ~.
57.18	Glanceʌ] ~.
57.20	Categoriesʌ] ~.
58.5	*metaphysics*] rom.
58.6	"which] ʌ~
58.6	desirable] desireable *Also* 59.6, 59.26
58.7	knowledge,"] ~,ʌ
58.7–8	pre|eminent] preëminent
58.8	othersʌ] ~.
58.8	(Aristotle *Metaphysics* 1.2.7).] (Arist. Metaph. i.2)ʌ
58.10	viz.] ~ʌ *Also* 77.2
58.14	§1. On] ~ʌ|~
58.20	believe] beleive *Also* 58.22, 76.17, 78.16, 78.25, 78.29–30
58.28	b.] ~ʌ
58.33–34	*Critique of Pure Reason*] rom.
58.34	"Doctrine of Method,"] ʌ~~~~ʌʌ
58.34	Ch. 1,] ~ʌ ~.
59.3	thing.] ~ʌ
60.3	chapter.] ~ʌ
60.4	meditationʌ] ~,
60.16–17	metaphysician.] ~ʌ
60.18	§2. On] ~ʌ|~
60.28	*Noumenon*] Neumenon
60.29	reason),] ~,)
60.33	these.] ~ʌ
60.34	*a.*] ~ʌ
60.34	*noumenon*] neumenon
60n.1	chanceʌ] ~,
60n.1	impossibility.] ~ʌ
61.2–3	noumenon] neumenon

61.21(3)	it∧] ~,
61.30	can∧only] ~-|~
61n.1	*Phaedrus*] rom.
63.11	belief] beleif *Also* 72.25, 77.8, 78.15
63.16	§3. On] ~∧|~
64.31	molasses.] ~∧
65.5	*Odi Profanum Vulgus*] rom.
65.13	metaphysics] metaphisics
65.20	rationalism.] ~∧
66.8(1)	given.] ~∧
66.10	¶∴The] ∧∴~
66.18	¶∴These] ∧∴~
66.19	¶To] ∧~
66.24	¶*Proof*] ∧~
66.37	it.] ~∧
67.9	realities.] ~∧
67.10	being.] ~∧
67.32	subject).] ~.)
68.17	III.] ~∧
68.27	¶In] ∧~
68.36	Conceptions.] ~∧
69.5	of.] ~∧
69.13	precedes] preceeds
69.13	science.] ~∧
69.15	consciousness.] ~∧
69.16	subject.] ~∧
*69.26	Dialectics] Dialects
*69.30	cannot] can
70.3	measurable] measureable
70.8	*à priori*] rom.
70.23	seasons,] ~∧
70.29	3.] ~∧
71.13	.60.] .~∧
71.15	.93.] .~∧
71.16	.75,] .~∧
71.17	.68.] .~∧
71.22	fundamentally] fundmentally
71.22	reasons.] ~∧
71.26	trifling.] ~∧
71.27	§3. Inference] ~∧|~
72.12	§∧1.] ~. ~.
72.16	Transcendentalism∧] ~,
72.16	Criticism),] ~,)
73.1	fact;] ~,
73.3	extended).] ~.)
73.16	I.] ~∧
74.6	true∧] ~,

74.14	III.] $\sim_\wedge$
74.25	supposable] supposeable
74.26	unrealizable] unrealizeable
74.31–32	*Faith*$_\wedge$|A.] $\sim$. $\sim$.
75.2	trustworthy] trust-worthy
75.4	cognition.] $\sim_\wedge$
75.8–9	proposition).] $\sim)_\wedge$
75.10	sense.] $\sim_\wedge$
75.11	¶∴Every] $_\wedge$∴$\sim$
75.14	¶∴Every] $_\wedge$∴$\sim$
75.14	data.] $\sim_\wedge$
75.15	inference.] $\sim_\wedge$
75.20	¶*Proof*] $_\wedge\sim$
75.23	&c.] $\sim_\wedge$ *Also* 76.28(1), 76.33
75.29	Form] Foorm
76.3	*Substantia et Accidens*] rom.
76.3	Impossibility] Imposs.
76.4	Non-existence] Non-ex.
*76.7	Reason.] *stet*
76.8	1.] $\sim_\wedge$
76.9	Soul.] $\sim_\wedge$
76.12	2.] $\sim_\wedge$
76.15	3.] $\sim_\wedge$
76.27	Impressions] Impression
76.28	love,] $\sim_\wedge$
76.28	remembrances,] $\sim_\wedge$
76.28	&c.).] $\sim_\wedge)_\wedge$
76.29	Impressions.] $\sim_\wedge$
76.30	¶*Proof*] $_\wedge\sim$
76.30	premisses.] $\sim_\wedge$
77.8	$_\wedge\alpha$.] ¶$\sim$.
77.10	$_\wedge\beta$.] ¶$\sim$.
77.18	III.] $\sim_\wedge$
77.18	Mansel] Mansell
77.19	Mansel's] Mansell's
77.31	realm.] $\sim_\wedge$
77n.3	body's] bodies
78.2	itself.] $\sim_\wedge$
78.3	advantages.] $\sim_\wedge$
78.6	attainment] attain$_\wedge$|ment
78.10	I.] $\sim_\wedge$
78.11	$_\wedge$1.] ¶$\sim$.
78.13	over-anxious] $\sim_\wedge\sim$
78.31	II.] $\sim_\wedge$
78.38	moved.] $\sim_\wedge$
79.2	useless.] $\sim_\wedge$
79.8	*METAPHYSICAL*] *METAPH.*

79.16	open.] ~;
79.22	*True*] rom.
79.32	example∧)] ~,)
80.5	conceptions.] ~∧
80.23	∧1.] ¶~.
80.27	qualities.] ~∧
80.34	§2.] ~∧
81.1	*notion*] rom.
81.4	absent),] ~,)
81.26	be] by
81.27	distinct] dinctinct
81.29	it] is
82.10	it is] is
82.12	actuality.] ~∧
82.13	§3.] ~∧
82.14	*Proposition.*] ~∧
82.24	Cor.] ~∧ *Also* 82.26, 82.28, 82.31, 83.1, 83.3
82.26	*noumena*] *neumena*
82.31	IV.] ~∧
82.34	true.] ~∧
82.37	*Idealism.*] ~∧
83.24	*Proposition.*] *Prop.*
83.25	*Proof.*] ~∧
83.25	parts.] ~∧
83.26	conceptions] conception
83.27	not.] ~∧
83.31	*Proposition.*] ~∧
83.33	are] is
83.35	other∧] ~.
83.36	third.] ~∧
84.2	compounded.] ~∧
84.4	moment.] ~∧
84.17	∴All] ∴There all
84.18	thoughts.] ~∧
84.19	*Proposition.*] *Prop.*
84.19	extensive.] ~,
84.22	others.] ~,
84.23	conceptions.] ~∧
84.25	complicated] complicate
84.26	other.] ~∧
84.27	the] The
84.36	Ego.] ~∧
84.38	Dynamical] Dynam.
84.38	Physical.] Phys.
84.39	§3.] ~∧

Analysis of Creation

Copy-text for "Analysis of Creation" is MS 71. All emendations for this item have been supplied by the editors and appear to the left of the square brackets. The readings to the right of the brackets are rejected readings from the copy-text.

85.5	and] & *Also* 85.9, 86.2, 86.7, 86.24, 87.3, 87.14, 87.16, 87.17, 88.8, 88.18, 88.27, 88.29, 88.36, 89.1, 89.2, 89.11, 89.19, 89.31, 89.36, 90.17
85.6	accidental,] ~∧
86.4	mere] meer
86.20	at] At
86.21	mind's] minds
86.23–24	Language,] ~∧
86.24	man,] ~∧
87.2	action.] ~∧
87.3	7.] ~∧
87.14	breadth] bredth
87.18	&c.] ~∧
87.18	service,] ~∧
87.18	speech,] ~∧
87.20	mechanism] machanism
87.20	perfect] pefect
87.21	Normality.] ~∧
87.22	or] Or
87.27	breadth.] ~∧
87.28	plurality,] ~∧
87.29	body] mody
87.29	inertia.] ~∧
87.33	3.] ~∧
87.35	4.] ~∧
88.1	5.] ~∧
88.2	6.] ~∧
88.3	7.] ~∧
88.16	*per se*] rom.
88.17	wholly] wholy
88.17	influenced] influences
88.26	everything] every∧|thing
88.32	breadth] breath
88.32	think] to think
88.34	force.] ~∧
89.6	5] 6
89.6	being.] ~∧

89.7	6] 7
89.8	7] 8
89.15	made] reduced made
89.23	resistance] resitance
89.29	runs] run
90.1	introduction.] ~∧
90.3	arrow-head,] ~-~∧
90.3	conception,] ~∧
90.3	conveyed,] ~∧
90.11	intimate] intimite
90.14	state∧it] ~. It
90.14	become] be∧|come
90.18	regulation.] ~∧

SPQR

Copy-text for "SPQR" is MS 72. All readings to the left of the bracket are emendations supplied by the editors. All readings to the right of the bracket are rejected readings from MS 72.

91.5	we must] must
91.17	are] Are
91.23	indicate] Indicate
91.25	Perception,] ~∧
92.7	¶Quantities] ∧~
92.7	Transcendentally] Trancendentally
92.8	and] & *Also* 92.13, 92.16(2), 92.17, 92.20, 92.23, 93.2, 93.4, 93.12, 93.14, 93.16, 94.14, 94.17
92.8	thing.] ~∧
92.9	¶Real] ∧~
92.9	relations?] ~.
92.11	¶Now] ∧~
92.21	*perpetually*] *pepetually*
92.23	a] &
92.28	Community] Com.
92.28	Causality] Caus. *Also* 94.7
92.28	Influx] Infl. *Also* 94.7
92.30	fact∧] ~.
92.30	Possibility] Poss.
92.30	Actuality] Act.
92.30	Necessity] Nec.
92.33	Influxual] Influal
93.24	¶The] ∧~
93.26	dependence.] ~∧

93.28	¶Plurality] ∧~
93.28	series.] ~∧
93.30	∧I] ¶~
94.1	∧Or] ¶~
94.2	In] in
94.2	previous∧] ~,
94.2	but] But
94.3	constitutes] consitutes
94.5	¶In] ∧~
94.7	Community] Comm.
94.10(2)	of] of of
94.17	Absoluteness] absoluteness

The Chemical Theory of Interpenetration

Copy-text is the only previous publication of this article in *American Journal of Science and Arts* 2d ser. 35(January 1863):78–82. All readings to the left of the bracket are emendations supplied by the editors. All readings to the right of the bracket are rejected readings from the copy-text. The particular journal copy used for collation purposes and copy-text is from Indiana University Library, Bloomington.

96.6	Proportions] proportions
96.18	Points] points
96.25	7.01;] ~,
100.7	even-] ~∧

The Place of Our Age

Copy-text is the only previous publication of this article in the *Cambridge Chronicle*, 21 November 1863, p. 1. All readings to the left of the bracket are emendations supplied by the editors. All readings to the right of the bracket are rejected readings from the copy-text.

101.25	Age∧] ~,
101.26	Jamestown).] ~.)
102.19	wind."] ~.∧
103.7–8	*Tracts for the Times*] rom.
103.15	Descartes∧] ~,
103.16	doubt,"] ~;"

104.22	*Kritik*] *rom.*
104.30–31	*Life of Jesus*] *rom.*
105.13	Barbarians] Barbarian
105.35	candid,] ~∧
106.37	Scholasticism] Scolasticism
108.15	over-] ~∧
108.19	*Othello*] *rom.*
108.22	Roderigo,] ~∧
108.37	nature] uature
111.7	tendency.] ~,
111.24	strengthened,] ~∧
111.37	*a priori*] *rom.*
113.10(2)	things] tbings
113.25	tuistical] tuisical
113.28	preceding] preceeding

Peirce to Chase

Copy-text for this item is L 82a. All emendations have been supplied by the editors and appear to the left of the square brackets. The readings to the right of the brackets are rejected readings from L 82a.

115.6	∧*Intellectual Symbolism*∧] "Intellectual Symbolism"
115.12	Kant's] Kants'
115.16	the matter] matter
115.25	views∧] ~,
115.25	which is] which
115.26	"which] ∧~
115.26	desirable] desireable
115.27	knowledge,"] ~,∧
115.27–28	pre|eminent] preëminent
116.3	and] & *Also* 116.5, 116.7

Shakespearian Pronunciation

Copy-text is the only previous publication of this article in *North American Review* 98(April 1864):342–69. All emendations have been supplied by the editors and appear to the left of the square brackets. All readings to the right of the square brackets are rejected readings from the copy-text.

117.5   "Orthoepical . . . English."] ∧Orthoepical . . . English.∧
117.7–8   "Memorandums . . . Era."] ∧Memorandums . . . Era.∧
119.1–2   De recta . . . Dialogus] rom.
119.3–5   On Orthographie: . . . nature] rom.
119.6–13   Booke . . . etc.] rom.
119.15–17   Æsops Fables . . . etc.] rom.
119.18–20   Writing Schoolemaster; . . . Writing] rom.
119.21–22   Logonomia . . . addiscitur] rom.
119.23–24   The English . . . tongue] rom.
119.25–29   The Feminin' Monarchi' , . . . experienc'] rom.
120.13   Reader] rom.
120.21–28   extract
120n.2   Feminine Monarchy] rom. Also 137n.3
120n.4   Elementarie] rom. Also 140n.3, 140n.5, 141n.5
120n.4   English Schoole-Master] English School-Master
120n.6   Shakespeare] rom. Also 121n.1, 127.23, 137n.22, 138n.19
120n.6   VII,] ∼.
120n.7   Logonomia Angl.] rom.
120n.7   IX,] ∼.
121.6   ∧Alvearie,∧] "Alvearie,"
121.10–16   extract
121n.1   II,] ∼.
121n.1   XII,] ∼.
121n.3   Alvearie] rom. Also 122n.1, 130n.1
121n.3   Gatakerus de Diphthongis] rom.
121n.4   Grammatica Linguæ Anglicanæ] rom.
121n.5   IX,] ∼.
122.2   Bullokar] Bulloker
122.6   ∧English Schoole-Master,∧] "English Schoole-Master,"
122.8–12   extract
122.17–23   extract
122.17   SMITH. I say that] "I say," says Smith, "that
122.24   &c.,] ∼.∧
122.28   extract
122n.1   IX,] ∼.
122n.9   English of Shakespeare] rom.
123.4   ∧Defence of Poesie,∧] "Defence of Poesie,"
123.10–12   extract
123.14–16   extract
123n.2   Elem.] rom.
123n.4–5   Spanish Grammar] rom.
123n.5   Spanish Dictionary] rom.
123n.6   French Dictionary] rom.
123n.7   England's Perfect School-Master] English Perfect School-Master
123n.8   1675. pp. 28–30.] 1675.
124.14   Atlantic Monthly] rom.
124.15   III,] ∼.

124.19–27	*extract*
124.19	T] *rom.*
124.19	*Theta*] *rom.*
124.22	D] *rom.*
124n.1	*Essay towards a Real Character*] *rom.*
124n.2	∧*Playhouse to be Let*,∧] "Playhouse to Let,"
124n.2	∧*Irish Mask*∧] "Irish Mask"
125.23	silent∧] ~,
125.24	*l*"),] ~,")
125n.5	*Ibid.*] *rom. Also* 142n.1
126.17	II∧] ~.
126n.2	*Ib.*] *rom. Also* 126n.4, 126n.5, 126n.6, 126n.7, 126n.8, 126n.9, 126n.10, 126n.11, 126n.12, 126n.14, 126n.19, 126n.20, 129n.5, 129n.6, 129n.7, 129n.11, 129n.12, 129n.13, 136n.16, 136n.18, 136n.19, 136n.20, 136n.21, 136n.22, 136n.23, 137n.11, 137n.31, 137n.32, 137n.33, 137n.36, 138n.8
126n.17	19.] ~∧
127.2	tu] *ital.*
127.17	IX,] ~.
127.23	IV,] ~.
127.33–34	*extract*
127n.1	*Lectures*] *rom.*
128.1	∧*Short Treatise*,∧] "Short Treatise,"
128.1	orthoëpy∧] ortho|epy,
128.1	1767),] ~,)
128.8	soot∧] ~,
128.9	wool∧] ~,
128n.1	*Essay . . . Character*] *rom.*
128n.1	363.] ~∧
128n.2	*Log. Angl.*] *rom.*
129.1	*extract*
129.2	*extract*
129.13	*Unabridged Dictionary*] *rom.*
129.14	etc.,] ~.∧
129n.2	IX,] ~.
129n.2	*Elem.*] *rom.*
130.4–9	*extract*
130.13–16	*extract*
131.2	etc.,] ~.∧
131.14	1] 7
‡131.16	*Fat*] *Fal*
131.25	*L'Art . . . Français*∧] L'Art . . . Français,
131.26	ed.),] ~.,)
131.26	I,] ~.
131.29	*French Grammar*] *rom.*
131.29	ed.,] ~.∧

131n.5	usuall." (p. 29).] usuall."
132.20	Richard] Rich.
132.20	*Spanish Grammar*] rom.
132.20–21	*Dictionary*] rom. *Also* 132.25, 132.35
132.27	ed.,] ~.ₐ
133.7	*Wegwyzer*] rom.
133.9	8).] ~.)
133.12	*Royal French Dictionary*] rom.
133.15	VIIIₐ] ~.
134.13–14	ₐ*An Introductorie . . . trewly,*ₐ] "An Introductorie . . . trewly,"
134.16–17	*extract*
134.29–135.8	*extract*
134n.1	*English Schollar's Assistant*] rom.
134n.2	*Korte Wegwyzer*] rom.
134n.3–4	*Perfect School-Master*] Perfect SchoolₐMaster
135.12–15	*extract*
135.18–25	*extract*
136.16–137.2	*extract*
136n.6–9	*extract*
137n.15	p.] pp.
137n.18	etc.,] ~.ₐ
137n.20	*ib.*] rom. *Also* 137n.26
137n.22	XII,] ~.
138.9	etc.,] ~.ₐ
138.12–14	*extract*
138n.19	XII,] ~.
138n.22	*Reader.*] Readerₐ
139.13–27	*extract*
139.13	tong hath] tong," says this author, "hath
139.13	soundyngesₐ] ~"
139.13	[:1.]] :(~.)
139.13	ₐLike] "~
139.14	"a] '~
139.15	rewarde"] ~'
139.16	us.ₐ] ~."
139.16	[2.]] (~.)
139.16	ₐIf] "~
139.18	"by] '~
139.19	awry,"] ~,'
139.21	diphthonges] dipththonges
139.23	"a] '~
139.23	twyne"] ~'
139.31	ₐremarks] '~
139n.2	*Logonomia*] rom. *Also* 141n.1
139n.2	16.] ~ₐ
140.28–34	*extract*
141.13–14	ortho|epy] orthoëpy

141.24–27	*extract*
141.28–34	*extract*
141n.3	*Elements of Orthoëpy*] rom.
142.10–12	*extract*
‡142.10	sound;] sound, or;
142.19–20	*extract*
142.34–143.2	*extract*
‡143.1	*niwter*] *niwty*

Analysis of the Ego

Copy-text for "Analysis of the Ego" is MS 78. All readings to the left of the bracket are emendations supplied by the editors. All readings to the right of the bracket are rejected readings from MS 78.

144.12(1)	subjects$_\wedge$] ~.
144.12	subjects.] ~$_\wedge$
144.18	exist] exists
145.20	*substance*$_\wedge$] ~.
145.21	heaven$_\wedge$] ~.
145.22	room$_\wedge$] ~.
145.23	"Scott$_\wedge$"] "~."
145.25	me$_\wedge$] ~.
145.28	retort$_\wedge$] ~.
145.29	&c.] ~$_\wedge$
145.31	body).] ~.)
146.6	¶*Idea*] $_\wedge$~
146.6	γ.] ~$_\wedge$
146.8	¶*Idea*] $_\wedge$~
146.8	δ.] ~$_\wedge$
146.11	¶*Idea*] $_\wedge$~
146.12	*instrument*.] ~$_\wedge$
146.13	¶*Idea*] $_\wedge$~
146.15	¶*Idea*] $_\wedge$~
146.15	η.] ~$_\wedge$
146.16	¶*Idea*] $_\wedge$~
146.18	¶*Idea*] $_\wedge$~
146.19	doubtful).] ~.)
146.21	¶*Idea*] $_\wedge$~
146.21	κ.] ~$_\wedge$
146.21–22	representation.] ~$_\wedge$
146.23	¶λ.] $_\wedge$~.
146.26	historical.] ~$_\wedge$

146.26	Subjective.] ~∧
147.4	and] & *Also* 149.22, 149.27(1)
148.3	metaphysical] metaphysycal
148.13	*idea*] rom.
148.13	*Function*] rom.
148.16	things,] ~∧
148.17	that] That
148.17	motions,] ~∧
148.17	etc.,] ~∧∧
148.26	moves,] ~∧
148.34	¶§2.] ∧~.
149.2	meaningless] meaning∧|less
149.9	it is] it
149.10	elastic.] ~∧
149.19	marks] mark
149.26	¶*The*] ∧~
149.29	¶*The*] ∧~
149.29	*Earth.*] ~∧
149.32	¶*The*] ∧~
149.32	material] matterial
149.37	¶*C.*] ∧~.
149.37	*Peirce.*] ~∧
149.40	¶*The*] ∧~
150.1	partial] purtial
150.1	put] but
150.8	¶*The*] ∧~
150.9	quality.] ~∧
150.13(1)	is] it
150.22–23	condition.] ~?
150.25	must be] must
150.27	material] matial
150.28–29	different] dif. *Also* 150.29
150.29	applications] appl.
150.31	PIANO.] ~∧
150.32	plates∧] ~,
151.8	SCALE.] ~∧
151.14(1)	which] will
151.23	legislature.] ~∧
151.24	ORBIT.] ~∧
151.24	application] appl.
151.27	CONCEPTION.] ~∧
151.28	attention.] ~∧
151.29	PEIRCE.] ~∧
151.33	are] a
151.36	be] by

Major Premisses of Natural Science

Copy-text for this item is MS 80. All readings to the left of the bracket are emendations supplied by the editors. All readings to the right of the bracket are rejected readings from MS 80.

152.7	to beg] beg
152.15	&c.] ~∧
152.16	Aristotle] Arist.
152.16	*Analytica Posteriora*] Anal. Post.
152.16	1.9.428).] i.9.)∧
152.18	1.] ~∧

Immediate Perception

Copy-text for "Immediate Perception" is MS 81. All emendations have been supplied by the editors and appear to the left of the square brackets. The readings to the right of the square brackets are rejected readings from the copy-text.

153.1	the] The
153.3	Doctrine] Docrine
153.6	Gibraltar] Gibralter
153.12	corner-stone] ~∧~
153.28	overrides] over rides
154.1	*fate,*] ~∧
154.1	&c.] ~∧
154.17–18	dogmatize,] ~∧
154.20	two-thirds] ~∧~
154.26	inferential] inferrential
154.30	contains] contain

Peirce to Abbot

Copy-text for this letter is the only extant copy deposited in the Harvard University Archives (Abbot Papers). All emendations have been supplied by the editors and appear to the left of the square brackets. The readings to the right of the square brackets are rejected readings from the copy-text.

156.4   Feb.] ~ₐ
156.8–9   re|examine] reëxamine
156.11   and] &   Also 156.17, 156.20, 156.27(2), 157.7, 157.22,
                157.28, 158.2(1), 158.7, 158.14, 158.17, 158.26, 158.32,
                159.14, 159.15, 159.37, 160.4, 160.17
156.13   Metaphysical Principles of Natural Science] rom.
156.17   Rosencrantz' Ed.,] Rosecratz' Edₐₐ
156.18   p. 236),] ~ₐ~)ₐ
156.24   (p. 103)] ₐ~ₐ ~ₐ
156.29   Kritik] rom.
156.29   p.] ~ₐ   Also 157.1, 157.27
156.29   wonderfully] wondefully
156.30   manner,] ~ₐ
157.13   (pp. 122–130)] ₐ~ₐ ~–~ₐ
157.19   "Axioms of Intuition"] ₐ~ ~ ~ₐ
157.19   (p. 761)] ₐ~ₐ ~ₐ
157.21(3)   space.] ~ₐ
157.36   says,] say'sₐ
157.37–158.6   extract
158.2   conception] conₐ|ception
158.10   defective;] ~ₐ
158.10   mistakenₐ] ~;
158.14   be] (which be
158.26   (p. 101)] ₐ~ₐ ~ₐ
158.27   knowledge.] ~ₐ
158.36   He] His
158.37   Werke] rom.
158.38   et seq.).] ~ ~.)ₐ
159.4   quod ponit . . . oppositi] rom.
159.12   (p. 104)] ₐ~ₐ ~ₐ
159.14   necessity],"] ~]ₐ"
159.14   you] You
159.16–17   principles] principle
159.18   and] &
159.23   believe] beleive
159.33   (p. 98)] ₐ~ₐ ~ₐ
159.34   irremediably] irremedially
159.34   This is] This
159.38   it?] ~.
160.6   receptacle] recepticle
160.20   Realität] rom.
160.20   Daseyn] rom.
160.24   so,] ~ₐ
160.26   (Kritik] ₐKritik
160.26   p. 258)] ~ₐ ~ₐ

Harvard Lecture I

Copy-text for "Lecture I" is MS 94. All readings to the left of the bracket are emendations supplied by the editors. All readings to the right of the bracket are rejected readings from MS 94.

162.6	piddling] *reinstate*
162.12	(see Aphorism XI)] ∧see Aph xi∧
162.24	character of] character
162.26	believe] beleive *Also* 173.37
162.31	ratiocination.] ~∧
163.1	degree] degee
163.1	character] "
163.2	principles.] ~∧
163.4	logic.] ~∧
163.6	Gratry,] ~∧
163.7–8	Mill.|4th] Mill. 4th
163.23	*Encyclopaedia Britannica*] Encyclopedia Britanica
163.27	Augustine] Augustin
163.28	*renaissance*] *rennaissance*
163.32	eyesight,] eye-sight∧
163.37	Ramus.] ~∧
164.3	"ars] ∧~
164.3	rerum."] ~.∧
164.7	and] & *Also* 167.23, 167.26, 168.6, 168.8, 168.11, 168.24, 174.23
164.18	"Logic] ∧~
164.20	evidence."] ~.∧
164.20	Duval-Jouve] Douval∧Jouve
164.23	"branch] ∧~
164.24	considered."] ~.∧
165.26	*substance*] *rom.*
166.4	three.] ~∧
166.14–15	symbols.|¶2.] ~. ∧~.
166.15	it] is
166.16	convenient] convienent
166.17	logic:] ~∧
166.21	Mill's] Mills
166.22–23	*Essay Concerning Human Understanding*] Essay on the Human Understanding
166.27	*debtor*] *Dr.*
166.34–35	Kantians] Kantian's
167.3–4	whatever.|¶The] ~. ∧~
167.10	correct, these forms] correct, we may just as well study these forms

167.21	produces] poduces
167.25–26	self-knowledge] self∧|knowledge
167.28	concerned,] ∼∧
167.28	something] some thing
167.34	self,] ∼∧
167.34(2)	world of] world
168.19	remembered] rememembered
168.20	And] &
168.21	when] When
168.24	time;] ∼∧
169.3	archetypal] architypal *Also* 169.7
169.3	Arithmetic,] ∼∧
169.10	says,] ∼∧
169.25	*horse*] *rom.*
169.26	unsaid,] ∼∧
169.35	Locke's.] ∼∧
170.11–12	*superscription*] supersciption
170.24(1)	an] a
170.30	acquired.] ∼∧
170.31	*symbol.*∧] ∼..
170.35	Locke.] Locke [Book iii Ch 2. §§4.5.6.7]
170.36–172.2	§4. *Words* . . . insignificant noise.] *supplied*
172.16	account] accounts
172.20	intelligible] intellegible
172.27	Locke∧] ∼,
172.30	says,] ∼∧
173.1	Secondly] Secondy
173.19	not—] ∼,
173.25	parables,] ∼∧
173.25	&c.,] ∼∧∧
173.32	correspond] corresponds
173.32	are] is
173.39	exercise] excercise
174.9	representations] representation
174.14	THOU∧)] ∼,)
174.17	translatable,] ∼∧
174.28	nonsense∧] ∼—
174.32	in itself] intelf
174.33(2)	the] The
175.3	the law] the
175.5(1)	true.] ∼∧
175.9	symbol's] symbols

Harvard Lecture II

Copy-text for "Lecture II" is MS 95. All readings to the left of the bracket are emendations supplied by the editors. All readings to the right of the bracket are rejected readings from the copy-text.

175.20	believe] beleive *Also* 179.28(1,2)
175.20	successfully] sucessfully
175.28	Mansel] Mansell
176.2	inasmuch∧] ∼,
176.15	[Repeat]] ∧∼∧
176.15	*carnivora*] rom.
°176.16	extensive and] extensive ∧ and *Also* 176.17
176.16	*vertebrates*] rom.
176.17	*mammals*] rom.
176.28	cloven-footed] ∼∧∼ *Also* 176.36
176.31	of the whole] whole
176.37	herbivora∧] ∼.
177.4	*neat and deer*] neat & deer
177.5	*cloven-footed*] ∼∧∼
177.13	and] & *Also* 177.15, 177.17, 177.18, 177.26, 179.32, 179.34, 180.1, 182.5(1), 182.6, 182.8, 182.10, 183.2, 185.24, 187.33, 187.37(1,2), 187.38, 188.1, 188.8, 188.37, 189.1
177.13(1)	long-lived] ∼∧∼ *Also* 177.19, 177.20
177.13(2)	long-lived] longlived *Also* 177.17(2)
177.15(2)	Man∧] ∼,
177.15(2)	horse∧] ∼,
177.18	says,] ∼∧
177.22	right-hand] ∼∧∼
177.22	thus,] ∼∧
177.25	premiss].] ∼]∧
177.26	thus,] ∼∧
177.26	if] is
177.34	equal] a equal
177.34	refuted.] ∼∧
178.17	enumeration] enumation
178.18	*particular*] rom.
178.31	successively] sucessively
178.36	apply] applies
179.33	form.∧The] ∼.; the
180.16	example.] ∼∧
180.21	table.] ∼∧
180.23	*inductive*] rom.
180.28–29	so-called] ∼∧∼
180.29	principles in this way] principles
°180.30–31	with empirical] with∧empirical

181.5	Juppiter] *ital. Also* 181.10
181.5	*on*] *one*
181.6	*Juppiter*] *rom. Also* 181.11, 181.13
181.15	ellipse] ellipe
181.26–27	performed;] ∼∧
181.27	proposition,] ∼∧
181.30	without] with out
182.25	t ⎫ s, ⎬ ∼∧ m ⎭
182.25	t ⎫ m, ⎬ ∼∧ s ⎭
182.26	*Felapton*] *Fesapo*
183.5	clear] clearly
184.17	of] Of
184.38	repeat∧] ∼,
185.2	Their] There
185.8	symbolizable] symbolizeable *Also* 185.15, 185.16
185.23	*à posteriori.*] ∼ ∼∧
185.24	'giving] "∼
185.31	is] does is
185.32	is] If is
185.37	animals,] ∼.
185.39	objects,] ∼∧
186.1	it;] ∼∧
186.1	valid,] ∼;
186.15	*Hypotheses non fingo*] *rom.*
186.22	nine-tenths] ∼∧∼
186.34	A'] ∼∧
187.1	A] a
187.5	object,] ∼∧
187.6	object,] ∼∧
187.19	embodied in] embodied
187.22	impracticability] impracticablity
187.31	things;] ∼∧
187.32	knowledge;] ∼∧
187.33	*distinctness.*] ∼∧
188.5	classes∧] ∼,
188.20	&c.] ∼∧
188.21	synthesis] syntheses
188.25	All] all
188.25	has] as
188.26	as] to
188.28	*P* ⎫ *p*; ⎬ ∼∧
188.30	S,] ∼;

188.35   S] Σ
188.36   extension,] ∼.
189.3   gives] give
189.8   such and such] such and

Harvard Lecture III

Copy-text for this lecture is MS 96. All emendations have been supplied by the editors and appear to the left of the square brackets. The readings to the right of the brackets are rejected readings from MS 96.

189.20   the] The
189.26   ones,] ∼;
190.2 $h,$] ∼ₐ
190.2 $b,$] ∼ₐ

190.9 $\left.\begin{array}{c} .. \\ ... \\ .. \end{array}\right]$ ∼ₐ

190.15   Capital] Capitol
190.16   United States] united states
190.16   capital] capitol
190.17 $= u,$] $=$ ∼ₐ
190.20   naught] nought
190.20   same.] ∼ₐ
191.4   ¶Now] ₐ∼
191.4   Logic,] ∼ₐ
191.5   doₐnot] ∼-|∼
191.10   one] *rom. Also* 191.21
191.13   &c.] ∼ₐ *Also* 191.20, 192.25
191.22   classes] class
191.23   one] *One*
191.28   is.] ∼ₐ
191.29   horses,] ∼ₐ
191.29   cows,] ∼.
192.6 $+ a,$] $+$ ∼ₐ
192.15   1 (unity)] ₐunityₐ
          1
192.15   0 ∧ (zero)] ₐzeroₐ
          0.
192.19   nothing,] ∼ₐ
192.28   Zeroₐdivided] ∼-∼
193.5 $= c-$] $=$ ∼;

193.5   and] & *Also* 193.16, 193.17, 193.36, 197.16, 197.29(1), 203.26, 203.34(1,2), 203.35(1,2)

193.6   class $c-$] $\sim \sim_\wedge$

193.6 $= b,$] $= \sim_\wedge$

193.8 $= 1,$] $= \sim_\wedge$

193.9   everything;] $\sim_\wedge$

193.10   1,] $\sim_\wedge$

193.15   equation,] $\sim_\wedge$

193.16   or that] that

193.18   equation,] $\sim_\wedge$

193.20 $= 0.$] $= \sim_\wedge$

193.20 $= 0,$] $= \sim_\wedge$

193.24   benefit] benifit

193.34   men,] $\sim_\wedge$

193.35(2)   dead,] $\sim_\wedge$

193.36(1)   women,] $\sim_\wedge$

193.36(2)   women,] $\sim.$

193.37   stands for] stands

194.8   nothing,] $\sim_\wedge$

194.9   *some,*] $\sim_\wedge$

194.9   *all,*] $\sim_\wedge$

194.10   *some,*] $\sim_\wedge$

194.10   *all,*] $\sim_\wedge$

194.10   any] and

194.26   meaning] mean

194.27 $\dfrac{a}{m},$] $\sim_\wedge$

194.27 $\dfrac{w}{w+m},$] $\sim_\wedge$

194.27 $\dfrac{1-d}{a+wd},$] $\sim_\wedge$

194.29 $\dfrac{m}{m}$ or]$\dfrac{m}{m}$

194.31 $(1-m)$] *ital.*

194.34 $\dfrac{1}{1}m,$] $\sim_\wedge$

194.34 $\dfrac{0}{1}m,$] $\sim_\wedge$

194.34 $\dfrac{1}{0}m,$] $\sim_\wedge$

194.34 $\dfrac{1}{1}(1-m),$] $\sim(\sim)_\wedge$

194.35 $\dfrac{0}{1}(1-m),$] $\sim(\sim)_\wedge$

194.35 $\dfrac{1}{0}(1-m),$] $\sim(\sim)_\wedge$

194.35   for.] $\sim_\wedge$

195.3(1)	some,] *some*$_\wedge$
195.3(1)	all,] *all*$_\wedge$
195.3(2)	some,] $\sim_\wedge$
195.3(2)	all,] $\sim_\wedge$
195.9	means.] $\sim_\wedge$
195.10	*some,*] $\sim_\wedge$
195.10	*all,*] $\sim_\wedge$
195.13	which,] $\sim_\wedge$
195.14	these,] $\sim$.
195.19(1)	on] one
195.19	0] *ital.*
195.21	Now] now
195.24	*B.*] $\sim_\wedge$
195.24	*m,*] $\sim_\wedge$
196.2	some,] $\sim_\wedge$
196.2	all,] $\sim_\wedge$
196.3	$= m,$] $= \sim_\wedge$
196.4	men.] $\sim_\wedge$
196.5	$= \dfrac{m}{m},$] $= \sim_\wedge$
196.6	therefore] there$_\wedge$|fore
196.11	for?] $\sim_\wedge$
196.15	For] for
196.15	$\dfrac{0}{0}$] $\dfrac{0}{1}$
196.15	same;] $\sim_\wedge$
196.17	¶Now] $_\wedge\sim$
196.17	letters.] $\sim_\wedge$
196.18	letter.] $\sim_\wedge$
196.24	letter.] $\sim_\wedge$
196.29	mean?] $\sim_\wedge$
197.1	$\dfrac{0}{w}(1 - m).$] $\sim(\sim)_\wedge$
197.2	some,] $\sim_\wedge$
197.2	all,] $\sim_\wedge$
197.3	¶Now] $_\wedge$now
197.7	some,] $\sim_\wedge$
197.7	all,] $\sim_\wedge$
197.12	times.] $\sim_\wedge$
197.15	This] this
197.16	Then] then
197.16(1,2)	wherever] where ever
197.16	one] *rom.*
197.17(1,2)	And] and
197.20	process.] $\sim_\wedge$
197.22(1,2)	$m = 1$] $\sim_\wedge\sim$
197.22(1,2)	$m = 0$] $\sim_\wedge\sim$

197.23(1,2) $a = 1$] $\sim_\wedge\sim$
197.23(1,2) $a = 0$] $\sim_\wedge\sim$
197.29(1,2) $y,$] $\sim_\wedge$
198.5 exists,] $\sim;$
198.5 it] It
198.13 exists.] $\sim_\wedge$
198.14 numerator] num.
198.15 denominator] denom.
198.18 women " "] women
198.19 kings " "] kings
198.20 now] not *Also* 199.6
198.21 strike] stike
199.15 believes] beleives
199.21 detecting] dectecting
199.22 believe] beleive
199.32 beginning] begginning *Also* 199.36
199.35 that] the
200.6 exceedingly] exceeding it
200.7 are commonly] commonly
200.9 rule,] $\sim_\wedge$
200.21 speak, we] $\sim.$ We
200.25 expression of] expres-|of
200.30 $I,$] $\sim_\wedge$
200.35 *necessary*] rom.
201.1 things.] $\sim;$
201.7 has] as
201.10 therefore] there
201.19 Stuart] Stuarat
201.19–20 by$_\wedge$adducing] $\sim$-|$\sim$
201.20 ancients] ancient
201.34 *antipodes*] rom.
201.37 follows.] $\sim_\wedge$
202.3 whatever has] has
202.5–22 constitutes a nation . . . the result.] *reinstate*
202.7 instants] instances
202.25 true$_\wedge$] $\sim.$
202.31 true,] $\sim_\wedge$
202.31 is that what] what
203.4 true,] $\sim_\wedge$
203.14 $_\wedge$and] ¶$\sim$
203.14 moreover] more over
203.33 line;] $\sim_\wedge$
203.33 it is] it
203.35 side.] $\sim_\wedge$
*203.36 blue] green *Also* 204.12, 204.13, 204.14, 204.15
204.1 neither.] $\sim_\wedge$
204.7 surface.] $\sim;$

204.9	sheet;] ~ₐ
204.21	this is] this

Harvard Lecture on Whewell, Mill, and Compte

Copy-text for this lecture is MS 99. All readings to the left of the bracket are emendations supplied by the editors. All readings to the right of the bracket are rejected readings from MS 99.

205.1	the] The
205.11	and] & *Also* 205.12(1,2), 205.14, 205.23, 206.3, 206.6(1), 206.9, 206.32, 206.37, 207.39(1), 208.14, 209.5, 209.27, 209.36, 210.33, 210.39, 211.2, 211.21, 211.23, 211.27, 211.32, 212.10, 212.21, 212.22, 213.11(1), 213.33, 213.34, 214.2, 214.3(1,2), 214.25, 214.34, 215.2, 215.5, 215.10, 215.35, 216.3, 216.7, 217.7, 217.10, 218.21, 219.25, 219.34, 220.17, 221.36, 223.24
205.16	Kantian:–] Kantian:–p 6 Aph V.
205.17–20	*Fact . . .* Ideas is.] *supplied*
205.29	"the] ₐ~
206.2	*Facts."*] ~.ₐ
206.2	process,] ~ₐ
206.3	facts,] ~ₐ
206.4	process,] ~ₐ
206.4–5	conceptions,] ~ₐ
206.9	conception."] conception Also read 71 Aph XV."
206.10–13	An Induction . . . Induction.] *supplied*
206.15	inductionₐ] ~;
206.23(2)	died,] ~ₐ
206.26	carry] carries
206.26	and] And
206.30	Mill's] Mills'
206.31	Dr.] ~ₐ
206.37	*Idea*] rom.
206.37	*Conception*] rom.
206.38	conceptions–] ~ₐ
206.38	representations–] ~ₐ
207.2	*Ideas,"*] ~,ₐ
207.2	"to] ₐ~
207.10–11	following:–] following:–p 187 when Hipparchus
207.12–25	when Hipparchus . . . this star.] *supplied*
208.5–6	*Limits of Religious Thought*] rom.
208.31	logic.] logic. Read p 97. 98. Aph XVII & XXI.
208.32–35	The *Logic . . .* is manifest.] *supplied*

208.37–209.2   The relation . . . highest.] *supplied*
209.6   example.] ~∧
209.9   says,] ~∧
209.30   the] *reinstate*
209.37   exercise] excercise
210.11   "often] ∧~
210.16   believe] beleive *Also* 211.22, 212.11
210.20   same, there] ~. There
210.32   that] that that
210.38   it's] its
210.39   number] numbe
210.39   it's] its
211.25   cannot consider] cannot
211.33   quiddities] quidities
211.35   *Course*] *rom.*
211.38   which] whis
211.39   researches] researhs
212.8   standpoint] stand-point
212.11   and who] who
212.23(1)   the] they
212.24   Hegel's] Hegels'
212.28   science.] ~∧
212.28   exploded.] ~;
212.37   hypothesis.] ~∧
212.38   Cuvier's] Cuviers
212.39   class] class him
213.4   is] *reinstate*
213.6   essence] essense
213.13   follows.] follows Vol ii p 434.
213.14–31   The method . . . leads us astray.] *supplied*
213.40   is,] ~∧
214.12   now.] ~;
214.14   separately] sepately
214.25   demonstratively] demonstatively
214.25   a] as
214.38   can,] ~∧
214.39   imagine] Imagine
215.3   board,] ~∧
215.7   *System of Logic*] *rom.*
215.11–12   *System of Logic*] system of logic
215.15   shown] show
215.23   William] Wm
215.23   Hamilton,] ~∧
215.28   a] A
215.36   *inference*] *rom.*
216.10   unless] unless unless
216.17   &c.] ~∧ *Also* 216.18, 216.23, 216.24

216.28	comprehended] comphended
217.4	otherwise,] ∼ₐ
217.5	*conditio sine qua non*] rom. Also 217.9
217.6	No.] ∼ₐ
217.8	All] all
217.21	*Kritik*] rom.
217.21	follows:] ∼ₐ
217.23	their] there
217.37	*à priori*] rom.
218.2	is] are
218.3	by] be
218.13	affected.] ∼ₐ
218.14	The] the
218.32	that] that that
219.6	*Logic*] rom.
219.7	"On . . . Induction,"] ₐ∼ . . . ∼,ₐ
219.7–8	"Of the Evidence of the Law of Universal Causation."] ₐOf the Evidence of Universal Causation.ₐ
219.9	"an] ₐ∼
219.10	induction."] ∼.ₐ
219.12	thisₐ] ∼.
219.13	there] There
219.15	induction.] ∼ₐ
219.26	valid.] valid; See p 187.
219.27–31	Before . . . scientific inquiry.] *supplied*
219.33	value,] ∼ₐ
219.36	enumeration.] ∼ₐ
220.2	Instances] Intances
220.7	latter] latters
220.12	p.] ∼ₐ
220.12	"an] ₐ∼
220.13	induction."] ∼.ₐ
220.15	Mill's] Mills
220.21	causation.] causation p 203.
220.22–29	It is . . . unconditional.] *supplied*
°220.30–34	¶This is . . . the mind. I cannot] I cannot
220.35	*necessity.*] ∼ₐ
220.36	evidence.] evidence p 341.
220.37–221.20	The truth . . . itself.] *supplied*
221.31	[Rap at blue]] ₐ∼ ∼ ∼ₐ
221.33	S] *ital.*
221.36	we] We
221.36	are the striking] the striking
221.37	ruleₐ] ∼.
221.37	law of] law
221.38	of.] of. [Read on 341]
221.39–222.12	I apprehend . . . we are.] *supplied*

222.15–16	discernible] discernable
222.16	amounts] amount
222.17	discernible.] discernible. [Read on 341]
222.18–31	Besides this . . . observation.] *supplied*
222.33	no] No
222.40–223.16	The progress . . . studying.] *supplied*
223.17	∧Here] ¶[Read on 342] Here
223.20	established it;] established;
223.24	Gratry,] ∼∧

Harvard Lecture VI

Copy-text for "Lecture VI" is MS 100. All emendations have been supplied by the editors and appear to the left of the square brackets. The readings to the right of the brackets are rejected readings from the copy-text.

223.26	VI: Boole's] ∼. |∼
223.30–31	∧*An Investigation . . . Thought, . . . Mathematical Theories . . . Probabilities.*∧] "An Investigation . . . Thought∧ . . . mathematical theories . . . Mathematics."
224.2	*Organon*] rom.
224.11	and] & *Also* 224.12, 224.14, 224.16, 224.19, 224.36, 225.3, 225.10, 225.13, 225.22(2), 225.30, 226.1(1,2), 226.4, 226.8, 226.9, 226.15, 226.16, 226.18, 226.19, 226.22, 226.33, 226.35(1,2), 227.1, 227.2, 227.5, 227.25, 227.26, 227.30, 227.35, 227.36, 228.22, 228.26, 228.27, 228.30, 229.19, 229.24, 229.25, 229.28, 229.35, 230.29, 230.34, 231.23, 231.29, 231.30, 231.33, 232.2, 232.3(1), 232.17, 232.25, 232.26(1,2), 232.29, 233.5, 233.15, 233.17, 233.18, 233.25, 233.28, 234.13, 235.31, 236.12, 237.23(1,2), 238.6, 238.17, 238.24
224.12	∞.] ∼∧
224.26	subject,] ∼∧
224.29	non-distribution] ∼∧∼
224.32	of] Of
224.35	write] white
224.35	thus,] ∼∧
224.35	*Mc.*] ∼∧
225.1	connected.] ∼∧
225.5	Hamilton's] Hamiltons
225.6	Ploucquet] Plouquet
225.6	thus,] ∼∧
225.6	*E.*] ∼∧

225.7	ϵ.] $\sim_\wedge$
225.12	Some] some
225.12	Ethiopian] Ethiopean
225.18	beforehand] before hand
225.18	do,] $\sim_\wedge$
225.23	and] and and
225.35	agreement] agrement *Also* 225.36
226.1	*b*] *c*
226.1	*c*] *d*
226.4	objects,] $\sim$.
226.5	animal,] $\sim_\wedge$
226.7	classes;] $\sim_\wedge$
226.17	*minus*] rom. *Also* 226.24
226.21	*x*,] $\sim$.
226.21(2)	*y*] *Y*
226.21	extension,] $\sim_\wedge$
226.32	christian,] $\sim_\wedge$
227.8	some,] $\sim_\wedge$
227.8	all,] $\sim_\wedge$
227.26	¶Exponentials] $_\wedge\sim$
227.32	All] all
227.33	*Y*.] $\sim_\wedge$
227.36	*X*] *x*
227.36	*Y*] *y*
228.7	class-character] $\sim_\wedge\sim$
228.8	Then] then
228.15	in so$_\wedge$far] $\sim \sim\text{-}|\sim$
228.19(1,2)	*vel est*] rom. *Also* 228.23
228.23	*vel non est*] rom.
228.23	*B*, then] $\sim$. Then
228.26	non-existent] $\sim_\wedge\sim$
229.4	thing, *A*] thing, there is *A*
229.5	non-existent] nonexistent
229.5	not-*A*;] $\sim\text{-}\sim_\wedge$
229.5	the] the the
229.7	$= 0$.] $= \sim_\wedge$
229.15	deficiencies$_\wedge$that] $\sim$. That
229.17	supplied.] $\sim_\wedge$
229.24	Hypothetical,] $\sim_\wedge$
229.28	*a* $_\wedge$ express] $\sim = \sim$
229.29	The] the
229.29	mean] means
229.36	terms.] $\sim_\wedge$
230.5	if griffins] if though griffins
230.6	four-sided$_\wedge$triangle] foursided-|triangle
230.17	If$_\wedge$] $\sim$,
230.17	smooth$_\wedge$] $\sim$,

230.24	believe] beleive
230.25	non-smooth$_\wedge$to] $\sim$-$\sim$. To
230.33	Quantity] Quanitity
231.1	$v_\wedge$ denotes] $\sim = \sim$
231.1	*some*] rom. *Also* 231.14
231.9	Four-legged] $\sim_\wedge\sim$ *Also* 231.10
231.12	negative$_\wedge$] $\sim$,
231.14	Some] some
231.24	shows] Shows
231.24	$y,$] $\sim$.
232.4	$a(1-b),$] $\sim(\sim)_\wedge$
232.4	$b(1-a).$] $\sim(\sim)_\wedge$
232.6	$= a,$] $= \sim_\wedge$
232.6	$= 0.$] $= \sim_\wedge$
232.9	them,] $\sim_\wedge$
232.9	$x,$] $\sim_\wedge$
232.10	$x(1-y).$] $\sim(\sim)_\wedge$
232.19	$x_0.$] $\sim_\wedge$
232.22	disappears;] $\sim_\wedge$
232.27	$= xf1$] $= xf1_1$
232.28	formula$_\wedge$] $\sim$.
232.29	$\dfrac{1-(a-b)^2.}{a}$] $\dfrac{1-(a-b)^2}{a} = u_\wedge$
232.31	$= af(1,b)$] $= a(f1,b)$
233.1	$_\wedge$Developing] ¶developing
233.7	$= 1$ and] $= 1$
233.9	$= 0$ and] $= 0$
233.11	$= 0$ and] $= 0$
233.16	$x,$] $\sim_\wedge$
233.16	$= x;$] $= \sim_\wedge$
233.18	*some,*] $\sim_\wedge$
233.19	*some,*] $\sim_\wedge$
233.19	*all,*] $\sim_\wedge$
233.21	another,] $\sim_\wedge$
233.21	$\dfrac{x}{y},$] $\sim_\wedge$
233.26	$= y;$] $= \sim_\wedge$
233.26	$= 0,$ while] $= \sim_\wedge$ While
233.28	$\dfrac{1}{0},$] $\sim$.
233.31(2)	either] Either
233.31	$= 0.$] $= \sim_\wedge$
233.32	$= 0.$] $= \sim_\wedge$
234.1	$= 0.$] $= \sim_\wedge$
234.2	$= 0.$] $= \sim_\wedge$
234.3(1,2)	$= 0.$] $= \sim_\wedge$
234.11	positive.] $\sim_\wedge$

234.17 (1,2)	$= 0.] = \sim_\wedge$
234.19	$= 0,] = \sim_\wedge$
234.21	¶Since] $_\wedge\sim$
234.21	*zero,* either] $\sim$. Either
234.21	$= 0;] = \sim_\wedge$
234.22	$= 0,] = \sim_\wedge$
234.26 (2)	the] the the
234.28	$= 0.] = \sim_\wedge$
234.29	$= 0$ and] $= 0$
234.29	$= 0;] = \sim_\wedge$
234.30	*zero,*] $\sim_\wedge$
234.30	$= 0$ and] $= 0$
234.31	$= 0,] = \sim_\wedge$
234.31	$= 0$ and] $= 0$
234.32	$=0.] = \sim_\wedge$
235.4	$= b(1 - a).] = \sim (\sim)_\wedge$
235.10	Negroes] negroes *Also* 235.13, 235.18
235.12	Negroes] negoes
235.13	There] there
235.14	Monkeys] monkeys
235.14	monkeys.] $\sim_\wedge$
235.15	$= 0.] = \sim_\wedge$
235.17	$= 0,] = \sim_\wedge$
235.18	$= 0;] = \sim_\wedge$
235.18	None] none
235.28	let it] let Give the prob. that one or both of two events happen; let it
235.31	$y.] \sim_\wedge$
235.35–36	happens).] $\sim)_\wedge$
235.37	$x).] \sim)_\wedge$
236.5	$= 0.$ When] $= \sim_\wedge$when
236.5	it] It
236.6	$= 0.] = \sim_\wedge$
236.6	general] geneneral
236.7	$= 0.] = \sim_\wedge$
236.19	we] We
236.22	$= 1$ and] $= 1$
236.25	When] when
236.25	$= 1$ and] $= 1$
236.28	When] when
236.28	$= 0$ and] $= 0$
237.2	When] when
237.2	$= 0$ and] $= 0$
238.7	$= \dfrac{X}{q},] = \sim_\wedge$
238.7	$= \dfrac{X}{p}.] = \sim_\wedge$

238.12	which] Which
238.14	p. Let the] p the
238.15(1)	probability] probility
238.15	and] $\&$
238.15	q.] $\sim_\wedge$
238.16	X.] $\sim_\wedge$
238.17(1)	hails.] $\sim_\wedge$
238.17	Let y be] y
238.17	thunders.] $\sim_\wedge$
238.17	u be] u
238.17(2)	hails.] $\sim_\wedge$
238.18	$= xy$ and] $= xy$
238.19	$(1 - y)$.] $(\sim)_\wedge$
239.1	as] a
239.6	hypothesis.] $\sim_\wedge$
239.9	appear$_\wedge$] $\sim$.
239.9	for.] $\sim_\wedge$
239.14–15	subject:] subject$_\wedge$ [p 365] ¶Next lecture—
239.16–32	These problems . . . inclusive.] *supplied*

Harvard Lecture on Kant

Copy-text for the "Lecture on Kant" is MS 101. All readings to the left of the bracket are emendations supplied by the editors. All readings to the right of the bracket are rejected readings from MS 101.

240.4	science,] $\sim_\wedge$
240.4	valid,] $\sim_\wedge$
240.14	then] Then
240.14(2)	and] & *Also* 240.26, 240.29, 240.30(1), 241.1, 241.13(2), 241.14(2), 241.37, 242.2, 242.10, 242.12, 242.21, 243.3, 243.7, 243.12, 243.13, 243.20, 243.21, 243.31, 243.34, 244.2(2), 244.28, 245.5(1), 246.16, 246.30, 248.30, 248.33(1), 248.34, 248.35, 248.36, 248.38, 249.1, 249.4, 249.7, 249.17, 249.18, 249.21, 249.24, 249.25, 249.26(1,2), 249.29, 249.30, 249.35, 249.38, 250.3, 250.5, 250.6, 250.8, 250.11, 250.14, 250.15, 250.19(1), 250.25, 250.28, 250.29, 250.30, 251.5(1), 251.17, 251.35, 252.8, 252.10, 252.29, 252.31, 252.36, 252.37, 252.39, 253.5, 253.15, 253.32, 253.38, 254.3, 254.23, 254.24, 254.25, 254.30, 255.1, 255.8, 255.16, 255.22, 255.26, 256.9
240.16	inference] inferrence
240.17	consciousness,] $\sim$.

240.19	opinions] opinion
240.21	transcendentalism.] ~ₐ
240.21	And] &
240.21	with] With
240.23	technical] technically
240.27	them,] ~;
241.5	says:] ~ₐ
241.6–16	*extract*
241.19	his] His
241.21	*Critic's*] Critics
241.32	beliefs] beleifs
241.32	*necessary,*] ~ₐ
241.33	*forms,*] ~ₐ
242.2	it,] ~ₐ
242.2	*form*] *Form*
242.20	"The] ₐthe
242.21	Time"] ~ₐ
242.21	*North American Review*] rom.
242.22	says:] ~ₐ
242.23–29	*extract*
242.30	Kant's] Kants
242.34	*Critik der reinen Vernunft*ₐ] Critik der reinen Vernunft.
242.35	(p. 125).] (~ₐ ~)ₐ
242.38	reviewer's] reviewers
243.1	(p. 122):] (~ₐ ~)ₐ
243.1	"How] ₐ~
243.8	broadest] brodest
243.8	features] feautures
243.15	mightₐ] ~,
243.15	instanceₐ] ~,
243.16	critic's] critics
243.17	barely] bareₐ|ly
243.17	referred] refferred
243.23	inconsistency] inconsitency
243.24–25	*Critic of the Pure Reason*] rom.
243.29	Don Quixote,] ~ ~ₐ
243.32	it] is
243.36–244.5	*extract*
244.6	*Critic of the Pure Reason*] critic of the pure reason
244.10	Wolff] Wollf
244.13	man's] mans
244.14	*Critic*] critic *Also* 244.27, 247.38, 250.19, 250.24, 251.24
244.16	schemes] shemes
244.17	besieged] beseiged
244.33	positivist] posivist
245.4	"Transcendental Logic."] ₐ~ ~.ₐ

245.4	"Analytic"] ∧~∧ *Also* 245.5
245.5	"Dialectic"] ∧~∧
245.5	"Analytic of Concepts"] ∧~ ~ ~∧
245.6	"Analytic of Judgments."] ∧~ ~ ~.∧
245.8	&c.] ~∧
245.30	infers] inferrs
246.3	it;∧] ~;;
246.5	Hence∧] ~;
246.10	consciousness (or] ~. Or
246.11	consciousness)] ~∧
246.13	belief] beleif
246.15	is] are
246.17	*à priori.*] ~ ~∧
246.19	material] matterial
246.29	is∧] ~;
247.12	A] An
248.1	possible.] ~∧
248.4	transcendental] trans-|scendental
248.6	*objective validity*] rom.
248.22	a] an
248.25	of time] time
248.26	space,] ~∧
248.29	of space] space
249.1	then are] are then are
249.21	infer] inferr *Also* 250.11
249.28	soul:] ~∧
249.28	Sensibility,] ~∧
249.29	Understanding,] ~∧
249.29	Feeling.] ~∧
249.30	class-concepts] ~∧~
250.2	its] it
250.6	time,] ~∧
250.12	*form*] rom.
250.39	class-conceptions] ~∧~
250.40	appearance,] ~;
251.2	appearance,] ~∧
251.6	say] says
251.13	things-in-themselves] ~∧~∧~ *Also* 251.16, 251.19–20
251.17	he] He
251.19	phenomena,] ~∧
251.19	therefore,] ~∧
251.21–22	consistently. ¶We] consistently. ¶Nearly ten minutes more. ¶We
251.38	William] Wm.
252.8	Kant's] Kants
252.12	says:–] says:–p 72

252.13–28	Logicians . . . each other.] *supplied*
252.30	number.] ~ₐ
252.31	Universal] a Universal
252.32	coincide] coincides
252.35(1,2)	All] all
252.36(1,2)	All] all
252.37	All] all
252.37(2)	men are] men
252.38	up;] ~ₐ
252.38	Some] some
252.38	Negroes] negroes *Also* 252.39(1), 253.1, 253.2(1)
252.39(1,2)	Some] some
252.39(1)	men are] men
252.39(2)	Negroes,] negroesₐ
253.1	*some*] rom.
253.1	Some] some
253.2(1,2)	No] no
253.2	Negroes,] negroesₐ
253.4	proposition.] ~ₐ
253.5	Old] old
253.5–6	Washington is mortal] Washington
253.12	*homo non est quadrupes*] homo non est quarupes
253.13	[REPEAT.]] ₐ~·ₐ
253.14	*homo est non quadrupes*] rom.
253.18	*infinite*] rom.
253.18	Aristotle's] Aristotles
253.18	ἀόριστος] ἀορίστος
253.19	says:—] says:—p 72. "In the same way, infinite Judgments must be distinguished from Affirmative &c.
253.20–28	In like manner . . . knowledge.] *supplied*
253.32	Thomson's] Thompson's
253.33	Substitutives, their] ~. Their
253.39	hypothetico-disjunctive] ~ₐ~
254.1(2)	prohibited] probited
254.2	it] It
254.22	*or*] rom.
254.24	predicate.] ~ₐ
254.25(2)	This] this
254.27	This] this
254.27	berryₐ] ~.
255.1	productsₐ] ~.
255.14	all;] ~ₐ
255.17	a true] true
255.18	hypothetico-disjunctives] ~ₐ~
255.24	contradict,] ~ₐ
256.1	has] as

Harvard Lecture VIII

Copy-text for "Lecture VIII" is MS 105. All emendations have been supplied by the editors and appear to the left of the square brackets. The readings to the right of the brackets are rejected readings from the copy-text.

256.11	VIII: Forms] ~. |~
256.12	and] & *Also* 256.19, 257.3, 257.11, 257.15, 257.20, 257.23, 257.25, 257.26, 257.28, 257.38, 258.4, 258.5, 258.15, 259.8, 259.10, 259.16, 259.18, 259.20, 259.22, 259.24, 259.26, 259.36, 259.37, 259.38, 259.39, 260.6, 260.8(1,2), 260.15, 260.27, 261.2, 261.11, 261.12 , 261.16, 261.23, 261.26, 261.33, 262.6, 262.27, 263.11, 263.18, 263.25, 264.16, 265.34, 269.9, 269.10(1), 269.18(1,2), 270.11, 270.21, 270.22, 270.23, 270.27, 271.1, 271.2, 271.13, 271.19
256.24	independent] independant
256.30	signalize—] ~ₐ
257.4	*Representation*] *rom.*
257.5	general] geneneral
257.6	a perfect] perfect
257.13	representations.] ~ₐ
257.18	is] is is
257.32	¶We] ₐ~
257.34	agreement] agre-|ment
258.4	representable] representible
258.21	inferences, to] ~. To
258.28	And] &
258.34	terms:] ~.
258.34	*animals*] *rom.* *Also* 258.37, 259.3, 259.9
258.37	*men*] *rom.*
°259.2	*stones*] pigs
259.9	twice-predicate] ~ₐ~ *Also* 259.10, 259.26
259.9	subject-predicate.] ~-~ₐ
259.10	twice-subject] ~ₐ~
259.10	*Stones*] *rom.*
259.14	propositions:] ~;
259.15	*premisses;*] ~ₐ
259.24	predicate-subject] ~ₐ~
259.34	the 2nd] 2nd
260.3(1,2)	Subsumption] Subsum
260.3	Result] Res.
260.4	Subsumption] Subs.
260.8	AB,] ~ₐ
260.8	predicate,] ~ₐ

260.10(1,2,3)	Fig.] ~∧ *Also* 260.22(1,2,3), 261.7
260.15	rule.] ~∧
261.3	*Darapti*] *darapti*
261.3	universals] univer∧|sals
261.18	they] the
261.19	well-established] ~∧~
261.19	conceptions;] ~∧
261.23	*rule,*] ~∧
261.33	result∧] ~.
261.33	the subsumption] subsumption
261.35(2)	the] the the
261.35	*reductio*] rom.
262.2	Negroes] negroes *Also* 262.3, 262.6, 262.7, 262.9, 262.10
262.4	We] we
262.13	Result] Res *Also* 262.14, 262.15
262.14(1,2)	Subsumption] Sub *Also* 262.15
262.18	mule∧] ~,
262.18	long-lived] longlived *Also* 263.11, 265.3, 265.5
262.20	animal] an.
262.20	long-lived] ~∧~ *Also* 262.26, 262.28, 263.10–11, 263.15, 265.13
262.25	left-hand] ~∧~
263.2	*Prior Analytics*] rom.
263.6	*long-lived*] ~∧~
263.18	thus:] ~∧
264.20	so-called] ~∧~
264.36	probability] probabi∧|lity
264.38	is.] ~?
264.39	Aristotle's] Aristotles
265.13	believe] beleive *Also* 265.14, 265.16, 267.39
265.20–21	system, it] ~. It
265.29	into] in to
265.33	cloven-hoofed] ~∧~ *Also* 266.3, 266.4, 266.6, 266.16, 267.5, 267.7
265.34	Presence.] ~∧
265.35	and] in
266.1	herbivora.] ~∧
266.2	exhibited] Exhibited
266.4	&c.] &
266.5	&c.] ~∧ *Also* 270.18, 271.2, 271.7, 271.11
267.2	acknowledged] acknowledge
267.5	and] & *Also* 267.7
267.16	fringes] frings
267.26	or] of
267.27	*à priori*] rom.
267.27	*à particularis*] rom.
267.28	*a posteriori*] rom.

°267.29   critically.] critically. ¶And first let me specify &c.
267.35   that in] that
268.13   conditions] condition
268.30   premiss,] ~∧
268.31   premiss,] ~∧
269.3(1)   est] rom. Also 269.14
269.3   non-B] ~∧~
269.3   non est] rom. Also 269.13
269.9   middle,] ~∧
269.11   proposition.] ~∧
270.9   Now] No
270.11   red,] ~∧
270.13   denied),] ~)∧
270.14   denied),] ~)∧
270.20   admitted,] ~∧
270.20   that] that that
270.23   Deductions,] ~∧
270.23   Inductions,] ~∧
270.23   Hypotheses,] ~∧
270.35   Venus] The earth
271.10   No carnivora] no Carnivora
271.11   cloven-footed] ~∧~ Also 271.12
271.25   Juppiter] rom. Also 271.26

Harvard Lecture X

Copy-text for this lecture is MS 106. All readings to the left of the brackets are emendations supplied by the editors. The readings to the right of the brackets are rejected readings from MS 106.

272.1   X: Grounds] ~. |~
272.4   and] & Also 272.10, 272.11, 272.12, 272.13, 272.16, 272.26,
                 273.15, 273.17, 273.19, 273.20, 273.21, 273.22, 273.25,
                 273.26, 274.11, 274.20(1,2), 274.21, 274.37, 275.1(1,2),
                 275.2, 275.7, 275.8, 275.9, 275.15, 275.19, 275.23, 275.26,
                 275.27, 276.4, 276.5, 276.8, 276.9, 276.11, 276.16, 276.21,
                 277.11, 277.14, 277.29, 277.35, 278.1, 278.3, 278.6,
                 278.8(1), 278.13, 278.19, 278.23, 278.24, 278.29, 278.30,
                 278.37, 279.3, 279.11, 279.14, 280.1, 280.2, 280.25, 281.22,
                 281.31(1,2), 281.37, 282.8, 282.13, 282.15, 282.20, 283.4,
                 283.24, 283.28, 284.24, 284.27, 284.28, 284.31, 284.34,
                 285.10, 285.11, 285.13, 285.19, 285.28(1,2), 285.32(1,2),
                 286.10(1), 286.14, 286.15, 286.16, 286.20
272.6(2)   its] it

272.18	intensive] Intensive
273.3	all.] ~∧
273.6	*Analytic*] *Anal.*
273.6	Fig.] ~∧ *Also* 273.9, 273.12
273.7	Predicate] Pred *Also* 273.10, 273.13
273.8	Subject] Subj
273.9	*Synthetic Intensive*] *Syn Int*
273.11	Subject] Sub.
273.17	*vice versa,*] ~ ~.
273.25	kind,] ~∧
273.26	right-handed] ~∧~
273.26	left-handed] ~∧~
273.38	Man] man
274.1	infer] inferr
274.2	All] all
274.21	representation] rep.
274.32	Symbols] Sym∧|bols
274.33	*conditio sine qua non*] *rom.*
274.36(1)	Universal] Univ.
275.15–16	connotative] cononative
275.18	animal, then] ~. Then
275.22	connotation] conotation
275.25	*man∧non-risible*] ~-|~-~
275.27	risible∧man] ~-~
276.1	+ *B′*] + *B*
276.5	*animal,*] ~;
276.11	instead] in stead
276.22	is] are
276.31	a concrete] concrete
276.32	information] inform.
276.33	"What] '~
277.12	determined;] ~∧
277.13	connotation,] ~∧
277.13	denotation,] ~∧
277.22	connotation.] ~∧
277.31	connotative] con.
277.32	denotative] den.
278.5	proposition,] ~∧
278.6–7	be green . . . unripe fruit.] *reinstate*
278.10	describe] descibe
278.13	denotation.] ~∧
278.14	*homo*] *rom.*
278.15	man, the] ~. The
278.18	immediately] immed.
278.20	Propositions] Props.
278.20	immediately determinative] immed. det. *Also* 278.22–23

278.21	denotation] denot.
278.21	denotative] denot.
278.22	Propositions which] Props. wh.
278.23	denotation] den.
278.23	connotation] con.
278.23	information] inf.
278.29	Deduction,] ∼ʌ
278.29	Induction,] ∼ʌ
278.29	Hypothesis] Hy.
278.31	understandʌ] ∼,
279.6	possesses] possess
279.35	parts:] ∼ʌ
280.2	depends,] ∼ʌ
280.34	symbolizability] symbolizeability *Also* 281.3–4, 281.18, 282.1, 284.31–32, 284.34
280.37	state] state to
281.1	information] implication
281.9	definition.] ∼ʌ
281.31	*and*] &
282.5	symbolizable] symbolizeable *Also* 282.7, 282.11, 282.12, 282.30, 282.31, 282.34–35, 283.3, 283.6, 283.8, 284.10
282.13	of things] things
282.20	denotationʌ] ∼;
°282.28	every collocation] everyʌcollocation
283.1	fact,] ∼;
283.8	Q.E.D.] ∼ʌ∼ʌ∼.
283.18–19	Hypothesis.] ∼ʌ
283.28	testedʌ] ∼;
283.28	kinds] kind
284.25	subsumption] subsumtion *Also* 284.27
284.28	A,] ∼ʌ
284.29	these,] ∼ʌ
285.15	theory,] ∼ʌ
285.19	is,] ∼ʌ
285.19	*vice versa.*ʌ] ∼ ∼. .
285.21	proposed,] ∼ʌ
285.27	a] as
285.28	*sheep,*] ∼ʌ
285.28	*deer–*] ∼,
285.30	preferred] prefered
286.6	hypothesis,] ∼ʌ
286.8	has,] ∼ʌ
286.12	destitute] Destitute
286.14	absolutely,] ∼ʌ
286.14	relatively,] ∼ʌ

Harvard Lecture XI

Copy-text for "Lecture XI" is MS 107. All readings to the right of the bracket are emendations supplied by the editors. All readings to the left of the bracket are rejected readings from the copy-text.

287.15   nature,] ~;
287.16   one, so] ~. So
287.21(1,2) and] & *Also* 287.24, 287.28, 288.8, 288.14, 288.16, 288.18, 288.20, 288.22, 288.23, 289.6, 289.13, 289.17, 289.19(2), 289.35, 290.27, 291.7, 291.9, 291.10, 291.14, 291.19, 291.28, 291.29, 291.32(1,2,3), 291.34(1,2), 291.35, 291.36, 292.2, 292.7, 292.12, 292.13, 292.14, 292.17, 292.33, 293.7(1,2), 293.9, 293.11, 293.23, 293.24(1), 293.26, 294.30, 294.34, 295.4, 295.5, 295.9, 295.15, 295.22, 296.20, 296.24, 296.25, 296.28, 297.11, 297.13, 297.17, 297.19, 297.20, 297.27, 297.34, 298.12, 298.13, 298.21(1,3), 298.23, 298.29(1), 299.6, 299.13, 299.25, 299.27, 299.29, 299.32, 300.8(1,2), 300.17(1,2), 300.18(1,2,3), 300.23, 300.27, 300.29(1,2), 301.22, 301.25, 301.30, 301.37, 302.7, 302.8, 302.9
287.29   intention$_\wedge$] ~;
287.29   *whiteness*] *rom.*
287.30   *nonentity,*] nonentity$_\wedge$
*287.39–288.2 information. To say . . . connotation.] information.
288.4   symbols,] ~$_\wedge$
288.4   logic,] ~$_\wedge$
288.8   things,] ~;
288.24   judgments.] ~$_\wedge$
288.28   informative,] ~$_\wedge$
288.32   denotative,] ~$_\wedge$
289.7   image$_\wedge$] ~.
289.8   copy$_\wedge$] ~.
289.10   objects$_\wedge$] ~.
289.11   hypothesis$_\wedge$] ~.
289.13   strictly$_\wedge$] ~.
289.14   propositions;] ~$_\wedge$
289.30   demonstration] demonstratration
289.34   symbolizable] symbolizeable *Also* 292.12, 302.31
289.34   symbolization] symbolizeation
290.12(2)   the] they
290.15 $_\wedge$*Nota notae*$_\wedge$] "Nota notae"
290.16   the affirmative] affirmative
290.29(2)   the] The
290.39   (it] $_\wedge$~
291.1   fortification)—] ~$_{\wedge\wedge}$
291.6   ¶We] $_\wedge$~

291.7   term—] ~;
291.7   deer—] ~;
291.7   it] It
291.14   well-known] ~ₐ~
291.15   unity,] ~ₐ
291.18   earth, the] ~. The
291.20   Mercury] mercury
291.26   hypothesis, because] ~. Because
291.27(1)   the] The
291.31   extension,] ~ₐ
292.10   corollary] corrolary
292.11   the] thes
292.15   probability] probality
292.36   J.] ~ₐ
293.1   induction] inₐ|duction
293.3   are] is
293.7   in] In
293.11   J;] ~ₐ
293.18   hypotheses] hypothesis
293.22   ¶It] ₐ~
293.31   against] aganist
294.2   from] as
294.6   sets] setts   *Also* 294.16
294.6   facts, it] ~. It
294.7   instance,] ~ₐ
294.18   But the] But of the
294.36   may be] may
294.39(1)   Hamilton—] ~ₐ
295.3   that] the
295.10   good,"] ~,ₐ
295.11   quantification,] ~ₐ
295.12   it,] ~ₐ
295.15   1.] ~ₐ
295.15(3)   All] all
295.16   2.] ~ₐ
295.16   i.e.] ~ₐ~ₐ   *Also* 295.18, 295.19, 295.20, 295.21, 295.22,
            299.27
295.17   3.] ~ₐ
295.17   i.e.] ~ₐ~.   *Also* 299.29
295.18   4.] ~ₐ
295.20   6.] ~ₐ
295.21   7.] ~ₐ
295.22   8.] ~ₐ
296.19   first,] ~ₐ
296.19   B,] ~ₐ
296.20(2)   All] all
296.24   Hamilton's] Hamiltons

296.24	innovations,] $\sim_\wedge$
296.25	*B*,] $\sim_\wedge$
296.27	this is] this
296.35	we] We
297.3	*some*] rom. *Also* 299.13
297.4	*virtuous*] rom.
297.7	Some] some
297.27–28	individual, that] $\sim$. That
297.30	too] to
297.34	result,] $\sim_\wedge$
297.34	*Darapti*] rom.
298.1	*Felapton*] rom.
298.1	syllogism,] $\sim_\wedge$
298.2	notation.] $\sim_\wedge$
298.10	¶This] $_\wedge\sim$
298.15	Deduction,] $\sim_\wedge$
298.15	Induction,] $\sim_\wedge$
298.28	scheme] sheme *Also* 301.17
298.29	clear,] $\sim_\wedge$
298.29	distinct,] $\sim_\wedge$
299.13	*all*] rom.
299.24	&c.] $\sim_\wedge$ *Also* 299.26, 299.28, 301.3, 301.6, 301.7
299.25(2)	Some] some
299.27(2)	Some] some
299.31	quality–] $\sim_\wedge$
299.31	indistinct–] $\sim_\wedge$
299.33	set] sett
299.35	other:] $\sim_\wedge$
299.35	Coëxtension,] $\sim_\wedge$
299.35	Subordination,] $\sim_\wedge$
299.35	Intersection,] $\sim_\wedge$
300.13	nor] or
300.19	superordination).] $\sim$.)
300.22–23	co|extensive] coëxtensive
300.26	or] &
300.27	go] goe
300.34(2)	*β*] B
301.15	anything] any$_\wedge$|thing
301.19	propositions] proposition
301.22	*B*,] $\sim_\wedge$
301.22	*C*,] $\sim_\wedge$
301.28	negative–] $\sim_\wedge$
301.30	infinites,] $\sim_\wedge$
301.31	*Non omnis*] rom.
301.31	*est*] rom. *Also* 301.34(1,2)
301.33	*Non omnis*] non omnis
301.34	*Aliquis*] rom.

301.34	non-*B*] ~ₐ~
302.1	contradicting,] ~ₐ
302.4(2)	Assertion] Ass.
302.4(1)	Contradiction] Cont.
302.7	only,] ~ₐ
302.8	are] is
302.10	proposition.] ~ₐ
302.19	lectures,] ~;
302.21	studied,] ~ₐ

Teleological Logic

Copy-text is MS 108. All emendations have been supplied by the editors and appear to the left of the square brackets. The readings to the right of the square brackets are rejected readings from the copy-text.

303.7	symbols.] ~ₐ
303.10	representations.] ~ₐ
303.17	and] &
304.1	1.] ~ₐ
304.2	2.] ~ₐ
304.6	¶By] ₐ~
304.8	mind,] ~ₐ
304.16	symbol] symol

Unpsychological View of Logic

Copy-text for the two variants of "Unpsychological View of Logic" is MS 109. All emendations have been supplied by the editors and appear to the left of the square brackets. The readings to the right of the brackets are rejected readings from MS 109.

305.7	and] & *Also* 305.13, 305.14, 306.15, 306.18, 306.27, 307.1, 307.4, 307.19, 308.4, 308.23, 309.17
305.7	Moodsₐ] ~.
305.8	Hypothesisₐ] ~.
305.9	Implicationₐ] ~.
305.10	Propositionsₐ] ~.
305.11	Inferenceₐ] ~.
305.19	Hypothesesₐ] ~.

305.21	*I.*] ~ₐ
305.25	third] and third
306.3	mind's] minds
306.5	But in a] But as in
306.9	Kantₐ] ~;
306.11	mind's] minds
306.22	such] a such
306.27–28	believe] beleive
306.29	colour,] ~;
306.32	from which] from
306.36	none] no
306.38	anti-redness] antiredness
307.17	noumenon,] ~;
307.18	there] theses
307.22	else.] ~;
307.26	similar] simar
307.35	or,] ~ₐ
307.36	mind,] ~ₐ
307.38	realization] realisation
308.5	consistsₐ] ~,
308.10	sorts.] ~ₐ
308.11	*Marks,*] ~.
308.15	*Analogues,*] ~.
308.16	which is] which
308.17	everything] everthing
308.20	*Symbols,*] Symbols.
306.36	symbols?] ~.
309.1	qualitiesₐ] ~;
309.2	logic;] ~ₐ
309.4	thing,] ~ₐ
309.6	words as] words
309.6	*creation,*] ~ₐ
309.10	inference is] inference
309.13	true."] ~ₐ"

Unpsychological View of Logic

310.1	Logicₐ|to] ~; ~
310.5	Logicₐ] ~.
310.6	Formsₐ] ~.
310.7	Forms of] Forms
310.7	Hypothesisₐ] ~.
310.8	Implicationₐ] ~.
310.9	Propositionsₐ] ~.

310.12	I₍ₐ₎] ∼.
310.12	Machinery] Machiery
310.13	II₍ₐ₎] ∼.
310.14	III₍ₐ₎] ∼.
310.14	Memory₍ₐ₎] ∼.
310.15	IV₍ₐ₎] ∼.
310.16	V₍ₐ₎] ∼.
310.16	Emotion₍ₐ₎] ∼.
310.17	Life₍ₐ₎] ∼.
310.18	VII₍ₐ₎] ∼.
310.18	Freedom₍ₐ₎] ∼.
310.19	VIII₍ₐ₎] ∼.
310.20	IX₍ₐ₎] ∼.
310.21	I.] ∼₍ₐ₎
311.3	surprising] surprizing
311.6	have to do] have
311.7	*Thought*₍ₐ₎] ∼,
311.13	and] & *Also* 312.32, 313.19(1), 313.27, 313.33, 313.37, 313.38, 314.8, 314.9, 314.12, 314.25(1), 314.32, 315.7(2), 315.10(2), 315.11, 315.21, 315.26, 315.29, 315.34, 315.37(1,2), 316.15, 316.17, 316.19(1), 317.7, 317.13, 317.14, 318.2, 318.4, 318.7, 318.12(1), 318.17, 318.19, 318.25, 319.15, 319.31, 320.8, 320.13, 320.20(1,2), 321.3(1,2), 321.6, 321.12
311.16	quantities,] ∼;
311.23	entanglements] entangements
311.27	long-extinct] ∼₍ₐ₎∼
311.27	syllogism be] syllogism to be
311.27–28	syllogism,] ∼₍ₐ₎
311.31	seen₍ₐ₎] ∼;
311.39	roundabout] roudabout
312.13	Mill₍ₐ₎] ∼,
312.15	is,] ∼;
312.20	B,] ∼₍ₐ₎
312.24	By a] By the a
312.25	which,] ∼₍ₐ₎
312.26	analyzable] analyzible *Also* 313.27
312.26	experience,] ∼₍ₐ₎
312.27	as] is
312.31–32	perceived,] ∼₍ₐ₎
312.32	discriminated,] ∼₍ₐ₎
312.34	generalized] genalized
312.39	sense₍ₐ₎] ∼,
312.39	in] it
313.1	reader's] readers
313.3	facts] fact
313.4	fact;] ∼.

313.15	imagination;] ~–
313.16	thought,] ~∧
313.19(1,2)	us,] ~∧
313.22	induce] induces
313.25	a] A
313.32	¶Corresponding] ∧~
313.35	elements;] ~∧
313.36	the] The
313.37	accidental,] ~∧
313.39	noumenon,] ~∧
314.2	*accidents,*] ~∧
°314.2–3	*qualities. Having*] *qualities.* It will be observed that I always use object & subject in their ancient sense, the former to signify——— Having
314.5	that an] that if an
314.10	representation] represtation
314.11	the thing] thing
314.11	represents–] ~,
314.11	representation–] ~∧
314.17	color∧] ~,
314.18	*locomotive*] rom.
314.30	are,] ~∧
314.31	reaches,] ~;
314.32	*object,*] ~∧
314.34	*II.*] ~∧
315.11	*Y,*] ~∧
315.16	corollaries] corrollaries
315.17	drawn;] draw∧
315.17–18	non-existence] ~∧~ *Also* 315.18, 315.19, 315.20
315.20	corollaries] corrolaries
°315.22	diagrams on p. 316.] following diagrams.
315.24	Syllogism.] ~∧
315.25	rule,] ~∧
315.25	case,] ~∧
315.26	denote] denotes
315.30	proposition.] ~∧
315.33	line;] ~∧
315.34	premiss,] ~∧
315.34	minor,] ~∧
316.2–3	Predicate] Pred
316.3	Subject] Sub.
316.17	rule,] ~∧
316.17	case,] ~∧
316.18	we] We
316.20	than] that
317.9	rule∧] ~,
317.9	result is] result

317.11   the] The
317.15(1,2)   rule,] ~∧
318.1   figure,] ~;
318.2   O,] ~∧
318.2   rejected upon] rejected for upon
318.6   figure.] ~∧
318.13   variations] varieties
318.14   permutation,] ~∧
318.15   variations] no variations
318.19   extremes,] ~∧
318.23(1)   the] The
318.26   Conversion.] ~∧
318.30(1,2)   Some] some
319.1   Some] some
319.8   This gives] *reinstate*
319.12   ¶There] ∧~
319.15   second,] ~∧
319.15   third,] ~∧
319.16   difference of] difference
319.31   second,] ~∧
320.4   side,] ~∧
°320.5–6   top. ¶There] top. ¶In the ordinary logic, each proposition & term of the syllogism has one name. In the present system each must have three names in order to connote different attributes. Here follow their definitions ¶There
320.12   inferred,] ~∧
320.13   is believed] beleived
320.13   others,] ~∧
320.14   are] or
320.15   apodictically] a apodically
320.17   propositions containing the subject] subject
320.18   propositions containing the predicate] predicate
320.19–20   *grammatically, logically*] rom.
320.20   *rhetorically, medial, sinister*] rom.
320.20   *dexter*] rom.
320.23(1,2,3)   affirmation] aff.
320.24(1)   denial] den.
320.24(2,3)   denial] den
320.25(3)   proposition] prop.
320.34(2)   conclusion] con.
321.2   grammatically] gram.
321.3(1)   result∧] ~.
321.4   predicate] pred.
321.5(1,2)   logically] log.   *Also* 321.7
321.5(3)   logically] log
321.6   predicate] pred
321.9   rhetorically] rhet.

321.10(2)   conclusion∧] ∼.
321.12(1)   rule,] ∼∧

Logic of the Sciences

Copy-text for "Logic of the Sciences" is MS 113. All readings to the left of the bracket are emendations supplied by the editors. All readings to the right of the bracket are rejected readings from the copy-text.

322.3   §1.] ∼∧
322.8   otherwise,] ∼∧
323.9   *representation*] rom.
323.10   cognition] cog∧|nition
323.15   only∧] Only,
323.23   truth of] truth
323.29   and] &   *Also* 324.9, 325.5, 325.7, 325.14, 325.24(1,2),
             326.9, 326.35, 326.36, 327.14, 328.15, 328.17, 328.18,
             328.21, 328.31, 328.37, 329.9, 329.15, 329.17, 329.18,
             329.20, 330.12, 330.23, 330.31, 330.35, 331.6, 331.10,
             331.24, 333.13, 334.12, 335.6, 335.9, 335.13, 335.19, 335.28,
             335.34, 335.39, 336.3, 336.6(1), 336.10, 336.26
324.18   self-contradictory] ∼∧∼
324.21   constituent] constitutent
324.35   indicates] idicates
325.2   viz.] ∼∧   *Also* 325.4, 335.33
325.4   1st∧] ∼,
325.11(1,2) thing,] ∼∧
325.18   Being] being
325.21   *b*.] ∼∧
325.22   *I. Definition*] *I.* |*Definition*
325.24–25   *proximum genus*] rom.
325.25   *genus summum*] rom.   *Also* 325.26
325.26   *Being*] rom.
325.28   *summum genus*] rom.
325.32(2)   being] be
325.33   representations).] ∼.)
326.15   instances] intances
326.38   *Summum Genus*] rom.
326.39   ascertain these] ascertain
327.2   2nd] 3rd
327.5   subject] subjet
327.24   marks;] ∼∧
327.30   Object∧] ∼.
327.31   2nd] 2

327.31   It determines] " "
327.31–32   representation to refer] " " "
327.33–34   It determines that representation to refer] " " " " " "
328.8   1.] ~ᴧ
328.14   2.] ~ᴧ
328.16   representationᴧ] ~;
328.18–19   It is] It
328.23   representationᴧ] ~,
328.25   are] a
328.26   objects,] ~ᴧ
328.31   prescinded.] ~ᴧ
328.36   1.] ~ᴧ
328.37   2.] ~ᴧ
328.38   3.] ~ᴧ
329.9   truth–] ~ᴧ
329.10   reason–] ~ᴧ
329.10   copy,] ~ᴧ
329.11   objects,] ~ᴧ
329.12   least,] ~ᴧ
329.22(2)   are] is
329.31   objects] objets
330.2   cloven-footed] ~ᴧ~
330.17   is] or
330.26   two;] ~ᴧ
330.31   refers] referrs
330.36   *matter,*] ~.
331.19   one wherein this] one which wherein which this
331.31   suffering).] ~.)
332.9   *portrait*] rom.
•332.9–10   sitter and painter . . . form and color.] &c.
332.19   Church "] Church
332.19   Frenchman "] Frenchman
332.20   Frenchman "] Frenchman
332.20   Eglise "] Eglise
332.29   hypothesis,] ~.
333.12   everything] everythything
333.14   something] somewhich
333.21   its] it
333.25   or] of
333.27   if] If
333.30   points.] ~ᴧ
333.31   relation.] ~ᴧ
333.38   be] *reinstate*
334.7   place] places
334.7   things] thing
334.7   of which] which
334.8   two,] ~ᴧ

334.12	not.] ~∧
334.19	itself] themselves
334.26(1)	one's] ones
335.6(2)	such∧] ~,
335.15	purpose,] ~∧
335.15	effect,] ~∧
335.26	conceptions,] ~∧
335.27	phases:] ~∧
335.30	*This.* Then] ~; then
335.32	suffering] sufferering
335.34	suffering] suffereing
335.37	barbarize] barbize
335.39(1,2)	object,] ~;
336.26	indefinite] indef-|ite

Logic Notebook

Copy-text for the "Logic Notebook" is MS 114 for the year 1865 and MS 117 for the year 1866. All emendations have been supplied by the editors and appear to the left of the square brackets. The readings to the right of the square brackets are rejected readings from the copy-text.

337.9	question.] ~∧
337.10	1.] ~∧
337.11	2.] ~∧
337.12	3.] ~∧
337.15	2.] ~∧
337.15	Affirmative.] ~∧
337.15	Yes.] ~∧
337.15	exist.] ~∧
337.16	3.] ~∧
337.18	and] & *Also* 339.4, 339.12, 339.17, 339.27, 339.31, 339.32, 339.37, 340.5, 340.8, 340.20, 340.31, 341.4, 341.6, 341.12, 341.13, 341.15, 341.17, 341.25, 342.3(1,2), 342.4, 342.8, 342.9, 342.12, 343.7, 343.16(1,2), 344.1, 344.12, 344.13, 344.16, 344.17, 344.23, 344.26, 344.31, 345.4, 345.7, 345.10, 345.12, 345.18, 345.19, 346.4, 346.9, 346.17, 346.19, 346.34, 347.2, 347.7, 347.9, 348.8, 348.20, 348.32, 349.9, 349.13, 349.16, 349.20(1,2), 349.21, 349.25, 349.27(1,2), 349.28, 349.29, 349.30, 349.32, 349.36, 349.39, 350.1, 350.2, 350.6, 350.8, 350.9, 350.14(1,2,3), 350.16(1,2), 350.19, 350.24, 350.26, 350.29, 350.30, 350.36(1,2)

338.5   character,] ~∧
338.7   remain:] ~∧
338.7   *acd.*] ~∧
338.8   Nov.] ~∧ *Also* 338.20, 339.1
338.10   Induction " " "] Induction
338.11   Hypothesis " " "] Hypothesis
338.23   insufficient] insuffient
339.6   everything] every thing
339.6   particular;] ~∧
339.6   it] must it
339.8   Dec.] ~∧ *Also* 339.13, 340.17, 340.26, 344.19, 348.23,
               349.7
339.22   congeries of] congeries
339.26   for] with
339.33   this,] ~∧
340.12   hypotheses∧] ~,
340.14   incapable] in∧|capable
340.31   1.] ~∧
340.31   cointensive.] ~∧
340.32   2.] ~∧
341.1   3.] ~∧
341.2   subordinate,] ~∧
341.2   superordinate,] ~∧
341.4   there] There
341.5   extension.] ~∧
341.6(1)   in] &
341.9   *B*, we] ~. We
341.10   subordinate,] ~∧
341.10   superordinate,] ~∧
341.15   4.] ~∧
341.17   subordinate,] ~∧
341.17   superordinate,] ~∧
341.19   intension;] ~∧
341.21–22   intersection] in∧|tersection
341.26–27   *Summum Genus,*] Summum Genus.
341.27–28   *Infima Species*] *rom.*
341.30   extension.] ~∧
342.3   intension, their] ~. Their
342.4   *being.*] ~∧
342.7   being.] ~∧
342.34   *sign,*] ~∧
342.35   would] Would
343.5   isn't] is n't
343.5–6   anything;] ~∧
343.9   = ∞.] = ~∧
343.17   manifest,] ~∧
343.17   mind that] mind

343.19	only,] ~ₐ
343.25	comprehensionₐ] ~'
343.26–27	somewhat] some what
344.12	1.] ~ₐ
344.17(2)	if] of
344.24	Two] 2
344.28	both,] ~ₐ
345.2	And] &
345.2	*vice versa*] rom.
345.12	*B*] be
345.12	*sentient.*] ~ₐ
345.20	subsists] subsist
345.24–25	The reverse . . . not *B*] *reinstate*
346.14	proposition, then] ~. Then
346.20	*nothing*] rom.
346.27	*Critic of the Pure Reason*ₐ] Critic of the Pure Reason.
346.27	("Transcendental Stoicheiology,"] ₐₐ~ ~ₐₐ
346.28	Part,] ~.
346.28	Division,] ~.
346.28	I,] ~ₐ
346.28	Ch. 2,] ~ₐ ~ₐ
346.28	Section 2,] ~ ~.
346.28	No. 2,] §2.
346.28–29	second paragraph)] Second Paragraphₐ
347.4	No.] ~ₐ
347.12	Those] those
347.13	*greater.*] ~ₐ
347.15	*killed.*] ~ₐ
347.16	symbols] symols
347.16	*terms,*] ~ₐ
347.19	destroyed.] ~ₐ
347.21	destroyed.] ~ₐ
347.24	1.] ~ₐ
347.27	knowledge,] ~ₐ
347.27	it.] ~ₐ
347.28	3.] ~ₐ
347.29	1.] ~ₐ
347.32	2.] ~ₐ
347.33	object.] ~ₐ
347.34	3.] ~ₐ
348.1	1.] ~ₐ
348.1	Disquiparants] Diquiparants
348.1–2	equiparants.] ~ₐ
348.3	Disquiparants of the] " " "
348.7	$\frac{0}{0}\cdot$ₐ] ~..
348.11	multiple.] ~ₐ

348.14	*fact.*] ~∧
348.24	∧*Principles of Human Knowledge*∧] "Principles of Human Knowledge"
348.32	matter,] ~∧
348.32	qualities,] ~∧
348.34	*facts,*] ~∧
348.34	*ideas,*] ~∧
349.11	∧1st] ¶~
349.13	¶*Proof.*] ∧~∧
349.14	its] Its
349.22	distribution.] ~∧
349.23	∧2nd] ¶~
349.23	That] that
349.23–24	once.| ¶If] ~. ∧~
349.24	subject-predicate] ~∧~
349.26	occurring] occuring
349.31	∧3rd] ¶~
349.31–32	concluded.|¶As] ~.∧~
349.33	neither∧] ~,
350.2	particular.] ~∧
350.3	affirmative.] ~∧
350.10	conclusion.] ~∧
350.17	below.] ~∧
350.18	affirmative.] ~∧
350.19	Otherwise,] ~∧
350.19	before,] ~∧
350.19	quality.] ~∧
350.20	quantity.] ~∧
350.21	¶If] ∧~
350.21	this] This
350.22	particular;] ~,
350.22	not,] ~∧
350.22–23	premisses.] ~∧
350.24	particular;] ~∧
350.26	particular;] ~∧
350.28	former,] ~∧
350.29	negative;] ~∧
350.32	the major] major

Logic Chapter I

Copy-text for "Logic Chapter I" is MS 115. All readings to the left of the bracket are emendations supplied by the editors. All readings to the right of the bracket are rejected readings from MS 115.

351.7	and]& *Also* 351.9, 351.13, 351.22, 353n.2, 354.7, 354n.4 (2)
351.14	of the categories] categories
351.15	merely₋] ~,
352.14	optical] opitical
352.27	practice.] ~₋
352.29	the force] force
352.34	mind,] ~₋
352.34	character,] ~₋
353.14	representable] representible
353.17(2)	the] the the
353.21	correspondent] correspondent
353n.3	to reproduce] reproduce
354.4	a correlate] correlate
354.11	separable] sepable
354.12	representations] relations
354.13	separable] seperable
354.14	¶Every] ₋~
354.16	involved, the] ~₋ The
354.25	as₋] ~,
354.25	approaching,] ~₋
354.27	merely,] ~₋
354.27	&c.] ~₋
354.35	Agreement₋] ~,
354.35–355.1	involves] since involves
354n.1	to be] to
355.2	if no] if there no
355.6	things] it things
355.9	argument's] arguments
355.35–36	represents] repraesents
355.37	*sign,*] ~₋
356.2	part,"] ~,₋
356.2	says] say
356.2	"especially] ₋~
356.5	believing] beleiving

Lowell Lecture I

Copy-text for this lecture is MS 122. All readings to the left of the bracket are emendations supplied by the editors. All readings to the right of the bracket are rejected readings from MS 122.

358.11	believe] beleive *Also* 360.27, 361.17, 362.1, 362.2, 370.4, 370.19

358.12	eclipse] ecclipse
358.16	it is] is
358.19	and] & *Also* 359.11, 359.32, 360.28, 360.29, 360.38, 361.1(2), 361.3, 361.4, 361.16, 362.3, 362.8(1), 362.13, 362.14, 363.18, 363.30, 363.33, 364.11, 364.21, 364.24, 365.15, 365.20, 365.28, 366.18, 366.21, 366.28, 367.1, 367.7, 367.8, 367.18, 367.23, 367.27, 368.8, 370.12, 370.15(1,2,3), 370.27, 370.31, 371.1(1), 371.2(1), 371.4, 371.6(1,2), 371.10, 371.14, 371.16, 371.22, 371.23, 371.26, 371.29(1), 371.30, 371.32, 372.1, 372.22, 373.24, 373.25, 373.26, 373.32, 374.6, 374.7(2), 374.9, 374.12, 374.23, 374.24, 374.25(1,2), 374.29, 374.31, 375.9
358.19	we] We
358.30	value,] ~∧
359.13	nor] no
359.19	bank-notes] ~∧~
359.22	analyst's] analysts
359.26	scrutinize] scrutinise
359.29	research] reseach
360.2	Whately] Whateley
360.4	grandfathers'] grandfathers
360.15	same time] same
360.15	taken] added taken
360.27	man,] ~∧
360.28	animals,] ~∧
360.28	humanity,] ~∧
360.29	animality,] ~∧
360.29	words] word
360.30	men,] ~∧
360.30	animals,] ~∧
360.30	*et cetera,*] ~ ~∧
360.30	appellations] appelations
360.39	Ockham] Occham
361.37	belief] beleif
362.8	foundation,] ~.
362.25	free∧agents] ~-~ *Also* 362.27, 362.33–34, 363.17, 363.33, 364.29, 364.32, 365.9, 366.8, 366.9
362.35	language] languge
362.36	*subsumption*] rom.
362.37	to] to to
363.5	men,] ~–
363.6	–in] ∧~
363.7	thing,] ~–
363.9	*rule,*] ~∧
363.22	otherwise] other wise
363.33	All] all
364.4	master] mast

364.9	There,] ~ₐ
364.9	servant,] ~ₐ
364.11	Yes,] ~ₐ
364.14	[Slow]] ₐ~ₐ
364.20	two-legged] ~ₐ~ *Also* 364.22
364.26	all;] ~,
364.33	subsumption] subsuption
365.3	make] may
365.8	rule;] ~ₐ
365.18	Affirmative,] ~ₐ
365.18	Negative,] ~ₐ
365.18(3)	for] For
365.21	οὐδέν] οὐδὲν
*365.23	*affirmo*] affirmo
*365.23	*nego*] nego
366.1	circular,] ~;
366.2	peace,] ~ₐ
366.2	war,] ~ₐ
366.3	army,] ~ₐ
366.3	E.] ~,
366.17	universal,] ~;
366.17	affirmative,] ~ₐ
366.23(1)	the] The
366.26	the rule] rule
366.28	*vice versa*] rom.
366.32	A ⎤ A. ⎥ ~ₐ A ⎦
367.9	A–A ⎤ A . ⎥ ~ₐ A ⎦
367.12	E ⎤ I , ⎥ ~ₐ O ⎦
367.14	figure.] ~ₐ
367.16	beings] being
367.18	Hereₐ] ~,
367.18	beginₐ] ~,
367.20	It] If
368.6	moods.] ~ₐ
*368.15	In this case . . . symmetrically.] All the letters in lines
369.8	Seaₐ] ~,
369.14–15	be admitted] admitted
369.19	Some] All
369.20	principle,] ~ₐ
370.3	another's] anothers
370.4	predecessors] predicessors
370.8–9	arguments.] ~;

370.11	different] defferent
370.11	kinds–] ~;
370.16(1)	which] with
370.26	question,] ~;
370.29	case;] ~∧
370.32	some, we] ~. We
370.32	$\left.\begin{matrix} MP \\ SM \\ SP \end{matrix}\right\}.\ \Big]\ \sim\ \Big\}_\wedge$
370.32	mood.] ~;
370.33(2)	$P_\wedge$] ~;
370.34	Some] some
370.34(2)	$M_\wedge$] ~;
370.35	Some] some
371.6	is] it
371.14	¶Firstly] ∧~
371.18	without] with out
372.5	there are] there
372.9	that in] in
372.28(1,2)	Some] some
372.29	thus:] ~∧
373.4	which] Which
373.7	tends] is tends
373.17	constant] const.
373.17	temperature] temp.
373.21	believed] beleived
373.23	Rule,] ~∧
373.24	rule,] ~∧
374.16	case,] ~;
°374.26	moods, as shown . . . next page.] moods:–
374.29	these.] ~∧
374.31	first] fist
375.14	uncolored] un-colorled

Lowell Lecture II

Copy-text for "Lecture II" is MS 123. All emendations have been supplied by the editors and appear to the left of the square brackets. All readings to the right of the brackets are rejected readings from the copy-text.

376.11	two] to
376.16	and] & *Also* 376.20, 376.24, 377.13, 377.21, 377.24, 378.12, 378.30, 379.3, 379.5, 379.10, 380.20, 382.24, 384.20, 384.26,

384.27, 385.1, 385.24, 385.28, 385.31(1,2,3), 386.3(2), 386.6(1,2), 386.9, 386.20, 387.10, 387.19, 387.26, 388.1, 388.8, 388.29, 389.10, 389.22, 389.29, 389.30, 390.1, 390.20, 390.37, 391.19, 391.30, 392.9, 392.25

377.8	&c.] ∼∧
377.15	said:] ∼;
377.15	"He] ∧∼
377.16	God."] ∼.∧
377.22	terms,] ∼∧
377.32	And] and
378.2	other, you] ∼. You
378.6	God–] ∼∧
378.12	¶The] ∧∼
378.13	if] that if
378.28	¶Having] ∧∼
378.29	universal, the] ∼. The
378.29	*affirmative,*] ∼;
379.2	God. This] ∼∧this
379.4	follow] follows
379.5(1,2)	Ye] ye
379.8	*parva logicalia–*] ∼ ∼∧
379.9	immeasurably] immeasureably
379.10(1)	the] the the
379.10	XIIIth] XIII
379.10	XIVth] XIV
379.14	¶Take] ∧∼
379.18	into] in to
379.29	equivalent] equivelent
380.10	east"∧] ∼",
380.14	barometer's] bar.
380.25(1)	N∧] ∼;
380.25	(that] ∧∼
380.25	N)] ∼∧
381.12(1)	M] N
381.18	Particular,] ∼;
381.22	results,] ∼∧
382.5	is false] false
382.21	kindly. And] ∼∧and
382.21	*result:*] ∼.
382.30	the him] the *the* him
383.vertical	[Diagram]] ∧∼∧
383.33	benefactor,] ∼;
383.34	John,] ∼∧
383.36(2)	benefactor] benefactors
384.9	propositions,] ∼∧
384.11	[*Diagram*]] ∧∼∧
384.26	it] It

384.28	case.] ~:
384.31	leads] leads to
384.vertical	[diagram]] ∧~∧
385.2	four-hundred-fold] fourhundred∧fold
385.16	other."] ~∧"
385.17	3."] ~∧"
385.27	rule.] ~∧
385.28	it] is
385.28	3.] ~∧
385.31(1)	2.] ~∧
385.33	despised] dispised
386.16	three-fourths] ~∧~ Also 386.17, 387.22
386.18	two-thirds] ~∧~ Also 386.22
386.25	company] comany
386.32	hats,] ~∧
386.33	%,] ~∧
387.7	to] to to
387.8–9	be∧expressed] ~-|~
387.15	premiss.] ~∧
388.34	truly,] ~∧
388.37	said, So] ~∧ so
388.38	said,] ~∧
389.4	your] you
389.6	because∧] ~,
389.7	swearing] swear
389.19	Chrysippus] Chryssippus
389.21	don't] dont
389.30	whose] who
389.33	absurdities] absurdies
390.11	who] whom
390.14	arguments] aguments
390.15	standpoint] stand-point
390.21	philosophers∧] ~,
390.28	things,] ~∧
390.31	corner-stone] ~∧~
390.36	Parmenides;] ~∧
390.37	contemporary] contempory
390.37	Protagoras,] ~∧
390.40	said,] ~;
391.1	things,] ~∧
391.8	false.] ~∧
391.9	motion,] ~∧
391.10	motion,] ~∧
391.15	distance,] ~∧
391.16	⌠, before] ~∧ Before
391.16	can] case
391.19	of that] that

391.30	therefore] there fore
392.13	Mansel] Mansell
392.17	a] an
392.23	¶Zeno's] ∧~
392.25	But] Buf
392.26	in time] time
392.31	date∧] ~,
392.34	East] West

Lowell Lecture III

Copy-text for "Lecture III" is MS 124. All readings to the left of the bracket are emendations supplied by the editors. All readings to the right of the bracket are rejected readings from MS 124.

393.5	and] & *Also* 393.11, 393.12, 393.26, 393.29, 394.5, 394.6, 394.15, 394.22, 394.31, 394.38, 395.7, 395.8(1), 395.32, 395.40, 396.11(1), 396.25, 396.26, 396.36(2), 396.38, 396.39, 397.4(2), 397.7, 397.8, 397.11, 397.32, 397.33, 398.37, 399.17, 400.24, 400.25, 401.9, 401.18, 402.5, 402.13, 402.17(1), 402.18, 402.23(1), 402.24, 402.26, 403.15, 404.22, 404.36, 405.9, 406.2, 406.12, 406.15, 406.22, 406.38
393.6(1)	red.] ~∧
393.7	no doubt] doubt
393.18	*why* what] what
393.18	resembles what] what
394.5	use,] ~∧
394.15	one.] ~∧
394.17	to attribute] attribute
394.17–18	induction∧] ~,
394.26	provide] proide
394.33	us:] ~∧
394.33	asks] ask
394.33	what] What
394.36	that] that that
395.1	professed] proffesed
395.15(2)	occurrences] occurences
395.23	one-half] ~∧~ *Also* 403.2
395.24	occurrence] occurence *Also* 395.25
396.10	event.∧] ~..
396.25	one-sixth] ~∧~ *Also* 396.26, 396.27, 396.29
396.36	white,] ~.
396.37	another.] ~∧
397.15	ball?] ~.

397.17   a] an
397.17   twenty-seven] ~∧~
397.19   either a] a either an
397.29   independent] independant
398.11–12   black, then] ~. Then
398.17–18   nothing,] ~;
398.18   because∧] ~,
398.28   are] is
398.29   what] What
398.32(1)   *likely*] rom.   *Also* 398.36, 400.26, 400.38
399.15–16   at any rate] any rate
399.25   ultimate,] ~∧
399.31   Let me point out with] *reinstate*
399.39   so,] ~;
400.3   likelihood] liklihood   *Also* 400.20
400.10   Dr.] ~∧
400.13   sufficient] suffient
400.28   analyst.] ~,
400.29   *Essay Concerning Human Understanding*] Essay on the Human Understanding
400.29   says:–] says:– [iii p 149] Book iv Ch 15 §1.
400.30–37   As demonstration . . . contrary.] *supplied*
401.33   complete] comple
401.36   somewhat] some what
402.7   being] being being
402.7   light∧blue] ~-~
402.9(1)   ½∧] ~.
402.10(1,2,3)   blue,] ~∧
402.11   predominate,] ~∧
402.18   kinds] kind
402.18   *c.*] ~∧
402.22   Z∧] ~.
402.23   A] since A
402.29(1)   ½.] ~∧
402.29(2)   Answer:] ~∧
402.36   And as] & As
403.2   chance–] ~∧
403.3   *Logic*] rom.
403.6   original] oginal
403.14–30   We will suppose . . . in the bag.] *reinstate*
403.18   that] than
403.20   balls, they] ~. They
403.36   occurrence] occurence   *Also* 404.17
404.30   believing] beleiving
405.2   an] any
405.3   *Laws of Thought*] rom.
405.10   Englishmen,] ~∧

405.11	such] as
405.12	Channel] channel
405.19(1)	a] a a
406.16	them—] ~,
406.35	is] is is

Lowell Lecture IV

Copy-text for "Lecture IV" is MS 125. All readings to the left of the bracket are emendations supplied by the editors. All readings to the right of the bracket are rejected readings from MS 125.

407.12	and] & *Also* 407.22, 407.24, 408.11, 408.19, 408.28, 408.35, 409.5, 409.18, 409.27, 409.30(1), 409n.2, 410.33, 411.3, 411.16, 411.35, 412.13, 412.14, 412.22, 412.36, 413.4, 413.14, 413.15, 413.16(1,2), 413.30, 414.28, 414.31, 414.35, 414.38, 415.2, 415.4(1), 415.5, 415.7, 415.18, 415.20, 415.30, 415.36, 415.40, 417.11, 417.12(1), 417.13, 417.14, 417.16, 417.25, 417.34, 417.35, 417.36, 418.1, 418.2, 418.18, 418.23, 418.40, 419.7, 419.8, 419.14, 419.27, 419.33, 419.38, 420.21, 420.22, 421.12, 421.29, 421.32, 422.11, 422.24, 422.27, 422.39, 423.18, 423.22
407.19	mean,] ~;
407.23	it;] ~,
407.23	argument,] ~;
408.8	referred] refered
408.14	reflectₐ] ~,
408.22	imperil] imperril
408.30	*Logic*] logic *Also* 411.20
408.38	a sense] sense
*409.1	unknown."[1]] unknown."
409.6–7	believe] beleive *Also* 409.15–16, 411.20, 412.33, 413.29
409.8–9	inference] *rom.* *Also* 409.17, 410.13, 410.24
409.18	*illation*] rom.
409.20	William] Wm.
409.20	"the] ₐ~
409.21–22	judgments."] ~.ₐ
409.24	says] say's
409n.1	*Logic*] rom. *Also* 414.16
409n.2	Book,] ~ₐ
409n.2	Chapter,] ~ₐ
409n.2	Section.] ~ₐ
410.5	believed] beleived
410.28	man,] ~ₐ

410.28   case,] ∼∧
410.29   mortal–] ∼;
410.33   say that] say i 227 B2 Ch3 §6 that
410.34   ¶In] "∼
410.35   follows:] follows: [Read]
410.35–411.1–2   "My . . . evidence.] *supplied*
411.8   man)] ∼∧
411.16   Mill's] Mills'
411.18   Mill's] Mills'
411.19   infer] inferr   *Also* 413.5–6
411.23   phraseology∧] ∼.
411.23   (Vol. 1 . . . 232 note).] (i. 232 note) B 2 ch 3 §8 *note*
411.26   says,] ∼∧
411.26   "I] ∧∼
411.28   rests."] ∼.∧
411.29   *premiss*] rom.
412.12   is,] ∼∧
412.19   All] all
412.21   proposition] proposisition
412.22   All] all
412.28   Deduction.] ∼∧
412.29   believes] beleives   *Also* 413.4, 420.17
413.10   Mill's] Mills
413.13   1st,] ∼∧
413.13   XIV,] ∼∧
413.13   &c.,] ∼∧∧
413.28   than] then
413.29   contrary,] ∼;
413.33   Mill's] Mills
413.35   "In] ∧∼
413.38   validity."] ∼.∧
414.4   rule,] ∼;
414.16   Mill's] Mills'
414.24   this∧] ∼,
414.24   Mill∧] ∼,
414.vertical [Diagram]] ∧∼∧
414.25   difficulty.] ∼∧
415.8   argument,] ∼∧
415.19(1)   true∧] ∼;
415.28   question∧] ∼,
415.30   *regressus ad infinitum*] rom.
415.34   saying∧] ∼,
415.35(3)   of] a of
416.15   Mill's] Mills
416.20   horses] horse
416.27   belongs] belong
416.36   experience.] experience. [ii 105.] B 3 ch 21 §4

416.37–417.4	The latter . . . absolute.] *supplied*
417.5	that] that that
417.10	uniformity,] ~∧
417.10	mention∧] ~,
417.10	hundred,] ~∧
417.16	apple-tree] ~∧~
417.27–28	observe∧that] ~. That
417.34	*locomotives.*] ~∧
*417.36–37	locomotives] steam engines
417.38	age,] ~∧
418.3(2)	long∧heads] ~-~
418.8	matter:] matter; (i. 135). Book 1 ch 7 §4
418.9–16	It is . . . together.] *supplied*
418.19	class∧] ~,
418.24(1)	of] *reinstate*
419.3–4	*everything's*] everythings
419.8(3)	men,] ~∧
419.9	classes,] ~—
419.10	one,] ~∧
419.10	men,] ~∧
419.16	every∧man] ~-|~
419.30	¶Suppose] ∧~
419.31	these] These
419.32	around] arond
419.40	irregularity∧] ~,
420.5	this that] this [i 343] Book 3 Ch 3 §1 That
420.6	"is] ∧~
420.7	description."] ~.∧
420.14	is found] found
420.15	comets'] comets
420.15	reverse,] ~∧
420.25	devices∧] ~,
421.3	propositions] proposition
421.15	who] which
421.20	touchstone] touch-stone
421.26	or,] ~∧
421.26	matter,] ~∧
421.26	principle?∧] ~??
422.2	abrogate.] ~;
422.13	furnished] funished
422.15	known] know
422.16	mentioned,] ~∧
422.16	the sample] sample
422.30	formal,] ~;
422.40	not] no
423.8	says,] says (ii 97) "I am convinced &c.
423.9–16	I am convinced . . . case.] *supplied*

Lowell Lecture V

Copy-text for "Lecture V" is MS 126. All readings to the left of the bracket are emendations supplied by the editors. All readings to the right of the bracket are rejected readings from the copy-text.

424.8	probability] propability
424.11	premisses—] ~ₐ
424.19	inference] infence
424.21	cloven-hoofed] ~ₐ~ *Also* 424.24, 425.8, 425.9, 425.27, 425.28, 426.13, 427.18, 427.20, 427.24, 427.25, 428.32, 429.14, 433.4, 433.16, 433.22, 434.23, 434.23–24
424.21	neatₐ] ~,
425.1	polarizable] polarizeable *Also* 425.2, 425.31, 425.33, 426.17, 426.18, 427.6, 427.30, 427.31, 427.33, 428.1, 428.3, 428.4, 435.3, 435.7
425.12–13	whatever.] ~ₐ
425.27	All] all
425.28	Neat] neat
425.29	Neat] neat
425.30	And] and
425.34	to bring] bring
426.10	cloven-hooved] clovenₐhoved
426.12	particular] paticular
426.13	herbivora] herbora
426.14	-hoofed] *reinstate*
426.21–22	inferred] infered
426.25	inferenceₐ] ~,
426.25	facts,] ~ₐ
426.30	neatₐ] ~,
426.35	classification.] ~ₐ
427.1	classification, because] ~. Because
427.23	this:] ~ₐ
427.33	ₐThe] ¶~
428.5	conclusion,] ~ₐ
428.13	forces,] ~ₐ
428.14	Physicsₐ] ~—
428.15	&c.,] ~.ₐ
428.16	Geology,] ~ₐ
428.23	and] & *Also* 432.2, 432.24, 435.31, 437.15(1), 437.31, 438.5(1,2), 438.6(2), 438.33(2), 438.34(2)
428.33	and] are
429.13	herbivorous] herbivous *Also* 433.6(2)
429.14	carnivorous,] ~ₐ
429.20	boxes.] ~ₐ
429.20	box.] ~ₐ

429.25	conclusion?] ~∧
430.9	both,] ~∧
430.11	three figures are] 1st figure is
430.17	we] We
430.20	premisses,] ~∧
430.23	black,] ~;
430.24	black,] ~;
430.31	all] All
431.2	obviously∧] ~,
431.3	induction,] ~∧
431.19	upon] up
431.32	the third] third
431.34(1)	asserted] ass. *Also* 431.35(1), 431.36(1), 432.4(1), 432.18
431.34	Result] Res *Also* 432.5, 432.16, 432.17, 434.29, 434.30, 434.31, 435.33, 435.34, 435.35
431.34(2)	asserted] ass *Also* 431.35(2), 431.36(2), 432.4(2), 432.16, 432.25, 434.29(1,2), 434.30(1,2), 434.31, 435.33(1,2), 435.34(1,2), 435.35
432.3	Result] Res:
432.3(1)	denied] den. *Also* 432.26, 432.27
432.3(2)	denied] den *Also* 432.5(1,2), 432.16, 432.17(1,2), 432.18, 434.29, 434.30, 434.31(1,2), 435.33, 435.34, 435.35(1,2)
432.6	one.] ~∧
432.25	Result] Res.
433.3	at] by
433.3	neat∧] ~,
433.3	swine∧] ~,
433.3	deer∧] ~,
433.5	instance] instant
433.10	to reason] reason
433.16	we] We
433.24	Some] some
434.3	induction,] ~;
434.3	explanatory;] ~,
434.8	failed. Let] ~∧let
434.10	premisses,] ~∧
434.11	induction∧] inductions,
434.14	matter. Let] ~∧let
434.15	cloven-hoofed∧] ~-~;
434.16	and Neat] Neat
434.16	to avoid falsity] to avoid falsity to avoid
434.17	herbivora,] ~;
434.21	cloven∧hoofs] ~-~
434.26	syllogisms are] syllogisms
434.30(2)	Case] Cass
435.5	result,] ~;

435.7	light] lights
435.7–8	unpolarizable] unpolarizeable
435.14	believe] beleive
435.15	out?] ~.
435.21	that] the
435.27	rests—] ~∧
435.28–29	conclusion.∧This] ~,–this
435.31	of] or
435.36	the third] third
435.36–37	inferred, we have deduction.] inferred.
436.3	to solve] solve
437.3	valid.] ~;
437.6	it] It
437.15–16	Negative] negative
437.28	sufficient] suffient
438.5	deduction] Deduction
438.5(1)	C,] ~;
438.5(2)	C,] ~∧
438.8	deduction,] ~∧
438.10	strength,] ~∧
438.11	valid,] ~∧
438.12	hereafter.] ~∧
438.28(1)	something] some thing
439.7	find∧] ~,
439.8	discover∧] ~,
439.12	err generally] *reinstate*
439.14	to close] close
439.17	without] with out
439.18	*non-existent*] *nonexistent*
440.9	the same] same
440.13	the same] same

Lowell Lecture VI

Copy-text for this lecture is MS 128. All emendations are supplied by the editors and appear to the left of the square brackets. The readings to the right of the brackets are rejected readings from the copy-text.

440.19	1.] ~∧
441.6	¶I] ∧~
441.7	and] & *Also* 441.21(1), 441.22(1,2), 441.24(1), 441.25, 441.33, 442.8, 442.24, 442.26, 442.29, 443.23, 444.2, 445.34,

446.1, 446.24, 446.26, 446.35, 446.36, 447.8, 447.9, 447.23, 447.33, 447.37(1), 447.38, 448.12, 448.17, 449.9, 449.14, 449.16, 449.21, 450.19, 450.30, 450.31, 451.3, 452.5(1,2), 452.12, 452.14, 453.22, 453n.2, 454.4, 454.5

441.8	say,] ~–
441.13	¶We] ∧~
441.27	which] wh. *Also* 442.25
441.30	conclusion, the] ~. The
442.1	¶In] ∧~
442.8	say,] ~–
443.34	¶The] ∧~
443.34	first maxim] first
444.5	hypothenuse] hypotheneuse
444.9	Pythagorean] pythagorean
444.13	scrutinize] scrutinise
444.24	Declaration of Independence] declaration of independence
444.24	"self-evident] ∧~-~
444.25	equal."] ~.∧
444.27–28	Negroes] negroes
444.30	¶It] ∧~
444.30–31	Declaration] declaration
444.35(2)	the] it the
445.3	described or] described
445.10	instance.] ~∧
445.18	contains] is contains
445.18–19	everyone] every one
445.21	Bible] bible *Also* 445.22
445.30	anyone's] any ones
445.33	man's] mans
446.5	it is] is
446.19	believe] beleive
446.30	fool,"] ~."
447.9	points] poinst
447.10	said:] ~.
447.22–23	definition∧] ~?
447.23	disputed?] ~.
448.4	required–] ~∧
448.5	facts∧] ~–
448.5	account–] ~,
448.18	remarks] remarks [i 172 note] Book 1 ch 8 §7 note American Ed. p. 105
448.19–33	Few people . . . over.] *supplied*
449.18	medicine] medine
449.23	requisites] resquisites
449.39	made] maked
449.39	Galens] Galen's

450.1	disease] desease
450.1	*diphtheria*] *diptheria*
450.2	diphtheria] diptheria
450.30	have] & have
450.34	to be] to
450.35	one.] ~∧
450.36	in] In
451.5	Inference.] Inference [Kant iii 262] (2½ pages MS?)
451.6–452.2	A *hypothesis* . . . indispensable.] *supplied*
452.23	not] no
453.11	intensity.] ~∧
453.26	Spiritualists:–] Spiritualists:–[393.]
453.27–30	The spiritualists . . . other.] *supplied*
453n.5	remarked.] remarked∧[388]
453n.5–7	" 'See,' said she . . . medium' "] *supplied*
454.3	bad as] bad & as
454.7	world∧] ~–
454.7	lies.] lies–"Certainly there be," says Lord Bacon &c.
454.8–22	Certainly there be . . . nature.] *supplied*

Lowell Lecture VII

Copy-text for "Lecture VII" is MS 129. All emendations are supplied by the editors and appear to the left of the brackets. The readings to the right of the brackets are rejected readings from MS 129.

455.6	and] & *Also* 455.14, 455.27, 455.29, 455.32(1,2), 455.33, 455.37, 455.38, 455.39, 456.15(2), 456.16, 456.29, 457.8, 460.1, 460.12, 461.11, 461.27, 461.29, 462.3(1), 462.4, 462.15, 463.20, 463.22, 464.15(2), 464.19, 464.20, 464.28, 464.33(1), 467.9, 467.33, 468.9, 469.10, 470.28(1,2), 471.3, 471.5, 471.6
455.11	it] It
455.13	Abbot,] ~∧
455.13	writers,] ~∧
455.18	are] and
455.24	manner,] ~–
455.29	Frenchman,] ~∧
455.29	Englishman,] ~∧
455.30	German,] ~∧
455.31	*Plantes,*] ~∧
456.4	national] National

456.5	Bismarck] Bismark
456.5–6	Prussian] prussian
456.9	becomes] become
456.11	evident,] ~∧
456.12	admitted,] ~∧
456.21	philosophy;] ~∧
456.21	when] which, when
456.21–22	mastered it] mastered
456.24	possess] posess
456.26	believe] beleive
456.39(1)	Philosophy] Phi-|lophy
457.2	Hickok] Hickock
457.4	Absolutes] Absolute's
457.10	¶We] ∧~
457.15	abstract] abstact
457.18	of] *reinstate*
457.20	*Analytics*] rom.
457.33	itself,] ~∧
458.3	syllogisms?] ~.
458.8	system;] ~∧
458.9	*that,*] ~∧
459.2	meant∧] ~.
459.3	important] immortant
459.3	word:] ~∧
459.7	*man*] rom. *Also* 459.9, 466.1
459.10	language,] ~∧
459.10	&c.,] ~∧∧
459.11	Negro] negro *Also* 459.12, 465.30(1,2), 465.33
459.18	extension.] ~∧
459.32	Sphere∧] ~.
460.2	another;] ~∧
460.8	spheres] sphere
460.20	diminished] dimished
460.24	synonyms] synonymes
460.30	terms∧] ~,
460.32	terms∧] ~,
460.34	innumerable] innummerable
461.1	sense–] ~,
461.4	not.∧] ~. .
461.21(3)	is] his
461.22	simple;] ~∧
461.22	that] the
461.26	Hence∧] ~;
461.26	one] on
461.32	it] It
461.33	*horse.*] ~–
462.16	perfect.∧] ~. .

462.34	*class*] rom.
463.1	random—] ~;
463.2	principle,ʌ] ~;—
463.9	explainʌ this,] ~, ~ʌ
463.10–11	deduction—] ~ʌ
463.20	A,] ~ʌ
463.20	B,] ~ʌ
463.24	diminution] dimunition *Also* 465.14–15
463.29	unchanged,] ~ʌ
463.37	*vice versa,*] ~ ~ʌ
464.3	not-blue,] ~-~ʌ
464.20	and] &
464.23–24	*crossed and dotted circle*] rom.
465.3	surrogates,] ~—
465.3	interpreters] interpretors
465.18	term—] ~,
465.29	these:] ~ʌ
465.30	Every] every
465.30	The] the
465.33	manʌ] ~—
465.33	zoölogy,] ~—
465.34	religion,] ~—
465.34	politics.] ~ʌ
465.35	every man] everyman
466.2(1)	that] the
466.11	propositionʌ] ~—
466.12	thing,] ~ʌ
466.30	what the] what the what the
466.37	term's] terms
467.10	twoʌlegs] ~-~
467.10	rational,] ~ʌ
467.10	&c.] ~ʌ
467.17(2)	*non-blue*] ~ʌ~
467.29	by] by by
467.32	likenesses] likeness
467.33	*hieroglyphics,*] ~ʌ
468.3	Likenesses] Likeness
468.5	They] The
468.32	symbols,—] ~,ʌ
469.1	the] the the
469.1	term—] ~,
469.3	whale—] ~ʌ
469.8	whale,] ~ʌ
470.11	fruit,] ~ʌ
470.12	orange,] ~ʌ
470.29	are] and
470.32	well-grounded] ~ʌ~

Lowell Lecture IX

Copy-text for "Lecture IX" is MS 130. All readings to the left of the brackets are emendations supplied by the editors. All readings to the right of the brackets are rejected readings from MS 130.

471.16	and] & *Also* 472.8, 472.12, 472.28, 472.33, 473.8, 473.13, 473.16, 473.22(1,2), 473.35, 474.3, 474.11, 474.20, 474.24, 474.26, 474.27, 474.35, 474.37, 475.1, 475.2, 475.5, 475.7, 475.9, 475.28, 475.32, 475.34, 476.3, 477.9, 477.20(1,2), 477.21, 477.31, 478.4, 478.27, 478.31, 479.10, 480.9, 480.23, 481.1(1), 481.5, 481.15(2), 482.12, 483.1(1,2), 483.20, 484.18, 484.19, 484.22(2), 484.23, 484.26, 484.28, 485.27, 485.32, 485.34(1,2), 486.1, 486.2, 486.3, 486.4, 486.5, 486.22, 486.28, 486.30, 486.31, 487.2, 487.5, 487.6, 487.11, 487.18, 487.20, 487.22(1), 487.30, 487.35, 488.12(1), 488.20(2)
471.23	possessing] posessing
472.17	man] rom.
472.19	mortal,] ~∧
472.21(1)	that] that that
472.25	pleasurable] pleasureable
472.27	do,] ~∧
473.1	Sensation∧] ~,
473.1	is,] ~∧
473.14–15	intelligible∧] ~,
473.15	possesses∧] ~.
473.15	itself.] ~,
473.19	" " " Correlate] Correlate
473.20	" " " Interpretant] Interpretant
473.25	separation:] ~,
473.25	*dissociation,*] ~∧
473.29	colour.] ~;
474.4	occasion] occassion
474.12	conception,] ~∧
474.15	¶We] ∧~
474.17	substance,] ~∧
474.17	Quality.] ~∧
474.28	order∧] ~.
474.37	manifold;] ~∧
474.38	substance,] ~∧
474.39	general,] ~∧
*475.6	¶Reference] ∧~
475.7–8	Interpretant,] ~∧
475.8	Correlate,] ~∧
475.10	Likeness,] ~∧

475.16   disquiparant] diquiparant
475.27   Quality] Qulity
475.31(1)   Quality‸] ∼–
475.31   proper)–] ∼)‸
476.2(1)   Relation‸] ∼–
476.17   scheme] sheme
476.19   2 ”] 2
476.20   3 ”] 3
476.21   Quality,] ∼‸
476.21(1)   relation,] ∼‸
476.21   representation.] ∼‸
476.23   representation:] represen-|tion,
476.24   1 ⎤
                2; ⎬ ∼‸
                3 ⎦
476.25(2)   separable] separble
476.26   ⎛1 ⎤
                ⎝2; ⎬ ∼‸
                 3 ⎦
477.2   symbols‸] ∼–
477.2   intention,] ∼‸
477.10   imputed;] ∼–
477.17   nothing;] ∼‸
477.19   "Aristotle"] ‸∼‸
477.22(1)   a] A
477.23(1)   what] in what
477.23   thing,] ∼‸
477.23   Quale‸] ∼.
477.24   same,] ∼‸
477.26(2)   object] objects
477.30   ground,] ∼‸
477.30   meaning,] ∼‸
477.31   ground,] ∼‸
477.35   represents] is represents
478.1   statement,] ∼–
478.6   argument,] ∼–
478.9   the] to
478.14   intended to refer to a] ” ” ” ” ”
478.16   whose object is formally a] ” ”
478.17   intended to refer to] ” ” ” ”
478.18   whose object is formally a] ” ”
478.20   shows] show
478.31   object‸] ∼–
478.32(3)   the] The
478.35   object‸] ∼–
478.36   *connotation,*] ∼‸
479.6   ” *Denotation*] *Denotation*
479.7   ” *Implication*] *Implication*

479.14	relate;] ~ₐ
479.17	*man*] rom.
479.17	*white.*] white_ₐ
479.23	the required] required
479.27–28	*whiteness,*] ~ₐ
479.28	character,] ~ₐ
480.2–3	object of] object
480.10	being,] ~ₐ
480.11	So] so
480.16	representation] represention
480.19	Moon,] ~ₐ
480.21	up,] ~ₐ
480.33	term.] ~ₐ
481.8	one] on
481.19	a] an
481.22	required:] ~ₐ
481.22	object;] ~–
481.23	ground,] ~ₐ
481.30	kind.] ~–
481.33	propositions.ₐ] ~.–
481.34	*Jehovah*] rom. *Also* 482.6
482.11	proposition,] ~ₐ
482.11	term,] ~ₐ
482.14	are;ₐ] ~,–
482.14	so,] ~ₐ
482.16	intoₐ] ~;
482.16	terms,] ~ₐ
482.30	proposition.] ~–
482.30	Thus,ₐ] ~:–
482.32	not-*A*ₐ–] ~-~.–
483.1	Negative,] ~–
483.15	predicate] pred.
483.16	*B*–] ~ₐ
483.16	is,] ~ₐ
483.17	*B*'s–] ~ₐ
483.17	the] to
483.17	*B*–] ~ₐ
483.17	is,] ~ₐ
483.19	logicians,] ~ₐ
483.23	as] is
483.25	predication,] ~ₐ
483.27	*B*'s] 'Bs
483.28	*B*'s.] ~ₐ
483.29	meaning,] ~ₐ
483.29	*B*,] ~.
483.32	William] Wm *Also* 484.15
483.33–34	notₐsomeₐ*B*] ~-|~-~

483.37	A's] As
483.38	Some] some
484.2	that] That
484.4	that,] ∼−
484.6	logic,] ∼∧
484.8	it:] it−[Quote.]
484.13	empfangen,] ∼∧
484.15	proposition,] ∼∧
484.16	Some] some
484.16	B,] ∼∧
484.25	false.] ∼−
484.28	truth.] ∼−
484.34	Likeness-terms,] ∼-∼∧
484.34	Index-terms,] ∼-∼∧
485.1	independently] independantly
485.5	Predicate] Pred
485.6(2)	Simple∧] ∼−
485.7	Simple∧] ∼−
485.7	Contingent] Conting.
485.8	Necessary] Necess.
485.14	Hypothesis,] ∼∧
485.14	Induction,] ∼∧
485.17	Extension,] ∼−
485.18	Extension;] ∼−
485.21–22	comprehension,] ∼−
485.23	comprehension,] ∼∧
485.24	which] of which
485.33	or] Or
485.34(1,2)	correlate,] ∼∧
485.34	ground,] ∼∧
485.35	interpretant.] ∼∧
486.3	likenesses,] ∼∧
486.3	indices,] ∼∧
486.4	symbols,] ∼∧
486.4–5	prescindible,] ∼∧
486.5	prescindible,] ∼∧
486.7	terms,] ∼∧
486.8	propositions,] ∼∧
486.10	disquiparance,] ∼∧
486.11	hypotheses,] ∼∧
486.11	inductions,] ∼∧
486.21	intelligible,] ∼∧
486.24	perfection∧] ∼.
486.25	led.] ∼∧
486.25	classes.∧] ∼.−
486.26	subdivision,] ∼∧
486.26	two,] ∼∧

486.27	subdivision,] ~ₐ
486.28	three,] ~ₐ
487.1	reasons:] ~ₐ
487.1	everything,] ~—
487.2	mechanics] mechancs
487.2	chemistry,] ~ₐ
487.11	things,] ~ₐ
487.24	Logicₐ] ~,
487.30	mathematics,] ~ₐ
487.30	Law,] ~ₐ
487.34	haveₐ] ~—
487.34	Historyₐ] ~;
487.35	(or] ₐ~
487.35	Botany,] ~ₐ
487.35	Mineralogy),] ~ₐ.
487.39	—as] as—as
488.1	Electricity,] ~ₐ
488.1	And] &
488.2	object—] ~ₐ
488.6	the] this
488.8	other's] others
488.8	too] to
488.20	searches] seaches
488.20	derived] deived

Lowell Lecture X

Copy-text for "Lecture X" is MS 131. All emendations have been supplied by the editors and appear to the left of the brackets. The readings to the right of the brackets are rejected readings from the copy-text.

488.29	and] & *Also* 489.8, 489.9, 489.12, 489.13, 490.1, 490.5(1, 2), 490.7
489.8	conclusion,] ~ₐ
489.8	identical;] ~ₐ
489.11	it].] ~]ₐ
489.12	lively.] ~]
489.13	itself] itₐ|self
489.18	futile,] ~ₐ
489.20	inferences,] ~ₐ
489.22	premise, since] ~. Since
489.26	prejudice] predjudice
489.26	all] the all

489.27	of cognition] cognition
489.28	¶The] ∧~
489.31	themselves,] ~∧
489.32	*feelings,*] ~∧
489.32	believing] beleiving
489.36	cognitions,] ~∧
490.3	whatever.] ~∧

Lowell Lecture XI

Copy-text for this lecture is MS 132. All emendations have been supplied by the editors and appear to the left of the brackets. The readings to the right of the brackets are rejected readings from MS 132.

490.10–11	Ladies—¦¶Philosophy] ~—∧~
490.11	attempt—] ~;
490.14–15	philosophy∧] ~—
490.15	they are] they
490.18	vise] vice
490.20	enthralled] inthralled
490.26	successful] succes-¦ful
491.3	inference:] ~;
491.4	varieties—] ~∧
491.4	Induction,] ~∧
491.4	and] & *Also* 491.11, 493.35, 494.1, 494.19, 495.18, 496.15, 496.19(1,2), 496.33(1,2), 497.13, 497.14, 497.16, 497.17, 497.26, 498.4, 498.19, 498.33, 499.1, 499.17, 499.18(1), 499.20, 500.12, 500.13, 500.20, 500.29, 500.30, 500.34, 501.2, 501.4, 501.5, 501.7(1,2), 501.30(1), 501.32(2), 501.40, 502.1, 502.5(3), 502.17, 503.1, 503.25, 503.29, 503.30, 503.33, 504.3, 504.6
491.4	Deduction;] ~.
491.6	comprehension;] ~,
491.7	Habits∧] ~;
491.8	consciousness:] ~;
491.9	comprehension,] ~∧
491.9–10	extension,] ~;
491.19	people∧] ~,
491.19	belief] beleif
491.22	Most] most
491.23	His] his
491.29	itself∧] ~,
491.32	believe] beleive *Also* 495.2, 498.3, 498.29, 499.10, 504.4
491.37	and] And

492.3	Psychology.] Psychology [Lines of Sir John Davies. Hamilton's Reid p 203]
492.4–35	For her . . . have taught.] *supplied*
493.22–23	antecedence∧–] ~;–
493.36	of them] them
494.4	for] from
494.9–10	*Liberty and Necessity*] rom.
494.10	Carleton] Carlton
494.22	is] in
494.25	What] what
494.28	let us] let
494.29	a man] man
494.30	mechanism,] ~∧
495.3	possession] pos-|ession
495.7	an] a
495.8–9	constitutes] consitutes *Also* 503.8
495.10	*think,*] ~∧
495.11	symbolization–] ~;
495.12	(the] –~
495.12	*being*)] ~–
495.15	sensation,] ~∧
495.19–20	*extract*
‡495.19	we're] we
495.24	Man,] man∧
495.25	sensationalists,] ~∧
495.31	*feeling*] rom.
495.37	sees,] ~∧
495.37	hears,] ~∧
495.37	Yes,] ~;
495.37	true;] ~∧
496.7	*planet*] rom.
496.7–8	of Hipparchus] Hipparchus
496.8	have] has
496.9	difference–] ~∧
496.9	since∧] ~–
496.10	word,] ~∧
496.11	mean,] ~∧
496.20	them] then
496.27	spiritual,] ~∧
496.27	rational,] ~∧
496.28	all–] ~;
496.29	grammar] gramnar
496.30–31	satisfactory,] ~∧
496.34	hand,] ~∧
496.38	also.] ~∧
497.11	Metaphor–] ~;
497.12	in the first] the first

497.13	stage,] ~∧
497.13	hands,] ~∧
497.16	word. The] ~; the
497.16	*metaphysician*] rom.
497.16–17	*metaphor*] rom.
497.19	metaphor∧] ~—
497.20–21	instead] in stead
497.22	fox—] ~,
497.24	language. But] ~; but
497.27	metaphor. That] ~—that
497.28	Cuvier's] Cuviers
497.33	symbols,] ~∧
497.34	be∧] ~;
497.34	∧our] (~
497.35	positively,∧] ~,)
497.36	so,] ~∧
498.2	*feelings,*] ~∧
498.4	concentration,] ~∧
498.4	effort,] ~∧
498.6	been∧] ~,
498.6	think,] ~∧
498.12	cognition,] ~∧
498.13	other] another
498.16	Why,] ~∧
498.16	the] thee
498.24	there;] ~∧
498.24	feeling,] ~∧
498.24	thought,] ~∧
498.25	something] some-thing
498.28	*six six*] rom.
498.36	Someone] Some one
498.38	these.] ~∧
498.39	sense.] ~∧
499.2	hypothesis.] ~∧
499.2	instant.] ~∧
499.3–4	attention.] ~,
499.4	thought,] ~∧
499.5	general,] ~∧
499.5	intuition.] ~∧
499.6	symbol.] ~∧
499.8	interpretant,∧] ~,—
499.9	himself] him-self
499.14	When∧] ~,
499.15	enter] enters
499.16	self;] ~,
499.16	the part] part
499.17	if] If

499.17	essence,] ~ₐ
499.20	men,] ~ₐ
499.20	carried] carries
499.21	soul,] ~ₐ
499.23	class,] ~ₐ
499.27	perhaps–] ~,
499.28 (1,2)	artisans] artizans
499.35	"the] ₐ~
499.36	upon,] ~ₐ
499.36	sufferance] sufference
499.37	dies."] ~.ₐ
499.38	who,] ~ₐ
500.7	*six*] rom. *Also* 500.8, 500.14(1,2)
500.10	unwritten?] ~.
500.26–27	immortal,] ~;
500.29	sentiments–] ~;
500.29	sympathy,] ~ₐ
500.29	love–] ~;
500.30	man's] mans
500.30	worth,] ~–
500.32–33	symbolization,] ~–
500.34	existence] ex-|tence
°500.37	of *vision*] of hearing *vision*
°500.37	for colors] for sounds & colors
500.40	*Jove,*] ~ₐ
501.5	its] is
501.11–12	idiosyncrasyₐ] ~–
501.12	man,] ~;
°501.13	existence.] existence.ᴬ
501.14	idiosyncrasy] idiosyncracy
501.19	*Harper's Magazine*] rom.
501.28	speak,–] ~,ₐ
501.35	child's] childs
501.40	until,] ~ₐ
502.4	anything:] any thing;
502.12	Aristotle–] ~;
502.15	No,] ~ₐ
502.26	corollary] correlary
502.28	*being,*] ~ₐ
502.30	*substance,*] ~ₐ
502.36	personal,] ~ₐ
503.3	is,] ~ₐ
503.6	symbol,] ~ₐ
503.6	respects,] ~ₐ
503.15	*ground,*] ~ₐ
503.16	thatₐ] ~,
503.19	anyone] any one

503.27   father's] fathers
503.29   response] reponse
503.30   father's] fathers
504.10   out of] out

Aristotelean Syllogism

Copy-text for this item is the only previous printing during Peirce's lifetime. The copy used for collation purposes and for the copy-text is from the Boston Public Library. All emendations have been supplied by the editors and appear to the left of the square brackets. The readings to the right of the brackets are rejected readings from the copy-text.

506.5   III$_\Lambda$] $\sim$.
506.6   III$_\Lambda$] $\sim$.
°506.11   following] above
°506.19–507.4   *diagrams completed*
°508.5   Light Roman] black letter
°508.6   Medium Roman] script
508.8   reasons.] $\sim$,
508.16   William of Shyreswood] William Shyreswood
508.35   syllogism] syllogysm
508.37   *some*] rom.
509.1   So$_\Lambda$] $\sim$,
°509.21   pages 506–7] the second page
510.22   *not-P*] rom.
510n.3   *Hispanus*] *Hisp.*
511.9   *some-S*] rom.
511.26   some-S] Some-S
512.8   Fig.] $\sim_\Lambda$
512.10   some-S] Some-S
513.26   P;] P;
                not P;] ot P;

Searching for the Categories

Copy-text is MS 133. All readings to the left of the brackets are emendations supplied by the editors. All readings to the right of the brackets are rejected readings from MS 133.

515.5	§1.] ~ˏ
515.6	consent] consents
515.24	legitimate] legitemate
515.29	and] & *Also* 518.17, 518.20, 518.36, 520.14, 520.26, 523.9, 525.6(2), 526.13(1), 526.24, 526.26, 526.27, 526.38, 527.29(2), 527.30, 527.38, 528.1, 528.18, 528.19, 528.21, 528.26(1)
516.8–9	be reduced] reduced
°516.24	§2] §3
517.19	cognitions),] ~,)
°517.21	§3.] §4:
517.31(1)	griffinˏ"] ~;"
518.7	tailedˏman] ~-~
518.8	supposable] supposeable
°518.20	§4] §2
518.35	discriminateˏ] ~,
518.36	prescindˏ] ~,
519.1	believe] beleive
519.2	page),] ~,)
519.25	general] gen
520.1	§5.] ~ˏ
520.18	conception,] ~ˏ
520.24	itself] it-self
520.24	together,] ~ˏ
520.24	andˏ] ~,
521.1	§6.] ~ˏ
521.14	independently] independantly
521.20	given,] ~ˏ
521.34	different,] ~;
521n.1	*De Generibus et speciebus,*] De Generibus et speciebus.
522.11	§7.] ~ˏ
°522.11	Correlate²] Correlate
522n.1	section] §
522n.1	rewritten.] ~ˏ
523.1	is] as
523.12	fulfills] fulfulls
523.12	interpreter] interpretor
523.13	foreigner] foreignor
523.21	simplyˏ] ~,
523.24	unanalyzable] unanalyzible
524.10	§9.] ~ˏ
524.20	objectˏ] ~,
525.13	§12.] ~ˏ
°525.14	A] But a
525.19	equiparant] equiparants
525.24	interpretantˏ] ~,

525.25	ground$_\wedge$] $\sim$,
525.26	object$_\wedge$] $\sim$,
526.5	of equiparance] equiparance
526.6	equiparants] equipants
526.6	correlates."] $\sim_\wedge$"
526.12	comprehension,] $\sim_\wedge$
526.12	intension,] $\sim_\wedge$
526.25	besides,] $\sim_\wedge$
°526.27	ratio] ratio°
526.29	———.] $\sim_\wedge$
526.30	*disquiparant*] *disquipant*
526.31	equiparance.] $\sim_\wedge$
526.33	disquiparance] disquipance *Also* 527.1, 527.33
526.37	hippopotamus] hippopotomus *Also* 526.38, 527.3(1,2), 527.4
527.2	equiparance,] $\sim_\wedge$
527.4–5	hippopotamus-like] hippopotomus$_\wedge$like
527.14	"A] $_\wedge\sim$
527.15	B"] $\sim_\wedge$
527.15	"A] $_\wedge\sim$
527.16	less,"] $\sim_{,\wedge}$
527.16	disquiparance] diquiparance
527.17	$_\wedge$A equals B$_\wedge$] '$\sim$ $\sim$ $\sim$'
527.19	$_\wedge$A] "$\sim$
527.19	exceeded$_\wedge$] $\sim$"
527.21	¶[Kind] $_\wedge$[$\sim$
527.28–29	disquiparance] disquiparace
527.29	C] B
527.33	ground of] ground
528.4	grounds,] $\sim$;
528.5	measurable] measureable *Also* 528.11–12
528.5(2)	is] Is
528.7	are] is
528.9–10	*exclusion in extension*] rom.
528.10	*opposition*] rom.
528.14	intention,] $\sim_\wedge$
528.14–15	comprehension,] $\sim_\wedge$
528.24	relation,] $\sim_\wedge$

Word-Division

The following list records the editors' resolutions of compounds or possible compounds hyphenated at the end of a line in the copy-texts.

2.9	frog-pond
26.6	class-mates
45.18	self-supported
47.28	conjoined
50.6	far-distant
74.12	self-contradictory
74.27	self-contradictory
82.39	thought-of
87.12	interspace
88.6	inworking
95.8	arrow-shaped
100.28	vapor-density
102.17	sack-cloth
107.12	override
117.29	forefathers
122.25	dissyllabic
130.30	vowel-sound
151.39	class-characteristic
170.11–12	superscription
206.12	superinduced
226.21	subordinate
226.26	non-existence
244.15	world-shattering
244.19	anti-dogmatical
245.24	household
266.13	cloven-hoofed
300.19	superordination
341.2	superordinate
359.18	bank-notes
360.33	fourteen-sided
363.32	subsumption

364.33	subsumption
405.9	madcaps
427.22	cloven-hoofed
429.5	cloven-hoofed
434.15	cloven-hoofed
437.13	overlooked
439.17	non-existent
450.2	sore-throat
453n.7	extraordinary
458.13	hodge-podge
485.20	cloven-hoofed
502.37	well-spring
506.2–3	subsumption
511.24	Some-*S*
512.12(1)	not-*P*

The following is a list of those words which were broken at the end of a line in the present text and which should be transcribed as hyphenated. All other ambiguously broken compound words or possible compound words should be transcribed as single words.

14.4	self-confidence
42.2	four-sided
48.30	self-dependent
83.7	of-thinkable
100.7	odd-basic
124.3	semi-vocals
134n.3	*School-Master*
167.25	self-knowledge
177.23	long-lived
180.28	so-called
185.36	cloven-footed
210.31	blue-green
231.10	Four-legged
241.14	air-castles
249.21	class-concepts
251.16	things-in-themselves
251.19	things-in-themselves
263.10	long-lived
281.36	*yellow-green*
315.17	non-existence
342.7	self-contradictory
352.9	starting-point

433.21	cloven-hoofed
434.23	cloven-hoofed
449.38	sick-room
460.17	*non-black*
472.18	two-legged
485.2	Likeness-term

Index

Abbot, Francis Ellingwood, 156, 455; "The Philosophy of Space and Time," 242

Abduction, xxxiii

Absoluteness: world of, 47

Abstraction, 145–46, 518, 522; world of, 47, 70, 84; composition of, 83; related to the nature of the perfect, 84; combined with manifold of sensation, 85; judgment of, 168; kind of, 353; as a kind of mental separation, 473

Accident: of the noumenon, 313–14; and logic, 338; conception between being and substance, 520. *See also* Categories

Actuality, 18, 47; degree of modality, 38; a category of the It, 530

Aesthetics, 10–12. *See also* Schiller

Affection, 4

Affirmatives, 229–30, 301, 315, 365, 374, 482–83, 505

Affirming: and asserting, difference between, 18

Agassiz, Louis, xvii, xix–xx, xxi, xxii, 218

Agassiz School for Young Ladies, xxxi

Algebra, 173, 306, 404, 528

American Academy of Arts and Sciences, xxii

American Association for the Advancement of Science, xvi, xix

American Ephemeris and Nautical Almanac, xvi

Analogue, xxxiii; as a kind of representation, 308

Animal kingdom: four branches of, 150

Anselm: argument concerning reality of abstractions, 67; proof of the existence of God, 446–47; book in favor of the fool, 447

Antecedent: inferred *a posteriori*, 180; sign of the consequent, 337; internal and necessary, 493

Anticipations, 152

Apelt, Ernst Friedrich, 163, 205

A posteriori, a priori: as terms used by Kant, 159, 245–46. *See also* Antecedent; Axioms; Cognition; Conception; Consequent; Inference; Judgments; Knowledge; Metaphysics; Object; Propositions; Reasoning; Representation; Thought

Application, 150–51

Aquinas. *See* Thomas Aquinas

Argument, 370, 443, 445; three kinds of, xxxiv–xxxv; and syllogism, 268, 478; elements of, 268; hypothetic, 283, 435,

442; inductive, 283, 430, 433–34, 442; as symbol, 347, 485; producing knowledge, 347; validity of, 363, 437–38; common character of, 394; deductive, 437; divisions of, 437, 485–86; ambiguity of, 447–48; Mill's view on, 448; reference to an interpretant, 478; and representation, 478, 486

Aristotle, xxvi, xxviii, 93, 302; on the categories, xxiv, 351; *Organon*, xxiv, 224; on definition, 58; *Metaphysics*, 58; on metaphysics, 58, 115, 152; as viewed by Francis Bacon, 103; *Posterior Analytics*, 152; definition of logic, 163; on induction, 163, 176–77, 179, 263; on syllogisms, 177, 262, 376–78; on validity of inductive inference, 177; and the Sophists, 199, 390; on fallacies, 200; on sophisms, 200; his term *indefinite*, 253; *Prior Analytics*, 263; evolution of theory of induction, 264–65; analysis of propositions, 351, 418; and logic, 351; reply to Zeno's third argument on motion, 392; *Analytics*, 457; on philosophy, 490; the "what" and the "why," 504

Asserting: and affirming, difference between, 18

Assertion: of rule, case, and result, 378

Association Philosophy: English, 457

Assumption: science of, 152

Astronomy, xx; and mechanics, 9

Atheism, 20, 21

Attention: definite conception or supposition, 518–19

Augustine, 163

Axioms, 56, 71, 152, 154, 218; of intuition, 31–33; *a priori*, 217; as representation, 217; Zeno's, 391; of geometry, 444

Bache, Alexander Dallas, xix, xx

Bacon, Francis, xxiii, xxiv, 21, 101, 103, 162; Baconian method, 70–71, 211; his view of Aristotle, 103; on the goal of science, 113; on the reform of logic, 162; on induction, 163, 265–66; compared to Comte, 211; his three tables of instances, 220; on truth, 454

Bailey, Nathan, 132

Bain, Alexander, 495

Bales, Peter, 119

Barbarians: age of migrations of, 106

Baret, John, 121–22, 123n, 130, 139, 142

Beauty: and the soul, 6; Schiller's definition, 10; the idea or sense of, 10–12;